NORWICH
Medieval and Early Modern Art, Architecture and Archaeology

General Editor   Alixe Bovey

NORWICH
Medieval and Early Modern Art, Architecture and Archaeology

Edited by
T. A. Heslop *and* Helen E. Lunnon

The British Archaeological Association

Conference Transactions XXXVIII

Cover illustration: John Adey Repton, *The Ethelbert Gate, Norwich Cathedral,*
watercolour *c.*1803
Reproduced by permission of the Society of Antiquaries of London

Published with the aid of a generous subvention from the
Norfolk and Norwich Archaeological Society

ISBN Hardback 978-1-909662-77-3
Paperback 978-1-909662-78-0

PUBLISHED FOR THE BRITISH ARCHAEOLOGICAL ASSOCIATION
BY MANEY PUBLISHING, JOSEPH'S WELL, HANOVER WALK, LEEDS LS3 IAB, UK
PRINTED AND BOUND BY CHARLESWORTH PRESS, WAKEFIELD, UK

Contents

List of Abbreviations

Antiq. J.	*Antiquaries Journal*
Archaeol. J.	*Archaeological Journal*
BAA Trans.	*British Archaeological Association Conference Transactions*
BAR	British Archaeological Reports
B/E	N. Pevsner et al., The Buildings of England (Harmondsworth, London various dates)
B/E, *Norfolk*, I & II	N. Pevsner and B. Wilson, The Buildings of England: *Norfolk,* second edition, 2 vols: I, *Norwich and the North-East* (London 1997); II, *North-West and South* (London 1999)
Blomefield, *Norfolk*	F. Blomefield and C. Parkin, *An essay towards a topographical history of the County of Norfolk,* 11 vols (London 1805–10)
Bull. mon.	*Bulletin monumental*
Cattermole and Cotton, 'Church Building'	P. Cattermole and S. Cotton, 'Medieval Parish Church Building in Norfolk', *Norfolk Archaeology*, 38 (1983), 235–79
EAA	East Anglian Archaeology
EH	English Heritage
Fernie, *AHNC*	E. Fernie, *Architectural History of Norwich Cathedral* (Oxford 1992)
Gilchrist, *Close*	R. Gilchrist, *Norwich Cathedral Close* (Woodbridge 2005)
HBMC	Historic Buildings and Monuments Commission
JBAA	*Journal of the British Archaeological Association*
Med. Archaeol.	*Medieval Archaeology*
Medieval Norwich	*Medieval Norwich*, ed. C. Rawcliffe and R. Wilson (London 2004)
Mon.	W. Dugdale, *Monasticon Anglicanum*, ed. J. Caley et al., 6 vols in 8 (London 1846)
NA	*Norfolk Archaeology*
NMR	National Monuments Record
NRO	Norfolk Record Office
Norwich Cathedral 1096–1996	*Norwich Cathedral: church, city and diocese, 1096–1996,* ed. I. Atherton, E. Fernie, C. Harper-Bill and H. Smith (London 1996)
ODNB	*Oxford Dictionary of National Biography* (Oxford 2004–2014)
PRO	Public Record Office
RCHME	Royal Commission on the Historical Monuments of England
TNA	The National Archives
VCH	Victoria History of the Counties of England
VCH, *Norfolk*, I & II	Victoria History of the Counties of England: *Norfolk*, 2 vols: I, Westminster 1901; II, London 1906

Preface

FOR FIVE SUMMER DAYS in 2012, more than 100 speakers, delegates and guests attended the British Archaeological Association's annual conference. Held between 7 and 11 July, the conference was convened in the medieval city of Norwich and based at the cathedral hostry. The resources of the city are incredibly rich, in terms of extant and archaeologically known religious houses, parish churches and secular buildings from a broad range of social rankings, and in addition Norwich is widely recognized as an artistic centre of considerable repute and influence. The conference sought to bring together themes concerned with production as well as reception of medieval art and architecture in the second most populous and wealthy city in medieval England. We sought to encourage new work, as well as providing a platform for finalizing research not previously made available, and for revising or reconsidering some that had.

The programme of lectures, presented in the Weston Room at the cathedral hostry, opened on Saturday afternoon with Brian Ayers providing an excellent introduction to the development and topography of the medieval city, the results of recent archaeology, and potential subjects for future research. With the stage set, a subsequent twenty-three formal papers were delivered during half-day sessions on Sunday, Tuesday and Wednesday mornings. We are grateful to all speakers for offering such varied and stimulating presentations. We also extend our sincere thanks to Simon Abel and the team at the cathedral hostry for their efficient and generous provision of facilities and refreshments which contributed greatly to the smooth and convivial running of the event.

Of the formal papers presented at the conference, nineteen are published in the present volume, and we are grateful to all the contributors for their efforts and patience through the editorial process. Among the papers not included in this volume, several have been or will be published elsewhere, but we wish gratefully to acknowledge the contributions made by Miri Rubin, Claire Daunton, Sue Hedge and Penny Wallis.

It is customary for the Association's conferences to be remembered as much for the site visits as for their formal papers, and the Norwich conference was no exception. Half of the programme was given over to site visits within the city and there was a day trip further afield. Site visits began in the cathedral on Saturday evening, and continued on Sunday afternoon. A number of speakers generously gave talks on facets of the cathedral, including Nicola Coldstream (nave), Eric Fernie (transepts), Veronica Sekules (Salmon's porch), Charles Tracy (choir stalls), Jill Franklin (Romanesque sculpture) and Roland Harris (triforium). We extend our thanks to the Dean and Chapter for their generosity and hospitality in welcoming the Association's visit, to Roland Harris for his role in facilitating access to parts of the cathedral which are normally off limits, and to the Right Reverend Graham James, bishop of Norwich, for allowing (and to Coralie Nichols for arranging) our visit to Salmon's porch, the only standing part of the 14th-century bishop's palace.

On Sunday evening we were welcomed in the remarkable late medieval Great Hospital located on the north side of Bishopgate east of the cathedral. Professor Carole Rawcliffe kindly introduced us to the site and in small groups we visited 'Eagle Ward' to see the late 14th-century painted timber ceiling adorned with the imperial double-headed eagle, probably referring to Anne of Bohemia's visit in 1383. A reception and dinner were served in the hospital's medieval refectory and Birkbeck Hall, and we express our gratitude to the Master, Air Commodore Kevin Pellatt, and all who made possible a wonderfully convivial evening in exceptional medieval surroundings.

Through artistic commissions, architectural emulation and patronal ambition glimpses of Norwich are identifiable across Norfolk. In order to capture this aspect of the city's medieval art and architectural history, a full day of the conference was devoted to site visits in north Norfolk where the legacy is particularly well represented. The route took us to East Dereham, North Elmham, Cley-next-the-Sea, Blakeney, Wiveton and Binham, and we extend our thanks to all of the key holders and custodians who made these visits possible. We also wish to thank those who, with such good grace and humour, willingly undertook the challenge of speaking to a hundred people in the churches and graveyards of north Norfolk, including Dominic Summers, Andrea Kirkham, Christopher Wilson, David King, Neil Batcock and Matthew Champion. The day produced two of the most memorable experiences of the conference: coffee and cakes so generously provided and served by the WI in North Elmham were delicious and plentiful beyond all our expectations, challenged closely by tea at the church in Blakeney. The magical setting of Binham Priory, bathed in evening sunshine, provided for an unforgettable champagne reception hosted by English Heritage and the Friends of the Priory. Such is the centrality of on-site study to the Association's ethos and practice that as editors we decided to include, for the first time, short reports on several of the sites visited and studied during the conference. We hope this addition to the format of the Transactions volume is welcome to our readers and may be continued by editors of future conference volumes.

Norwich is unsurpassed for the number of its medieval buildings which survive and continue in use today. Discussion of aspects of civic and parochial Norwich was presented in a number of papers and site visits, including the remains of the Norman house beneath the present day Magistrates Court (Brian Ayers), the Guildhall (David King), Blackfriars Hall (John Goodall) and the parish churches of St Peter Mancroft (Frank Woodman), St Giles (Helen Lunnon), St Laurence (Julian Luxford), St Andrew (Jonathon Piesse), St Peter Hungate (Sandy Heslop). As a direct result of sharing conversations and discussions at the conference about the national and international importance of the city, the Leverhulme Trust has provided funding for a three-year research project on the parish churches, which began in September 2014, and which aims to enhance public understanding of this unique corpus of buildings and sites.

Such a complicated and varied conference programme could not be achieved without exemplary organization, and for this we wholeheartedly thank Kate Davey (conference organizer) and Abigail Wheatley (conference administrator). Together Kate and Abigail calmly and efficiently ensured that the programme was both stimulating in its variety and achievable and that everyone was kept informed of where to be and when. For this and much, much more we are in their debt.

Our final thanks go to the student scholars and those who gave generously to the bursary fund which makes it possible to award conference scholarships. The lively, bright, engaging and spirited nature of the event was enhanced by the number and calibre of students who attended. The conference and the resulting Transactions volume have undoubtedly benefited from their participation, and it is hugely encouraging that the British Archaeological Association is so committed to bringing together new and established scholars in our ongoing study of medieval art, architecture and archaeology in Britain.

T. A. Heslop and Helen E. Lunnon
Conference Convenors

The Development of an Urban Landscape: Recent Research in Medieval Norwich

BRIAN AYERS

This paper presents a review of recent progress in the study of medieval Norwich, a city of European importance, examining its urban landscape, buildings, institutions, and commerce and industry. Evidence is drawn from survey, excavation, building recording and analysis, artefact studies and palaeo-environmental data. Much of the information is derived from work of the last forty years, starting with the ground-breaking initiatives of the Norwich Survey in the 1970s, continuing through large-scale excavations conducted by the Norfolk Archaeological Unit — notably at the Magistrates' Courts, Castle Mall and the Franciscan friary, all now published — and from research undertaken by other scholars at the cathedral, on the elite houses of the city, and in the surviving parish churches (thirty of these still stand out of a medieval total of over sixty). The paper concludes with an assessment of potential for future research.

NORWICH, probably the fourth largest town in England in 1066, grew rapidly after the Norman Conquest to become a regional capital, housing the only royal castle for Norfolk and Suffolk until the mid-12th century, the seat of the diocese of East Anglia and, by the late 13th century, an impressive range of crafts, trades and mercantile activity.[1] By the 1340s, the city occupied a walled area greater than that of London and Southwark combined. Its population had perhaps reached 30,000 in the decades preceding the Black Death.[2]

Attempts to provide an appraisal of the development of the city, drawn from a range of sources, have a fine lineage. In 1963, for instance, a ground-breaking exhibition was held at Norwich Castle Museum, entitled 'Norwich: The Growth of a City'.[3] This incorporated archaeological material into an assessment of the documentary and built inheritance of Norwich, and proved to be the precursor of the considerable archaeological and allied research which has deepened understanding of the medieval development of the city in the years since. One successor has been a recent review which examines the origins of the settlement and its growth prior to 1066.[4] This work built on an earlier appraisal published by the late Alan Carter in 1978, wherein he attempted to summarize new discoveries within a context of developing hypotheses and methodologies concerning urban growth.[5]

The current paper, exploring understanding of Norwich between 1066 and the Reformation, also takes Carter's lead as a starting point. Carter was the director of the (now defunct) Norwich Survey, an interdisciplinary organization established in the early 1970s to examine the documents, historic buildings and buried archaeology of the city. Confronted with an extraordinary task and armed with only modest resources, he and his colleagues necessarily had to be selective. In consequence, their research agenda concentrated mainly (but not exclusively) on three key areas: excavation sought primarily to understand the early development of Norwich prior to 1270; documentary research focused on the remarkable collection of enrolled property deeds of the later 13th and early 14th centuries; and building survey sought to explore how the known dramatic expansion of the early post-medieval population was housed within an urban area which did not itself expand. Carter set out the problems and the methodological approaches in a second paper, also published in 1978.[6]

Perhaps as a consequence of the broad split of research endeavour, Carter never produced an appraisal for the post-Conquest period as he had for the origins of Norwich. The Norwich Survey, always designed as a finite project, largely ceased to excavate in 1978 and was finally wound up in the mid-1980s. Archaeological work thereafter, until the mid-1990s, was exclusively undertaken by the Norfolk Archaeological Unit which initially adopted the research strategy of the Norwich Survey, but began to broaden this, partly under the pressure of events (such as the necessity for responding to development on an unprecedented scale within the scheduled areas of Norwich Castle, some two hectares needing comprehensive excavation[7]) and partly due to the increased challenges and opportunities afforded by the introduction of Planning Policy Guidance 16 in 1990.[8] A further development in the late 1990s led to the establishment of a Regional Research Framework for the East of England with chapters specifically directed to urban studies.[9] More widely, emphasis upon the potential for archaeology to explore towns of all dates was summarized in a national framework document.[10] Each of these documents has had an impact upon research within Norwich, particularly for those projects initiated as reactions to development pressure, newly identified research themes helping to focus resources within an increasingly competitive archaeological environment.

The potential for a range of reactive research centred on medieval Norwich (and its role in the regional and wider economy) has been increasingly recognized in recent years with major archaeological projects — now published — at Norwich Castle, the Franciscan friary and Dragon Hall, all deepening knowledge and understanding of the administrative, ecclesiastical and commercial framework underpinning much of the city.[11] There has, however, also been a concomitant growth in pure research, undertaken by academic institutions and individuals. Detailed study of surviving late medieval houses has led to greater awareness of the economic and social roles of the mercantile elite of Norwich.[12] A thorough appraisal of the cathedral close has examined not only its function and meaning within the medieval city, but also revealed the wealth of information latent within the surviving buildings.[13] Ongoing research is exploring the important painted glass industry.[14] The study of cemetery assemblages, particularly that of a cemetery associated with executed criminals, has broadened knowledge of the urban population.[15]

All this work has been, and is being, undertaken within a widening methodological framework. Urban growth was necessarily part of a social and economic development cycle which took in the various hinterlands of the city: the immediate rural environment; that hinterland comprising other settlements which were either competitive or complementary (such as Great Yarmouth, a town that was both); and an extensive network of commercial and cultural contacts in the eastern region and beyond.

This paper therefore seeks to review recent progress in the study of medieval Norwich, a city of European importance, examining its urban landscape, buildings, institutions, and commerce and industry. The compass of a short paper is too constrained to permit either a detailed discussion of these individual elements or a strictly chronological approach; a recent treatment of the latter is available elsewhere.[16]

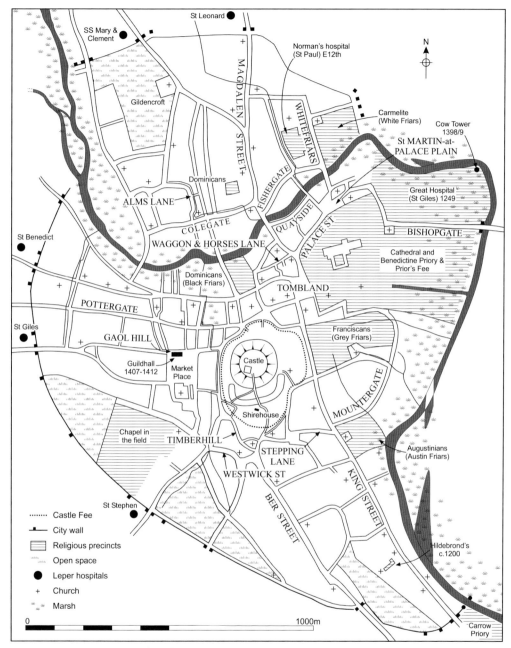

St Leonard

SS Mary & Clement

Norman's hospital (St Paul) E12th

N

Gildencroft

MAGDALEN STREET

WHITEFRIARS

Carmelite (White Friars)

Cow Tower 1398/9

St MARTIN-at-PALACE PLAIN

Dominicans

ALMS LANE

FISHERGATE

Great Hospital (St Giles) 1249

St Benedict

COLEGATE

QUAYSIDE

PALACE ST

BISHOPGATE

WAGGON & HORSES LANE

Dominicans (Black Friars)

TOMBLAND

Cathedral and Benedictine Priory & Prior's Fee

POTTERGATE

St Giles

GAOL HILL

Franciscans (Grey Friars)

Guildhall 1407-1412

Market Place

Castle

MOUNTERGATE

Shirehouse

Chapel in the field

TIMBERHILL

STEPPING LANE

Augustinians (Austin Friars)

WESTWICK ST

KING STREET

St Stephen

BER STREET

Hildebrond's c.1200

Castle Fee

City wall

Religious precincts

Open space

Leper hospitals

Church

Marsh

0   1000m

Carrow Priory

FIG. 1.   Map of medieval Norwich with street-names mentioned in the text

David Dobson

Furthermore, this appraisal is largely confined to the city as encircled with walls by the mid-14th century. Nevertheless an attempt will be made to provide an overview of a range of initiatives, concluding by seeking to identify potential areas for future work. Street names mentioned in the text are shown on Figure 1.

THE URBAN LANDSCAPE

NORWICH is situated in the valley of the Wensum, a river which rises in mid-Norfolk and flows eastward to the sea, having a confluence with the River Yare south-east of the city before running to its outfall at Great Yarmouth. Early settlement benefited from locations either on well-drained river-edge gravel terraces or on more elevated ground generally of Norwich crag (fine-grained marine sands with some gravels and clay) and chalk. The river was bridged by the end of the 11th century, and quite probably in the mid-10th century.[17] The likely extent of the Anglo-Scandinavian town on the eve of the Norman Conquest has been mapped.[18] The immediate impact of the Conquest was seen in the construction of the great castle (perhaps from 1068) with the laying out of a borough to the west for the *Franci de Norvic* following on between 1071 and 1075.[19] This latter settlement was established by the king and Earl Ralph, the earl only holding the office for four years. Norman domination of the central part of the city was completed by the establishment of the cathedral close, traditionally from the 1090s, but perhaps in preparation from as early as the 1070s.[20]

While such institutional additions to the urban environment are well known, infilling of what was to become the walled city has always been less clear. Attempts to characterize development utilizing documentary evidence have been attempted (most ingeniously — and convincingly — by Carter using landgable rent data to map areas probably developed by 1130).[21] It has, however, needed the results of archaeological excavation to provide physical evidence of urban growth away from the central riverside belt. As examples, it is now clear that, contrary to early hypotheses, timber buildings occupied the foreshore of King Street south of Mountergate/Stepping Lane by the time of the Conquest (that is, outwith of a probable formal boundary to the Anglo-Scandinavian borough marked by a ditch found in 2000[22]). These structures were precursors of more substantial development in the 12th century. Slight traces of a so-called sunken-featured (or cellared) timber building of probable 11th-century date were uncovered west of the street in 2012.[23] North of the river, excavation at Alms Lane, immediately outside known early-10th-century Anglo-Scandinavian defences, identified low-grade industrial working extracting iron ore from river gravels into the 13th century, but thereafter the area was occupied by housing (of poor quality).[24] Further north still, the churchyard of St Margaret *in combusto* was probably founded very late in the 11th century, or early in the 12th.[25]

Urban development also included colonization of marginal areas within the central area, namely the banks of the river. Excavation has demonstrated that infilling of low-lying marshy deposits started well before the Conquest.[26] This process accelerated from the 12th century onward. Recent work at the Great Hospital on Bishopgate indicates that the institution was extended across what appears to have been grazing pasture.[27] Streets such as Westwick Street, which appear to have originated as river-edge thoroughfares with perhaps a single row of buildings between them and the floodplain, became isolated as urban activity — such as the requirements of industry for ready access to water — led to dumping of refuse material and the construction of houses and workshops.

An inter-connectability of activity can be detected as the post-Conquest settlement grew. Numerous excavations in recent years have uncovered quarry pits, normally for sourcing sands and gravels, but chalk and flint were also extracted. The steep eastern slopes of the Ber Street escarpment are testimony to relict medieval quarries, and nearby, at Cannon Wharf off King Street, evidence was uncovered for deposition of over a metre of chalk, flint and gravel in the 15th century before the site was finally free of flood risk.[28] Similar discoveries at Whitefriars north of the river and of chalk floors at locations such as the Ferry Boat Inn and Dragon Hall on King Street suggest that, in excavating pits for flint, the chalk by-product was then used for infilling and floor consolidation.[29]

Infilling of the river margins can also be linked to possible straightening of the Wensum; it has been pointed out that the north bank bend opposite the site of the Dominican friary ought to have a corresponding bend on the south bank. It does not; thus implying that the friars, when infilling, straightened the river.[30] In doing so, they probably also contained the outflow of the Great Cockey, a stream flowing north-ward into the river at this point. Other small estuaries of cockeys were canalized and obscured by infilling, as can be surmised for the outflow of the Dalymond off Fisher-gate.[31] Others were even diverted, as suggested for the Muspole whose original estuary is probably indicated by the alignment of Water Lane off Colegate and the parish boundary between St George Colegate and St Clement, as well as by the 4 m deep deposits located on St George's Street in 1986.[32]

Riparian infilling could have a dramatic effect on extant buildings; a stone house, constructed *c.* 1170 adjacent to the river foreshore at St Martin-at-Palace Plain, was cut into the north-facing slope of Bichil, creating ground-level access to its principal floor from the street frontage and similar ground-level access to the floor below from the lower part of the slope. By the early post-medieval period such 'cellared' access was only possible via a preserved sloping passage, effected between two retaining walls which held back accumulated layers of infill.[33]

Norwich is not a city necessarily considered to be hilly, but it does have several dramatic breaks of slope and other areas where long, gentle slopes clearly inhibited building. This led to the construction of vaulted undercrofts which acted as building platforms and as locations of secure storage,[34] and to landscape manipulation, as seen in excavations on the site of the Dominican friary where infilling of the river foreshore provided a level platform on a sloping site for the massive claustral buildings, which largely still survive.[35] Similarly, at the Franciscan friary, evidence for terracing was found. Here, changes in level were accommodated by use of parallel walls, one con-structed with a batter, helping to enclose an area containing deposits of compacted clay, probably preparatory to laying of a paved floor.[36]

Such landscape modification was minor compared to the topographical impact brought by the imposition of major post-Conquest institutions. The creation of the castle and the cathedral in the 11th century had profound implications for the local environment. The physical geography was altered substantially by the earthworks of the castle where excavation revealed ditches in excess of 9 m in depth, features which would once have been commanded by upstanding earth ramparts of presumably similar dimensions.[37] Both the castle and the cathedral truncated routes within the pre-Conquest street plan as, later, did friaries such as those of the Dominicans and Fran-ciscans. Evidence of pre-institutional roads have now been published from both the area of the cathedral close and that of the Franciscan friary (hoof-prints being recorded on the latter) while the alignment of Mountergate seems to have been readjusted in order to accommodate the Augustinian friary off King Street.[38]

Some truncated streets continued to exist throughout the medieval period, only to be lost subsequently. One such was uncovered off Palace Street in 2006. Running north-ward towards the river, it was bounded by the flint-built rear ranges of substantial houses dating to the 13th or 14th centuries. Sufficient height survived in one wall to include remains of a blocked window.[39] Elsewhere, the recovery of tenement bound-aries through excavation, when linked to documentary evidence, enabled a correlation to be drawn between 12th-century re-planning of part of the city with the rental income derived thereby.[40]

URBAN BUILDINGS

FLINT-BUILT houses were not the norm in the centuries immediately following the Norman Conquest. Although such buildings were introduced in the 12th century, their numbers remained small and their distribution limited. Only one such house has sur-vived relatively intact, the Music House on King Street, perhaps originally constructed about 1140 and then extended c. 1175. Careful examination in recent decades has concluded that it consists of a chamber block above a shop (the latter vaulted with moulded ribs of Caen stone) and a more private office (with unmoulded ribs), supple-mented later by an aisled hall (the one surviving aisle pier bearing a close relationship to the c. 1180 infirmary piers at the cathedral).[41] This documented building was in Jewish ownership by the third quarter of the 12th century, its most notable occupant being Isaac, a financier of national repute who, in the 1220s, had £1,647 in transactions recorded in the rolls known as the Norwich Day Book, the next highest individual being recorded at £258.[42]

Substantial elements of a second stone house were excavated in 1981 at St Martin-at-Palace Plain and are now preserved beneath the late-20th-century Magistrates' Courts (Fig. 2).[43] This undocumented structure lies next to the river, as does the Music House, and at least two further houses are documented as having been in similar locations on Quayside. Riverside buildings therefore seem to form one group of such prestigious houses; a further group is provided by those structures known to have existed around the market-place in the French borough. In all, some eighteen stone houses are recorded, primarily from documentary references, although excavations such as that at the Forum site west of St Peter Mancroft church are beginning to indicate the locations of stone structures, even if only rammed gravel foundations survive.[44]

Such footings may seem relatively inconsequential, but they are substantial com-pared to the scanty evidence for poorer housing, such as the clay-walled, indeed un-heated, homes excavated in peripheral parts of the city centre. At Alms Lane in 1976, urban expansion across earlier areas of iron ore extraction resulted in the construction of clay-walled single-storey structures. As well as documenting and publishing these discoveries, the excavator went on to review the typology of such mean houses across the city, charting their rebuilds every forty to fifty years and exploring their varying types and scale. He noted that the technique had ceased to be used by the 16th century and found it remarkable that evidence of its use had been 'eradicated so completely in the city. Its rediscovery is one of the most significant results of the recent programme of excavations'.[45]

More commonly, houses utilized wood and, increasingly from the 13th century onward, some flint and brick, although often such materials would only be used for

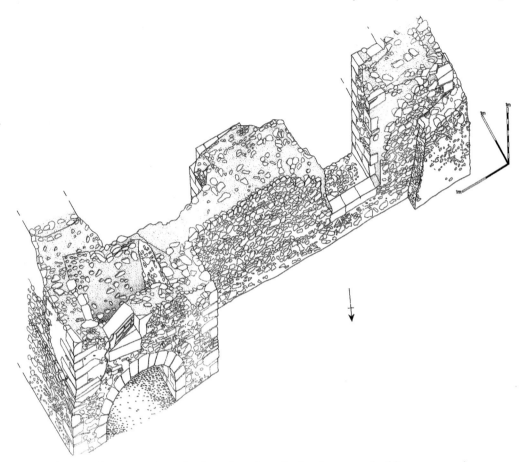

Fig. 2. Axonometric projection of north wall of 12th-century building excavated at
St Martin-at-Palace Plain, Norwich
Norfolk Archaeological Unit

footings, gable ends or ground-floor walls with timber above. Norwich is poorly
furnished with surviving medieval buildings of this type, mainly as a result of significant
fires in the 16th century, and those that do still exist tend to be structures which were
houses of the most affluent in the city. Buildings which were occupied by the middling
sort are largely lost, but excavation in 1976 did recover a terrace of such buildings on
Pottergate, destroyed by fire in 1507 but with brick cellars surviving intact, often with
the contents of the kitchens which had been located above. These structures and their
assemblages remain one of the best-recovered examples of urban housing in the
country, the artefacts revealing much about the aspirant sensibilities of the occupants
as well as the precocious nature of an urban society closely linked to developments in
continental culture.[46]

The mercantile elite of the late medieval city occupied substantial building com-
plexes, a good sample of which survive, albeit often in changed and occasionally
mutilated form. Such buildings have frequently been subjected to architectural and

archaeological appraisal seeking to understand their function and use, both in Norwich and elsewhere.[47] More recent assessments have sought to demonstrate that it is also possible to extend such analysis to explore 'the role of the built environment in the constitution of social identities and relationships [...]'.[48] Specifically, it is argued that the elite houses were configured, adapted and used to express wealth, power and status for

FIG. 3.   Excavations at Dragon Hall, King Street, Norwich
Norfolk Archaeological Unit

social gain and control. The late medieval context of Norwich, a city notable for its lack of individual mercantile guildhalls, meant that the elite private house achieved a functional status within the wider community not seen elsewhere. In addition, 'Norwich is characterized by an early adoption of 'closed' architectural forms within the houses of the middling sort …[who negotiated] their social position, through an increasing investment in domestic material culture and the development of new modes of formal domestic life and sociability'.[49]

The application of techniques such as access analysis to some of the houses has led to a greater understanding of day-to-day usage of buildings, suggesting how they were viewed, entered and, on occasion, configured to restrict entry to certain groups. The mercantile/domestic complex at Dragon Hall, excavated and surveyed in 1997–98, is a good example of this (Fig. 3). It is a location where access 'can be categorized at various levels: public, semi-public, commercial and storage, and private'.[50] Control of access also implies social control and it can be argued, therefore, that archaeology in Norwich is recovering in part something of the social 'rules' which governed medieval society.

URBAN INSTITUTIONS

WHILE the impact of stone dwellings upon the urban environment may have been dramatic, the impact of institutional developments such as the castle and the cathedral during the late 11th and early 12th centuries would have been considerably greater. The castle has been investigated thoroughly over the last three decades, partly as a result of developer-led excavation and partly through art-historical and archaeological approaches to extant masonry structures. The excavations, primarily undertaken between 1989 and 1991, were able to explore the pre-castle landscape, the south bailey and part of the motte of the castle itself, together with neighbouring elements of the borough (Fig. 4).[51] Occasionally the work, as well as uncovering substantial lost defensive works such as impressively deep ditches and part of a major stone gateway, also revealed surprising discoveries concerning known buildings. Notably, the great bridge leading to the motte was shown to be largely early 12th century in date with an arch some 15 m in height — now halved by ditch infill — and a diameter of some 12 m, favourably comparable in width to the great arch at Castle Hedingham, reputedly 'the broadest surviving Romanesque arch in Britain'.[52]

It can be argued, though, that the greatest single contribution of the excavations to understanding has been in the information now available about the inter-relationship of the castle complex and the urban area which surrounded it. Although the castle only had an active life as a military institution until 1345 at the latest, it nevertheless received several alterations and additions to its defensive arrangements. Similarly, urban tenements adjoining the castle precinct, in an area known as the Castle Fee (essentially an unfortified zone of royal land between the royal castle and the borough), underwent considerable change from the 12th century onwards. Such developments could be explored both through a comprehensive reappraisal of the surviving documentary evidence and through excavated features, deposits and artefacts. In consequence, the physical, social and economic relationships between the royal fortification and the surrounding community are now much better understood than hitherto, while the nature of the Castle Fee or Liberty itself has been further discussed with the support of a comprehensive overview of the available documentation.[53]

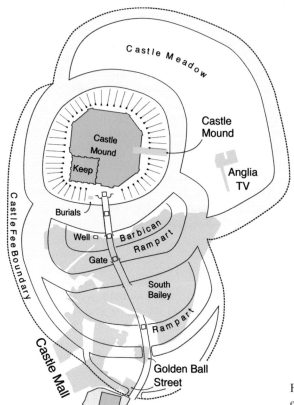

FIG. 4.   Plan showing extent of
excavations at Castle Mall
Norfolk Archaeological Unit

Considerable work has been undertaken on Norwich Castle keep in recent years, from study of its design aesthetic to excavation within the building. Understanding of the structure is hampered by loss of all its internal walls in the 18th century and unsympathetic exterior refacing in the 1830s. Nevertheless, considerable progress has been made by detailed study of the surviving fabric — and of the more recent work — with new discoveries such as a lost arcade in the southern compartment and an assessment of a previously unregarded but probably 14th-century door to the south-west stair.[54] In addition, the apparently anomalous location of the keep within the fortress can perhaps now be seen to be a result firstly of the earthwork history, an earlier mound beneath the keep being extended at the end of the 11th century, and secondly of a deliberate policy of providing a dramatic approach to the key building of the complex.

The civic defences of the city have not received the same attention as the castle. A summary overview was published recently, drawing together archaeological, architectural, documentary and illustrative references to the city walls, and an architectural survey, incorporating an assessment of early images of the walls, was undertaken between 1999 and 2002.[55] However, the only detailed archaeological survey has been that carried out on the Cow Tower. Here, examination of the interior wall fabric was accompanied by an assessment of the building accounts and enabled the published account to amplify earlier recognition of the monument as an early and rare artillery bastille.[56] Nearby, the fine ashlar stonework of the lower south face of the Bishopgate gate has been revealed by excavation and now remains exposed to public view, the only extant element (aside from Bishop's Bridge itself, of which it formed part) of the twelve medieval city gates. A thorough reassessment of the city walls, incorporating examination of innovative features such as 14th-century gun-loops as well as consideration of their relationship to both the urban and suburban environment, is overdue.

Increased awareness of the importance of a landscape context within the medieval environment has borne fruit with study of the great cathedral church and its attendant close. Documentary survey in the 1980s explored the manner in which the future bishops of Norwich acquired urban land in the late 11th century, land which formed the cathedral close and an extramural area known as the Prior's Fee.[57] Subsequently, a major survey of the growth and use of the cathedral close, utilizing both appraisal of extant buildings as well as documentary and illustrative records, provided an overview of a cathedral precinct seen as 'an exemplar for the contextual study of changing sacred space in a single institution'.[58] As a result of this work, it is now possible not only to view the cathedral church and its environs as a sacred site but also as a location divided into spaces with varying degrees of public, private and functional access. While the introduction of concepts such as 'boundedness' can be challenging, it is also useful to be reminded that the inherited topography of the close owes much to changing function, such as that enforced by the Reformation when, from the 1560s onwards, houses for prebends (now often married men rather than celibate ones) were fashioned out of buildings within the inner court such as the former infirmary chambers. These buildings were divided both horizontally and vertically, smaller rooms were created and large stacks were inserted.

Detailed archaeological survey prior to modern re-use has not only enabled a greater understanding of the medieval organization of such buildings (the hall and camera of the infirmarer were identified in 2001, for instance) but has also located other features such as the great drain of the cathedral precinct (some 2 m high and 1 m wide, barrel-vaulted in flint) and an early-16th-century painted ceiling.[59] Excavation in advance of works within the ruins of the refectory and the hostry has resulted in increased knowledge of the use and probable internal arrangements of the former, both in its monastic and post-monastic phases.[60] At the hostry, rebuilding of the Romanesque structure after a riot in 1272 could be identified.[61] Work at the hostry also uncovered part of the lay cemetery and, in further excavation within the precincts of Norwich School, the probable east boundary wall of the cemetery was found to have fallen, its flint-coursed structure fragmenting along the lines of constructional 'lifts' but otherwise surviving to its full height, capped with 17th-century pan-tile coping.[62]

Survey during conservation work of the cathedral church itself ensured that the original Romanesque design of the north transept could be elucidated, as could the 'design, construction and subsequent history' of the tower and spire.[63] Excavation has uncovered such details as a probable masons' yard and a painter's oyster shell palette.[64] Although found in a 16th-century pit, this object is likely to date to the 14th century or earlier and is paralleled by a further such palette of c. 1300 recovered from the Franciscan friary.[65] These discoveries, especially when they contain traces of the expensive pigments azurite and vermilion, as in the friary example, complement other work such as the paint analysis undertaken in the ante-reliquary chapel at the cathedral which established the use of significant quantities of these colours.[66]

Detailed study of the cathedral church has produced a range of works in recent years, notably Eric Fernie's magisterial assessment.[67] This has been supported by studies of the Romanesque building, its sculpture and the architectural influence of the building.[68] Coupled with revised understanding of the design aesthetic of the castle keep, the centrality of Norwich to architectural development in late-11th-century and early-12th-century England becomes ever more clear. The influence of the cathedral was naturally also felt locally; recent research argues that the distinctive quadrant pilasters on the cathedral church were probably the prototypes for the smaller versions found on many of the round-towered churches of Norfolk.[69]

The cathedral is a great church which survives, but Norwich had several other great churches which are lost. Carrow Priory, a 12th-century foundation for nuns, boasted the second-largest building after the cathedral church. Its footings were uncovered in the 19th century, but further work in 1981 consolidated the east end, slype, chapter-house and dormitory undercroft while also recording the graves of several nuns and a priest.[70] This was small-scale work, but more extensive excavation at both the Franciscan friary and the Carmelite friary has explored extensive areas of the claustral buildings of these institutions. Landscaping associated with the Franciscans has already been mentioned, but excavation also recorded a complex water management system which both distributed water through the precinct and removed waste from it.[71] At the Carmelite friary, the recovery of quantities of rare 14th-century window glass, together with lead cames and sculptural fragments, has enabled a discussion of the glazing of the friary, some of the glass quite possibly originating from a window known to have been donated by John of Gaunt.[72]

Another major church which has survived is that of St Helen, the building associated with the Great Hospital. This institution, originally established in 1249 and re-founded at the Reformation, uniquely retains most of its medieval structures and much of its archive. This fortunate happenstance has enabled ground-breaking research which exploits this juxtaposition of site and record, and establishes the Great Hospital as an exemplar for studies of medieval hospitals elsewhere.[73] The work also incorporates consideration of the setting of the hospital within the urban landscape, further increasing understanding by demonstrating how a medieval mentality could associate the location of the hospital on the road east towards a river bridge with the role of the institution as a broker between this life and the next.

Such insights into medieval mentality drawn from the built environment have been gleaned at the cathedral where it has been pointed out that Carnary chapel, once the location of an ossuary, is an architectural expression of a reliquary shrine, reinforcing linkage between corporeal existence and spiritual belief.[74] Similarly, recent assessment of the bosses in the east walk of the cathedral cloister suggests that the images were intended to prepare the viewer for judgement after death.[75] Further, it has been argued convincingly that the sculptural reliefs on the exterior of the Ethelbert Gate reference Isaiah's prophecies regarding the overthrow of Babylon, an apposite illustration when the cathedral priory was in conflict with the city.[76] Parish churches can also carry symbolic messages, such as the spandrels on the porch of St George Colegate where the saint is being armoured by angels, just as people entering the church will take on spiritual armour.[77] Interesting recent research has focused upon the responses of women to their environment and has highlighted the importance in the city of specific cults pertinent to female concerns, those of St Anne and St Margaret of Antioch (the former associated with conception and pregnancy, the latter with women in labour).[78] Images of both saints survive in the 15th-century painted glass at St Peter Mancroft, while

St Margaret is depicted in a panel painting from St Michael-at-Plea church, a cathedral wall-painting, a boss and a bench end at St Helen's church, and in the spandrels of the porch of St Margaret Westwick.

Notwithstanding such observations from parish buildings, in general the parochial churches of the city have not received the detailed attention afforded to the larger institutions. Of some sixty parish churches in the Middle Ages, thirty survive above ground for study and, within them, new discoveries and insights continue to be made. Two recent examples of increased knowledge concern the discovery of wall-paintings showing the four doctors of the church in St Gregory (a building already renowned for a large painting of St George)[79] and a major assessment of the glass of St Peter Mancroft.[80] However, an overarching assessment of the churches, providing an architectural and art-historical study linked to exploration of their development and inter-relationships, remains to be undertaken.

Comprehensive excavation has only been conducted on one church, the bombed and now demolished church of St Benedict.[81] Partial excavation at two others, St James and St Martin-at-Palace, has revealed details of the origins and development of the buildings, with reassessment of the discoveries in St Martin suggesting an alternative model for urban growth adjacent to the river.[82] Otherwise research has concentrated on particular aspects of the buildings: their location, their monuments and their porches among others.[83] Architectural assessments include a recent overview which incorporated evidence from both observation and documentary evidence[84] with occasional more detailed appraisals such as that published for St Peter Mancroft.[85]

Study of the parish churches therefore remains an under-utilized resource, but large-scale excavation of one churchyard, that associated with the lost church of St Margaret *in combusto* at the northern end of Magdalen Street, has greatly increased knowledge of the medieval urban population (Fig. 5). The church also bore the sobriquet *ubi sepeliunter suspensi* (where those who have been hanged are buried) because those executed outside Magdalen Gates had right of burial there. In consequence, excavation revealed a significant number of burials which were clearly associated with execution victims. Perhaps unsurprisingly, palaeopathological analysis indicated that the bulk of these individuals were relatively healthy young men.[86]

At Chapelfield, in the south-western quarter of the city, excavation uncovered a deep pit or well within which some seventeen individuals had been buried hastily in the 12th century. Eleven of these individuals were children, with two of them being under two years, a further three under five years, and three more under ten years. The circumstances of the burials indicated either poverty or crisis. Recent DNA analysis has suggested that five individuals shared a familial link and that this may have been Jewish.[87] The work indicates the potential of new forensic techniques when applied to medieval human bone assemblages.

Cemeteries can also suggest patterns of previously unknown urban development. Two discoveries in the vicinity of Tombland illustrate this. Excavation in 1988 uncovered part of a 13th-century graveyard which subsequent documentary research revealed to be an overspill area for the constrained churchyard of SS Simon and Jude, overspill actually established within the parish of St George Tombland.[88] Later work in 2007 located an unsuspected cemetery north of St George itself, almost certainly associated with the foundation of this church *c.* 1100.[89] It has long been supposed that the church took advantage of the truncation of the east-to-west line of Holmestrete, a Roman road cut by construction of the cathedral.[90] The 2007 work indicated that its

FIG. 5. Excavation of prone burials at the churchyard of St Margaret in combusto, Magdalen Street, Norwich

Norfolk Archaeological Unit

likely churchyard was originally much more extensive than previously envisaged, occupying the entire quadrant formed by the north-western part of Tombland, Waggon and Horses Lane and the truncated Holmestrete, although development seems to have crept over the excavated site by the late 1200s. Evidence for further development with three substantial townhouses was also discovered, paralleling the encroachment of presumed commercial stalls and subsequently shops on that part of St George's churchyard immediately east of the church (buildings which still stand albeit nearly all in a later form).

URBAN COMMERCE AND INDUSTRY

ARCHAEOLOGICAL discovery has contributed significantly to knowledge of the medieval urban economy, its infrastructure and products in recent decades. A summary of Norwich's industrial activity, drawing predominantly upon excavated material, was published in 1996.[91] Several key sites are the subject of individual reports. A dyeworks was excavated next to the river in the 1970s, dyeing being one of the cloth-finishing processes critical to the important textile industry of the city.[92] Other processes can be seen in ecofacts, artefacts and features recovered: seeds of *Reseda luteola* or Dyer's Rocket from St Martin-at-Palace Plain; iron woolcombs from Pottergate; a probable carding comb from Whitefriars; and possible retting of flax at Whitefriars Street (a pre-Conquest activity here).[93] Analysis of the late-13th- to early-14th-century enrolled deeds revealed some sixty-eight distinct crafts, industries, trades and services within Norwich.[94] Excavated evidence has been located for a number of these either through recovered products or working waste: iron slags, horn cores and a wooden mandrel or central core from turning a wooden bowl are three examples; or features specific to industrial activity, for instance a limekiln which was discovered off St Peter Street.[95]

The quality of Norwich products can still be assessed in a number of cases. Glass is the most obvious, with examples of high-quality window glass surviving in both city and county churches, most spectacularly in the east window of the church of St Peter Mancroft on the market-place. Indeed, the quality here is such that it can be argued that the glass gave the donor, the affluent cloth merchant Robert Toppes, 'an opportunity to illustrate his wares', the rich apparel of figures such as that of St Elizabeth being clearly depicted.[96] Other high-quality ecclesiastical production can be seen from the recovery of a large 14th-century Walsingham pilgrim badge mould fragment (Fig. 6), an artefact which was not only used to produce an intact badge found in London but one wherein the craftsmanship suggests an individual or workshop also responsible for badges commemorating the shrine of St Thomas Becket at Canterbury. The concept of Norwich production of localized material for a diverse national market has implications for broader understanding of the mechanics of the medieval economy, 'a further complication for those who would seek the simplest pattern of production locations for each variety of badge'.[97]

A major Norwich industry was the production of bells with numerous examples surviving in churches throughout Norfolk and beyond. Evidence for bell production has been uncovered at several locations, with bell pits located at Bishopgate, the Franciscan friary and within the graveyard of St John Timberhill. This church lies in an area of the city noted for the number of bell founders from the 13th century onwards.[98] A pit used for casting a bell was shown to date to the late 14th or early 15th century and bell-mould fragments confirmed that the process adopted was the false bell technique.[99] The Franciscan bell pit, which also used the false bell process and contained the *in situ* remains of a pedestal for casting, was located in a foundry together with metallurgical debris which suggested the casting of a range of vessels as well as bells. Archaeo-magnetic dating of 1490 to 1525 was sufficiently precise to suggest that the bell founder responsible was either Richard Brasyer the younger (who died in 1513) or his former apprentice, John Aleyn, who was active thereafter until at least the 1540s.[100]

As with industrial activity, archaeological evidence for commerce has also been summarized in a synthetic paper.[101] Excavated material has produced ceramics from Germany, the Low Countries and France, as well as Continental artefacts, such as a 16th-century German decorated powder-horn.[102] Contact with the Low Countries, clear from pottery finds, can perhaps also be surmised if the recent identification of the 15th-century building known as the Britons Arms on Elm Hill as a probable beguinage is correct.[103] Dendrochronological work in 2012–13 has established that the roof timbers of this building date to the first two decades of the 15th century and are fashioned from Baltic timber, a further example of commercial contacts.[104]

15

FIG. 6.   Pilgrim badge mould fragment
depicting the Annunciation excavated at
Cinema City, St Andrew's hill, Norwich
NPS Archaeology

Most of the trans-North Sea trade of Norwich was probably undertaken through shipping at Great Yarmouth.[105] Norwich did, however, retain its importance as a riverine port. The situation and orientation of Dragon Hall is sufficient to illustrate this, its 15th-century owner Robert Toppes having considerable estates in north-east Norfolk, and his warehouse complex was thus well situated to take advantage of the local, coasting and international trade. Indeed, archaeological evidence in such form, from either above-ground structures or below-ground discoveries, is necessary for an understanding of the relative importance of such trade as documentary records are poor, Norwich merchants being exempt from local customs accounts.[106] Revetments of willow and oak have been seen at Cannon Wharf, King Street, used to retain land-raising materials.[107] Regrettably, to date discoveries of waterfront installations remain minimal and comprehensive excavation of riverine commercial areas has not yet proved possible.

This lack of excavation is unfortunate; the anaerobic conditions of such riverine locations have potential for considerably enhancing understanding both of the background environment and of changes wrought by urban industrial and commercial activity. As examples of the potential, small-scale work at Whitefriars Street in 1979 uncovered evidence for early importation of both hop and walnut.[108] Information on transport might also be available; a 'rather wonderful eccentrically-perforated polygonal object of ash, probably a block from ship's rigging found within an early-to-mid 12th-century context' was located at Cannon Wharf and re-used boat timbers in an evaluation excavation at St Anne's Wharf, both off King Street.[109] In one instance, however, a small 'keyhole' excavation has proved very informative about the urban topography; work on Quayside, the only city-centre street now adjacent to the river, demonstrated that it not only owes its origin to a wharf constructed in the river marsh, but that its alignment was probably fixed as early as 1146.[110]

Management and control of trade within the city has long been explored within documents, while studies have also been made of buildings associated with governance as well as commerce, such as the Guildhall.[111] Reference to the extant corpus of mercantile undercrofts has been mentioned above, although the only detailed study to date remains an 'interim statement' and there is potential for further research.[112] Recently, elements of a medieval shop-front have been located in cellars below retail premises on Gaol Hill.[113] The building above has been identified as the early-18th-century Goldsmiths' Hall.[114] The courtyard complex quite probably reflects the footprint of its medieval predecessor, the goldsmiths having occupied the site since the 13th century.

POTENTIAL FOR FUTURE WORK

NORWICH was an exceptionally large medieval city by English standards, with diverse institutions and contacts and, accordingly, its potential for future research is wide-ranging. This research encompasses buried archaeology, consideration of the topography and townscape, standing buildings, architectural aesthetic and detailing, artefact investigation, palaeo-ecology and more.

The buried archaeology of the city, while rarely capable of exceptional preservation due to the well-drained and acidic soils, retains considerable potential for enhancing understanding of the demography, economy, social differentiation and culture of the city. The location of Norwich, close to the influence of Continental Europe, means that innovation — technological and environmental as well as cultural — can often be explored archaeologically, as can evidence for immigration as a factor in economic growth. Study of the development cycle is one for which archaeology is particularly suited, as has already been noted from the city where localized urban decay can be shown to have existed side-by-side with 'economic buoyancy'.[115] Other research themes, such as underlying structural change, population density and economic sustainability can also be informed by archaeological data.[116]

As importantly, there is considerable scope for broadening awareness of the influence and contribution of the various hinterlands of Norwich to the urban economy and society. An example might be found with the relationship of the cathedral to its estates. Recent publication of an assessment of the provisioning of the cathedral priory drew attention, inter alia, to the network of ecclesiastical landed estates and the likely manner in which this resource was exploited by the priory.[117] Archaeological evaluation of material located within the estates themselves (such as data collated from metal-detecting) might reveal unsuspected contacts between the urban and rural cultures. Night-soiling between urban and rural contexts is an as yet little-explored area but is starting to yield results in the hinterland of towns such as medieval Deventer in the Netherlands where waste disposal clearly placed urban-derived artefacts into rural deposits. Exploration of the wider rural area here has also enabled examination of the relationship between rural hop production and urban beer consumption in Deventer itself.[118]

Within Norwich, more specific research areas include a greater focus upon the extraordinary corpus of churches still extant in the city, the greatest concentration of medieval parish churches north of the Alps, with similar numbers now lost. A recently commissioned study of the setting of both standing and lost churches within the urban environment, linked to an examination of the chronology of church development and their stylistic interdependence, has great potential for enhancing understanding of their social, economic and civic roles.[119] Exploration of other aspects of church development of relevance to development elsewhere within the city can also be followed: the acquisition and use of raw materials; plotting of wealth distribution; the impact of corporate activity; and the effects of the Reformation (for example excavation of secular buildings off Palace Street in 2006 recovered a Papal Bulla, a stone ecclesiastical stoop and a collection of 16th-century glassware, 'objects that seem to have been jettisoned at the Dissolution'[120]).

The impact of corporate activity is a factor to be considered in looking at the city's defences and other urban infrastructure. Further, the development and use of specialized markets must have grown from the variety of goods for sale, and archaeological work can therefore examine urban influence on commerce and wider society. Industrial productivity and product distribution can be explored as can urban specialization and the dissemination of urban values. Indeed, as has been demonstrated above, exploration of medieval urban mentalities themselves are possible given the rich diversity of the urban archaeological resource within and around Norwich.

Finally, archaeological methodologies themselves need to be explored, examined, dissected and reconstructed to ensure that new understandings can emerge from accumulated data. Scandinavian colleagues have been early adopters of such practice; an assessment of waste disposal management, for instance, was undertaken for medieval Norwegian towns some twenty-five years ago.[121] More recently, Larsson has expanded discussion of potential with an essay examining such concepts as the nature of urban power, moving from an archaeological position which merely describes the effects of power to one where power relationships are investigated. His example is the town of Lund, where study of prominent buildings and the urban topography has led him to suggest 'a bounding and regulation of space' as 'a way of mediating the hierarchy of social order'.[122] A similar approach has already been adopted for Norwich Cathedral close by Gilchrist[123] and exploration through material culture of the concepts of community, status, power, values and spirituality is the subject of a paper by the present writer.[124] Norwich is well placed for enhanced study of its medieval past in such areas. It has a rich archaeological environment, previous examination of which is well published in comparison to many towns, a diverse tradition of exploration, and hinterlands with much untapped information. Study of the city continues to reveal much that is new and which contributes to a wider appreciation of the complexity of medieval society.

NOTES

1. J. Campbell, 'Norwich', in *Historic Towns*, ed. M. D. Lobel (London 1974), 8ff.; S. Kelly, 'The Economic Topography and Structure of Norwich c. 1300', in *Men of Property: An analysis of the Norwich enrolled deeds 1285–1311*, ed. U. Priestley (Norwich 1983), 13–39.

2. E. Rutledge, 'Immigration and population growth in early fourteenth-century Norwich: evidence from the tithing roll', *Urban History*, 15 (1988), 15–30.

3. B. Green, *Norwich: the growth of a city* (Norwich 1963; rev. edn 1981).

4. B. Ayers, 'The growth of an urban landscape: recent research in early medieval Norwich', *Early Medieval Europe*, 19/1 (2011), 62–90.

5. A. Carter, 'The Anglo-Saxon Origins of Norwich: The Problems and Approaches', *Anglo-Saxon England*, 7 (1978), 175–204.

6. A. Carter, 'Sampling in a medieval town: the Study of Norwich', in *Sampling in Contemporary British Archaeology*, ed. J. F. Cherry, C. Gamble and S. Shennan, BAR British Series 50 (Oxford 1978), 263–77.

7. E. Shepherd Popescu, *Norwich Castle: Excavations and Historical Survey, 1987–98*, EAA, 132 (Dereham 2009).

8. Planning Policy Guidance 16: Archaeology & Planning (1990); now superseded and archived at: http://webarchive.nationalarchives.gov.uk/20120919132719/http://www.communities.gov.uk/publications/planningandbuilding/ppg16.

9. B. Ayers, 'Anglo-Saxon, Medieval and Post-Medieval (Urban)', in *Research and Archaeology: A framework for the Eastern Counties, Part 1 resource assessment*, ed. J. Glazebrook, EAA Occasional Paper, 3 (Norwich 1997), 59–66; B. Ayers, 'Anglo-Saxon, Medieval and Post-Medieval (Urban)', *Research and Archaeology: A framework for the Eastern Counties, Part 2 research agenda and strategy*, ed. N. Brown and J. Glazebrook, EAA Occasional Paper, 8 (Norwich 2000), 27–32.

10. D. Perring, *Town and Country in England: frameworks for archaeological research*, Council for British Archaeology, Research Report 132 (York 2002).

11. Shepherd Popsecu, *Norwich Castle* (as in n. 7); P. Emery, *Norwich Greyfriars: Pre-Conquest Town and Medieval Friary*, EAA, 120 (Dereham 2007); A. Shelley, *Dragon Hall, King Street, Norwich: Excavation and Survey of a Late Medieval Trading Complex*, EAA, 112 (Norwich 2005).

12. C. King, 'House and Society in an English Provincial City: The Archaeology of Urban Households in Norwich, 1370–1700' (unpublished Ph.D. thesis, University of Nottingham, 2006).

13. Gilchrist, *Close*.

14. D. King, *The Medieval Stained Glass of St Peter Mancroft Norwich*, Corpus Vitrearum Medii Aevi (Oxford 2006).

15. A. Stirland ed., *Criminals and Paupers: the Graveyard of St Margaret Fyebriggate in combusto, Norwich*, EAA, 129 (Dereham 2009).

16. B. Ayers, *Norwich: Archaeology of a Fine City* (Stroud 2009).

17. Ayers, 'Growth' (as in n. 4), 83.

18. Ibid., 70, fig. 4.

19. *Domesday Book: Norfolk*, ed. P. Brown (Chichester 1984), 118a.

20. M. Tillyard, 'Documentary Evidence', in *Excavations at St Martin-at-Palace Plain, Norwich*, ed. B. Ayers, EAA, 37 (Dereham 1987), 134–50.

21. Carter, 'Anglo-Saxon Origins' (as in n. 5), 185, fig. 4.

22. Ayers, 'Growth' (as in n. 4), 83; B. Ayers, 'The Urban landscape', in *Medieval Norwich*, 10.

23. David Adams, pers. comm.

24. M. W. Atkin, 'Excavations on Alms Lane (Site 302N)', in *Excavations in Norwich Part II*, ed. M. W. Atkin, A. Carter and D. H. Evans, EAA, 26 (Norwich 1985), 149ff.

25. B. Ayers, 'Archaeological and Historical Context', in *Criminals and Paupers* (as in n. 15), 36.

26. B. Ayers, *Excavations at Fishergate, Norwich, 1985*, EAA, 68 (Dereham 1994), 4–7 and fig. 4.

27. D. Adams, 'Archaeological Evaluation at Site of Proposed Community Hall, adjacent to the Medieval Cloisters, The Great Hospital, Bishopgate, Norwich' (unpublished NAU Archaeology Report No. 2180b, 2012), context 59 on fig. 6, and 12 and 27.

28. A. Shelley, 'An Evaluation at Cannon Wharf, King Street, Norwich' (unpublished NAU Archaeology Report No. 296, 1997).

29. David Adams, pers. comm.

30. Fran Green, pers. comm.

31. Ayers, *Fishergate* (as in n. 26), 76–77 and 80.

32. B. Ayers, *Digging Deeper* (Norwich 1987), 10.

33. Ayers, *St Martin-at-Palace Plain* (as in n. 20), 58 and fig. 52.

34. R. Smith and A. Carter, 'Function and Site: aspects of Norwich buildings before 1700', *Vernacular Architecture*, 14 (1983), 5–18.

35. B. Nenk, S. Margeson and M. Hurley ed., 'Medieval Britain and Ireland in 1991', *Med. Archaeol.*, 36 (1992), 253.

36. Emery, *Norwich Greyfriars* (as in n. 11), 65–66 and figs 3.8 and 3.16.

37. Shepherd Popescu, *Norwich Castle* (as in n. 7), 418.

38. H. Wallis, *Excavations on the site of Norwich Cathedral Refectory, 2001–3*, EAA, 116 (Dereham 2006), 9–10 and figs 9 and 10; Emery, *Norwich Greyfriars* (as in n. 11), 26ff., fig. 2.20 and pls 2.6 and 2.7; A. Shelley, 'The Austin Friars', *Current Archaeology*, 170 (2000), 84–85.

39. D. Adams, 'An Archaeological Excavation at the former Bussey's Garage, Palace Street, Norwich' (unpublished NAU Archaeology Report No. 1376, 2008), 40–48 and pl. 6.

40. Ayers, *St Martin-at-Palace Plain* (as in n. 20), 153.

41. R. Smith, 'The Music House', Vernacular Architecture Group Papers for the Spring Conference 1997 (unpublished).

42. V. D. Lipman, *The Jews of Medieval Norwich* (London 1967), 106.

43. Ayers, *St Martin-at-Palace Plain* (as in n. 20), 26ff.

44. E. Rutledge, 'The Early Stone House in Norwich: the documentary evidence', in *La Maison Médiévale en Normandie et en Angleterre/The Medieval House in Normandy and England*, ed. D. Pitte and B. Ayers (Rouen 2002), 103–10 and fig. 1; A. Hutcheson, 'The French Borough', *Current Archaeology*, 170 (2000), 67.

45. Atkin, 'Alms Lane' (as in n. 24), 144–260; M. Atkin, 'Medieval Clay-Walled Building in Norwich', *NA*, 41 (1991), 171–85.

46. D. Evans and A. Carter, 'Excavations on 31–51 Pottergate (Site 149N)', in *Excavations in Norwich Part II* (as in n. 24), 8–85.

47. A. Quiney, *Town Houses of Medieval Britain* (New Haven and London 2003); J. Schofield, *Medieval London Houses* (New Haven and London 1995).

48. C. King, 'The interpretation of urban buildings: power, memory and appropriation in Norwich merchants' houses, c. 1400–1660', *World Archaeology*, 41/3 (2009), 484–85.

49. C. King, '"Closure" and the urban great rebuilding in early modern Norwich', *Post-Medieval Archaeology*, 44.1 (2010), 73–74.

50. B. Ayers, 'Understanding the Urban Environment: Archaeological Approaches to Medieval Norwich', in *Medieval East Anglia*, ed. C. Harper-Bill (Woodbridge 2005), 78.

51. Shepherd Popescu, *Norwich Castle* (as in n. 7); H. Wallis, 'Excavations in Norwich Castle Mound' (in prep.)

52. A. Shelley, 'Norwich Castle Bridge', *Med. Archaeol.*, 40 (1996), 217–26 and figs 7 and 8; J. Goodall, *The English Castle* (New Haven and London 2011), 121.

53. Shepherd Popescu, *Norwich Castle* (as in n. 7), 459ff. and 1054ff.; E. Shepherd Popescu, 'Norwich Castle Fee', *Med. Archaeol.*, 48 (2004), 209–19.

54. T. A. Heslop, *Norwich Castle Keep: Romanesque Architecture and Social Context* (Norwich 1994); P. Drury, 'Norwich Castle Keep', in *The Seigneurial Residence in Western Europe AD c. 800–1600*, ed. G. Meirion-Jones, E. Impey and M. Jones, BAR International Series 1088 (Oxford 2002), 211–34; P. Dixon and P. Marshall, 'Norwich castle and its analogues', in ibid., 235–43; B. Ayers, '"... traces of the original disposition of the whole". Excavated Evidence for the Construction of Norwich Castle Keep', in *Proceedings of 2012 Conference at Norwich Castle*, ed. J. Davies (Norfolk Museums Service, forthcoming); O. Rackham, 'Door in Norwich Castle' (unpublished assessment report 1999).

55. B. Ayers, 'The fortifications of medieval and early modern Norwich', in *Lübecker Kolloquium zur Stadtarchäologie im Hanseraum VII: Die Befestigungen*, ed. M. Gläser (Lübeck 2010), 29–46; the city walls survey is located at http://www.norwich.gov.uk/apps/CityWalls/.

56. B. Ayers, R. Smith, and M. Tillyard, 'The Cow Tower, Norwich: a detailed survey and partial reinterpretation', *Med. Archaeol.*, 32 (1988), 184–207; A. D. Saunders, 'The Cow Tower, Norwich: an East Anglian bastille?', *Med. Archaeol.*, 29 (1985), 109–19.

57. Tillyard, 'Documentary Evidence' (as in n. 7), 134–36 and fig. 96.

58. Gilchrist, *Close*, 11.

59. J. Bradley and M. Gaimster, 'Medieval Britain and Ireland in 2001', *Med. Archaeol.*, 46 (2002), 195; Ayers, *Norwich* (as in n. 16), 80.

60. Wallis, *Norwich Cathedral Refectory* (as in n. 38).

61. S. Morgan, 'An Archaeological Excavation at The Hostry, Norwich Cathedral' (unpublished NAU Archaeology Report No. 1266a, 2008), available at http://hbsmrgateway2.esdm.co.uk/norfolk/DataFiles/Docs/AssocDoc6110.pdf.

62. D. Gurney ed., 'Excavations and Survey in Norfolk in 2006', *NA*, 45 (2007), 268–69.

63. R. Gilchrist, 'Norwich Cathedral: a biography of the north transept', *JBAA*, 151 (1999), 107–36; R. Gilchrist, 'Norwich Cathedral Tower and Spire: Recording and Analysis of a Cathedral's Longue Durée', *Archaeol. J.*, 158 (2001), 291–324.

64. J. Bown, 'Excavations on the North Side of Norwich Cathedral, 1987–88', *NA*, 43 (1998), 428–52; S. Cather, 'Oyster shell palette', in Wallis, *Norwich Cathedral Refectory* (as in n. 38), 72–73.

65. H. Howard, 'Medieval oyster shell palette', in Emery, *Norwich Greyfriars* (as in n. 11), 139–43.

66. D. Park and H. Howard, 'The Medieval Polychromy', in *Norwich Cathedral 1096–1996*, 379–409.

67. Fernie, *AHNC*.

68. S. Heywood, 'The Romanesque Building', in *Norwich Cathedral 1096–1996*, 73–115; J. A. Franklin, 'The Romanesque Sculpture', ibid., 116–35; M. Thurlby, 'The Influence of the Cathedral on Romanesque Architecture', ibid., 136–57; J. A. Franklin, 'The Eastern Arm of Norwich Cathedral and the Augustinian Priory of St Bartholomew's, Smithfield, in London', *Antiq. J.*, 86 (2006), 110–30.

69. S. Heywood, 'Towers and Radiating Chapels in Romanesque Architectural Iconography', in *Architecture and Interpretation: Essays for Eric Fernie*, ed. J. A. Franklin, T. A. Heslop and C. Stevenson (Woodbridge 2012), 99–110.

70. M. Atkin and S. Margeson, 'A 14th-century pewter chalice and paten from Carrow Priory, Norwich', *NA*, 38 (1983), 374–79.

71. Emery, *Norwich Greyfriars* (as in n. 11), 75–79 and 83.

72. R. Clarke, 'Norwich Whitefriars: Medieval Friary and Baptist Burial Ground. Excavations at Jarrold's Printing Works, Norwich 2002–03' (EAA forthcoming).

73. C. Rawcliffe, *Medicine for the Soul: the Life, Death and Resurrection of an English Medieval Hospital* (Stroud 1999).

74. Gilchrist, *Close*, 250.

75. S. Mittuch, 'The Norwich Book of the Dead', *British Archaeology*, 92 (2007), 46–49.

76. V. Sekules, 'Religious Politics and the Cloister Bosses of Norwich Cathedral', *JBAA*, 159 (2006), 284–306.

77. B. Ayers, 'Status, Power and Values: archaeological approaches to understanding the medieval urban community', in *Lübeck und der Hanseraum: Festschrift für Manfred Gläser*, ed. M. Schneider (Lübeck and Kiel 2014), 223–33.

78. C. Hill, *Women and Religion in Late Medieval Norwich* (Woodbridge 2010).

79. Ayers, *Norwich* (as in n. 16), pl. 24.

80. King, *Mancroft Glass* (as in n. 14).

81. J. P. Roberts and M. Atkin, 'St Benedict's Church (Site 157N)', in *Excavations in Norwich 1971–1978 Part I*, EAA, 15 (Norwich 1982), 11–29.

82. M. Atkin, 'St James' Church, Pockthorpe (Site 415N)', in *Excavations in Norwich 1971–1978 Part I* (as in n. 81), 130–37; O. Beazley, 'Excavations in St Martin-at-Palace Church, 1987', in *Two Medieval Churches in Norfolk*, EAA, 96 (Dereham 2001), 63; D. Stocker and P. Everson, 'Erratics and Enterprise', in the present volume.

83. B. Ayers, 'Understanding' (as in n. 50), 75–76; J. Finch, *Church Monuments in Norfolk before 1850: An Archaeology of Commemoration*, BAR British Series 317 (2000); H. E. Lunnon, 'Defining Porches in Norwich, *c*. 1250–*c*. 1510', in the present volume.

84. J. Finch, 'The Churches', in *Medieval Norwich*, 49–72.

85. F. Woodman, 'The Rebuilding of St Peter Mancroft', in *East Anglian Studies: Essays presented to J. C. Barringer on his Retirement*, ed. A. Longcroft and R. Joby (Norwich 1995), 290–95.

86. Stirland, *Criminals and Paupers* (as in n. 15), 129.

87. Press report at http://www.bbc.co.uk/news/uk-1385523800.

88. D. Gaimster, S. Margeson and T. Barry ed., 'Medieval Britain and Ireland in 1988', *Med. Archaeol.*, 33 (1989), 203.

89. J. Ames, 'An Archaeological Excavation at Samson and Hercules House, Tombland, Norwich' (unpublished NAU Archaeology Report No. 1681a, 2008). Available at http://hbsmrgateway2.esdm.co.uk/norfolk/DataFiles/Docs/AssocDoc4821.pdf.

90. B. Ayers, 'The Cathedral Site before 1066', in *Norwich Cathedral 1096–1996*, 65.

91. B. Ayers, 'Craft industry in Norwich from the 12th to the 18th century', in *Lübecker Kolloquium zur Stadtarchäologie im Hanseraum V: Das Handwerk*, ed. M. Gläser (Lübeck 2006), 27–46.

92. M. Atkin, 'The Industrial Features', in M. Atkin, 'Excavations on The Bottling Plant, Westwick Street (Site 159N)', in *Excavations in Norwich 1971–1978 Part III*, ed. M. W. Atkin, A. Carter and D. H. Evans, EAA, 100 (Norwich 2002), 151.

93. P. Murphy, 'Industry', in Ayers, *St Martin-at-Palace Plain* (as in n. 20), 133; S. Margeson, *Norwich Households: The Medieval and Post-Medieval Finds from Norwich Survey Excavations 1971–1978*, EAA, 58 (1993), 182 and fig. 134; J. Huddle, 'Medieval Long-tooth Comb', in B. Ayers and P. Emery, 'Excavations at Jarrold's Printing Works, Whitefriars, Norwich, 1992', *NA*, 43 (1999), 283–84; B. Ayers and P. Murphy, *A Waterfront Excavation at Whitefriars Street Car Park, Norwich, 1979*, EAA, 17 (Dereham 1983), 47.

94. Kelly, 'Economic Topography' (as in n. 1), 16.

95. Ayers, 'Craft industry' (as in n. 91), 31–43; A. Hutcheson, 'The French Borough', *Current Archaeology*, 170 (2000), 64–68.

96. B. Ayers, 'Lifestyle! Luxury in medieval Norwich', in *Lübecker Kolloquium zur Stadtarchäologie im Hanseraum VI: Luxus und Lifestyle*, ed. M. Gläser (Lübeck 2008), 36.

97. G. Egan, 'Stone Moulds from Pit [57]', in H. Wallis, 'Excavations at Cinema City, Norwich, 2003–06: Late Saxon and Medieval Occupation', *NA*, 45 (2009), 478–82 and fig. 9.

98. Shepherd Popescu, *Norwich Castle* (as in n. 7), 555.

99. T. Jennings and C. Mortimer, 'Bell Mould Fragments', in Shepherd Popescu, *Norwich Castle* (as in n. 7), 580 and figs 8.22 and 8.23.

100. Emery, *Norwich Greyfriars* (as in n. 11), 122–25 and fig. 3.18.

101. B. Ayers, 'Archaeological evidence for trade in Norwich from the 12th to the 17th centuries', in *Lübecker Kolloquium zur Stadtarchäologie im Hanseraum II: Der Handel*, ed. M. Gläser (Lübeck 1999), 25–35. This work appeared prior to more recent work such as the monograph on Dragon Hall, the 15th-century mercantile complex on King Street of which the main building still stands, see Shelley, *Dragon Hall* (as in n. 11).

102. S. Jennings, *Eighteen centuries of pottery from Norwich*, EAA, 13 (Norwich 1981), 30–35; Shepherd Popescu, *Norwich Castle* (as in n. 7), 888–89 and fig. 10.71.

103. King, 'House and Society' (as in n. 12), 6.3.2.

104. Information from Rory Quinn and Janet Jury, pers. comm.

105. P. Dunn, 'Trade', in *Medieval Norwich*, 225.

106. Ibid., 228.

107. M. Gaimster, C. Haith and J. Bradley, 'Medieval Britain and Ireland in 1997', *Med. Archaeol.*, 42 (1998), 146; A. Shelley, pers. comm.

108. Ayers and Murphy, *Waterfront Excavation* (as in n. 93), 40–42.

109. A. Shelley, pers. comm.

110. Ayers, *Growth* (as in n. 4), 20.

111. H. Sutermeister, *The Norwich Guildhall* (Norwich n.d.).

112. Smith and Carter, 'Function and Site' (as in n. 34), 5.

113. Robert Smith, pers. comm. and observation by the writer.

114. C. Garibaldi, 'The guildhall of the Norwich company of goldsmiths', in *East Anglian Silver 1550–1750*, ed. C. Hartop (Cambridge 2004), 31–35.

115. K. D. Lilley, 'Decline or decay? Urban landscapes in late-medieval England', in *Towns in Decline AD 100–1600*, ed. T. R. Slater (Aldershot 2000), 250.

116. Ayers, 'Anglo-Saxon, Medieval and Post-Medieval (Urban)', Part 2 (as in n. 9), 27–32.

117. P. Slavin, 'Bread and Ale for the Brethren: The provisioning of Norwich Cathedral Priory 1260–1536', *University of Hertfordshire Studies in Regional and Local History*, 11 (2012).

118. T. A. Spitzers, 'Archaeological evidence and models on waste disposal and the infrastructure of Deventer', in *Lübecker Kolloquium zur Stadtarchäologie im Hanseraum IV: Die Infrastruktur*, ed. M. Gläser (Lübeck 2004), 117–20 and fig. 2; M. Bartels, 'De Hopplantage op de Rielerenk en de Consumptie van Hopbier in Middeleeuws Deventer', *Rapportages Archeologie Deventer*, 21 (2007), 95–112.

119. The project, funded by the Leverhulme Trust, is being undertaken through the University of East Anglia from September 2014.

120. Adams, *Palace Street* (as in n. 39) and pers. comm.

121. P. Molaug, 'On the representativity of artefacts found during excavations in Norwegian medieval towns', in *Archaeology and the urban economy. Festschrift to Asbjørn E. Herteig*, Arkeologiske Skrifter 5 fra Historisk Museum Universitetet i Bergen (1989), 229–44.

122. S. Larsson, 'Theoretical and Methodological Directions in Urban archaeology: the Case of Lund, Sweden', in *Archaeology of Medieval Towns in the Baltic and North Sea Area*, ed. N. Engberg, A. N. Jorgensen, J. Kieffer-Olsenm, P. K. Madsen and C. Radtke, Publications of the National Museum Studies in Archaeology and History 17 (2009), 167–79.

123. Gilchrist, *Close*.

124. Ayers, 'Status, Power and Values' (as in n. 77), 223–33.

Erratics and Enterprise: Lincolnshire Grave-Covers in Norwich and Thetford and Some Implications for Urban Development in the 10th Century

PAUL EVERSON and DAVID STOCKER

This paper identifies a group of fragments of late Anglo-Scandinavian stone sculpture excavated at the church of St Martin-at-Palace-Plain in Norwich in 1987 as known grave-cover types imported from Lindsey. It is suggested that they can be seen as monuments erected by an alien merchant community to mark burials in distinctive fashion. The analogy is drawn with a number of major trading centres of northern and eastern England, including Lincoln and York, where this phenomenon has been observed. Similar monument types from late Anglo-Scandinavian Thetford are then also identified, and it is noted that all these comparable towns exploit their local topography in very similar ways. Returning to Norwich, it is noted that St Martin's church occupies a similar contemporary topography to these other examples, and that we can therefore suggest revisions to the received understanding of the development of the pre-Conquest town.

It takes a long time for the details of archaeological research to enter the mainstream of debate. Scholars take time to catch up with their reading and often remain unaware of important discoveries long after they are first made. Such an oversight was committed by the two authors of this paper in respect of the excavations undertaken by Olwyn Beazley at the parochial church of St Martin-at-Palace-Plain in Norwich in 1987. These exemplary excavations were duly written up and published, as one would expect, within ten years of the excavation finishing.[1] Unfortunately, the importance of two particular stone finds from the site was not recognized at the time by either of us, even though they turn out to be of more than local significance. This paper is intended to put the record straight: to draw attention to their importance and to discuss the contribution they might make to understanding the development of Norwich in the 10th century. In the process we can compare Norwich's development with contemporary towns in eastern and northern England, and in particular with Thetford, 25 miles to the south west, with which it is so closely linked historically.

THE STONES

THE stones in question are five fragments from two monumental grave-covers. They are carved from Jurassic limestone from the Lincoln Edge, probably from the quarries surrounding the city of Lincoln itself, as they contain distinctive fossil bivalves which are unique to this zone of quarries.[2]

The first grave-cover is represented by four fragments. It actually retains the entire thickness of the original slab of stone, as well as part of one original long side and a fragment of one end, though whether the head or the foot it is not possible to say. The upper surface was originally decorated with interlace sculpture in low relief. It retains a short length of single 'cable' moulding along the surviving long edge and it is likely that such a border moulding once surrounded the interlace decoration on all sides. Within the cabled border moulding, the whole of one sculpted figure-of-eight interlace unit survives along with much of a second. The interlace strands are of pronounced 'U' section and the interstices are broad flat tables, making the strands themselves stand out clearly against the background, in a manner that is characteristic of the many other members of the monument group to which this stone clearly belongs. The surviving figure-of-eight unit is of a size comfortably within the close range found in the group. Based on the twenty-three other examples known, we have reconstructed the likely original appearance of the monument from which this fragment comes (Fig. 1). As this shows, the original monument would have been a rectangular slab of stone about 1500 mm long by 500 mm wide, and with a thickness of 125 mm. Any taper within the stone would have been marginal.

The second early monument recovered from St Martin's has the same petrology and is also probably from a grave-cover. It is somewhat more problematic to interpret, although it seems highly unlikely to us that Sue Margeson's published understanding of the fragment can be correct.[3] She interpreted the curving lines within the cable-moulded border as 'drapery', but there are no examples of grave-covers decorated with figures of the type she apparently envisages for another four centuries. Rather, this stone too seems to be a fragment from a second well-understood grave-cover type produced at the Lincoln quarries, and the curving lines, we suggest, represent the distinctive 'splayed foot' of the cross depicted on many of these monuments (Fig. 2).[4] This type of cover, we suggested in our Lincolnshire *Corpus*, would have been approximately contemporary with the first cover, although its date-range is somewhat broader and probably extended right up until the Norman Conquest, if not to the end of the 11th century.

In that same *Corpus* volume, our detailed consideration of the distinctive group of grave-covers to which the first of the new stones from St Martin's belongs drew attention to the uniformity of design across the group as a whole, with its three columns of 'figure-of-eight' interlace motifs.[5] We were able to demonstrate that the minor differences in border and grouping of units permitted the identification of three sub-types within the group. With its single-cabled border, the grave-cover from St Martin's belongs to what we termed 'sub-type b', which now numbers nine examples. Through an extended discussion of the typology of the late Anglo-Saxon grave-covers of Lincolnshire, we were able to date this entire group of monuments to the period between the later 10th and early 11th centuries. The output may have spanned the period from *c*. 975 to *c*. 1025. While it is not possible to be precise, its production probably post-dated the restoration of a bishopric of Lindsey in 953 and the stone may have derived from quarries under the bishop's control in Lincoln. These monuments represent a distinctive and interesting group of sculptures, but the most salient fact about them is their restricted geographical distribution. When we wrote up the group in the early 1990s, stones from Coates in Nottinghamshire (just over the Trent, here

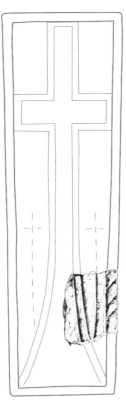

FIG. 1.   (*left*) Reconstruction of stone fragments from St Martin-at-Palace-Plain, Norwich, as a Lindsey cover of type 'b'

FIG. 2.   (*right*) Reconstruction of stone fragment from St Martin-at-Palace-Plain, Norwich, as a Lincoln type of grave-cover

the Lindsey boundary) and Thetford, were not known to us, though they had been discovered *c.*1900 and in the 1950s or 1960s respectively. Consequently, all of the examples we had registered were located within the bounds of the former kingdom and later bishopric of Lindsey. As a result, we called the entire monument type the 'Lindsey covers'; a name which has now found its way into the literature more widely.[6] Furthermore, the pattern is not broken locally by the finds from Coates, since — arriving as imported rubble for a secular reuse in the early 19th century — they most probably derive from one of the demolished medieval churches and reoccupied graveyards in Torksey, just across the river on the Lindsey bank.[7]

Discovery of the second grave-cover that appears to come from the same group of quarries at the same Norwich church enhances the interest of the more complete example. Despite the fact that the form of this second monument is less certain, and that the group to which it belongs is less distinctive or easily mapped, its origin in the same distant group of quarries as the first stone must nevertheless raise a number of important questions about the geographical reach of early Norwich citizens and thus about the establishment of trade in this place in the late 10th and early 11th centuries.

First, we need to understand the archaeological context of these discoveries. Of the five stones that make up these two monuments, one came from an unstratified context whilst a further three were discovered in the backfill of various grave-cuts and other features in the church floor, mostly of medieval date. One fragment of the Lindsey cover, however, was reused in the packing material around one of the posts in the phase II building that pre-dates the earliest stone church on the site. This was considered by the excavators to represent its timber predecessor and to be of 11th-century date.[8] The context of this one stone establishes the presence of the whole monument at St Martin's in its earliest phases.

All freestone had to be imported into Norwich. One possible means by which the stones were carried from Lindsey is as broken rubble — 'small ballast' — in the hold of a ship; a phenomenon of which Paul Buckland has taught us to be aware.[9] Such ballast might have been abandoned in Norwich in favour of a more commercial cargo on the return leg, such as pottery. However, according to Buckland, such ballast was usually dumped in a single location at or near the quayside. Had this material arrived in Norwich in this manner, mixed and pre-broken, the likelihood that adjoining fragments of the same original monument would have remained together during a second or third transportation to the site of St Martin's seems highly questionable. Furthermore, the St Martin's grave-covers bear the marks of deep and localized calcination, and this suggests that they were first broken up using the method of lighting a fire on the upper surface and then dousing it with water to make the stone split. This method appears to be more typical of systematic recycling of stone *in situ*, especially in cases — as here — where we have adjoining stones from both sides of the fracture.[10]

The more obvious interpretation of the St Martin's finds is therefore that these scrappy remains of two large stone grave-covers indicate that there was a graveyard on this site prior to the construction of its 11th-century timber church and that its monuments were cleared and broken up to construct the timber church of that date. Indeed, this graveyard might have been associated with an even earlier timber church, traces of which the excavators discovered further to the south. This graveyard itself, it seems, was even earlier in date, and may originally have been established in the 9th century, before burials here were marked with stone markers.[11] It is just possible that these stones came to St Martin's from another local graveyard; but, in the absence of any evidence or inherent likelihood to that effect, we presume that the graves that the covers originally marked lay in the pre-existing graveyard of St Martin's, and that they were broken up by fire in this vicinity about the time of the construction of the phase II timber church here in the mid-11th century.

All this suggests that, at some moment early in the history of St Martin's as a burial ground, two important Norwich residents were interred beneath expensive, imported monuments of distinctively 'Lindsey' or Lincoln type. In Lincolnshire, we have interpreted this sort of occurrence of one or two early stone monuments, mostly in rural situations, as the evidence of 'founders' graves' of new churches and graveyards, on the pattern revealed in the excavations at Raunds Furnells site in Northamptonshire.[12] Stone monuments were certainly imported into rural Norfolk and can be found in small numbers at individual sites in just this way; and in those cases we should undoubtedly wish to propose a similar interpretation.[13] But at St Martin's an alternative understanding of the circumstances, we suggest, is preferable. This form of burial, beneath a substantial sculpted stone grave-cover, was most unusual in 10th-century Norwich. These are the only grave-covers — or indeed stone funerary sculpture of the second half of the 10th century of any sort — that have emerged from the town. There is only one other stone of comparable pre-Conquest date from here, namely the so-called 'St Vedast stone', now displayed at the Castle Museum (accession number 1896.75).[14] Fashioned in a reddy-brown Pennine gritstone, this too is an import; this time of a distinctively Anglo-Scandinavian monument from the North Midlands or Northumbria. Through the conventional typologies for such things it would usually be dated a couple of generations earlier than the two covers from St Martin's.[15] We are less certain where this item originally came from. It was recovered when a domestic building at the north-west corner of the junction of Rose Lane and Cathedral Street South was demolished to allow street widening in 1896. Hudson reports that the house itself was 'not a very old one', but, wishing to associate the stone with the lost church of St Vedast, proposes that the wall incorporating it was older and possibly formed the enclosing wall of the abandoned churchyard of St Vedast's, which was itself demolished in the 16th century and its cure absorbed into St Peter Parmentergate.[16] Brian Ayers, for one, is not convinced that this important monument came from the church of St Vedast;[17] and once it is freed from that association it might have come from anywhere in the city, and might as well fall into the context discussed below for the covers from St Martin's.

Like the 'St Vedast' monument, the St Martin's grave-covers are very distinctive. So distinctive and, within England, so clearly do they belong to Lindsey, that the use of such a monument in Norwich must surely imply that the deceased (or more correctly the deceased's kin?) wished to be commemorated as originating in these remote parts. That is, they were not simply residents of the developing town, but more specifically they were resident aliens: that is to say, merchants.[18]

ST MARTIN'S AND THE EARLY TOWN

THE topographical location of St Martin's and its associations lends crucial support to the proposition that these monuments might represent early members of Norwich's mercantile community. In another paper, and building on observations first made in our Lincolnshire *Corpus*, one of us has considered the relationship between notable concentrations of simple late Anglo-Scandinavian monuments of the type represented by the Lindsey covers and the social elite represented by the free merchants, who we know were to be found at certain contemporary trading places.[19] St Martin's was arguably located in relation to just such a waterside trading location along the south side of the River Wensum, at a point where the riverside marshes on both sides give way to hard land (Fig. 3).[20] There is early evidence for meeting and gathering here. A recent attempt at plotting Middle Saxon finds from Norwich produced a concentration of mid-Saxon material on the gravel terrace to the north of the cathedral, including buildings which produced an 8th-century radiocarbon date.[21] We have already seen that the St Vedast cross fragment, discovered 500 m to the south of St Martin's, but probably *ex situ*, is decorated in a style of animal ornament in an architectural frame which, in the North Midlands and Yorkshire, would be associated with the early part of the 10th century.

North of the river, 10th-century occupation has a somewhat different character. St Clement's is evidently an early church and lies close to concentrations of 10th-century pottery at Fishergate.[22] Both lie within the boundary of the D-shaped enclosure, whose ditch (though not dated precisely) is known to have been in existence at least from the 10th century. This is the 'Anglo-Danish burh' perhaps first established by the Danes, but whose 10th-century character Brian Ayers has associated with Edward the Elder or Æthelstan and linked with the creation of a mint, with earliest issues dating to the 930s. We should note that Æthelstan's decree of Grateley (Hants.) of *c.*935 regarding the establishment of mints specifically relates them to trading centres and markets.[23]

Thanks largely to Ayers's work, then, the picture of 10th-century Norwich is starting to exhibit a recognizable pattern. There was an enclosure to the north of the river,

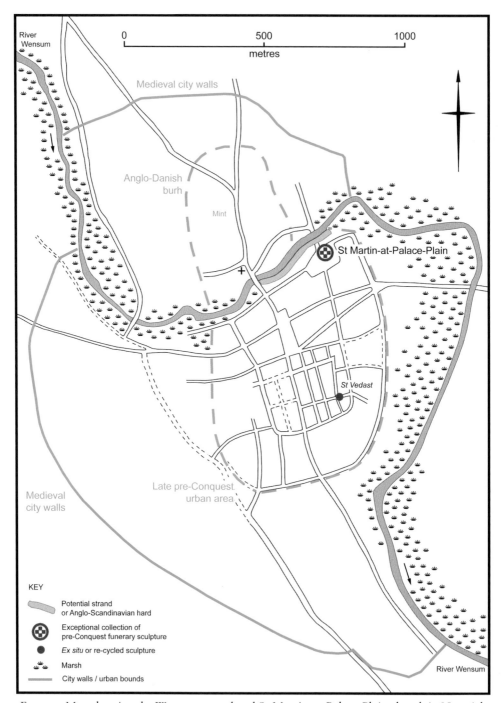

FIG. 3.   Map showing the Wensum strand and St Martin-at-Palace-Plain church in Norwich
(based on Popescu, *Norwich Castle* (as in n. 26), Part I, fig. 4.2)

on the inside of the bend of the Wensum, which appears to have had aristocratic and military patronage. To the south-east, on the outside of the Wensum bend, was a settlement which we may suspect functioned as a trading and manufacturing centre. Specifically, the strip along the waterfront, on the outside of the bend, lent itself to trade: the foreshore here would have been a gently shelving 'hard', traces of which have been recovered, again by Ayers, in excavations along the modern river. Here the water-front was consolidated by small wickerwork fences, with dumping behind to create a surface on which boats could be beached: there is also evidence for boat-building.[24] It is this riverside zone with which St Martin's church is topographically connected, and this trading function that lends weight to our interpretation of our two imported grave-covers. They were brought specially from Lindsey to make a distinctive display of two burials in the churchyard that stood just behind the trading hard, marking the deceased (presumably) as distinguished incomers to the city. They surely must imply trading links, and a likely 'alien' merchant community of resident merchants from Lindsey.

This suggestion certainly sharpens the picture of 'hints of trade', and rather tenuous arguments about the dedication of the church of St Vedast — a Flemish saint and therefore a possible indicator of trading contacts — or debates whether a Ringerike-style mount from St Martin's might also suggest exotic trading contacts in the early 11th century, that have featured in recent discussions.[25] Even the quantitative analysis now possible of the massive collections of early medieval pottery from excavations in the city does not signal high levels of trade through the presence of exotic imports. The late pre-Conquest pottery is overwhelmingly dominated by Thetford-type ware from local Norwich kilns; products from East Midlands sources are typically confined to St Neots-type ware and Stamford coarse and fine wares, but occurring in very small quantities and only slightly more commonly than the contemporary Continental imports of Badorf-type, Pingsdorf-type, and Blue-Grey wares.[26]

'MONUMENTS AND MERCHANTS' ELSEWHERE IN EASTERN ENGLAND

MORE importantly, the situation we are now glimpsing at Norwich is directly comparable with several other 10th-century towns in eastern England, where this relationship between early sculpture and trade has been explored in greater depth. At York, for example, the reserved and partly ecclesiastical enclosure on the inside bend of the Ouse looked across the river towards what we now think was a 10th-century trading settlement on the outside bend (Fig. 4).[27] Just as we are now suggesting at Norwich, the trading settlement at York was focused on a strand on the river: the later Skeldergate. Furthermore, at York, this area has produced large numbers of Anglo-Scandinavian graveyard monuments, from the church of St Mary Bishophill Senior situated close behind the strand. While quantities of sculpture from Norwich are much smaller, nevertheless we have seen that the sculpture has come from a very similar relative location in this town also. A similar picture can be seen in 10th-century Lincoln, with a reserved enclosure on the north bank of the river and hards on the river to the south (Fig. 5). Once again it is from the churches adjacent to these hards, St Mark's and St Mary le Wigford, that 10th-century sculpture has come in considerable quantity.[28]

There are other, similar examples;[29] but, as we are exploring Norfolk, we should also draw attention to the situation at Thetford. The town has much the largest concentration of Anglo-Scandinavian funerary sculpture in Norfolk, numbering, at present understanding, at least nineteen stones representing a minimum of thirteen original monuments (Fig. 6). They have come mostly from state-sponsored excavations between

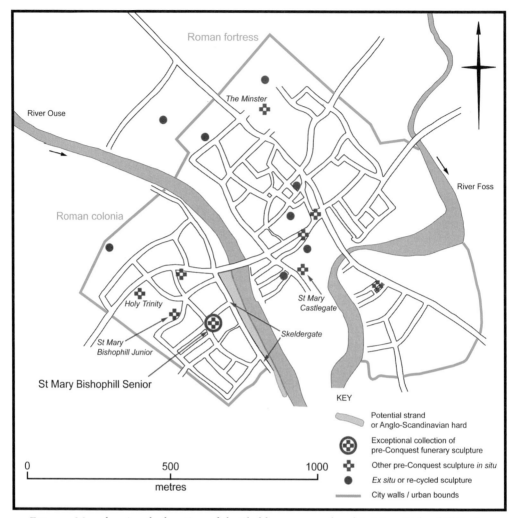

FIG. 4. Map showing the location of the Skeldergate strand and St Mary Bishophill Senior church in York (based on Stocker, 'Monuments and merchants' (as in n. 19), fig. 12)

the 1930s and the 1970s.[30] As a group, they are mostly monuments from the quarries of South Lincolnshire and southwards towards Barnack and Peterborough. At least one of them, however, is from the quarries around Lincoln and is undoubtedly a Lindsey cover (Fig. 7). It has the characteristic three rows of repetitive figure-of-eight interlace, and three surviving edges are ornamented with double cabling, which makes it an example of the stylish 'sub-type a'.[31] This monument at least, then, represents a close parallel for the example from St Martin's church in Norwich.

Discovering the likely locations of the burials originally marked by these Thetford stones, however, has proved surprisingly complex, but investigation points overwhelmingly in one direction. Ten or eleven of the Anglo-Scandinavian stone funerary monuments from Thetford are known to have come from a single source: the Cluniac Priory

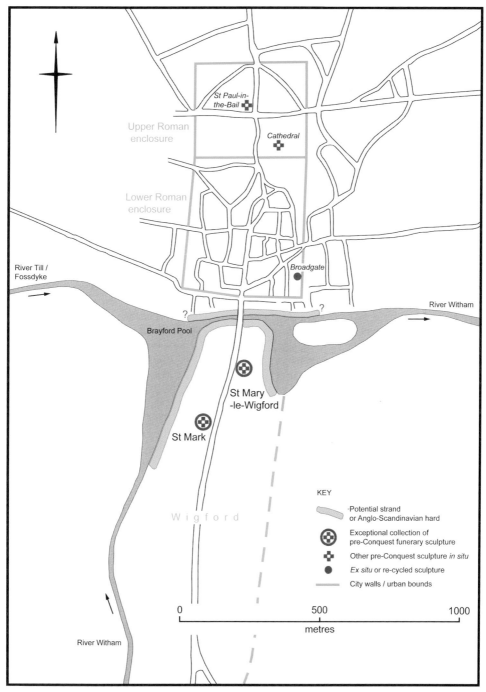

FIG. 5.   Map showing the location of the Wigford strand and the churches of St Mary and
St Mark in Lincoln (based on Stocker, 'Monuments and merchants' (as in n. 19), fig. 8)

	Other Catalogue Number	Location 2012	Short Description	Stone Type	Where found	Reuse	Reference
1	English Heritage (EH) 78102145	Wrest Park	Half of a Lindsey grave-cover (type a)	Lincoln	Probably St Mary's Priory, discovered 1956		Fig. 7 = Cramp photo in CASSS archive; Med. Archaeol., 1 (1957), 153
2	EH 78101370	Wrest Park	Cross-head of disc form: debased South Kesteven cross	Barnack	Probably St Mary's Priory [unless the same as No.3 below]		Cramp photo in CASSS archive
3		not known	Cross-head mentioned by Knocker in 1960s	?	'a cross-head from the same site [i.e. St Sepulchre's?]'		Knocker notes in EH archive
4	EH 78101391	Wrest Park	Fenland grave-cover fragment	Barnack	St Mary's Priory	Recut with large curving rebate in its rear face	
5	EH 78101716	Wrest Park	Fragment with interlace [possibly part of 4?]	Barnack	? St Mary's Priory, since in EH archive catalogue	Reused as a voussoir	
6	EH 78101395	Wrest Park	Fenland grave-cover fragment	Barnack	St Mary's Priory	Reused as chevron-decorated arched lintel	
6a	EH 78101715	Wrest Park	Part of 6	Barnack	St Mary's Priory	Reused as chevron-decorated arched lintel	
7	EH 78101419	Presumed to be at Wrest Park	Fenland grave-cover	Barnack?	St Mary's Priory	Reused as chevron-decorated monolithic arched lintel	
8	EH 78101420	Wrest Park	Presumed Fenland grave-cover fragment?	Barnack	St Mary's Priory	Reused as chevron-decorated arched lintel	
9	EH 78101421	Wrest Park	Fenland grave-cover fragment	Barnack	St Mary's Priory	Reused as chevron-decorated arched lintel	
10	EH 781 01685	Wrest Park	Fenland grave-cover fragment	Barnack	St Mary's Priory	'Recut as neat square block'	

11		Gressenhall store	Near-complete double-ended Fenland grave-cover, Cambridge Castle type	Barnack	Queensway Primary School (TL8672829) in 1964; *in situ* over burial	No reuse? [Unless indicated by unusual evidence for its man-handling]	*Med. Archaeol.*, 19 (1965), 173; EAA, 22 (1984), 53
12	THEHM1979.181	Thetford Ancient House Museum: 'under the table'	Part of Fenland grave-cover, Tallington type	Barnack	Probably seen by Knocker at St Sepulchre's pre 1969; museum catalogue suggests link with St Mary's Priory in 1950s	Reused as chamfered set-off	Knocker notes in EH archive; Ancient House Museum catalogue
13		Gressenhall store? [not found 2012]	Small interlace-decorated fragment	?	Williamson Close in 1949; stone a	Reused in burial cist?	EAA, 22 (1984), 53
14		Gressenhall store? [not found 2012]	Small interlace-decorated fragment	?	Williamson Close in 1949; stone b	Reused in burial cist?	EAA, 22 (1984), 53
15	Not in curated collection	Built into east wing-wall at King's House	Fenland grave-cover fragment	Barnack	Presumably St Mary's Priory, like the other stonework recycled here		
16	Not in curated collection	Built into east wing-wall at King's House	Interlace fragment	Barnack	Presumably St Mary's Priory, like the other stonework recycled here		
17	SF 738 (3116)	Gressenhall store	Fragment of Fenland grave-cover or a South Kesteven shaft	Barnack	Brandon Road (site 12) in 1966	Recut as later C12 voussoir; found, unstratified, with many other C12 & C13 frags	EAA, 62 (1993), 133–58, illus.
18	Not yet accessioned	Gressenhall store	Fragment of mid-Kesteven cover?	Ancaster?	Deposited by S. Heywood in 2012; said to be from St Mary's Priory	Recut as one of a pair of C16/C17 socles/corbels	
19	Not in curated collection	Built into wall, south of Grammar School	Grave-marker or standing cross, with cross pattée & inlay	Barnack	Suggested St Mary the Great		NA, 44/4 (2005), 726–27, illus.

Note Two sculptured fragments built into the east gables of Thetford Grammar School, though sometimes said to be pre-Conquest, seem rather to be tympana – and therefore not funerary – and probably of 12th-century date. They may be from St Mary's Priory.

FIG. 6. Table of known items of Anglo-Scandinavian funerary sculpture from Thetford

of St Mary. There is direct evidence that a considerable number of them were recovered from clearance and consolidation work at this site: Professor Rosemary Cramp photographed several in the Ministry of Public Buildings and Works site hut in the 1960s, and the discovery of one large cover fragment embedded in the priory's domestic buildings — perhaps the Lindsey cover pictured by Cramp (Fig. 7) — was reported in the first volume of *Medieval Archaeology*.[32] At least four pieces of early grave-cover were recut for decorative elements in the first phase of the priory's buildings. Furthermore, two stones built into the eastern wing-wall of King's House, next to St Peter's church, occur as part of much larger collections that are also known to have been robbed from the Priory ruins in the post-Dissolution centuries. As it carries a 12th-century moulding from a window rerearch, we also suspect that the fragment from another 'Fenland cover' discovered in the site clearance before excavations at Brandon Road in 1966[33] also represents *spolia* from the Priory and that it arrived on this site for reuse in building fabric in the 18th or 19th century. It may belong with a further group of stylish 12th-century fragments recovered nearby in those investigations, as part of a load of stone en route for commonplace reuse.[34] The fragment of a Tallington-type cover now preserved in the Ancient House Museum also bears the clear evidence of recutting, as a chamfered set-off, and the trail of its acquisition points to its discovery at the priory site in 1954.[35] Finally, un-accessioned on a pallet in the Norfolk Museums Service store at Gressenhall, and reportedly recovered from the Priory site, are two substantial stone fragments in Lincolnshire Limestone of Ancaster type: one has part of a Romanesque half-shaft on one face and a 17th-century base or capital on the other, but the second has a similar base or capital plus interlaced surface decoration of strands with median incisions of a type characteristic of the mid-Kesteven group of grave-covers, which were produced in quantity by the later pre-Conquest Ancaster quarries.[36]

The Cluniac Priory of St Mary at Thetford was only founded in 1103–04. Fortunately, as we have noted, a significant proportion of the Anglo-Scandinavian monuments show unmistakable signs of having been recut for use in the first phase of Romanesque building here, demonstrating that the newly-arrived monks' builders were exploiting masonry from an existing graveyard in the town for the construction of their elaborate new buildings. This clearly contained a major collection of burials marked with distinctive and expensive imported stone covers and other types of sculpted monuments. Where was it located? The early history of the Priory offers the strong implication that this graveyard was one associated with the church of St Mary the Great, sited immediately south of the presumed ford, and at the eastern end of Thetford's presumed strand (Fig. 8). St Mary's is known to have been in existence in the Anglo-Scandinavian period as it was adopted by the bishop for use as the 'temporary' cathedral of the diocese between 1071 and 1094.[37] The cathedral at Thetford was said to be 'of another person's possessions' and not to belong to the bishopric at all.[38] Yet, although the bishop evidently transferred his seat to Norwich in 1094, even so he retained the use of St Mary's at Thetford until about 1103 when the site was adopted, in a rather similar fashion, by the newly arrived Cluniacs. But neither the bishop nor the Cluniacs appear to have built a new stone church here; it was only in 1107 that the monks started work on their new church north of the river, moving the short distance to that site in 1114. In doing so, it is presumed that they took masonry from their temporary site.[39] That statement appears to be borne out by the Anglo-Scandinavian monuments that were reused to provide stone for Romanesque architectural ornament in the first half of the 12th century.

FIG. 7. The substantial section of a Lindsey cover of type 'a' recovered from Thetford Priory (Figure 6 no. 1), photographed by R. J. Cramp in the Ministry of Public Buildings and Works site hut there in the 1960s

Corpus of Anglo-Saxon Stone Sculpture archive, University of Durham (photographed by Rosemary Cramp)

It is not necessary for our purposes that we demonstrate that all early stone sculpture in Thetford originated in the same graveyard, just that an 'exceptional' quantity did.[40] A more-or-less complete cover of a well-recognized 'Fenland grave-cover' type, for example, was excavated *in situ* over a burial at the Primary School off Queensway in 1964.[41] A nearby burial was a 'weapon grave', and, as Andrew Rogerson argues, this limited grouping of interments, nearly 1 km south of the river crossing and at the periphery of the settlement area, need not be a church-related burial ground. The early church of St Mary the Great, however, stood south of the river and part way to this location, so just possibly this cover was recruited from its graveyard, when it was cleared.[42] Alternatively, but less plausibly, these burials belong to the same cemetery represented by the considerable number of burials that have been discovered a little to the north west, around Icknield Way, Williamson Crescent and Nelson Crescent. These may be associated with the church of St Margaret, formerly situated to their south, but many of them are undoubtedly of later date than the Anglo-Scandinavian monuments, and the two fragments from a second Fenland grave-cover found here were recycled scraps of masonry used randomly in lining a cist, and could also have come from St Mary the Great.[43]

At Thetford, then, St Mary the Great had an 'exceptional' collection of pre-Conquest funerary stone sculpture within its graveyard. This graveyard went back at least as far as the late 10th century, as indicated by the stylish Lindsey cover and probably by the mid-Kesteven grave-cover fragment, too. The site had an eminence that fitted it briefly as the seat of a bishop, albeit one who would rather have been seated at Bury and did in practice soon move on to Norwich. Yet it is of critical importance that the bishop was

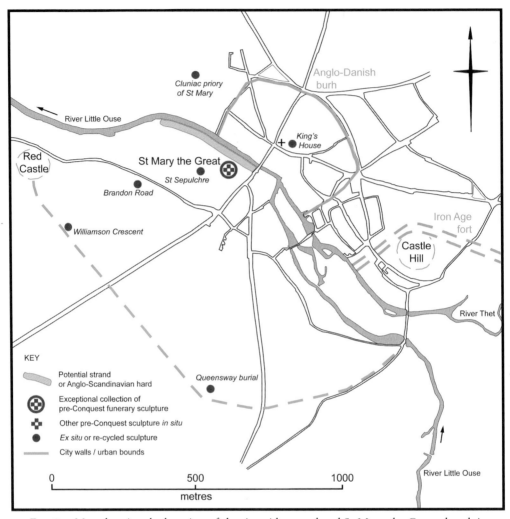

FIG. 8.   Map showing the location of the riverside strand and St Mary the Great church in
Thetford (based on Everson and Jecock, 'Castle Hill and the early medieval development
of Thetford' (as in n. 45), fig. 39)

not considered to be the church's lord. Though Herfast had assumed it by the end of
the 11th century, that honour belonged to descendants of the founders of the graveyard, we might suggest; that is, to the heirs of those commemorated by the earliest of
the elite monuments here.[44] The graveyard's key characteristic, however, was that it
was located adjacent to the extended riverside hard, which hosted the trade that fuelled
the town's growth and prosperity. It was apparently the only church with that proximity and perhaps stood alone on an open marketing zone behind the hard. As at
Norwich, the particularly distinctive decoration of the Lindsey cover signalled the
affinity with distant Lincoln by a resident alien merchant and/or his family. Other,
more numerous, monuments reflected the waterborne trade networks of the Welland,

Ouse and Nene river systems. In summary, Thetford's Anglo-Scandinavian monuments offer good evidence for a similar pattern of early urban zoning to what we see at Norwich, Lincoln and York, indicating burial of (and presumably occupation by) alien merchants on and near the strand. At Thetford, at some stage in the later 10th century, the 'foreign' traders at the strand became permanent residents and buried together in a churchyard that was associated specifically with it. At Thetford, too, as at these other centres, the strand and its community of traders were located opposite a fortified enclosure on the north bank, the Anglo-Danish burh, as well as the lowering presence of the prehistoric promontory fort, within which the Viking Great Army had presumably over-wintered in 870 and within which the Norman castle was subsequently planted.[45]

Stocker's study exploring this link between trading places with hards and early sculpture and early churches showed that there appears to be a relationship between many of the largest groupings of 10th-century sculpture in northern and eastern England and this type of trading place.[46] That study explored, too, the likelihood that incoming merchants would either be inclined to establish their own settlements around the hards themselves, for convenience, or would be compelled to do so by the indigenous secular authority. No doubt such settlements were originally temporary, only subsequently becoming more permanent. It is very notable that all such settlements were established outside, but adjacent to, the gates of major aristocratic enclosures, and there may have been many other legal restrictions on the traders' freedom of movement, at least initially. Such a group of incoming merchants — on the one hand wealthy and honoured guests, but on the other hand definitely 'other', and kept under tight official control — would surely be quite likely to mark their burials in a distinctive fashion.[47] In doing so, it was natural that they and their kin should express their individuality through emphasizing their own origins.

This, we suspect, is also the lesson of the two Lindsey covers from St Martin's in Norwich. They represent, perhaps, two incoming traders from remote Anglo-Scandinavian Lincoln, in the former kingdom of Lindsey, who traded about the year 1000 or perhaps a little earlier with the former kingdom of East Anglia, and who were buried here in distinctive style deliberately recalling their origins.

THE EARLY DEVELOPMENT OF NORWICH

WITHOUT presuming to venture far into the legitimate domain of experienced local colleagues, then, the limited point we wish to make is that the two grave-covers from St Martin's might represent the burials of two early alien merchants trading from Norwich's earliest strand. This leads to a sharper characterization of the immediate southern riverside frontage at Norwich in the 10th century as a waterfront trading zone.[48] In its turn, this observation might provide helpful pointers to understanding the city's early urban development south of the river. Already Elizabeth Popescu, in summarizing current thinking after the massive Castle Mall excavations, has borrowed the phrase 'incipient urban network' or loose settlement arrangement — an assessment applied twenty-five years ago to the results of urban excavations in Northampton — to characterize Norwich's urban development in the 10th century.[49]

We should say, more positively, that we should expect — both in the practical functioning of the trading facility we have described and by comparison with other urban examples in eastern England — that there would be manufacturing and processing activity in an extensive zone behind the riverside hard and its market area. This, indeed, is what the earliest documentation for Norwich implies. The first reference to the town, in *Liber Eliensis* in the late 10th century, states that 'If anyone bought land there he did not require sureties',[50] which implies a well-established, residential manufacturing and trading place, and it includes Norwich amongst trading centres in the region such as Thetford, Ipswich and Cambridge. We might anticipate that such manufacturing was rather loosely organized (as excavations at Thetford have amply demonstrated), but perhaps would be zoned by product specialism. There seems to be growing evidence of this, too, in Norwich (Fig. 9). Most obviously, local Thetford-type ware pottery production was located to the south west, but significantly has now been found inside as well as outside the formal urban boundary that is often mapped. At Castle Mall, there was good evidence of discrete distributions of craft waste (including antler-, horn- and metalworking) and of grain storage and processing.[51] At the Greyfriars, signs of the working of precious metals, notably silver, were encountered.[52] All these indications, as Popescu has noted, argue against the proposition that Norwich south of the Wensum had its origin in a formally bounded enclosure with a formally planned internal street pattern, on the Wessex model, as some scholars have been inclined to suggest, pointing to the residual grid of streets in the city plan. The arguments we have put forward here — both *specific* about the key role of a trading strand-like waterfront and *general* in the comparisons we have drawn with the trading centres of eastern England — also speak against that model of development. The formal boundary and the grid of streets must be a superimposition upon an earlier, more informal settlement against the strand, which were in turn modified by post-Conquest developments driven by the arrival of castle and cathedral.

Yet that later grid of streets may still have something to tell us of the early urban layout on which we have been trying to cast light. Its location and limited extent, lying wholly to the south of an early east–west street — in fact the line of the Roman road, whose continuation is later Princes Street and which was truncated by the new Close wall in the years around 1100 — contrasts with the area to the north of that east–west alignment. The latter has no such formality of historical street pattern and includes not only the immediate riverside trading zone that we have proposed above, but also fragments of the open areas of Palace Plain and Tombland. Perhaps, rather than a sequence which might see Tombland as a discrete market created separately and sustained in later centuries by replacing the riverside trading strand, we should rather consider that the early, open, marketing space connected with the strand occupied the whole of this area north of the east–west alignment (Fig. 9). Both Palace Plain and Tombland might then in different degrees be residual fragments of that early much larger marketing space, which became defined as market places of a later type by encroaching streets and properties. Tombland in effect moved and was re-formed in front of the main city-facing gates of the new cathedral Close, in a recasting of urban space that saw the demolition of at least the church of St Michael and adjacent major residences.[53] Both the name 'Tombland' (OE *tōm*, 'free from', ME *tōm* 'empty'/'open'; but considered to be of Scandinavian origin)[54] and results of recent excavations in this area (as Brian Ayers advises us) may offer some support to this proposition. The medieval name for the topographical area, latterly Palace Plain, within which St Martin's church and its graveyard sat was *Bichill* (probably OE *bic* or *biccan* 'beak' in a topographical sense, but specifically referring to the hard where shipping offloaded around St Martin's).[55] This name is shared with several riverine market places in Yorkshire: Knaresborough, Wakefield and York, where its form from the later 13th century is 'Bishophill', precisely the early trading focus discussed above.[56] It is probably also

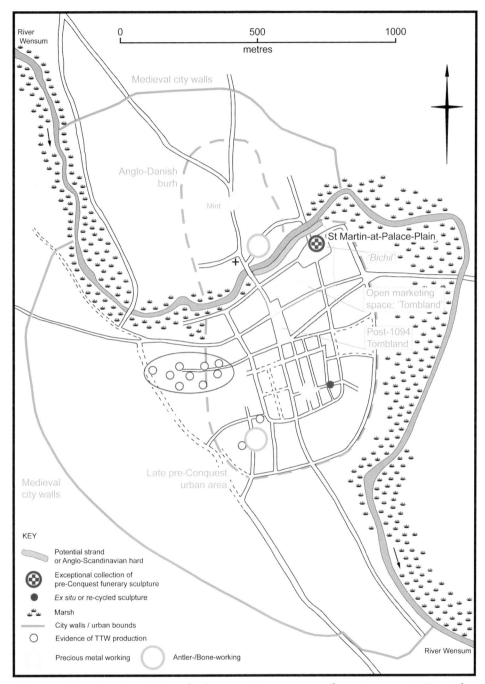

River Wensum

0   500   1000
metres

Medieval city walls

Anglo-Danish burh

Mint

St Martin-at-Palace-Plain

'Bichil'

Open marketing space: 'Tombland'

Post-1094 Tombland

Medieval city walls

Late pre-Conquest urban area

KEY

Potential strand or Anglo-Scandinavian hard

Exceptional collection of pre-Conquest funerary sculpture

Ex situ or re-cycled sculpture

Marsh

City walls / urban bounds

Evidence of TTW production

Precious metal working   Antler-/Bone-working

River Wensum

FIG. 9.   Map showing evidence for later pre-Conquest manufacturing zones in Norwich and suggesting the location and extent of an open riverside market and trading area behind the hard (based on Popescu, *Norwich Castle* (as in n. 26), Part I, fig. 4.2)

worth noting that just such a large early market space has been recently been proposed on the hillside at Lincoln, to the north of the regular street grid of the area of earliest settlement, in the detailed analysis of the development of that city by Alan Vince and David Stocker.[57] As at Norwich, this Lincoln market space had already begun to infill and be subdivided by the 12th century, and probably by the later 11th. Also as at Norwich, it was probably dominated by at least one church that stood on an 'island' graveyard in its midst.[58] It would not be unreasonable to anticipate that the infilling of this large marketing area at Norwich was a gradual process, perhaps beginning significantly before the Conquest and even including elements that projected the southern street grid. As Brian Ayers again informs us, recent excavation results in this area hint at such complexity.[59]

Finally, this small study of Norfolk's two principal Anglo-Scandinavian urban centres at Thetford and Norwich also reflects light back on the contemporary urban centre of Lincoln. It demonstrates that this town's trade at an early date was not wholly focused through its important out-port at Torksey and the waterway networks of the Trent and Humber basin. That orientation of interest and influence from the Hiberno-Norse kingdom of York is perhaps clearest in the archaeological record, not least in the early stone sculpture.[60] However, the early covers at Thetford and Norwich indicate that, as in later centuries, the Witham waterway to the Wash was just as important and just as early a route of trade, serving not only coastal networks but also linking into the river systems that penetrated to the heart of East Anglia. Just as Lindsey and mid-Kesteven covers marked the burials of the superior sort of merchant in the waterside trading communities at St Mary and St Mark in Lincoln itself, and perhaps at the city's out-port at Torksey, in a similar way Lindsey and mid-Kesteven covers were imported as permanent and emblematic markers of merchant burials at both St Mary the Great in Thetford and at St Martin's in Norwich. But also, and more significantly, they point to the substantive connections in place between the main towns of East Anglia and the Five Boroughs as urban growth transformed English society in the 10th century.[61]

Successive editions of Brian Ayers's fine book about the city's archaeological development clearly demonstrate how a continuous flow of new information results in new debates and new understanding; and our offering here is intended to support and stimulate our archaeological friends in Norwich in that continuing quest for a clearer understanding of the city's origins and urban development. Our note also demonstrates that an artefact type — early stone sculpture — still most commonly discussed in style-critical terms can make significant contributions to much wider agendas. In this case to issues of 'urban development', 'urban living', 'social organization', 'demography: population movement and immigration' and 'economy', to quote from the main priorities of the Regional Research Agenda and research objectives of (for example) the Castle Mall project.[62] We cannot tell what our putative Lincoln merchants resident in Norwich traded in (not pottery or anything conveyed in ceramic vessels, clearly; the city's fine coloured cloth might be the best conjecture). But surely they were here and part of a vibrant trading community which contributed to Norwich's wealth and size and status in its late pre-Conquest boom era.

ACKNOWLEDGEMENTS

We are deeply grateful to Brian Ayers, David Adams and Tim Pestell, who have all read this paper as it has developed, and have offered information, correction and encouragement, and friendly reassurance to us as scholarly outsiders to Norwich and Norfolk. The section on Thetford would have been impossible without the cordial cooperation of our friends in sculptural and ecclesiastical studies — Derek Craig, Jackie Hall and Stephen Heywood — whose generosity in sharing information helped us assemble a plausible first listing of the important collection of early sculpture from that town and a way into its complex history, though they may not share all of our conclusions. Our adventures in Anglo-Saxon sculpture studies owe much to the Corpus of Anglo-Saxon Stone Sculpture project, and to the manner in which Professor Emerita Rosemary Cramp has pursued its national completion and promoted the wider archaeological relevance of the material.

NOTES

1. O. Beazley and B. Ayers, *Two Medieval Churches in Norfolk*, EAA, 96 (2001).
2. B. C. Worssam, 'Regional Geology', in P. Everson and D. Stocker, *Corpus of Anglo-Saxon Stone Sculpture Volume V: Lincolnshire* (Oxford 1999), 17–21.
3. Beazley and Ayers, *Two Medieval Churches* (as in n. 1), 39–40.
4. Everson and Stocker, *Lincolnshire* (as in n. 2), illus. 188–89, 231, 244, 254.
5. Ibid., 51–57.
6. Ibid., fig. 15; J. Blair, *The Church in Anglo-Saxon Society* (Oxford 2005), 467–70.
7. P. Everson and D. Stocker, *Corpus of Anglo-Saxon Stone Sculpture Volume XII: Nottinghamshire* (Oxford forthcoming).
8. Beazley and Ayers, *Two Medieval Churches* (as in n. 1), 5–13.
9. P. C. Buckland and J. Sadler, 'Ballast and Building Stone: A Discussion', in *Stone: Quarrying and Building in England AD 43–1525*, ed. D. Parsons (Chichester 1990), 114–25.
10. D. Stocker with P. Everson, 'Rubbish Recycled: A Study of the Re-use of Stone in Lincolnshire', in ibid., 83–101, esp. 85–86.
11. B. Ayers, 'The Urban Landscape', in *Medieval Norwich*, 4 and n. 22.
12. D. Stocker and P. Everson, 'Five towns funerals: decoding diversity in Danelaw stone sculpture', in *Vikings and the Danelaw. Select Papers from the Proceedings of the Thirteenth Viking Congress*, ed. J. Graham-Campbell, R. Hall, R. Jesch and D. Parsons (Oxford 2001), 223–43, esp. 224–29.
13. Our friend, Dr Derek Craig, is currently assembling a *catalogue raisonnée* of pre-Conquest stone sculpture in Norfolk as a contribution to the work of the Corpus of Anglo-Saxon Stone Sculpture project, based at Durham University. We are extremely grateful for the help he has extended towards us in respect of early monuments from Thetford.
14. London, British Library, MS Add. 37552, fol. 9; W. Hudson, 'The stone bridge in St Faith's Lane, Norwich', *NA*, 10 (1888), 117–42, esp. 140 n. 9; idem, 'On a sculptured stone recently removed from a house on the site of the church of St Vedast, Norwich', *NA*, 13 (1898), 116–24; J. R. Allen, 'Early Christian Art', in VCH, *Norfolk*, II, 555–63, esp. 558; S. Margeson, *The Vikings in Norfolk* (Norwich 1997), 24–25. It was said that two fragments of sandstone from the excavations in the north-east bailey of Norwich Castle in 1979 were from an 'arcaded screen' of pre-Conquest date (S. Heywood, 'The Stone Fragments', in *Excavations within the North-East Bailey of Norwich Castle, 1979*, ed. B. Ayers, EAA, 28 (Dereham 1985), 41–44. Objections were raised to this identification at the time, and subsequent studies (e.g. P. Everson and D. Stocker, 'A note on the fonts of Wharram', in *A History of Wharram Percy and its Neighbours*, ed. S. Wrathmell, Wharram, A Study of Settlement on the Yorkshire Wolds, XIII (York 2012), 260–62) have demonstrated that stone fragments of precisely this decoration, form and petrology derive from the rims of Romanesque fonts.
15. Hudson, 'Stone from St Vedast' (as in n. 14), 117 conveying the opinion of G. F. Browne; Allen, 'Early Christian Art' (as in n. 14), 558; Margeson, *Vikings in Norfolk* (as in n. 14), 24.
16. Hudson, 'Stone from St Vedast' (as in n. 14), 116–17, 120–21; N. Groves, *The Medieval Churches of the City of Norwich* (Norwich 2010), 147. Residual stonework perhaps from the construction, modification or demolition of St Vedast's church has been reported in recent excavations of the Norwich Greyfriars: see P. Emery, *Norwich Greyfriars: Pre-Conquest Town and Medieval Priory*, EAA, 120 (Dereham 2007), 42, 98–99.
17. B. Ayers, 'The cathedral site before 1096', in *Norwich Cathedral 1096–1996*, 59–72, esp. 68 and n. 37; B. Ayers, *Norwich: archaeology of a fine city*, rev. 3rd edn (Stroud 2009), 35. Tim Pestell, too, opines (pers. comm.) that the association made with St Vedast church by the stone's traditional name might be lazy.
18. We are aware that superficially this looks like an old-fashioned 'pots = people' argument, now properly challenged by modern theoretical approaches. But, whereas subscription to a widely dispersed monument type, like the South Lincolnshire and Barnack covers, by the family of the deceased might imply that they were merely following a local fashion prevalent across large areas of eastern England, we feel that subscription to

such a distinctive and emblematic monument type as the Lindsey covers, which have such a tightly restricted — yet remote — distribution, must imply that the occupants of these graves (or their families) wanted to associate themselves specifically with Lindsey.

19. Everson and Stocker, *Lincolnshire* (as in n. 2), 76–77; D. Stocker, 'Monuments and Merchants: Irregularities in the Distribution of Stone Sculpture in Lincolnshire and Yorkshire in the Tenth Century', in *Cultures in Contact. Scandinavian Settlement in England in the Ninth and Tenth Centuries*, ed. D. M. Hadley and J. D. Richards (Turnhout 2000), 179–212.

20. For the result of recent work on the marshy foreshore of the Wensum to the west of this zone, and the steep fall of the river bank behind it (now masked by tipping and infill), see D. Adams, 'Report on window sampling at the former Eastern Electricity offices, Duke Street, Norwich' (unpublished NAU Archaeology Report No. 1249, 2007; available online through Norfolk Heritage Explorer, NHER no. 49778).

21. Ayers, *Norwich* (as in n. 17), 27, 29; B. Ayers, 'The growth of an urban landscape: recent research in early medieval Norwich', *Early Medieval Europe*, 19/1 (2011), 62–90, esp. 70–76.

22. For St Clement, see Ayers, *Norwich* (as in n. 17), 31; B. E. Crawford, *The Churches Dedicated to St. Clement in Medieval England: a hagio-geography of the seafarers' saint in 11th century North Europe*, Scripta Ecclesiastica, 1 (St Petersburg 2008), esp. 94–100. For Fishergate, see Ayers, 'Growth of an urban landscape' (as in n. 21), 76–79.

23. A. Carter and J. P. Roberts, 'Excavations in Norwich — 1972. The Norwich Survey — second interim report', *NA*, 35 (1973), 443–68, esp. 445.

24. B. Ayers and P. Murphy, 'A waterfront excavation at Whitefriars Street car park, Norwich, 1979', in *Waterfront excavation and Thetford ware production, Norwich*, ed. P. Wade-Martins, EAA, 17 (Dereham 1983), 1–60, esp. 55–60; B. Ayers, *Excavations at St Martin-at-Palace-Plain, Norwich, 1981*, EAA, 37 (Dereham 1987).

25. Ayers, *Norwich* (as in n. 17), 30, 35, 50.

26. E. S. Popescu, *Norwich Castle: excavations and historical survey, 1987–1998*, EAA, 132 in 2 vols and CD (Dereham 2009), II 'c. 1345 to Modern', fig. 13.10, table 13.28; and see earlier J. Bown, 'Pottery: English Wares', in Ayers, *St Martin-at-Palace-Plain* (as in n. 24), 74–80, esp. 75.

27. Stocker, 'Monuments and merchants' (as in n. 19), 203–05; R. A. Hall et al., *Aspects of Anglo-Scandinavian York*, The Archaeology of York 8/4 (York 2004), 495–96.

28. Everson and Stocker, *Lincolnshire* (as in n. 2), 198–210, 211–17; Stocker, 'Monuments and merchants' (as in n. 19), 183, 187–89; A. Vince and D. Stocker, 'The new town: Lincoln in the High Medieval Era (c. 850–c. 1350)', in M. J. Jones, D. Stocker and A. Vince, *The City by the Pool. Assessing the archaeology of the city of Lincoln*, Lincoln Archaeological Studies 10 (Oxford 2003), 159–302.

29. Stocker, 'Monuments and merchants' (as in n. 19).

30. For practical reasons to do with changes in their long-term storage, we were unable to view the stones in the custodianship of English Heritage in time for this paper, and have had to make assessments of stone type from photographs, where such exist. Thus we are enormously grateful to Jackie Hall, who has given us full access to her notes on, and photographs of, the collection, made whilst it was accessible at Beeston.

31. Everson and Stocker, *Lincolnshire* (as in n. 2), 51–57.

32. Corpus of Anglo-Saxon Stone Sculpture archive in Durham; *Med. Archaeol.*, 1 (1957), 153.

33. C. Dallas, *Excavations in Thetford by B. K. Davison between 1964 and 1970*, EAA, 62 (Dereham 1993), 153–58.

34. Ibid.

35. Ancient House Museum records, reference THEHM 1979.18; for the cover type, see Everson and Stocker, *Lincolnshire* (as in n. 2), 262–63.

36. Access and information by courtesy of Tim Pestell; for the cover type, see Everson and Stocker, *Lincolnshire* (as in n. 2), 36–46, updated in Everson and Stocker, *Nottinghamshire* (as in n. 7).

37. B. Dodwell, 'Herbert de Losinga and the Foundation', in *Norwich Cathedral 1096–1996*, 36–43, esp. 39–41.

38. *The First Register of Norwich Cathedral Priory*, ed. H. W. Saunders, Norfolk Records Society, 11 (1939), 22.

39. For the priory itself, see F. J. E. Raby and P. K. Baillie-Reynolds, *Thetford Priory Norfolk* (London 1979). We have encountered no contemporary evidence recording the removal of stone from Great St Mary to the Priory, and the notion that the Cluniacs took stone from the site of Great St Mary appears to be an assumption based on the discovery of fragments of worked stone from the earliest buildings at the Priory which have been created from earlier Anglo-Scandinavian monuments. The assumption is, however, very well founded.

40. What might constitute an 'exceptional' collection of such stone monuments in such circumstances is considered in Stocker, 'Monuments and merchants' (as in n. 19), 183 and n. 2.

41. *Med. Archaeol.*, 19 (1965), 173; A. Rogerson and C. Dallas, *Excavations in Thetford 1948–49 and 1973–80*, EAA, 22 (Dereham 1984), 53; for the cover type, see Everson and Stocker, *Lincolnshire* (as in n. 2), 46–50.

42. Rogerson and Dallas, *Excavations in Thetford* (as in n. 41), 189. The Queensway cover exhibits in its edges unusual evidence of seatings for tackle to assist in manhandling it. No radiocarbon determinations were sought for the burials, which is unfortunate in view of the combined interest of both the associated artefacts — the cover and the sword, nominally of an approximately contemporary type. It is an omission that, with the possibility of modern dating enhanced by Bayesian statistics, might usefully be revisited, if the bones survive.

43. Ibid., 53.

44. Dodwell, 'Herbert de Losinga and the Foundation' (as in n. 37), 39.

45. P. Everson and M. Jecock, 'Castle Hill and the early medieval development of Thetford in Norfolk', in *Patterns of the Past. Essays in Landscape Archaeology for Christopher Taylor*, ed. P. Pattison, D. Field and S. Ainsworth (Oxford 1999), 97–106.

46. Stocker, 'Monuments and merchants' (as in n. 19).

47. The tension sometimes surfaces in official documentation, notably when the king asserted his interest: e.g. P. Sawyer, *Anglo-Saxon Lincolnshire*, History of Lincolnshire, 3 (Lincoln 1998), 183–84. For early examples of the topographical relationship, as at London or Rouen, and the possibility that this forms a common pattern, see T. Pestell, 'Markets, emporia, wics, and "productive sites"', in *The Oxford handbook of Anglo-Saxon archaeology*, ed. H. Hamerow, D. A. Hinton and S. Crawford (Oxford 2011), 556–79.

48. Because it would lie within this strand and downstream of most of it, we suggest — *contra* Ayers, *Excavations at St Martin-at-Palace-Plain* (as in n. 24) — that there was no early bridge immediately north of St Martin's, even though the parish of St Martin crosses the river here. What became Whitefriars Bridge might have been a part of the development and infilling of the strand-and-market area envisaged below.

49. J. H. Williams, 'A review of some aspects of Late Saxon urban origins and development', in *Studies in Late Anglo-Saxon Settlement*, ed. M. L. Faull (Oxford 1984), 25–34; Popescu, *Norwich Castle* (as in n. 26), II, 1056–58.

50. *Liber Eliensis. A History of the Isle of Ely from the Seventh Century to the Twelfth*, ed. and trans. J. Fairweather (Woodbridge 2005), II, 26, 122; Ayers, *Norwich* (as in n. 17), 37.

51. Popescu, *Norwich Castle* (as in n. 26), II, 1023–32, 1057.

52. Emery, *Norwich Greyfriars* (as in n. 16), 40–41, 42–43, 122.

53. Groves, *Medieval Churches of Norwich* (as in n. 16), 147.

54. K. I. Sandred and B. Lindström, *The Place-Names of Norfolk. Part 1, The place-names of the city of Norwich*, English Place Name Society, 61 (Nottingham 1989), 148; E. Björkman, *Scandinavian Loan-Words in Middle English*, Studien zur Englischen Philologie, 7 (Halle 1900–02), 256.

55. Sandred and Lindström, *Place-Names of Norwich* (as in n. 54), 137–38. It may be relevant that in the later Middle Ages 'beak' was a technical term for the bows of a ship, and perhaps earlier — on the principle of part for whole — for a ship; see B. Sandahl, *Middle English Sea Terms*, Essays and Studies on English Language and Literature, VIII (Uppsala 1951), Part 1, 26–27.

56. A. H. Smith, *The Place-Names of the West Riding of Yorkshire*, English Place Name Society, 30–37 (Cambridge 1961–63), Part 2, 166; Part 5, 111; idem, *The Place-Names of the East Riding of Yorkshire*, English Place Name Society, 14 (Cambridge 1937), 282. For Bishophill, see also D. M. Palliser, 'The medieval street-names of York', *York Historian*, 2 (1978), 2–16, esp. 5.

57. Vince and Stocker, 'The new town' (as in n. 28), 204–07, 260–64, RAZ 9.22, 9.60.38.

58. D. Stocker, 'Aristocrats, burghers and their markets: patterns in the foundation of Lincoln's urban churches', in *Everyday Life in Viking Towns: Social Approaches to Towns in England and Ireland c.800–1100*, ed. D. M. Hadley and L. ten Harkel (Oxford 2013), 119–43.

59. See D. Adams, 'An Archaeological Excavation at the former Bussey's Garage, Palace Street, Norwich' (unpublished Norfolk Archaeology Unit Archaeology Report No. 1376, 2008; available online through Norfolk Heritage Explorer, NHER no. 26442).

60. Everson and Stocker, *Lincolnshire* (as in n. 2), 80–84; Sawyer, *Anglo-Saxon Lincolnshire* (as in n. 46), 178–84.

61. Tim Pestell makes the wider point that 10th- and 11th-century metalwork finds in Lincolnshire and East Anglia might suggest other links between the two areas, perhaps relating to the construction and maintenance of identities deriving from a shared Viking/Scandinavian heritage; see 'Imports or immigrants? Reassessing Scandinavian metalwork in late Anglo-Saxon East Anglia', in *East Anglia and its North Sea world in the Middle Ages*, ed. D. Bates and R. Liddiard (Woodbridge 2013), 230–55.

62. N. Brown and J. Glazebrook ed., *Research and Archaeology: a framework for the Eastern Counties, 2. Research agenda and strategy*, EAA Occasional Paper, 8 (Norwich 2000); Popescu, *Norwich Castle* (as in n. 26), II, 1054–71.

Norwich Cathedral Revisited: Spiral Piers and Architectural Geometry

ERIC FERNIE

The paper has two parts. The first discusses the spiral piers in the nave of the cathedral, chiefly in terms of the different ways in which they have been explained. The argument that their location formed part of the overall design of the building is preferred to the view that they are the result of a change of mind occasioned by a break in the building programme. It is suggested that the widespread preference for the second type of explanation for non-uniform piers, especially in the late 19th and early 20th centuries, can in some respects be attributed to reactions to the Darwinian revolution. The second part examines the case for the use of a particular geometrical formula in the designing of the building, and asks why it should have had a notable status in Antiquity and the Middle Ages.

This paper re-examines two aspects of the Norman cathedral which were of special interest to me when I was working on the building some years ago, namely its spiral piers and its geometry.[1]

THE SPIRAL PIERS

THE cathedral has a system of alternating major and minor piers. Two of the pairs of minor piers near the east end of the nave take the form of cylinders with spirals, differing from the other minor ones, which are of compound form (Fig. 1). The traditional explanation for these was that they represented the original design for the whole nave, in Bishop Herbert's building works between 1096 and 1119, and that the different minor piers to the west were the result of a change of plan in Bishop Eborard's time, between 1121 and 1145. This view is supported by clear evidence of a break in building immediately to the west of the western pair of spirals.

However, against it are the following three observations. The first minor piers in the nave are of the same design as the minor piers in Eborard's bays (Fig. 2). Therefore, if the change-of-plan theory is right, there were two changes, not one. That is, Herbert started the nave with minor pier type A and immediately changed it to type B. Then Eborard decided he preferred type A. Such things are of course possible, but this is beginning to sound somewhat complicated as an explanation. The second observation is that all the piers have their centres, as would be expected, in line with the centre of the wall, except for the spiral piers, which are set 130 mm in towards the nave. The deviation is so small that the effect is subliminal, but it makes the spirals just that fraction more prominent as the worshipper approaches from the west end of the nave (Figs 1 and 2).[2] The last observation is that the First Register of the cathedral says that

FIG. 1.   Norwich Cathedral: the nave looking east
University of East Anglia

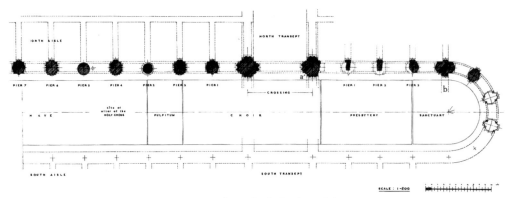

FIG. 2.   Norwich Cathedral: plan of the piers

A. D. Johnson

Herbert built 'up to the altar of the Holy Cross'.[3] Given the position of the building break in the fabric, the spiral piers can therefore be seen as marking this sanctuary.

The spiral piers act as markers not only because they are different and striking but because they have an iconographic significance. What I have been calling spiral piers would probably have been thought of by the patrons, masons and others as columns, and as such they can be seen as referring to the spiral columns marking the tomb of St Peter in his church in Rome (Fig. 3).[4]

The study of Norwich led me to examine a number of other buildings with non-uniform supports, whether they are spirals or not, among which the early Gothic cathedral at Laon was particularly rewarding.[5] In doing this, I noticed a pattern in the explanations for the odd supports. The instances in some Continental buildings have been identified as markers, as for example in Malmström's study of 12th-century churches in Rome, whereas in Britain the explanation from a change of plan was almost exclusively applied.[6] The abbey church of Romsey provides a telling example (Figs 4 and 5). Here, Charles Peers, in his study for the Victoria County History of 1911, explained the single giant-order column at the east end of each nave wall as part of an alternating system originally intended for the whole length of the nave, but altered to a non-alternating system from the third pier on.[7] Yet his own evidence, presented in the same article, placed the building break a bay west of where it would need to be for the change-of-plan explanation to work.

How is this difference of approach to be explained? I have a suggestion which takes me completely out of my areas of expertise, both chronologically and in terms of subject. I think that what we are seeing is a result of an application of the British empirical tradition as opposed to the broader philosophical traditions of the Continent. Thus explanations based on changes of plan may be attractive because they make use of random or extraneous events, such as a change in leadership, and therefore appear to be more scientific. Events such as the death of a bishop or the collapse of a tower are concrete and hence more acceptable than the slippery business of divining artistic intention. And that in turn makes me think of the most prominent argument of the late 19th and early 20th centuries, that over Darwinism, between accident, that is mutation, which was a scientific explanation, and design, which required faith. This hypothesis may sound far-fetched, but it should be placed beside the difficulty of explaining how

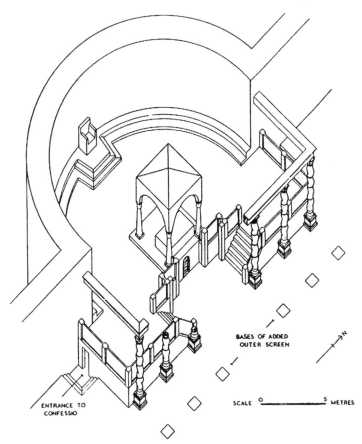

FIG. 3. Rome, St Peter's:
sanctuary as reconstructed
by Ward Perkins, 1952
(as n. 4)

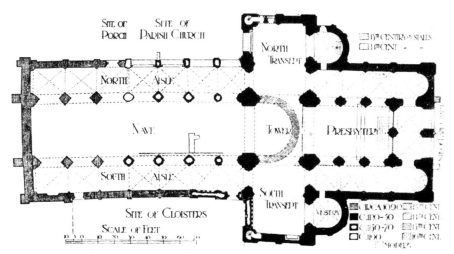

FIG. 4. Romsey Abbey: plan, from Peers, 1911 (as n. 7)

FIG. 5.   Romsey Abbey: the nave looking west
Malcolm Thurlby

as serious and careful a scholar as Charles Peers, writing in the VCH, could adopt a solution which simply sets aside his own detailed evidence. The explanation has I think to come from a cultural inclination of some importance.

THE GEOMETRY

THE geometrical proportion which I think was used in the designing of the cathedral is that between the side of a square and its diagonal (Fig. 6a). As right angles were needed for setting out the great majority of masonry buildings, the square was always available and the proportion simplicity itself to establish. In what follows, I shall present the evidence for its occurrence at Norwich, then discuss how that has been received, and finally I shall address the question of why it was used.[8]

While there is evidence throughout the building, one of the clearest areas for purposes of exposition is the relationship between the width of the aisle and the thickness of the arcade wall (Fig. 7). The side of the square forming the aisle bay has a diagonal which equals the side of the square plus the thickness of the arcade wall (Fig. 6b). In terms of dimensions, the average side of the aisle bays is 4.56 m and the aisle plus the arcade wall is 6.44 m, while a square with a side of 4.56 m has a diagonal of 6.45 m.

The relationship between the side of the cloister square and the length of the nave shows the same proportion as that between the width of the aisle and that width plus

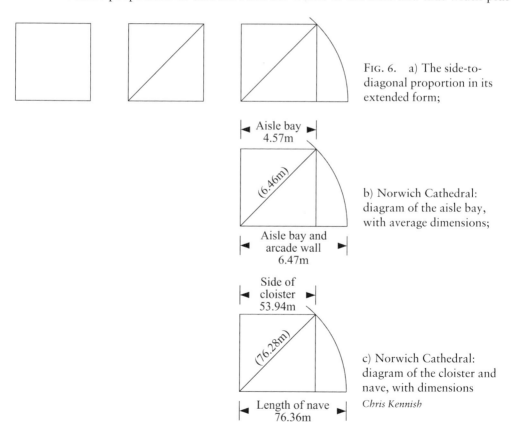

FIG. 6.   a) The side-to-diagonal proportion in its extended form;

Aisle bay
4.57m

(6.46m)

Aisle bay and
arcade wall
6.47m

b) Norwich Cathedral: diagram of the aisle bay, with average dimensions;

Side of
cloister
53.94m

(76.28m)

Length of nave
76.36m

c) Norwich Cathedral: diagram of the cloister and nave, with dimensions

Chris Kennish

49

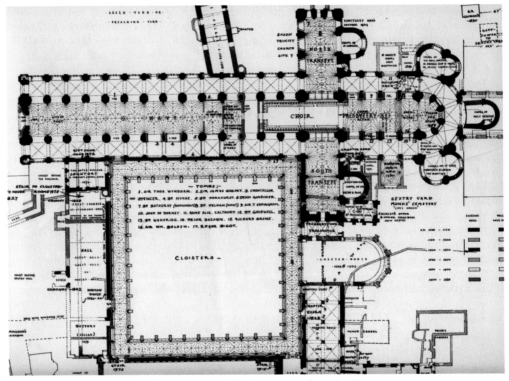

FIG. 7.   Norwich Cathedral: plan, detail
Arthur Whittingham

the arcade wall (Fig. 7). That is, the average length of the four sides of the cloister is 53.94 m and the length of the nave from the west face of the crossing to the east face of the façade is 76.36 m, while a square with a side of 53.94 m has a diagonal of 76.28 m (Fig. 6c). Longer dimensions are, of course, less trustworthy than shorter ones, as they may have been laid out less accurately, there is less certainty about which points were used for the measurements, and there is also a greater likelihood of those points having been reworked. The last consideration is relevant here in that the walls of the cloister were refaced in the 14th century.[9]

There is, however, an indication — in the numbers of bays — that the side-to-diagonal proportion was the one intended. In arithmetic terms a square with a side of 1 unit will have a diagonal which is 1.4142 etc. units long (that is, the square root of 2) and consequently a side of 10 units will have a diagonal of 14.142 etc. units. As the cloister is the equivalent of ten bays of the nave and the nave is fourteen bays long, the two are a round-number version of the 1 to 1.4142 etc. or side-to-diagonal proportion. This could, of course, be a coincidence, but another support for the proposed use of the side-to-diagonal proportion is its apparent occurrence in the layout of other Norman churches of the late 11th century, and in particular in a quirk in some examples at the point where the west wall of the cloister meets the wall of the aisle. At the cathedrals of Winchester and Worcester and the abbey church of Tewkesbury the west wall of the cloister meets the aisle wall within the length of a bay, with difficult consequences because the west cloister doorway into the south aisle is restricted or even excluded altogether (Fig. 8). If the designers were not using a particular proportion, then why would they do this? It would surely be simpler to make the cloister wall line up with the nearest bay divider. Acceptance of the difficulties suggests that they wanted to apply a particular proportion.

How has the claim that the side-to-diagonal proportion was used at Norwich been received? It has been accepted and used by Sandy Heslop, Roger Stalley and Hugh McCague, though I must here stress that Peter Kidson's fundamental thesis of 1956 lies behind all our approaches.[10] How the designer's ideas were translated into the actual building, an aspect of the subject previously neglected, has been taken up by David Yeomans, in an article in the 2011 volume of *Architectural History*. In the course of his study he uses my work on Norwich as an example. He accepts it as correct for the widths of the nave, aisles and arcade walls, but says that whether the processes proposed for the longer dimensions, such as cloister to nave, are correct remains a moot point.[11]

It has been criticized by Nigel Hiscock, in that, while he accepts the use of the side-to-diagonal proportion in the Middle Ages, he does so only in the form of a rotated square, not that of the diagonal used to extend the square, the formula I have tried to

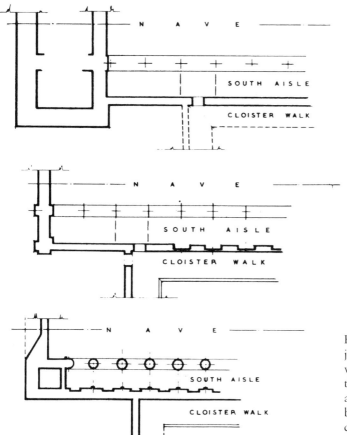

FIG. 8. Diagrams of the junction between the west wall of the cloister and the wall of the aisle at a) Winchester Cathedral, b) Worcester Cathedral, and c) the abbey of Tewkesbury

A. D. Johnson

demonstrate in the aisle bays and between the cloister and nave.[12] I cannot, however, see any reason for excluding the extended version, both because it is such a straightforward way of using the diagonal and because it was known to Vitruvius, who describes it as follows.

In width and length, atriums are divided into three classes. The first is laid out by [...]; the third, by using the width to describe a square figure with equal sides, drawing a diagonal line in this square, and giving the atrium the length of this diagonal line.[13]

Documentary references to the use of geometric forms in buildings before the 13th century are rare. The single mention in Vitruvius may not sound like much, but it puts the form into a special category in being mentioned at all.

Hiscock has questioned the relevance of the reference in Vitruvius, saying, 'Were there to be no more justification than this, it would be difficult to understand why large numbers of medieval abbey and cathedral plans should have been based on the atrium of a Roman house [...]'.[14] It had not occurred to me that citing Vitruvius's application of the extended diagonal could be taken to mean that the masons read Vitruvius and chose his third atrium as the model for their church designs. My intention was, rather, only to note Vitruvius's description as evidence that the proportion was in use. Similarly, noting the occurrence of the side-to-diagonal ratio (in both rotated and extended forms) in Insular manuscripts of the 1st millennium does not imply that the masons perused the manuscripts, only that the instances provide more evidence of its occurrence, the differences in place, time and medium adding weight to the view that its use was wide-spread.[15]

Hiscock also questions having the cloister begin the sequence of the larger dimensions, on the grounds that it is of less importance than the church. If one wants to think of the sequence in these terms, then the obvious consideration is that the cloister, if thought of as the portico of Solomon, is almost exquisitely appropriate as a starting point. More to the point, however, is that I have not made myself clear: I did not intend the cloister-to-nave proportion to be seen as a sequence beginning with the more important element, but only as evidence for the use of the proportion in these parts of the building. Indeed the sequence could as easily begin with the length of the nave and that then be taken as the diagonal of the cloister.[16]

The use of the side-to-diagonal ratio, in its extended as well as rotated form, has been proposed at numerous other buildings of the 11th and 12th centuries, such as York Minster, the chapel in the Tower of London, and the cathedral of Modena.[17] Why was the proportion used? The main possibilities can be categorized as the practical, the aesthetic and the symbolic. This is not the place for a discussion of the relative likelihood of these explanations, and in fact I want to restrict myself to a fourth, to do with what one might call association or perhaps reputation, the view that there was something about this proportion which could have made it attractive to geometers and by extension to masons.

There are two pieces of evidence for this, in the portfolio of Villard de Honnecourt and in Vitruvius. The first comes in one of the drawings on folio 20r of the portfolio, that accompanied by a text saying 'How to divide a stone so that each of its halves is square' (Fig. 9). The diagram shows a square containing a smaller square with its corners at the mid-points of the sides of the larger one, and the smaller square provided with its two diagonals. The four triangles in the smaller square are the equivalent of the four outside it, so that dividing up the initial square into the eight triangles provides the components for two smaller squares each half the area of the larger one. The other

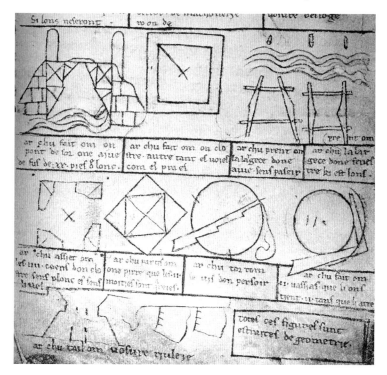

FIG. 9.   Villard de Honnecourt (as n. 18), fol. 20r, fourth row, second diagram from the left

drawings on the page present practical solutions to specific problems, such as how to establish the diameter of a column where only a small part of its circumference is visible, how to find the centre of a circle, and how to measure something which is not accessible. In the case of the square slab of stone it is not clear what problem is being solved. Why would a mason want to divide a square slab into two halves each of which is square? There are no obvious circumstances in which this might be required, and even if there were, the process of dividing the slab into eight triangles and then reconstituting them as two squares seems unnecessarily laborious, compared with simply cutting two squares to the required size out of separate pieces of stone. As Carl Barnes says,

A stone could be so cut, and the four triangular pieces on the outside reassembled to form a block of approximately the same mass as the stone remaining from the cutting. However, this would be a very impractical approach to a stereometric problem.[18]

This looks instead as if it is a mental exercise. It has landed in Villard's practical page presumably because he did not know where else to put it. Why, then, did he include it? The answer may be just because he was a magpie, but it is also possible that he or the masons who advised him knew it was important, without understanding why.

Vitruvius provides an explanation, or at least a step toward one. In paragraphs 4 and 5 of the introduction to book IX he presents the reader with the following.

First of all, among the many very useful theorems of Plato, I will cite one as demonstrated by him. Suppose there is a place or a field in the form of a square and we are required to double it. This has to be effected by means of lines correctly drawn, for it will take a kind of calculation not to be made by means of mere multiplication. The following is the demonstration. A square place ten feet long and ten feet wide gives an area of one hundred feet. Now if it is required to double the square, and to make one of two hundred feet, we must ask how long will be the side of that square so as to get from this to the two hundred feet corresponding to the doubling of the area. Nobody can find this by means of arithmetic. For if we take fourteen, multiplication will give one hundred and ninety-six feet; if fifteen, two hundred and twenty-five feet. Therefore, since this is inexplicable by arithmetic, let a diagonal line be drawn from angle to angle of that square of ten feet in length and width, dividing it into two triangles of equal size, each fifty feet in area. Taking this diagonal line as the length, describe another square. Thus we shall have in the larger square four triangles of the same size and the same number of feet as the two of fifty feet each which were formed by the diagonal line in the smaller square.[19]

This is the same form as Villard's diagram but going up in size rather than down, and, while it is practically easier to carry out, as with Villard's slab it is difficult to think of any circumstances in which it would be required. This is especially so given the way in which Vitruvius introduces the account (in paragraph 3): 'Since, therefore, these great benefits to individuals and to communities are due to the wisdom of authors, I think that not only should palms and crowns be bestowed upon them, but that they should even be granted triumphs [...]'. What on earth is there about Plato's solution which deserves such praise? The answer lies in the fact that the side-to-diagonal relationship cannot be accurately stated in whole numbers. If Vitruvius were to take a square with a side of 100 feet the diagonal would measure 141 feet and a fraction of a foot, a side of 1,000 feet would have a diagonal of 1,414 feet and a fraction over, and so on to any length, no matter how great. The diagonal is therefore an irrational magnitude, which is not a number at all.

The importance of Plato's solution lies in the problem which this concept of irrational magnitudes posed for the Pythagorean view that the structure of the universe is based on numbers, as with the musical scales and the right-angled triangle with sides of 3, 4 and 5 units. Irrational magnitudes undermine that system. The story goes that one of Pythagoras's disciples discovered the phenomenon, made it public and (it is implied, because of this) subsequently died in a shipwreck. Between the time of the discovery in the late 6th or 5th century BC and that of Plato in the early 4th, the Pythagorean system therefore remained in doubt. In the *Meno*, Plato has Socrates asking a young slave a series of questions in order to demonstrate innate knowledge, in the process solving the problem of how to double the area of a square in a form which is also square, as follows. Socrates gets the boy to agree that a square with sides 2 feet long will be 4 square feet in area (Fig. 10a) and that a square double the area will have 8 square feet.

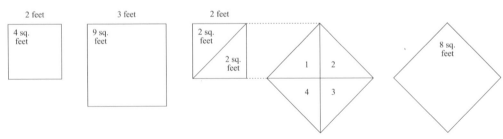

FIG. 10. Diagram illustrating the doubling of the area of a square in a form which is itself square, as described in Plato's Meno (as n. 20)

Chris Kennish

How to achieve it? A square with sides of 3 feet will contain 9 square feet, which is obviously too large (Fig. 10b). Rather than continuing by trial and error with lengths shorter than 3 feet, Socrates gets the boy to divide the square in half using its diagonal, each of the two triangles therefore being 2 square feet in area (Fig. 10c). He then in a series of steps puts together four of these triangles, using what had been the diagonal as the side of a new square, which will consist of four shapes of 2 square feet each, or 8 square feet in total (Fig. 10d). Socrates has therefore made the transition by a series of discrete steps, and therefore by whole numbers, thereby re-establishing the validity of the Pythagorean system. The order of the universe was restored, Plato warranted the highest honours, and the side-to-diagonal proportion was given an air of huge if rather vague importance which lasted not only through Greek and Roman antiquity, but the Middle Ages as well.[20]

CONCLUSION

THERE are other aspects of the design of the cathedral which can be explained by the side-to-diagonal ratio, such as the angles of the bishop's palace and the north-east and south-east radiating chapels.[21] Equally, the spiral forms are only one of a number of subtleties in the piers of the building, especially those of the crossing, the east arm and the apse. Taking these elements together with such things as the symbolism of the slope of the floor on the aisles in the eastern arm, the inventiveness of the vaults of the bays of the ambulatory around the apse, and the handling of the spiral staircases in the elevation of the east wall of the transept, Herbert de Losinga's cathedral can indeed be considered, as John Onians once called it, an intelligent building.

NOTES

1. Fernie, *AHNC*.

2. E. Fernie, 'The Romanesque piers of Norwich cathedral', *NA*, 36 (1977), 383–86. The plan in Fig. 2 is the work of the architect, the late Don Johnson, who gave me unstinting support — in both measuring and drawing — in my work on the cathedral and many other buildings, and also to other members of staff in the School of Fine Art and Music, University of East Anglia.

3. H. W. Saunders, *The First Register of Norwich Cathedral*, Norfolk Record Society, 11 (1939), fol. 8r.

4. J. B. Ward Perkins, 'The shrine of St Peter and its twelve marble columns', *Journal of Roman Studies*, 42 (1952), 21–33.

5. E. Fernie, 'The use of varied nave supports in Romanesque and early Gothic churches', *Gesta*, 23 (1984), 107–17. This interpretation of the non-uniform supports in the nave of Laon as intended markers is accepted by A. Sturgis, 'The Liturgy and its relationship to Gothic cathedral design and Ornamentation in late 12th- and early 13th-c France' (unpublished Ph.D. thesis, University of London, 1991), 162–63. Peter Draper, *The Formation of English Gothic: Architecture and Identity* (London 2006), 198, says Sturgis has established that there were no liturgical reasons for the form of the architecture at Laon. Sturgis did come to that conclusion, but concerning the eastern extension of the building, whereas his approval of the link in the case of the nave piers is unequivocal. In conversation Draper has agreed that this is the case. For further examples of non-uniform supports which appear to have a design function, see M. Thurlby, 'Articulation as an expression of function in Romanesque architecture', in *Architecture and Interpretation*, ed. J. Franklin, T. A. Heslop and C. Stevenson (Woodbridge 2012), 42–59, and J. Mitchell, 'Believing is seeing: the natural image in late antiquity', *Architecture and Interpretation*, 16–41, and for the subject of iconographic supports on the broadest canvas, J. Onians, *Bearers of Meaning* (Princeton 1988).

6. R. E. Malmström, 'The colonnades of high medieval churches at Rome', *Gesta*, 14/2 (1975), 37–45. See also J. Habich and C. Timm, *Handbuch der Deutschen Kunstdenkmäler, Hamburg, Schleswig-Holstein* (Munich, 1971), on the church at Bad Segeberg.

7. C. Peers, VCH, *Hampshire*, 4 (London 1911, reprinted 1973), 460–64.

8. E. Fernie, 'The ground plan of Norwich Cathedral and the square root of two', *JBAA*, 129 (1976), 78–86, and Fernie, *AHNC*, 94–100.

9. The dimensions of all the aisle bays, the sides of the cloister, and many other parts of the cathedral are available in Fernie, *AHNC*, appendix 3.

10. P. Kidson, 'Systems of Measurement and Proportion in Early Medieval Architecture' (unpublished Ph.D. thesis, 2 vols, University of London, 1956); T. A. Heslop, *Norwich Castle Keep: Romanesque Architecture and Social Context* (Norwich 1994), and 'Orford castle: nostalgia and sophisticated living', *Architectural History*, 34 (1991), 36–58; R. Stalley, 'Gaelic Friars and Gothic Design', in *Medieval Architecture and its Intellectual Context: Studies in Honour of Peter Kidson*, ed. P. Crossley and E. Fernie (London 1990), 191–202. H. McCague, 'Learning from the Medieval Master Masons: A Geometric Journey through the Labyrinth', in *Historical Models in the Mathematics Classroom*, ed. A. Shell-Gellasch (Washington 2007), 1–15, and 'A Mathematical Look at a Medieval Cathedral', *Math Horizons*, X/4 (Mathematical Association of America, April 2003), 11–15, 31.

11. D. Yeomans, 'The Geometry of a Piece of String', *Architectural History*, 54 (2011), 23–47.

12. N. Hiscock, 'A schematic plan for Norwich Cathedral', in *Ad Quadratum. The practical application of geometry in medieval architecture*, ed. N. Wu (Aldershot and Burlington 2002), 83–121.

13. Vitruvius, *Ten Books on Architecture*, trans. M. Morgan (Harvard 1926), VI, III, 3; see also the translation of F. Granger, Loeb Classical Library, 2 vols (Cambridge, Massachusetts 1970).

14. N. Hiscock, *The Wise Master Builder: Platonic Geometry in Plans of Medieval Abbeys and Cathedrals* (Aldershot, Brookfield USA, Singapore and Sydney 2000), 7. There is another criticism Hiscock makes of something I have written which is not to do with Norwich Cathedral. Ibid., 208, he says, 'It is often held to be essential, however, that each building study should be supported by measurements taken from the building in question by the person studying it', with a reference to E. Fernie, 'A beginner's guide to the study of architectural proportions and systems of length', *Studies in Honour of Peter Kidson* (as in n. 10), 229–38 at 230. What I say there is this: 'The investigator on the other hand should always conduct the exercise by means of calculations, using measurements derived from the building itself and not by the inaccurate if more romantic method of drawing lines on a plan'. There is nothing in these words which suggests that the investigator has to take the measurements with their own hands — which would be a marvellous piece of New Age nonsense. The point I was making is also made by Robert Bork in *The Geometry of Creation: Architectural Drawing and the Dynamics of Gothic Design* (Farnham and Brookfield 2011), 11: 'Three closely linked methodological problems have undercut the authority of most publications on Gothic geometry: imprecision, ambiguity, and wishful thinking [...] Another sort of imprecision can arise in the testing of geometrical hypotheses if, for example, the testing method involves drawing candidate lines manually across the underlying survey drawing'.

15. On the insular manuscripts, see R. D. Stevick, 'The art of radically coherent geometry', in *Villard's Legacy: Studies in Medieval Technology, Science and Art in Memory of Jean Gimpel*, ed. M.-T. Zenner (Aldershot 2004), 211–28.

16. Hiscock, 'Norwich Cathedral' (as in n. 12), 84; W. Dynes, 'The Medieval cloister as Portico of Solomon', *Gesta*, 12 (1973), 61–69.

17. C. Norton, *Archbishop Thomas of Bayeux and the Norman Cathedral at York* (York 2001); R. B. Harris, 'The structural history of the White Tower', in *The White Tower*, ed. E. Impey (New Haven and London 2008), 90–92; E. Casari, 'Osservazioni sulla planimetria del Duomo di Modena: Lanfranco, i quadrati, le diagonali', in *Lanfranco e Wiligelmo: il Duomo di Modena*, ed. E. Castelnuovo, V. Fumagalli, A. Peroni and S. Settis (Modena 1984), 223–27.

18. C. F. Barnes, *The Portfolio of Villard de Honnecourt* (Farnham 2009), 136; H. Hahnloser, *Villard de Honnecourt: Kritische Gesamtausgabe* (Graz 1972), 111–12 and pl. 39 (the equivalent of Barnes's fol. 20r).

19. Vitruvius, *Ten Books on Architecture* (as in n. 13).

20. Plato, *Meno*, 82a7–85b6, trans. R. W. Sharples (Chicago 1985), 67–77. On the theoretical problems, see T. Heath, *A History of Greek Mathematics*, 2 vols (Oxford 1921), I, 65, and for those and the shipwreck, A. Wasserstein, 'Theaetetus and the History of the Theory of Numbers', *Classical Quarterly*, new series, 8(3/4) (1958), 165–79, especially 165–66, nn. 2 and 3. Concerning the discovery of incommensurables, see also K. R. Popper, *Conjectures and Refutations* (London 1972), ch. 2, esp. 83-87. The new square in Socrates's demonstration relates to the initial one as illustrated in Fig. 10e, producing squares which relate in the same way as the larger and smaller squares in Villard's diagram (Fig. 9). I would like to thank Sandy Heslop for pointing out that, in distinguishing between measure and number in addition to weight, the Vulgate contains elements of the Pythagorean-Platonic strain of thought represented by the side-to-diagonal problem. (*Sed omnia mensura et numero et pondere disposuisti*. Wisdom 11.21.)

21. Fernie, 'The ground plan of Norwich Cathedral' (as in n. 8).

Reconstructing the Cathedral-Priory at Norwich: Recent Research on Lost Parts of the Romanesque Church

ROLAND B. HARRIS

Although it saw considerable neo-Romanesque re-styling in the 19th century, Norwich Cathedral remains one of the more complete Romanesque great churches in England. In part this reflects continuity from the medieval cathedral priory to the post-Dissolution secular cathedral, but it is also a product of the comparatively modest scale of the Gothic additions and alterations. Significant parts of the building constructed between 1096 and 1145 have been lost, however, and this article presents recent research on several of the missing — as opposed to remodelled or restored — elements of the cathedral, comprising the axial chapel, the presbytery clerestory and the roofs.

INTRODUCTION

NORWICH Cathedral is a substantially complete Romanesque building, effectively the most intact late-11th- and 12th-century great church in England. This degree of survival means that analysis of the original form of the cathedral is more straightforward than is the case with many of its contemporaries. Later medieval and post-medieval losses of primary fabric, however, are significant, and previous studies of the Romanesque cathedral have sought to establish the form of missing or heavily altered elements of the building to better understand the overall design. For example, in his lecture of 1847, Robert Willis presented graphical reconstructions of the original form of the axial chapel and the presbytery internal elevation, and discussed the alterations to the gallery walls and roofs and the belfry interior.[1] More recent studies of the Romanesque building by Eric Fernie and Stephen Heywood have amplified and developed this analysis of the missing primary fabric,[2] and have been supplemented by detailed studies of individual parts of the cathedral: Philip McAleer has examined the evidence for the original form of the west front and its neo-Romanesque development in the 19th century,[3] and Roberta Gilchrist has discussed the evidence for the primary form of the exterior of the central tower and the north elevation of the north transept.[4] Despite such attention, problems remain in that evidence for several missing elements of the Romanesque cathedral has been misinterpreted, under-examined, or, even, largely ignored. This paper considers the evidence for three of the more significant lost parts of the primary fabric: the axial chapel, the roofs, and the presbytery clerestory.

THE AXIAL CHAPEL

THE building of Norwich Cathedral in 1096 — as recorded in the later account by the Norwich monk Bartholomew Cotton, who began writing his chronicle in 1292 —

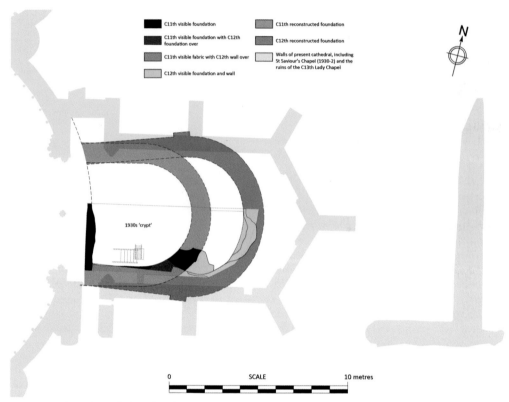

C11th visible foundation

C11th visible foundation with C12th foundation over

C11th visible fabric with C12th wall over

C12th visible foundation and wall

C11th reconstructed foundation

C12th reconstructed foundation

Walls of present cathedral, including St Saviour's Chapel (1930-2) and the ruins of the C13th Lady Chapel

1930s 'crypt'

N

0   SCALE   10 metres

FIG. 1.   Plan of axial chapels, showing foundations set within outline of St Saviour's Chapel and with reconstructed form

started with the laying of foundation stones in what was evidently the axial chapel, dedicated to the Holy Saviour and located at the eastern extremity of the church.[5] The present axial chapel (St Saviour's chapel), which projects eastwards from the Romanesque ambulatory, was built in 1930–32 to the design of Sir Charles Nicholson.[6] Its foundations sit inside those of Bishop Walter Suffield's 13th-century Lady chapel, which had been demolished, possibly following neglect, in the late 16th century.[7] The extent of the 1240s chapel was revealed by excavation in 1871,[8] and remains of the east and part of the south walls survive as low ruins in the ground to the east of the present chapel. The scarring of its former abutment with the cathedral is plainly visible externally, while the 13th-century double-arched entrance to the Lady chapel was unblocked in 1930–32 to provide access to the new St Saviour's chapel from the ambulatory. Excavations for the construction of Nicholson's building exposed remains of foundations pre-dating the work of the 1240s, which were left accessible in a concrete-roofed space created under the new floor. The flint-rubble foundations exposed during the building works represent just over half the area of an apsidal axial chapel: only the southern part of the chapel foundations survived in 1930–31, and an east–west concrete wall was inserted to form the northern wall of the new 'crypt'.

The late-11th-century Romanesque foundations (Figs 2 and 3) are of exceptional interest, and have been the subject of some discussion. A false start to building the

FIG. 2.   Remains of ambulatory and west part of axial chapel foundations

FIG. 3.   Remains of east part of axial chapel foundations

cathedral has been proposed by Fernie, who reinterpreted remains of what Dean Cranage had suggested, in 1931–32, was evidence for a smaller Saxon chapel found within the remains of a larger horseshoe-shaped Norman chapel.[9] Fernie discounted Cranage's Saxon dating of the lower western foundations, suggesting instead that work began in 1096, that the smaller chapel had external walls of an oblong plan, and that this start on foundations was followed almost immediately by a change in design, which resulted in the building of a larger axial chapel on a different, more northerly, axis.[10] Subsequently, Heywood developed the idea and argued that this putative aborted Romanesque chapel, and more widespread works on foundations on this different axis, may have pre-dated the 1096 foundation by as much as five years, which he later modified to a start date of c. 1094.[11] Even ignoring Barbara Dodwell's more substantive argument, on documentary grounds, that preparations for the new building began in 1095,[12] Heywood's proposed chronology is suspect: for Herbert to have laid his foundation stone in 1096 only at the start of works on a second axial chapel requires, rather implausibly, that the beginning of the first chapel, and any other building work at this time on the eastern arm, was not seen as the start of works proper, but as some experimental exercise.[13] More importantly, however, recent metric survey of the foundations of the supposed aborted axial chapel[14] shows that the plan made by Sir Charles Nicholson in 1932 (published by Cranage and then reproduced uncritically by Fernie and Heywood) is highly inaccurate, and that the lower western foundations are not off-axis when compared with the Romanesque chapel as built or, indeed, the cathedral itself. The modern survey also shows that the supposedly aborted axial chapel was substantially wider than Nicholson's plan indicates, at c. 5.6 m rather than c. 3.8 m (Fig. 1). The fact that the western apse-like foundations are not off-axis is significant, as the hitherto supposed change in axis is central to Heywood's argument for a radical redesign of the chapel and the eastern arm early in the construction of the cathedral.[15] The revised actual width of the chapel is also noteworthy, as Fernie and Heywood's comparison of the dimension to that at Bury (which they give as c. 3.7 m) no longer stands as evidence of an exact parallel between this element of the two designs.[16]

This leaves the question as to what other conclusions can be drawn from the excavated foundations? What is clear is that the lower, or western, foundation is generally consistent with that of the adjoining ambulatory outer wall, and the two are bonded: the large flint cobble courses run through and the mortar is consistent and seamless. The straight part of the side foundation of this part of the 11th-century chapel is approximately parallel to the axis of the cathedral. The curved eastern part of this strongly suggests an apse, but it must be noted that in 1930–32 no evidence was found for a continuation of the apse wall. Although Fernie and Heywood both state that the fabric of the putative earlier apse exactly matches the work above and to the east,[17] there is, as Cranage noted, considerable difference:[18] the lower, western work has clearly defined courses of flint rubble, with evidence of banding in the foundations, while that to the east and above has a heavily mortared — almost rendered — face, giving a much smoother finish and making the individual flints hard to distinguish. The mortared face of the higher work is not surprising since, being offset, it presumably marks the lower part of the wall proper as distinct from the wider foundation. Where the mortared finish is used in the foundations of the eastern apsidal wall, however, it does represent a different technique from the foundations to the west. The mortar of the two types of work is also rather different, and, significantly, the junction of the two types is evident in the mass of foundation to the east of the smaller western apse wall: the curved outer face of the small apse wall (*c.* 1.10 m thick) is abutted by a mass of later rubble work that formed part of the works of the eastern apse.

The sequence of foundation construction is clear. First, the foundations of the smaller apsidal chapel were built at the same time as those of the ambulatory. The internal apse of this early work was matched by a curved outer face, not the squared form suggested by Fernie. These foundations were then succeeded, and partly overlain, by those of a larger chapel, of horseshoe plan. What is less clear is whether the first chapel was completed or whether the design was revised at foundation level. As we have seen, both Fernie and Heywood argue that the modification was at foundation level. This is almost inevitable given their suggestion that the initial chapel was built off-axis to the present cathedral, and given apparent support by their contention that the fabric of the two phases of work is identical. With neither argument standing up to scrutiny, it is evident that the answer lies in the date of the second foundations. Of course, this flint-rubble offers little in the way of datable features, beyond the general horseshoe and apsidal form, together with what appears to be the foundation for a respond of an arch opening into its apse. Given this form and the replacement of the chapel by Bishop Suffield's Lady chapel in the 1240s, there is little doubt that the second phase of foundations is Romanesque. However, the very different technique of the foundations from those of the smaller apse and the ambulatory means that it is very difficult to argue that the secondary foundations represent a modification made at foundation level. Indeed, with the cathedral's rubble foundations in the style of those of the western apse and ambulatory (i.e. with banding and very visible large courses of flint) continuing through to the building of the cloister outer walls (as observed most closely in the Hostry excavations of 2007) in the early 12th century,[19] it is most likely that the secondary foundations under Nicholson's chapel post-date the initial construction of the entire cathedral and its conventual buildings. In short, it is most likely that the earliest foundations excavated in the 1930s are those of a fully realized axial chapel of the 1090s, which was replaced at some point during the 12th century.

PRESBYTERY CLERESTORY

ALTHOUGH the Romanesque clerestory survives in the nave (Fig. 4) and the transepts, that in the presbytery was destroyed or substantially damaged by the collapse of the spire in 1362, which fell through the presbytery roof.[20] The new clerestory was built in 1364–86, replicating the bay divisions of its predecessor, but rising 5.2 m higher. This higher clerestory was probably provided with flying-buttresses, which were replaced with the present ones when a stone vault was added in 1472–99.[21] Despite such complete rebuilding, the western ends of both the north (Fig. 5) and south clerestory passages are marked by a Romanesque respond (the southern one is heavily restored), which is consistent with the form of the surviving Romanesque clerestories in the other arms of the cathedral. Further Romanesque masonry is found *in situ* in the rear, or outer wall, of the presbytery clerestory passage; it includes the base of a nook shaft for a window in the western bay of the southern passage and ashlar that shows the abutment of groin vaulting over the clerestory passage in what was otherwise solid walling between each bay (Fig. 6). Thus, like the intact Romanesque clerestory in the rest of the cathedral, each of the straight bays in the eastern arm had a large central arch corresponding with the window, flanked by small arches opening into a continuous wall passage, with the bays separated by wall shafts rising from ground level. The taller central

FIG. 4.   Surviving Romanesque clerestory in nave

arches spring from an upper tier of small nook, or stilt, shafts that sit on top of the
more substantial lower shafts from which spring the minor arches.

A graphical reconstruction of the original form of the presbytery clerestory was first
presented by Willis in 1847, and Fernie's analysis subsequently came to similar conclusions.[22] Fernie's reconstructed elevation of a single bay, however, includes details that
differ from the surviving Romanesque clerestory to the west and for which there is no
evidence: the freestanding lower shafts are shown with pronounced entasis, and the
upper nook shafts are depicted without bases. Conversely, there is no reference to a
significant difference: the outer wall of the presbytery passage is of ashlar, while, other
than a single bay (immediately joining those of the eastern arm) in each of the transepts,
the passage wall is of rubble construction. The presbytery clerestory passage is further
distinguished from that in the rest of the cathedral by the consistent use of groin
vaulting for the low passages behind the minor arches. Although there are occasional
occurrences of such groin vaults elsewhere in the cathedral (most notably in the eastern
part of the nave north passage), the majority of the clerestory uses plain barrel vaulting.
It is possible that the presbytery clerestory had other details that distinguished it from
that in the transepts and the nave.

Fernie refers to the earliest example of the tripartite clerestory as being that at
Winchester (begun 1079) and identifies the particular form with stilted nook shafts as
distinctively East Anglian.[23] Heywood's subsequent paper on the Romanesque architecture of Norwich Cathedral develops the discussion of the sources of the clerestory,
identifying the tripartite arrangement here as having 'its immediate source at Ely',
begun in 1083.[24] While the key role of Winchester is evident, marking the departure

FIG. 5. Surviving Romanesque north-west respond of presbytery clerestory

from the equal arches of early examples of clerestory passages in Normandy, at St Etienne, Caen (1060s), and at Cerisy la Forêt (*c.* 1080), the clerestory at Norwich actually finds its closest parallel — not least in the upper level of nook shafts to support the impost of the main arch — in the equally, if not more, sophisticated example at Westminster Hall (Fig. 7).[25] With Westminster Hall first used by William Rufus for a feast at Whitsun (29 May) 1099 and under construction in 1097,[26] this suggests that it was begun in the mid-1090s. Whatever the exact start date, it is highly probable that the building of the windows and wall passage at Westminster Hall predates the clerestory at Norwich Cathedral. The influence of secular Westminster Hall is hardly surprising as it was one of the pre-eminent Anglo-Norman buildings of the late 11th century, and, more specifically, Herbert de Losinga was a court favourite of William Rufus (and then Henry I), and one of the principal patrons of architectural projects of his time. Although Westminster Hall was, as seems almost certain, the immediate source for the

FIG. 6.   Ashlar rear wall
of Romanesque presbytery
clerestory, which shows
former presence of groin-
vaulting

clerestory at Norwich, the cathedral was very probably the key influence on the subsequent adoption of similar clerestories elsewhere in East Anglia, at Binham Priory (from *c*. 1100) and Peterborough Abbey (now Cathedral: begun 1117–18). Fernie's argument that the example at Waltham Abbey (from *c*. 1125) also derives from Norwich is unnecessary (Losinga died around six years before it was begun), and, given the royal patronage at Waltham, it again ignores the potential influence of Westminster Hall.[27] Moreover, the type is found in a sophisticated form at Romsey *c*. 1140, with no East Anglian connection, although again with a direct royal link via its patron, Henry of Blois. Subsequently, as Lawrence Hoey has noted, the 'stilt shaft' survived in Gothic form in the North in the clerestories of Ripon Minster, Nun Monkton, Coldingham Priory and Hexham Abbey.[28]

The four straight bays of the presbytery at Norwich end at the apse chord, where opposing responds with double-shafts rise from ground-level to capitals at the level of

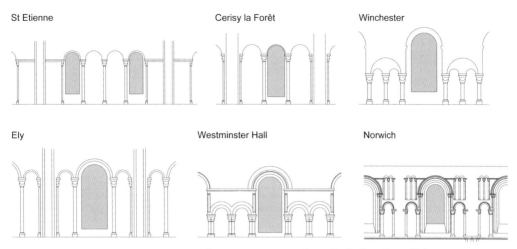

FIG. 7.   Romanesque clerestories: Norwich Cathedral and parallels

the floor of the clerestory passage. There can be little doubt that these responds carried a transverse, or diaphragm, arch at clerestory level, rising above this to form a gable, and buttressed by the former solid walls with arches at this point at gallery level (see below). Just to the east of the southern respond a Romanesque base survives at the level of the clerestory passage, which is today 790 mm lower than that of the straight bays. Its northern counterpart dates from the 19th century, rather than *c.* 1100 as hitherto assumed,[29] but it is not clear whether this reconstruction was based on surviving fabric or was simply designed to match the southern respond. On both sides of the presbytery, the lowest courses of the outer walls of the Romanesque clerestory passage survive sufficiently, before being superseded by the straight walls of the 14th-century polygonal east end, to show that the passage continued into the Romanesque apse. These details suggest that the eastern arm terminated in a masonry semi-dome, penetrated at its base by a wall passage with low arches rather than the tripartite arrangement of the rest of the cathedral. Fernie and Heywood propose that the arches of the apse matched the smaller arches of the straight bays, with two arches to each bay, forming a continuous run of arches, or arcade, around the apse. Two small arches to each bay of the apse are indeed more likely than single arches (which, at 2.21 m wide, would have approached the scale of the main clerestory openings in the straight bays), although the position of the surviving bases show that the apse arches would have been separated by substantial areas of solid masonry (albeit penetrated by the passage) approximately 700 mm wide, excluding the responds or half-shafts (Fig. 8): the widths of the apse bays and the location of the surviving bases preclude the continuous row of equal-sized arches shown in Fernie's reconstruction.[30] This reconstructed sectional elevation also depicts the semi-dome springing above the level of the clerestory arches, which accurate survey data of the cathedral shows is rather implausible: a true semi-dome with a radius of 4.3 m rising to the apex of the straight bay wall heads at *c.* 25.1 m OD, would have sprung from 20.8 m OD, which is only *c.* 1.1 m above the apse clerestory passage floor and, thus, below the likely apexes of the arches in the clerestory passage around the apse. This implies that the semi-dome was squat or, more likely, that it was cut by groining to allow for the clerestory arches. Such groining is found elsewhere in the cathedral, in

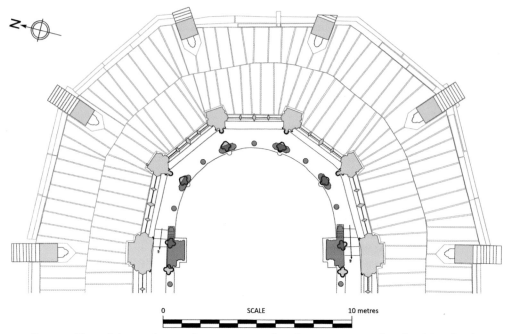

FIG. 8.   Plan of the presbytery clerestory apse, showing reconstructed arches (tinted red)

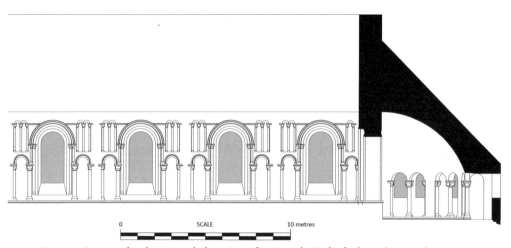

FIG. 9.   Longitudinal sectional elevation of Norwich Cathedral presbytery clerestory
(reconstruction)

the semi-domes of the apses of the Romanesque vaults in the ground-level Jesus chapel, St Luke's chapel and St Andrew's chapel. Christopher Wilson suggests an umbrella vault, with the surviving gallery-level shafts continuing as vault ribs up to the apex of the semi-dome, and this certainly makes more sense if groining was required to accommodate the clerestory arches .[31] Similar shafts survive at Cerisy la Forêt, although the umbrella vault here is a Gothic replacement and does not follow the 11th-century bay divisions below. Of course, at Norwich more localized, low level, groining would not preclude rib vaults extending to the apex of a smooth semi-dome, as appears to have been the case originally at Cerisy la Forêt and which survives from the 12th century at St Georges de Boscherville.

ROOFS

No parts of the Romanesque roofs survive at Norwich Cathedral. Although renewal of the roofs in 1955–70 saw the destruction of almost all the medieval roof carpentry,[32] it is unlikely that any Romanesque timbers survived into modern times. In part, this was ensured by later medieval events (most notably the destruction of the presbytery roof by the falling spire in 1362) and alterations, such as the heightening of the galleries throughout the cathedral in the 15th century. It might be expected that the introduction of high vaults to all four arms of the church in the 15th and early 16th centuries saw replacement of any earlier roofs (especially in the case of the transepts, where vaulting followed a fire in 1509[33]), although the scant records of the roofs prior to their removal in the 20th century suggests that this was not the case. The roofs recorded by Repton *c.*1800[34] and by Bernard Feilden in 1955 and 1965, in the nave, north transept and south transept,[35] were of steep-pitched scissor-braced form most closely associated with 13th-century works (Fig. 10) and, thus, are unlikely to date from as late as the introduction of vaulting. As with William of Wykeham's more substantial remodelling of the nave at Winchester Cathedral,[36] the insertion of stone vaults in the transepts and

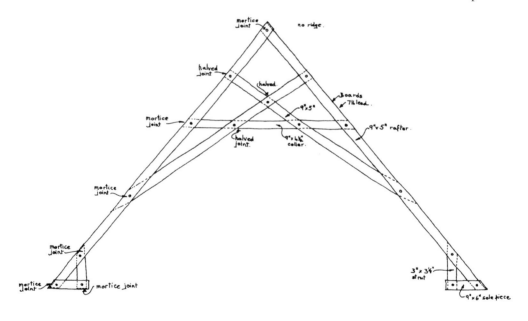

FIG. 10.   Drawing of scissor-braced roof truss (from nave), by Feilden & Mawson architects (1965)

nave at Norwich left the existing roofs seemingly intact, although the fire damage to the transept roofs in 1509 may have required significant repair. While almost certainly predating the high vaults, the scissor-braced roofs evidently did not date back to the initial roofing of the Romanesque cathedral, as the roof type first appeared at the very end of the 12th century, and, thus, represents later re-roofing, very probably during the 13th or early 14th century.

The general form of the main Romanesque roofs at Norwich Cathedral has been explored previously, drawing on the pitch of surviving gables and the evidence of abutments against the faces of the crossing tower. In particular, both Fernie and Heywood focus on the evidence for the presbytery roof, which takes the form of a trapezoidal painted border to an area of fictive masonry on the east face of the crossing tower (Fig. 11). While recognizing that the painting itself represents restoration, they note that it coincides with disturbed masonry and conclude that it represents the outline of the Romanesque roof, with the horizontal upper border marking the location of the roof collars. Certainly, a small area of scarring is visible, along with a more extensive area of plaster or render patching on the northern pitch, which suggests that the painted outline (19th-century restoration or overpainting) does constitute important evidence of the roof destroyed by the collapse of the spire in 1362. That it represents evidence for the Romanesque roof, however, is less convincing. The scissor-braced roofs of the transepts and nave suggest major re-roofing in the 13th or the early 14th century, and it is likely that this included the eastern arm. In this regard it is highly significant that the soffits of the collar of the nave and transept scissor-braced roof trusses, as recorded in

FIG. 11.   Fictive masonry at west end of presbytery (east side of crossing)

1955 and 1965, exactly match the upper horizontal border of the painted area in the presbytery. Moreover, the origins of the painted fictive masonry and border are not Romanesque, but almost certainly lie as part of a decorative scheme of wall painting much in evidence elsewhere in the eastern arm, which, on stylistic grounds, dates from the second half of the 13th century and which may have followed damage in the 1272 riots.[37] It is quite likely that the riot, which saw extensive burning,[38] also instigated, or even necessitated, the replacement of the Romanesque roofs.

Fernie identifies a steep original pitch from the outset for the transept and nave roofs on the basis of the masonry of the respective faces of the crossing tower.[39] There is no clear evidence of this; rather there are areas of patching that suggest a lower-pitched roof than at present. Equally, his assumption that the surviving north transept gable represents the Romanesque roof pitch is mistaken.[40] Although not remodelled like the

0   SCALE   5 metres

FIG. 12.   Elevation of north transept gable, showing original lower pitch (red), blocked niches by present facework (green) and reconstructed upper window (blue), arising from analysis of the elevation by the author during works in 1996–97

west front or south transept gables in the 19th century, recording by the author during conservation works in 1996–97 revealed significant earlier remodelling of the gable showing that its present pitch of 52.5° is significantly steeper than the gable of *c.* 1100, which had a pitch of *c.* 47.0°.[41] Gilchrist suggests that the remodelling occurred in the 16th century,[42] when the transept vaults were inserted, but it is much more likely that the pitch of the gable was steepened when the scissor-braced roof was inserted, probably in the 13th or early 14th century. The lower pitch of the north transept Romanesque gable is consistent with what is known of 11th- and early-12th-century roofs, and provides further confirmation that the much steeper painted 'scar' on the east wall of the crossing tower (with a pitch of 52.3°)[43] relates to a subsequent Gothic roof.

Reconstructing the minor roofs of the Romanesque cathedral is, for the most part, less complex. One exception is the roofing of the two-storey radiating chapels of the eastern arm, for which no evidence survives, but which may well have seen different ridge heights and alignments for the two parts of the upper chapels.[44] The roofs of the two-storey apsidal chapels of the transepts were rather simpler, and, although both of the upper chapels have been removed, the form can be determined from the roof scars. In both cases there were roofs on an east–west axis, pitched at 47.5°: this closely matches the pitch of the Romanesque north gable of the transept (see above). Immediately below the roof scars are blocked semi-circular arches, which formerly were open to the transepts. In the case of the north transept example, Gilchrist interpreted the arch as representing the remains of a primary barrel vault.[45] There is, however, insufficient room between the soffits of the arches and the upper surfaces of the roofs above for such vaults: the space, which would have had to include rafters and the roof covering (probably lead on boards), measures as little as 415 mm. Quite clearly, the upper chapels were open to their roof timbers.

The most extensive minor roofs comprised those of the galleries of the nave and eastern arm, removed during heightening of the outer walls in 1454–62 and 1472–99 respectively.[46] The low-pitched 15th-century roofs were in turn almost completely replaced in 1973–75.[47] The scars of the Romanesque lean-to roofs remain plainly visible in the north and south galleries of the eastern arm, and the north gallery of the nave, and show the pitch to have been *c.* 37.5°. More interestingly, substantial evidence survives to show that the gallery roofs relied on the support of masonry quadrant-arches (Fig. 13). The lower parts of the outer walls of the galleries retain the Romanesque fabric largely intact. In the eastern arm and the nave south gallery the bays of the outer wall are separated by responds with two half-shafts, which rise to the level of the abaci and imposts of the Romanesque windows and blind arcading. In the nave north gallery the responds were removed when the gallery was heightened in the 15th century or, perhaps, subsequently, leaving scars and patching. The responds in both the nave and the presbytery galleries carried quadrant arches that rose to the surviving higher responds on the inner, or arcaded, side of the gallery. There is, however, an exception at the point of the apse chord in the eastern arm, where lower inner responds reflect the fact that here there were solid walls with semicircular arches, similar to those found where the galleries meet the transepts. Although almost entirely removed, it is possible to reconstruct the form of the quadrant arches themselves as some *in situ* fragments of the arches survive. In the nave removal of the inner ends of the arches has been almost complete, with only a few blocks of ashlar surviving above the abaci in the south gallery. These blocks have been incorporated within more substantial brick piers that support the principal members of the gallery roofs. Where the nave outer responds survive, in the south gallery, the springing points of the

FIG. 13.   Presbytery south gallery showing reconstructed quadrant arches

Romanesque quadrant arches have been removed throughout, except in the case of the third respond from the east. Here, the lowest voussoir of a quadrant arch survives intact, along with a stub of masonry bonding it to the south wall, and provides important evidence of the profile of the arches. In the eastern arm the reuse of the lower outer responds by the later flying buttresses saw removal of any Romanesque masonry above the capitals, but the fact that the 15th-century roof did not reuse the inner responds to support its principal members has led to the survival of remains of the upper ends of the quadrant-arches. This comprises four courses of horizontally-coursed ashlar and areas of rough flint-rubble core work above the capitals of the responds and below the ashlar remains of pilaster buttresses that articulate what would have been the exterior of the Romanesque clerestory. In one case, in the third respond from the west on the south side, sufficient ashlar survives to show that the soffit of the quadrant arches coincided with the top of the respond abaci. The evidence of these *in situ* remains can be combined with that of the scars of the Romanesque aisle roofs where they abut the transepts to give the exact form of the quadrant arches (Fig. 13). The delicate Norwich examples are very similar to the quadrant-arches in the nave galleries at Durham, begun *c.* 1110, in their lightweight form (i.e. *c.* 400 mm deep) before being thickened for raising of the roof in the 15th century and addition of orders of arches in 1914.[48] Similar quadrant arches are also found in the later work at Cerisy la Forêt (north choir gallery) of the early 12th century. Like the quadrant-arches at Norwich, these other examples were also designed as roof supports, not as buttressing for high vaults.

While the pitch of the Romanesque roofs at Norwich Cathedral can be determined and, in the case of the gallery roofs, the masonry components can be reconstructed, there is little evidence for the form of the carpentry. Heywood's reconstruction of the presbytery roof is determined by the misapprehension that the form of the roof had to reflect the later painting on the east face of the crossing tower,[49] but also — in such details as tie-beams corresponding to the bay divisions below — fails to take into account what is known in terms of contemporary roofs in Normandy and elsewhere on the Continent,[50] and, to a more limited extent, in England:[51] the most relevant English example is the early-12th-century roof at Ely Cathedral reconstructed from reused timbers by Gavin Simpson.[52] This evidence suggests that as first built Norwich Cathedral had a common tie-beam roof, with multiple hangers angled between the tie-beams and the rafter couples, allowing comparatively lightweight construction: it was this lighter construction that appears to have necessitated such frequent replacement of Norman roofs in the later medieval period. Ceilings to the roofs are a possibility, although appear to be ruled out by the presence of blind arches, flanking and set slightly higher than central doorways, or openings, on the faces of the tower above tie-beam level overlooking each arm of the cathedral. The blind arches in particular seem implausibly sophisticated decoration for a ceiled roof space. The openings are accessed from the lower wall passage of the lantern stage of the crossing tower and are at the level of a 30 mm offset and *c.* 540 mm above the Romanesque wall head: this corresponds reasonably well with the upper level of the assumed common tie-beams. If not simply providing access to a roof space or a smaller boarded area (such as a catwalk along the roof), the doorway may have had a ceremonial or liturgical function.

CONCLUSION

MUCH remains to be discovered about the form of the Romanesque cathedral at Norwich and this is likely to be linked to future works programmes. By reviewing just three lost elements of the primary building, it is possible to advance our broader understanding of the history and design of the cathedral. In terms of the historical significance, it is clear that the remains of the first axial chapel do not provide the basis to argue for a false start to Herbert de Losinga's new cathedral. Equally, the remains do not match those of the axial chapel at Bury St Edmunds, and this is a theme amplified by the presbytery clerestory (and the subsequent — and surviving — clerestory of the rest of the cathedral): the immediate sources and parallels for Norwich Cathedral have been identified too readily in East Anglia, with the connection to Rufus's hall at Westminster in particular offering a fresh insight into the design of Losinga's church. Close parallels for the roofs are, inevitably, harder to make given the complete loss of all the carpentry elements, although the evidence reviewed here suggests that the Norwich examples were consistent with contemporary roofs in England and Normandy, and were not of the quirky and anachronistic form previously suggested.

NOTES

1. D. J. Stewart, 'Notes on Norwich Cathedral', *Archaeol. J.*, 32 (1875), 16–47.

2. Fernie, *AHNC*; S. Heywood, 'The Romanesque Building', in *Norwich Cathedral 1096–1996*, 73–115.

3. J. P. McAleer, 'The Romanesque Façade of Norwich Cathedral', *The Journal of the Society of Architectural Historians*, 25/2 (May 1966), 136–40; J. P. McAleer, 'The Façade of Norwich Cathedral: the Nineteenth-Century Restorations', *NA*, 41/4 (1993), 381–409; J. P. McAleer, 'The Façade of Norwich Cathedral as it might have been', *NA*, 42/4 (1997), 481–91.

4. R. Gilchrist, 'Norwich Cathedral: a Biography of the North Transept', *JBAA*, 151 (1998), 107–36; R. Gilchrist, 'Norwich Cathedral Tower and Spire: Recording and Analysis of a Cathedral's *Longue Durée*', *Archaeol. J.*, 158 (2001), 291–324.

5. Fernie, *AHNC*, 13; B. Dodwell, 'Herbert de Losinga and the Foundation', in *Norwich Cathedral 1096–1996*, 36–43, at 41.

6. D. H. S. Cranage, 'Eastern Chapels in the Cathedral Church of Norwich', *Antiq. J.*, 12 (1932), 117–26.

7. NRO DCN 24/2.

8. Cranage, 'Eastern Chapels' (as in n. 6), 118.

9. Ibid., 117–26.

10. Fernie, *AHNC*, 19–22. N.B. Fernie elsewhere (ibid., 16) refers to the priory being 'begun in or after 1091', although nowhere in his preceding summary of the documentary history does he give grounds for this conclusion.

11. Heywood, 'The Romanesque Building' (as in n. 2), 73–74, 84; S. Heywood, 'Aspects of the Romanesque Church of Bury St Edmunds Abbey in their Regional Context', in *Bury St Edmunds: Medieval Art, Architecture, Archaeology and Economy*, ed. A. Gransden, BAA Trans., xx (1998), 16–21, at 20.

12. Dodwell, 'Herbert de Losinga and the Foundation' (as in n. 5), 41.

13. Heywood, 'The Romanesque Building' (as in n. 2), 84.

14. HBRU metric survey (Dr Roland B. Harris and Philip Thomas, 1998). Given the importance of the remains, the measurements for crypt were re-checked by Dr Roland B. Harris (17 October 2010) and were indeed accurate, although the opportunity was taken to add additional detail to the HBRU base survey.

15. Heywood, 'Romanesque Church of Bury St Edmunds' (as in n. 11), 20.

16. Fernie, *AHNC*, 19; Heywood, 'Romanesque Church of Bury St Edmunds' (as in n. 11), 20.

17. Fernie, *AHNC*, 22, n. 4; Heywood, 'The Romanesque Building' (as in n. 2), 84; Heywood, 'Romanesque Church of Bury St Edmunds ' (as in n. 11), 20.

18. Cranage, 'Eastern Chapels' (as in n. 6), 120.

19. D. Adams, 'Archaeological Excavation at The Hostry, Norwich Cathedral, Norwich, Norfolk' (unpublished NAU Archaeology Report No. 1289b, 2012), 25–26.

20. Gilchrist, 'Norwich Cathedral Tower' (as in n. 4), 297.

21. F. Woodman, 'The Gothic Campaigns', in *Norwich Cathedral 1096–1996*, 189–90.

22. Stewart, 'Notes on Norwich Cathedral' (as in n. 1), facing 24; Fernie, *AHNC*, 34–36.

23. Ibid., 144, 152.

24. Heywood, 'The Romanesque Building' (as in n. 2), 111.

25. R. B. Harris and D. Miles, 'Romanesque Westminster Hall and its roof', *Westminster: Medieval Art, Architecture and Archaeology*, ed. W. Rodwell and T. Tatton-Brown, *BAA Trans.*, xxxix (for 2013, forthcoming).

26. D. Whitelock, D. C. Douglas and S. I. Tucker ed., *The Anglo-Saxon Chronicle: A Revised Translation* (1961), 175; F. Barlow, *William Rufus*, 3rd edn (2000), 400.

27. Fernie, *Norwich Cathedral* (as in n. 2), 152.

28. L. Hoey, 'The Design of Romanesque Clerestories with Wall Passages in Normandy and England', *Gesta*, 28 (1989), 78–101, at 91–94.

29. Fernie, *AHNC*, 36; Heywood, 'The Romanesque Building' (as in n. 2), 85.

30. Fernie, *AHNC*, 24 (fig. 8).

31. C. Wilson, 'Abbot Serlo's Church at Gloucester (1089–1100): Its Place in Romanesque Architecture', *Medieval Art and Architecture at Gloucester and Tewkesbury*, ed. T. A. Heslop and V. Sekules, *BAA Trans.*, VII (1985), 52–83, at 64–65.

32. B. M. Feilden, 'Restorations and Repairs after World War II', *Norwich Cathedral 1096–1996*, 736–37, 742.

33. Fernie, *AHNC*, 193; Gilchrist, 'Biography of the North Transept' (as in n. 4), 110.

34. S. R. Pierce ed., *Norwich Cathedral at the End of the Eighteenth Century: John Adey Repton* (1965), pls 5 and 6; J. Britton, *The History and Antiquities of the See and Cathedral Church of Norwich* (1816), pl. 3.

35. Norwich Cathedral, Feilden & Mawson digital archive refs 393 and 438.

36. J. Hare, 'The Architectural Patronage of Two Late Medieval Bishops: Edington, Wykeham and the rebuilding of Winchester Cathedral nave', *Antiq. J.*, 92 (2012), 273–305, at 293.

37. D. Park and H. Howard, 'The Medieval Polychromy', *Norwich Cathedral 1096–1996*, 379–409, at 383–90.

38. N. Tanner, 'The Cathedral and the City', in *Norwich Cathedral 1096–1996*, 255–80, at 259–61.

39. Fernie, *AHNC*, 41.

40. Ibid.

41. Gilchrist, 'Biography of the North Transept' (as in n. 4), 120–26.

42. Ibid., 125–26.

43. Fernie, *AHNC*, 41, gives the pitch at 'about 55°', whereas the value here was defined by REDM total station measurement by the author in 2013, and represents a mean of the two pitches (51.67° and 52.84°).

44. Heywood, 'The Romanesque Building' (as in n. 2), 89.

45. Gilchrist, 'Biography of the North Transept' (as in n. 4), 112.

46. Woodman, 'The Gothic Campaigns' (as in n. 21), 187.

47. Feilden, 'Restorations and Repairs' (as in n. 32), 742.

48. S. Gardner, 'The Nave Galleries of Durham Cathedral', *Art Bulletin* , 64/4 (December 1982), 564–79.

49. Heywood, 'The Romanesque Building' (as in n. 2), 86–87.

50. E.g. F. Épaud, *De la charpente romane à la charpente gothique en Normandie*, 2nd edn (2011).

51. Harris and Miles, 'Romanesque Westminster Hall and its roof' (as in n. 25).

52. G. Simpson and C. Litton, 'Dendrochronology in Cathedrals', in *The Archaeology of Cathedrals*, ed. T. Tatton-Brown and J. Munby (Oxford 1996), 183–201.

The Romanesque Apse of Norwich Cathedral: A Re-examination of the Bishop's Throne Platform and its Supposed Relic Niche

JOHN CROOK

This is a study of the remains of the medieval bishop's throne platform in the apse of Norwich Cathedral and its relationship to the so-called relic niche in the ambulatory with its associated shaft. The documentary, graphical and archaeological evidence for the development of the complex masonry structure is examined. The notion that the niche was intended to house relics for the benefit of the bishop seated above it is questioned, and consideration is given to the possibility that the massive substructure of the throne was originally designed as a reliquary platform connected with the new cult of St William of Norwich in the 1150s, but that the saint's shrine was in fact never placed there. Consequently, the bishop's throne, originally intended to have been located lower down on the intermediary platform, was raised to the top of the structure.

INTRODUCTION

THE curved stone steps behind the high altar of Norwich Cathedral, leading up to the bishop's throne, are a dominant feature of the Romanesque apse of that great church (Fig. 1, left). In 1959, charged with creating something more appropriate than the steep flight of wooden steps that had provided access to the throne for the previous thirty-five years, the architect Stephen Dykes Bower, assisted by former Chapter surveyor Arthur Bensley Whittingham, designed a grandiose semi-circular podium redolent of the architecture of the London Olympic Games of a decade earlier. The throne is reached by means of eleven vertiginous steps without a handrail: a challenge to the equilibrium of any robed prelate seeking to ascend, let alone descend, them. In its present form the throne was first occupied by Bishop Lancelot Fleming, and a photograph taken at his enthronement in January 1960 shows him sitting uneasily some seven feet above the congregation, flanked by his suffragans and chaplains who stand behind desks at a lower level.[1]

At the rear of the 1950s podium, in the ambulatory, we are transported to a gentler world of Romanesque serenity and there, set within evidently inserted masonry in the central arch of the apse, is an unusual feature, the so-called 'relic niche' (Fig. 1, right). Briefly described — for the structure will be more fully analysed later in this paper — this is a round-headed recess, its floor on the same level as the original 11th-century stylobate, 785 mm above the ambulatory pavement. The niche is 1,545 mm high from its floor to the apex of its vault and 1,140 mm deep, and in its rear wall, just below the apex, is a small rectangular opening into a narrow rectangular shaft which rises up to a modern pierced stone in the throne platform at the bishop's feet.

FIG. 1.   (*left*) The bishop's throne and podium; (*right*) south-west view in ambulatory showing the 'relic niche'

A recent notice sets out the received wisdom concerning this ensemble. 'This recess is directly beneath the Bishop's Throne, behind the High Altar, and may once have contained holy relics. It was thought that the essence of these relics could rise up through the "flue" and give the Bishop divine aid and assistance.' The idea is attractive, but medieval parallels for such an arrangement are hard to find — and in this paper I consider another possibility, namely that the structure was originally intended as a shrine-base for the emerging cult of St William of Norwich.

THE ARCHITECTURAL SETTING

The presbytery floor

IN its present form the presbytery floor comprises a single flat surface east of the crossing.[2] This results from a late-19th-century restoration of the level of the 1090s pavement. Probably by the mid-12th century the floor in the eastern third of the presbytery had been raised by 880 mm above its original level. Consequently, when in the 1470s Bishop Goldwell encased the Romanesque piers as a support for his new vault, the Perpendicular pier bases at the west end of the first straight bay were set at a level consistent with that raised floor. When the original floor level was reinstated 400 years later, the Romanesque bases were revealed once more and fortunately were not tidied away (Fig. 2). They are characterized by scorching above the level of the secondary floor (evidenced by a surviving line of mortar); the fire which caused this damage was

FIG. 2. Norwich Cathedral: north side of presbytery. Perpendicular bases of the 14th-century vaulting responds set on the level of the secondary raised floor (indicated by a surviving line of bedding mortar) and unweathered Romanesque masonry beneath. The scorching caused by a fire after the floor was raised is evident

so severe that it even penetrated the floor slabs. The same horizon is also discernible on the apse chord piers. Coincidentally, the context of Goldwell's works may have been another recorded fire in 1463 which scorched the masonry of the 14th-century clerestory (this had been rebuilt by Bishop Percy probably after damage caused by the destructive gale that brought down the spire in 1362).[3] But the fact that the Romanesque bases show no signs of scorching below the level of the evidenced floor, their cleanness, and the crisp character of their tooling, suggest that they had been submerged from a much earlier date, certainly before the fire of 1463, and probably before those of 1171 and 1272.[4] The latter conflagration, resulting from local riots, is said to have reduced the cathedral church to ashes, apart from the Lady chapel. Although this must be an exaggeration, it does suggest that the 1272 fire was particularly severe.

The floor level at the east end of the presbytery is unlikely to have been altered before 1120, when stone screen walls were inserted between the arches of the apse, given that they are set on the original stylobate. The raised floor must therefore have been built against those inserted screens so that they served as retaining walls. If a similar screen wall occupied the central bay for a time, it was rapidly replaced by a mid-12th-century phase comprising the presumed throne platform, relic niche and shaft, and probably the access steps as well. I demonstrate below, using observations made by Whittingham in 1958–59, that the heights both of these steps and of the throne platform, with its niche and shaft, are carefully related to the level of the secondary floor. The raising of the floor appears therefore to be contemporary with these modifications of *c.* 1150.

It is regrettable that the stratigraphical relationship between the inner wall faces of the apse bays and the higher floor was not recorded when the floor was lowered to its 11th-century level in the 1870s. The wall face in the bays flanking the throne was, between that time and 1959, normally concealed by curtains. The works of 1959 were no better recorded than those of the 1870s, and we have only Whittingham's testimony that the west faces of the flanking screen walls comprised 'rubble walling'. His account implies that they were similar in appearance to the west face of the central bay, which is depicted in photographs, and indeed looks like rubble that has been very roughly mended and pointed, rather than dressed stone. In the case of the flanking bays this appearance could have resulted from the demolition of stone steps and platforms and the cutting back of the wall face, which as originally built presumably comprised coursed facing masonry that was intended to be seen. Unfortunately, all this evidence was covered over or refaced in 1959 without being drawn or photographed.

The exterior of the apse, seen from the ambulatory

IN the north-east and south-east bays of the apse are the inserted stone screens mentioned above, flanking the rear of the throne platform. These were refaced on the presbytery side in 1959, but their original masonry survives on the ambulatory side. They are decorated with blind arcading, and the arches have capitals whose form is neatly paralleled by those on similar arcading in the upper levels of the lantern tower (Fig. 3). The same carvers might well have been involved, but unfortunately it is not possible to date the capitals with precision. Somewhat similar capitals, though lacking the leaf vein detail, are found in the nave north gallery arcade on the piers flanking the third bay from the east. These are more reliably datable, having been set in place just before the building break that occurred just before or at the death of Bishop Herbert de Losinga in 1119.[5] The most likely context for the screens in the ambulatory, however, is the resumption of work c. 1121 and the enthronement of Bishop Everard.

The outer face of the axial bay in the ambulatory is different. It is in this wall that the so-called relic niche is located. The niche itself and the shaft behind are analysed more fully below, but it is clear from the stylistic detail of the shafts of its entrance arch that the niche is later than the blind arcading of the flanking bays. The carving is somewhat rustic in character (Fig. 4), suggesting local imitation of stylistic features observed elsewhere rather than innovation. With its scallops, separated by daggers or truncated cones, this detail would more appropriately be placed a couple of decades later, perhaps as late as c. 1150, and this would also better suit the more developed character of the arch moulding. The date receives some local support from the chunky truncated cones between scallops that are found in the capitals of the upper arcade of the belfry, dating from the 1140s.[6]

FIG. 3. (left) Capitals of the blind arcading in the ambulatory; (right) capitals of the blind recesses in the upper level of the lantern tower

Photo (right): Dr Roland Harris

FIG. 4. Capitals of the 'relic niche' in the ambulatory

To summarize the analysis so far: the surviving medieval fabric of the apse is of three phases. The first comprises the late-11th-century stylobate and the arcade into which the screens and throne platform are manifest insertions, together with the original floor level (as now reinstated). Next are the flanking screens which, from their architectural style, arguably date from the early 1120s. The third phase comprises the masonry of the throne platform, niche and relic shaft, and probably also (as argued below) the raised floor level of the apse and masonry platforms on the west sides of the flanking screens, perhaps of the period 1145–55. Had all the original fabric of these three phases survived, analysis would be simple enough. In fact, what one sees today is the product of post-Reformation changes which must now be passed in review. In this account I first assemble the documentary and graphical evidence for the development of the area, then I study the physical evidence in detail, drawing again where necessary on the documentary and graphical records to support my analysis.

DOCUMENTARY AND GRAPHICAL EVIDENCE FOR THE DEVELOPMENT OF THE APSE AND THE 'OLD BISHOP'S THRONE'

THE apex of the apse would not have been readily accessible to early antiquaries. Probably at the Reformation, a screen had been inserted between the apse chord piers, partitioning off an area that served as a vestry behind the high altar.[7] It was described by the Norfolk historian Francis Blomefield *c.* 1743 as 'a late partition [. . .] now disused', and is indicated in his plan of the cathedral (Fig. 5) by reference letter *c*.[8] The same plan also indicates (*b*) 'The old Throne', with a flight of four or five steps leading up to it, though in his text he refers to 'The ancient bishop's THRONE, ascended by three steps'.[9] Had there been only three steps, they would each have been 386 mm high, which is implausible.

The screen was removed by order of Chapter dated 3 June 1766: 'That the Screen or Sept now behind the Communion Table, be taken down; & the Choir continued to the East Wall of the Church'.[10] A slight raising of the pavement west of the altar steps was

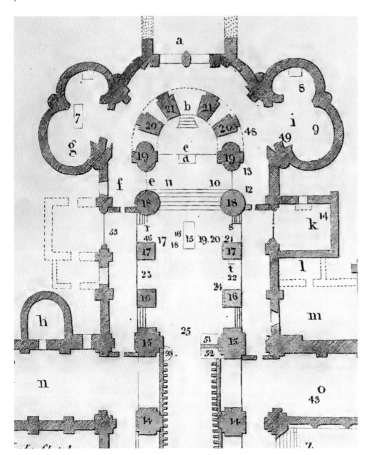

FIG. 5. Detail from the 'Ichnographical plan' dated 1743, published by Blomefield. Reference letters indicate *b* 'The old Throne' and *c* 'The Old Vestry'

also envisaged at this time, but graphical evidence suggests it was not carried out. The *memoranda* of Dean Lloyd give a fuller account of what was actually done:

At the time of making this Repair, the Skreen which cut off the lower part of the semicircle [...] was removed, & a beautiful termination given to the Choir; all the ornamental Pillars, of the Arches which were thus restored to the Choir, were new built of Stone, Capitals were added to them of Plaister, and the whole East End enclosed by a Gothic Fluting [...][11]

The arrangement is depicted in various contemporary views of the presbytery. The earliest is a painting in the deanery by Joseph Browne, a Norwich coal heaver with artistic talent, dated 1781.[12] From a decade or two later are John Adey Repton's important pen-and-wash survey drawings of the cathedral.[13] His eastward view in the choir (Fig. 6) shows the screens, adorned with narrow stone panels, and the 'Plaister' (presumably stucco) volute capitals that had replaced the fire-damaged original cushion capitals, as well as the way the arch heads were filled with sub-arches, also with volute capitals, completely blocking off the apse from the ambulatory.

Repton's plan and section (Figs 7–8) are also crucial evidence for this stage in the apse's development and for their depiction of the so-called 'relic niche' in the ambulatory, a feature not shown in Blomefield's earlier plan. The section does not, however,

FIG. 6.   J. A. Repton, *East View in Choir*, 1790s. Detail from north–south section through crossing
Society of Antiquaries of London, Norfolk Red Portfolio, p. 17

show the shaft, which is surprising as the opening into it seems still to have been in place at this date, even though the west side of the niche appears to have been truncated by the insertion of the 1760s screens, which evidently cut into the mid-12th-century masonry.

The final transformation of the presbytery took place in the early 1870s under Dean Goulburn, who paid for most of the work himself. First the central arch was opened up in 1871–72, then the floor at the east end was lowered more or less to its original level as agreed in Chapter:

June 3 1873. That permission be given to the Dean to reduce the whole of the Presbytery to the present level of the Apse at his own expense on condition of his not interfering with any Norman bases which may be found at the foot of the Perpendicular shafts.[14]

There is a hint here that the Romanesque bases had been discovered during preliminary investigations, and they were presumably used to determine the final floor level. It is regrettable that no archaeological descriptions of the works appear to have been made. This deficit is partially compensated by the fortunate survival of a drawing of the apex of the apse and the old bishop's throne by Robert Farren, published in 1883 (Fig. 9).[15] Crucially, it shows an unusual view of the shaft below the throne which he identifies as a 'squint'. This can never have been its function; a squint would not have required a shaft above it. Furthermore, as explained below, the shaft would originally have been closed off on the west side by the stairs leading up to the platform. When these were removed the shaft was exposed to view, as was the rubble wall face mentioned by

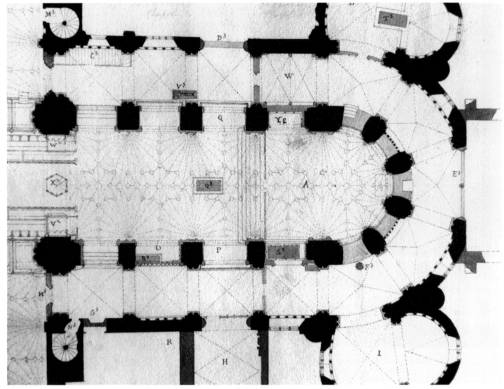

FIG. 7.   Detail from J. A. Repton's plan of Norwich Cathedral, 1790s
Society of Antiquaries of London, Norfolk Red Portfolio, p. 13

Whittingham and shown in *c*. 1930 photographs; it was covered over by the new steps in 1959.

One piece of evidence suggests that, despite leaving no written record, the Victorians were sensitive to archaeology. In 1941 Dean Cranage noted,

In front of the Staircase a line of circular curvature will be noticed on the pavement. This represents foundations discovered when the tessellated pavement, given by Dean Goulburn, was put down in 1878. The curvature, unlike that at Torcello, does not align with that of the apse but is contrasted with it.[16]

According to Whittingham, the line, which is not visible in contemporary photographs, was incised in the tessellated pavement.[17] Its curve projected towards the west, in contrast with the border of the pavement, which is concentric with the apse. In 1959 Dykes Bower used the line to determine the position of the bottom step of the new podium.[18]

It is unfortunate that Cranage does not state at what depth the curved 'foundations' were found during the works of the 1870s. If they were at the level of the late-11th-century pavement, they must relate to a step within the apse built off that original floor level. More probably the Victorians found evidence for a curved step higher up, that is, built off the raised floor in the east end of the presbytery, which appears to be contemporary with the 'throne'.[19] Whittingham merely made the ambiguous comment,

FIG. 8.   J. A. Repton, section of east end of presbytery, 1790s
Society of Antiquaries of London, Norfolk Red Portfolio, p. 16

'It may have been an original flight of semi-circular steps to the throne or raised when the floor was raised'.[20]

The west side of the lower part of the central bay as depicted by Farren was clearly unsightly, and was probably usually concealed by a curtain. In the 1870s consideration was given to inserting a 'podium' in the apse, and William Butterfield was engaged to design it — but the Dean and Chapter felt that it would obscure too much of the Romanesque arcading.[21] An alternative scheme by Reginald Blomfield was not adopted either.[22]

The works of the 20th century are better recorded. In 1924–25 the throne was 'restored' at the expense of Bishop Bertram Pollock, having been hailed as a 'discovery'.[23] A flight of eight uncomfortably high wooden steps was provided, giving access to a rather simple throne. The arrangement may be seen in several photographs, amongst the earliest being by Norfolk historian and photographer George Plunkett,[24] together with an undated postcard by H. Coates of Wisbech (Fig. 10). These clearly show that the eight steps and intermediate wooden platform were set against a wall that appears to be of poorly pointed rubble and certainly not good facing masonry — in his drawing Farren seems to have embellished the appearance of the wall face. The 'squint' illustrated by Farren was concealed behind the upper steps or stair carpet; in January 1958 Whittingham observed that the shaft needed 'a new west wall', implying

FIG. 9.   Robert Farren, 'Bishops Throne & Squint', seen from the west

it was still open on that side.[25] He mentioned, too, that the opening from the rear of the niche into the shaft had been blocked since the Second World War; and that is how it is shown in a photograph by another prolific local photographer, E. C. Le Grice.[26]

The decision to replace the wooden steps by a stone podium was taken in 1957–58 following a bequest.[27] The Dean and Chapter engaged Stephen Dykes Bower as project architect, assisted by Arthur Whittingham, who had already studied the bishop's throne and relic niche. Another interested party was Gilbert Thurlow, vicar of Great Yarmouth, who had written an article on the throne for the Friends of Norwich Cathedral and followed this up with a new account after the construction of the podium in 1959.[28] Thurlow wrote to Whittingham at the end of 1957, when the re-furbishment project was presumably already under discussion, and Whittingham commented that 'Your letter induced me to look into the problems of the Bishop's Throne again, & I feel I now have a more thorough understanding of them than ever before'. Whittingham's detailed response to Thurlow's enquiry is important primary evidence, being by far the fullest surviving description of the apse before the works, and the relevant paragraphs are quoted here:[29]

5. The THRONE stands on a platform 6′ 5″ above the present floor & was approached by a flight of 4 STRAIGHT STEPS from a Lower Platform 4′ above the floor. The mark of the top step survives on the N, showing that they were of stone, 7″ high & extending the full width of the arch.

FIG. 10. (*left*) Bishop's throne and wooden stair of 1928, by George Plunkett, taken in April 1938; (*right*) postcard of similar date by H. Coates of Wisbech

(left) © George Plunkett; (right) Warburg Institute Picture Library

6. Across the adjoining arch on each side is a TABLE 3′ high which had a 6″ moulded stone capping along the top. The marks of this are clear on the R in the N arch, & along the back of BOTH in the supporting rubble. These tables stand on the same Lower Platform (at 4′ above the floor) which also shows on the face of both arches. These tables may have served for the display of relics or have supported relic-chests [...]

7. The LOWER PLATFORM was presumably approached up 2 steps which spread out into a semicircle in front of the centre bay. The rest of the APSE (& to just W of the altar) was floored at 3′ above the present floor. The marks can be seen in the W corners of the apse & the adjoining responds. The floor then dropped another 2 steps & ended with a flight at the present Communion Rail.

8. One of the more interesting features is the SHAFT [...] provided so that the Bishop could be in communication with the RELICS of the saints in the arch below his throne (like the shaft still leading down into St Peter's grave). The shaft was about 18″ × 6″ & provided with a grating at the Bishop's feet. Parts of the frame were found in situ in Victorian times. [...] The lower outlet is still there and has only been blocked since the war, because it provided a meaningless view down the Choir. The shaft needs a new west wall. It might be best to provide it with a door top & bottom, as its purpose is obsolete.

It was some ten years before Whittingham published an account of the throne. Quicker off the mark was Ralegh Radford, who in 1959 published an article on the two fragments of stone that he identified as 8th-century work from the original East Anglian cathedral at North Elmham, brought to Norwich via the subsequent cathedral at Thetford.[30] Most of his paper was, however, concerned with parallels for the *synthronon* arrangement which he believed had existed at North Elmham. His discussion of the architectural setting of the throne at Norwich, notably the niche (which he thought was 'presumably intended to hold relics'), occupied but three paragraphs. He believed that the medieval position of the throne was 'part of the rearrangement carried out after the fire of 1171'.

Whittingham's own contribution to the debate was published in 1979.[31] It is above all an art-historical study of the stylistic influences of the sculpture on the throne arms, which he was able to decipher to his own satisfaction despite its burnt and weathered condition. By then the tentative interpretation of the architectural setting that he had advanced in 1958 had become certainty: 'A stone table for relics or for a relic chest was constructed in the adjoining arch on each side of the throne, and below the throne itself was the arch in which more relics were kept visible from the ambulatory'.[32] He dated this arch to 'soon after 1160'.

In the same paper Whittingham supplied some details of the archaeological discoveries made in 1959 and which are now concealed by the Dykes Bower podium:

In 1959 the rubble walling in the three apse arches and the fire marks on the piers supplied evidence to indicate what these later Norman arrangements were and where the steps came. All three arches were floored across in mortar raised 1.2 m above the original and present floor level. The Bishop's Throne was raised (as now) a further 0.76 m higher. A most interesting feature was a shaft (0.45 m × 0.23 m) connecting the bishop's feet with the relics in the arch below, as at St Peter's, Rome, a shaft connected the Papal throne with the saint's grave below. The Victorians found evidence that the Norwich shaft had been covered by an iron grating in an oak frame. (This has now been replaced by a pierced stone.) At Norwich the arch is severely burnt. It had two shelves, and a hole remains near the top of the back wall into the shaft behind. The north flank and rebated corners of the shaft have Norman tooling but no burning, so the fire was either caused independently by a light amongst the relics, or by burning debris spilling over from the throne into the ambulatory, a possibility, as the shafts had to be renewed below the arches of the Lady Chapel entrance opposite in the fifteenth century.

The works of 1959 were the last intervention in this area. They included the modification of the 'squint' shown by Farren into the shaft described by Whittingham, by reinstating its west wall. We turn now to an analysis of the surviving fabric (some of it covered in 1959).

ARCHAEOLOGICAL ANALYSIS

Floor levels, steps and access to the throne

BECAUSE almost all the evidence for the original floor levels and access to the platform are obscured by the masonry of 1959, analysis of features on the west side of the platform relies heavily on Whittingham's two brief descriptions.

Whittingham believed that by the time the throne platform was inserted the floor level of the east end of the presbytery had been raised by '3 ft'. Crucially, he observed evidence for what he called a 'lower platform' 4 ft above the present floor and he inferred that this was reached from the main apse floor level by means of two steps. The present intermediate platform for clergy seating that flanks the 1959 steps 1,262 mm above the present floor and corresponding to a wide fourth step from the top of the central flight seems to have been inspired by Whittingham's discovery.

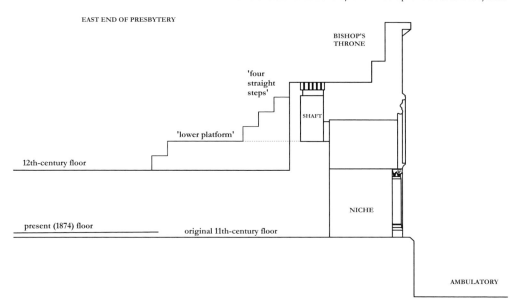

FIG. 11.   The steps to the throne platform; interpretation of Whittingham's description

When Whittingham's measurements are plotted accurately in the form of a section (Fig. 11), two interesting points emerge. Firstly, the floor of the relic shaft corresponds almost exactly with his 'lower platform'. Secondly, the heights of the risers in each of the two postulated flights of steps are identical to within 3 mm, which is perhaps a strong indication that the raised floor level at the east end of the presbytery was determined as part of the insertion of the throne platform. More practically, had the 'throne platform' (whatever its original purpose) been built when the floor was at its original level, steps springing from the line discovered in the 1870s would have been uncomfortably steep, as they are today.

The niche and throne platform

THE works of 1959 have obscured almost all medieval masonry within the apse. The modern steps conceal the lower parts of the 1120s screen walls in the flanking bays, and at higher level these walls have been refaced. In the central bay, behind the throne, the parapet has been rebuilt. The only possibly medieval fabric visible within the central bay of the apse is a small area of flint corework beneath the wooden throne, though this is pointed in modern cement.

Considerably more medieval fabric survives in the niche and shaft behind it, accessible from the ambulatory. The niche has side walls of ashlar, mostly original, though with a few obvious replacements. These walls abut the rear wall, whose coursing is independent of the side walls. The tunnel-vault has no impost. It retains early, perhaps 12th-century mortar. The masonry of the niche shows obvious signs of burning, but localized areas with a different degree of burning indicate that there were wooden shelves here at the time of the conflagration. They were supported on posts in the rear corners, and horizontal bearers at the level of the floor, at mid-height, and just below the springing level of the vault.

87

There are no indications either in the side walls or the floor that there was ever any kind of grille or door in front of the niche.[33] This has serious implications for the proposal that the niche was intended to contain relics. Relic theft was a feature of the cult of saints in the Middle Ages, the successful acquisition of a relic being taken as a sign of God's approval of the theft, and relic niches were invariably provided with grilles which both protected the contents and drew attention to their precious nature.

High in the rear wall, immediate below the vault, is a rectangular hole into the shaft behind, one of the thin slabs which separate the top of the niche from the shaft having been omitted. The masons' vertical setting-out lines for this operation are clearly visible on the course below. It is clear that the hole was created as part of the construction of the niche's rear wall; it was not hacked through later. The ashlar below must be a mere facing to the flint and rubble corework that was for a time exposed on the west side, but the stones either side of the opening are narrow slabs faced on both sides.

The shaft (Fig. 12) measures 407 mm wide by 341 mm deep.[34] Its floor is simply rendered, presumably over corework. As already noted, the level of this floor corresponds to the 'lower platform' for which evidence in the form of scorch patterns had been observed by Whittingham. The west face of the shaft is modern masonry, and to north and south parts of the junction with the ragged masonry depicted by Farren are visible, though it is mostly concealed by a partial continuation of the cement render that covers the west wall. Given Whittingham's comment in 1958 that 'The shaft needs a new west wall' the masonry here, like the pierced stone above, must form part of the works of 1959. No obvious signs of the evidence for the wooden frame and iron grille allegedly discovered in the 1870s are visible.

THE FUNCTION OF THE NICHE AND SHAFT

The throne fragments

IN order to determine the function of the niche and shaft, and indeed the platform as a whole, it is important to reassess the known history of the historic fragments

FIG. 12. View inside the shaft looking west and upwards

purporting to comprise parts of the Anglo-Saxon throne. That they are pre-Conquest in origin may perhaps be accepted, but both Radford and Whittingham, authors of the principal studies of the fragments, concurred that they were not a matching pair. The larger stone on the north does indeed appear to be the right-hand arm of a throne; that on the south seems to come from a different structure. As already noted, the latter is a broken, perhaps cut-down fragment. Whittingham postulated that this damage might have been caused by the insertion of an aumbry between the side of the throne and the adjacent apse pier in the 15th century,[35] but this improbable suggestion relied on a mis-reading of an article by Dean Beeching which mentions the possibility of a 'tabernacle' on the south side of the high altar.[36]

To add to the confusion, other related pieces of masonry are claimed to have been located. In 1975 a 'broken stone' was discovered beneath the tower floor and said to be decorated with animal motifs that Whittingham related to the north arm of the throne; he thought it had been 'discarded below the floor in probably 1101'. It showed no signs of burning. He identified other parts of the same structure as having been used as 'quoining in the Deanery garden wall near the transept and near the door of No. 63'.[37]

These chance discoveries could suggest that other pieces of pre-Conquest material survive within the cathedral and Close at Norwich. It is perhaps straining credulity to accept that a pre-Conquest episcopal throne was transported from Thetford to Norwich at the time the cathedral was under construction, and that parts of it were then discarded. To circumvent this difficulty Whittingham was compelled to suggest that what had come from Thetford was a complete *synthronon* comprising not only the bishop's chair but flanking seating for clergy, and that only the central portion had actually been used. This sounds like special pleading, and we must, I think, briefly consider the possibility that two fragments were in fact discovered in quite recent times, were identified as deriving from the 'ancient throne', and were placed on the apse platform because of a long tradition that it was here that the medieval throne had been located.

It is strange that there is in fact no absolutely conclusive evidence for the stones being in their present position before the 19th century. Blomefield's indication of 'the old throne' might simply have referred to the platform,[38] and it is surprising indeed that he did not mention or depict the two ancient stones which, then as now, could be regarded as an interesting antiquarian curiosity. Unfortunately, Blomefield was the only historian to have written to any extent about Norwich Cathedral before the throne platform was concealed behind the screen walls within the apse in the late 1760s. Thereafter the remains of the platform would have been accessible only from the ambulatory, requiring a ladder to look or climb over the parapet wall which rises above the east side of the platform, 3.6 m (just under 12 ft) above the ambulatory pavement, as J. A. Repton's 1790s section clearly shows. In his brief guide to Norwich Cathedral (mainly an abridgement of Blomefield), a later local historian, Philip Browne, stated that 'the Bishop's throne was formerly raised to a considerable heighth [*sic*], as appears by the old stone work, behind the new inclosure', but this also appears to refer only to the concealed remains of the platform.[39] More ambiguously Browne later asserted that 'whoever walks round the eastern aisle, can plainly discern the stone work of these seats; that of the bishop in the middle arch, behind the new screen of the present altar',[40] but again this must refer merely to the rear wall behind the throne, which is all that could be seen from the ambulatory.

In 1875 the Revd D. J. Stewart published a series of memoranda which Professor Robert Willis had made at the time of the Royal Archaeological Institute's visit to Norwich in July 1847.[41] These include the observation, presumably Willis's rather than Stewart's, that

On a small platform in the central severy of the apse of the presbytery there are the fragments of the original stone seat built for the use of the Bishop, and on the pavement and adjoining piers there are traces of the steps by which the throne was reached.

This may be the earliest reference to the fragments before the west side of the apse was exposed again, allowing Farren to draw the state of the remains in 1883.

All this is, of course, negative evidence, and in partial support of the fragments having been in place throughout the history of the cathedral is the fact that they show signs of burning like the architecture around them. Whittingham attributed this to the fire of 1463 and pointed out that the damage was differential; those areas of the throne stonework that had been submerged beneath the floor or rear wall were less reddened — though the stones would presumably have been similarly embedded in their original location if they derived from a throne brought from elsewhere. But for Ralegh Radford the fire damage preceded the stones' obvious weathering and he considered that the architectural masonry nearby was far less fire-damaged than the throne fragments.[42] He thought the damage, and the weathering, had both occurred *before* the fragments reached the present cathedral.

Another possible indication that the fragments might have occupied their present position from an early date is the fact that, although they clearly do not comprise the symmetrical left and right arms of a single throne, they have both been modified by means of a wide matching chamfer on the inner angles (only just discernible on the stone on the south side). This certainly looks like an adaptation of two dissimilar pieces for a single purpose. Furthermore, the chamfer on the north piece is noticeably fire-reddened. However, Radford implies that the adaptation of the two pieces might have occurred at North Elmham when the cathedral church was 'reconstituted' *c.* 950, and 'the two best preserved stones from the old furnishing of the apse were recovered and reset to form a new throne'.

There seem to be two possibilities. Either the two fragments were indeed in place from an early date, and were simply not mentioned or drawn by Blomefield when he undertook his antiquarian study of the cathedral, or they were introduced in quite modern times as an antiquarian curiosity in order to conform with a long-held belief that the platform in the apse was the site of the bishop's throne. This would, however, require the stones to have been inserted on the platform whilst it was still concealed by the 18th-century screens, in order to have been discovered by Professor Willis in 1847. Furthermore, a photograph of the larger (north) fragment before the works of 1959 seems to show it embedded in what could well be medieval corework.[43]

On balance, the likelihood would seem to be that the two stone fragments do indeed represent a medieval arrangement and derive from a functioning throne confected from older remains. This raises the question of when that arrangement came to an end. There is no record of the throne being smashed by Parliamentarians, though that would be a strong possibility. However, even if the fragments have been located in their present position since the 12th century, which seems the more likely scenario, this does not necessarily indicate that they formed part of the primary ensemble, and in the next part of this paper I propose an alternative interpretation.

90

A possible reliquary platform

IN the light of the uncertainties outlined above, other options for the original intended purpose of the structure within the central bay of the apse should be explored. I suggest here that although the structure was probably never used for any function other than a throne platform, it may originally have been designed and built with a different use in mind. This proposal springs from an observation that I first put forward in 2000,[44] that in its relationship to the ambulatory the closest contemporary parallel for the so-called 'relic niche' is the tunnel known as the 'Holy Hole' in the former Romanesque apse of Winchester Cathedral.[45] This vaulted passage extended westwards beneath, and was integral with, a 'feretory platform' that was inserted into the apex of the cathedral's late-11th-century apse in the 1150s by Bishop Henry of Blois. The purpose of this tunnel was, I have argued, to allow suppliants to crawl beneath the altar of St Swithun with its reliquary containing the saint's bones.[46] We cannot tell whether a shaft provided an even closer link between the tunnel and the reliquary altar because the platform was cut down at the Reformation, and the tunnel was truncated, the only surviving part being preserved within the Decorated screen which replaced the Norman apse in around 1315.

This parallel provides a possible clue to the original intended function of the niche in the Norwich ambulatory, not as a receptacle for relics, but to provide a measure of access to relics that were, as at Winchester, located on a platform above, possibly on their own shrine altar. The mid-12th century was a busy period in the development of the cult of saints and new arrangements were being made for the veneration of their relics. At about the same time that Bishop Henry was promoting St Swithun, Prior Alexander of Ely was doing much the same thing in his own church, raising up the earthly remains of several local benefactors into a new structure on the north side of the choir,[47] and at Rochester the cult of St Ithamar was being vigorously promoted with the creation of new *Lives* of the saint.[48] At Hexham Priory the cults of the local saints, including former bishops of Hexham Acca, Ealhmund and Eata, were being given a new lease of life with a major translation of their relics.[49] There seems to have been an element of competition amongst English prelates in this fervent promotion of local saints.

It is in this historical context that William 'Turbe', bishop of Norwich from *c.* 1146 to 1174, promoted the entirely new cult of the local boy-saint, St William, claimed to have been ritually murdered by 'the Jews' in 1144. The body was eventually moved into the cathedral in 1151, but it was some time before a suitable place was found for it, the main problem being lack of potential pilgrim access. As at Winchester, the monastic choir was not accessible to the laity and other arrangements had to be found. According to Thomas of Monmouth the relics were moved in 1154 from the south side of the high altar to an altar of the Holy Martyrs on the north side (perhaps to be identified as the Jesus chapel);[50] by the Reformation they appear to have moved again to the saint's own chapel, near the north end of the rood-screen.[51] Thus, the location at the altar of the Holy Martyrs might also have been regarded as a temporary staging-post in 1154.

Consideration should, I think, be given to the suggestion that Bishop William, during whose episcopate (to judge from its style) the platform in the apse was created, was attempting to create a prestigious location for the cult of his name-sake, perhaps inspired by the new architectural setting that Henry of Blois had created for St Swithun of Winchester. The purpose of the niche in the ambulatory would then have been, like the 'Holy Hole' at Winchester, to provide a measure of access to the relics of St William, which — had the scheme been fulfilled — would have been elevated behind the high altar, the normal position for a major reliquary at that date. The reliquary would have been visible only from afar, being located in the ritual choir that would normally have been out of bounds to the laity, but lay people could have walked around the ambulatory and placed their heads and shoulders into the niche in the knowledge that the holy emanations were passing down the shaft from the relics some 5 ft above their heads — performing a similar function to the niches provided in the sides of high shrines in the later Middle Ages.[52] The arrangement would have fulfilled two major criteria for a saint's cult in the high Middle Ages: that the reliquary should be raised on high in a prestigious position, and that there should be limited access for suppliants.

The interpretation does not preclude the episcopal throne also having been placed within the apse, for it could have been placed on the 'lower platform', which is otherwise unexplained. The lateral platforms which Whittingham thought were 'relic shelves' might in fact have provided seating for the bishop's assistants. Thus, the viewer from the choir would have seen the high altar, the bishop presiding behind it in what at that date was still the normal position at the head of the apse, and — higher still — the reliquary of the saint, framed by the central arch of that apse.

If the architectural ensemble in the apse was originally intended to be a shrine platform, the idea must have been abandoned before ever being fulfilled; there is certainly no documentary evidence that the reliquary of the saint was ever located here. The decision was perhaps then made to raise the bishop's throne to the top of the platform, giving the arrangement which in essence survives to this day. The shaft would have become redundant, and was later turned to a new, albeit unknown purpose with the insertion of wooden shelving.

The structure as an episcopal throne platform

I acknowledge that if the masonry structure within the axial bay was originally conceived as a shrine platform for St William, that intention must very quickly have been abandoned. Such archaeological evidence as survived the reconstruction of the structure in the 1950s seems to indicate that the two Anglo-Saxon 'throne arms' were in position from an early date. Unless new documentary evidence emerges to indicate that those fragments were a post-medieval insertion, the platform may well have supported the bishop's throne from the mid-12th century onwards, until the later Middle Ages when a new, wooden *cathedra* was provided in the more normal lateral position.

Whether the 1150s throne platform in the apse was designed as such from the start or resulted, as suggested above, from a modification of a shrine platform, it is likely to have perpetuated a similar arrangement that had been in place since the completion of the cathedral, comprising an episcopal throne at the lower original level of the east end of the choir, or maybe raised on a low platform set on the original choir floor. This putative earlier throne might well have incorporated the ancient fragments from the old cathedral, which would explain why they were still available at least half a century after the construction of the new cathedral. The retention of Anglo-Saxon *spolia* may perhaps be attributed to Herbert de Losinga and the transfer of the episcopal see from Thetford — it is surely far-fetched to imagine that William 'Turbe' belatedly sent workmen to the previous cathedral church in search of historic masonry. A number of other deliberately archaic features have been noted from the earliest phases of Norwich Cathedral, perhaps intended to provide a sense of institutional continuity, such as the 'St Felix' panel and the triangular arches in the north transept. William 'Turbe' may have shared the same view of the past. He had been associated with Norwich Cathedral all his life (he is thought to have entered the cathedral priory as an oblate), so he was presumably also deeply imbued with the traditions of the place; the retention of significant relics of the institution's earlier history might have appealed to him.[53]

The problem with the identification of the structure as a throne base from the outset is the so-called relic shaft, and the niche in the ambulatory. At Winchester, the tunnel provided pilgrims with a measure of contact with relics on the platform above. At Norwich, on the other hand, it has been argued since the 1950s that the bishop benefited from a similar link with relics in the niche below — an inversion of the Winchester arrangement. Dean Cranage had suggested in 1941 that 'the arched recess was for the reception of relics',[54] but the notion of holy emanations rising to the throne above appears to go back no further than Whittingham's letter of January 1958, already cited.[55] It is ironic that the idea was first promulgated by the very person who concealed so much of the archaeological evidence within the apse without, it would seem, leaving an adequate drawn or photographic record.

Whittingham invoked the parallel of St Peter's Rome, where a shaft or *cataracta* indeed linked the altar of the *Confessio* with the presumed tomb of the titular saint, an arrangement that survived two major remodellings of the church and was first described by Gregory of Tours's deacon Agiulf in the 590s.[56] At St Peter's, however, the papal throne both in the church as remodelled by Gregory the Great and in the present Renaissance basilica was located at the head of the apse, not over the apostolic tomb, so the parallel is slender.

Finally, there is a practical objection to the notion that relics were located within the niche, namely (as noted above) the apparent lack of any kind of grille. It is inconceivable that a reliquary would have stood unprotected on the floor of the niche; and even if the niche had been fitted with shelves from the outset in order to show off a relic collection, a protective grille would again have been expected. A wooden cupboard, even fitted with bars, would not have guarded against relic theft.

For these reasons, I very much doubt that the niche was ever intended as a relic cupboard. The presence of the shaft, on the other hand, so like the *cataractæ* which in earlier Christian architecture linked altars with the relics beneath them, implies a reliquary function which, I argue, is best explained if it had originally been provided as a means of contact between laity in the ambulatory and a shrine above.

CONCLUSIONS

GIVEN the paucity of the available evidence, interpretation reduces to two albeit related possibilities. Since the 1950s it has been held that the structure was designed from the outset as a platform for the episcopal throne, which made use of *spolia* retrieved at uncertain date from Thetford. The presence of the niche and shaft remains a problem for reasons advanced above. Firstly, there are no good parallels for such an association of an episcopal throne with relics; secondly, major relics (which, in any case, Norwich did not possess) would not have been housed in an ambulatory at this date; thirdly, even if the niche did house minor relics, they would have had to be protected.

The alternative, proposed in this paper, is that the structure was initially designed (though never used) as a high platform on which the shrine altar of Norwich's new St William would be displayed. This is the traditional position for the reliquary of a major saint, visible to all and 'giving light to the whole house' rather than being 'hidden under a bushel'. The niche and shaft would have functioned rather in the manner of the central corridor of a ring-crypt, allowing the faithful a measure of access to the shrine which otherwise was inaccessible in the monastic choir. Such an interpretation need not preclude the throne's having been placed on the intermediate platform, in a suitable hierarchy of high altar, bishop and shrine. There is insufficient evidence to prove decisively that the structure was originally intended to support the reliquary of St William as suggested in this paper, but such a solution does I think satisfy the physical evidence better than the anachronistic scenario proposed by Whittingham.

NOTES

1. *Friends of Norwich Cathedral, Thirtieth Annual Report* (1959), frontispiece.

2. The changing levels of the presbytery floor are the subject of two studies by E. C. Fernie, 'An architectural and archaeological analysis of the sanctuary of Norwich Cathedral', *NA*, 39 (1986), 296–305; idem, *AHNC*, 26–69. The levels are also discussed by S. Heywood, 'The Romanesque Building', in *Norwich Cathedral 1096–1996*, 73–115.

3. A. B. Whittingham, 'Norwich Saxon Throne', *Archaeol. J.*, 136 (1979), 60–68, at 60–61.

4. The fire of 1171 is chronicled in the *The First Register of Norwich Cathedral Priory*, ed. H. W. Saunders, Norwich Record Society, 11 (1939), fol. 14v, lines 20–27: *Tempore illius Willelmi fuit Ecclesia Sancte Trinitatis Norwyci fere combusta*; that of 1272 in Bartholomew Cotton, *Historia Anglicana*, ed. H. R. Luard (Rolls Series, XVI, 1859), 147. Unfortunately Luard used a defective text which suggested that the entire church except the Lady chapel was saved rather than the other way round. For clarification of this point, see D. J. Stewart, 'Notes on Norwich Cathedral', *Archaeol. J.*, 32 (1875), 16–47, at 28, n. 1.

5. Dr Roland Harris, pers. comm.

6. Dr Roland Harris, pers. comm.

7. The vestry is shown in the plan published by Blomefield, *Norfolk*, IV, facing 6, entitled 'Ichnography of the Cathedral Church of Norwich, made 1743'.

8. Ibid., 32.

9. Ibid.

10. NRO, DCN 24/5: Chapter Minute Book 1733–94, fol. 104v.

11. NRO, DCN 118/1: 'Dean Lloyd's Memoranda', 39.

12. Reproduced in G. Thurlow, 'Cathedral Picture, 1781', *NA*, 35 (1970), 1–5.

13. Society of Antiquaries of London, Norfolk Red Portfolio Nos 12–21, published as *John Adey Repton's Drawings of Norwich Cathedral at the end of the Eighteenth Century*, ed. S. Rowland Pierce (Farnborough 1965).

14. NRO, DCN 24/8: Chapter Minute Book 1857–78, fol. 227v.

15. *Cathedral cities, Ely and Norwich, drawn and etched by R. Farren, with introduction by Edward A. Freeman* (Cambridge 1883), pl. 29.

16. D. H. S. Cranage, 'The "Cathedra" of the Bishop of Norwich', *NA*, 27 (1941), 429–36, at 431.

17. Whittingham, 'Saxon Throne' (as in n. 3), 61 states that 'when the tesselated pavement was laid in 1877 a semi-circular incision was made in the surface to mark the line of a step that was found when lowering the sanctuary floor'. A. G. G. Thurlow, 'The Ancient Throne in Norwich Cathedral', *Friends of Norwich Cathedral, Twenty-Third Annual Report* (1952), 4–6, at 5, observed that the curve of the steps was 'marked by a line in the Victorian pavement'.

18. Ibid.: '[...] the podium of 1959 carefully follows the same curve'.

19. See below pp. 86–87.

20. Ibid.

21. NRO, DCN 24/8: Chapter Book 1857–78, 264, 6 July 1874: 'Mr Butterfield's plans for a new Altar, Sedilia, Bishop's Throne, and marble pavement in the Sacrarium of the Cathedral were produced and inspected but did not receive the approval of the Chapter'.

22. NRO, DCN 131/8: Letter to the Dean of Norwich from the Revd J. F. Wickenden, dated 12 February 1877.

23. NRO, DCN 160/3: Typewritten notes for an article, sent by the liturgist Percy Dearmer to Dean Cranage, 31 May 1929.

24. Plunkett's photographs are all available for download on http://www.georgeplunkett.co.uk

25. See paragraph 8 of the letter from Whittingham to Thurlow cited below, p. 85.

26. NRO, DCN 125/30.

27. *Eastern Daily Press*, 20 March 1958, announced that the throne was 'to be restored under the Will of Miss Mary Elizabeth Matthews of Swaffham'.

28. Thurlow, 'Ancient Throne' (as in n. 17); idem, 'The Throne of Norwich and the tradition behind it', *Friends of Norwich Cathedral, Thirtieth Annual Report* (1959), 5–7.

29. NRO, MC 186/93, 648X8: Letter from Whittingham to Thurlow dated 20 January 1958.

30. C. A. Ralegh Radford, 'The Bishop's throne in Norwich Cathedral', *Archaeol. J.*, 116 (1959), 115–32.

31. Whittingham, 'Saxon Throne' (as in n. 3).

32. Ibid., 62.

33. I owe this thought to Dr Charles Tracy.

34. This is 111 mm deeper than estimated by Whittingham when it lacked its west wall (see above, p. 86).

35. Whittingham, 'Saxon Throne' (as in n. 3), 61. The authority for this appears to have been the dean, H. C. Beeching, 'The Chapels and altars of Norwich Cathedral', *The Architect and Contract Reporter*, 3 and 10 December 1915, 434–37 and 452–55.

36. Ibid., 455.

37. Whittingham, 'Saxon Throne' (as in n. 3), 65.

38. See n. 8 above. *Pace* Ralegh Radford, 'Bishop's throne' (as in n. 30), 115, who confidently wrote that 'The first record of these stones dates from the 18th century, when they appear in their present position in the plan published by Blomefield'.

39. P. Browne, *An Account and Description of the Cathedral Church of the Holy Trinity, Norwich, and its Precincts* (Norwich 1785), 18.

40. Idem, *The History of Norwich, from the Earliest Records to the Present Time* (Norwich 1814), 365–66.

41. D. J. Stewart, 'Notes on Norwich Cathedral', *Archaeol. J.*, 32 (1875), 16–47, at 18.

42. Ralegh Radford, 'Bishop's throne' (as in n. 30), passim.

43. Ibid., pl. XIB. I have not been able to locate the original photograph.

44. J. Crook, *The Architectural Setting of the Cult of Saints in the Early Christian West* (Oxford 2000), 215.

45. The term has been used since at least the 15th century, when it is cited (in English) by local chroniclers of Winchester Cathedral.

46. J. Crook, *English Medieval Shrines* (Woodbridge 2011), 173–78; idem, 'The cult of St Swithun in Winchester Cathedral after 1093', in *Winchester Studies*, vol. 4.i, by B. Kjølbye-Biddle and M. Biddle, forthcoming.

47. Idem, '"Vir Optimus Wlfstanus": The post-Conquest commemoration of Wulfstan, Archbishop of York, at Ely Cathedral', in *Wulfstan, Archbishop of York*, Proceedings of the Second Alcuin Conference. Studies in the Early Middle Ages 10, ed. M. Townend (Turnhout 2004), 501–24.

48. Idem, 'The Medieval shrines of Rochester Cathedral', in *Medieval Art, Architecture and Archaeology at Rochester*, ed. T. Ayers and T. Tatton-Brown, *BAA Trans.*, XXVIII (2006), 114–29.

49. Idem, 'Medieval Saints' Cults at Hexham', in *Newcastle and Northumberland: Roman and Medieval Architecture and Art*, ed. J. Ashbee and J. Luxford, *BAA Trans.*, XXXVI (2013), 141–51.

50. *The Life and Miracles of St William of Norwich by Thomas of Monmouth*, ed. A. Jessopp and M. R. James (Cambridge 1986), 221.

51. According to Jessopp and James, ibid., p. xii.

52. Crook, *English Medieval Shrines* (as in n. 46), 257.

53. For this sense of archaism, see Heywood, 'The Romanesque Building' (as in n. 2), 91.

54. Cranage, 'Cathedra' (as in n. 16), 431.

55. See above, p. 85.

56. Crook, *Architectural Setting* (as in n. 44), 80–82.

Norwich Castle Keep: Dates and Contexts

JAMES F. KING

No contemporary documentation about the construction of the castle keep at Norwich survives, but discussion of the origin of the keep has been ongoing for centuries. Until now detailed research on the fabric of the building has been limited; legend and mis-interpretation having confused the subject. Comparison of carved decoration and other features of the keep with equivalents at Norwich Cathedral and elsewhere, together with a re-examination of the historical facts, suggest that work on the keep is unlikely to have commenced before the 1120s, and that the upper part of the keep was begun somewhat later, probably in the 1130s.

BACKGROUND

THE earliest known reference to a 'castle' in Norwich concerns the 1075 revolt of Earl Ralph Guader (also 'de Gael' or 'Wader'). While William I was in Normandy, forces loyal to the king quashed the rebellion, causing Ralph to flee abroad. His wife remained temporarily in the castle as the *Anglo-Saxon Chronicle* records: Ralph's *wif wæs innan þam castele*.[1] A letter from Archbishop Lanfranc to the king about this refers to *castrum Noruuich*.[2] Other near-contemporary chroniclers have similar wording. The *Waverley Annals*, for example, has *castello de Norwich*, while Orderic Vitalis uses *castrum suum* (the 'his' referring to Ralph) and Symeon of Durham gives *castello*.[3]

Domesday Book makes no reference to the events of 1075, saying only that the new French borough, which Ralph founded, was between (*inter*) himself and the king.[4] *Domesday Book* does record seventeen empty messuages in the occupation of the castle *c.* 1086 (*xvii. mansure vacue que sunt in occupatione castelli*) that were originally on land over which [King] Harold held soke. In the *burgo*, which was in the soke of the king and earl, it records that there were 190 empty messuages, and 81 messuages in the occupation of the castle (*in occupatione castelli*). In contrast to other sites listed in *Domesday Book*, the record for Norwich makes no reference to these being the result of castle building, stating only that many who had either fled or remained in Norwich were ruined, partly on account of Earl Ralph's forfeitures, partly because of fire, partly because of the king's geld and partly by Waleran. The king replaced Guader with Roger Bigot, but seems never to have made Roger an earl. In 1088, Roger entered the castle of Norwich, apparently laying waste to the surrounding countryside: *Roger het an of heom. se hleop into þam castele æt Nordwic* (*Anglo-Saxon Chronicle*); *Rogerus Bigot intravit castrum de Northwic* (Symeon of Durham); *Rogerus [...] venit in castellum de Norwich* (*Waverley Annals*).[5] Nevertheless, Roger remained in charge of Norwich throughout the reign of William II (William Rufus) and the early years of Henry I. Before Abbot Simeon of Ely's death in 1093 Simeon was released from his obligations to provide military support at Norwich but with no mention of a castle: *De custodia de Norewic abbatem Symeonem quietum esse dimittite, sed ibi munitionem suam conduci*

BAA Trans., vol. XXXVIII (2015), 96–117
© British Archaeological Association 2015

faciat et custodiri.[6] The next mention of a castle in Norwich comes with the survey of the land given for the city's new cathedral, land which was *apud Norwycum castrum*.[7] Not long after, Roger Bigot was obliged to remove his *palacium* west of the cathedral as it was blocking access to the site.[8]

In records surviving from Henry I's reign, there are few references to any castle in Norwich, though when Bishop Hervey of Ely was released from ward duty in 1130 it was specified that ward duty had previously been made *castello Norwici*.[9] In 1136, on rumours of King Stephen's death Hugh Bigot seized *castellum Norewic*.[10] In 1139/40, Stephen released the abbey of Bury St Edmund's of ward duties at *castellum meum de Norwico*.[11] And in 1153, a treaty between Stephen and Prince Henry (later Henry II), stated that the castle of Norwich (*castra scilicet et villas de Norwico*) was to be retained by Stephen's son William after Stephen's death (in 1157 the castle was taken back by Henry II).[12] In the *Pipe Rolls* of Henry II, there are numerous mentions of the castle (*castellum*, etc.).[13] A royal charter of 1157 (and other documentation thereafter) records the church of *sancti Johannis ante portam castelli*.[14] Specific reference to the castle keep, however, first occurs in 1175–76, when the *Pipe Rolls* list payment for repairs on the *turris Norwici*.[15]

In the 13th century, Matthew Paris repeated some of the previous chroniclers, but expressed the problems of 1075 (listed as 1074) as *in villa Norwicensi*.[16] He goes on to say about King Henry I's building works: *praeter turres et castella, XXV. opere construxit sumptuoso*.[17] Significantly, in the late 14th century Knighton states that William II *construere atque palacia, prout castra, Dorobernia, Wyndosora, Norwychi, Excestria & magna aula Westmonasterii*, making it clear that by that time it was believed that the castle at Norwich had been built by William Rufus, but without mentioning the keep.[18] Polydore Vergil, shortly before the Reformation, made no reference to its origins either.[19]

Most of the words used in medieval sources about the 'castle' at Norwich are based on *castele*, *castellum* and *castrum*, but it is clear that there is considerable disagreement about what these words imply, particularly during the earlier medieval period. All three words had been used before 1066 in England; none necessarily indicates the presence of a keep. Modern translations have further complicated the situation. While 'castle' is the usual translation in modern English, some have preferred 'fort', 'stronghold', 'fortification' or even 'town', which further confuses matters. A source of still greater confusion is that usage changes over time. What was meant in the late 11th and 12th centuries is therefore problematic. Eventually, 'Norwich Castle' tended to become synonymous with the keep itself, though during the medieval period a clear distinction was intended. In references to a 'castle' in Norwich in the early period we should therefore probably accept that the words *castele*, *castellum* and *castrum* signified little more than a fortified place.

After the Reformation, varying hypotheses concerning the keep's foundation emerged. In 1575 Alexander Neville wrote that the castle and keep had been built by Gurguntus and his successor Gutheline.[20] Ten years later, Holinshed (1585) remained silent on the subject,[21] but in 1607 Camden refuted Neville's argument, suggesting the castle [keep] had probably been built by Hugh Bigot around the time the Young King Henry (son of Henry II) promised it to him.[22] Woods (1623) translated Neville's work, but added no views of his own.[23] Though Baker (1674) made no reference as to who built the castle or keep,[24] Dugdale (1675 and 1682) stated that Roger Bigot 'fortified' the castle in 1088 and was given custody of Norwich Castle in 12 Henry II.[25] Dugdale further related that the cathedral had been built *apud Norwicense castrum*. Spelman (1695) said only that the keep was of Norman origin.[26]

The 1718 *History of Norwich* repeated Neville's theory of the origins of the castle.[27] But Gurdon (1728) was convinced the entire keep had been built by Canute.[28] Kirkpatrick (d. 1728) suggested the castle keep had been built just before 1066 or more likely soon afterwards.[29] Blomefield (1745) felt the first castle at Norwich had been built by King Uffa shortly after 575, but that the keep had most likely been built by Roger Bigot during Henry I's reign.[30] Of those who wrote after this, both Edward King (1777 and 1782) and William Wilkins (1796) thought that the main part of the castle keep had been built by Canute, with the fore-building being later.[31] For King the fore-building dated from the reign of Edward II, while Wilkins believed it was built by one of the Bigots, and so named it 'Bigod's Tower'. Significantly, King referred to the 'tradition' that the castle [keep] had been built by Roger Bigot about the time of William Rufus.[32] Woodward (1836) continued to believe that the keep was built by Canute, but Harrod (1857) argued that the castle had been built early in William I's reign and that the keep as well was early Norman.[33]

By the second half of the 20th century there was common agreement that the present castle and keep were post-1066, though a range of dates prevailed. Renn (1960) wrote that the keep had possibly been begun in 1094, but that the second phase (i.e. the decorated upper parts and fore-building) was constructed between 1119 and 1132.[34] Green (1970 and 1980) felt the keep was constructed between 1120 and 1130, while Faulkner (1971) suggested that the first phase of construction was *c.*1130 and the second phase *c.*1160, the whole of the keep completed *c.*1170.[35]

Whittingham, who first recorded the masons' marks in both the cathedral and the castle keep, changed the scholarly thinking. Although he followed a *c.*1130 date in a paper published in 1951, in 1980 and in unpublished papers he wrote that his study confirmed Knighton's statement that the castle had been built by William Rufus.[36] Moreover, Whittingham suggested that masons had moved from the cathedral to the castle in 1101 and that the keep was only just finished in time for Henry I to spend Christmas there in 1122 [*sic*]. Fernie (1993) suggested that the pre-1075 castle had probably been built of earth and timber, but that the stone keep might have been started during William Rufus's reign, with the upper parts of the keep constructed in the later years of Bishop Herbert's episcopacy (1091–1119), finished only during the time of Bishop Everard (1121–45).[37] In 1994, Heslop wrote that the motte had probably been built immediately after the Conquest, that the keep was begun by William Rufus and that it was finished by Christmas 1121 (referring both to Whittingham and also to the then unpublished work of Marner).[38] Excavations of the castle precincts between 1987 and 1998 showed not only that the motte had been constructed in the late 11th century, but that an extension to the motte had been made in order to build the present keep.[39] The research work highlighted that there had been substantial subsidence (most likely because the extension had not been given adequate time to settle), causing considerable damage to the lower part of the keep soon after it was started. In the excavation reports, Shepherd stated that a timber castle was probably built on the first motte between 1067/68 and 1070 and the stone keep built *c.* 1094–1122 on the enlarged motte. Her final report on the excavations in 2009 reiterated these dates, making it clear that this was based on Heslop.[40] Ayers (2000), Baxter (2004) and Goodall (2011) followed Heslop's theory.[41] Dominic Marner (2002) meanwhile published his article on the masons' marks of the castle and cathedral, proposing that the lower window splays in the basement of the keep had been built as early as *c.* 1098 and that other masons' marks in the upper parts showed that the keep had been finished by the mid-1110s.[42] In 1984, Drury suggested it was 'probable' that the keep had been finished in time for Henry I to spend Christmas there, but by 2002 seemed to have accepted Marner's argument.[43]

MASONS' MARKS AND MORTAR WIDTHS

ANALYSIS of the masons' marks on site does not support the theories of Whittingham and Marner, and shows that many of the marks previously stated as being the same were actually carved by distinct masons. A few other masons' marks said to be used exclusively within the east end of the cathedral appear in the nave, and several of the marks more comparable with those in the keep are only used towards the west end of the nave. Occasionally, Whittingham was not entirely accurate in his notes. For example, he states that one mark was found only 'in Eborard's early work', while his notes elsewhere show clearly that he found this mark only at the west end of the nave, a detail now verifiable on site. I have found no visible evidence for the claim that the east end of the cathedral and the castle keep are contemporaneous. In fact, stronger relationships exist between the masons' marks of the keep and the middle and western parts of the cathedral nave. However, no unambiguous evidence from masons' marks shows that the same masons worked at both sites or that they moved between the two, as the following table shows (Fig. 1). Although the figures are not drawn to scale and the cathedral's marks have not been exhaustively recorded, the table gives a fairer picture of what is presently visible.

One point previous scholars have overlooked is the fine mortaring in the keep, mostly about 5 mm thick. Not only does this appear in the upper levels, it is also found in the ashlared areas of the lower parts. This is in marked contrast to what is found at the east end of the cathedral, where mortar is 10 to 20 mm thick. A change occurs within the cathedral in work undertaken for Bishop Everard (consecrated March 1121),[44] where the mortar is thinner, generally 10 mm or less (though still not as fine as at the keep).

Around 1125 William of Malmesbury wrote that stonework at Old Sarum was so fine that it appeared like one piece of stone, implying a change in practice.[45] Indeed, surviving English buildings from this period seem to confirm this. Work undertaken during William Rufus's reign at Westminster, for example, both in the surviving monastic areas of the abbey and in the great hall of the royal palace the mortar is thick, mostly 10 to 30 mm (occasionally as much as 40 mm). Lanfranc's crypt at Canterbury Cathedral, the royal White Tower of London, Colchester Castle and Gundulf's Tower at Rochester all show this thick type of mortaring. At Ely Cathedral, whose diocese neighbours Norwich, mortar thicknesses generally range between about 20 and 30 mm (rarely as thin as 10 mm). Only in the west transepts (probably post-1150) is the mortar thinner (about 10 mm). The first evidence of change to a somewhat thinner mortar may be identified in the work begun about 1096 for Archbishop Anselm at Canterbury Cathedral, varying between about 8 mm and 12 mm (at times thicker, with an average of no less than 10 mm).[46] This was repeated regionally at places such as the royal keep of Canterbury and in the episcopal keep at Rochester. The thicker type continued to be used elsewhere for some time afterwards, as at the church of St Kyneburgha (Castor near Peterborough), with a carved dedication date of 1124, where mortar varies between 15 mm and 20 mm.[47]

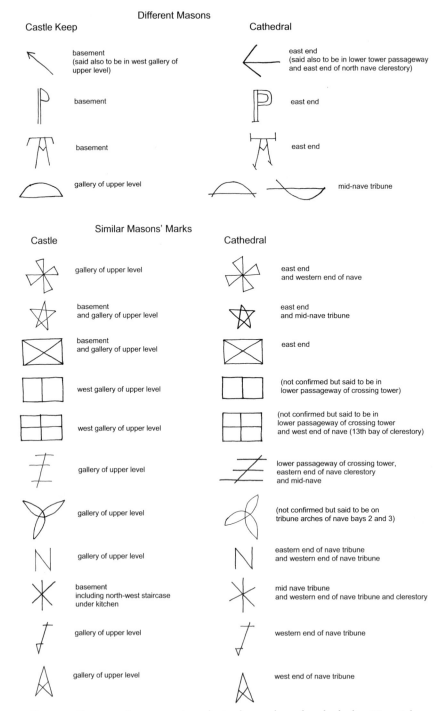

FIG. 1.   Comparative masons' marks in the castle and cathedral at Norwich

In the abbey (now cathedral) church of Peterborough, possibly overlapping in date with work at Castor, thin mortar was used from the start, generally less than 10 mm. This is possibly the earliest example of the type in this region. Castle Rising's keep (*c.* 1138), clearly dependent on that at Norwich, also has thin mortar (between about 5 mm and 15 mm), as does the nave at Wymondham Priory near Norwich (probably late 1120s or 1130s) with less than 10 mm. It is difficult to support an argument that any of the ashlar work on the keep at Norwich Castle could be earlier than the 12th century. Previous arguments for an early date for the keep at Norwich based on a supposed connection with work at the cathedral now seem untenable. Why would masons purportedly employed at both the cathedral and the castle change their marks as well as the thickness of their mortaring?[48]

CARVED STONEWORK

IN the early 19th century the keep was re-faced on the exterior, though changes had already been made in the 18th century and earlier.[49] The lower exterior of the keep was originally faced with flint and although Caen stone was used for quoins, window openings and a few other areas, no sculpted decoration was applied to this part of the building. However, a change in design occurred during construction, including a kitchen above a staircase which had already been begun. The upper part of the keep was to be fully faced with ashlared Caen stone (interior and exterior) and receive lavishly carved decoration, thus becoming one of the most ornate castle keeps anywhere. On the exterior, decorative wedges were used on many of the arches (Fig. 2). In the interior,

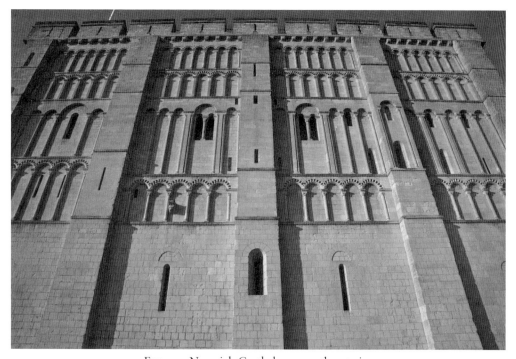

FIG. 2.   Norwich Castle keep: south exterior

FIG. 3.   Norwich Castle keep: entrance doorway

some original carving survives: on the chapel, upper passageways, fireplace, exterior of the garderobe wall, fore-building ground-floor level vault, and great hall ceremonial entrance (Fig. 3). There remains also an original corbel head supporting a drainage stone on the south exterior. Undoubtedly, there were other well-decorated areas, though these have now vanished. Norwich's keep was one of the largest Norman keeps ever built (33.6 m × 28.3 m including fore-building, 28.3 m × 29.3 m excluding fore-building), comparisons of known dimensions suggesting that it was third or fourth largest in ground plan, Colchester's keep (46 m × 33.5 m) and the Tower of London (36 m × 29.56 m) being the biggest.[50]

Since no contemporary documents state when the keep was built, it is imperative to look closely at carved details used on the keep. This shows that decoration used elsewhere in the 1120s and 1130s compares more closely with that on the keep than any found earlier in England. The most common motif on the keep is a trapezoidally shaped wedge extending onto an arch roll (Fig. 4). It is used on the upper exterior of the keep, the main doorway (originally also on the fore-building), several of the windows and lower arches of the upper interior, and the fore-building vault. There are two types used at Norwich, one shorter and one longer, the latter used only on jambs of the main doorway. This longer type, noted previously in association with standard beakhead, has led to references such as 'conventional beakhead' or 'geometric beakhead', the latter term used in this paper.[51] The shorter Norwich form has recently been nicknamed 'beaker moulding'.[52] Beakhead, including geometric beakhead, seems to have started in Britain in south-west England in the 1120s.[53] But in Norfolk and northern Suffolk there are few places using it, only one showing proper 'beakhead'. None

FIG. 4.   Norwich Castle keep: lower vault of forebuilding

FIG. 5.   Norwich Castle keep: outer wall of garderobe

appears to be earlier than the 1140s. The two north Suffolk examples at Westhall and Wissett (closely related to each other) are especially interesting since the floor of the west tower of the church at Wissett has been radio-carbon tested and given a suggested date of *c.* 1147.[54] The doorway of the church at Barton Bendish, whose jambs compare more closely with those on the doorway at Norwich, was probably carved in the second half of the 12th century, as the dogtooth decoration implies. The doorway arch at South Burlingham, not far from Norwich, has wedges related to Westhall, Wissett and Norwich, but it also has a series of circles with small central holes exactly like those found on the garderobe wall of Norwich Castle keep (Fig. 5). This motif is rare and suggests a connection between the two.

Early forms of geometric beakhead occur at Sherborne Castle (Dorset) and Romsey Abbey (Hampshire), but its origin seems to be western France.[55] Forms of beakhead without animal heads were also used about 1130 on the tower at Bury St Edmunds (Suffolk), but none of these are especially close to the Norwich type. Various geometric beakheads were carved elsewhere in the country, the main concentrations found in just two geographical areas: from Buckinghamshire and Berkshire to Wiltshire and Gloucestershire, and in Yorkshire. All forms of geometric beakhead sit proud of the roll (i.e. not carved within the same plane as the roll). The shorter form, in particular, contrasts with another type of decoration which has sometimes been associated with it, one found, for example, at Durham Cathedral carved within the main surface plane with no extension onto the roll. In fact, the short Norwich type may be understood as a combination of two forms, one from Sherborne Castle (Fig. 6), and another (not overlapping a roll) found primarily in Hampshire (possibly first used in Winchester).[56]

Beakhead on jambs, as seen in East Anglia at Norwich Castle and at Barton Bendish, is also found around Derbyshire and southern Yorkshire; but it is primarily used further south and west, where within England it surely originates. Examples include Avington (Berks.), South Cerney (Glos.), and Quenington (Glos.) (Fig. 7). What is extremely rare, though found at Norwich Castle, is beakhead (geometric or otherwise) overlapping a capital (Fig. 8). Only five places are known where this occurs: Quenington and South Cerney (Glos.), Chirton (Wilts.), Tutbury (Staffs.) and Kedleston

FIG. 6.   Sherborne (Dorset): carved fragment from castle

FIG. 7.   South Cerney (Glos.)

FIG. 8.   Norwich Castle keep:
entrance doorway

(Derbys.), most likely copying Tutbury.[57] The latter two (probably no earlier than the 1150s) seem to be later than the others, which may have been carved as early as the 1130s.[58] The edges of the Norwich jambs are also cusped, a feature that in this form is probably no earlier than the 1120s. Early instances occur on fragments from Old Sarum Cathedral (Wilts.), Sherborne Castle (Dorset) and Reading Abbey (Berks.), and are still *in situ* at such places as Shobdon (Herefs.), South Cerney (Glos.) and elsewhere.

More significant is the appearance at Norwich of a rib-vault under the waiting area of the fore-building decorated on both sides of the central roll with the shorter geometric beakhead/beaker clasp (Fig. 4). The roll itself is unusual in that it is three-quarters round, unlike the usual half-rolls found elsewhere. The concept of decorating rolls on both sides seems to have first occurred in the 1120s, with early examples yet again at Sherborne Castle, Avington, Winchester and also at Stowe (Lincs.).[59] Rib vaults within Norfolk seem to occur only at Norwich Castle and Castle Rising during this period; no rib vaults were used in Norwich Cathedral. Ely Cathedral also has no rib vaults and the closest geographical examples seem to be those of Peterborough, the earliest of which probably date from the 1120s,[60] though there devoid of additional decoration. The upper section of the rib vault at the keep has been cut back so it is no longer possible to determine its original decoration. However, the chapel vault of the related Castle Rising keep features devouring heads, suggesting the possibility for

Norwich as well. This feature forms another link with south and west of England, the only other region where it appears in Britain.[61]

A series of large flower-like shapes appears among the carvings on the doorway of the keep at Norwich on the enclosing arch over the main doorway. One form has four main petals (occasionally with subsidiary smaller petals), on top of which are secondary leaves with central vein of beading (Fig. 9). Within Norfolk, a related type is found at Chedgrave, which may have been inspired by Norwich. The Norwich form of flower, however, is rare, and the only other close British examples that have been identified are from Old Sarum Cathedral, Shaftesbury Abbey and Rochester Cathedral (chapter-house facade). The source for the beaded-leaf motif seems to be western France, where it appears frequently, as at Saint-Jouin-de-Marnes. Large flowers were used elsewhere in the British Isles after 1120, as at Kenilworth Abbey (Warks.), Dunfermline (Fife), Avington (Berks.) and Bury St Edmunds (Suffolk), but none is the same as at Norwich. Flower patterns were also used for the decoration of the cloister at Norwich Cathedral, most likely not before the 1120s at the earliest, but these, too, are not the same.[62]

A rather odd creature, two found on one capital in the chapel, is a bird with folded wings grasping the torus (Fig. 10). While the same type is found also at Liverton (Cleveland), where beakhead is also employed, there is otherwise no obvious parallel for this. It may be that some related type was used at the cathedral of Old Sarum, as north of this Great Durnford (probably copying motifs from Old Sarum) has winged animals clasping the torus in a similar manner, though neither of the birds there has folded wings.

Decorative nobs/cones are another feature used to ornament both the chapel arch and the doorway at Norwich's keep (Fig. 11). Although several 12th-century buildings built after 1120 used decorative nobs as one of the motifs, examples closest in type to those at Norwich are from Sherborne Castle, Reading Abbey and the churches of Avington (Berks.) and Old Clee (Lincs.). A series of sunken 'spaces', flanked by stylized leaves and decorative nobs is also found on the main doorway. Examples of similar 'spaces' were employed at both Old Sarum Cathedral and Gloucester Abbey (now the cathedral). Those at Bury St Edmunds and Saint-Georges-de-Boscherville in Normandy (related to each other) are distinctly different.

It is difficult now to make out a number of features carved on the capitals at Norwich, but one capital of the ceremonial doorway has small animal heads on the corners with large leaves emanating from their mouths (Fig. 12). This type, with large

FIG. 9.   Norwich Castle keep: entrance doorway

FIG. 10.   Norwich Castle keep: capital of chapel arch

FIG. 11. Norwich Castle
keep: entrance doorway

FIG. 12. Norwich Castle
keep: capital right of
entrance doorway

FIG. 13. Norwich Castle keep: capital of entrance doorway

leaves coming directly from the mouths rather than via long tendrils, is one that seems to appear first around the 1120s and is found frequently alongside beakhead. On another capital a figure is carved with a series of horizontal lines (Fig. 13). The source for this remains speculative, but comparisons may be made with figures from the church of Saint-Eutropes in Sainte (western France), Tournai Cathedral (Belgium), on various Tournai-marble baptismal fonts, and the cloister doorways of Ely Cathedral (Cambs.). Ordinarily, lines on the chests of such figures are curved and not straight. The carving of the Norwich Castle figure is certainly different from any carved work surviving from the cathedral precincts, as too are the dragons, with their distinctive snouts, on one of the arches above (Fig. 14).

FIG. 14. Norwich Castle keep: arch of entrance doorway

Although no direct connection may be made between the masons from the cathedral and the castle, one feature in the western area of the cathedral may provide a clue to the date of construction of the upper part of the keep. On one of the west wall interior capitals is a motif that resembles a string of pearls carved proud of the surface, similar to some found on the main doorway of the keep (Figs 15 and 16). Carved beading appears earlier in the cathedral, as on the two dragon capital of the north transept, but this type is not the same as at the keep, the earlier form being more 'common', with the beads set into a concave vein. The eastern bays of the nave were completed by the time Bishop Herbert died in 1119, and we know only that the nave of the cathedral was completed by the time Bishop Everard left in 1145. Suggestions that it was finished about 1140 seem not unlikely, which would indicate that the western parts were under construction in the 1130s, overlapping the early period of King Stephen's reign.

FIG. 15.   Norwich Cathedral: capital on west interior nave wall

FIG. 16.   Norwich Castle keep: arch of entrance doorway

HISTORICAL CONTEXT

NEITHER William I nor William II is known to have visited Norwich. References to William Rufus's involvements with Norwich cannot, however, be overlooked. He was responsible for giving land for a new cathedral to be built when it moved to Norwich, and it was during his reign that the palace of Roger Bigot was taken down to allow access to the cathedral. But just where Earl Ralph Guader's castle was located during William I's reign is unknown. References to the 1075 rebellion and later in the *Domesday Book* seem to indicate that Ralph's castle and the king's land were quite separate. Moreover, references to Ralph being in 'his' castle imply that the references to the siege in Norwich at that time may not actually be referring to a castle of the king. There does not, in fact, appear to be an unequivocal reference to a royal castle in Norwich by 1075, which leaves open the possibility that even if the motte was started/completed by William I (which is not entirely certain), the first buildings (wooden?) on the motte were those of William Rufus. There is no physical evidence that the present stone keep was started at this time, and excavations showing that the motte had to be extended in order to build the stone keep beg a number of questions about just who was responsible.

The date of the keep at Castle Rising (Norfolk) is important in this context, as it models itself on Norwich Castle's keep. It is believed to have been begun *c.*1138, when William II d'Aubigny married King Henry I's widow, Adeliza of Louvain.[63] It does seem unlikely that it would have been begun before this given the weight of evidence, including excavations showing previous buildings on the site prior to the present keep.[64] William II d'Aubigny's father (William I) died in 1139, when William II presumably inherited the lands in and around Castle Rising, though it is possible he received them when he married. In 1138/9 William II was made earl of Lincoln, changed in 1141 to earl of Sussex. In 1141, at the Battle of Lincoln, William was among King Stephen's most loyal supporters, though Stephen was captured and imprisoned in Bristol Castle. When in 1141, or more likely *c.*1145, a second official coinage was produced, it was minted exclusively on the east side of England including at a new mint set up at Castle Rising, which lasted until Stephen's death (or possibly the first of Henry II's issues in 1158).[65] It may be significant that Castle Rising's keep does not incorporate Caen stone, since chaos within England from 1140/1 onwards was not congenial for shipping great quantities of stone and Normandy ceased to be under royal control in 1144. Suggestions have also been made that the keep at Castle Rising was left unfinished, that William lost interest in it when his wife Adeliza died in 1151, and that he turned his attention more generally towards Sussex thereafter.[66] In 1146 he gave his castle at Old Buckenham to the Augustinians, a new castle having been established at New Buckenham. It is hard to imagine why anyone would want to build a keep like that at Castle Rising, so closely based on that of Norwich, if there were a twenty-year gap (or more) between the two, a suggestion that has previously been made.

It is noteworthy that the bulk of keeps built by Henry I, and certainly the most relevant ones, were erected in the years after *c.*1120, at which time a large range of stone keeps were under construction, both for Henry and for others. Examples include the royal castle keeps of Falaise (*c.*1123), Caen (*c.*1123), and Portchester (prob. 1130s), and other castles such as Old Sarum (work begun late teens, mentioned 1129–30), Sherborne (1120s–30s), Rochester (*c.*1127), Arundel (work paid for 1129–30), Bristol (1120s or 1130s), Newark (mentioned as recently built in 1139), Banbury (after 1123, probably 1130s), Sleaford (after 1123, probably 1130s), Castle Rising (probably after

1138), Hedingham (probably 1130s or 1140s), Castle Acre (creation of keep which was never finished, usually suggested as *c.* 1140), and the castle keeps of Bishop Henry of Blois (begun *c.* 1138).[67] In fact, contemporary chronicles suggest that between 1136 and 1140 there were many castles built.

Interactions between Henry I, Stephen and the city of Norwich are revealing. Henry I seems only to have visited Norwich around 1106, 1109, Christmas 1121, and possibly 1116.[68] Despite claims made that the keep was complete by late 1121 and that Henry and his new bride celebrated Christmas within it, there is no evidence to support them.[69] From Easter 1116 until late November 1120, Henry was at war in Normandy. His first wife Matilda died in 1118 while he was away. In November 1120, after conflicts in Normandy seemed at last to be over, Henry's only legitimate son, William, was drowned in the White Ship disaster, along with many of the first-born males of the leading families. Henry spent Christmas 1120 with his nephew Theobald of Blois at the royal manor of Brampton (near Huntingdon),[70] and just over a month later married Adeliza, daughter of the duke of Louvain, the announcement of his marital intentions being given at the beginning of January. Henry then departed from his normal routine for celebrating Christmas and Easter (and other feast days). Previously, unless away in Normandy, he had spent almost every Christmas and Easter in the south and south-west regions of the country, generally at Westminster and Winchester.[71] Following 1120, Henry spent these feasts traveling around his realm, probably a campaign to deliberately reassert his presence in England while breaking with the past. There is no apparent evidence, however, that when Henry spent Christmas 1121 in Norwich he held court there; there appear to be no surviving charters made at this time (contrasting with what usually happened at these events).[72] Shortly after his marriage, Henry founded Reading Abbey, and sometime between June and September 1122 he made his illegitimate son Robert earl of Gloucester, who then began constructing a stone keep in Bristol.[73] In the autumn of 1122 Henry was in Carlisle where he ordered that the city be strengthened and a castle built. Several castles in Normandy are listed under the year 1123 and most 12th-century stone English castle keeps seem to have been begun sometime thereafter.[74] The delay between the building of the castles in Normandy and those in England is easily explained. Renewed conflicts in Normandy obliged Henry to return to Normandy in June 1123, finally returning to England in September 1126 after negotiating peace with Louis VI of France. Only after this did the main surge in castle building in England take place. Henry spent Easter 1133 in Oxford in his new palace there (*in nova aula*).[75]

In Norwich, meanwhile, Bishop Herbert de Losinga had died in 1119 and was not replaced until June 1121, when Everard, previously royal chaplain and archdeacon at Old Sarum, was consecrated.[76] Records show that Bishop Herbert completed the cathedral church up to the altar of the Holy Cross.[77] It has also been speculated that the stone bishop's chair behind the main altar may have been installed for Bishop Everard's enthronement.[78] Christmas 1121 would have been an ideal time to visit the new bishop, see recently finished work on the cathedral, and attend the Christmas religious celebrations. There is no indication how long the king stayed in Norwich; but once he left he never returned. It is said, however, that about this time Henry issued to the citizens of Norwich a charter granting them the same liberties as those previously given to the citizens of London, the first grant or charter the city received, but there is some doubt about the authenticity of this statement.[79] In Henry I's one surviving pipe-roll (for 1129–30), nothing is recorded concerning work at the castle of Norwich.[80]

It has also been said that in 1122 Henry named Hugh Bigot (who had inherited the Bigot lands on the death of his brother William in 1120) constable of Norwich Castle and governor of the city, but there is no actual evidence for Hugh being either constable or governor at Norwich during the reigns of either Henry I or Stephen.[81] Hugh does appear as a charter witness for Henry I, as one of his many dapifers in 1123,[82] but it is only from 1128 that he is more frequently recorded in the presence of the king. In the pipe-roll of 1129–30 he is referred to simply as *Hugo bigotus*, no title being given.[83] Before 1141 Hugh witnessed numerous charters for Stephen and even fought with him in the Battle of Lincoln, but Hugh then changed over to the Angevin side and was made earl of Norfolk by Henry I's daughter, Matilda.[84]

Stephen, by contrast, seems to have had a strong relationship with Norwich throughout his reign. When in 1136 Hugh Bigot seized Norwich Castle on the rumour that Stephen had died, he refused to return it unless Stephen went to Norwich in person to retake it.[85] Between 1136 and 1137 Stephen gave land in Norwich at Carrow for nuns to build a church, a charter witnessed by *episcopo Sarum per Hugonem Bigod, et R. filio Ricardi*.[86] In 1139/40 Stephen issued a charter for Reading Abbey at Norwich,[87] and in 1140, perhaps on the same visit to Norwich, Stephen issued a document concerning the abbey of St Benet's Holme witnessed by several key magnates.[88] Later, about 1146, the king heard certain pleas in Norwich, granted a three-day fair in nearby Wymondham and re-founded Carrow Priory.[89] Between 1147 and 1153 Stephen was again in Norwich when he confirmed gifts to the abbey of Earl's Colne.[90] In the later medieval period it was documented, almost certainly copied from an earlier document, that in 1152 Stephen issued a new and significant charter for the town of Norwich.[91] Then between November 1153 and October 1154 Stephen was once again in Norwich and issued another confirmation relating to the abbey of St Benet Holme.[92] In the 1153 Winchester treaty between King Stephen and Duke Henry (later Henry II), it was declared that the king's surviving son, William, would keep Norwich Castle, the city and certain lands after Stephen's death.[93]

Other events may also be related: such as Stephen's nephew being made abbot of St Benet's Holme (near Norwich) in 1146, apparently at the direct intervention of the king,[94] and the decision that the abbot of Bury St Edmund's would undertake his castle-guard at Bury instead of Norwich (1139–45).[95] Numerous moneyers minted coins for Stephen in Norwich during this period,[96] and at some point not long after the death of Henry I the burgesses of Norwich built a new *fossatum*.[97] In 1150 a meeting of a joint shire court took place in Norwich in the bishop's garden under the jurisdiction of King Stephen's steward William Martel.[98]

Sometime between 1147 and 1149 Stephen's son William, then about twelve years old, married Isabel de Warenne, probably after her father left for the Holy Land.[99] For all or part of the period 1147–54/7, Reginald de Warenne, Isabel's uncle, may have been constable of Norwich Castle, acting for the young William and his bride until they came of age.[100] One theory suggests that the young William was given Norwich Castle as a kind of wedding present, his brother Eustace having been given the earldom of Boulogne.[101] It is certainly clear from the relevant charters that Reginald acted as regent for the Warenne lands during this period.[102] At the same time, between 1146 and 1157 there was also a break with the Chesney family's usual appointment as sheriffs of Norfolk.[103] Although Henry II took Norwich Castle and the associated lands back into royal hands in 1157, he knighted William in 1158 and William went on to fight with Henry in France, dying at Toulouse in 1159.[104]

Stephen's reign has often been characterized as a time of disruption, but it is clear that this was not widely felt until 1140/1. In fact, Henry of Huntingdon and others clearly state that Stephen ran a successful government in his early years, that finances in the first two years were good and in the third year moderate. Only in 1139 to 1140 were the revenues in less good shape.[105] Towards the end of 1139, Stephen seized the fortunes of Bishop Roger of Sarum, which were soon to be spent on continuing conflicts. It seems that it was this money that helped him make a French alliance through the marriage of his eldest son Eustace and Constance, sister of Louis VII of France.[106]

CONCLUSION

THE evidence discussed above indicates that the keep at Norwich was constructed between *c.* 1120 and 1157: there is nothing in Henry II's pipe-rolls that would account for such building work following 1157. The earliest possibility would allow for the extension to the castle mound at Norwich (essential for the keep) to have been undertaken before 1120, with a relatively brief period of time allowed for it to settle. The keep might have been ordered by Henry I when he visited Norwich at Christmas 1121, suggesting a start date no earlier than 1122, a date consistent with the construction of Henry's other related castle keeps. The pipe-roll for 1129–30 makes no mention of payments for work at Norwich, which one would not expect if the keep was either under construction or just finished, so the keep must have either been fully finished by then or there was a building break, which we know occurred between the lower and upper parts. However, the evidence given does not seem to support a conclusion that the entire keep was completed before *c.* 1130, especially considering the necessary major repairs to the lower part which had to be undertaken before the upper part was begun. This would mean that the upper part was begun in the 1130s. Another scenario, assuming that the extension to the mound was started on Henry I's command at Christmas 1121, leads to a similar conclusion: either the keep was started immediately after the work on the extension was accomplished and was finished by 1129/30, which seems rather unlikely given the evidence, or more likely that the 1129/30 break was due to work on the keep coming to a halt while problems due to subsidence were rectified, the upper part of the keep being constructed in the 1130s. Both scenarios leave open the possibility that the upper part of the keep might have been finished by, or even begun, by Stephen. An end date for work by 1140 is likely due to the large and distinguished council which met in Norwich in that year.[107] This suggestion explains more satisfactorily work undertaken at Castle Rising keep during Stephen's reign, a keep which followed closely on from that at Norwich. Whatever the precise chronology, the evidence does not support the theory that the upper part of the keep could have been built before the 1120s, at the earliest, and it seems more likely that it dates from the 1130s, which fits in better with related work undertaken throughout the realm during this period.

APPENDIX

It has been brought to my attention that Quarr stone from the Isle of Wight is found in a few places in the lower part of the basement of the keep (it does not seem to occur above this). Quarr seems to have ceased to be used outside its local area after *c.* 1120, a theory supported at Norwich Cathedral where it appears to have been used only until Bishop Herbert de Losinga's death in 1119.[108] But, unlike its use at the cathedral, the Quarr stone in the keep can only be found used as top stones for a few interior post-holes of uncertain date and in some areas where the walling seems to have been patched. It would be rash to jump to specific conclusions about these few stones, but the most likely scenario seems to be that these were reused from an earlier building or were left over from work at the cathedral. Since the Quarr quarries were under royal control, it is possible such stone may have been used on royal constructions for a while after 1120.

ACKNOWLEDGEMENTS

I would like to thank the following for their help and support: the dean and chapter of Norwich Cathedral, the curators and staff of Norwich Castle Museum, Dr Roland Harris, Tim Tatton-Brown, Dr John Crook and Dr Thomas Tolley.

NOTES

1. *The Anglo-Saxon Chronicle, A Collaborative Edition*, VII: MS. E, ed. S Irvine (Cambridge 2004), 91.

2. H. Ellis, *Original Letters Illustrative of English History*, 3rd series, rev. edn (London 1969), I, 9–10.

3. *Annales Waverleienses*, in *Historiae Anglicanae Scriptores Quinque*, 2 vols, ed. W. Fulman (Oxford 1684–91), II, 131; *The Ecclesiastical History of Orderic Vitalis*, ed. and trans. M. Chibnall, 6 vols (Oxford 1969–80), II, 310 and 316; *Symeonis Monachi Opera: Historia Regum*, ed. T. Arnold, Rolls Series, 75 (London 1885), 206.

4. *Little Domesday, Norfolk*, ed. A. Williams (London 2000), vol. 1, f. 118.

5. *Anglo-Saxon Chronicle* (as in n. 1), 99; Symeon of Durham (as in n. 3), 215; *Annales Waverleienses* (as in n. 3), 136.

6. *Liber Eliensis*, I, ed. E. O. Blake, Camden, 3rd series, 92 (London 1962), 206.

7. *First Register of Norwich Cathedral Priory*, ed. P. Millican and trans. H. Saunders, Norfolk Record Society, 11 (1939).

8. W. Dugdale, *Monasticon Anglicanum*, 3 vols (London 1655–73; 2nd edn of vol. I, 1682), I, 407.

9. *Liber Eliensis* (as in n. 6).

10. M. Paris, *Historia Anglorum*, 3 vols, ed. F. Madden (London 1866–69), I, 253; Henry of Huntingdon, *Historia Anglorum: The History of the English People*, ed. and trans. D. Greenway (Oxford 1996), 706–07.

11. *Regesta Regum Anglo-Normannorum 1066–1154*, 3, ed. H. A. Cronne and R. H. C. Davis (Oxford 1968), 279 no. 757.

12. *Regesta Regum* (as in n. 11), 98; Paris, *Historia* (as in n. 10), 307.

13. *The Great Rolls of the Exchequer, commonly called the Pipe Rolls, and other Documents Prior to the Year A.D. 1200*, 38 vols, Pipe Roll Society (London 1884–1925).

14. *The Charters of Norwich Cathedral Priory*, Pipe Roll Society, 40 part 1, ed. B. Dodwell (London 1974).

15. *The Great Roll of the Pipe for the Twenty-second Year of the Reign of King Henry the Second, A.D. 1175–1176*, Pipe Roll Society, 25 (London 1904), 60.

16. Paris, *Historia Anglorum* (as in n. 10), 19.

17. Ibid., 249.

18. H. Knighton, *Chronica*, in: *Historiae Anglicanae Scriptores X*, ed. R. Twysden (London 1652), 2373.

19. P. Vergil, *Anglica Historia* (Basel 1555), ed. and trans. D. F. Sutton, hypertext critical edn at http://www.philological.bham.ac.uk/polverg/ [updated 25 May 2010].

20. A. Neville, *Norvicus* (London 1575), 108–09.

21. R. Holinshed, *The Chronicles of England* (London 1585).

22. W. Camden, *Britannia*, 2 vols, 4th edn (London 1772), I, part 3, 378.

23. R. Woods, *Norfolke Furies and their Foyle* (London 1623).

24. R. Baker, *A Chronicle of the Kings of England* (London 1674).

25. W. Dugdale, *The Baronage of England*, 2 vols (London 1675–76), I, 132; Dugdale, *Monasticon* (as in n. 8), I, 407.

26. W. Spelman, 'Icenia: sive Norfolciae', *The English Works of Sir Henry Spelman* (London 1723), 133–62.

27. *The History of the City of Norwich*, printed by B. Lyon for R. Allen and N. Lemon (1718).

28. T. Gurdon, *An Essay on the Antiquity of the Castel of Norwich* (Norwich 1728), 36.

29. J. Kirkpatrick, *Notes Concerning Norwich Castle*, ed. W. Herring (London 1847), 11.

30. F. Blomefield, *An Essay Towards a Topographical History of the County of Norfolk: The History of the City and County of Norwich*, 2 (Norwich 1745), 3 and 6.

31. W. Wilkins, 'An Essay towards a History of the Venta Icenorum of the Romans, and of Norwich Castle, with remarks on the architecture of the Anglo-Saxons and Normans', *Archaeologia*, 12 (1796), 145, 162; E. King, 'Observations on Antient Castles', *Archaeologia*, 4 (1777), 396–97; E. King, 'Sequel to the Observations on Ancient Castles', *Archaeologia*, 6 (1782), 256.

32. King, 'Observations' (as in n. 31), 396.

33. S. Woodward, *The History and Antiquities of Norwich Castle*, ed. B. Woodward (London and Norwich 1847), 3; H. Harrod, *Gleanings among the Castles and Convents of Norfolk* (Norwich 1857), 145 and 150.

34. D. Renn, 'The Anglo-Norman Keep, 1066–1138', *JBAA*, 3rd series, 23 (1960), 17.

35. B. Green, *Norwich Castle, A Fortress for Nine Centuries* (Norwich 1969); B. Green, 'Norwich Castle', *Archaeol. J.*, 137 (1980), 358-59; P. Faulkner, 'Report on Norwich Castle Keep', Department of the Environment (September 1971), 1.

36. A. Whittingham, 'Norwich Castle', *Archaeol. J.*, 106 (1951), 77; unpublished notes of Arthur Bensley Whittingham, Norwich NRO, MC186/211, 649X3; A. Whittingham, 'Note on Norwich Castle' in 'Report of the Summer meeting at Norwich, 1979', *Archaeol. J.*, 137 (1980), 359–60.

37. Fernie, *AHNC*, 147.

38. T. A. Heslop, *Norwich Castle Keep: Romanesque Architecture and Social Context* (Norwich 1994), 4, 7–8.

39. E. Shepherd, 'Norwich Castle', *Current Archaeology*, 15.2 (October 2000), 55–56.

40. E. Shepherd-Popescu, *Norwich Castle: Excavations and Historical Survey, 1987–98; Part I: Anglo-Saxon to c. 1345*, EAA, 132 (Dereham 2009), 4 and 377.

41. B. Ayers, 'How Norwich Began', *Current Archaeology*, 15.2 (October 2000), 51; R. Baxter, 'Beakhead Ornament and the Corpus of Romanesque Sculpture', *Historic Churches. The Conservation and Repair of Ecclesiastical Buildings*, 11th annual edn, J. Taylor (Tisbury 2004), 8–11, at 9–10; J. Goodall, *The English Castle 1066–1650* (London 2011), 29.

42. D. Marner, 'The Mason's Marks of Norwich Castle Keep', *The Seigneurial Residence in western Europe AD c.800–1600*, ed. G. Meirion-Jones, E. Impey and M. Jones (Oxford 2002), 219–20.

43. P. Drury, 'Norwich Castle Keep, A Preliminary Report on the Evolution of the Fabric and the Internal Planning of the Building', unpublished, a copy at Norwich Castle Museum (1984); P. Drury, 'Norwich Castle Keep', *The Seigneurial Residence in Western Europe AD c.800–1600*, ed. G. Meirion-Jones, E. Impey and M. Jones (Oxford 2002), 211.

44. *English Episcopal Acta*, 6, *Norwich 1070–1214*, ed. C. Harper-Bill (Oxford 1990), xxxi.

45. William of Malmesbury, *Gesta Regum Anglorum: The History of the English Kings*, ed. and trans. R. A. B. Mynors et al., 2 vols (Oxford 1998), I, 739.

46. F. Woodman, *The Architectural History of Canterbury Cathedral* (London, Boston and Henley 1981), 45.

47. There is some uncertainty about whether the carved date should be read as 1124 or 1114.

48. Whittingham, unpublished notes (as in n. 36); Whittingham, 'Note on Norwich Castle' (as in n. 36), 359–60; Marner, 'Masons' Marks' (as in n. 42), 219.

49. Wilkins, 'Venta Icenorum' (as in n. 31), 152, 154; J. Kirkpatrick, *Notes Concerning Norwich Castle*, ed. W. Herring (London 1847), 4–5; D. Renn, *Norman Castles in Britain*, 2nd edn (London 1973), 259.

50. Wilkins, 'Venta Icenorum' (as in n. 31), 151; Woodward, *Norwich Castle* (as in n. 33), 12; Goodall, *English Castle* (in n. 41), 79.

51. J. Salmon, 'Beakhead Ornament in Norman Architecture', *The Yorkshire Archaeological Journal*, 36 (1944–47), 349; F. Henry and G. Zarnecki, 'Romanesque Arches Decorated with Human and Animal Heads', *JBAA*, 20–21 (1958), 19 n. 5.

52. Heslop, *Norwich Castle Keep* (as in n. 38), 16.

53. Salmon 'Beakhead Ornament' (as in n. 51), 349–56; Henry and Zarnecki, 'Romanesque Arches with Heads' (as in n. 51), 1–34; J. King, 'Sources, Iconography and Context of the Old Sarum Master's Sculpture', in *Medieval Art and Architecture at Salisbury Cathedral*, ed. L. Keen and T. Cocke, *BAA Trans.*, XVII (1996), 79–84.

54. A. Bayliss, C. Ramsay, D. Hamilton and J. van der Plicht, *Church of St Andrew, Wissett, Suffolk: Radio-carbon Wiggle-matching of the Second Floor of the Bell Tower*, English Heritage Research Dept. Report, 32 (Portsmouth 2006), 3–4.

55. Examples of related motifs can be found in Melle on the church of Saint-Hilaire, on the church of Saint-Jouin-de-Marnes, in Matha-Marestay on the church of Saint-Pierre, and in Parthenay on the church of Sainte-Croix, as well as at other places.

56. The Winchester example is found on a stone fragment, but, though the date for this stone must be 12th century, its original location is uncertain. The decoration compares favourably with that found still in St Peter's Church at Petersfield (Hants.) and St Mary's Church at Portchester (Hants.) which date from the second quarter of the 12th century, but the decoration there appears on only one side of a roll.

57. Kedleston, like Tutbury, has full beakhead on the jambs and overlapping the capitals. Kedleston is just a few miles from Tutbury and the medieval overlords for both were the de Ferrers.

58. J. Alexander and J. King, 'The Architecture and Romanesque Sculpture of Tutbury Priory', *Staffordshire Histories*, ed. P. Morgan and A. Phillips (Keele 1999), 41–46.

59. Ibid.; R. Stalley, 'A Twelfth-Century Patron of Architecture', *JBAA*, 3rd series, 34 (1971), 62–83.

60. According to the Peterborough Chronicle, a fire in 1116 destroyed the monastery, leaving only the chapter-house, dormitory and reredorter. In 1118, Abbot Martin began work on the new church and the monks moved into it in 1140. *The Peterborough Chronicle of Hugh Candidus*, trans. C. Mellows and W. Mellows, ed. W. Mellows (Peterborough 1966), 52, 53, and 59.

61. The vault heads at Cashel (Ireland) are related and probably derive from those in south-west England, though they are not of the devouring type.

62. Fernie, *AHNC*, 152, observes that churches in south-east Norfolk 'depending closely' on the cloister at Norwich date to the 1120s and 1130s.

63. R. A. Brown, *Castle Rising* (London 1978), 13.

64. B. Morley and D. Gurney, *Castle Rising Castle, Norfolk*, EAA, 81 (Dereham 1997), 14–18, 133.

65. W. Andrew, 'The Mints of Rye and Castle Rising in the Reign of Stephen', *British Numismatic Journal*, 20 (1932), 117–22; M. Blackburn, 'Coinage and Currency', *The Anarchy of King Stephen's Reign*, ed. E. King (Oxford 1994), 145–205.

66. Morley and Gurney, *Castle Rising* (as in n. 64).

67. *Chronicle of Robert of Torigni*, ed. R Howlett (London 1889), 106–07; *Rogeri de Wendover, Flores Historiarum*, II, ed. H. Coxe (London 1841), 203; *Annales Monastici*, II, ed. H. Luard (London 1865), 51; *Chronica Walteri Hemingford*, in *Rerum Anglicanum Scriptorum Verterum*, I (Oxford 1687), 482; J. Fowler, *Medieval Sherborne* (Dorchester 1951); A. Gomme, M. Jenner and B. Little, *Bristol, an Architectural History* (London 1979); Renn, 'Anglo-Norman Keep' (as in n. 34), 17–18; D. Renn, *Norman Castles in Britain*, 2nd edn (London 1973); M. Majendie, *Hedingham Castle* (Halstead 2005); S. Rigold, *Portchester Castle*, 3rd edn (London 1965); J. Coad, *Castle Acre Castle* (London 1984); M. de Bouard, *Le Chateau de Caen* (Caen 1979); R. A. Brown, *Rochester Castle* (London 1969); Goodall, *English Castle* (as in n. 41), 98–106.

68. W. Farrer, 'An Outline Itinerary of King Henry the First', *English Historical Review*, 34.135 (Oxford, 1919), 303–82.

69. Heslop, *Norwich Castle Keep* (as in n. 38), 8.

70. Farrer, 'Itinerary' (as in n. 68), 514.

71. Ibid.

72. This would not have been the first time this happened. It is recorded, for example, that King Henry did 'not wear his crown at Christmas' in December 1110. Farrer, 'Itinerary' (as in n. 68), 362.

73. *Reading Abbey Cartularies*, I, ed. B. Kemp (London 1986), 13; J. Green, *Henry I* (Cambridge 2009), 174.

74. *Chronicle of Robert of Torigni* (as in n. 67), 106–07, 126.

75. *Annales Waverleienses* (as in n. 3), 151.

76. *English Episcopal Acta*, 6 (as in n. 44), xxxi; Farrer, 'Itinerary' (as in n. 68), no. 430.

77. E. Fernie, 'Norwich Cathedral', *Archaeol. J.*, 137 (London 1980), 312.

78. Fernie, *AHNC*, 29.

79. Blomefield, *History of the County of Norfolk* (as in n. 30), 16. It is unclear what the source for Blomefield's statement is.

80. *The Great Roll of the Pipe for the Thirty-first Year of the Reign of King Henry I, Michaelmas 1130*, ed. and trans. J. Green, Pipe Roll Society, new series, 57 (London 2012).

81. Examples stating this as fact include Dugdale, *Baronage* (as in n. 25), 132; and *The Dictionary of National Biography*, ed. L. Stephen and S. Lee, 22 vols (London 1908–09), II, 484.

82. *Regesta Regum Anglo-Normannorum 1066–1154: Regesta Henrici Primi*, ed. C. Johnson and H. A. Cronne (Oxford 1956), no. 1391.

83. *The Great Roll* (as in n. 80).

84. R. H. C. Davis, *King Stephen*, 3rd edn (New York 1990), 138–39; *Regesta Regum*, 3 (as in n. 11), xxv fn. 3; *The Annals of Roger of Hoveden*, trans. H. T. Riley (London 1853), 243.

85. *Henry of Huntingdon* (as in n. 10).

86. Although no date is actually given, Hugh Bigod changed his allegiance to the Empress Matilda in 1141 and no longer acted for King Stephen following this. The only bishop of Sarum possible would be Roger, who died late in 1139, after whom there was no bishop of Sarum until 1142. 'Carrow Nunnery', in *Mon.*, IV, 70;

Regesta Regum, 3 (as in n. 11), 226–27 no. 615; W. Rye, *Carrow Abbey; otherwise Carrow Priory* (Norwich 1889), 1–2.

87. *Regesta Regum*, 2 (as in n. 82), no. 690.

88. Ibid., no. 399.

89. Ibid., no. 974; *English Episcopal Acta*, 6 (as in n. 44), no. 402.

90. *Regesta Regum*, 2 (as in n. 82), no. 241.

91. BL Cotton MS. Claudius D.XIII, *Registrum Cartarum Prioratus de Binham*, f. 199v. The main text of the Register was written in the 14th century, but the relevant text (later transcribed word-for-word by Dugdale in *Monasticon Anglicanum*) was copied on blank pages at the end of the manuscript in a later medieval hand between other copies of charters written by a variety of scribes; J. Margerum, 'An Edition of the Cartulary of Binham Priory with a Critical Introduction' (unpublished Ph.D. thesis, University of East Anglia, Norwich, 2000).

92. *Regesta Regum*, 2 (as in n. 82), no. 404.

93. Ibid., no. 272.

94. Ibid., no. 402; N. Vincent, 'New Charters of King Stephen, with Some Reflections upon the Royal Forests during the Anarchy', *English Historical Review*, 114 (1999), 899–928, at 901–02; *English Episcopal Acta*, 6 (as in n. 44), no. 154 and n.

95. *Regesta Regum*, 2 (as in n. 82), no. 757 and 757 fn; The transfer of castle guard from Norwich to Bury St Edmunds was not permanent and seems not to have been recognised by Henry II.

96. R. Mack, 'Stephen and the Anarchy 1135–1154', *British Numismatic Journal*, 35 (1967), 38–112.

97. *St Benet of Holme 1020–1210: The Eleventh Century Sections of Cott. M. Galba E.ii., The Register of the Abbey of St Benet of Holme*, transcribed J. West, Norfolk Record Society, 2 and 3 (1932), 1, no. 17 and 2, 188.

98. *Regesta Regum*, 2 (as in n. 82), xxvii.

99. J. Phillips, *The Second Crusade* (New Haven 2007), 201. William III earl of Warenne died during the Second Crusade in 1147.

100. J. Watson, *History of the Ancient Earls of Warren and Surry and their Descendants to the Present Time* (Warrington 1776), 73, 76; *The Chartulary of the Priory of St Pancras of Lewes*, part 2, ed. L. Salzman, Sussex Record Society, 4, (Lewes 1934), 25; 'Warenne, Reginald [Rainald] de', *Oxford Dictionary of National Biography*, 4, ed. H. Matthew and B. Harrison (Oxford 2004), 403.

101. Davis, *King Stephen* (as in n. 84), 103 and 139; Heslop, *Norwich Castle Keep* (as in n. 38), 9.

102. *The Chartulary of St Pancras of Lewes* (as in n. 100), 25; Watson, *Ancient Earls* (as in n. 100), 98; 'The Honour of Warenne', *Early Yorkshire Charters*, 8, ed. C. Clay, Yorkshire Archaeological Society Record Series (1949), 26 and 97 n. 49.

103. L. Salzman, 'Sussex Domesday Tenants. IV. The Family of Chesney or Cheyney', *Sussex Archaeological Collections*, 65 (1924), 20–53; J. H. Round, 'The Early Sheriffs of Norfolk', *English Historical Review*, 35.140 (1920), 481–96.

104. *Chronicle of Robert of Torigni* (as in n. 67), 193, 196 and 206.

105. Huntingdon, *Historia* (as in n. 10), 710–11.

106. Ibid., 720–21.

107. The list includes specific reference to fourteen dignitaries by name and says there were also '*aliorum multorum*'; *St Benet of Holme* (as in n. 97), 8–9.

108. R. Gilchrist, 'Norwich Cathedral: A biography of the North Transept', *JBAA*, 151 (1998), 122–25.

Steps to Lordship

PHILIP DIXON

Staircases have existed in major buildings for thousands of years, and their location and the linkage they provide has for generations been an element in the descriptions of these buildings. General studies of the development of staircases, however, are rare, and only recently has it been observed how they have been designed to add emphasis and grandeur to the process of entering a room. This paper attempts to set up a classification of staircases based on the various designs which developed in the 11th and 12th centuries in the case of major secular buildings. A few of these are simple vertical corridors, reaching the doors of superimposed floors. A more striking series of examples shows risers designed to emphasize the moment of entering the upper room, with the stair rising through the wall, or even rising within the upper chamber itself. In a rare final example, the entrance to a significant floor has been set above the floor, to give emphasis to the people appearing at the head of a short flight of steps, head and shoulders above the heads of those waiting their arrival in the room below.

INTRODUCTION

FOR over five millennia it has been the practice to change levels within sites by steps (more commonly than ramps), and remains of staircases are found, for example, in the Cretan palaces, or before them in the mud brick palaces of Mari. It is such a natural feature of sites with upper storeys, or steeply sloping terrain, that the variations in design of these building elements is seldom noticed, and even less frequently discussed.[1] This is true of the first secular stone buildings found in numbers during the Middle Ages in Britain, the Norman keeps or great towers. The present paper attempts to remedy some of this neglect by considering the various ways in which access was provided from the ground to the main entrance into the tower. It is not a catalogue: that must come later. Nor is it a complete explanation of the entrance phenomenon. That requires consideration of a much greater number of examples, and of the changing social and economic circumstances of their builders. It is, however, a first attempt to show that there were several clearly distinct ways of entering a keep, and there are categories which vary in date and social level. One element not considered in the following pages is defence. It is assumed throughout that this is fundamental to the design of the donjon, and that a little more interesting is the small variations in layout which show the different aspirations of the builders.

NORWICH CASTLE KEEP

CENTRAL to any discussion of the great tower during the Norman period, both in terms of its date between *c.* 1090 and *c.* 1120, and in terms of its importance, as a palace of Rufus and of Henry I, is the keep of Norwich Castle, one of the most significant of

BAA Trans., vol. XXXVIII (2015), 118–134
© British Archaeological Association 2015

the great towers of the early Middle Ages.[2] It is a matter of extreme regret that much of the interior has been removed by early modern rebuilding, and the exterior has been heavily restored, leaving remarkably little of the original intact. However, while there is some controversy about the reconstruction of the western parts of this donjon, the interpretation of the eastern side is fairly clear, thanks to late-18th-century drawings, and the main entrance to the keep is still reasonably well preserved.[3] So far so good, but for the purposes of the present paper, we are hamstrung by the restorations, since the staircase approach to this main entrance has been reconstructed at least twice, once perhaps in the Middle Ages, and again in the 19th century, and now owes little to its original design. In consequence, the exact form of the fore-building has been lost, in particular the level at which the landing at the head of the stairs was constructed (Fig. 1). The marks of vaulting in the roof of the modern cupboard below the stairs suggests that the original level of the top of the stairs was lower than now, and was raised, probably later in the Middle Ages. Some clues are given by Wilkins' elevation drawing of 1797. The drawings of this area show that the topmost landing before 1830 was lit by three large round-headed openings, which have been in part reproduced in the Victorian rebuilding. This upper landing was, before the restoration, reached from the ground by a straight flight of some thirty-two risers, supported on a round stone arch. It incorporated a pair of narrow landings where the steps passed through an intermediate defensible arch across the stair. At the head of these risers the elevation drawing shows a gap one bay broad, spanned by a drawbridge, shutting off the head of

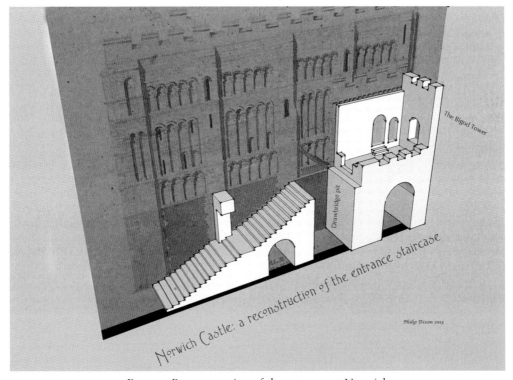

FIG. 1.   Reconstruction of the entrance at Norwich

the fore-building, by now called the Bigod Tower. This was itself open at ground-floor level, and its floor was supported on a round arch, the crown of which was higher than the drawbridge. The height of the top of this arch accordingly shows that the interior of the Bigod Tower above it (which is not visible in the drawing) was set a little higher than the drawbridge, at the level of the external string-course, or a little below. When one considers the present rather squat proportions of the main portal, it seems reasonable to suggest that the landing as we now have it, running level into the modern interior gallery which imitates the floor level of the original great hall, is a creation of the 19th century, and that originally the floor of the Bigod Tower was rather lower than this, perhaps by as much as 600 mm. If so, the portal was reached by one or more steps, to form what is termed below as the 'extended staircase entrance' (type 3). In brief, then, the visitor would arrive at the foot of a tall flight of broad steps, surmounted by an arch closed by a timber door, probably of two leaves. Through this the stair continued up to a timber drawbridge, which was raised against the face of the Bigod Tower. Beyond the bridge there must have been one or two more steps to allow clearance above the vault beneath. The visitor would now stand in a rectangular space, lit by four large windows, almost certainly unglazed. On his left was the main portal, lavishly decorated with carvings, and presumably painted, at the head of a short flight of steps, perhaps two or three.

How, then, would this approach to Norwich great tower fit into the context of contemporary buildings? To answer this question, I propose in the present paper to discuss the layout of a series of stairs in buildings of the 11th and 12th centuries, in order to identify different and sometimes apparently illogical expedients to achieve the simple purpose of entering the donjon. For the moment, to make the issues clearer, I have divided the entrance arrangements into four broad categories, with two variants of type 1:

1(a) The simple entrance (a) with the door at the head of a flight of external stairs
1(b) The simple entrance (b) with the door at the head of the stairs inside a fore-building
2   The internal fore-building with ground-floor doorway
3   The extended staircase entrance
4   The descent into the tower

The majority of the buildings under consideration were entered at the first-, or, in a few cases, second-floor level. This, of course, involves access from an external staircase or from another structure via a bridge, and various examples of this can be found in both England and France. A number of very early towers were probably entered directly from a timber or stone staircase. Examples can be seen at Mayenne (c. 900), or Beaugency (c. 1013–39), where the entrances led to upper storeys, without evidence for fore-buildings or protected stairs. It therefore appears that these were examples of type 1a, though it is not now possible to be certain.[4]

THE SIMPLE ENTRANCE

To illustrate these variations, one might consider the entrances of among the earliest known great towers, for instance the early-11th-century example at Loches (c. 1013–35),[5] which shows simple entrances of both type 1(a) and type 1(b) in contemporary use in the same building. Here access to the upper storey is gained by a stair which runs along the inner sides of a massive fore-building. This seems to be of the same date as the main structure, with identical pilasters, and regular courses of masonry linking both elements; a doorway, probably originally at the head of a few steps, gives access to the interior of the fore-building, within which the stairs run around the side walls, open in the centre, and finish outside the main door, with only a threshold to step over to change the levels. This is altogether the most logical manner to form a staircase entry to an upper room, with a protected entry and a reasonably impressive stair. A second small door in the narrow end of the keep seems intended for private access to the hall and the services. This was reached by a tall wooden stair, now gone but probably divided into two or more flights. Sockets in the walls show that the landing at the head of the stair was at the level of the doorway; this too, then, is an example of a simple entrance, but of the second class. Though this style (simple entrance types 1a and 1b) can be found elsewhere, it is remarkable in our series of early towers how rare these straightforward entrances actually are. Let us for the moment suggest that at Loches the main portal was designed to impress, with its divided stair and lofty fore-building, while the rear entrance simply allowed access to a platform at the level of the door.

After Loches, a good example of the simple entrance is to be found in the tower attached to the rectangular hall at Langeais of the period *c*. 1000.[6] Here a simple stair, probably at first a single straight flight, rose from the ground to the level of the entrance in the east wall, blocked in phase II. This would make the structure an example of 'simple entrance type 1a'.[7] Another example, a century later, and on a much grander scale, can be seen at the great tower at Rochester, of *c*. 1120–30. Access to the upper door is provided by a long stair, which rises from the ground, passes through a turret across the stair, and at almost the top of its course crosses a drawbridge and enters a rectangular fore-building, of the same date as the tower. This then so far resembles the slightly earlier work at the Bigod Tower at Norwich. Within the Rochester fore-building, however, the head of the stair is cranked through 90 degrees to arrive at the level threshold of the entrance doorway into the hall of the keep. Despite the complexity of the design of the fore-building, with various gates on the stair and further rooms, including a chapel arranged on the upper storeys above the stair itself, this is an example of a simple entrance, where the staircase provides immediate access to the entrance level of the tower.

An apparently similar example can be seen at the enormous tower of Colchester, of *c*. 1070 to 1100 and after.[8] Here complications have been introduced to the design of the entrance by the location of the 11th-century building on top of the Roman temple podium. This meant that the 'ground floor' entrance was already some 3 to 4 m above the contemporary ground level. This led to the creation of a raised ground-floor entrance, at first reached by an external stair (Fig. 2). The foundations of this stair which can now be seen post-date the original build, and the stair may at first have been a simple open wooden structure, similar to the one excavated by de Bouard at Doué-la-Fontaine, where it provided access to the first-floor doorway of the second phase of the hall, as a type 1a entrance.[9] Later alterations have made reconstruction of the primary entrance at Colchester difficult, but it seems that from the first this raised doorway into the keep led into an antechamber with a room on its east; the route ahead into the ground-floor storage chambers was closed by a door, while to the west a broad portal raised above one or two shallow steps gave access to a short passage which ran to the foot of a newel staircase of great size (among the three largest Norman staircases in England).[10] This size allows groups of two or even three abreast to mount the stair, and gives the impression that the entrance, brought into the building at rather too low a

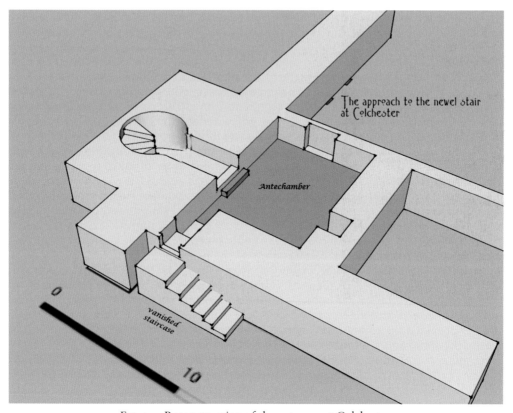

FIG. 2.   Reconstruction of the entrance at Colchester

level for the normal arrangements, is here being extended upwards by a stair broad enough to form simply an extension of the passage (Fig. 3). One might even say that the antechamber within the keep answers the same need as the fore-buildings of Loches and Rochester, with an external set of steps, closed by a portal, and beyond it a series of steps (here in a spiral) to the upper level, but in this case the 'fore-building' is set within the keep. The exposition is convoluted, but serves to emphasize the uniqueness of the entrance at Colchester. All this is perhaps no more than an expedient made necessary by the presence of the massive Roman undercroft.

This, the 'simple entrance', can be seen at a small number of 12th-century towers, for example at Orford of 1165–73.[11] Here the first-floor door is at present reached by a rebuilt flight of open steps, but the marks on the wall from the original stair seem to show that this was no more than a simple flight of steps, rising to a platform with a parapet at the level of the first floor inside. There may have been a small timber pentice at the head of the stairs.

At Castle Hedingham (c. 1140) the arrangement was at first similar.[12] Here the first-floor door of the tower is now reached by a shallow flight of steps in a stone fore-building similar to that described below at Scarborough. This fore-building, however, is clearly a secondary addition to the tower, and the location of an original loop (now blocked by the addition of the fore-building) immediately below the first-floor door

FIG. 3.   The inner side of the Colchester entrance, showing the wide passage and great and shallow staircase

shows that the original arrangement must have been an open stair, presumably of timber, similar to the one excavated at Doué-la-Fontaine. The outer entrance to the tower at Hedingham was accordingly one of the simple category, but as we shall see below there are considerable complexities in the internal entrance arrangements of its upper floor.

Simple entrances are by no means confined to early towers. Many keeps, such as that at Brough in Westmorland, *c.* 1180–1200, appear to have been entered by an external stair reaching up to the level of the first-floor doorway, as a type 1(a) entrance. Bowes Castle on Stainmore, a two-storeyed hall building on a massive scale, *c.* 1170–80, seems to have had a regular staircase in a small fore-building. Though this has now been reduced to its footings the scar on the face of the keep indicates that the stair reached up as far as, but no further than, the threshold block of the entrance door, thus making it a type 1(b) entrance. The donjon at Conisbrough, probably *c.* 1180–90, shows a similarly simple entrance. Here the stair is an external building ending in a platform at the level of the first floor. Additional protection is afforded by a wooden bridge linking the summit platform to the tower entrance. A very similar arrangement must have been made to reach the first-floor door at Pembroke, of *c.* 1190–1200, this time by a level bridge from the chemise wall beside the great tower.

THE INTERNAL FORE-BUILDING

Two castles display a variant form of this simple entrance: the towers at Carlisle and Bamburgh. Neither is dated, though it is likely that they belong to the first third of the 12th century, and the similarity between them, both in size and layout, suggests that they were structures from the same workshop, either that of David I of Scotland, or more probably of Henry I, who resumed control of the area in 1120.[13] More recent work suggests a date for Bamburgh in the 1110s and for Carlisle after 1121.[14] In each case the entrance is quite remarkably on the ground floor, leading to a passageway into the basement storage, with the broad straight staircase to the upper storeys immediately inside the door (Fig. 4). Both towers have been much altered in the Middle Ages and later, and the detailed interpretation of their first phases presents several issues. At Carlisle the portal seems to be of the 15th century, and the door is reached by a short flight of four steps; once past the internal stair, the entry continues with a descent of five steps into the storehouses of the interior. At Bamburgh, in contrast, the ground-floor entrance doorway is clearly original, and is reached by a short flight of three risers. Despite the alterations here and at Carlisle, it seems very likely that this method of access is part of the original and very unusual design, which takes the notion of a fore-building and incorporates it into the internal arrangements of the tower, setting its staircase within a thick wall. In this it resembles in part the design of the keep at Colchester, described above, and also that at Richmond, Yorkshire, of c. 1170, where the access from the first-floor level to the upper floors is provided by a straight staircase in the thickness of the wall. In each case the thick wall is set in the interior and protected side of the tower, facing into the bailey. Richmond, however, differs from the

FIG. 4.   Carlisle: the internal stair, showing some original masonry

earlier examples in being a rebuilding of an 11th-century gatehouse, which provides its basement storey, and so the design is a contrivance to permit a reasonably stately entrance to the important upper hall on the second floor. The first-floor entrance to the keep gives direct and level access to a chamber with viewing or display galleries facing into the town. All this is far removed from the massive solidity of the internal fore-buildings at Carlisle and Bamburgh, which remain anomalies in tower design.

THE EXTENDED STAIRCASE ENTRANCE

THE next category of staircase is what may be termed 'the extended staircase entrance', where the outside staircase, in stone or in timber, has been arranged to finish several steps below the level of the room into which the entrance gives access. On the face of it, this is a quite odd arrangement, since it requires an additional complexity to the design of the inner entrance passage. In almost every case the doors of a castle open inwards, sitting in hefty stone rebates formed in the outer face of the wall.[15] This has two consequences: with an extended staircase it is necessary to provide a level platform inside the walls, into which the doors can swing, and that it is normally necessary to divide the door into two leaves, to minimize the size of this platform, which makes this crucial defence weaker. Beyond this point, the entrance passageway continues into the keep with a series of steps to bring the passage to the level of the room inside. This arrangement can be seen in the White Tower, London, of the 1070s and after, where at least eight steps flanked by a pair of recesses for porters continue the rise of the external stair to reach the level of the first floor room (Fig. 5).[16] This shows also a third consequence, that the internal stair requires the construction of a sloping vault, to allow sufficient headroom above the stair. All this introduces an unneeded complexity into the layout of the significant element, the means of defence of the entry to the great tower, and must therefore have been a strongly desired part of the designed layout of the tower.

These extended staircase features can be seen at a number of 12th-century towers, for example at Scarborough, *c.* 1159–68.[17] The first-floor door is approached by a substantial external stair of twelve risers, which passes inside a fore-building in the form of a tower, with a door, and a movable platform or drawbridge to defend the entry, above the so-called 'prison pit' in the fore-building. The wooden floor which this stair reaches is about 1.8 m below the floor of the keep, and to reach this upper level the builders have contrived another flight of eight shallow steps within the thickness of the wall, with no closure except perhaps the lifted floor of the fore-building. At the top of this second stair access may have been blocked by a door set in rebates at the very entrance to the room, but little evidence of this remains. All this internal contrivance is clearly capable of defence if needed, since the outer door of the fore-building was closed by two leaves and overlooked by a *meutrière*, but the width of the stair is considerable: the first flight of steps is more than 2.7 m wide, while the apparently open flight through the wall of the keep is no less than 2.2 m wide, and it seems more likely that some other purpose than fortification was intended for this split entry, that is to say, it was the provision of a *mise-en-scène* for processions into the royal tower (Fig. 6).

Some further clue to this interpretation is provided at Castle Hedingham (probably *c.* 1140). Here the simple external stair has already been mentioned, but, once inside a lower hall, the newel staircase from this point is deliberately brought to a height about 7 ft (2.1 m) below the level of the main floor. A further nine risers would have allowed level entry, but this was ignored. From here a door at this lower point gives access to a

FIG. 5. The White Tower, London, showing the extended staircase into the keep from the outside

straight stair in timber within the room, forcing the guest to climb slowly into the presence of the castle's lord, the first earl of Oxford, sitting facing the stair. The earl was recently ennobled, and by this staircase contrivance was made more significant to the eyes of the visitor (Fig. 7). Further evidence for careful arrangement of the circulation in this donjon is given by the access to the upper gallery: here the newel stair continues to the level of the walkway, which is entered through a decorated door, plain on the inside. The walkway continues around the keep, giving views down into the second floor, until it reaches another decorated door and a short flight of steps back down to the newel stair, here some five steps below the entrance to the gallery. The circulation was thus intended to run anti-clockwise around the keep, and the design of the great building was intended to serve as a place of ceremonial for the new earl.[18]

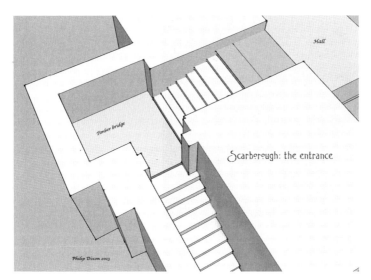

FIG. 6. Scarborough: sketch of the extended staircase into the keep

A few years earlier, at Castle Rising in Norfolk (*c.* 1138, and left unfinished *c.* 1170),[19] the approach is via a complex fore-building, highly decorated on its exterior with interlaced arcading and masks, which rises from a broad two-leaved door, up a broad staircase (Fig. 8). This is closed by two further two-leaved doors before arriving at a large square chamber at the stair head. This chamber has been considerably modified during the Middle Ages and after, but originally had four large, unglazed openings to the south and east. This was clearly intended to be an antechamber or waiting room, and was dominated by an elaborately carved door of four orders, covered in zigzag and broad rolls. This door sat at the head of a short flight of steps, probably four or five risers (now removed to insert a post-medieval fireplace) (Fig. 9). This brought the entrance up to the level of the hall beyond the door. The result of this design is that

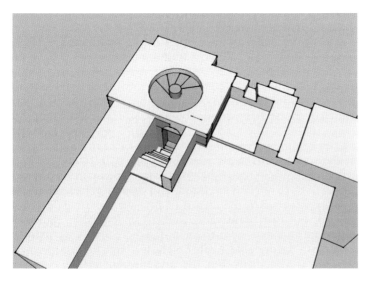

FIG. 7. Hedingham, Essex, showing the entrance into the main upper floor

FIG. 8. Castle Rising, Norfolk: view up the broad staircase in the fore-building

those arriving at the stair head had a bright (and probably cold) space in which to wait and admire the carved door, until it was opened to admit them up the steps into the hall, dominated by its pair of thrones under arched niches in the wall nearby. These were lighted by the largest window in the keep, high up on the southern wall. The management of the entrance to the keep was in order to provide a series of spaces in which the visitor was held in check until the final denouement of the opening of the doors, to allow an audience with the lord and his royal lady, now visible within the hall, but raised for the moment higher than the arriving guest, to emphasize the significance of their status.

Rising was the latest of a series of similar keeps built from the 1090s until the 1120s.[20] At Norwich, as discussed at the start of this paper, the 18th-century drawings show a straight stair rising to enter the fore-building at or below a large landing lit by a series of very large openings, which seem to have been unglazed, and open to the elements, in the same fashion as at Rising. In this regard, the layout of Norwich, perhaps c. 1120, was identical to that at the later but otherwise very similar Castle Rising, and was arranged to provide a waiting room and steps up into the hall, where niches were probably arranged in the now-vanished facing side wall.[21] Falaise, Henry I's donjon of the 1120s, perhaps had a similar arrangement, but the present concrete blockhouse

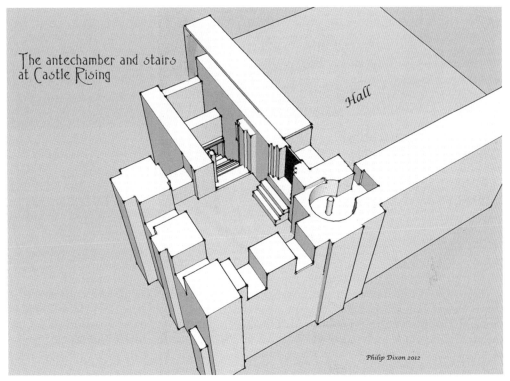

The antechamber and stairs at Castle Rising

Hall

Philip Dixon 2012

FIG. 9.   Castle Rising: sketch of the anteroom at the stair head

attached to its side has obliterated traces of the original arrangements. Photographs of the scars on the side of the keep, taken before this regrettable modern intervention, suggest a high vaulted stair turret ending a little below the entrance door.[22] Though certainty is not possible now, it is likely that all three of these palatial donjons were designed with a fore-building floor a little below that of the adjacent room. Thus these three closely linked great towers present us with instances of the opportunities for a procession, a check or pause outside the entrance in an antechamber, and a ceremonious entrance up a short flight of steps into the presence of the lord, already seated in the great hall.

A final and grand example of the 'extended staircase entrance' is provided by the great tower at Newcastle upon Tyne, *c.* 1168–79.[23] This was probably entered by a large portal at the foot of the fore-building, in a section of the structure now removed (Fig. 10). This door must have been reached by a staircase of about eight risers from the level ground. Once inside, a flight of about two-dozen steps led to the first closed arch across the staircase, and a further series of about two-dozen risers reached the level platform at the stair head, in the open air. At this point the stair was faced by a chamber, often called a porter's lodge but almost certainly a chapel, above the ground-floor level chapel at the foot of the fore-building. From this platform the stair turns inwards and rises a further nine steps to the main door of the keep, at the level of the second floor. Once inside, however, and clear of the swinging leaves of the door, the staircase continues a further three risers into the room (Fig. 11). The extended staircase,

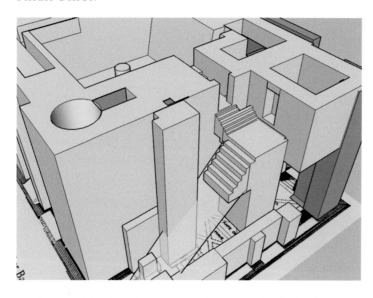

FIG. 10. Sketch of the arrangements at the head of the stairs at Newcastle

as discussed in the above examples, was clearly laid out to provide the experience of rising into the presence chamber even after the opening of the chamber door, emphasizing the status of the occupant, perhaps accentuated by a dais, a sitting niche, or simply by the guest arriving with his head at the level of the lord's knees.

DESCENT INTO THE CHAMBER

ONE final category can be illustrated here, and the comparison between the keep at Newcastle upon Tyne and that at Dover is instructive. Both were built within a short period by the same designer, Mauritius or Maurice, known as the Mason or *Ingeniator*.[24] They have some elements in common, most notably the placing of a chapel or large oratory on the staircase in the fore-building, presumably to allow prayers and thanks on completing or beginning a journey. Both rise up several flights of steps, through doors, or in the case of Dover doors and a drawbridge, to reach an open-air platform at the stair head, not at first-, but at second-floor level (Fig. 12). But here the similarities end. At Newcastle a further flight of steps runs upwards to the entrance door, which is elaborately carved like the earlier doorways of keeps with extended staircase entrances. At Dover, however, the door is remarkably plain, decorated with a simple roll, and stands at the level of the platform, like the most simple entrance of the first category. Furthermore, once through this doorway, the passageway continues through the wall to the head of a flight of steps which runs *downwards* into the level of the hall. This is a unique element in the design, and it underlines the purpose of the entrance arrangements of this great keep. Henry II ordered its construction immediately after it became obvious that the recently martyred (and soon to be sanctified) archbishop, Thomas Becket, was attracting numbers of foreign potentates, that these were travelling to Canterbury via Dover (rather than the earlier route via Southampton) and that the king had no suitable residence in which to greet them in Dover, only an old castle in poor condition, since Kent had few royal estates and no hunting forests, and until now had given the king no particular reason for spending money on its royal

Second Floor Plan

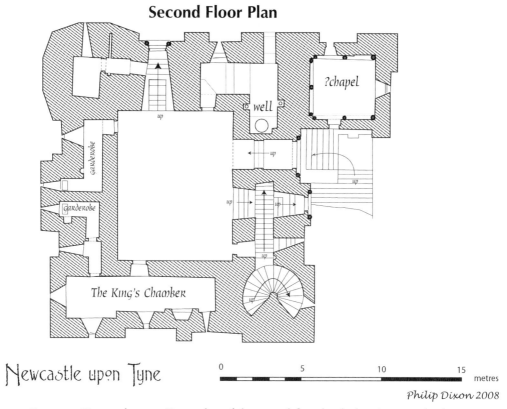

Newcastle upon Tyne

0   5   10   15
metres

Philip Dixon 2008

FIG. II.   Newcastle upon Tyne: plan of the second-floor level, showing complex layout of staircases

castle. The new keep at Dover was accordingly designed to provide this accommodation for the pilgrimages of kings and royal dukes, and among the surviving elements linked to this ceremony is a high balcony behind the dais, from which the arriving party could be observed by those waiting inside. The guest, once seen or perhaps greeted by the host from the balcony, could ascend the fore-building stair to reach a chapel built across the stairs, where prayers of thanks and greeting could be delivered, and then could climb again towards the upper platform outside the door of the keep at second-floor level. Here a stone bench was arranged outside the door, and most remarkably a flue from a ground-floor oven rose to heat this seat. This unique feature was presumably designed to be a stone seat for Henry II to stay warm in the open air, while awaiting his royal or ducal guest climbing up the stairs to meet him. The door at his side was small and completely plain, since it was necessary not to distract the guest from the grandeur of his host, sitting beside it. At this point host and guest turned into the door, walked through the entrance passage and appeared dramatically in front of the courtiers waiting inside, at the head of a short flight of steps down into the hall, where they could either progress to the dais in front of the balcony, or pass through to a throne room in the chamber beyond. Further ceremonies were clearly planned, since the dais at the end of the hall provided a timber staircase into a small withdrawing

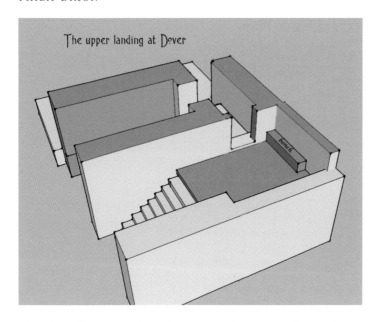

The upper landing at Dover

FIG. 12.   Dover: sketch of entrance at head of the stairs

chamber, from which a short spreading stair descended again to the chamber out-side the private chapel and royal pew. Here the host and guest, who had just passed into the withdrawing chamber, could be greeted by courtiers who themselves had risen from the dais table, and had passed through a door in the jamb of the balcony window into this large chamber at the foot of the stair. Host and guest were then allowed to proceed into the privacy of the royal pew.

SUMMARY

THIS brief account of a series of staircase entrances has shown a variety of expecta-tions by patrons and their masons. A summary of the results is shown in Figure 13, which tables the buildings concerned in terms of entrance type. Not all attributions are equally certain, as is shown in the table by a query against the class. The numbers involved are small, owing to rebuildings and demolitions in many of the great towers which have survived, and the conclusions must therefore be taken with caution. Simple staircases tend to be found in the early examples, but this is not really a function of the date since similar occurrences of the type are found to the end of the 12th century. The more complex entrance arrangements tend to occur a little later, but the very early example of Loches shows that this, too, is not the result of mere date. One significant difference does occur: the table indicates the status of the owner. All were built for men of great wealth, but there appears to be a genuine division between those who were baronial (earls, counts or lesser) and those who were royal. For the latter in particular, the elaboration of the extended staircase is appropriate for royal castles (the White Tower, Scarborough, Newcastle and probably Norwich), or for highly aspiring nobles (at Hedingham, the third de Vere, who was earl of Oxford, and at Castle Rising, the second husband of Queen Adeliza — Rising is a site at which further emphasis on the staircase is made by its extreme elaboration of decorative details). In these rare cases a ceremonial akin to crown wearing — coronet wearing — might be expected. Dover

	Approximate Decade	Class	Owner
Mayenne	*c.* 900		Baronial
Doué-la-Fontaine II	*c.* 940	1a	Baronial
Langeais	*c.* 1000	1b	Baronial
Loches	1010s	1b 1a	Baronial
Domfront	1090s	? 1a	Baronial
Castle Hedingham	1140s	1a	Baronial
Orford	1160s	1a	Royal
Conisbrough	1180s	1a	Baronial
Pembroke	*c.* 1200	1a	Baronial
Bridgnorth	1100s	? 1a	Baronial or Royal
Corfe	1100s	? 1b	Royal
Porchester	1120s	? 1a	Royal
Colchester	1070s	2 or 3	Royal
Carlisle	1110s	2	Royal
Bamburgh	1120s	2	Royal
White Tower	1074	3	Royal
Canterbury	1080s	3	Royal
Norwich	1095–1120	3 ?	Royal
Falaise	1120s	? 3	Royal
Rising	1138	3	Baronial
Scarborough	1150s	3	Royal
Newcastle	1168–78	3	Royal
Dover	1180s	4	Royal

FIG. 13. Table of classifications — the arrangement of entrance staircases

takes this one stage further, with a particular ceremony of royal greeting by the king dictating the layout of the masonry. The other donjons of type 1a or 1b display their grandeur more simply in terms of an entrance to a floor given status by being raised to first-floor level.

NOTES

1. The present paper extends the arguments, mostly concerning the later Middle Ages, in P. W. Dixon, 'Design in castle building: the controlling of access to the lord', *Chateau Gaillard*, 18 (1998), 47–57. The theme was taken up in P. Marshall, 'The ceremonial function of the donjon in the twelfth century', *Chateau Gaillard*, 20 (2002), 141–51.

2. The best account of Norwich is T. A. Heslop, *Norwich Castle Keep: Romanesque Architecture and Social Context* (Norwich 1994). For an alternative view of the first-floor layout, see P. W. Dixon and P. Marshall, 'Norwich Castle and its analogues', in *The Seigneurial Residence in Western Europe: AD c.800– 1600*, ed. G. Meirion-Jones, E. Impey and M. Jones, BAR International Series 1088 (Oxford 2002), 235–44.

3. For discussion of these sources, see Heslop, *Norwich Castle Keep* (as in n. 2), 15. Wilkins drawings were published in *Archaeologia*, 12 (1797); the original drawings are preserved in the Society of Antiquaries (Wilkins), and in the Norwich Castle Museum (Stone).

4. For Mayenne, see R. Early, 'Le premier édifice de pierre du Château de Mayenne', in N. Faucerre, *Tours seigneuriales de l'Ouest* (2004), 13–22; for Beaugency, see V. Mataouchek, 'La tour César', *Archéologie médiévale*, 30–31 (2000), 441.

5. J. Mesqui, 'La tour maitresse du donjon de Loches', *Bull. mon.*, 156 (1998), 65–125; C. Dormoy, 'L'expertise dendrochronologique du donjon de Loches (Indre-et-Loire): des données fondamentales pour sa datation', *Archéologie Médiévale*, 27 (1998), 73–89; Marshall, 'The ceremonial function' (as in n. 1), 143–45.

6. E. Impey and E. Lorans, 'Langeais, Indre-et-Loire: an archaeological and historical study of the early Donjon and its Environment,' *JBAA*, 151 (1998), 43–106.

7. A drawing of this is shown in Impey and Lorans, ibid., pl. VIA.

8. P. Drury, 'Aspects of the Origins and Development of Colchester Castle', *Archaeol. J.*, 139 (1982), 302–419; P. W. Dixon, 'The influence of the White Tower', in *The White Tower*, ed. E. Impey (New Haven and London 2008), 245–48.

9. M. de Bouard, 'De aula au donjon: les fouilles de la motte de la chapelle à Doué-la-Fontaine, xe–xie siècle', *Archéologie Médiévale*, 3–4 (1973-4), 5–110. The phasing of Doué has been challenged by Impey (see Impey and Lorans, 'Langeais, Indre-et-Loire' (as in n. 6)); this does not affect the interpretation of the stairs, but my own examination of the site rather coincides with de Bouard's views.

10. The others are Durham Cathedral, north transept stair, and Lincoln Cathedral, the processional palace stair in the west front.

11. Dixon, 'The influence of the White Tower' (as in n. 8), 268; T. A. Heslop, 'Orford Castle: Nostalgia and Sophisticated Living', *Architectural History*, 34 (1991), 36–58.

12. P. W. Dixon and P. Marshall, 'The Donjon of Hedingham Castle', *Fortress*, 18 (July 1993), 16–23.

13. See R. A. Brown, H. M. Colvin and A. J. Taylor, *History of the King's Works*, II (London 1963), 595, which would imply a date between 1136 and 1157. This is probably too late for the style of masonry of both towers.

14. Dixon, 'The influence of the White Tower' (as in n. 8), 265; M. R. McCarthy, H. R. T. Summerson and R. G. Annis, *Carlisle Castle: a Survey and Documentary History* (London 1990); C. J. Bates, *The Border Holds of Northumberland* (Newcastle 1891), 235–36.

15. A rare exception is at Rhuddlan, of 1277–83, where the great gates rather unexpectedly opened outwards.

16. E. Impey, *The White Tower* (New Haven and London 2008), 69ff.

17. J. A. A. Goodall, *Scarborough Castle* (London 2000).

18. Dixon and Marshall, 'Hedingham Castle' (as in n. 12).

19. R. A. Brown, *Castle Rising, Norfolk* (London 1978).

20. Dixon, 'The influence of the White Tower' (as in n. 8), 255ff.

21. Dixon and Marshall, 'Norwich Castle and its analogues' (as in n. 2).

22. R. Doranlo, 'Le Château de Falaise', *Congrès Archéologique* (1953), 184–200; J. Mesqui, *Châteaux et enceintes de la France médiévale: de la défence à la résidence*, 2 vols (Paris 1991–93), I, 123.

23. The most recent account is S. Brindle, 'Henry II, Anglo-Scots Relations, and the Building of the Castle Keep, Newcastle upon Tyne', in *Newcastle and Northumberland: Roman and Medieval Architecture and Art*, ed. J. Ashbee and J. Luxford, *BAA Trans.*, XXXVI (Leeds 2013), 90–115, esp. 103; earlier accounts are summarized in W. H. Knowles, 'The Castle, Newcastle upon Tyne', *Archaeologia Aeliana*, 4th series 2 (1926), 1–51.

24. Some of the following account is to be presented in a forthcoming multi-authored volume on Dover Castle, edited by S. Brindle and E. Impey.

The Romanesque Sculpture of Norwich and Norfolk: The City and its Hinterland — Some Observations

JILL A. FRANKLIN

This paper looks at the relationship between the Romanesque architectural sculpture in Norwich and that of the surrounding county by exploring four themes: the carved motifs on the cathedral church and castle keep in the city, the Romanesque fragments preserved at the cathedral, the decorated portals of south-east Norfolk, and the sculpture at Castle Acre Priory.

NORFOLK'S 12th-century architectural carving ought to constitute an ideal field of study, for several reasons. The county is ancient, its Domesday boundaries largely unchanged, other than by an encroachment into north-east Suffolk in 1974.[1] Although the seat of the Anglo-Norman see was transferred to Norwich c. 1095 and provided with a brand new cathedral church soon after, it was nevertheless in territory that had been an ecclesiastical entity for over four centuries, notwithstanding periods of devastation and documentary silence.[2]

Relatively little Romanesque sculpture escaped destruction or damage during Norfolk's late-medieval building boom, but 12th-century carving survives at almost a third of the county's 650 medieval churches. We can be fairly confident, moreover, given East Anglia's affluence in the late 11th and 12th centuries, that what remains is representative of the best that Anglo-Norman patrons could buy.[3] There is a wealth of published information — demographic, climatic, ecclesiastical and fiscal — relating to medieval Norfolk and its immediate surroundings, sufficient to make investigation into the development of its architectural sculpture a worthwhile activity.[4] Major patronage is particularly well documented during the period: Norwich's founding bishop, Herbert de Losinga (1094–1119), oversaw an extensive, county-wide building programme, while Domesday Norfolk's most prominent Norman tenants-in-chief — William de Warenne in the west of the county and Roger Bigod in the south-east — established a Cluniac priory apiece and much else besides.[5] Norfolk's other larger Romanesque abbey and priory churches — although ruinous and in some cases vestigial — are documented and retain original carved elements.[6]

As for the city of Norwich, although 12th-century sculpture is preserved at just three of its thirty-two medieval parish or lesser churches, the original design and decoration of its two major Romanesque monuments — the castle keep and the cathedral church — are intact or recoverable.[7] The sophistication of the historiated capitals thought to have come from the cathedral's 12th-century cloister testify, moreover, to a climate of high artistic aspiration in a city that then ranked second in the realm.[8] The dearth of

FIG. 1a.   Norwich Cathedral, north transept interior east wall: tympanum of stair door

FIG. 1b.   Marham, Holy Trinity: blocked north door tympanum

figure sculpture in the county as a whole is striking, however; there are just two figural reliefs of any size,[9] while of some forty-one Romanesque fonts, only a handful in the north-west are ornate and even fewer bear figure carving.[10] Tympana, so often a field for sculpture, are rare in the county. There are just three decorated examples *in situ* and the remains of a fourth.[11] The range of ornament they display could hardly be narrower; two bear an identical reticulated pattern, and the other two bear a simple emblem and again are similar (Fig. 1a and b).[12]

That said, a relatively varied and sizeable sample of good quality Romanesque carving in both the city and the county exists to enable us to trace features from one monument to another, to draw inferences, and to test hypotheses.[13] For example, that the cathedral and the castle keep shared a common workforce of stone masons,[14] or that in a county with over ninety Romanesque carved doorways, a regional workshop produced a small but distinctive group of them, concentrated in the south-east, largely in the adjacent Hundreds of Clavering and Loddon, in a triangle of territory defined by the rivers Yare and Waveney, held by the Bigods, one of Norfolk's influential Norman families.[15] Reaching conclusions about the character of Norfolk's sculpture, plotting the movement of motifs and testing the theory that design ideas migrate from major to lesser monuments are exercises that are, moreover, becoming easier with the growth of the Corpus of Romanesque Sculpture in Britain and Ireland, the nationwide digitized survey inaugurated in 1987 by Professor George Zarnecki and the British Academy.[16]

And yet, even with the emergence of a more comprehensive picture of the architectural carving in the county — and, equally importantly, in adjacent areas — the study of 12th-century stone sculpture in Norfolk is still bedevilled by intractable issues. The abiding problem of dating Romanesque architectural sculpture is undiminished, even when it is *in situ*, but especially where it is not, as with the capital and moulding fragments at Norwich Cathedral. And who, for example, can be thought of as the patron responsible for commissioning what appears to be a group of costly, carved doorways on small parish churches apparently clustered in the Yare valley? Surely the Bigods themselves are unlikely to have borne the expense of these simply because they were in their territory? Such are the questions considered below.

NORWICH CATHEDRAL AND CASTLE KEEP

NORWICH's two great Norman structures, the cathedral and the castle keep, were in building less than 500 m apart from each other in the first quarter of the 12th century, on a comparable scale, both partly using imported Caen limestone. Aspects of the external architectural sculpture of the upper levels of the keep — the panels of reticulated ashlar and the tiers of blank arcading — have been seen as reflecting the influence of the cathedral, assuming them to have occurred there earlier.[17] Yet the perceived affiliation between the two buildings is compromised, or complicated, by a marked difference in their basic sculptural vocabulary. For example, the dominant mouldings at the cathedral — chevron and billet — occur widely elsewhere in the British Isles on contemporary buildings, but are absent from the castle keep, as is the equally characteristic but more localized double-cone motif. By the same token, particular types of ornament selected for the keep do not appear at the cathedral, notably the small conical bosses found on the main portal of the castle keep and the geometric beakhead, or 'beaker' moulding, as T. A. Heslop has called it, also used on the portal and on the vault ribs of the forebuilding basement (Fig. 2a and b).[18] The keep, moreover, unlike the cathedral church, was adorned with historiated capitals.[19]

FIG. 2a.   Norwich Castle keep: detail of the entrance door to the hall at first-floor level

FIG. 2b.   Norwich Castle keep: detail of the vault rib beneath the entrance arch platform

This discrepancy between the decoration of a domesticated military building and a cathedral church is not explicable in terms of a 'secular versus ecclesiastical' divide, for the geometric motifs on both the castle keep and the cathedral are also found on the county's parish churches.[20] The beaker moulding used at the keep also occurs, for example, at Framingham Earl, Mundham, Gillingham, South Burlingham and Thwaite St Mary.[21] All five sites are geographically close, in a wedge of territory south and east of Norwich that was Bigod heartland.[22] Framingham Earl was in Bigod territory, and both the king and Bigod had jurisdiction in Mundham, while Gillingham, like Norwich Castle, was on royal demesne. Bigod seems to emerge as the possible link between the castle keep and the lesser churches, intimated by the incidence at both of the beaker motif. In neighbouring Suffolk, moreover, beaker moulding occurs at Kelsale, also held by Bigod, and again at Westhall (absent from the Domesday survey) alongside an arch order of large relief quatrefoils recalling those on the portal of Norwich keep, as well as at Little Glemham and, in a decorated version, at Wissett, both held by Count Alan.[23]

Throughout the 12th century, Norwich Castle was regulated by the sheriffs of Norfolk, who would have had some responsibility for supervising building operations and repairs at the keep.[24] Roger Bigod (d. 1107) was sheriff between 1081 and 1107, apart from a hiatus in 1087.[25] The question of whether Roger's agency is somehow demonstrated by the use of the beaker motif at both the castle and at some churches on his holdings — assuming Norwich to have been the motif's primary source locally — hinges on the construction date of the keep, traditionally set at *c.* 1100.[26] A later start date, after Roger's death, would cast doubt on Bigod involvement in the whole enterprise, however, as there is little to suggest that Roger's successors were much engaged with the castle. Although Roger's son, William (d. 1120), was appointed to it in 1114, the role of sheriff may have left Bigod hands as early as 1115–19.[27] It had certainly passed to Robert FitzWalter by 1129 and remained with his successors until at least the early 1150s, effectively circumventing Roger Bigod's younger son, Hugh (d. 1176/7).[28] Hugh Bigod became Norfolk's first earl by 1141, but he did not control the shrievalty, and his documented castle-building activity was in Suffolk.[29]

The grooved conical bosses on the main portal of the keep also occur on the exterior of the chancel of the Norfolk parish church of St. Margaret at Hales.[30] In England, this limpet-like motif is not confined to the eastern region, as is so ably demonstrated by the CRSBI: other instances can be found on the website in Berkshire at Ashbury St Mary and at Avington, for example, as well as in Warwickshire, at St Nicholas, Kenilworth. The ornament occurs in differing incarnations elsewhere in Romanesque Europe, for example in Normandy at Montivilliers towards the mid-12th century, and at Llo near Perpignan.[31] The motif recalls the head of a peg or nail and, as with other features of the keep at Norwich, could be an ornamental skeuomorph, derived from wooden construction or metalwork.[32]

THE ROMANESQUE FRAGMENTS AT NORWICH CATHEDRAL

THE carved Romanesque sculpture fragments housed at the cathedral came to light when repairs were carried out to the monastic cloister in 1900.[33] A number of 12th-century carved double and nook-shaft capitals and other decorated fragments were found to have been reused in the construction of the existing Gothic cloister, their carved faces squared off and turned inwards.[34] It is thought that the capitals came from the dismantled arcades of the cathedral's lost 12th-century cloister.[35]

Although it is often stated that the first cloister arcades were replaced as a consequence of the documented conflagration at the monastery of 1272, this is open to question. The Romanesque arcades were left standing for a quarter of a century after the fire,
and parts of the original cloister were still in good enough order to take a coat of
whitewash in 1292, five years before rebuilding started in 1297.[36] The 12th-century
arcades would have been dismantled gradually from the late 13th century onwards. The
cathedral's monastic customary survives in a 13th-century manuscript, but the claustral
processions and psalter-recitation it prescribes must have taken place in the Romanesque cloister alleys.[37] It seems more probable that the ancient arcades were replaced
because they were old-fashioned and impractical; unglazed, they afforded no protection
to the brethren in the much-frequented cloister walks.[38]

In one of a number of pivotal monographs on English Romanesque sculpture by
Professor George Zarnecki, the hand of an accomplished sculptor was identified in the
carving of the 12th-century cloister doorways at Ely Cathedral.[39] In the George
Zarnecki Memorial Lecture for 2012, delivered for the British Archaeological Association in London, T. A. Heslop convincingly reasserted the individual artistic person-
ality of this Ely master.[40] Sculpture as stylistically homogeneous and particular as his
was evidently not the work of a team. The Ely sculptor had a way of carving figures and
foliage that even a dedicated copyist would struggle to reproduce with consistency.
His foliage is especially recognizable: springy stems are divided into two strands. One
half widens into a smooth leaf, folded over onto itself as if pressed flat, leaving a con-
toured lower edge.

Zarnecki detected a stylistic connection between the Romanesque architectural
sculpture of Ely Cathedral and the capital fragments at Norwich, concluding that the
Ely carver had subsequently moved on to work at Norwich, some 45 miles to the north-
east, adding that little of his work survived there.[41] Above all, none of his trademark
leaves appear on the Romanesque carved fragments at Norwich, for example, and there
is nothing at Ely to compare with the finest figural carving on the Norwich capitals,
with its linear, pictorial quality.[42] Perceived connections between the sculpture at the
two cathedrals are probably attributable to their proximity and to the ease with which
popular motifs could be transmitted.

In suggesting that the Norwich fragments were carved slightly after the Ely sculpture,
Professor Zarnecki's relative dating of the two ensembles seems well judged. The
activity of the Ely sculptor is, as usual at this period, undocumented. Any date suggested for his cloister doorways will always be debatable, given that decorated portals
were invariably carved on a bench and inserted into standing or rising masonry, and are
thus not always closely dated by their architectural context. But the master sculptor's
work at Ely is also found inside the cathedral itself, in a setting that is more readily
datable. The capitals that he carved for both transept tribune arcades at Ely are situated
in a part of the building that we know was probably completed by c. 1110.[43]

The Norwich capital fragments are evidently not the work of the Ely sculptor. The
splendidly crafted figures and animals on the cloister portals at Ely are more conven-
tionalized and ornamental than anything at Norwich. The finest figure carving on the
Norwich capital fragments — seen on six of them — is likewise the work of a single
artist.[44] Unlike the Ely sculptor, the master carver at Norwich was not responsible for
the tiny amount of ornamental carving within the building itself. The quality that most
decisively sets the Norwich sculptor apart from his (older?) colleague at Ely is, however, his concern with naturalistic representation.

Moreover, the Norwich carver's work on the double capitals also introduces a concept that is not exploited in the Ely sculpture, namely that of story-telling. On one of the better-known Norwich capitals, a sequence of events is portrayed. If it were still *in situ* as part of an arcade, the capital would present us with a transformation as we walked past. One face bears a fully formed homunculus, straddling the vine and clinging to it with outstretched arms. On the next, only the head and upper body remain, for the legs have been turned into bifurcating stems. Lastly, on the third face, the figure has completely vanished, having been absorbed by the foliage.[45] A comparable metamorphosis occurs on the faces of a crypt capital, sometimes described as unfinished, at St Bénigne in Dijon.[46] The development of this story at Norwich is most clearly seen in a drawing showing the sculpture as a continuous frieze (Fig. 3).[47]

On another of the Norwich double capitals, two of the figures possibly represent a single warrior shown twice, performing the role of a 'hinge' character, moving the story forward through successive episodes (Fig. 4a).[48] The passage of time is indicated by the overlapping of legs and feet, a device that turns our attention from one moment in the narrative to the next. The pictorial device of duplicating a figure to portray a sequence of events within a single scene also occurs in the miniatures in a Durham manuscript of Bede's *Life of St Cuthbert*, dated *c*. 1100 (Oxford, Univ. Coll. MS 165).[49] Of particular relevance to the Norwich capital is the episode on page 153 of the manuscript, where the turned head of one of a pair of back-to-back figures — here apparently representing two separate individuals — and their superposed feet, invest the battle scene with drama and dynamic action (Fig. 4b). The treatment of anatomy and drapery are also remarkably similar on the capital and the drawing, but this is not to argue that the Norwich sculptor derived his composition directly from this Durham illumination, or from any other manuscript. What the analogies between the carving and the drawing reflect is a common, and probably contemporary, interest in communicating a sequence of events pictorially. It is his engagement with the mechanisms of story-telling that particularly characterizes the Norwich master's work and distances it from anything surviving at Ely.

In addition to the double capitals, some twenty-five decorated Romanesque voussoir and jamb fragments lodged at Norwich Cathedral are said to have come to light during repairs to the existing cloister in 1900.[50] As with the loose capitals, the disassembled voussoirs were cut down and reused as masonry, largely preserving their decorated

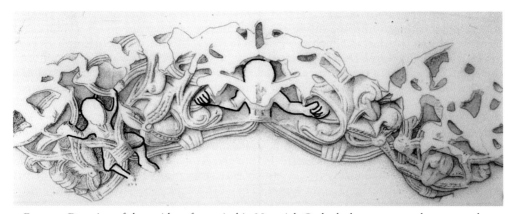

FIG. 3.   Drawing of three sides of a capital in Norwich Cathedral stone store, shown together

JILL A. FRANKLIN

FIG. 4a.   Norwich Cathedral stone store, capital: detail

FIG. 4b.   *Life of St Cuthbert*, illustration from Oxford, University College MS 165, p. 153, *c.* 1100

Reproduced by kind permission of the Master and Fellows of University College, Oxford

faces. They divide into five types, but all have features in common, and together they constitute a coherent stylistic group. All are decorated with variants of either chamfered, semi-circular billet, or squared 'dice' ornament, but with a carved leaf or flower in the hollows between the projecting mouldings, rather than the usual alternating voids. The projections themselves are chased, or decorated with drill-holes, and in the cases of types 1 and 2 they have a slightly keeled section. The illustrations show the four main types notionally reassembled (Fig. 5). It can be calculated that they formed arches with a diameter of between 2 m and 3 m, too wide for the arcades of the 12th-century cloister; bay widths of the few surviving or reliably reconstructed English Romanesque cloister arcades are far smaller than this.[51] The new Gothic east and south cloister walks at Norwich were probably finished by 1346–47.[52] The following year (1348–49), the cathedral sold off 159 voussoirs, conceivably from the Romanesque cloister arcades that had just been dismantled.[53] The surviving 12th-century voussoir fragments probably belonged to one or more of the doorways or openings into the cloister, all of which were replaced during the 14th and 15th centuries.[54]

If the surviving voussoirs were reused in the building of the south buttresses of the Gothic cloister, they may well have come from the triple openings of the 12th-century chapter-house, as this was dismantled before the Romanesque arcades of the south cloister walk were taken down.[55] In which case, they probably formed part of the original decoration of the chapter-house. They cannot be associated with the burial within it in 1150 of the faux boy-martyr William, who died in 1144.[56] The voussoirs were carved earlier than 1150, in any event, judging from their ornament; rounded

142

FIG. 5.   Notional reconstruction of four arch orders, from voussoirs at Norwich Cathedral

chamfered billet, without foliate inserts, was used inside Norwich Cathedral soon after 1096, in the presbytery apse arcade. Continuous keeled mouldings became common in England from around 1135 to 1140, but billet with a gently keeled profile made an appearance much before that in Normandy, at Cerisy-la-Forêt, a building usually dated to the late 11th century (Fig. 6).[57]

Some years ago, I suggested that work on the Romanesque cloister arcades at Norwich was underway in the second decade of the 12th century, before the death of the inaugural bishop, Herbert de Losinga, in 1119.[58] This conflicted with the widely accepted date of *c.* 1130–40 for the Norwich cloister sculpture.[59] A slightly earlier date of *c.* 1110–20 for that ensemble still seems reasonable in my view.

DECORATED PORTALS IN SOUTH-EAST NORFOLK

HAVING studied the voussoir fragments at Norwich Cathedral, I saw them as closely related to similar, though simplified, motifs on the carved portals on some parish churches in the south-east of the county.[60] At both Heckingham and Hellington, for example, an order of drilled dice on the doorways resembles some of the cathedral voussoir fragments, minus the carved foliage in the gaps (Fig. 7a and b). Might the missing foliate motifs have been depicted in paint in the hollow sections of the mouldings on the parish church doorways, perhaps as an economy measure? The south portal at Chedgrave church has an order of billet decorated with beaded straps that resembles the Type 5 voussoirs at the cathedral (Fig. 8a and b).

FIG. 6.   Cerisy-la Forêt Abbey, axial ground-floor window: detail
Photo: G. Zarnecki

Charles Keyser suggested in 1908 that these carved doorways constituted a stylistically coherent group.[61] The small, undated buildings they adorn mostly lie between the
rivers Yare and Waveney.[62] Keyser identified a discrete repertory of motifs on these
portals in addition to the decorated billet and dice mouldings, including two types that
he singled out as especially characteristic of the Eastern Counties: the double cone —
sometimes separated by scalloped cinches, as at Heckingham church — and a type
of ornament which he referred to as the 'cheese moulding' (now also called 'double
disc' or 'radial billet'), as at Hellington.[63] A feature that Keyser thought was probably
exclusive to south Norfolk and north Suffolk is the elevated plinth, often with a
pseudo-colonnette on the leading edge of the jamb, as for example at Hales church
(Fig. 9).[64] Other distinctive motifs found on these doorways are wheel-rosettes, beaded
trellis and confronted spirals.
     Are any of these motifs to be found in a dated context? Double cone (Fig. 10) occurs
first in the region on Norwich Cathedral, on the west face of the north transept, a
part of the building completed before Bishop Herbert de Losinga's death in 1119.[65]
Three small churches within the city of Norwich — one with an institutional date —
have carved doorways that link them to this 'Yare Valley' group: St Etheldreda's, which
was held by Norwich Cathedral priory, has two arch orders of decorated billet
(Fig. 11a).[66] A doorway at St Julian's, relocated from the lost church of St Michael-
at-Thorn, has large square-section dice, without drill holes (Fig. 11b).[67] The third
Norwich church, St Mary Magdalen (Lazar House), has a south doorway with an order
of badly weathered angled billet and grooved dice (Fig. 12a and b). It also has pseudo-
colonnettes on raised plinths, the feature Keyser thought exclusive to the region.
St Mary Magdalen was founded by Bishop Herbert de Losinga which might indicate
that, like the eastern arm of the cathedral, the building is datable before 1119.[68] As
such, therefore, it could be seen a key monument for the dating of the 'Yare Valley'
mouldings, and for the Norwich voussoir fragments.[69]

FIG. 7a.   Heckingham, St Gregory, south door: detail

FIG. 7b.   Hellington, St John the Baptist, south door: detail

FIG. 8a. Chedgrave, All Saints, south door: detail

FIG. 8b. Voussoirs from
Norwich Cathedral

    The accompanying table and map summarize the incidence and distribution of these
ornamental motifs exclusively within Norfolk, even though some of the motifs are
found outside its boundary (Figs 13 and 14). In neighbouring north Suffolk, for
example, the double disc/radial billet moulding was used on doorways at Mettingham,
Redisham and Kelsale, the last two held by Roger Bigod, while Mettingham and
Wissett also have jambs on a raised plinth.[70] Each church on the chart is related to the

FIG. 9.   Hales, St Margaret: north door

relevant tenant-in-chief cited in Domesday Book, though not necessarily in the hope of
assigning it to an individual patron. All of those named were dead by 1107, somewhat
earlier than the earliest date proposed for any of the sculpture, including that associated
with the episcopate of Herbert de Losinga, 1094/5–1119. However, as Domesday

FIG. 10.   Norwich Cathedral: window arch on nave gallery
Photo: S. Heywood

tenancy was generally heritable, it seems relevant to include the information, even though recorded in 1086.[71] As the motifs occur mostly on doorways, measurements in centimetres are shown for the height and width of an opening. Perhaps the most striking outcome of this exercise is the considerable variation and lack of correlation it reveals. The average height, for example, is about 2.155 m, but the range is between a

FIG. 11a.   Norwich, St Etheldreda, south door: detail

Photo: S. Heywood

148

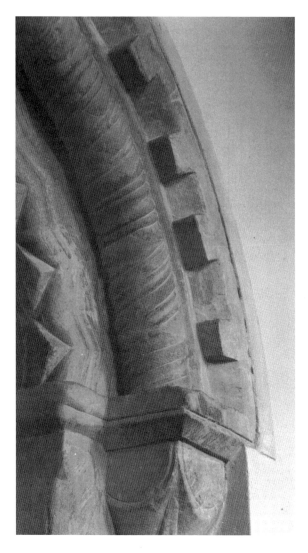

FIG. 11b.   Norwich, St Julian, south
door (ex Norwich, St Michael-at-
Thorn): detail
Photo: S. Heywood

maximum of 2.57 m and a minimum of 1.85 m. The Yare Valley 'school' evidently operated in all corners of the county in the 12th century, at the behest of a range of patrons. Sculpture motifs were not, therefore, the exclusive product of Bigod patronage; the frequency with which Bigod occurs doubtless reflects his wealth and position in the county.[72]

CASTLE ACRE PRIORY

IN his study of the carved motifs on the doorways of south-east Norfolk, Charles Keyser also included the sculpture of the monastic site at Castle Acre, even though this Cluniac priory was situated on the opposite side of the county, towards King's Lynn, some 50 miles from the Yare Valley portals. Now a magnificent ruin, the priory was

FIG. 12a.   Norwich, hospital of St Mary Magdalen: south wall

FIG. 12b.   Norwich, hospital of St Mary Magdalen: detail of door arch

	LOCATION	Hundred/Borough	Tenant-in-chief in 1086 and/or later	Doorway, unless otherwise shown:		Dec dice/square billet	Raised plinth	Dble disc/Rad billet	Cinched □	Dble cone	Dec billet	Beaded trellis	Spiral	Wheel/Rosette	Beaker	Limpet boss
1	Ashby St Mary	Loddon	Roger Bigod		S h214 w85		■		□							
2	Attleborough	Shropham	Roger FitzRainard	Int: tower openings				■	□							
3	Castle Acre Priory	Freebridge	Wm de Warenne	W. h 464 (max) w 299	S-W h245 w102			■ ex situ	■	□ (façade)		■				
4	Chedgrave	Loddon	Ralph Baynard	N h196 w98	S h210 w84		■	■ S				■ S				
5	Clippesby	West Flegg	King/sheriff	N h191 w80			■					■				
6	Easton	Forehoe	Count Alan	S **										■		
7	Framingham Earl	Henstead	Roger Bigod	N**	S h220 w79							■ S		■ S	■ S	
8	Gillingham	Clavering	King/sheriff	Ext. tower openings											■	
[9]	Gt Dunham:	*ex situ*										■		■		
10	Hales	Clavering	Roger Bigod	N h223 w98	S h225 101	■ S	■ S&N		□ N			■ N +ext		■ N		■ S +ext.
11	Heckingham	Clavering	Roger Bigod	N h135 w 91	S h199 w 94	■ S	■ S	■ S	□ S			■ S		■ S		
12	Hellington	Loddon	Roger Bigod	N h212 w84	S h257 w96	■ S	■ S	■ S	□ S							
13	*Hillington (lost)*	Freebridge	Wm de Warenne							■						
14	Kirby Cane	Clavering	Hugh of Avranches		S h226 w106		■									
15	Langford	S. Greenhoe	Hugh of Montfort	chancel arch	S **				□							
16	Larling	Shropham	de Warenne		S h218 w105	■						■				
17	L. Plumstead	Blofield	King/Godric					■								
18	Mundham	Loddon	King /Bigod		S h212w107		■	■					■		■	
19	Norwich Castle Keep	Norwich	King	+ f'building basement **											■	■
	Cathedral Priory	Norwich	King	N transept, W face, ext.						■						
	Cathedral Priory			*stone store*		■		■	■	■						
	St Etheldreda	Norwich	Cathedral Priory	**							■					
	St Julian	Norwich		*lost*		■										
	St Mary Magdalene	Norwich	Cathedral Priory	**			■				■					
	*St Michael-at-Thorn (lost)**	Norwich	King	*relocated* **		■										
20	Roydon	Freebridge	Bishop of Bayeux	N h227 w107	S h220w107				■ N							
21	Shingham	Clacklose	Ralph de Tosny		S h185 w94							■				
22	South Burlingham	Blofield	Bishop of Thetford	N h218 w147	S h234 w147										■ N	
23	South Lopham	Guiltcross	Roger Bigod	N h240 w102				■								
24	Thetford Priory	Thetford	*King/Bigod*	*stone store*				■		■ fragment noted in 1852						
25	Thurlton	Clavering	King / Wm de Noyers		S h193 w86			■					■			
26	Thurton	Loddon	Roger Bigod	N h156 w84	S h200 w91		■ S	■ S								
27	Thwaite St Mary	Loddon	not in Domesday Book		S h191 w85		■	■			■				■	

*church destroyed WWII, doorway relocated in 1950s to St Julian's, Norwich, which had lost its Norman doorway in WWII
**doorway unmeasured
N, S, W= north, south, west doorway
h=height w=width

FIG. 13.   Distribution of Romanesque sculptural motifs in Norwich and Norfolk

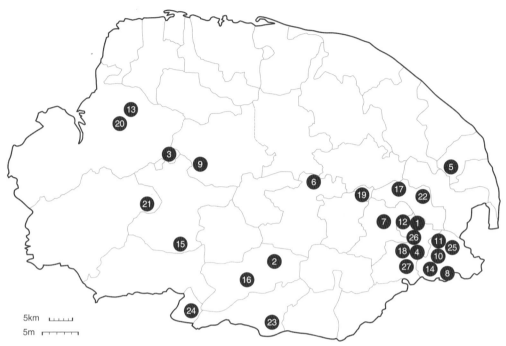

FIG. 14.   Location of buildings listed in Figure 13
Toby Montague

founded in or soon after 1089 by William II de Warenne.[73] Acquired by the Duke of
Norfolk after the Dissolution, the monastery was gradually dismantled and its freestone reused as building material.[74] Keyser speaks of 'two fine doorways to the refectory, and no doubt others, which have been destroyed, as till recent times, the place was
allowed to be a quarry to supply the needs of the surrounding district'.[75]

Keyser was wise to bring Castle Acre Priory into his discussion of the decorated
doorways in the Yare Valley, despite their geographical separation. Motifs such as the
beaded trellis on the church façade at Castle Acre (Fig. 15) occur on doorways almost
40 miles away at Clippesby, near Great Yarmouth (Fig. 16) and at Heckingham, which
also has the hallmark double-cone moulding. *Ex situ* fragments at Castle Acre include
— cemented in for safe-keeping — a variety of syncopated double disc (Fig. 17a),
another of Keyser's quintessential regional motifs, also used outside Bigod territory at
St Mary's, Attleborough.

About three miles east of Castle Acre, in the village of Great Dunham, many
decorated Romanesque fragments were reused in the construction of the 18th-century
house and barns of Rookery Farm and are still visible in the elevations (Fig. 18). A few
related carved fragments have been deployed as parking bollards around the lawn of
the Old Rectory in the village, while others have been lodged nearby at the important
'overlap' church of St Andrew's.[76] The Great Dunham sculpture fragments are said to
have come from the chapel of St Mary which belonged to St Andrew's and stood
nearby.[77] St Andrew's was in turn a possession of Castle Acre Priory.[78] Several of the
motifs on loose or reused fragments at Great Dunham also occur at Castle Acre,

however. For example, a readily identifiable through-voussoir with a floral motif on its soffit, flanked at either end by a chevron, occurs at two of the Great Dunham sites — one inside St Andrew's church, and many more as reused masonry at Rookery Farm. One more is (or was in 1985) on display at Castle Acre Priory, which is, I suggest, where all of these distinctive voussoirs came from originally. More significantly, ornamental motifs matching some on the Great Dunham fragments are still *in situ* at the priory. For example, the beaded trellis on reused fragments in the walls at Rookery Farm can still be seen *in situ* on the portals of Castle Acre priory church. All of the related Romanesque carved stones at the three Great Dunham sites are likely to have been quarried from Castle Acre Priory after the Dissolution, in my view, rather than from the lost chapel of St Mary.

FIG. 15. Castle Acre Priory: west façade, south door

FIG. 16.   Clippesby, St Peter, north door: detail

FIG. 17a.   Castle Acre Priory: double disc   FIG. 17b.   Norwich Cathedral: stone store,
moulding   double disc moulding

TO CONCLUDE

CONNECTIONS between the Romanesque sculpture at Norwich and that in various parts of the wider county seem clear. It appears that ideas and motifs used at the new cathedral and in city churches under Bishop Herbert were transmitted to the rural manors, sometimes reconfigured by the craftsmen into simpler and, perhaps, cheaper forms. Many of the parish churches in the Yare Valley were on territory held at the

FIG. 18.   Great Dunham, Rookery Farm: stones from Castle Acre Priory reused in barn wall

Conquest by Roger Bigod (d. 1107).[79] One of the carved motifs commonly used on the doorways of these churches, the double disc, is also to be found with the many loose stones said to have come from Bigod's monastic foundation at Thetford Priory (f. 1103/04; present site, 1107),[80] while another example survives among the fragments at Norwich Cathedral (Fig. 17b), with whose foundation Bigod was also involved.[81] The Bigods and the Norwich episcopate also appear to have liaised on an important project outside the county, in London.[82]

As we have seen, however, the sculptors trained in the 'Yare Valley' tradition employed on Bigod territory and by the bishop also worked for an equally powerful rival nobleman at Castle Acre, another Cluniac priory, 50 miles away. Moreover, the team who devised the Norwich 'Type 3' voussoir, with its square-section projections scored around the edge, seem to have devised something similar, if less expensive, for the jambs of the south doorway at Larling church where the projections are quirked in a comparable fashion (Fig. 19).[83] Larling lies to west of the Yare Valley group, in Shropham Hundred, held by William de Warenne, patron of Castle Acre. It seems clear, therefore, that sculptors active in the workshop tradition identified here were engaged first in Norwich and later also employed by other patrons in quite different parts of the county.

It seems improbable, however, that the Clavering and Loddon parish church doorways, decorated with elaborate geometric carving on costly, imported stone, would have been paid for by the Bigods. Late-11th-century Norfolk had an exceptionally high numbers of free men, especially in the south-east where the Yare Valley doorways survive.[84] Perhaps these relatively privileged tenants were prevailed upon to contribute to the costs of embellishing their local church.

Given that stone-carvers trained in the same workshop tradition were working in Norwich as well as in all corners of Norfolk in the first half of the 12th century,

FIG. 19.   Larling, St Ethelbert: south door

De Warenne at Castle Acre and the Bigods, or their parochial tenants, in the south-east, must have employed teams of itinerant carvers using a common repertory of decoration. Although Castle Acre may look like an outlier of the Yare Valley group now, there must once have been other churches in the intervening 50 miles with characteristic decoration on doorways that were replaced in more prosperous times, like the apparently isolated examples surviving at Langford, south of Swaffham, with double-cone on its portal, and Shingham, a few miles to the north-east, on the way to Castle Acre, whose doorway bears the tell-tale beaded trellis ornament (Fig. 20).

What appears to be a concentration of similarly decorated portals in the Yare Valley area is somewhat illusory, therefore, together with the notion of a localized team of masons. The parish churches for which the doorways were made were the product of a 12th-century building boom, particularly evident in the affluent south-east of the county. Their portals may have survived because the region's relative decline in the later middle ages made replacing them unaffordable; south-east Norfolk did not share in the prosperity enjoyed by the maritime and mercantile towns in the north of the county in the 14th century, testified by the mighty Gothic churches at Blakeney or Cley-next-the-Sea.

FIG. 20.   Shingham,
St Botolph, south door:
detail

Our commonly held assumption that apparently localized artistic practice is indicative of regional patronage may therefore need to be reconsidered in the case of Norfolk. Romanesque sculpture workshops were not necessarily exclusive to individual lords and their territory, or to particular religious houses, as this paper has attempted to show; the best carvers — perhaps imported from the European mainland like some of the stone they dressed — worked everywhere, for the richest patrons of whatever class, without allegiance to a single nobleman or institution. Motifs that appear to be local to a specific area because of an accident of survival can in fact be seen to occur, sporadically, across a wider area. We can probably still speak with reason of regional Romanesque sculpture workshops in an East Anglian context — specializing in particular types of ornament — provided the boundaries defining their activity are sufficiently widely drawn.

NOTES

1. B/E, *Norfolk*, I, 13.

2. J. Campbell, 'The East Anglian Sees before the Conquest', in *Norwich Cathedral 1096–1996*, 3–21.

3. The rural population of 11th-century Norfolk was the largest in England; H. C. Darby, *Domesday England* (Cambridge 1977/86), 336 Appendix 1. Norfolk and Suffolk accommodated between them almost a quarter of the country's population; E. Miller and J. Hatcher, *Medieval England: Rural Society and Economic Change 1086–1348* (London and New York 1978), 5.

4. Only two of the projected VCH volumes for Norfolk were published, but the second contains a translation of the county's Domesday survey and a documented gazetteer of its religious foundations; VCH, *Norfolk*, II, 39–203 and 315–466 respectively. Norfolk's comprehensive antiquarian record, e.g. Blomefield, *Norfolk*, is supplemented by the collected illustrations of Dawson Turner (1775–1858); London, BL Add. MSS 23024–52, 23053–62, including several of the Romanesque portals, a number of which are also recorded in J. S. Cotman, *Architectural etchings of old English Buildings, chiefly in Norfolk* (London 1838). Historic sites are covered by the dedicated volumes of B/E — in two editions, both entailing two volumes — and *Norfolk Archaeology*. Other relevant studies include C. Harper-Bill, *English Episcopal Acta VI: Norwich 1070–1214* (Oxford 1990) and T. Williamson, *The Origins of Norfolk* (Manchester and New York 1993). A valuable digitized photographic record of Norfolk's monuments is: http://www.georgeplunkett.co.uk/.

5. Fernie, *AHNC*, 207–09; D. Wollaston, 'Herbert de Losinga', in *Norwich Cathedral 1096–1996*, 22–35, at 33–34. De Warenne founded Castle Acre Priory in or soon after 1089; London BL MS Harley 2110 (Castle Acre Cartulary), *Mon.*, V, 49–54; VCH, *Norfolk*, II, 356–58; B. Cherry, 'Romanesque Architecture in Eastern

England', *JBAA*, 131 (1978), 1–29, at 12–14; Fernie, *AHNC*, 147–49. Bigod's foundation at Thetford Priory was established on its present site in 1107; *Mon.*, V, 141–55; VCH, *Norfolk*, II, 363–69; Cherry, 'Romanesque Architecture', 11–12; B/E, *Norfolk*, II, 705–07.

6. Late-11th-/12th-century structure or fragments survive of the abbey at Wymondham (*Mon.*, III, 323–41; VCH, *Norfolk*, II, 336–43; S. Heywood, 'The Romanesque Church', in *Wymondham Abbey*, ed. P. Cattermole (Wymondham 2007), 69–83), the priories of Binham (*Mon.*, III, 341–53; VCH, *Norfolk*, II, 343–46; Fernie, *AHNC*, 148–51), Bromholm (*Mon.*, V, 59–64; VCH, *Norfolk*, II, 259–63; B/E, *Norfolk*, I, 373–74), Carrow (*Mon.*, IV, 68–73; VCH, *Norfolk*, II, 351–54. See also Richard Halsey's paper in these transactions), St Nicholas, Great Yarmouth (*Mon.*, VI, 465; VCH, *Norfolk*, II, 330; B/E, *Norfolk*, I, 494–97) and St Margaret's, King's Lynn (*Mon.*, VI, 462–63; VCH, *Norfolk*, II, 328–29; B/E, *Norfolk*, II, 465–66) and the significant ruined church at North Elmham (S. Heywood, 'The Ruined Church at North Elmham', *JBAA*, 135 (1982), 1–10).

7. The three city churches are St Etheldreda, St Julian (housing the portal from the lost city church of St Michael-at-Thorn) and St Mary Magdalen; B/E *Norfolk*, I, 233, 241, 247, 330; Fernie, *AHNC*; T. A. Heslop, *Norwich Castle Keep* (Norwich 1994).

8. J. A. Franklin, 'The Romanesque Cloister Sculpture at Norwich Cathedral Priory', in *Studies in Medieval Sculpture*, ed. F. H. Thompson, Society of Antiquaries of London Occasional Paper, New Series, III (London 1983), 56–70; Williamson, *Origins* (as in n. 4), 178.

9. For the relief panel of the bishop from the north wall of the north transept of Norwich Cathedral, see J. A. Franklin, 'The Romanesque Sculpture', in *Norwich Cathedral 1096–1996*, fig. 48, and for the seated figure above the south doorway at Haddiscoe church, see B/E, *Norfolk*, II, fig. 15.

10. Fonts with figural reliefs are at Burnham Deepdale, with the Labours of the Months, and Fincham, with rustic Old and New Testament scenes. A stylistic group of three richly carved fonts, with corner colonnettes and decorated supports, are in churches at Sculthorpe — also with full-length figures in relief — Shernborne and Toftrees. The first paid tithes to Cluniac Lewes Priory in Sussex — established by William Warenne, founder of the influential Norfolk dynasty — while the last two were possessions of Binham Priory. The carving on the font at Castle Rising church, belonging to Lewes, and on the font base at Hautbois, is related but coarser; F. Bond, *Fonts and Font Covers* (Oxford 1908), frontispiece, 156–57, 189–99; S. Margeson, F. Seiller and A. Rogerson, *The Normans in Norfolk* (Norwich 1994), 65, nos 73, 74, 75. Less ornate examples can be seen at http://www.crsbi.ac.uk/site/720/, http://www.crsbi.ac.uk/site/739/, http://www.crsbi.ac.uk/site/735/ and http://www.crsbi.ac.uk/site/734/.

11. The decoration on the tympanum in the east wall of the north transept of Norwich Cathedral is generically the same as that on the north door at Marham; Franklin, 'Romanesque Sculpture' (as in n. 9), 120–21, fig. 50 and n. 18. The county's other *in situ* carved tympanum at Tottenhill bears a motif of a cross within a looped cable; C. Keyser, *Norman Tympana and Lintels* (London 1904), 51, fig. 12.

12. Fragments survive at King's Lynn Museum of the tympanum from Mintlyn, described by Charles Keyser as 'formerly over the south door but lying broken in the ruined church, bearing a circular cable band as at Tottenhill but no cross within it'; C. Keyser, 'The Norman Doorways in Norfolk', in *Memorials of Old Norfolk*, ed. H. J. Dukinfield Astley (London 1908), 188; Keyser, *Tympana and Lintels* (as in n. 11), 29; Margeson, et al., *Normans in Norfolk* (as in n. 10), 67–68, fig. 77; B/E, *Norfolk*, II, 544.

13. For an account of the architecture of the region in the late 11th/12th century, see Cherry, 'Romanesque Architecture' (as in n. 5).

14. A. Whittingham, 'Note on Norwich Castle', *Archaeol. J.*, 137 (1980), 359–60; Heslop, *Norwich Castle* (as in n. 7), 7, 12 and n. 14.

15. Keyser, 'Norman Doorways' (as in n. 12); J. A. Franklin, 'The Romanesque Cloister Sculpture of Norwich Cathedral' (unpublished MA dissertation, UEA, 1980), 38; J. A. Franklin in *Medieval Sculpture from Norwich Cathedral*, ed. A. Borg et al. (Norwich 1980), 23–26; J. A. Franklin, 'Romanesque Cloister Sculpture' (as in n. 8), 67 and n. 19; A. Harris, 'Late Eleventh- and Twelfth-century Church Architecture of the Lower Yare Valley, Norfolk' (unpublished M.Phil. dissertation, UEA, 1989).

16. www.crsbi.ac.uk.

17. M. Thurlby, 'The Influence of the Cathedral on Romanesque Architecture', *Norwich Cathedral 1096–1996*, 136–57, at 150–51 and n. 43.

18. Heslop, *Norwich Castle* (as n. 7), fig. 10, 16, 31–32.

19. Only one capital in the cathedral, in the north transept blank arcading, has figural decoration on its three exposed faces, in the form of a pair of winged dragon-like beasts with beaded bodies. The font base at Hautbois, north of Norwich, bears a similar beast; J. A. Franklin, 'The Romanesque Sculpture', in *Norwich Cathedral 1096–1996*, 116–35, at 121, fig. 52.

20. Heslop, *Norwich Castle* (as in n. 7), 64.

21. Framingham Earl, Thwaite St Mary and Gillingham are cited in Heslop, *Norwich Castle* (as in n. 7), 64.

22. A. Wareham, 'The Motives and Politics of the Bigod Family c1066–1177', *Anglo-Norman Studies*, 17 (1994), 223–42, at 227.

23. For the Suffolk sites, see www.crsbi.ac.uk.

24. N. J. G. Pounds, *The Medieval Castle in England and Wales. A Social and Political History* (Cambridge 1990), 96.

25. Wareham, 'Motives' (as in n. 22), 225.

26. The date of the construction of the keep at Norwich is discussed elsewhere in this volume by James King.

27. Wareham, 'Motives' (as in n. 22), 229, 231.

28. J. A. Green, *The Government of England under Henry I* (Cambridge 1989), 66 n. 56; J. A. Green, 'Financing Stephen's War', *Anglo-Norman Studies*, 14 (1991), 99; Wareham 'Motives' (as in n. 22), 234.

29. J. A. Green, *The Aristocracy of Norman England* (Cambridge 2002), 304 n. 217; A. F. Wareham, 'Bigod, Hugh (I), first earl of Norfolk (*d.* 1176/7)', *ODNB*, online edn, http://www.oxforddnb.com/view/article/2376 [last accessed 28 March 2015].

30. S. Heywood, *St Margaret's Church, Hales, Norfolk* (London 2004), 4.

31. At the abbey church of Montivilliers, grooved bosses occur in the interstices of the planar confronted lateral chevrons on the soffit of the transverse arch introduced with the rib-vaulting of the transept arms towards the mid-12th century; L. Musset, *Normandie Romane: II La Haute Normandie*, La nuit des temps 41, 2nd edn (La Pierre-qui-Vire 1985), 134–35, figs 55 and 56. For the late-11th-century church, see J. A. Franklin, 'The Romanesque Sculpted Arch at Montivilliers: Episodes from the Story of David', in *Medieval Art and Architecture at Rouen*, ed. J. Stratford, *BAA Trans.*, XII (1993), 36–45. For the Romanesque portal of the church in the lost village of Llo, see A. Duprey, *Itinéraires romans en Roussillon* (La Pierre-qui-Vire 1977), 84, fig. 32.

32. Heslop, *Norwich Castle* (as n. 7), 30–31. The shell-like appearance of the motif is intriguing, given that the zoological name for a limpet, *patella*, appears to be the diminutive of *patera*, the small roundel occurring in Classical architecture.

33. A. B. Whittingham, surveyor to the fabric at Norwich Cathedral (1932–63), pers. comm. to the author, 1979; Franklin, 'Romanesque Cloister Sculpture' (as in n. 15), 10, 68 n. 1.

34. Franklin, *Medieval Sculpture* (as in n. 15), 7–27.

35. Ibid., 7.

36. Ibid,, 6.

37. Franklin, MA dissertation (as in n. 15), 6. The surviving manuscript of the customary was compiled between 1257 and 1265; J. B. L. Tolhurst ed., *The Customary of the Cathedral priory Church of Norwich*, Henry Bradshaw Society, 72 (1948), vii.

38. Franklin in *Medieval Sculpture* (as in n. 15), 6.

39. G. Zarnecki, *Early Sculpture of Ely Cathedral* (London 1958), 17, 26–27, 29–31, 33, 35–36.

40. Presented at Burlington House, London, on 4 April 2012.

41. Zarnecki, *Ely* (as in n. 39), 33, 36.

42. One capital bearing foliate carving somewhat resembling an Ely type of leaf occurs inside the cathedral itself, in the tribune gallery arcade, south side of the presbytery: capital 2 in bay 3 (counting W to E), north face (towards the central vessel).

43. Franklin, 'Romanesque Cloister Sculpture' (as in n. 8), 67 and n. 24; Zarnecki, *Ely* (as in n. 39), 16–17, where it is argued that the capitals, only partly carved, were decorated *in situ c.* 1130 as an afterthought, using scaffolding erected for the construction of the crossing tower. However, the undecorated parts of the soffit capital in the south transept tribune are accessible from the gallery — and visible from the ground — and could also have been carved, without using scaffolding, had the decision to carve been an afterthought.

44. Franklin, 'Romanesque Cloister Sculpture' (as in n. 8), 57.

45. Ibid., figs 59a, b and c. 'But that's narrative!' was Professor Michael Kauffmann's comment when I showed him this progression in 1994.

46. Franklin, 'The Romanesque Sculpture' (as in n. 9), figs 62 and 63.

47. Based on a drawing commissioned for, and first published in, Franklin, 'The Romanesque Sculpture' (as in n. 9), fig. 56c.

48. O Pächt, *The Rise of Pictorial Narrative in Twelfth-Century England* (Oxford 1962), 15; J. J. G. Alexander, *Medieval Illuminators and their Methods of Work* (New Haven and London 1992), 85.

49. Possibly copied from a lost, late-11th-century model; Pächt, *Pictorial Narrative* (as in n. 48), 14–21; C. M. Kauffmann, *Romanesque Manuscripts 1066–1190* (London 1975), no. 26; M. Baker, 'Medieval Illustrations of Bede's Life of St Cuthbert', *Journal of the Warburg and Courtauld Institutes*, 41 (1978), 16–49; A. Lawrence-Mathers, *Manuscripts in Northumbria in the Eleventh and Twelfth Centuries* (Oxford 2003), 89–108.

50. Franklin, *Medieval Sculpture* (as n. 15), 25–27; Franklin, 'Romanesque Cloister Sculpture' (as n. 8), 58, 67–68, pls XVb, XVIa and XXIa.

51. The colonnettes of the reconstructed arcades at Bridlington Priory are set at 89 cm centres and those of Reading Abbey are slightly narrower, while the width of the standing bays of the infirmary cloister arcade at Canterbury Cathedral is 122 cm; J. A. Franklin, 'Bridlington Priory: an Augustinian Church and Cloister in the Twelfth Century', in *Medieval Art and Architecture in the East Riding of Yorkshire*, ed. C. Wilson, *BAA Trans.*, IX (1989), 44–61, at 46; T. Tatton-Brown, 'The Cloister Arcades at Canterbury Cathedral Priory', in *The Medieval Cloister in England and Wales*, ed. M. Henig and J. McNeill, *JBAA*, 159 (2006), 91–104, at 93; R. Baxter and S. Harrison, 'The Decoration of the Cloister at Reading Abbey', in *Windsor: Medieval Archaeology, Art and Architecture of the Thames Valley*, ed. L. Keen and E. Scarff, *BAA Trans.*, XXV (2002), 302–12.

52. V. Sekules in *Medieval Sculpture from Norwich Cathedral*, ed. A. Borg et al. (Norwich 1980), 4.

53. Franklin, in *Medieval Sculpture* (as n. 15), 26, 48 n. 53.

54. Franklin, in *Medieval Sculpture* (as n. 15), 26, 48 n. 55; F. Woodman, 'The Gothic Campaigns', in *Norwich Cathedral, 1096–1996*, 158–96, at 163, 177–78.

55. E. C. Fernie and A. B. Whittingham, *The Early Communar and Pittancer Rolls of Norwich Cathedral Priory*, Norfolk Record Society, 41 (1972), roll 1030; Franklin, MA dissertation (as in n. 15), 36, 75 n. 7.

56. Thomas of Monmouth, the Norwich monk responsible for promoting William's cult, says nothing in his crypto hagiography about the building's being redecorated to commemorate the boy. The decision to bury William in the chapter-house was unpopular with the prior. Within a year, the child's remains had been relocated to the cathedral; Thomas of Monmouth, *The Life and Miracles of St William of Norwich*, ed. A. Jessop and M. R. James (Cambridge 1896), 123–25, 127, 167, 185–89. Franklin, 'Romanesque Cloister Sculpture' (as in n. 8), 56 and notes.

57. Franklin, 'Romanesque Cloister Sculpture' (as in n. 8), 67, pl. XXIb.

58. Ibid., 68.

59. For example, *English Romanesque Art 1066–1200*, ed. G. Zarnecki et al. (London 1984), nos 126, 134a, 134b; Heywood, *Hales* (as in n. 30), 7.

60. Franklin, MA dissertation (as in n. 15), 37–40 and n. 10, where the list of churches given is expanded in the table in the present paper; Franklin, 'Romanesque Cloister Sculpture' (as in n. 8), 58, 67 and n. 19, pl. XXIa. One addition, the lost church at Hillington (Freebridge hundred) — illustrated in the Dawson Turner Collection but not recorded by Pevsner — had an arch order of the distinctive double cone motif on its south doorway; Keyser, 'Norman Doorways' (as in n. 12), 197.

61. Keyser, 'Norman Doorways' (as in n. 12), 188–89.

62. Harris, 'Lower Yare Valley' (as in n. 15), where the connection between the motifs on the doorways and the cathedral voussoir fragments is not noted.

63. Keyser, 'Norman Doorways' (as in n. 12), 188, 189. The double-cone motif is sometimes carved on an individual voussoir where two cones appear to be joined at their bases. It can also be formed on a row of voussoirs, each of which bears a single 'diabolo' shape.

64. Keyser, 'Norman Doorways' (as in n. 12), 189.

65. Heywood, *Hales* (as in n. 30), 6. The double-cone mouldings *in situ* in this location are restorations, but three original double-cone voussoirs were noted in the cathedral stone store in 2012.

66. Norwich Cathedral priory held the rectory of St Etheldreda's; VCH, *Norfolk*, II, 317–28, at 318.

67. Keyser, 'Norman Doorways' (as in n. 12), 198, 199; B/E, *Norfolk*, I, 241, 247.

68. *Mon.*, VI, 768; VCH, *Norfolk*, II, 448–49; *The First Register of Norwich Cathedral Priory*, ed. H. W. Saunders, Norfolk Record Society XI (1939), fol. 7, 33–36.

69. The two damaged portals at St Mary Magdalen stand in disturbed flint masonry. That on the south side certainly appears reinserted. However, given the vicissitudes of the building since the 16th century, the Romanesque doorways could represent the vestiges Herbert's building, even if they are no longer in precisely their original positions; B/E, *Norfolk*, I, 333.

70. Keyser, 'Norman Doorways' (as in n. 12), 189. All of the Suffolk sites can be found on www.crsbi.ac.uk.

71. 'Of 596 families with an ancestor in Domesday Book, 437 can be identified in the *Cartae Baronum* of 1166. The number would be higher if there were no gaps in the surviving *Cartae* returns'; K. S. B. Keats-Rohan, *Domesday Descendants. A Prosopography of Persons Occurring in English Documents 1066–1166. II: Pipe Rolls to Cartae Baronum* (Woodbridge 2002), 5.

72. Roger Bigod held 187 manors in Norfolk at the time of the Domesday Survey — vastly more than any other tenant-in-chief in the county — valued in 1086 at £281 18s.; G. Munford, *An analysis of the Domesday Book of the County of Norfolk* (London 1858), 21. Only William de Warenne, calculated to have held fewer manors (145) but with a higher valuation of £329 4s., was comparable; ibid., 19.

73. For the sculpture at Castle Acre Priory, see: http://www.crsbi.ac.uk/site/724/.

74. VCH, *Norfolk*, II, 356–58.

75. Keyser, 'Norman Doorways' (as in n. 12), 191–92.

76. For the Romanesque fragments at Great Dunham, see: http://www.crsbi.ac.uk/site/1870/ and http://www.crsbi.ac.uk/site/1871/.

77. B/E, *Norfolk*, II, 365.

78. Harper-Bill, *Episcopal Acta* (as in n. 4), no. 29.

79. Harris, *Lower Yare Valley* (as in n. 15), which does not mention the related voussoir fragments housed at Norwich Cathedral. For Bigod's proximity to Henry I, see Orderic Vitalis, *Ecclesiastical History*, ed. and trans. M. Chibnall, 6 vols (Oxford 1969–80), V, 298; W. Hollister, *Henry I* (New Haven and London), 59 and n. 143.

80. Thetford Priory accession no. 7810 1656; J. Hall, 'Scan of Collection of Loose Stone from Thetford Priory for English Heritage' (unpublished 2004), 15. I am most grateful to Dr Hall for providing me with information from her inventory of Thetford Priory stone fragments.

81. *First Register* (as in n. 68), fols 1d, 2, 4d, 5, 5d; Fernie, *AHNC*, 11–13.

82. J. A. Franklin, 'The Eastern Arm of Norwich Cathedral and the Augustinian Priory of St Bartholomew's, Smithfield, in London', *Antiq. J.*, 86 (2006), 110–30.

83. http://www.crsbi.ac.uk/site/1824/.

84. Williamson, *Origins* (as in n. 4), 116–25. The highest density of free men in the county in Domesday Book was in the Hundred of East Flegg, where they constituted 74 per cent of the recorded inhabitants; T. Hawes, *Norfolk in 1066 and 1086. Domesday Book Rearranged*, Norfolk Historical Aids, 18 (Cringleford 2001), 24, 28.

Carrow Priory Church, Norwich and the Introduction of Gothic Architecture to Norfolk

RICHARD HALSEY

A Benedictine priory for nuns was founded at Carrow in 1146 with the patronage of King Stephen, possibly on the site of a previous hospital. It remained an important monastery in Norwich until dissolution in 1538 when the west range became the house of Sir John Shelton and the remainder was demolished. The site is now within a Unilever factory. Excavations by J. J. Colman in 1880–81 revealed a substantial late-twelfth-century church, initially built with Norfolk Romanesque details. A second phase has some early Gothic features originating in northern France that by comparison with the cathedral infirmary can be dated to the 1180s. Without Cistercian 'missionaries of Gothic' in Norfolk, the adoption of such details as waterleaf and crocket capitals presumably came about from individual acquaintance with French, or possibly other English buildings. However, such features are used decoratively in a Romanesque context, suggesting that without the example of Cistercian and reformed order churches the Gothic style took time to be adopted in Norfolk. Parallels are drawn with work in other monasteries in Norfolk, particularly the remains of Bromholm Cluniac priory.

THE name Carrow is now most widely associated with the Norwich City Football Club stadium on Carrow Road. It stands next to the river Wensum below an escarpment, just outside the line of the city walls. In the Middle Ages, this area was dominated by the Benedictine nun's priory that stood on the hill, 'about a furlong from Southgates', as Francis Blomefield says.[1] Although the site is now widely called Carrow Abbey, it never achieved this status.[2] Nevertheless, it was an independent house and until the coming of the friars, had the second largest church in Norwich after the cathedral.[3]

DOCUMENTARY EVIDENCE

A lost cartulary seen and partly copied by Bishop Tanner stated that in 1146 Seyna and Lescelina, nuns of the hospital of St Mary and St John in Norwich, founded the nunnery of St Mary of Carhowe.[4] Previously, in a charter of 1136/7 King Stephen had granted

in perpetual alms to God and the Church of St Mary and St John of Norwich and to the nuns there serving God all that arable land which he possessed in Norwich in open lands [. . .] and I will that on that land they may build their church.[5]

BAA Trans., vol. XXXVIII (2015), 162–180
© British Archaeological Association 2015

Stephen's charter does not mention a hospital as such,[6] and there is no other reference than the lost cartulary to a 'hospital of St Mary and St John'. Whether the new priory subsumed it (as Blomefield thought) or whether the women came here from a lost nunnery (as Walter Rye suggests) is not known.[7] Tim Pestell has suggested that the position of Carrow Priory beyond the city gate across King Street could well have been the site of a hospital and draws a parallel with the nunnery of St George at Thetford.[8] The creation of Benedictine nunneries after the Conquest can be obscure, but they were sometimes a regularization of existing arrangements involving devout women informally attached to male monasteries, such as may have existed at the cathedral priory.[9]

Nothing ecclesiastical earlier than the mid-12th-century priory buildings has been found on the site, neither is the priory recorded as having any hospital function, though the 15th-century cellarer's accounts and visitations suggest that there were many guests of various sorts resident in the priory.[10] The nuns also provided a priest for the parish church of St James the Apostle, Carrow, apparently on or adjacent to the priory site. It had disappeared by Blomefield's time, though he reports its site was an area called the Churchyard.[11] The origin of the name Carrow is disputed; it might refer to the bend in the river, a 'carr', beside the hill or howe,[12] but Blomefield gives six alternative spellings, including Kairo.[13] It is certainly a hilltop site, and unless there were as many trees as today, the church must have been very visible from the city below.

Although reputedly pious and thought to be sympathetic to the reformed orders, Stephen was not a renowned ecclesiastical patron.[14] His principal foundation at Faversham in 1148 was for Cluniac Benedictine monks and he intended it to become a dynastic mausoleum.[15] He was the sole founder of Savignac Furness Abbey, Lancashire, in 1127, when Count of Boulogne and Mortain (the latter county includes Savigny), and then with Queen Mathilda he founded Savignac Coggeshall Abbey, Essex, in 1140.[16] His only other nunnery, the Benedictine Higham Priory in Kent, seems to have been founded for his daughter Mary, its first prioress.[17] Smaller foundations include the Augustinian priory of Thornholme in Lincolnshire[18] and the Templar preceptory at Eagle in the same county.[19] Little survives of any of the buildings built in his lifetime, so no clear conclusions can be drawn on Stephen's architectural interests, though it can be surmised that Faversham was much more decorated and grandiose than Furness or Coggeshall (which both follow Savignac austerity). His promotion of the reforming Savignacs might simply be due to their mother house being in his county of Mortain.[20] Stephen had no obvious connection with Norwich and it would be interesting to know how Seyna and Lescelina attracted his attention and patronage. Perhaps they were known to his daughter Mary?[21] Whatever the circumstances, Stephen's benefaction quickly attracted many more small-scale donations from the citizens of Norwich, and Carrow Priory continued to receive support from the citizens throughout its existence.[22]

Following Blomefield, it is often stated that Carrow was originally founded for a prioress and nine nuns, but no further authority is given for these numbers.[23] On his visitation in 1492, Bishop Goldwell questioned a prioress and twelve mainly elderly nuns. At the Dissolution in 1536, there was a prioress and eight nuns.[24] Blomefield describes the priory running a successful girls' school for the wealthy families of Norwich and Norfolk, but with no other evidence, this seems to be one of his creative inventions. The anchoress St Julian of Norwich might have been a nun there as a number of documents refer to anchoresses at Carrow and the church of St Julian had been appropriated by the priory.[25]

The 1535 *Valor Ecclesiasticus* reckoned the priory was worth £64 16s. 6d., a lot less than Norwich at over £1,000 and about a fifth of the value of male monasteries of similar scale and age like Castle Acre or Thetford. It was much wealthier, though, than the other four Norfolk nunneries at Blackborough and Thetford (Benedictine), Marham (Cistercian) and Crabhouse (Augustinian).[26] The Suppression Commissioners found there were eight religious persons at Carrow in 'a priory of very good name', with seventeen other persons: two priests, seven male and eight female servants. The house was in very good repair, the bells and lead worth £145 and the moveable goods £40 16s. 11d.[27] The site was sold to Sir John Shelton in 1538; he made his house out of the prioress Isobel Wygun's west range buildings that still survive, but he dismantled the rest to sell as building materials. In the 1730s, Blomefield thought 'the site within the walls contained about ten acres, the church was large, tho' so far demolished that it was with difficulty I found its site' — but clearly enough did survive for him to locate it.[28]

EXCAVATION HISTORY

A visit in 1879 by the British Archaeological Association to the Shelton house then called Carrow Abbey (occupied by J. H. Tillett Esq. MP), prompted an excavation of the priory church.[29] It was undertaken by J. J. Colman MP of the mustard family, owner of the adjacent property Carrow House. He gave the job to Mr A. S. King, an assistant in the Building Department of his Carrow mustard works that had occupied the riverside site below since the 1850s.[30] King cleared the meadow of soil to a depth of several feet, reportedly 'allowing nothing to be disturbed or destroyed'. The Colman family papers include photographs of the excavations in progress. Comparing them with what survives on site today strongly suggests that the surviving ruins have not been rebuilt or reassembled.[31]

On behalf of J. J. Colman, the BAA's Honorary Secretary E. Loftus Brock then read a paper on the excavations to the Association in December 1881. When this was published in the *Journal* the following year,[32] it was illustrated with drawings of the exposed piers and arcading clearly based on the excavation photographs (compare 'Fig. 3' in Figs 1 and 2), some sketches of architectural details (Fig. 3) and included a fulsome description of the site.[33] Loftus Brock also published a small-scale plan 'prepared with very great care by Mr King that may be relied on' (Fig. 3).[34] The original of this plan or indeed any other large-scale plans have not been located — a pity, as the dimensions Loftus Brock gives in the article do not accord with those given in the second article published by the Diocesan Surveyor, Richard Makilwaine Phipson in *Norfolk Archaeology* in 1884. Phipson's plan was drawn up by his 'old friend W G Wallis' in November 1881 and is described as a 'most accurate plan of all that has been exposed'.[35] However, Phipson also states 'on this skeleton, I have tried to build up in the best way I can, some of the parts wanting'.[36] This second plan needs to be used with caution but has been the basis of most published plans since. Phipson also illustrated mouldings, sections and stones; comparison with pieces of stonework visible on site confirms the accuracy of the detail drawings in both articles.

Loftus Brock reports that the church had been recovered 'except a portion of the nave and west end, where the whole had been removed'.[37] Phipson reports that 'part of the west wall has been rebuilt', but the blind arcading of the aisle walls 'returned round the west end'.[38] A third account by Tillett and Rye written in 1882 disputes the line drawn by Phipson.[39] These different interpretations might explain the discrepancy of some of the architectural dimensions between the authors. Like everyone else, Phipson

FIG. 1.   Carrow Priory: illustration from Loftus Brock article in *JBAA*, 38 (1882). 'Fig. 3' the
south-east nave pier is the only one found, presumed to survive under grass; 'Fig. 4' the south-east
crossing pier viewed from the south-west; 'Fig. 5' the bases of the sanctuary arch south respond

noted that only one pier of the nave was left, 'the south east one' and 'no foundations of
the rest remained'. Nevertheless, 'after consideration and comparison with other
churches of the same date' he created a nave arcade of seven bays.[40] As the south aisle
wall apparently had no responds, this must be an informed guess based on the distance
between the south-east nave pier and the remains of the south-west crossing pier. That

FIG. 2.   Carrow Priory: 1881 excavation
photograph of the south-east nave pier
*Reproduced by kind permission of Unilever from
an original in Unilever Archives*

165

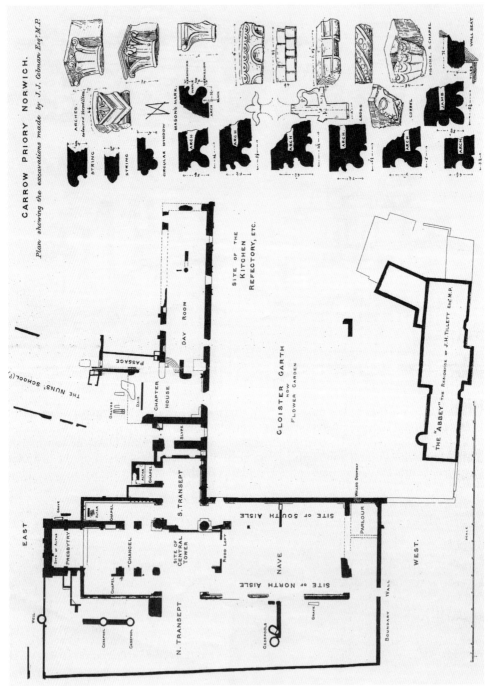

FIG. 3.   Carrow Priory: Loftus Brock plan and details from *JBAA*, 38 (1882)

'very perfect' south-east nave pier (Fig. 2) should still survive below the grass beyond the Abbey Dining Room 'built as a light structure without foundations, occasioning no harm to the remains' of the nave in 1968.[41] Although numerous artefacts (including a 13th-century acoustic jar) were recovered from the site of the nave, no account of any archaeological work seems to have been written.

A measured plan that also shows the dimensions given by Phipson was published by Eric Fernie for the Royal Archaeological Institute's 1979 Summer Meeting in Norwich.[42] It is acknowledged to be based on the 1881 plan by Wallis.[43] In 1981 the ruins (having become a scheduled ancient monument) were again exposed and consolidated under the archaeological supervision of the Norwich Survey (Fig. 4). Eleven burials uncovered but not disturbed in 1881 were excavated. All proved to be females except one, whose contents showed it to be a 14th-century priest's burial.[44]

THE 12TH-CENTURY CONTEXT

In his article, Loftus Brock states the total internal length 'within the walls' is 175 ft 9 in., but measured on his (small-scale) plan, the figure is nearer 197 ft. This is close to the total figure of 195 ft 6 in. that Phipson's measurements suggest. Unfortunately, the two authors' other measurements also differ by inches, but they were interpreting

FIG. 4.   Carrow Priory: view looking south-east towards the south transept in 2013
Photo: author

ruined walls and foundations. The stated Loftus Brock measurements are probably the more accurate (despite the discrepancy described above) as they were presumably taken by the site excavator, Mr King. They give an overall internal width of the nave and aisles as 53 ft 3 in. and the internal width of the south transept 23 ft 3 in. These dimensions and proportions are similar to the churches of the Romanesque Cluniac priories at Thetford (210 ft, 60 ft, 23 ft) and Castle Acre (190 ft, 56 ft, 24 ft); as these are both of an earlier generation they have an apsidal rather than square end to the sanctuary and chapels. The Carrow dimensions are also similar to the contemporary churches of the Augustinian priories of St Augustine, Bristol, founded 1140 (210 ft, 58 ft and 29 ft) or St Frideswide, Oxford being built around 1160 (203 ft, 54 ft and 21 ft). Both the latter have square east ends with a sanctuary projecting beyond an aisled chancel, short transepts with eastern chapels and aisled naves.

It is possible that at least the two eastern protruding bays of the east end at Carrow functioning as the sanctuary were covered by a vault. The present ruins and both post-excavation plans show that the wall between the chancel and St John's chapel to the south was solid east of the two choir bays next to the crossing with a width of at least 5 ft, certainly thicker than the aisle outer wall which was under 4 ft. The plinth for blind arcading at dado level survived on the south.[45] Both plans also show four bases for wall masts towards the chancel (and on the first free-standing choir pier), but there is now little evidence on site for them. This strongly suggests that at least the four easternmost rectangular bays, if not the whole east end, were vaulted. Phipson concluded that there was no 'stone groining' because 'I cannot find any signs of abutments strong enough to resist such a thrust and the walls themselves are comparatively thin'.[46] However, there are external pilaster buttresses behind the existing sanctuary wall responds which, with the wall width and by comparison, would surely be good enough to support main space vaulting at a modest height.[47]

The external east wall is divided into three equal bays which could imply an elevation like the transept ends of the cathedral. However, three thinner buttresses on the exterior east wall of St Nicholas, Castle Hedingham, Essex of c. 1180 sit below a wheel window, the buttresses terminating at mid-wall height.[48] St Frideswide's Oxford had rib vaults over rectangular bays at a height of about 38 ft with pilaster buttresses and a wall width of about 4 ft. It also had a round east window. The lack of comparative material in East Anglia is frustrating; the great abbey churches appear to have had only apse and aisle vaults, with rib vaults appearing in Peterborough aisles by 1120. Perhaps the squaring off of apses in the mid-12th century as at Colne Benedictine Priory, Essex and Ely Cathedral might indicate the use of rib vaults allowing larger, even circular, east windows.[49] Loftus Brock draws a section through a small 'circular window' (Fig. 3). The only surviving main space late-12th-century vaults in East Anglia are those at the west end of Peterborough Cathedral (where aisles were rib-vaulted from c. 1120), with smaller c. 1175 rib vaults over the sanctuary of the monastic infirmary chapel at Ely and over the east bay of St Thomas' parish church at Ramsey, a building associated with the adjacent Benedictine abbey.[50] A small rib vault can be found in the fore-building, 'Bigod's Tower', at Norwich Castle,[51] and the undercroft of Wensum Lodge Norwich also has large rectangular rib vaults of about 1130. There is enough evidence, admittedly only at ground level, to suggest that the sanctuary of Carrow was rib vaulted c. 1150. No stonework from such a vault has been certainly identified, but the east range undercroft was vaulted and there are large amounts of lightweight tufa stone on site.

Superficially, the Carrow plan is reminiscent of the Bernardine plan used by the Cistercians from the 1140s. Surviving mid-12th-century abbey churches like (Savignac) Buildwas (Shropshire) and Kirkstall (Yorkshire) have vaulted sanctuaries over solid walls with a single unaisled east bay. The nearest Cistercian houses were at Sibton (Suffolk, f. 1150), Sawtry (Cambs., f. 1147) and Tilty (Essex, f. 1153), all three daughter houses of Warden Abbey (Beds.), itself founded from Rievaulx Abbey (Yorks., c. 1140). Sawtry and Tilty had two chapels to each transept flanking a short chancel with solid walls. However, Carrow had just one transept chapel (from the evidence of the south) and this was originally separated from the choir aisle by an open space.[52] The plan was therefore more like an early-12th-century plan, such as Thetford, but with a single square rather than apsidal chapel to the east of each transept arm. This, with the distance between Carrow and these Cistercian houses and their apparently later 12th-century builds, makes clear that the Carrow plan was not influenced by a Cistercian model.

More importantly, perhaps, Carrow was a nunnery and would have employed priests to celebrate mass for the nuns. There was therefore no need for chapels as in a male monastery where some monks would have been priests and needed altars to fulfil their obligation to celebrate Mass daily. Quite how many priests were engaged is not known; two are listed at the Suppression and Carrow was responsible for St James' parish church in the precinct and for supplying chaplains for the cross in Norwich market place.[53] No clear parallels can be found in the plans of other 12th-century English nun's churches with transepts, though most seem to have chapels flanking the chancel.[54] The south choir chapel was dedicated to St John the Baptist, the north chapel to St Catherine.[55]

As it had bells in 1538, there was probably a crossing tower, as the plan precludes western towers.[56] The south-east crossing pier is the only one to remain with sufficient details to determine its form ('Fig. 4' of Fig. 1). It belongs to the East Anglian compound pier type that incorporates a substantial segmental column, here on the east towards the south choir arcade and more unusually to the south, facing into the south choir aisle. Sufficient of the corresponding south aisle respond survives to see that it, too, was a column segment. The west face of the crossing pier is formed of three equal but separated half-shafts; the same forms can be seen on the crossing piers at Binham Priory and Attleborough. The north face towards the choir is reconstructed by Phipson as a segmental column because the surviving flintwork (now outlined in concrete) extends to a similar depth as the east face. This would be unique[57] and the more cautious Loftus Brock does not attempt a reconstruction. He also reports evidence for the nuns' stalls subsequently running across the architectural crossing.[58] I suggest, then, that there was a flat face at ground level, but, like the pier in the same position at Castle Acre, shafts rose from a corbel above the stalls.

Wall arcades seem to have lined all the internal walls, another feature common to the major churches of East Anglia,[59] but at Carrow they stand on a substantial bench with a prominent moulded string-course — unlike the cathedral, for instance, where the arcades stand on a low plinth. Romanesque church doorways in Norfolk often place their jamb shafts on a high plinth (Hales, Chedgrave) and this practice continues into the 13th century (the wall arcading of Burgh-next-Aylsham chancel). Phipson claimed the arcading 'returned around the west end',[60] but Loftus Brock only reported it along the south nave aisle (though his plan indicates a bench on the north aisle wall, too). No responds interrupt this arcading in the surviving St John's chapel, so any vault there or in the nave aisles would have risen from corbels. The chancel, south chapel and south transept wall arcading share the same moulding to their plinth and this also appears in the north-east corner of the cloister. Wall shafts or responds in the chancel and south transept stand in front of the wall bench, but their plinth moulding is simpler and corresponds to the plinth moulding of the arcade and crossing piers. There is therefore a discontinuity at the junctions of these plinth mouldings, but this is not to be interpreted as a building break as the masonry above courses through.[61]

The surviving bases suggest two successive phases of work, probably without much of a time lapse between them. The base of the sanctuary bay arch respond has an upright profile which is widely used in Norfolk (Fig. 5 and 'Fig. 5' of Fig. 1). The base of the smaller shaft of the adjacent wall arcading is a 'reversed capital': an upside-down cubic capital.[62] Similar reversed capitals can also be seen on the nook shafts to the external pilaster buttresses of the sanctuary and south chancel walls, St John's chapel and the south transept chapel. These bases might be a form of the *congé* feature as described by Viollet-le-Duc in his *Dictionnaire*[63] and usually seen on small engaged shafts.[64] However, bases formed with reversed capitals are seen on a number of Romanesque fonts in Norfolk, such as Toftrees and Burnham Norton, and in minor architectural contexts such as the throne of the seated figure over the south door at Haddiscoe.[65] Architecturally, they start to appear in mid- to late-12th-century work like the tribune gallery openings at Binham Priory nave and the slype at Thetford Priory (where they sit on a moulded plinth very like that at Carrow). The consistent use of these bases therefore suggests that the whole east end is of one build started around the time of the reported founding in 1146.

The sole wall arcade base to survive inside St John's chapel belongs to the type defined by Stuart Rigold as 'the quintessential neo-Attic form'[66] present in the early Gothic buildings of the Ile de France by 1140: the base mouldings of the south-east crossing pier and respond are also of this group.[67] For Rigold, 'Christ Church Canterbury in 1174 might not have been the first English work of high patronage to use it' (and he notes similar bases at St Augustine's Canterbury, rebuilding after 1168) 'but from about that time there was no self-respecting alternative in either country'.

The profile of the surviving south respond of the arch to the south nave aisle is also of this type, but its scotia contains vertical nicks (Fig. 6). These nicks are also present on the wall arcade bases of the east wall of the south transept, probably indicating a slightly later phase of work. Although prominently used on the bases of the Portail Royale on the west front of Chartres Cathedral, such nicked scotias are otherwise

FIG. 5.   Carrow Priory: upright base of the sanctuary arch south respond and reversed capital base of the adjacent blind arcading (and see Fig. 1.5 above)
Photo: author

FIG. 6.   Carrow Priory: nicked
scotia base of the south aisle
respond at the junction of the
south nave aisle and south
transept
Photo: author

FIG. 7.   Wensum Lodge: base of
arcade respond
Photo: author

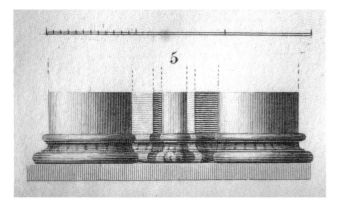

FIG. 8.   Norwich Cathedral:
infirmary pier base 1804 by
Repton
*Reproduced by kind permission of the
Society of Antiquaries*

rather rare.[68] In England, there are examples at St Frideswide's Priory Oxford, *c.* 1160 (west respond, south chancel arcade), Rousham in north Oxfordshire (south nave arcade) and Southwark Cathedral (south west respond, south nave arcade and excavated cloister bases). More pertinently for Carrow, examples can be seen in the arcades of the infirmary of Norwich Cathedral and Wensum Lodge (the Music House) in King Street (Fig. 7). The date of the latter is not known, and assertions that it was built for the Jewish merchant, Jurnet, just before 1177 have been questioned.[69]

According to the First Register, the infirmary was built by Bishop John of Oxford by 1183 to replace that burnt down in 1171.[70] It was demolished in 1804 and so only some of the piers of its south arcade remain in a car park. Repton (who drew it soon after it was demolished) records paint and gilding to the capitals and arches and his drawings show that the bases have been correctly restored (Fig. 8).[71] A few stones remain in the cathedral stone collection[72] and some mouldings are incorporated into a garden feature erected by Dr Philip Martineau, now in the grounds of County Hall.[73] The infirmary arch mouldings incorporate keeling often accompanied by a sharply undercut hollow, a combination found on a number of mouldings recovered at Carrow (Fig. 3). No mouldings or capitals survive at Wensum Lodge, but the base measurements are similar to both the infirmary and Carrow, and its heavy shaft rings are similar to those on some

FIG. 9.   Norwich Cathedral: infirmary pier 2013
Photo: author

infirmary piers. Given the use of the rare nicked scotia, it must be presumed that all three buildings are by the same workshop working in Norwich around 1180.[74] It would not be unreasonable then to think that the east end of Carrow was built from 1146 to *c*. 1180, with the eastern nave and south transept west wall following on without a break and to the original plan.[75]

The only known nave pier base at Carrow, now apparently buried under grass, is probably later in date than the infirmary piers but continues their creative use of shafts (Figs 2 and 9). This square pier is composed of eight shafts, three per side, separated by wide hollow mouldings; the smaller central shaft was keeled.[76] Its base moulding is deeper and so more waterholding than those of the south-west transept bases (Fig. 6) and it has no nicks; the leaf spurs are clearly of stiff leaf. It was surely in place well before 1244 when two bishops were consecrated in the church.[77]

FROM ROMANESQUE TO EARLY GOTHIC

THESE conclusions are of course drawn from — at most — the lowest 4 ft of the building. The excavations recovered a number of later 12th-century mouldings and capitals, though it is not recorded where they were found and only a selection was drawn for the two publications (Fig. 3). An 1881 photograph of a stone pile (Fig. 10) and an NMR photo of 1952[78] show all these drawn details and others. Given the poor level of information retrieved in the nave and north transept, it would seem likely that these stones

FIG. 10.   Carrow Priory: 1881 excavation photograph of stones piled on top of the south-east crossing pier

Reproduced by kind permission of Unilever from an original in Unilever Archives

FIG. 11. Selection of stones in the garden dump of the Abbey Conference Centre, 2013
Photo: author

come from the east arm and probably the south transept and crossing area where most architectural remains survive. Unfortunately, these stones are now distributed around the garden beds and in the gardener's dump of the Abbey Conference Suite (Fig. 11). Of the capitals, only the broken waterleaf capital drawn by Loftus Brock is now visible (Fig. 3), but the small (roughly 150 mm square) scalloped capital of a pillar piscina survives (Figs 3, 10).[79] Just one of the many excavated foliated lateral chevron voussoirs which Loftus Brock notes as 'coloured vermilion' remains on site (Figs 3, 11). The surviving decorative stonework includes typical Norfolk Romanesque features like radial billet, cusped hood moulding, foliated and plain lateral chevron and a plain version of the enlarged billet used in the cathedral cloister.[80]

However, the survival of many late-12th-century mouldings and the discovery of waterleaf and crocket capitals (that from their size are likely to come from the dado arcading), suggests that the south transept at least was built with early Gothic details. At least six stiff leaf crocket capitals are visible in the 1952 photo alongside some waterleaf and cubic capitals.[81] A very similar early Gothic vocabulary can be seen in the outer porch of the Prior's Lodgings at Castle Acre, dated to *c.* 1180–90 (Fig. 12).[82] The crocket capitals, lateral chevron and deeply hollowed and keeled mouldings are much like those at Carrow. Some of the tribune arches of Binham nave have similar mouldings, attic bases and leaf spur bases, but the crocket capitals are crudely carved. The same vocabulary (without chevron) is used and developed in the ruined north transept of Bromholm Cluniac Priory, 20 miles north-east of Norwich, probably built by the time formal independence from Castle Acre came in 1195.[83] The eastern wall at Bromholm is slightly earlier than the rest, but it is noticeable that the pointed arches to the east transept chapel and to the north nave aisle opposite rise from scalloped corbels, both flanked by crocket capitals (Fig. 13). Round and pointed arches are used side by side on the east and west wall clerestories and, though it appears that the east transept chapel and the north choir aisle were vaulted, the main space was not.

The Cistercians have long been credited as the 'missionaries of Gothic', bringing the new style from northern France to England before the rebuilding of Canterbury

FIG. 12.   Castle Acre Priory: outer porch of the Prior's Lodgings
Photo: author

Cathedral choir by William of Sens after 1174.[84] The only Cistercian abbey in Norfolk, for nuns, was not founded at Marham until 1246; neither are there any houses of reformed Augustinian canons.[85] The nearest Cistercians to Norwich were 30 miles to the south at Sibton Abbey, Suffolk. The big Benedictine houses had a monopoly in the county — indeed, most of East Anglia — by the middle of the 12th century and they had, by and large, completed their churches by 1150. There was nevertheless great wealth in the county and, as elsewhere, there must have been many late-12th-century building projects in parish churches, but hardly anything survives. A re-sited pointed arch door at Shipdham is of about 1170 and its nook shafts stand on a high base with a prominent moulding in Norfolk fashion and have late Romanesque capitals. A good generation later, the south door of East Tuddenham has mature stiff leaf on its capitals and hood moulding, but includes an order of highly attenuated chevron with a fine fillet to the central roll moulding; a similar chevron might have existed at Carrow, from a stone visible in the 1952 photo.[86]

The main parallels quoted for Carrow are located in monastic and secular buildings, and again there were major projects in Norfolk now only known from documentary sources. William Turbe (bishop of Norwich 1146/7–74) built a new chapter-house in 1148 and completed his palace with a great hall amongst other works following the 1171 monastery fire. His successor John of Oxford (1175–1200) built the infirmary

RICHARD HALSEY

FIG. 13.   Bromholm Priory: pointed arch of the north choir aisle rising from scalloped corbels
with the blocked clerestory windows and small pointed arch in the west wall of the north
transept beyond

Photo: author

before 1183. Both men were well travelled in northern Europe on State and Church business, and Turbe especially was closely associated with the royal court.[87] Henry II was a prolific builder and, having lived in France before his accession, might be expected to be aware of architecture there. The Norwich infirmary arcades and that at Wensum Lodge may be looking for inspiration to one of his aisled stone halls, such as Clarendon or Woodstock.[88] A major loss for eastern England in this period is Henry's enormous extension of Waltham Abbey after 1177, although the Exchequer seemed to have stopped funding it after 1184.[89] Another ancient Benedictine house, the abbey of St Benet Holme east of Norwich, built a new cloister, chapter-house and dormitory in the decades after 1151.[90]

Bromholm appears to be the largest surviving example of late-12th-century architecture in Norfolk, which from its illogical use of round and pointed arches, corbels decorated with scallops alongside crocket capitals and early Gothic mouldings, can with hindsight be termed 'Transitional'.[91] There are other instances of old and new forms being used together in the region in the last decades of the 12th century. At Denny Abbey (Cambs.), scallop and waterleaf capitals face each other across window jamb shafts. At Binham, some tribune arches have a scallop capital facing a crocket. Little is known of

176

the buildings of Cistercian Sibton Abbey (f. 1150), but an arch to the refectory rises from scallop corbels much like Bromholm and the refectory windows had round arches. An excavated capital from Sibton has fleshy broad leaf decoration with beading, not unlike the Norwich infirmary capitals.[92] This type of leaf may have been developed locally rather than being imported from France; capitals at St Bartholomew's Orford, *c*. 1165, are quite similar.[93]

Their random use suggests that features we now associate with the early Gothic architecture of northern France (waterleaf and crocket capitals, keeled and deeply hollowed mouldings, leaf spurs to neo-attic bases) were simply seen as new decorative forms rather than as parts of a new architectural style. This use of architectural details suggests that it was masons aware of new features who started to introduce them, rather than patrons wanting to emulate the architecture of the reformed orders or adopt a whole new style using rib-vaulted main spaces. In Norfolk, then, these details apparently arrived from France through work at individual buildings. Canterbury Cathedral may have become a source after 1174: Bromholm and Carrow show the bell rim and tight corner crockets seen in the smaller capitals there. However, whilst the repertoire of moulding profiles is broadly similar, neither of the Norfolk priories use dogtooth, chevron or billet decoration or (as far as can be seen) Purbeck marble, which seems to rule out Canterbury as a model.[94] From the Carrow evidence, it looks likely that such details were coming to Norfolk before Canterbury made any impact.

The paucity of evidence means that Norfolk is not seen as a place to study the introduction of early Gothic architecture, but that does not mean that it did not happen. Here (as perhaps elsewhere in England), without the Cistercians to show the way, it seems that details from northern France came to East Anglia piecemeal, initially as new sources of decoration. We now surmise that the Early English style of Lincoln and then Ely were most influential, but there are clear signs that Benedictine houses like Carrow and especially Cluniac Bromholm were already looking across the Channel for ideas in the 1170s and 1180s.

ACKNOWLEDGEMENTS

I am grateful to Mike Canham, Conference and Dining Rooms Manager of Unilever, for arranging access to the Carrow Priory site and to Jonathan Deane for granting access to Bromholm Priory. Josette Reeves, Assistant Archivist at Unilever Archives and Records Management, was most helpful in identifying and arranging for the licence to reproduce the photographs of the 1881 excavations. Stephen Heywood, Brian Ayers and Tim Pestell willingly answered my often obscure questions and efficiently pointed me in the right direction for the answers. My thanks to Graham Phillips for preparing the figures.

NOTES

1. Blomefield, *Norfolk*, IV, 524–30.

2. Ibid., 524, 'In 1388, John Downe was buried in the *abbey* church as it was even then called'.

3. Although often said to be the second biggest church in Norwich after the cathedral, e.g. B. Ayers, *Norwich: Archaeology of a Fine City* (Stroud 2009), 87, the whole of Blackfriars church was 215 ft long, even if formed of two spaces separated by the passageway.

4. Quoted by W. Rye, *Carrow Abbey* (1889) Appendix i, from Tanner MS 342 f. 149v. 'Sorores moniales de hospitalis' has been taken to mean two blood sisters, e.g., E. A. Tillett, *Norwich Hamlets IV, Carrow*, 21 (Norwich Local Studies Collection, unpublished scrapbook, *c*. 1905).

5. H. A. Cronne and R. H. C. Davis ed. *Regesta Regum Anglo-Normannorum* (Oxford 1968), III, no. 615.

6. C. Rawcliffe, *The Hospitals of Mediaeval Norwich* (Norwich 1995), 142.

7. Ibid., 41–47 and Rye, *Carrow Abbey* (as in n. 4), 2. The leper hospital of St Mary Magdalene was founded by Herbert de Losinga before 1119 to the north of the city; its infirmary is now Sprowston branch library. For the Norman Norwich hospitals, see also Ayers, *Norwich* (as in n. 3), 82–83.

8. T. Pestell, *The Establishment of Religious Houses in East Anglia c.650–1200* (Woodbridge 2004), 193.

9. R. Gilchrist, *Gender and Material Culture: The Archaeology of Religious Women* (London and New York 1994), 33. It is possible that Bishop William Turbe promoted the priory, perhaps from personal knowledge of the nuns as he was a monk of Norwich and was 'particularly solicitous of the welfare of nuns'. C. Harper-Bill, 'William [William Turbe] (*c.*1095–1174)', *ODNB*, online edn, 2004, http://www.oxforddnb.com/view/article/29466 [accessed 3 December 2013].

10. C. Harper-Bill and C. Rawcliffe, 'The Religious Houses', in *Medieval Norwich*, 73–119 at 95–101.

11. Blomefield, *Norfolk*, IV, 524. In 1880 this referred to the field containing the foundations of the priory church (E. Loftus Brock, 'On the excavations of the site of Carrow Abbey, by J. J. Colman Esq. M.P. in 1880–81', *JBAA*, 38 (1882), 168), so the church of St James was probably in the priory precinct. By his will of 1449, Robert Everard, chaplain of Carrow, directed that he be buried in the 'parish church of Carrowe, in front of the altar of St James' (Rye, *Carrow Abbey* (as in n. 4), Appendix IX, xxix).

12. Tillett, *Norwich Hamlets* (as in n. 4), 14 who points out that carr and hoh can both mean a rock or hill.

13. Blomefield, *Norfolk*, IV, 525. Carhoe, Carrow, Kairo, Carhow, Car-hou 'and sometime Car-Dieu'.

14. E. King, *King Stephen* (New Haven and London 2010), 301–03.

15. VCH, *Kent*, II, ed. W. Page (London 1926), 141.

16. VCH, *Essex*, II, ed. W. Page and J. H. Round (London 1907), 128.

17. VCH, *Kent*, II (as in n. 15), 145–46.

18. VCH, *Lincolnshire*, II, ed. W. Page (London 1906), 166–68.

19. Ibid., 210.

20. Edmund King, 'Stephen (*c.*1092–1154)', *ODNB*, online edn, September 2010, http://www.oxforddnb.com/view/article/26365 [accessed 3 December 2013].

21. S. P. Thompson, 'Mary, suo jure countess of Boulogne (*d.* 1182)', *ODNB*, online edn, October 2006, http://www.oxforddnb.com/view/article/54455 [accessed 3 December 2013].

22. Harper-Bill and Rawcliffe, 'Religious Houses' (as in n. 10), 88–101. See also n. 9.

23. VCH, *Norfolk*, II, 352 goes as far as to say 'originally nine [...] afterwards increased to twelve'.

24. Ibid.

25. Ibid.

26. Blackborough £42 6s. 7½d., St George Thetford £40 11s. 2½d., Marham (Cistercian) £39 0s. 1¾d., Crabhouse (Augustinian) £30 6s. 2d. VCH, *Norfolk*, II.

27. Ibid., 354.

28. Blomefield, *Norfolk*, IV, 527.

29. Proceedings of the Great Yarmouth Congress, *JBAA*, 36 (1880), 346–47 and Loftus Brock, 'Excavations' (as in n. 11), 165–66.

30. R. M. Phipson, 'Notes on Carrow Priory, Norwich', *NA*, 9 (1884), 216. Carrow Abbey and the Priory site belonged to the Martineau family until J. & J. Colman Ltd bought it in 1878. The house was converted into the Abbey Conference Centre in 1968 and since 1995 the whole site has belonged to Unilever.

31. Unilever Archives and Records Management, Colman's collection, Acc. 1996/127. A small area of the east cloister wall appears to have been rebuilt as it includes stones inscribed with modern initials and numbers.

32. Loftus Brock, 'Excavations' (as in n. 11).

33. Another paper by Canon Edmund Venables, Precentor of Norwich Cathedral was delivered to the Royal Archaeological Institute in May 1882, but not published.

34. Loftus Brock, 'Excavations' (as in n. 11), 176.

35. Phipson, 'Notes' (as in n. 30), 217.

36. Ibid.

37. Loftus Brock, 'Excavations' (as in n. 11), 169 and 176.

38. Phipson, 'Notes' (as in n. 30), 220.

39. Rye, *Carrow Abbey* (as in n. 4), 26, reprinted from *The Norfolk Antiquarian Miscellany*, vol. II, pt ii (1883), 465–98.

40. Phipson, 'Notes' (as in n. 30), 219.

41. E. Fernie, 'Carrow Priory, Norwich', *Archaeol. J.*, 137 (1980), 291. However, a deep basement was created beyond the west and north walls of the nave.

42. Ibid.

43. A typo credits 'Willis' as the plan's author.

44. M. Atkin and S. Margeson, 'A 14th century pewter chalice and paten from Carrow Priory, Norwich', *NA*, 38 (1983), 374–80.

45. Visible in an 1881 photograph but no longer extant.

46. Phipson, 'Notes' (as in n. 30), 220.

47. The pilaster buttresses have nook shafts, following the example of Norwich Cathedral and other Romanesque churches in Norfolk.

48. B/E, *Essex*, ed. J. Bettley and N. Pevsner (New Haven and London 2007), 195. A very large round west window exists at St Botolph's Priory church in Colchester, which, if contemporary with the door below, is mid-12th-century and so 'the earliest major round window in England', ibid., 271. It could have supplied the model for Castle Hedingham.

49. E. Fernie, *The Architecture of Norman England* (Oxford 2000), 251–52, notes that the sort of square ended sanctuary bay seen at Carrow existed in Anglo-Saxon English churches and exceptionally at Rochester Cathedral *c.* 1083 and Southwell Minster *c.* 1110. A. W. Clapham, *English Romanesque Architecture after the Conquest* (Oxford 1934), 75, suggests that square-ended chapels and chancel are 'more economical to build and easier to roof than the usual apsidal form' and 'the square ended presbytery extending a bay or more beyond the aisles was the favourite type [of plan] in the churches of the Austin Canons', 92.

50. The aisled chancel of the church at Orford (Suffolk) begun around 1165 had rib-vaulted aisles and the protruding unaisled east bay could have been rib vaulted too.

51. This may have been in place for the king's visit in 1121. T. A. Heslop, *Norwich Castle Keep: Romanesque architecture and social context* (Norwich 1994), 8.

52. The external plinth of the south aisle survives in what is now a 'small compartment of later construction, approached from the south transept'. Rye, *Carrow Abbey* (as in n. 4), 26. Unfortunately, the south chapel is labelled 'sacristy' on most plans, following Phipson's interpretation.

53. Rye, *Carrow Abbey* (as in n. 4), 5. See also Atkin and Margeson, 'chalice and paten' (as in n. 44).

54. Both Barking and Romsey Benedictine abbeys rebuilt in the early decades of the 12th century had a single apsidal chapel to each transept, but contiguous with the choir aisle. A. W. Clapham, 'The Benedictine Abbey of Barking', *Essex Archaeological Transactions*, 12 (1913), 69–89. Romsey plan in Fernie, *Architecture of Norman England* (as in n. 49), fig. 136. Other nun's church plans in Gilchrist, *Gender* (as in n. 9).

55. At first sight, St John the Baptist might seem an odd dedication for a nunnery, but it was quite common. See R. Gilchrist and M. Oliva, *Religious Women in Medieval East Anglia*, Studies in East Anglian History, 1 (Norwich 1993), 26–27. The great majority of pre-1200 nunneries are dedicated to St Mary sometimes linked (as here) with a male saint. Both Godstow (Oxon.) Benedictine abbey and Wintney (Hants.) Cistercian priory add St John Baptist, but Kilburn (Middlesex) Benedictine priory and Haliwell (Middlesex) Augustinian priory are dedicated to St John the Baptist alone.

56. Phipson, 'Notes' (as in n. 30), 220 describes the triangular lump of stone where a north-west tower pier might be expected as a 'lump of the original wall [...] pitched down [...] when the priory was destroyed'.

57. A large segmental column is recessed into the post-1107 crossing piers at Winchester, but rises from a corbel, leaving the lowest few feet flat to accommodate stalls.

58. Loftus Brock, 'Excavations' (as in n. 11), 174.

59. At Thetford, the exterior walls had similar arcading too.

60. Phipson, 'Notes' (as in n. 30), 220.

61. See base sections illustrated by Phipson, ibid.

62. S. E. Rigold, 'Romanesque bases, in and South-east of the Limestone Belt', in *Ancient Monuments and their interpretation; essays presented to A. J. Taylor*, ed. M. R. Apted, R. Gilyard-Beer and A. D. Saunders (Chichester 1977), 108.

63. Viollet le Duc, *Dictionnaire raisonné de l'architecture française du XIe au XVIe siècle* (Paris 1856). Illustrated in Rigold, 'Romanesque bases' (as in n. 62), 109 no. 3.

64. The use of this feature to terminate an arch moulding can be seen in the south arcade at Castle Hedingham church of about 1180 and in the wall arcading of the north transept of Bromholm Priory.

65. Further Norfolk examples are listed by M. Thurlby, 'The Influence of the Cathedral on Romanesque Architecture', in *Norwich Cathedral 1096–1996*, 136–57, at 146. The list includes small examples in the transept and nave clearstory of the cathedral, work presumably completed before 1119.

66. Rigold, 'Romanesque bases' (as in n. 62), 128.

67. See n. 59.

68. Rigold, 'Romanesque bases' (as in n. 62), 128.

69. Ayers, *Norwich* (as in n. 3), 66–67. E. A. Kent, 'Isaac's Hall or the Music House, Norwich', *NA*, 28 (1945), 31–38 was the first to suggest that these shafts formed the respond for a doorway into the Hall.

70. Gilchrist, *Close*, 166.

71. S. R. Pierce, *J. A. Repton: Norwich Cathedral at the End of the Eighteenth Century* (Farnborough 1968) is a large-scale reproduction of the original drawings. Repton also wrote an illustrated article 'XXXII. Description of the ancient Building at Norwich', etc., in *Archaeologia*, 15 (1806), 333–37, recording his visit shortly after demolition in 1804 that includes his reconstruction drawings. Gilchrist, *Close*, reproduces some of these and drawings by others.

72. Some described by Gilchrist, *Close*, 173.

73. List description for Archway at County Hall, Norwich, English Heritage Building ID 228738.

74. Kent, *Isaac's Hall* (as in n. 69), 35 thought the use of the nicked scotia here and in Wensum Lodge made it 'difficult to resist the conclusion that the two [...] were constructed by the same lodge of masons'. He also noted the same nicks at Carrow.

75. The same simple external plinth can be seen around all the extant church walls.

76. Phipson's drawing indicates an ogee keel, but this is not readily visible in other drawings or the 1881 photograph.

77. VCH, *Norfolk*, II, 352.

78. NMR photograph AA98/12708, dated 31 January 1952.

79. Loftus Brock, 'Excavations' (as in n. 11), reported it to be from the south transept east chapel.

80. A. Borg et al., *Mediaeval Sculpture from Norwich Cathedral*, Catalogue of 1980 exhibition at the Sainsbury Centre for Visual Arts, University of East Anglia, Norwich, entry 21 by J. Franklin. There are no other parallels in the decorated Romanesque stonework from Carrow and the cathedral.

81. The cubic capitals have astragals and so would not have been used as bases.

82. E. Impey, *Castle Acre Priory and Castle*, English Heritage guidebook (2008), 19. Rigold, 'Romanesque bases' (as in n. 62), 125, no. 199 shows the base moulding.

83. VCH, *Norfolk*, II, 359. Bromholm was founded April 1113 as a dependency of Castle Acre (itself founded 1089 from Lewes Priory), but from 1195 was dependent on Cluny itself.

84. C. Wilson, 'The Cistercians as "missionaries of Gothic" in Northern England', in *Cistercian Art and Architecture in the British Isles*, ed. C. Norton and D. Park (Cambridge 1986), 228–55. Professor Wilson has revised his views in 'Gothic Architecture Transplanted; the Nave of the Temple Church in London', in *The Temple Church in London; history, architecture and art*, ed. R Griffith-Jones and D. Park (Woodbridge 2010), 19–44, esp. 38 and n. 59. Research at York Minster by Christopher Norton and Stuart Harrison is also demonstrating that early Gothic features from northern France were present independently of Cistercian influence. S. Harrison and C. Norton, 'Reconstructing a lost cathedral; York Minster in the eleventh and twelfth centuries', *Ecclesiology Today*, 40 (July 2008), 53–59. Others like David Stocker and Glyn Coppack have also questioned this established view of the Cistercians in their studies of non-Cistercian sites.

85. Only Walsingham and Pentney of the pre-1189 Augustinian priories in the county were of any scale in the mid-12th-century. The earliest Premonstratensian house was at West Dereham, f. 1188.

86. A south nave arcade arch at Binham shows how the Carrow fragment could have been used.

87. See their entries in the *Oxford Dictionary of National Biography* by C. Harper-Bill.

88. R. A. Brown, H. M. Colvin and A. J. Taylor, *The History of the King's Works, The Middle Ages*, II (London 1963), 910–11, 1010.

89. Ibid., I, 88–89.

90. VCH, *Norfolk*, II, 330.

91. For the use of this term, see E. Sharpe, *The Seven Periods of English Architecture Defined and Illustrated* (London 1851); also F. Woodman, 'Transitional style', in *The Dictionary of Art*, ed. J. Turner, 34 vols (London and New York), XXXI, 283–85.

92. W. H. St J. Hope, 'Sibton Abbey', *Proceedings of the Suffolk Institute of Archaeology and Natural History*, 8 (1894), 54–60.

93. Further examples can be seen on the doors of Ubbeston and Cookley, all illustrated on the website of the Corpus of Romanesque Sculpture in the British Isles. A fleshy broad leaf can be seen in isolated examples throughout southern England such as the singular capital to the 1175 west respond of the south choir arcade at Canterbury.

94. The use of a few foliage capitals inspired by Canterbury in the north tribune of Peterborough Cathedral might be explained by the appointment of the Canterbury prior, Benedict, as abbot of Peterborough in 1177. However, his fully rib-vaulted west end uses scalloped capitals and makes extensive use of complex chevron, with marble only used for the west door trumeau.

Bishop John Salmon's Architectural Patronage at Norwich Cathedral

VERONICA SEKULES

The role of Bishop Salmon in the communal and spiritual development of Norwich Cathedral in the early 14th century promoted a new phase in its architecture and design, which brought Norwich into line with the latest developments and fashions. This paper considers the impact of contemporary events on his patronage and the ways they might have influenced relationships beyond the monastery and thus governed his policies. It also considers the extent to which his priorities served to bring the cathedral into the artistic mainstream, in terms of relationships within the East Anglian region, and how that plays a part in the development of a national 'court' style.

JOHN SALMON was bishop of Norwich from 1299 to 1325, as well as having onerous state duties as one of the Ordainers for Edward II from 1310 and chancellor of England from 1319. Surprisingly, he was one of only two Norwich bishops who was a monk, the other having been founding bishop, Herbert de Losinga. He was also one of only two bishops of the see who were venerated after their deaths, the other being Walter Suffield, the builder of the cathedral's Lady chapel and the Great Hospital.[1] Bishop Salmon clearly achieved something significant at Norwich, which earned him a posthumous claim to sanctity. One of the issues to be examined is the extent of his involvement in the development of the priory, given that he also had heavy administrative duties in royal service. Although his episcopate can be seen as permissive, with the bishop presiding over developments at the cathedral which were already in train, I shall argue for his more active and creative role, one where he had a vision for what Norwich could become and deliberately set out to rethink and expand the role of the cathedral priory, transforming current programmes of architectural renewal and initiating others.

John Salmon was a native of Ely, probably born in Meldreth. His father, sometimes called Solomon, was a goldsmith, who died in 1307.[2] John Salmon became prior of Ely in 1290, the year William of Louth acceded as bishop there. On the death of Bishop William, Salmon was elected by the majority of monks to succeed him but there was a dispute, as a minority preferred John Langton. The archbishop of Canterbury intervened immediately in 1299, moving Langton to Chichester, translating Bishop Walpole to Ely from Norwich (where he had been bishop 1288–99), and instating Salmon in Norwich. Subsequent to his appointment, Salmon was drawn into the royal service under Edward II. He was certainly part of a court circle, being both an official whom the king trusted, yet able to maintain a certain political detachment. He travelled often, to Rome as ambassador to the pope three times between 1305 and 1309, and to Avignon in 1316. He negotiated at the French court for the king's marriage in 1307 and was involved in diplomacy over Gascony and Aquitaine between 1310 and 1313. He was chancellor from 1319 to 1323, when he had to resign through ill health. He died in 1325 at Folkestone Priory on return from an ambassadorial trip to France.[3]

The primary role of any bishop was to be the head of his diocese, but for a monastic cathedral priory he could also play a key role as the head of the community, in effect acting as its abbot.[4] Broadly speaking, the bishop regulated the monastery's wider context both locally and for the diocese as a whole. He had overall responsibility for admissions of clergy and ordinations, undertook visitations to ensure the proper conduct of religious business and presided over the consistory court. The prior managed the priory, exercising day-to-day control, but it was the bishop who engaged in public service and made sure that mandates issued by the archbishop, the royal court and the papacy were properly enacted.

How this translated into the balance of responsibility for the physical development of the monastery is a moot point for there does not seem to have been any overall consistency of practice. At Norwich, the position of the bishop in relation to the monastery, as exemplified by its physical layout, has been represented as a power balance or a power struggle between bishop and prior. Roberta Gilchrist has highlighted their opposition as represented by the physical entities either side of the cathedral: with the prior's hall to south and the bishop's palace to north.[5] This point is worth emphasizing as, in the literature on Norwich, the bishops are credited with all the initiatives for building and might well have taken a particular interest and an unusual degree of responsibility.[6] This was not invariably the case elsewhere. At Ely, for example, significant building work gets both administered by and attributed to the sacrist under the prior: in the early 14th century those credited with architectural projects were respectively Alan of Walsingham and John Crauden.[7]

On the other hand, many bishops had, like Salmon, diplomatic roles to play nationally and internationally both within the Church but also in secular politics. There was, of course, a difference in the role and influence of the bishop depending on whether he presided over a monastic or a secular cathedral at the heart of the diocese, but generally bishops could play a powerful enabling role in major development projects, sourcing money for building work as well as raising aesthetic ambitions. Nicola Coldstream attributes the impetus for the growth of the Decorated style to the desire of bishops to enlarge, aggrandize and modernize.[8] Jean Bony had previously argued a similar point, but more in terms of a group of English bishops in the late 13th century whose patronage established a court style which in his view was both disseminated by and developed from French Rayonnant.[9] His view was that bishops enabled the development of a regional version of mainstream court taste which was manifest alike in large-scale projects, furnishing and tombs. The experience at Norwich under Bishop John Salmon seems to corroborate this view and is entirely consistent with the kind of ambition a bishop would gain as a leader of a large community in a wide area of the country, while simultaneously engaged in national politics, royal service and foreign travel. However, Salmon's origins as a monk who was the son of a goldsmith add an extra level of interest and knowledge. In early life he would have been both steeped in ritual devotion and acquainted with high-level making skills, which may well have given an additional edge to his experience and perhaps to his taste.

At Norwich during the first quarter of the 14th century, John Salmon is directly associated with three major building projects and campaigns:

- He commissioned and paid substantially towards the Carnary chapel, founding a college and perpetual chantry there
- He extended the bishop's palace

- He left a legacy for the continuation of the cloister, paying for part of the east and the south walks.

There were in addition other projects undertaken during his episcopate, with which he is likely to have been closely connected, although officially they would have been the province of the prior. This included continuing repair work necessitated by the 1272 riots, some of which became very much more ambitious than mere replacement building. For example, the belfry and the Ethelbert gate in the western close concerned the precinct's public face and, given the history of the bishops' engagement in town-monastery politics, would have involved him to some degree. There is also a substantial amount of undocumented work on the north aisle of the nave of the cathedral itself. It is likely that this work was undertaken during Salmon's episcopate as part of a wider campaign to provide and enhance access to the north of the cathedral towards what was to become the preaching yard, adjacent to the bishop's palace. With this I associate the vault paintings for the so-called ante-reliquary chapel. Their date is uncertain and, although a direct connection with Salmon's patronage is not demonstrable, their quality, style and subject matter are certainly consistent with ideas he was promoting in his other commissions.

Throughout this period there were clearly a number of different groups of masons employed at Norwich, among them great masons with court and London connections who must have contributed in no small measure to the quality and ambition of the work undertaken. Richard the Mason, otherwise Richard Curteys, was master in 1285–90. He was a king's servant and is likely to have worked on Norwich chapter-house.[10] He was father of William Ramsey I (master at Westminster), who was in turn the father of John Ramsey I. John Ramsey I is recorded as master in charge during the building of the belfry in 1303–04.[11] John also worked on the cloister in the early 1320s alongside his son, William Ramsay II, and between them they went on to execute the most significant work of all at St Paul's Cathedral in London.[12]

THE PRIORY AND THE TOWN: RELATIONSHIPS AND DEVELOPMENTS AT THE BEGINNING OF JOHN SALMON'S EPISCOPATE

There were a number of reasons historically why it became imperative to address the character of the area bordering Tombland, in order to define its boundaries and designate it more clearly as a religious area. Strictly speaking, the perimeter walls and enclosure on the south side of the close were the responsibility of the prior. It seems that the basic job of repairing the enclosure was achieved fairly promptly after the Tombland riots of 1272, as the renewed fabric was dedicated in 1278. However, the more ambitious and grandiose aspects of the rebuilding all happened after 1300, and relate to Salmon's wider ambitions to bring Norwich up to date architecturally and spiritually.

John Salmon became bishop over twenty years after the riots which represented the culmination but not the end of particular circumstances of strife at Norwich between the townspeople and the monastery over rights of common land and trading between the city and the priory.[13] While Bishop Roger Scarning had resolved the immediate problems and punished the aggressors, including the prior, their repercussions were still keenly felt.[14] For example, wider trading disputes remained, and it fell to Bishop Salmon to negotiate a settlement in 1306 over an agreement between priory and townspeople about the jurisdiction and management of commercial activity in Tombland.[15] It is highly likely, therefore, that he became acutely aware not only of the need for continuing to reduce tensions between the priory and the town, but of the importance of creating some kind of secure yet permeable boundary which would make clear that the cathedral was still a holy place which maintained strong religious values akin to those of God-fearing citizens.

There are a number of other very good reasons why Bishop Salmon might have wished to strengthen the precinct perimeter and approach and improve its outward face. One of these emerged following his visitation of 1308. A major concern was clearly the regulation and order of the monastery, its timekeeping, cleanliness and decorum. While this could have been a routine matter following his visitation, Salmon showed a firm hand, aware of the need to follow through and execute plans rather than just admonishing. In his injunctions of 1309, Salmon, who was a monk after all, expressed anxiety about the amount of time devoted to administration, taking monks away from the choir. But much worse than that, he had clearly found an extreme degree of inefficiency and poor practice which necessitated much more than the kind of routine corrections normally required by bishops following their visitations. He noticed an unacceptably high level of absenteeism: only six monks out of sixty attended church at any time. Inattentiveness and inappropriate behaviour during services resulted apparently in all classes of people jostling for space in the choir when monks ought to have maintained proper religious ritual.[16] Salmon, who in his later concerns showed himself to be a stickler for decorum, was especially exercised that the nobility would have been shocked at the lack of cleanliness and even the squalor. Vestments were in tatters and, much worse, the buildings stank, having been kept in an untidy and insanitary condition. Texts were poor and not standardized and timekeeping was terrible. He decreed in 1309 that monks should always attend services, and should be universally present on feast days. Mass books should be standardized, and a new clock should be provided.[17]

The clock was the prior's responsibility, along with the regulation of the monastery, maintenance of its religious routines and its administration. It proved to be his undoing. Prior Henry of Lakenham has gone down in history for seeing to the restoration of the library and for promoting the intellectual development and scholarship of the monks, making sure they had access to a university education.[18] He was also a keen administrator and fundraiser for the priory estates. It was during his period of office that Norwich developed an unusually sophisticated method of book-keeping.[19] But evidently the religious aspects of life, the regulation of church services and attendance were another matter. For the clock, clearly an important instrument of such regulation and a symbol of order, Salmon set a deadline of one year. Were it not in place by Easter of the following year, there would be dire consequences.[20] But by the end of that year, nothing had happened, and by February 1310 Henry of Lakenham had resigned as prior.[21] There is a strong possibility that Salmon forced him to step down, holding him responsible for the over-emphasis on administration and the spiritual decline of the monastery, using the clock deadline as a tactic to oust him. Lakenham was immediately succeeded as prior by Robert de Langley, with whom Salmon was to collaborate closely for the remainder of his episcopate.[22] Eventually, an extraordinarily elaborate astronomical clock arrived some sixteen years later, in 1324.[23]

DEVELOPMENT OF THE WESTERN CLOSE AND THE NORTH SIDE OF THE
CATHEDRAL c.1300–c.1320

WHILE there was clearly a long-term cultural problem to be addressed both within the monastery and at its perimeter, throughout the time of Salmon's episcopate, power over the spiritual welfare of citizens was also being seriously challenged by the rapidly expanding numbers of mendicant friars. As Rawcliffe and Harper-Bill have noted, the Blackfriars, having established over twenty years a strong following for their preaching in Norwich, had a substantial building underway shortly after 1310 and the Franciscans followed suit, having a great church, cloisters, a walled and gated enclosure and cemeteries by 1324. By the time of Salmon's death there were at least 140 friars established in these two places alone, as against some sixty monks at the priory.[24] Any ambitious leader in the Church, especially one responsible for spiritual leadership for the whole diocese, would have seen this at least as a challenge to be met with energy.

The mendicant challenge might have provided increased impetus for the reconstruction of the spiritual heart of the monastery, the cloister. This was already underway before Salmon arrived, but he promoted the project, adding to it from his own personal resources towards the end of his life and posthumously.[25] He could have left it entirely to the prior and the monks, but, perhaps because he was a monk himself, his benefaction demonstrates his concern, perhaps his determination, to make it an exemplary project. While Salmon did not live to see the majority of its building, what must have been happening during his term of office was the laying out, the planning and the decisions about its elements, especially its decorative repertoire, the imagery of its doorways and bosses.[26] The building of the so-called Prior's doorway and adjacent part of the east range were coeval with his term of office. It is tempting to suggest that he might have played a role in strengthening its message in the light of contemporary politics, which he would have been in a unique position to observe and respond to. It is the first of the great 14th-century building projects at the cathedral to use figurative vault bosses. The Passion sequence of the northern bays of the east walk, together with the radial figurative imagery of the Prior's doorway centred on Christ in Majesty displaying his wounds, and flanked by representatives of the Old Law and the New, is unique among surviving cloisters. I suggested elsewhere that another important context was the desire for a strong restatement of the stories of Christian redemption following the recent expulsion of the Jews in 1290.[27] Stylistically, also, this sculpture has a wider East Anglian context. Combining religious scenes with combats, struggles, caprices and jokes, such as the man defecating over the slype doorway, it echoes the work of the Ormesby Psalter, illuminated at or near Norwich and given to the cathedral by Robert Ormesby, a monk there. The cloister project demonstrates more than anything the need for coherence of overall vision in the light of the complex range of factors which had to come into play, between benefactors, account holders, masons, monks and imagery, let alone in terms of the internal and external political contexts to be considered.

At the other side of the Close, on the western perimeter, was another kind of important symbol of the continued importance of the monastery. In the early 14th century several major buildings at its frontier with the town were rebuilt, and enhanced. Highly symbolic among them was the free-standing belfry, built in 1303–04, with John Ramsey I documented as its builder.[28] As was the case at Rochester, St Albans, and probably York, there had been a pre-existing free-standing belfry among the buildings of the Norman period. The Norwich one, situated at the boundary of the western close, had been used as a fortification by the prior during the 1272 riots and as such provoked the citizens to counter-attack and raze it to the ground.[29] So its rebuilding as a grandiose structure would have been a clear restatement of the priory's presence and power, but also of its right to regulate the hours audibly for the entire community both lay and religious. The belfry project was succeeded by another priory commission, the completion of the Ethelbert gate as the principal grand entrance to the close between *c.* 1314–16. Presenting a façade to the town which is both decorative and thought-provoking with its combative sculptures of a man and dragon in spandrels above the main doorway, surmounted (originally) by Christ displaying his wounds, it stands as a symbol not only for the religious power of the monastery, but as an example of the highest quality and latest fashion in contemporary architecture. With its lierne vault, very early for its date, the exquisitely carved bosses, fine examples of flushwork, and façade detailing which includes blind-arcading, tracery and relief sculpture, it was very much in the vanguard of courtly architectural fashion. It demonstrates the fusion of style and substance that characterized the next phase of Salmon's patronage.[30]

During the first decades of the 14th century, attention seems to have been dedicated more consistently to the northern side of the church and the western and northern areas of the Close. There may have been a number of reasons, as this was adjacent to the site of the lay cemetery, but also significant was the fact that this was to become the main route of access to the cathedral's preaching yard, its own counterpart to the preaching provision of the mendicant friars.[31] While this area was not to be acknowledged in the records formally until later in the 15th century, when it is referred to as the Green Yard, much of what Salmon was to effect enhanced the surrounding area, and provided connections and routes to it from within and without the church, and to an expanded bishop's palace.[32] More than that, I would suggest that Salmon used this whole area, its architecture and iconography, to signal the status and power of the bishop, and the history of bishops at Norwich, the bishopric in general and their responsibility for the laity as well as the monastery.

After the rebuilding of the belfry, the next substantial development, datable stylistically between *c.* 1310–15, but unfortunately undocumented, is the whole rebuilding of the north nave aisle of the cathedral (Fig. 1). This aisle is fenestrated with simple three-light intersecting tracery windows. These continue into the west face of the transept, where there is a much more elaborate window as part of the same series (Fig. 2). This is also of three lights, but the centre portion flares towards the top to frame a five-petalled flower form made of four-cusped mouchettes around a central four-lobed figure. The stylistic details of the windows, with fine plain shafted mouldings rising into the intersecting cusped tracery at the head, are clearly different from any of the known work by the Ramseys, whose window moulding shafts tend to have capitals and bases, and tracery which is curvilinear and multi-cusped. Intersecting tracery windows of this type in the Norwich aisle may relate ultimately to the family of tracery designs associated with the court style whose early appearance *c.* 1290, at Merton College chapel, Oxford, shows mouldings which are fine-shafted and rise without capitals carrying their cusped arches into the window head. The Norwich design is less vertical and has deeper cusping and more pronounced ogee-formed mouchettes, so relates to a later phase of design. There is no obvious parallel for the window in the north transept executed in the richer design, but again one might look for its basis to the court phase of the 1290s, such as the east window of Exeter Cathedral Lady chapel which has a version of a similar tracery design, but without the fluidity. Simple intersecting tracery windows can be found from the early 14th century in a number of parish churches locally in Norfolk and Suffolk, and extending westwards into Lincolnshire, where for example similar windows may be found at St Wulfram's parish church, Grantham.[33] It has a subsequent echo in the three-light subsidiary tracery design of the very much more complex east window of Ely Lady chapel, which also has a central panel opening at the head into a five-petalled form, two narrow mouchettes of which form the head of the lower light and link it with

FIG. 1.   Norwich Cathedral: nave north aisle, including blocked door

FIG. 2.   Norwich Cathedral: north transept, west wall, window tracery

the three larger quatrefoils which span the head of the window. This demonstrates above all that there were a number of different teams of masons at Norwich, who could be called on for different purposes when there were several large building campaigns underway. It also shows how there might be a number of different stylistic influences operating, emanating from different regional centres, and that there was not necessarily a master plan, or central control of the overall consistency of appearance.

A doorway (Fig. 3), now blocked, in the north aisle of the nave gave access through to a courtyard area west of Losinga's original palace, the area which subsequently became the preaching yard. This doorway is of some interest stylistically in relation to Salmon's other commissions. There is an obvious relationship with the sculpture of the spandrels of the Ethelbert gate in that it shows two hybrid figures facing towards one another across the arch head, both of them engulfed in vine-like foliage trails. The sculpture is less crisp and refined and the finial in particular has the appearance of being squashed down so that it will fit in the limited space above it. However, it is clearly in the same family and, I suggest, by the same mason as sculpture for the porch of Bishop Salmon's new hall to be discussed below. Further evidence for the fact that Salmon's patronage might be identified with this phase of work on the church, and of his continuing attention to the importance of its ceremonial and ornaments, is the fact that he gave a tabula for the high altar in 1314, which, according the prior's thank-you letter, he had acquired in London.[34]

This gift might well have marked the culmination of the north aisle project, but also indicates a further connection with work on the north side further to the east, namely the now much damaged and faded paintings on the vault of the so-called ante-reliquary chapel, adjacent to the high altar. This work is undocumented and its dating, style and potential wider context and history have been much discussed. Park and Howard established in 1996 that the paintings of the apostles on the western arch soffit and the litany grouping of twelve saints on the vault, three in each of four vault cells, were all of the same period.[35] They related these stylistically both to paintings for St Faith's chapel at Westminster in the first decade of the 14th century and to more local paintings

FIG. 3. Norwich Cathedral: nave north aisle, detail of spandrel carving of blocked door

c. 1300 at Little Wenham, Suffolk. Paul Binski has subsequently suggested a date towards the end of the 13th century relating the programme tentatively to Norwich's possession of a relic of the Holy Blood, which might be the most significant focus of honour in such a chapel. As had Park before him, he suggested that the most unusual of the sainted confessors represented was Bishop Richard of Chichester. Not only had Bishop Walter of Suffield (1245–57) received a legacy from him, but Binski suggests that his presence was part of the continuing campaign at Norwich to reinforce Suffield's canonization and to promote the cause of saintly bishops at Norwich.[36] Stylistically, the reliquary arch paintings are indeed very much in the Westminster family. I would concur with Park in that the closest comparisons are with the slender formalized figures of St Faith's chapel paintings at Westminster Abbey, and even more so with the sedilia there, which is dated 1308. In both cases, and in common with Norwich, the figures lean back gently rather than sway. Their draperies tumble in rippling folds ending in points and swirl out in graduated layers splaying around their feet. The canopies over the apostles are also stylistically related to the Westminster sedilia, albeit without crockets, but then the Norwich paintings are altogether more spare and compressed into a limited space.

Binksi convincingly and appropriately invoked both the importance of the Holy Blood relic and the promotion of the cult of bishops. In my view, the most likely time for these two initiatives to coincide was in the early 14th century, for reasons further amplified below. It is perhaps not a coincidence that the largest donations at Suffield's tomb were in the years from 1296–1305, around the beginning of Salmon's episcopate.[37] I suggest that the impetus for the campaign of vault painting would have been entirely characteristic of Bishop Salmon, more so than of his immediate predecessors. He appears to have been in the course of a programme of work at the cathedral which was both reinforcing the visible expression of its religious authority, and also attending to the status of its bishops. But there was a further devotional development. It was also a time of the rethinking of the Easter sepulchre as a new kind of monument honouring the body as well as the blood of Christ, a movement which I have suggested elsewhere, seems particularly to have taken hold among the court chaplains and ecclesiastics associated with Edward II, circles in which Salmon was moving.[38] The reliquary chapel is above what must have been the Easter sepulchre, a significant factor in its embellishment.[39] I suggest therefore that it performed a function, not so much as a reliquary chapel, but as a bishop's chapel for honouring the sacrament, and that it was undertaken as part of the north aisle refurbishment and complete by 1314, as Salmon's painting was placed on the high altar which it overlooked.

THE CARNARY CHAPEL

The fact that John Salmon was aware of London artists and artistic developments in court circles is also of great relevance to the next phase of his patronage. Almost as the Ethelbert gate was being completed in 1316, he established a chantry foundation in memory of his parents (his father had died in 1307) and previous bishops of Norwich.[40] This became the Carnary College with its chapel sited west of the façade of the cathedral between the lay cemetery, which its site partly displaced, and the preaching yard (Fig. 4). It was dedicated to St John the Evangelist, and functioned partly as a charnel chantry for the bones of the laity, kept in its lower storey. Possibly the dedication prefigures the later interest in the Apocalypse which emerged in the south cloister range to which Salmon's testamentary legacy contributed.[41] The initial chantry for four priests

FIG. 4.   Carnary chapel, Norwich Cathedral close: exterior from the south

was paid for out of profits of Westhall rectory, Suffolk, and was later augmented to six priests in 1322.[42] Salmon, following what emerges repeatedly through his statements and benefactions as his belief in ritual and religious regulation, stated explicitly that the priests should live and eat and drink together as a community. It was given its own library. Already in 1317, it was open and aiming to attract pilgrims, as Carnary chapel visitors secured 100 days' indulgence.[43]

In terms of the form and type of building, it has a number of different kinds of parallels and precursors. Frank Woodman described it as Norwich's answer to St Stephen's Westminster, a two-storey palace chapel, begun in the 1290s.[44] Eric Fernie alluded to the well-known royal tradition for two-storey chapels: the palace chapel at Aachen and St Louis's Sainte Chapelle in Paris which have often been cited as the most obvious models for all casket-like two-storey reliquary chapel buildings.[45] Salmon knew Paris well by 1316, and was without doubt alert to a wide range of models elsewhere. In terms of bishops' chapels, there is equally a long history, not least for the emulation of the palace chapel at Aachen; William of Malmesbury mentions it in relation to the chapel built by Bishop Losinga at Hereford (1079–95) to the north of his palace.[46] The

13th-century buildings for the abbot's palace at St Augustine's Canterbury included a two-storey chapel abutting the north side of the nave.[47] There were other potential models and contemporaries in London, notably in Old St Paul's churchyard, which had a charnel chapel in the late 13th century, when a modestly endowed chantry was established, served by one priest.[48] The Norwich Ramsey family of masons went on to work at St Paul's, so these similar chapels may represent more of a pre-existing connection.[49] It is possible that there was a growing trend, which especially seems to be manifest in London, as excavations in Spitalfields have revealed another charnel house probably built in the period immediately following 1280–1310.[50]

In its form and its decorative character, Norwich's Carnary chapel is a remarkable building which will always have stood out distinctively in the western Close. The principal floor is designed as a four-bay structure, punctuated by tall three-light traceried windows with a pair of proto-Perpendicular style formalized budding flower designs in the head, with a pronounced vertical emphasis owing to the fact that they are formed by the continuation of the lines arising from the mullions and arches below. The lower floor is illuminated by circular traceried and deeply cusped windows. This had also been a feature of the belfry, connecting the design again with the Ramsey family of masons. In the Carnary context, these lower windows would have enabled worshippers to glimpse the bones in the crypt chapel, much as in the manner the faithful would have been able to approach relics in a shrine base. This analogy is a particularly compelling one and, given Salmon's father's profession as a goldsmith, he might indeed have been familiar with the micro-architecture of shrines and their bases. It is more in the shrine bases, in particular that of St Albans, 1305–08, where one can see the similarity.[51]

These connections do suggest that Salmon's foundation was keeping up to date with current developments, both in its intention as well as in its design. The question remains as to whether, by being 'up to date', it is bringing a new kind of contemporary impetus to Norwich and to what end? Salmon was fortunate in having the services of excellent mason-architects in John Ramsey and his son William Ramsey II, the principal masons already resident in Norwich, with close connections over the years with the king's works. In its stylistic detail, the Norwich Carnary is modestly innovative. The tracery designs have no clearly identifiable precedents, but they are echoed subsequently in a number of other buildings, notably the octagon at Ely which is another project by the Ramsey family, and even more notably the south transept window at Gloucester Abbey as already noted by John Harvey in 1961 and Jean Bony in 1979,[52] and in the arcades of the cloister of Old St Paul's, regarded by Christopher Wilson as William Ramsey's masterpiece. Norwich was clearly where these influential styles were being formed, and perhaps where the reputations of the Ramseys were established, possibly helped by Salmon's patronage and influence. Other London relationships and parallels can be drawn. Inside the chapel, the carved head corbels can still be seen through the caked layers of repainting as being of remarkably fine quality. The largest head towards the west over the position of the entrance is of a bishop and this must surely be a representation of Salmon himself (Fig. 5). Stylistically, it is similar to the carved wooden heads on the Westminster Abbey sedilia, so much so that they could almost be by the same artist.

While it has been noticed before that the position Salmon chose for his foundation straddled the lay cemetery and the priory lands, the significance of this choice needs to be emphasized further. For Salmon to create a space to honour the bones of the townspeople in such a prominent site was a masterstroke of diplomacy, given the history of civic strife he inherited. But it was also signalling a new axis to the precinct, connecting

FIG. 5.   Carnary chapel, Norwich
Cathedral close: headstop of bishop

the area which was to be increasingly developed as the preaching yard, to the north side
of the cathedral, and the area he was to develop next to enlarge his palace.

THE BISHOP'S PALACE

ALTHOUGH Salmon travelled a great deal in royal service, he seems to have been
largely based in England, if not in Norwich, for the few years in the mid-teens of the
14th century. His plans for greatly extending the bishop's palace show that he took his
local commitments seriously. Immediately following the completion of the Carnary
chapel, Salmon set about acquiring land to begin the expansion of his palace surrounded by its own grounds. In 1318 he gained a licence to purchase 47 perches and
4 feet × 23 perches and 12 feet of land to enlarge its site.[53] This enabled him to open up
a new access gate to the north of the Close, so it was potentially more public facing on
the side towards Palace Plain. Salmon's work within the new boundaries was substantial, including a great hall, outer offices, kitchens and at least one chapel.

It is characteristic of Salmon that he was not content to follow convention too
rigidly, but he commissioned the largest bishop's palace hall known — 110 ft × 60 ft.
It had its own kitchens and outer offices and remains of undercrofts exist from more
substantial buildings surrounding it. Eric Fernie has criticized the 'impunity' with
which he extended the palace, pointing out that for Salmon to have refurbished it following the problems between the priory and the town showed lack of sensitivity.[54]
However, this might have been calculated impunity for reasons which were legitimate
for and expected of bishops. Given the ways in which bishops' palaces had been

developing for some fifty years, with aisled halls and kitchens for hospitality, chapels for consistory courts and meetings of parliament, the palace of the founding bishop, Herbert Losinga, was by then seriously old-fashioned. Even now one can tell from its remains that it was somewhat forbidding and dark, with high walls and relatively small windows.[55] It is also evident from the rebuilding of the north aisle of the cathedral and the complete replacement of the cloister at Norwich that 12th-century work was considered out-dated and even its fine sculpture was treated in cavalier fashion.[56]

Models for palace and great hall enlargements had already offered themselves from the early 13th century at Canterbury and Lincoln. The 13th-century building works at St Augustine's Canterbury, which had possibly been influential on the Carnary chapel, included a substantial development of the abbot's lodgings and provision for entertaining which signalled a new emphasis in monastic life on the importance of hospitality, which he may have been echoing. Bishop Thomas Bek (1280–93) of St David's began the process of enlarging the palace there with a new chapel and hall, which was continued and further extended after the date of Norwich, by Bishop Henry de Gower in 1328–47. At Bishop Auckland, the residence of the bishops of Durham, the 12th-century great hall was apparently altered and augmented by Bishop Anthony Bek

FIG. 6a.   Bishop Salmon's Hall porch, Norwich bishop's palace: view from the south-east

(1284–1310), brother of Thomas, or after his death, a little later in the 14th century. A new great hall was built in 1294 for his castle at Acton Burnell, Shropshire, by Robert Burnell, bishop of Bath and Wells and chancellor to Edward I.[57] Burnell had also rebuilt the palace in Wells itself between 1275 and 1292, with a new chapel and hall.

There is no known reason why great halls became required in so many bishops' palaces at this time, beyond speculation that the households had grown larger and more lavish, especially in the context of royal service.[58] Philip Dixon thinks that it was considered appropriate for them to be prepared for royal audiences and visits.[59] Bishop Salmon did not become royal chancellor until 1319–20, during the course of his building, but there is little doubt that being in the court circle already would have raised his ambitions at least to bring Norwich into line with prevailing taste and practice for his position and class. Clearly, there were ambitions by Salmon to update and modernize, to create an impact and, in an impetus consistent with his concerns throughout his episcopate, to observe correct ceremonial.

Few remains of his palace are extant. These include undercrofts and kitchen offices which are now part of Norwich School, the porch to the great hall (Figs 6a and 6b) and windows which are part of what is now known as Bishop Reynolds' chapel (Fig. 7). The remains demonstrate, however, that the buildings shared generic characteristics with all the buildings of this time at Norwich: large traceried windows with stained glass (only a few tiny grisaille fragments remain in the Ethelbert gate), lierne vaults both for the

Fig. 6b.   Bishop Salmon's Hall porch, Norwich bishop's palace: detail of blind tracery

FIG. 7. Bishop Reynold's chapel, Norwich bishop's palace: window tracery

Ethelbert gate and Bishop Salmon's porch, rich niches and mouldings and an abundance of decorative sculpture — with bosses and corbels, foliage, finials, crockets. In short, this is the characteristic repertoire of the Decorated style brought to Norwich.

The Reynolds chapel is generally acknowledged as being part of, or at least incorporating Salmon's build.[60] Its tracery is clearly medieval and has close parallels in Lincolnshire, especially at Sleaford and Heckington. The chancel windows at Heckington are almost identical and share such a distinctive device, of the foliage from capitals spreading onto adjacent mouldings, that they may be by the same group of masons. Heckington is also a building created in the court ambit, having been commissioned in the first quarter of the 14th century by its rector, one of Edward II's chaplains, Richard de Potesgrave, and with aristocratic patrons as Lords of the manor, Henry and Alice de Beaumont and Henry's sister, Isabella de Vesci.[61]

The porch to Salmon's hall shares with the Reynolds windows the device of foliage spreading across mouldings, but it has a number of other distinctive quirks which link it to the other building projects, especially to the north doorway leading out from the nave, which must have been designed and carved by the same masons. It is quite a bulky, heavy structure and there are signs of small variations and adaptations to mouldings, the use of little tricks, such as wedge-shaped insertions, as if the design of the building was developing as it went up. Other characteristic tracery types are found here, such as teardrop ogees framed within outer ogee mouldings, which can be found in gallery windows at Ely Cathedral, aisle windows at Great Walsingham, in north Norfolk, as well as at Beeston and Mileham in central Norfolk.[62] Richard Fawcett pointed out that the porch's early examples of sub-tracery within shapes which approximate to reticulation units which anticipate the tracery designs of the west end of the north walk of the cloister.[63] Figure styles are closely related across all of the work associated with Salmon and show a number of sculptors, up to three, working simultaneously. The crouching figure corbels in the lower storey of Carnary chapel, the spandrel reliefs of north aisle doorway of the cathedral and the corbels and roof bosses in bishop's hall porch are somewhat stocky robust figures and are all likely to be by the same mason. They are different in style from the roof bosses in the cloister at Norwich but rather are stylistically similar to corbels and head-stops which can be found in conventual buildings in Ely, and this may be a common regional school.[64] There is also carving in a similar style among aisle corbels at St Margaret's Cley parish church, which is also sometimes associated with the Ramsey workshop.[65] Another, different, very fine carver who may be a mason of London origin, as mentioned above, made corbels and roof bosses in the Ethelbert gate, and probably also the head-stops of the upper chapel of the Carnary.

In terms of subject matter, there are consistent themes developed in the porch and gate bosses, the corbels of the hall porch, the north aisle doorway, and the Ethelbert gate, to do with confrontations between man and beast, which can be read as symbolizing forces of control, of nature, or as good and evil. The hall porch has a preponderance of images of women, female busts as corbels and roof bosses featuring a scene of Tutivillus and the Gossips and what appears to be the figure of a woman and a priest in some sort of close communication (Fig. 8). Most of the bosses are foliate, and overall it

Fig. 8. Bishop Salmon's Hall porch, Norwich bishop's palace: detail of vault boss

comes across as a collection of stock images which a good team of masons familiar with current styles of building would produce for that kind of context. However, the very fact that it is elaborately vaulted and has a variety of sculptural detail shows its ambition and gives a tantalizing idea of what kind of grandeur it prefaced in the main buildings.

OVERALL CONCLUSIONS

IN discussing the patronage of Bishop John Salmon, this paper has sought to raise matters which were particular to him, and also some of the generic issues pertaining to the role of a bishop in relation to building projects. These concern especially the ways in which it was necessary for him to maintain a strong cosmopolitan vision for his building while being absent for large amounts of time and how this entailed his having to be reliant on this being matched by local talents and capabilities, people able to carry out his wishes in an exemplary fashion. There are also concerns addressed here about the stereotyping of a place like Norwich in terms of questions of localism versus centrism: the relationships between regions and metropolitan centres, the ever-present possible stigma of it being regarded as a provincial backwater. The interpretation of his projects here shows Salmon as a patron to be operating at a grand scale, raising ambition, having vision. Through his court role and travels, Salmon had the opportunity to widen his sense of what was needed and what was appropriate for Norwich. His building projects and developments undoubtedly connected Norwich with the current, fashionable courtly style repertoire both in terms of the types of buildings — grand entrances, chapel, palace — and the manner in which they were executed, mindful of the latest fashions in construction and decorative details. His works gave a new coherence to the route through the precinct and buildings, from the western Close via the Carnary and the north aisle development of the cathedral to the bishop's palace. The extension of the palace to create the biggest of bishops' halls was, I suggest, as much about audience as it was about show and grandeur. Equally, his palace is perhaps the most important example of how his knowledge of the wider world led him to create what was expected of his class and status; he cared about ceremonial, for him it was important that Norwich could equal the best in the hospitality, grandeur and solemnity that the bishop could provide.

There were up to three, concurrent large building projects at any one time throughout this period at Norwich, and for their physical execution they drew from a number of sources, some of them from the immediate locality, some from the wider eastern region, some from London. Norwich had retained a number of very good mason-craftsmen, especially in the Ramsey family, and their involvement with the Norwich building programmes of course helped to establish their reputation, but the effect was mutual. While Salmon's projects in Norwich were undoubtedly helped in their creation by a family of masons who were strongly connected to the royal court, it was possibly through his good offices that they moved on so successfully from Norwich to develop their reputations in London. The overall impression is of a pluralist culture of patronage which dips in and out of regional and metropolitan engagement. Salmon and his masons consistently showed awareness of certain contemporary tendencies and parallels for artistic styles and may indeed have been in the vanguard of creating new trends.

John Salmon seems to have been a generous and convivial person, keen on order and control but fond of luxuries and known for his gifts, his alms-giving, his donation of pictures, vestments and ornaments to the church.[66] He was buried probably in the cathedral and for a generation after his death, his tomb was venerated and received modest offerings.[67] He stipulated in his will that on his anniversary one mark be given to the poor. But the convent was to have two marks for 'exceedings' at dinner.[68] The delivery of his commissions was a matter of balancing possibilities and opportunities which, whatever the institutional rivalries, had to be a matter of teamwork between the offices of the bishopric and the priory. Salmon's works seem to have corrected some of the inefficiencies and ill-judgements of the priory, especially in its relationships with the city, but also in their own regulation and spiritual development. Roberta Gilchrist said that Norwich's first bishop, Herbert de Losinga, wanted to give Norwich a sense of Christian antiquity.[69] I would say that John Salmon, who in some ways did much to undo, or redo, what Losinga had provided, was the first bishop since the founder to have an overall vision of what was needed to improve the spiritual and physical environment, and that it was to give Norwich as a city and diocesan centre a sense of Christian modernity.

ACKNOWLEDGEMENTS

I would like to extend my thanks especially to John Walker, archivist of Norwich School, and to Roland Harris, cathedral archaeologist, for opening up hidden areas of the site, for providing me with plans and maps, and for invaluable advice and discussions.

NOTES

1. J. R. Shinners, 'The Veneration of Saints at Norwich Cathedral in the Fourteenth Century', *NA*, 40 (1987–89), 133–44, at 137–38.
2. Blomefield, *Norfolk*, I, 497.
3. M. C. Buck, 'Salmon, John (*d.* 1325)', *ODNB*, online edn, January 2008, http://www.oxforddnb.com/view/article/24553 [accessed 9 May 2014]; Blomefield, *Norfolk*, I, 497, 497 ff.
4. B. Dodwell, 'The Monastic Community', in *Norwich Cathedral 1096–1996*, 239. D. Greenaway, *Fasti Ecclesiae Anglicanae 1066–1300; II, Monastic Cathedrals*, online edn, http://www.british-history.ac.uk/report.aspx?compid=33866 [accessed 9 May 2014]. VCH, *Norfolk*, II, 317–28, online edn, Version 4, November 2013, http://www.british-history.ac.uk/report.aspx?compid=38258 [accessed 9 May 2014].
5. Gilchrist, *Close*, 143–48.
6. Ibid., 76. Most building work at Norwich was funded by its bishops, following from its founder.
7. J. Maddison, *Ely Cathedral Design and Meaning* (Ely 2000), 61–82.
8. N. Coldstream, *The Decorated Style* (London 1994), 134–45.
9. J. Bony, *The English Decorated Style* (London 1979), 9–18.
10. J. Harvey, *English Medieval Architects. A Biographical Dictionary down to 1550*, revised edn (Gloucester 1987), 77.
11. Fernie, *AHNC*, 180.
12. Harvey, *Medieval Architects* (as in n. 10), 239–45; C. Wilson, *The Gothic Cathedral, The Architecture of the Great Church 1130–1530* (London 1990), 207, 212, 215.
13. These had involved persistent disputes over trading rights, such as those of priory tenants assuming priority over the citizens, and had been complicating the situation politically and culturally at repeated intervals throughout the 13th century. The 1272 eruption had involved considerable violence and killing by both monks and citizens and, in what must have been a shocking breach of clerical trust, resulted in Prior Burnham marching on the citizens with an army recruited from Yarmouth. In assuming control, Bishop Roger Scarning had to issue an interdict and excommunicate the city bailiffs and town clerk. He imprisoned the prior in the bishop's jail, whereupon he resigned and was replaced. There seems to have been some progress in making good the damage on both sides. VCH, *Norfolk*, II, 317–28, online edn, Version 4.0, November 2013, http://www.british-history.ac.uk/report.aspx?compid=38258 [accessed 9 May 2014].

14. Ibid.

15. Any tolls were to be sorted out directly between the priory and the city bailiffs — the bailiffs no longer had power to charge directly. The only markets were to be the priory's Whitsuntide fair and a market on Sundays when there was a synod, when food could be sold at the priory gates. On those market days, the citizens could have first choice as to which half they wanted for their stalls and they would not be charged a toll. The other half was for the prior's use (ibid.).

16. E. H. Carter, *Studies in Norwich Cathedral History* (Norwich 1935), 19–24; C. Harper-Bill and C. Rawcliffe, 'The Religious Houses', in *Medieval Norwich*, 83.

17. Carter, *Studies* (as in n. 16), 29; J. Geddes, 'The Medieval Decorative Ironwork', in *Norwich Cathedral 1096–1996*, 431.

18. The restocking of the library, for example, was overseen by Prior Henry Lakenham, who was apparently a learned man who saw to it that Norwich monks got a university education. Dodwell, 'Monastic Community' (as in n. 4), 244; and B. Dodwell, 'The Muniments and the Library', in *Norwich Cathedral 1096–1996*, 325–38.

19. R. Virgoe, 'The Estates of Norwich Cathedral Priory', in *Norwich Cathedral 1096–1996*, 351.

20. Salmon's injunction states: 'In the said Church of Norwich let there be a reliable and goodly clock by which the brothers may be governed both day and night, [...] we wish and command to be begun before Easter, and to be completed as soon as possible afterwards: and this on him or on those who hold office we enjoin in virtue of his obedience and we command it under pain of removal from office'. Carter, *Studies* (as in n. 16), 29.

21. Greenaway, *Fasti* (as in n. 4), online edn, http://www.british-history.ac.uk/report.aspx?compid=33866 [accessed 9 May 2014].

22. Carter, *Studies* (as in n. 16), 12–14, implies that Lakenham's inefficiency in regulating the priory was due to infirmity.

23. J. Geddes, 'The Medieval Decorative Ironwork' (as in n. 17), 441–42 for details.

24. Harper-Bill and Rawcliffe, 'The Religious Houses' (as in n. 16), 103–07.

25. The cloister rebuilding was already underway, initiated by Bishop Walpole in 1297. Fernie, *AHNC*, 167. Salmon's contribution to it seems to have been made at the end of his life, from 1325, and then principally in the form of a legacy and posthumous offerings at his tomb from 1326–30, though no doubt this indicates his continued support and interest in the project whose beginning antedated his financial contribution. His money paid towards the completion of the east walk and substantially for the south walk. However, we know that offerings at his tomb were not huge (at its peak in 1328 it was £2 7s. 8d.), so his donations were likely to have been more symbolic than substantial: Shinners, 'Veneration of Saints' (as in n. 1), 137–38.

26. V. Sekules, 'Religious Politics and the Cloister Bosses of Norwich Cathedral', *The Medieval Cloister in England and Wales*, ed. M. Henig and J. McNeill, *JBAA*, 159 (2006), 288–92.

27. Ibid., 292.

28. Harvey, *Medieval Architects* (as in n. 10), 240–41.

29. N. Tanner, 'The Cathedral and the City', in *Norwich Cathedral 1096–1996*, 259–61.

30. V. Sekules, 'The Gothic Sculpture', in *Norwich Cathedral 1096–1996*, 197–209.

31. Gilchrist, *Close*, 94–96; Roland Harris told me that recent excavations have revealed that the lay cemetery extended further to the south within the western Close than had previously been supposed.

32. Gilchrist, *Close*, 101; Dodwell, 'Monastic Community' (as in n. 4), 247.

33. E.g. Eriswell, Suffolk; Carlton Rode and Winfarthing, Norfolk. D. Start and D. Stocker ed., *The Making of Grantham: the medieval town* (Sleaford 2011).

34. D. King, 'The Panel Paintings and Stained Glass', in *Norwich Cathedral 1096–1996*, 413; C. Norton, D. Park and P. Binski, *Dominican Painting in East Anglia* (Woodbridge 1987), 79, n. 87; Binski subsequently conjectured that the painting may have been of Italian origin, in P. Binski, *Westminster Abbey and the Plantagenets* (New Haven and London 1995), 182.

35. D. Park and H. Howard, 'The Medieval Polychromy', in *Norwich Cathedral 1096–1996*, 390–400.

36. P. Binski, 'The Ante-Reliquary Chapel Paintings in Norwich Cathedral: the Holy Blood, St Richard and All Saints', in *Tributes to Nigel Morgan. Contexts of Medieval Art: Images, Objects & Ideas*, ed. J. M. Luxford and M. A. Michael (Turnhout 2010), 241–61, suggested that the four groups of three figures representing Virgins, Confessors, Apostles and Martyrs, accorded with the account of All Saints as outlined in the Golden Legend, representing the four corners of the world.

37. Shinners, 'Veneration of Saints' (as in n. 1), 137.

38. V. Sekules, 'The Tomb of Christ at Lincoln and the Development of the Sacrament Shrine: Easter Sepulchres Reconsidered', *Medieval Art and Architecture at Lincoln Cathedral*, ed. T. A. Heslop and V. A. Sekules, *BAA Trans.*, VIII (Leeds 1986), 118–31, at 123–25.

39. T. A. Heslop, 'The Easter Sepulchre in Norwich Cathedral: ritual, transience and archaeology', in *Echoes mainly musical from Norwich and around: local studies for Michael Nicholas, organist at Norwich Cathedral*, ed. C. Smith (Norwich 1994), 17–20.

40. Fernie, *AHNC*, 181–82; A. J. Whittingham, 'The Carnary College, Norwich', *Archaeol. J.*, 137 (1980), 361–64; A. Stephenson, 'The Carnary College', *Archaeol. J.*, 106 (1949), 88; *Calendar of Patent Rolls: Edward II, 2, A.D. 1313–17* (London 1898), 525. P. Cattermole, *Norwich School Chapel and School House*, ed. B. Cattermole (Norwich 2011): Cattermole says he did not provide for it sufficiently and the priory had to step in to augment the living.

41. Gilchrist, *Close*, 105, makes a connection with the Carnary chapel and apocalyptic imagery/death.

42. Cattermole, *School Chapel* (as in n. 40).

43. *Calendar of Entries in the Papal Registers Relating to Great Britain*, ed. W. H. Bliss, 17 vols (London and Dublin 1893), II, 142.

44. F. Woodman, 'The Gothic Campaigns', in *Norwich Cathedral 1096–1996*, 178.

45. Fernie, *AHNC*, 182; St Stephen's chapel at the Palace of Westminster was begun in 1292, but when the Norwich Carnary was finished it was still probably little more than a third through its lengthy building and decorating campaigns, even though it was clearly a later work involving the same family of Norwich masons — the Ramseys.

46. H. J. Böker, 'The Bishop's Chapel of Hereford Cathedral and the question of Architectural Copies in the Middle Ages', *Gesta*, 37.1 (1998), 44–54; R. Krautheimer, 'Introduction to an iconography of medieval architecture', *Journal of the Warburg and Courtauld Institutes*, 5 (1942), 1–33.

47. M. Sparks, *St Augustine's Abbey*, English Heritage (1988/93), 32–33; T. Tatton-Brown, 'The Abbey Precinct, Liberty and Estate', in *St Augustine's Abbey Canterbury*, ed. R. Gem (London 1997), 129–31.

48. G. H. Cook, *Medieval Chantries and Chantry Chapels* (London 1948), 116–17.

49. Ibid., 116; I am grateful to Christopher Wilson for reminding me of the likely importance of the St Paul's charnel chapel and connection with Norwich.

50. http://www.museumoflondonarchaeology.org.uk/Education/Archaeology-on-location/CharnelHouse.htm, ref. online, Museum of London [accessed 9 May 2014].

51. N. Coldstream, 'English Decorated Shrine Bases', *JBAA*, 129 (1976), 15–34.

52. Bony, *English Decorated* (as in n. 9), p. 60, pls 340, 341, 342. He implies that it was William Ramsey who designed the Carnary chapel.

53. Blomefield, *Norfolk*, I, 498; A. Whittingham, 'The Bishop's Palace', *Archaeol. J.*, 137 (1980), 365–68.

54. Fernie, *AHNC*, 182.

55. Losinga's palace had led directly into the church. For Salmon's buildings, a passageway to the church was built later. I am grateful to John Walker archivist for Norwich School and Roland Harris cathedral archaeologist for going over this ground with me.

56. A. Borg et al., *Medieval Sculpture from Norwich Cathedral* (Norwich 1980), 7.

57. Coldstream, *Decorated Style* (as in n. 8), 140, pl. 86.

58. T. B. James, *The Palaces of Medieval England* (London 1990), 97–104; M. H. Thompson, *The Medieval Hall* (Aldershot 1995), 117–19.

59. Pers. comm.

60. Bishop Reynolds (1660–76) repaired the bishop's palace and completed the chapel in 1672, reusing masonry and tracery 'from Salmon's destroyed chapel', Gilchrist, *Close*, 231; T. Browne, 'Repertorium, or some account of the Tombs and Monuments in the Cathedral Church of Norwich', 1680, in *The Works of Thomas Browne*, ed. G. Keynes (London 1954), III, 134.

61. V. Sekules, 'Beauty and the Beast: Ridicule and Orthodoxy in architectural marginalia in early fourteenth-century Lincolnshire', *Art History*, 18.1 (1995), 37–62.

62. R. Fawcett, 'The Influence of the Gothic Parts of the Cathedral on Church Building in Norfolk', in *Norwich Cathedral 1096–1996*, 214, fig. 101.

63. Ibid., 215.

64. Coldstream, *Decorated Style* (as in n. 8), pl. 62.

65. Fawcett, 'Influence in Norfolk', (as in n. 62), 211–14; and see Christopher Wilson in this volume.

66. Blomefield, *Norfolk*, I, 498.

67. Ibid., 498, thought he was buried in his palace chapel; according to Shinners, 'Veneration of Saints' (as in n. 1), 137 and n. 31, the site of his tomb is unknown but, as separate donations were received in the Carnary chapel and at his tomb, it was more likely to have been sited in the cathedral.

68. Blomefield, *Norfolk*, I, 498.

69. Gilchrist, *Close*, 252.

The Norwich Cathedral Passion Altarpiece ('The Despenser Retable')

T. A. HESLOP

The choice of subject matter and detailed iconography of the five scenes on the altar-piece demonstrate a remarkable degree of particularity. It is clear that the artist was both original and inventive in bringing together and transcending ideas from a range of sources in England and on the Continent. Very similar conclusions can be drawn from the painting techniques and accomplished style of execution which indicate that the painter was well versed in recent artistic developments in Italy and northern Europe, though he was clearly trained in England and apparently based in Norwich. The altar-piece is too small for the high altar of a major church such as Norwich Cathedral, and the suggestion is made that it was intended for the north-eastern ambulatory chapel which housed the relics of the boy-martyr St William. The date c. 1385 corresponds with the completion of building work in the presbytery and renewed interest in the saint's cult. These factors distance the altarpiece from the often cited connection with the Peasants' Revolt of 1381 and Bishop Despenser's part in its suppression.

THE Norwich Cathedral Passion Altarpiece (Fig. 1) is 8 ft 6 in. long and its restored height is 3 ft 9 in. It dates from the last quarter of the 14th century, and is an oil painting on a chalk ground laid on an oak support of four horizontal planks, embellished with gilded *pastiglia* backgrounds. It was 'discovered' in the cathedral in 1847, where it was apparently being used face downwards as a table or shelf.[1] The engraving published in 1851 and early photographs show where square-section legs were attached at the corners.[2] Despite this damage, most of the painted surface is well preserved, the major loss being at the top of the Crucifixion, where Christ's head and arms had been removed; what is there today was painted by Pauline Plummer. Although the original height of the altarpiece is unknown, St John Hope noted the even spacing of the armorials at the side and argued reasonably enough that one unit was missing.[3] Supplying it gives the height as now reconstructed. The result is generally pleasing, and each scene has the proportions of a double square 15½ in. × 31¼ in. The additional height would allow the figure of Christ in the Ascension to be completed. Though the Crucifixion is rather cramped at the top, other English panel paintings of the period also show this rather abrupt upward curtailment of the Cross, and the absence of the inscribed titulus board.[4]

Earlier painted altarpieces in England, at Westminster and Thornham Parva, are rectangular and that also serves to justify the form chosen when the Norwich altarpiece was restored.[5] However, the more numerous surviving English medieval alabaster altarpieces, many of which are now to be found in churches and museums on the European continent, usually have a central panel taller than those surrounding them.[6] Even when these altarpieces do not survive complete, it is clear this was the standard

FIG. 1.   Norwich Cathedral, St Luke's chapel: the Passion altarpiece
Andy Crouch

arrangement because most surviving individual Crucifixion and Trinity panels in this material are between about 19 and 22 in. in height, whereas other narrative subjects such as the Annunciation, Flagellation or Ascension are from 16 to 18 in. tall.[7] In other words there was, on average, a 3 in. or 4 in. discrepancy between the height of central and flanking panels. While it is true that panels with the Crucifixion or Trinity are also usually wider than the flanking narrative panels, which is not the case with the Norwich altarpiece, the possibility should still be borne in mind that the Crucifixion was once taller than the scenes around it.

The corpus of surviving alabasters also allows an assessment of the choice of scenes on the Norwich altarpiece. There are about 120 alabaster Crucifixion panels known, the other frequent Passion subjects being the Resurrection (143) and Betrayal (107), followed by the Flagellation and Entombment.[8] The complete alabaster Passion retable at Ecaquelon (Monfort-sur-Risle, near Rouen) is thus likely to represent the most popular configuration of main panel subjects in the sequence Betrayal, Flagellation, Crucifixion, Entombment and Resurrection. The same four flanking scenes can be found on the Nottingham Museum retable, where the central subject is the Trinity, of the Gnadenstuhl type with Christ on the Cross.[9] By the mid-15th century it seems a consensus had been reached, with the essential narrative running from Christ's capture in the Garden of Gethsemane to his Rising from the Tomb. Thus both the starting (Flagellation) and finishing point (Ascension) of the Norwich altarpiece are apparently unusual. What about the choice of scenes in general?

Forty-six alabaster panels of the Ascension were noted by Cheetham. However, as the Ascension is also used in the context of Marian (Joys of the Virgin) retables, such as the Swansea Altarpiece in the Victoria and Albert Museum,[10] it is legitimate to infer that others among those now separated from their original context may not come from Passion sequences either. Some support may be adduced from the rarest subject on the Norwich altarpiece, Carrying the Cross, of which Cheetham listed a mere twenty-one.[11] Supposing the Ascension was as unusual as Christ Carrying the Cross on alabaster Passion retables (arguably on only about 20%), the occurrence of these two subjects on the Norwich altarpiece is worth noting both for their inclusion and for what in consequence had to be omitted: the much more popular Betrayal and Entombment. It is, however, worth noting that the roof bosses at the northern end of the east walk of the cloister at Norwich have five Passion subjects also beginning with the Flagellation and Carrying the Cross, the Crucifixion and Resurrection — only the final scene, the Harrowing of Hell, is different and may be explained by its location.[12]

The Norwich altarpiece is demonstrably unusual in the iconography of individual scenes.[13] The Flagellation includes an authority figure, presumably Pilate, supervising the torment (Fig. 2). No doubt he is there in part to remind viewers at whose command this was done. Whereas in narrative sequences beginning with the Betrayal, the Flagellation appears as a result of Christ's arrest in the Garden, that context was missing on the Norwich altarpiece, and Pilate's presence indicates some of the back story. The inclusion of Pilate is not, however, unprecedented. It occurs in England in the so-called St Albans Psalter, around 1130, and elsewhere in English Romanesque illumination, but as has been noted Pilate also appears in this scene in Italian paintings, such as Duccio's *Maesta*, based on Byzantine prototypes.[14] However, rather than being a seated supervisor as in earlier English representations, on the Norwich altarpiece Pilate stands and reaches out to grasp Christ's hair, presumably to implicate him directly in the physical torment; this may well be unique and indicative of a localized perception of Pilate's character and his role in the Passion.[15] Christ's pose, with his wrists tied to the column above his head, his legs crossed and feet hanging downward in 'dancing step', occurs in the earlier St Omer Psalter, made in Norwich *c*. 1340. However, there Christ is shown behind the column. In the Lytlington Missal, from Westminster 1383–84, he is in a similar pose and in front of the column, as on the altarpiece, but without the elegant leg position.[16] The vilification of the tormentors on the altarpiece is extreme, particularly the wild-eyed and bestial figure to the left, whose contorted features and ungainly, staccato pose imply vicious or even imbecilic cruelty. This has been taken as indicative of changing attitudes to the lower social orders in response to the Peasants' Revolt of 1381, but neither the presence of Pilate nor the details of the other pictures on the altarpiece fit comfortably with such a reading.[17]

Christ carrying the Cross is shown already stripped of his garments wearing only a cloth round his hips. Although relatively rare on the Continent, particularly in Italy, this had been the commonest way of depicting him in English art since around 1100.[18] The gate of Jerusalem to the left was also a recurrent feature. Most unusual, however, is the stress on the cavalcade emerging from it, normally it would have been the holy women and other 'daughters of Jerusalem', whom Christ addresses in Luke's gospel (Luke 23.27–31). The soldiery, in their exotic costume detail and two with their faces close together as though in conversation (Fig. 3), find their closest parallels in recent Italian paintings of the Passion, especially the Crucifixion, as represented for example in Padua by Altichiero in the 1370s and 1380s.[19] It is as though they have been added to draw attention to the painter's awareness of this development. Given the space at his disposal, he could not put them in the Crucifixion itself and this was a good alternative. There is, however, some continuity between Christ Carrying the Cross and the next panel, as the man framed in the gate of Jerusalem reappears in the Crucifixion still wearing his distinctive, green conical hat.

The Crucifixion, with John supporting the swooning Mary, is representative of a long-established tradition which was becoming more prevalent from the mid-14th century.[20] Moving John to the same side of the Cross as Mary alluded to Christ's words that henceforth Mary should take John as her son, but it also made room to the right of the Cross for the centurion and at least one companion (here there are two) to whom he

FIG. 2.   Norwich Cathedral, St Luke's chapel: detail of the Flagellation panel
of the Passion altarpiece

FIG. 3.   Norwich Cathedral, St Luke's chapel: detail of the Carrying the Cross
panel of the Passion altarpiece

utters the words 'truly this man was the son of God'. This utterance by a disinterested and pagan bystander was given particular emphasis during the second half of the 14th century, perhaps because it was an unsolicited, eyewitness response to the event from a figure of authority, emphasized here by his rich tunic and expensively fur-lined cloak and matching hat. The two men listening to him show by their expressions that they are taking his statement seriously; the one who wears a green hat and has a short, neat brown beard had apparently followed Christ along the *via crucis*. It is not clear who he is but one possibility is Nicodemus, the sympathetic Pharisee.[21]

The picture of the Resurrection is remarkable in a number of ways (Fig. 4). The sleeping soldiers are ambitiously angled to display sophisticated attempts at foreshortening their faces. The head of the old soldier at the back of the composition nods forward to his right so the tip of his nose is in front of his lips, and this motif can be found in the Arena Chapel in Padua, painted by Giotto.[22] But it is the open-mouthed man in the right foreground who is most remarkable, his face is seen from above in less than three-quarter view, showing one and a half eyebrows and slightly more than half his lower lip (Fig. 6). The same scene from the Wittingau altarpiece in Prague, of around the same date, shows a similar approach but without the crisp delineation of the Norwich altarpiece.[23] The superb figure of Christ steps out of his tomb onto one of the sleeping soldiers, a motif that was to become increasingly common in English art. It is perhaps intended to indicate his triumph, trampling on his enemies as though they were a footstool; he arises from death while they sleep in life. He looks out of the picture with a remarkable expression of transcendent serenity on his face, engaging the viewer's gaze directly, in a way not found in the other scenes, and raising his right hand in blessing. These three elements: looking at the viewer, blessing and stepping onto a soldier occur in northern art, especially in Germany, from the 1230s onwards.[24] The pink and blue of his cloak brings the colouring of the early morning sky into the heart of the painting, implying a reference to the rising sun. The contrast with the harder colours of the soldiers' garments adds to this effect. There are other allusions: above Christ to either side is a golden bird, perhaps a phoenix, with wings outstretched, supporting round its neck a shield bearing instruments of the Passion.[25] On one shield the column, staff and sponge and lance are set against an ermine field, not of the usual tincture, black on white, but painted red on white so as to turn each configuration of marks into splashes of blood, a wonderfully inventive idea. On the dexter shield are the Cross with the nails still in place, Crown of Thorns and whips surrounded by a red border, no doubt also an allusion to blood. This display of the *arma Christi* in the manner of a funeral 'achievement' is complemented by the representation of Christ still wearing the Crown of Thorns. This motif was to become commonplace on alabaster panels of the Resurrection in the 15th century, but was rare before 1400. The Norwich altarpiece is thus an early example of this phenomenon.[26]

Most unusually Christ's tomb has a canopy, and its design is significant. With its two vaulted bays it directly recalls the space in the cathedral used as the Easter sepulchre, under the so-called reliquary arch (Fig. 5). Although refashioned in 1424–25, the vault and its internal supports date from 1278, so were in place well before the altarpiece was painted.[27] However, the chances are good that the sepulchre at Norwich had this form much earlier since it already appears on the cathedral's seal in the second quarter of the 12th century.[28] Clearly, devotion to the Resurrection was of long-standing at Norwich, and the conception of this episode on the altarpiece is a deliberate reference to the locus for the Easter ceremony in the north ambulatory.

FIG. 4.   Norwich Cathedral, St Luke's chapel: the Resurrection panel from the Passion altarpiece
Andy Crouch

FIG. 5.   Norwich Cathedral: presbytery north aisle, the site of the Easter sepulchre

The Ascension shows Christ, vested in the same pink and blue cloak, surrounded by a radiant mandorla. Below him, but on a much larger scale, the apostles and Mary kneel in prayer. Several contemporary images from Cologne and the surrounding area show very similar compositions: Mary and the apostles kneeling around the base of the Mount of Olives with a diminutive figure of Christ, in an aureole of light, almost centrally placed above them.[29] With the exception of the Mount, no doubt omitted because of the narrower proportions of the panel, the Norwich version is so similar in conception to suggest both a north German source and that originally Christ's figure and mandorla were seen in full, and this makes it likely that some painting is also missing from the tops of each of the other subjects flanking the Crucifixion.

This analysis of the Passion pictures indicates the wide range of motifs and iconography that the Norwich painter was aware of: from Italy in the south to Westphalia in the north, and possibly as far east as Bohemia. Just as significantly, much of it is of recent origin. Indeed, some characteristics, such as the foreshortening of the soldiers' faces in the Resurrection scene (Fig. 6), show him to be working with the emerging concerns of the best contemporary artists. Quite how he knew about these developments is a matter of speculation, but it seems unlikely that they could have been so fully and confidently absorbed at second hand. An Italian Crucifixion painting with mounted soldiers may have been accessible in England,[30] but for the northern European elements it seems as likely that he had travelled across the North Sea and engaged directly with work being produced there. All that said, there are more than enough characteristics of distinctly English lineage to indicate that our painter's training and formation was primarily in England and quite possibly in eastern England in the third quarter of the 14th century.

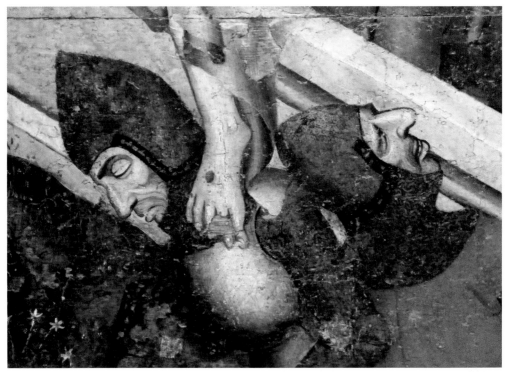

FIG. 6.   Norwich Cathedral, St Luke's chapel: detail of the soldiers in front of the tomb, from the
Resurrection panel of the Passion altarpiece

FIG. 7.   Palace of Westminster: wall paintings from St Stephen's chapel
British Museum

General evidence for this comes from the fragments of the Old Testament narratives painted in St Stephen's chapel in Westminster Palace from 1350 to 1363 (Fig. 7). The range of colours and the sharp white highlighting are similar, so too the 'perspectival' architectural settings with slender columns, monochrome exteriors and red vaults or ceilings inside. Many of the painters working at Westminster were recruited from Norfolk and Suffolk; by the end of the project the master in charge was one William of Walsingham.[31] St John Hope suggested that the painter of the altarpiece was also responsible for the two earliest of the panels from the collection once held at St Michael-at-Plea in Norwich, or, as he sagely added, 'at any rate by an artist of the same school' (Figs 8 and 9).[32] If it is agreed that the altarpiece and Plea panels are by the same hand, or even just 'the same school', and the visual evidence is compelling, then it is virtually certain that the work was done in Norwich for a local clientele. The artist would probably have to be a freeman in order to practice in the city beyond the confines of the cathedral close.[33] There is a view, which I support, that the Plea panels are later than the cathedral's altarpiece, perhaps by a decade or so, hence it is possible to see how the artist developed over time.[34] In the later work, his highlighting is more muted, the

Fig. 8.   The Crucifixion panel from St-Michael-at-Plea, Norwich, now Norwich Cathedral, St Andrew's chapel
Andy Crouch

FIG. 9.   Detail from the Betrayal panel from St-Michael-at-Plea, Norwich, now Norwich
Cathedral, Innocents' chapel

Andy Crouch

modelling softer, the overall effect richer. St John's cloak has been painted scarlet, as
was becoming common in northern European painting around 1400, rather than a
crimson highlighted in white of earlier decades. However, the artist is still using the
same models. Christ is recognizably the same type, with an almost cylindrical head,
high forehead, small mouth and fine eyebrows. Furthermore, the Crown of Thorns has
the same proportion and manner of painting, and Christ's halo design, too, is virtually
identical, with a diamond on the splayed ends of each arm of the cross and scalloping in
between. Two of the soldiers at the Resurrection appear again in the St Michael-at-Plea
Betrayal seen from different angles (Figs 6 and 9). It seems that the artist was using life
drawings of the same models in both works.

    A general comparison of the two Crucifixions is informative in other ways. The Plea
panel (Fig. 8) has two devotees at the foot of the Cross, probably the man and woman
(husband and wife?) who paid for the altarpiece from which it comes. They may have

stipulated that only Mary and John should be shown beside the Cross, and perhaps also that angels should fly above, with chalices to catch the blood from Christ's wounds. Along with bunches of grapes on the *pastiglia* background, this presents a much more 'Eucharistic' conception than that on the altarpiece, where the emphasis is on Christ as man and son of God. Hence Mary swoons and is supported by John, rather than looking to Christ as though for salvation as she does on the Plea panel. It is also worth remarking that, on the basis of the surviving panels from alabaster retables of the Passion mentioned above, it is likely that the Plea altarpiece had more conventional subjects beginning with the Betrayal.[35] At 18 in. across and apparently at least 36 in. high, these panels also come from a larger ensemble, perhaps 10 ft in length, a point of significance for the likely location of both altarpieces.

A dating of the cathedral's altarpiece indicated by comparisons with artistic developments in England and the Continent is well borne out by the evidence of the surviving heraldry on the frame of the painting, which appears in rectangular panels set behind glass. The appearance of Henry Despenser's arms indicates the painting comes from the period of his episcopate, 1369–1406, but others help to narrow the range to the 1380s. Most recently, David King has identified the other six legible 'banners' as belonging to men who were implicated in suppressing the Peasants' Revolt in Norwich diocese in 1381, largely under Bishop Despenser's leadership.[36] That might seem to point to his direct involvement in the commission, though the position of Despenser's arms on the upper part of the left side frame should caution us against regarding the work as a specific celebration or thank offering made by the bishop for success in quashing the rebellion. Unfortunately, the heraldry under the central Crucifixion, which might have related most directly to the patronage of the altarpiece, has been lost without trace.[37]

There are also reasons other than historical commemoration for Norwich Cathedral wanting new altar furnishings at this date. The work of rebuilding the presbytery was being completed around 1386 (following the fall of the spire of the central tower in 1362), and this seems a more likely stimulus for the commission as the renewed eastern arm of the church was brought back into service.[38] However, it seems improbable that the altarpiece was intended for the high altar.[39] For one thing, it does not focus on the Trinity, which is the cathedral's and thus the high altar's dedication. For another, by late medieval standards it is relatively modest in size. Both the earlier examples at Westminster and Thornham Parva are considerably longer, 11 ft and 12 ft 6 in. respectively as against 8 ft 6 in. These are from the high altars of great churches, Westminster Abbey and Thetford Dominican priory, and the size of the latter is indicative of the increase in high altar lengths between c. 1270 and c. 1340.[40] It follows that, unless the cathedral was way behind the times, its high altar or even the main nave altar is likely to have been 13 ft or 14 ft in length, and the Norwich altarpiece would have looked quite out of scale in such a context. It would have been better suited for a side chapel, either in the transept or ambulatory, rather than a main space.

Given the late-14th-century renovation of the presbytery, the obvious sites would be the radiating chapels to either side. The altarpiece is currently housed in St Luke's chapel (originally St John the Baptist's chapel), and its scale is very appropriate for that setting. However, for various reasons, its counterpart on the north side, now known as the Jesus chapel (originally apparently St Stephen and All Martyrs, sometimes referred to as the Holy Innocent's chapel), seems more likely.[41] In the 14th century this was the site of the shrine of St William of Norwich, the skinner's apprentice thought to have been 'crucified' by members of the local Jewish community in 1144. Because of the supposed nature of his martyrdom, a Passion altarpiece would be particularly appropriate. Furthermore, in 1376, the Norwich furriers' guild had adopted St William as their patron and the site of his shrine became the setting for an annual requiem mass for deceased members. This may help account for the dramatic rise in offerings made at the shrine, from just over 4s. in 1368 to nearly £20 in 1386, a one hundredfold increase.[42]

For reasons that are not yet clear, the idea that the altarpiece came from the Jesus chapel has a history. In Bell's Cathedral series on Norwich, first published in 1898, Charles Quennell wrote, 'This was formerly the altar-piece to the Jesus chapel', though without explaining why.[43] Representations of the chapel in the early 19th century, such as a watercolour by Cotman (Fig. 10), show that there was indeed a space of about the right size for the altarpiece made by cutting away the Romanesque blind arcading in the apse.[44] The medieval brackets for sculpted images which survive to either side would have allowed sufficient width to accommodate a reredos up to 9 ft across. Whether such empirical observations lay behind the determination that the altarpiece was from this chapel is never stated, but is perhaps the most likely explanation unless, of course, that was where it had been located prior to its 'discovery' in 1847. The table covered by a cloth shown in Cotman's watercolour is the right size to have had the altarpiece as its top.[45]

Apart from the appropriateness of a Passion altarpiece for the cult of St William, the location would have been particularly resonant as it was within a few feet of the two-bay canopy over the site of the Easter sepulchre in the ambulatory. Indeed, it is likely that visitors to William's shrine passed through the sepulchre space on their way to the Jesus chapel. If it were ever possible to prove that this was the intended location for the altarpiece, the likeliest date for the commission would be between its adoption as a guild chapel in 1376 and the dramatic upsurge in the popularity of the cult of St William evident in the offerings being made there by 1386, when the presbytery renovation was being completed. The generally accepted dating of the work to the time of the suppression of the Peasants' Revolt in 1381 and the visit of King Richard and Anne of Bohemia in 1383 is therefore a good approximation, even if neither of those events was the direct stimulus for its creation.

SUMMARY

THE Norwich Cathedral Passion Altarpiece was the work of a locally based artist with a wide-ranging and up-to-date knowledge of developments in European painting. He used compositions and motifs borrowed from the Rhineland and Italy and techniques, such as the foreshortening of faces and the creation of architectural stage space, also with antecedents both north and south of the Alps. However, in most respects his greatest debt was to earlier English traditions, and that no doubt indicates where he received his training. The survival of two later panels apparently by his hand, from another dismembered altarpiece in Norwich, show how inventive he was and that he adjusted his style to take account of changing tastes in the use of colour, which favoured darker tones and softer transitions in modelling forms.

Although the date generally proposed for the altarpiece in the mid-1380s seems very likely, the emphasis normally placed on Bishop Despenser's patronage in the context of the suppression of the Peasants' Revolt of 1381 is neither fully convincing nor necessary. The bishop's arms are not in a prominent position on the frame, and there are no internal indications that the painting was made as a thank offering following this event. Implicating the lower orders in Christ's Passion might, for example, have been

FIG. 10.   John Sell Cotman, *The Jesus chapel in Norwich Cathedral*, watercolour *c.* 1807
The Higgins Bedford

exploited in a depiction of the Betrayal (omitted) or the substitution of ordinary people for the soldiers depicted in Carrying the Cross. Accordingly, I suggest that the altarpiece was commissioned as part of the refurbishment of the east end of the cathedral after the building of the new clerestory and more particularly that it was made for the chapel which contained the relics of St William.

Future researches among the rich available archival sources for the cathedral and a close technical examination and analysis of the altarpiece itself have the potential to clarify much that remains uncertain. It is beyond doubt that the cathedral's Passion altarpiece merits this attention both as a rare survival of English medieval panel painting but also as the work of an outstanding artist whose output sheds light on the reception of ideas from the Continent and their repurposing for an East Anglian clientele in the late 14th century.

NOTES

1. The first publication by A. Way, 'Notice of a Painting of the 14th Century, Part of the Decorations of an Altar: Discovered in Norwich Cathedral', *Proceedings of the Archaeological Institute, Norwich 1847* (London 1851), 198–206, was superseded by W. H. St John Hope, 'On a painted table of the fourteenth century in the Cathedral Church of Norwich', *NA*, 13 (1898), 293–342. P. Plummer, 'Restoration of a Retable in Norwich Cathedral', *Studies in Conservation*, 4 (1959), 106–15, gives an account of its condition and some analysis of materials. The fullest art historical study remains J. Symonds, 'A Study of the Painted Altarpiece now in St Luke's Chapel, Norwich Cathedral' (unpublished MA dissertation, University of East Anglia, 1970).

2. Way, 'Notice of a Painting' (as in n. 1), 198, and Hope, 'On a painted table' (as in n. 1), pl. 1.

3. Hope, 'On a painted table' (as in n. 1), 296–99.

4. Such as the Berger and later St Michael-at-Plea Crucifixions: respectively T. A. Heslop, 'Attending at Calvary: an early fifteenth-century English panel painting', *Tributes to Nigel Morgan. Contexts of Medieval Art: Images, Objects and Ideas*, ed. J. M. Luxford and M. A. Michael (London and Turnhout 2010), 279–92, and J. Mitchell in *Gothic. Art for England 1400–1547*, exhib. cat., ed. R. Marks and P. Williamson (London 2003), 392–93, cat. 277.

5. *The Westminster Retable: History, Technique, Conservation*, ed. P. Binski and A. Massing (Cambridge and London 2009), and *The Thornham Parva Retable: technique, conservation and content of an English medieval painting*, ed. A. Massing (Cambridge and London 2003).

6. For example, F. Cheetham, *English Medieval Alabasters, with a Catalogue of the Collection in the Victoria and Albert Museum* (London 1984), figs 11, 12, 15 and pl. 1.

7. The figures derive from the measurements given in F. Cheetham, *Alabaster Images of Medieval England* (Woodbridge 2003), 74–79, 115–18, 120–27, 142–44 and 147–53.

8. Ibid., 134–41 and 109–14.

9. For Ecaquelon, ibid., fig. 4, and for Nottingham, F. Cheetham, *Unearthed: Nottingham's Medieval Alabasters* (Nottingham 2004?), 64–70.

10. Cheetham, *English Medieval Alabasters* (as in n. 6), 70–71.

11. Cheetham, *Alabaster Images* (as in n. 7), 119–20.

12. The sequence is unusual as the Harrowing of Hell normally precedes the Resurrection. The explanation may be the desire to bring Christ rescuing souls from Limbo as close as possible to the Judgement iconography on the prior's door.

13. Symonds, 'A Study of the Painted Altarpiece' (as in n. 1) offers the only detailed analysis of the iconography.

14. C. Hourihane, *Pontius Pilate, Anti-Semitism and the Passion in Medieval Art* (Princeton 2009), 199–200, 272–89.

15. S. Stanbury, *The Visual Object of Desire in Late Medieval England* (Philadelphia 2008), 85.

16. The relevant pages of the St Omer Psalter and Lytlington Missal are reproduced in R. Marks and N. Morgan, *The Golden Age of English Manuscript Illumination 1200–1500* (London 1981), pls 21 and 25. It is perhaps worth noting that Abbot Lytlington was a kinsman of Bishop Henry Despenser and bore the same armorials.

17. Stanbury, *Object of Desire* (as in n. 15), 76–94, esp. 80–85.

18. T. A. Heslop, 'St Anselm, Church Reform and the Politics of Art', *Anglo-Norman Studies*, 33, ed. C. P. Lewis (Woodbridge 2011), 103–26, at 119–21 discusses this iconography.

19. J. Richards, *Altichiero, an Artist and his Patrons in the Italian Trecento* (Cambridge 2000), 160–64 and pl. 42 for the Crucifixion in the Chapel of St James in the Santo in Padua, dating from the 1370s.

20. A. Neff, 'The Pain of Compassion: Mary's Labor at the Foot of the Cross', *Art Bulletin*, 80 (1998), 254–73.

21. For his possible presence also on the Berger Crucifixion painted in East Anglia (quite probably in Norwich) *c.* 1415, and now in Denver, Colorado, see T. A. Heslop, 'Attending at Calvary' (as in n. 4).

22. For example, Joseph in the Adoration of the Magi: F. Basile, *Giotto, The Arena Chapel Frescoes* (Milan 1993), 129.

23. This comparison between the Norwich altarpiece and Bohemian painting is made in K. M. Swoboda, *Gotik in Böhmen: Geschichte, Gesellschaftsgeschichte Architektur, Plastik und Malerei* (Munich 1969), 229 and pls 154–55.

24. See G. Schiller, *Ikonographie der Christlichen Kunst*, 5 vols (Gütersloh 1968–91), III, 75–77, and pls 201, 204–05, 212, 214, 216 and 228.

25. Or perhaps griffins, as they have ears, though the mouths are more dragon-like than beaks. Bishop Despenser's crest was a griffin; see T. Sims, 'Aspects of Heraldry and Patronage', in *Norwich Cathedral 1096– 1996*, 451–66, at 453 and fig. 169.

26. Cheetham, *English Medieval Alabasters* (as in n. 6), 272–73, dates two Resurrection panels in which Christ wears the Crown of Thorns in the Victoria and Albert Museum 'late 14th century', and it becomes standard practice in this medium, as does showing the Crown on Christ at the Entombment. The motif is also found in a Resurrection in the Sherborne Missal. So far as I know the origins of this phenomenon have not been explored.

27. C. H. B. Quennell, *The Cathedral Church of Norwich. A Description of its Fabric and a Brief History of the Episcopal See* (London 1900), 72; T. A. Heslop, 'The Easter Sepulchre in Norwich Cathedral: ritual, transience and archaeology', in *Echoes mainly musical from Norwich and around: local studies for Michael Nicholas, organist at Norwich Cathedral, 1971–94*, ed. C. Smith (Norwich 1994), 17–20.

28. T. A. Heslop, 'The Medieval Conventual Seals', in *Norwich Cathedral 1096–1996*, 443–50 at 444–46.

29. B. Corley, *Painting and Patronage in Cologne 1300–1500* (Turnhout 2000), pls 61, 79, 80, though all are a few years later than the date of the Norwich altarpiece.

30. In his will of 1361, the painter Hugh of St Albans left 'a six-piece Lombard panel painting which cost me £20' to his wife, Agnes: P. Binski, *Medieval Craftsmen: Painters* (London 1991), 12–13.

31. R. A. Brown, H. M. Colvin and A. J. Taylor, *History of the King's Works*, I (London 1963), 518–19.

32. Hope, 'On a painted table' (as in n. 1). This view is, however, contested by A. Martindale in *Medieval Art in East Anglia 1300–1520*, exhib. cat., ed. P. Lasko and N. Morgan (Norwich 1973), 37–38, cat. 52.

33. City ordinances from 1374–75 suggest that the status of freeman was increasingly necessary for those trading in the city and remained the case when trade guild organization was formalized in 1449: W. Hudson and J. C. Tingay, *The Records of the City of Norwich*, 2 vols (Norwich and London 1906–10), II, xxxiv– xxxix, xlii–xlix.

34. D. King, 'Panel Paintings and Stained Glass', in *Norwich Cathedral 1096–1996*, 410–30, at 414.

35. In the 19th century panels with the Flagellation, Entombment and Ascension survived at St Michael-at-Plea and may have formed part of the same altarpiece: *Medieval Art in East Anglia* (as in n. 32), cat. 52.

36. King, 'Panel Paintings' (as in n. 34), 410–13.

37. A. Martindale in *Medieval Art in East Anglia* (as in n. 32), 36–37, cat. 51 suggests that the most important heraldry would have been on the lost upper frame.

38. F. Woodman, 'The Gothic Campaigns', in *Norwich Cathedral 1096–1996*, 158–96, at 179–82.

39. As suggested by P. Tudor-Craig in *Age of Chivalry: Art in Plantagenet England 1200–1400*, exhib. cat., ed. J. Alexander and P. Binski (London 1987), 516–17, cat. 711.

40. J. Gardner, 'Some Franciscan Altars of the Thirteenth and Fourteenth Centuries', in *The Vanishing Past: Studies in Medieval Art, Liturgy and Metrology present to Christopher Hohler*, ed. A. Borg and A. Martindale, BAR International Series 111 (Oxford 1981), 29–38 discusses the increase in altar sizes from the mid-13th century.

41. For the changing dedications, see J. R. Shinners, 'The Veneration of Saints at Norwich Cathedral in the Fourteenth Century', *NA*, 40 (1988), 133–44, at 134 and n. 5.

42. Ibid., 135–36.

43. Quennell, *Cathedral Church of Norwich* (as in n. 27), 92.

44. Now in The Higgins Bedford, *John Sell Cotman*, ed. M. Rajnai (London 1982), cat. 65, dated 1807–08.

45. The location of the 'discovery' was contentious: Hope, 'On a painted table' (as in n. 1), 293–94, thought it had been found at gallery level above the Jesus chapel, but Dr Bensly understood it was in the southern equivalent, above St Luke's chapel.

Ranworth and its Associated Paintings:
A Norwich Workshop

LUCY WRAPSON

In this paper, the medieval screen at Ranworth is associated with other surviving works from the same painting workshop using technical and stylistic means. The basis for this study is the surviving screenwork of Norfolk and Suffolk, which has been surveyed as a whole.[1] As part of this, paintings from the same workshop as those at Ranworth have been attributed and dated using technical means, including dendrochronology, and also on the basis of design, style and jointing techniques. The related works having been established, the Ranworth workshop is then examined in the light of recent work by David King concerning a multi-media workshop in Norwich responsible for brass, glass and rood-screen paintings. The paper concludes that it is indeed highly likely that the Ranworth painters were Norwich-based and that they were associated with crafts-men and workshops also responsible for brass-making and stained glass design.

INTRODUCTION

THE history of the screen at St Helen's, Ranworth, since its construction involves defacement and dismantling, 19th- and 20th-century renown, and a lucky escape from destruction by fire.[2] Ranworth's is probably the best known rood-screen in the country and features prominently in both academic and popular studies of church history.[3] Following the 1865 survey of Norfolk's screens instigated by the Norfolk and Norwich Archaeological Society, Ranworth, or Randworth as it was then known, was the first of five screens to be the subject of an illustrated monograph by Winter, as well as the subject of an article by Morant and L'Estrange.[4] Another short monograph was written about the screen by Strange in 1902, the sale of which funded restoration of the church.[5] In 1910, Pearson published a set of drawings of the Ranworth screen.[6]

The Norfolk Broads' status as a popular holiday destination by the late 19th century enhanced the wider popularity of Norfolk screens. Numerous late Victorian and Edwardian picture postcards of screens testify to this. Dutt, whose 1903 guidebook to the Norfolk Broads was one of the less derivative tomes, said:

Ranworth is not the least delightful of the Broads lying between Acle and Wroxham; but the parish is more famous for having in its church one of the finest and best-preserved rood-screens in the county. Indeed, the committee of the Society of Antiquaries assert that as a whole there is 'nothing of the sort remaining to equal it in England.'[7]

In this vein, the screen at Ranworth has received more attention than any other in England, its unrecorded painters variously described as English, Swabian and Catalan.[8] This attention is, arguably, justified; Ranworth's screen is unusually elaborate in format and is well preserved, retaining much of its loft coving, though not its parapet or

BAA Trans., vol. XXXVIII (2015), 216–237

FIG. 1.   Ranworth rood-screen
Lucy Wrapson, Hamilton Kerr Institute, University of Cambridge

rood group (Fig. 1). It is well executed both in terms of its carpentry and painting: the best of its 15th-century paintings are among the finest surviving in England. The incorporation of nave altars into the scheme is relatively rare and the depiction of the Holy Kinship indicates that the whole was coherently conceived, and as such may reflect specific patterns of local use, such as the churching of women at an altar on the south side.[9] Technically, there is no reason to suggest that Ranworth represents anything other than a single, coherent scheme of painting, although it involved more than one painter and would have taken several years to complete.[10]

ESTABLISHING THE RELATED WORKS

THERE are other paintings on other screens soundly attributable to the Ranworth group of artists, although the exact paintings have been a matter for debate, as no known documentation ties named painters to any painted works. Long, writing in 1931, identified Ranworth, North Elmham, Old Hunstanton, Thornham and the central 'Apostles' panels at Southwold as being by the same hand.[11] Briggs, writing in 1934, related almost every figurative screen of any note to Ranworth, including screens as divergent in date as Gooderstone (with a will bequest of 1446) and Potter Heigham with bequest dates of 1494 and 1501.[12]

Baker developed genuine stylistic connections further identifying Ranworth, Old Hunstanton, Thornham, Filby, Southwold (centre screen), North Elmham, St James Pockthorpe (Norwich), North Walsham, Attleborough and Pulham St Mary the Virgin as the 'Ranworth group'.[13] In 2000 Mitchell outlined a slightly smaller set of paintings attributable to the Ranworth artists, omitting Attleborough, North Walsham and Pulham St Mary the Virgin, which had been included by Baker.[14] Plummer additionally identified the single panel of St Apollonia from St Augustine in Norwich (now in St Peter Hungate) as an unfinished painting from the Ranworth group.[15] Nichols terms the group the 'damask workshop' on the basis of the brocade patterns found on the garments of the figures.[16] I consider the Ranworth group to consist of ten screens and fragments from screens, of which nine are extant (Ranworth, Old Hunstanton, Thornham, Filby, Southwold [centre screen], North Elmham, St James Pockthorpe [Norwich], North Walsham and the St Apollonia panel). The lost screen is that from Great Plumstead, which is known only from illustrations, having been burnt in 1891.

These paintings have typically been compared on a stylistic basis. Baker was the first to outline the use of brocade patterns mimicking imported textiles as being indicative of the Ranworth group, as well as comparing the style of the figure painting.[17] Many of the brocade patterns found at Ranworth are indeed found at the other related sites (Fig. 2). Like the brocade patterns, which have been shown to relate to Italian silks,

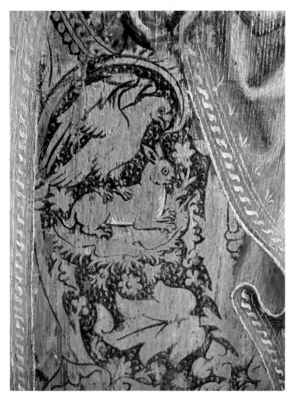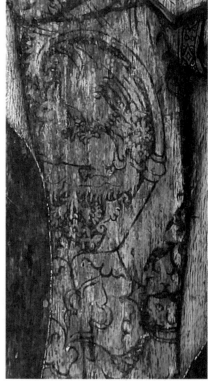

FIG. 2.   Brocade patterns in the Ranworth group at Ranworth (left) and Filby (right)

Lucy Wrapson, Hamilton Kerr Institute, University of Cambridge

Baker also pointed out the proximity of tiles beneath the saints' feet as typical of Ranworth group paintings (Fig. 3).[18] These tiles are also a Continental-derived motif and can be seen from the early 15th century, for example in stained glass, but their role in defining recessional space was either not understood or not considered desirable by the Ranworth painters. Instead of being arranged perspectively, they are used decoratively.

Beyond those paintings ascribable to the Ranworth group, parti-coloured tiling is only found on a further five rood-screens of the surviving examples in the region, at Walpole St Peter, Beeston Regis, Great Barton, Wickmere (panels now in the pulpit) and Cawston.[19] In these cases the pattern is used within a spread of other designs of flooring. At Beeston Regis, it appears better understood perspectively, as might be expected given that the screen dates to *c.* 1519, by which time Continental influence through printed sources was even more evident than in the mid-century.[20] At Cawston, the design of the saints' foreground on the panels of the north side appears influenced by the work of the Ranworth group, though less well handled. Notably, three of the

FIG. 3.   Floor tiling in the Ranworth group at (left to right, top to bottom): St James Pockthorpe, Norwich, Ranworth, Old Hunstanton, Filby, North Elmham, St Augustine, Norwich, Southwold, North Walsham, Great Plumstead (from Vallance)

Lucy Wrapson, Hamilton Kerr Institute, University of Cambridge, except where stated

five, Walpole St Peter, Beeston Regis and the north side panels at Cawston (which emulate Ranworth), are the output of the same workshop.[21]

As well as floor tiles and brocades, many of the paintings attributed to the Ranworth group also share the use of the same stencils. A stencil is a discrete and original tool, specific to a particular workshop, therefore where it is found on different screens it means that the artist had to travel to the site with the self-same tool. As can be observed repeatedly from barbs of paint adjacent to uprights and lacunae behind applied tracery, screens were painted *in situ*. Stencils evidently could have significant longevity, as the same stencils can be found on many of the works of the Ranworth group, though they could also be replaced and updated. Stencils of other patterns are widely found on painted screens in East Anglia.

Although no known stencils from panel paintings survive, there are survivors from the wall-paintings context. One example is a lead rosette stencil found at Meaux Abbey in Humberside, dating to the 14th century.[22] Lead may have been too heavy and malleable for some of the delicate stencils used on East Anglian screens, but leather, paper or parchment might have been stiff and tough enough. When applying mordant gilding through a stencil to reconstruct a section of the Thornham Parva Retable, modern tracing paper worked successfully.[23]

Five of the Ranworth group screens, Ranworth, Old Hunstanton, Filby, Thornham and North Elmham, share the use of the same stencil tool and, as can be seen in Figure 4, there are crossovers with more than one pattern between the screens of the group. A virtually identical version of the pattern can be seen on the panels derived from St James Pockthorpe in Norwich, evidence that workshops liked to replace favourite patterns (as there are other compelling points of comparison, such as the figure style and the particoloured flooring which make the St James Pockthorpe panels assuredly members of the group). The evidence for workshops replacing favoured patterns is strengthened by a further example at North Walsham (Fig. 5). It looks almost identical to the first example which occurs on five screens. However, it is a different stencil of extremely similar design, most likely postdating the more widespread stencil, but replacing it within the same workshop. The basic design of the two stencils is the same, although the spray of flowers at the top are distinct and the leaves are bunched and bound in a different way just above the base. Notably, there is a greater perspectival sense in the North Walsham version. Certainly, there is no stencil so proximate in paintings outside the Ranworth group.

Pauline Plummer considers the Ranworth group paintings the output of two generations of artists, placing Ranworth, Old Hunstanton and North Walsham as earlier than North Elmham, Filby and Norwich St James Pockthorpe.[24] The principle is correct, the paintings by the Ranworth group workshop do appear to be the work of more than one generation, but the division may not lie where Plummer suggests.

The evidence from the stencils makes for some subdivided groupings. The central screen at Southwold, North Walsham and St James Pockthorpe share some overlap, while Ranworth, Old Hunstanton and Filby use near identical sets of stencils, insofar as it is possible to tell at the heavily overpainted Filby. Thornham and North Elmham again share stencils. Stencils can therefore be used convincingly to interrelate most members of the group — Ranworth, Filby, North Elmham, St James Pockthorpe, Southwold, North Walsham, Old Hunstanton and Thornham. Three putative members of the group cannot be assessed on this basis. They are the destroyed screen from Great Plumstead, the unfinished St Augustine panel and the overcleaned and overpainted screen at Pulham St Mary the Virgin.

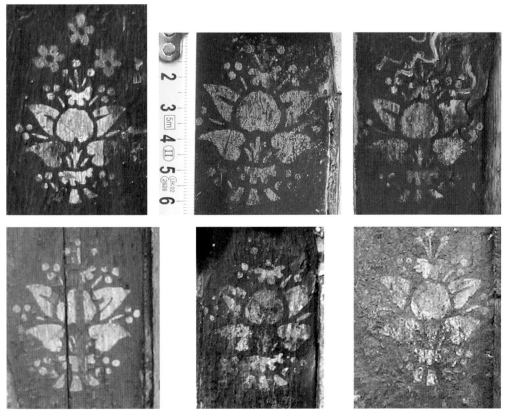

FIG. 4.   Shared stencil patterns at (left to right, top to bottom): Ranworth, Thornham, Filby,
Old Hunstanton, North Elmham, St James Pockthorpe, Norwich

Lucy Wrapson, Hamilton Kerr Institute, University of Cambridge

While the screen at Great Plumstead, destroyed by fire in 1891, can only be assessed
through illustrations from the Dawson Turner collection, the flooring, inscriptions,
figure style and stencils (which, despite being impossible to examine closely, are visually
very similar) all indicate that it was part of the group. So, too, is the unfinished panel of
St Apollonia from St Augustine in Norwich and now at St Peter Hungate, which is of
unknown origin. The panel is unusual because it is unfinished and also because, instead
of having applied tracery, it has painted tracery, a further indication that the carpentry
of the structure onto which it was painted was also unfinished, or was of 14th-century
design. Despite this, the panel must have been on view in the 16th or 17th centuries, as
it has been subjected to iconoclasm. This consists of scratching targeting St Apollonia's
face and saintly attribute. A barb of paint around the edge of the painting indicates that
it abutted other wood when it was painted, *in situ* as part of a screen structure.

St Apollonia's attribution to the Ranworth group cannot be based upon stencil
patterns or brocades, as these gilded features were not completed on the painting, on
which only the underdrawing and basic dead colouring were finished. The figure style
can be seen to be very close to that of St Cecilia at North Elmham, even down to the

FIG. 5.   Stencils from Old Hunstanton (left) and North Walsham (right)
Lucy Wrapson, Hamilton Kerr Institute, University of Cambridge

detail of the foot position (Fig. 6), although the designs differ in size and were probably copied freehand from a pattern book, rather than using a traced cartoon.

The unfinished painting of St John the Baptist at Ranworth also makes for a pertinent comparison. On the north side nave altar there are four saints, St Etheldreda, a palimpsest figure of St John the Baptist, which has sometimes been termed St Agnes, an unfinished panel of St John the Baptist and St Barbara. Infrared photography shows that beneath the finished St John the Baptist there is the underdrawing of an archbishop saint (Fig. 7). The planned archbishop saint was converted to St John the Baptist at a late stage, probably, as Duffy has suggested, because a reliquary or statue of the Baptist was to be placed on the altar in front.[25]

The upper angel of the 'original' St John the Baptist was painted out, and the rest left incomplete and probably painted out, only to be revealed by later restoration. The existence of this other unfinished work makes for close comparison with St Apollonia. Both share the use of dead colouring after the initial painting has been completed and the style of the painting and hatching is similarly skilled. Furthermore, the layout of the ground on which Apollonia stands lies ready for the tiling and inscriptions seen on so many other members of the group.

The Ranworth group painters were evidently at the higher status end of rood-screen painting in Norfolk. The quality of the drawing and painting speaks for itself. However, technical study using X-ray fluorescence and analysis of paint samples indicates that the Ranworth group painters used among the fullest range of pigments found on East Anglian screens. This includes both silver and gold leaf, two blue pigments, azurite and indigo, and a range of red lake pigments including both madder and a darker red lake. A unifying feature of the Ranworth group paintings is the absence of the use of white priming layers over the ground, seen in many screens elsewhere (for example, at Carleton Rode in Norfolk). Another typical feature of the Ranworth workshop output

FIG. 6.   St Cecilia, North Elmham compared with the unfinished St Apollonia panel from
St Augustine, Norwich

Lucy Wrapson, Hamilton Kerr Institute, University of Cambridge

FIG. 7.   St John the Baptist/bishop saint, Ranworth in normal light and infrared photographs
Lucy Wrapson, Hamilton Kerr Institute, University of Cambridge

is the application of indigo flowers to decorate the white frameworks which surround the panels.

Taken together, all these features build a strong picture of continuity and consistency in design and technique between a sequence of related works. On the basis of technical as well as stylistic evidence Baker's larger Ranworth grouping can be accepted, excluding the screens at Pulham St Mary and Attleborough. Although badly damaged, over cleaned and much overpainted, the Pulham screen is of high quality; but the figures are thicker set, where visible the paint can be seen to be modelled in a different way, and there are none of the distinctive curly locks favoured by the Ranworth artists (Fig. 8). The scheme at Pulham St Mary more closely resembles paintings of the 1460s, and relates to the painting at Attleborough. Furthermore, there is no evidence of characteristic stencil patterns, indigo flowers, brocades, or the distinctive floor pattern seen in other members of the group. I suspect that the paintings at Attleborough have been related to Ranworth as much on the basis of the screen's having nave altars as for their stylistic similarities. This in turn comes from a misunderstanding of the typically divided nature of screen carpentry and painting.[26]

FIG. 8.   St Andrew and St John the Evangelist, Pulham St Mary the Virgin
Lucy Wrapson, Hamilton Kerr Institute, University of Cambridge

DATING THE RANWORTH GROUP PAINTINGS

THE testamentary bequests relating to the various screens or related work at churches within the Ranworth group are set out in Table 1. Rood-lofts were large, expensive, composite structures, so were often the product of parish fundraising and could take decades to complete. Where screens are dated by painted inscription, this marks the end of a long story of construction and decoration, which were typically separate processes involving distinct craftsmen. This separation of the crafts can be seen clearly at St Catherine's, Fritton in Norfolk, where the painters had to respond to the unfinished tracery carving by cramming St Jude beneath an un-carved tracery head. However, the distinction is also borne out when grouping related screens. While there are groups of works by both the same carpenters and the same painters, the groupings do not interrelate.

As a general rule, related works of carpentry tend to cluster around specific localities, whereas related works of painting, particularly the Ranworth group paintings, are more disparate. An examination of rood-screen paintings demonstrates that, with the exception of those on paper at Lessingham, Cawston and Aylsham, they had to be painted on site. Therefore artists had to be itinerant.

The surveying of screens has demonstrated a significant change in the jointing technique of the transom to uprights that can be given a chronology through comparison of will bequest dates to surviving objects (Table 2).[27] Comparing the joint types used at this junction with dating evidence for over a hundred screens reveals a pattern in which

225

TABLE 1.   Will Dates for Ranworth Group Rood-Screen Paintings[28]

Location	Dating
Filby	1471 William Tebbe left church a pulpitum. 1503 bequest by Walter Lemanton to paint Crucifix, Mary and John.
Great Plumstead	Unknown.
North Elmham	Blomefield's notebooks record an inscription formerly on the doors of the screen which had the date 1474.[29] There was also a 1457 donation to the pulpitum before the rood loft.
North Walsham	No bequests, but there was extensive building work c. 1460–80.
Norwich St Augustine	Unknown.
Norwich St James Pockthorpe	1479 William Blakdam to paint screen.
Old Hunstanton	Unknown.
Ranworth	1479 screen above the altar of St Mary to be painted of his goods, Robert Iryng.
Southwold	1459 John Colton/Golcorn £20 to making new candlebeam. 1459 John Talyour 20s. 'ad trabem'. 1461 William Grantham 20d. 'ad factur particu'. 1470 Robert Scolys 22s. to decorate rood. 1474 Thomas Sewall to paint reredos behind rood. 1481 Henry Burgese 40s. to paint candlebeam.
Thornham	Donors John and Clarice Miller (John d. 1488). Inscription formerly on screen.

'scribed joints' supersede the 'mason's mitre' (Fig. 9). This examination of jointing techniques on screen transoms is relevant here because there has been diversity of opinion over the date of the Ranworth screen. There have been four traditionally ascribed dates for Ranworth, c. 1417, c. 1430, c. 1450 and c. 1479.[30]

Once Ranworth's related screens are taken into account and their will bequests and jointing techniques examined, it becomes clear that the group spanned the period of transition between mason's mitre and scribed joints. On the basis of the wider body of screens in Norfolk and Suffolk this indicates a 1470s–1500 date for the output of this workshop.

This late-15th-century date for the Ranworth group has been further corroborated by the results of dendrochronology undertaken by Ian Tyers.[31] Two sets of Ranworth group screens were examined: the panels originally from St James Pockthorpe and the single panel depicting St Apollonia from St Augustine in Norwich (now in Hungate). All of these panels are detached from their original structures.

In the case of the St Apollonia panel, the board has been much trimmed, meaning that the latest discernible year ring was 1393. However, given the trimming, the date-range c. 1401–1500 can be established. Unfortunately, this does not assist in discerning the plausibility of any of the dates traditionally assigned to Ranworth. The panels from St James Pockthorpe were more tightly datable. It was possible to examine more

TABLE 2. Jointing Types in the Ranworth Group

Screen	Joint Type (Transom to Uprights)	Dating from Wills
Filby	Scribed	1471 to pulpitum; 1503 to painting rood.[32]
Great Plumstead	Unknown	Unknown.
North Elmham	Scribed	1474 dated inscription.
North Walsham	Mason's mitre	After *c.* 1470.
St Augustine	Unknown	Unknown.
St James Pockthorpe	Unknown	1479 will bequest.
Old Hunstanton	Mason's mitre	Unknown.
Ranworth	Mason's mitre	1479 altar of St Mary.
Southwold	Scribed	Construction in 1450s–60s. 1474 painted tympanum, 1481, to painting candlebeam.
Thornham	Scribed	Donors John and Clarice Miller (John d. 1488). Inscription formerly on screen.

FIG. 9.   A mason's mitre transom joint at Ranworth and a scribed transom joint at Southwold
Lucy Wrapson, Hamilton Kerr Institute, University of Cambridge

panels, several of which still retain their sapwood, and a date range of 1459–94 could be ascribed to the felling of the tree and its use in the screen.[33]

The only recorded donor for the screen from St James Pockthorpe is William Blakdam, a worsted weaver who gave 10 marks for the painting of the screen in 1479.[34] The inclusion of a St Johanna on the screen has been used to date it to after 1505, on the basis of the saint's identification as St Joan of Valois, but this identification is uncertain.[35] The tree-ring dating evidence indicates that the 1479 will date is accurate in this case.

In general, dating screens from wills is not without its pitfalls, as is the case at Southwold where there are five screens. The three which cross the church are richly painted and can be considered to form the rood-screen; the other two screens run east/west and separate chapels from the chancel. The rood-screen is in turn decorated with angels, apostles and prophets. The surviving will bequests for the Southwold screen are outlined in Table 1.

While the central apostle screen at Southwold can be seen to be a member of the Ranworth group, it differs in design from the other members. Southwold is the only screen in Suffolk where applied glass decorations survive, although this technique was very long-standing in medieval English art.[36] It is also the only Ranworth group screen where the repeat cast method tin-relief is found, and where the stencilled decoration on a red or green background gives way to the use of a gilded cloth of honour motif. Despite the apparently early date from documentary evidence, an average of the wills puts it at 1469, both the screen structure and the painted design of the central screen indicate a date of c. 1500. On physical evidence, the date 1469 much more closely reflects the design and decoration of the two parclose screens to either side. The two parcloses have mason's mitre joints, whereas the central screen is scribe-jointed.

An examination of the profile of the surviving four hundred or so East Anglian screen transoms has demonstrated how they change over time.[37] This reflects general trends in design change, and identical complex transoms can furthermore be demonstrated to be the products of the same carpenters. Transoms of the 14th century are often variations on simple square or rectangular sections, there is a substantial design change with the shift to Perpendicular-style screens in the early 15th century with an elaboration in form. In the mid- to late 15th century, designs become more complex still — and those of the 16th century are generally the largest, most complex and elaborate forms.

The two parclose screens at Southwold fit into the mid- to late-15th-century category. In fact, the moulding profiles and tracery design of the two parcloses are nigh on identical to those at nearby Woodbridge where an average of dates from its will bequests comes to 1454. The proximity in design is close enough to propose a shared workshop origin. On the other hand, the central screen at Southwold has the heavy, elaborate transom, and design details of a 16th-century screen.

This likely date is reiterated by the painting. The Ranworth group 'Apostles' screen at Southwold has details which show a different approach to painting from what must be earlier works — for example, in the depiction of St Philip's bread basket. At Ranworth itself this basket is painted using a black paint over silver leaf, the preciousness and significance of the bread being emphasized by the materials chosen to depict its container. At Southwold, the saint's basket is rendered without precious leaf, but instead modelled three-dimensionally in paint (Fig. 10). This more modern rendering was inspired no doubt by northern European painting technique. As Mitchell has shown, from about 1500 the influence of the northern Renaissance came to be felt in East Anglian screen painting. It is at this date that cloth of honour backgrounds like

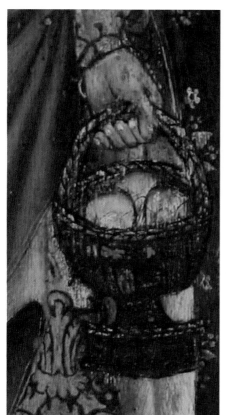

FIG. 10. St Philip's bread basket at Ranworth (left) and Southwold (right)

Lucy Wrapson, Hamilton Kerr Institute, University of Cambridge

those at Southwold become more widespread, alongside depictions of perspectival spaces, landscapes and even portraiture.[38] Southwold's central screen may have come from elsewhere or, more likely, the replacement of the central section of the 1460s screen is not documented.[39] Either way, there is sound evidence, from style, motifs such as tiling and brocades, and the use of stencils found on other Ranworth group screens to show that it represents the last surviving work of the Ranworth painters and dates to *c.* 1500.

THE RANWORTH GROUP PAINTINGS: A NORWICH-BASED WORKSHOP?

THE foregoing discussion raises questions: who might have painted the Ranworth screen and did the same generation paint Southwold? How many members of the workshop were there at any one time? A look even at the designs of floors at Ranworth indicates there was more than one hand there (Fig. 11), although the consistency of stencils indicates that the screen was the product of one campaign of painting. Did they work only as painters, or were they also responsible for other artistic output? Where was the workshop based?

FIG. 11.   Ranworth floors, probably by more than one hand
Lucy Wrapson, Hamilton Kerr Institute, University of Cambridge

Mitchell has suggested that as many as four hands can be identified within the Ranworth group.[40] Differentiating between different hands in a workshop aiming for uniformity is difficult, and the Ranworth workshop figures can seem elongated or robust, depending on the scale of the panels on which they are painted. Furthermore, it is only at Ranworth itself where the less formulaic nave altars and parclose wings allow the painters to work with greater freedom than when painting awkward dado saints on their knees. Nonetheless, the workshop undoubtedly comprised more than one hand, and the division of labour rather than being straightforwardly delineated between panels may instead be found in the execution of different paint passages or areas.[41]

A 2008 paper by David King builds on and refines work done in the 1970s by Greenwood and Norris concerning Norwich glazier William Heyward.[42] Greenwood and Norris suggested that there was a multi-media workshop based in the Norwich parish of St Peter Parmentergate which was responsible for making stained glass, brasses and possibly rood-screen panels, although they were not aware of the itinerant nature of screen painting.[43] Greenwood and Norris identified a series of related brasses termed N3, and tied their design to stained glass at East Harling and St Peter Mancroft. Evidence used to support this association was the will of John Ayleward, the rector of East Harling who in 1503 ordered his marble stone and brass from leading Norwich glazier William Heyward, who became a freeman in 1485 and died in 1505. Only the indent for the brass survives, and the association of what must have been a high-quality Norwich brass with high-quality Norwich glass at East Harling formed the basis of the attribution.

King's work on the glass of East Harling has led to the modification of the specifics of the attribution. He has shown that the glass Greenwood and Norris associated with N3 brasses at East Harling is most likely the earlier output, *c.* 1465–80, of John Wighton. King instead ties the design of N3 brasses to the *Te Deum* glass in the east window of

East Harling (Figs 12 and 13). The patron of this window was Anne Harling. It contains glass from as many as four different workshops and it is datable to *c*. 1491–98.

King's stylistic attribution is based on two key N3 group brasses, the 1495 brass of William de Grey and family at Merton, and the 1496 brass of Henry Spelman and his wife at Narborough. Notably, the Spelmans were close family friends of Anne Harling. King ties his proposed multi-media workshop to the Ranworth group by relating the two elaborate brasses and the *Te Deum* window to the screen paintings. He also makes the point that the period when most screens were being made, which, as Duffy has shown, was between *c*. 1450–1530, was the time at which the names of painters are less numerous.[44] Counting the named painters and stainers, King shows that nineteen names are from the first half of the 15th century, seven from the second half and only two from the early 16th century. He suggests two possible explanations for this: that

FIG. 12.   Part of the *Te Deum* window at East Harling including Ranworth-type floor
Lucy Wrapson, Hamilton Kerr Institute, University of Cambridge

231

FIG. 13.   Angel from the East Harling *Te Deum* window compared with St Michael, Filby
Lucy Wrapson, Hamilton Kerr Institute, University of Cambridge

much of the work on screens was undertaken outside the city, where craftsmen did not have to be enrolled as freemen and are unrecorded, and that the dearth of named painters may be due to the presence of a multi-media urban workshop which practised several crafts.[45]

Indeed, there are close links between the design of the East Harling *Te Deum* window and Ranworth group painting, particularly in terms of the depictions of the faces of angels. It is possible to go further: the *Te Deum* window also has one of comparatively few instances in Norfolk stained glass of the characteristic flooring seen on the painted screens. It can be seen in two other examples of Norfolk stained glass, at St Peter Hungate in Norwich and at Warham. At Warham, as well as a fragmentary example of Ranworth-style flooring in the stained glass, there is also an attributed N3 brass, the group of brasses attributed by Greenwood and Norris to William Heyward.

Two further N3 brasses can be found at Ranworth itself; one is the earliest of the N3 brasses, the other probably a late example, although it bears no date. Strikingly, the early brass may be the memorial for the only known benefactor to the screen, or a close relative. The tomb, situated in front of the altar on the south side, commemorates Roger Erying and the accompanying brass is dated 1484. The 1479 will of Robert Irying records what may be the only surviving bequest to the Ranworth screen. It records his instruction for 'the screen above the altar of St Mary to be painted of my goods'.[46] The other brass, that of Alice, daughter of John Berney, also with an N3 attribution, may reflect a continuing relationship between the workshop and the church.[47]

The relationship between screens and tomb monuments was often intimate. Luxford has shown how the cadaver panels at Sparham may have functioned as a surrogate tomb monument.[48] Ralph Segrym, mayor of Norwich, was buried close to a screen which had highly personalized decoration — his merchant mark and initials as well as a choice of saints that reflected his personal charitable interests.[49] The situation is repeated at other sites: at Aylsham the screen is inscribed (in paint) to Thomas Wymer and his brass lies in close association with it. Within the Ranworth group itself, at Thornham the donor John Miller's tomb now lies at the west end of the south aisle but is recorded by Blomefield as having formerly been near the screen.[50] Miller's will was proved at Norwich in 1489.[51]

Although the evidence is circumstantial, the presence of N3 brasses at Warham and Ranworth strengthens King's suggestion. The implication is that it was possible to order funerary monuments, glass and screen painting from a single source. William Heyward's will indicates activity in both brass making and glass painting, as he left his glazing tools to his brother.[52] He also made a bequest for an obit to be said for a 'Mother Marbler and her husband'. Tax returns in Norwich in 1489 list a Marion Marbler, widow of marbler Thomas Sheef, who may well be Heyward's 'mother marbler'.[53] Marbler was the term for a brass maker as their main products were the marble stones into which brasses were set. In his will, William Heyward may have been offering thanks for those who taught him an allied trade, or close colleagues for whom he acted as a designer and to whom he subcontracted work.

In fact, William Heyward's dates mean he is unlikely to have been personally responsible for those rood-screen paintings which appear to have been done in the 1470s, as he was made free in 1485 and made his will in 1505/6. However an examination of his wider family and professional connections is extremely instructive (Table 3). Heyward had an elder brother, Nicholas, who was also a glazier. The brothers came from Knapton, near Paston in Norfolk, and Nicholas was made free as a glazier in Norwich in 1469/70.[54]

Nicholas Heyward was apprentice to Thomas Goldbeater, who died in 1467. Goldbeater's surname, as King has suggested, implies a panel-painting origin, and a property of his in St Peter Parmentergate in Norwich was previously owned by painter Stephen Frenge and later by Nicholas Heyward.[55] Notably, Goldbeater's other apprentices included John Tompson who was made free as a glazier, but also Richard Steere who, like Nicholas Heyward, was made free in 1469, but was made free as a painter, although he too later worked as a glazier. It is possible that the panel-painting aspect of the wider workshop was managed by painter Richard Steere.[56]

William Heyward was the most prominent figure of the four and was one of only two glaziers to become an alderman of Norwich.[57] It is unlikely, therefore, that Heyward would have been in charge of an itinerant painting workshop with its origins in the city. Richard Steere, a painter trained by a glazier with a panel painter's surname, would appear a more likely candidate.

The brass and screen combination at Thornham also supports this hypothesis. Donor John Miller's name is recorded as having been on the screen and, while his brass has since been moved, his slab previously lay in front of the screen. An examination of Miller's plaque, not explicitly grouped by Greenwood and Norris, reveals it to be of their N2 type. Critically, brasses of the N2 variety, made in Norwich, are thought by Greenwood and Norris to be the direct workshop precedent to the N3 group.[58] Whereas N3 brasses are associated with William Heyward and begin only in 1484, the N2 brasses are associated with the earlier workshop under Marion Sheef ('Mother Marbler') and those who may have worked for her, Richard Foxe and possibly Thomas Storme. At this point, the relationship between the brass, glass and screen workshop may have been different than under William Heyward, but the alliances and possible

TABLE 3. Craft Associations[59]

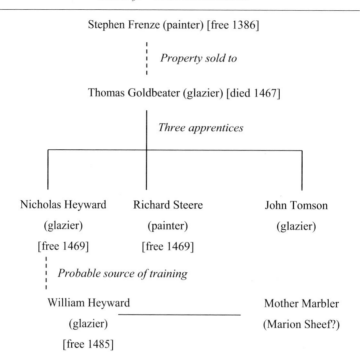

Stephen Frenze (painter) [free 1386]

Property sold to

Thomas Goldbeater (glazier) [died 1467]

Three apprentices

Nicholas Heyward	Richard Steere	John Tomson
(glazier)	(painter)	(glazier)
[free 1469]	[free 1469]	

Probable source of training

William Heyward   Mother Marbler

(glazier)   (Marion Sheef?)

[free 1485]

Nicholas Heyward was apprentice to a Thomas Goldbeater, who died in 1467.

subcontracting that led to a close relationship between the Sheef brass workshop and the Ranworth painters may have already been in place.

Documentary evidence as well as other figures in stained glass suggest that the workshop responsible for Ranworth may not have been the only one operating in painting and designing stained glass. Norwich/Dutch glazier William Mundeford's trade as a currier or leather dresser implies a link with painting: painters in Utrecht belonged to the Saddler's guild.[60] Between 1382 and 1388 there are references to a painter-glazier called John Alunday/Glazier for painting fireplaces, gates and banners for the city of Norwich.[61] Once again, the craft boundaries can be seen to have been fluid.

The post-Renaissance tendency to see painting as pre-eminent among the crafts can accord anachronistic significance to medieval painters over the practitioners of other crafts. However, it seems likely that the painters of screens were also the painters of glass and the designers of brasses. It would make sense for a benefactor planning for their soul after death to order their brass and screen decoration at the same time from medieval tradesmen clubbed together into workshops offering a variety of services. Although screens were often community ventures, subdivisions and localized inscriptions to individuals often remain in evidence. Given the relationship between screens and tombs, the leap from brass-making to glass and screen painting might not be as strange as it first appears, particularly when one considers that in Norwich craftsmen of each type were members of guild of St Luke.[62]

NOTES

1. The survey was funded by the Leverhulme Trust and undertaken at the Hamilton Kerr Institute, University of Cambridge.

2. The screen, and church, was nearly lost in the early 1960s when the then thatched roof caught fire from a cigarette dropped from the tower. Following on from wood conservator Joe Royal, Pauline Plummer and her team undertook conservation on the screen seasonally from 1962 until 1975, during which time the screen was visited by the Queen.

3. Ranworth featured, for example, in *Churches: How to Read Them*, a 2011 BBC television series.

4. G. A. F. Plunkett, 'Norfolk church screens 1865 survey', *NA*, 37 (1979), 178–89; W. Morant and J. L'Estrange, 'Notices of the church at Randworth, Walsham Hundred', *NA*, 7 (1872), 178–211; C. J. W. Winter, *Illustrations of the Rood-screen at Ranworth* (Norwich 1867).

5. E. F. Strange, *The Rood-screen of Ranworth Church* (Norwich 1902).

6. R. O. Pearson, *Ranworth Rood Screen* (Norwich 1910).

7. W. A. Dutt, *The Norfolk Broads* (London 1903), 174–75.

8. Fox considered Ranworth English (and was probably right); Strange thought it was painted by Swabians; Vallance favoured a Catalan origin. G. E. Fox, 'Medieval Art', in *The Victoria History of the Counties of England: Norfolk*, ed. W. Page, vol. 2 (London 1906), 529–54; Strange, *Rood-screen* (as in n. 5); A. Vallance, *English Church Screens* (London 1936).

9. Women were habitually segregated in the north side of the church, but there are a number of churches where this was reversed. For the separation of the genders in church, see M. Aston, 'Segregation in church', in *Women in the Church: papers read at the 1989 Summer Meeting and the 1990 Winter Meeting of the Ecclesiastical History Society*, ed. W. J. Sheils and D. Wood (Oxford and Cambridge 1990), 237–94. M. Naydenova-Slade, 'Images of the Holy kinship in England, c. 1170 to c. 1525' (unpublished Ph.D. thesis, Courtauld Institute of Art, 2008), 148–50. Nave altars were previously part of the screens at Attleborough, South Burlingham and Wellingham (all in Norfolk), among other places.

10. Churchwardens' accounts, such as those for Yatton in Somerset, sometimes reveal the payments made to painters over several years for the painting of rood lofts. The drying time of oil paint should also be taken into account when considering the time that screen painting might take. E. Hobhouse ed., *Churchwardens' Accounts of Croscombe, Pilton, Yatton, Tintinhull, Morebath and St Michael's, Bath, ranging from A. D. 1349–1560*, Somerset Record Society, 4 (London 1890).

11. E. T. Long, 'Screen paintings in Devon and East Anglia', *The Burlington Magazine for Connoisseurs*, 59.393 (1931), 168–71. Long perceptively noted that, on stylistic observation, Southwold appeared to be the latest screen.

12. O. M. Briggs, 'Some painted screens of Norfolk', *JRIBA*, 3rd series, 41.19 (1934), 997–1016. Dates come from S. J. Cotton, 'Mediæval roodscreens in Norfolk, their construction and painting dates', *NA*, 40/1 (1987), 48, 50.

13. Baker also relates Attleborough, partially on a structural basis. However, this is based on a misunderstanding of how the structure and painting relates, on the assumption that they are the work of the same workshop. A. M. Baker, *English Panel Paintings 1400–1558: A survey of figure paintings on East Anglian rood screens* (London 2011), 37–38.

14. J. Mitchell, 'Painting in East Anglia around 1500: the continental connection', in *England and the Continent in the Middle Ages: studies in memory of Andrew Martindale*, ed. J. Mitchell (Stamford 2000), 365–80.

15. Plummer in Baker, *English Panel Paintings* (as in n. 13), 15–32, 169.

16. A. Eljenholm Nichols, *Early Art of Norfolk: A Subject List of Extant and Lost Art Including Items Relevant to Early Drama* (Kalamazoo 2002), 321–22.

17. Baker, *English Panel Paintings* (as in n. 13), 13.

18. Ibid., 14.

19. It is also found on the St Etheldreda panels, now in the Society of Antiquaries and thought to have an Ely provenance, but by Bury painter Robert Pygot.

20. Mitchell, 'Painting in East Anglia' (as in n. 14), 365–80.

21. L. J. Wrapson, 'Patterns of production: a technical art historical study of East Anglia's late medieval screens' (unpublished Ph.D. thesis, University of Cambridge, 2013), 423–25.

22. E. Howe, 'Wall painting technology at Westminster Abbey c. 1260–1300', in *Medieval Painting in Northern Europe: Techniques, Analysis, Art History*, ed. J. Nadolny et al. (London 2006), 91–113.

23. A. Tavares da Silva, 'Reconstructing the decorated background', in *The Thornham Parva Retable: Technique, Conservation and Context of an English Medieval Painting*, ed. A. Massing (Cambridge and Turnhout 2003), 129–33.

24. P. Plummer, 'The Ranworth rood screen', *Archaeol. J.*, 137 (1981), 292–95.

25. E. Duffy, 'The parish, piety, and patronage in late medieval East Anglia: the evidence of screens', in *The Parish in English Life, 1400–1600*, ed. K. L. French, G. G. Gibbs and B. A. Kümin (Manchester 1997), 156–58.

26. Baker, *English Panel Paintings* (as in n. 13), 37–38.

27. First pointed out by Hugh Harrison and developed by Tim Howson in relation to Suffolk screens. T. Howson, 'Suffolk church screens: their production in the late middle ages and their conservation today' (unpublished Diploma in Buildings Conservation, Architectural Association, 2009).

28. Except where indicated, all of the bequest information comes from Cotton, 'Mediæval roodscreens' (as in n. 12), 44–54.

29. Oxford, Bodleian Library, MS Gough, Norfolk 4, f. 179r: 'On ye screen many sts and Orate p(ro) a(n)i(m)ab(us) roberti pynnis & margarete uxoris sue et omnium benefactorum eor(um) qui hoc opus fecerunt pingi an(n)o d(omi)ni $M^o ccc^o lxxiiij^o$.' I am grateful to David King and Simon Cotton for this reference.

30. Morant and L'Estrange first associated the 1419 will of Thomas Grym and its reference to the 'cancelli' with Ranworth's screen, and their early dating was followed by Pevsner, but altered in revision by Wilson. Tudor-Craig also supported the 1419 will date, but proposed a delay until *c.* 1430. Lasko and Morgan suggested *c.* 1450. Howard and Crossley were the first to date Ranworth late 15th century, and this is supported by Mitchell. Morant and L'Estrange, 'Notices' (as in n. 4), 178–211; B/E, *Norfolk*, II, 642–43; P. Lasko and N. J. Morgan, *Mediæval art in East Anglia 1300–1520* (London and Norwich 1973), 49; F. E. Howard and F. H. Crossley, *English Church Woodwork: A Study in Craftsmanship during the Medieval Period A.D. 1250–1550* (London 1927), 242; P. Tudor Craig, 'Medieval paintings from St Michael at Plea, Norwich', *The Burlington Magazine*, 642.98 (1956), 333–34; Mitchell, 'Painting in East Anglia' (as in n. 14), 371.

31. I. Tyers, 'Tree-ring analysis of a rood screen fragment: St Apollonia, from St Augustine's Church, Norwich' (unpublished report 504, 2012). The painting may have been applied to an earlier screen without tracery, hence the early date and fictive painted tracery head.

32. The bequest information comes from Cotton, 'Mediæval roodscreens' (as in n. 12), 44–54. See Table 1 for further details.

33. I. Tyers, 'Tree-ring analysis of the rood screen at St Mary Magdalene, Silver Road, Norwich, formerly from St James Pockthorpe, Norwich' (unpublished report 505, 2012). The boards used to make up the dado of the St James Pockthorpe screen were shown to derive from oak trees in Norfolk, that from St Apollonia from the eastern Baltic.

34. Cotton, 'Mediæval roodscreens' (as in n. 12), 50.

35. W. W. Williamson, 'Saints on Norfolk Rood-Screens and Pulpits', *NA*, 31 (1957), 312; Eljenholm Nichols, *Early Art* (as in n. 16), 204–25.

36. In Norfolk, the screen at Cawston also features this technique.

37. Wrapson, 'Patterns of production' (as in n. 21), 78–88.

38. Mitchell, 'Painting in East Anglia' (as in n. 14), 365–80.

39. The screen is cut down by a half-bay at each side. Local architect John Bennett has speculated that the screen may come from Covehithe church (pers. comm.).

40. Mitchell, 'Painting in East Anglia' (as in n. 14), 371.

41. For the theme of individual hands and workshop practice, see L. F. Jacobs, *Early Netherlandish carved altarpieces, 1380–1550: medieval tastes and mass marketing* (Cambridge 1998), 209–37; S. Kemperdick, '"Meister" und Maler. Was sind die Kölner Werkgruppen um 1400?', *Die Sprache des Materials — Kölner Maltechnik des Spätmittelalters im Kontext, Zeitschrift für Kunsttechnologie und Konservierung*, 26.1 (2012), 114–26; N. Peeters and M. P. J. Martens, 'A cutting edge? Wood carvers and their workshops in Antwerp 1453–1579', in *Constructing Wooden Images. Proceedings of the symposium on the organization of labour and working practices of Late Gothic carved altarpieces in the Low Countries* (Brussels 25–26 October 2002), ed. C. van de Velde, H. Beeckman, J. van Acker et al. (Brussels 2005), 75–92, and U. Schäfer, 'Is it possible to describe the personal style of an Antwerp carver?', in *Constructing Wooden Images. Proceedings of the symposium on the organization of labour and working practices of Late Gothic carved altarpieces in the Low Countries* (Brussels 25–26 October 2002), ed. C. van de Velde, H. Beeckman, J. van Acker et al. (Brussels 2005), 27–50.

42. D. King, 'A Multi-Media Workshop in Late Medieval Norwich — A New Look at William Heyward', in *Lumières, formes et couleurs: Mélanges en hommage à Yvette Vanden Bemden*, ed. C. De Ruyt, I. Lecocq, M. Lefftz and M. Piavaux (Namur 2008), 193–204; see also D. King, 'The Indent of John Aylward: Glass and Brass at East Harling', *Monumental Brass Society Transactions*, 18.3 (2011), 251–67.

43. R. Greenwood and M. Norris, *The Brasses of Norfolk Churches* (Holt 1976), 31.

44. E. Duffy, 'The Parish, Piety, and Patronage in Late Medieval East Anglia: The Evidence of Screens', in *The Parish in English Life, 1400–1600*, ed. K. French, G. Gibbs and B. Kümin (Manchester 1997), 138.

45. King, 'Multi-Media Workshop' (as in n. 42).

46. This has been associated with a cloth hanging, as the Latin is somewhat ambiguous, 'Item volo quod quid. Pann' pendent' coram altarem Sce Marie in eadem ecclesia erit pictat' de bonis meis propiis'. Morant and L'Estrange, 'Notices' (as in n. 4), 195. If Robert/Roger Erying were not the same man, then a family connection seems highly probable.

47. Greenwood and Norris, *Brasses* (as in n. 43), 49.

48. J. Luxford, 'The Sparham corpse panels: unique revelations of death from late fifteenth century England', *Antiq. J.*, 90 (2010), 1–42.

49. Specifically his charitable interests concerning prisoners is reflected in the presence of St Leonard. For Segrym's patronage of a women's prison in Norwich, see R. B. Pugh, *Imprisonment in Medieval England* (Cambridge 1968), 358.

50. Blomefield, *Norfolk*, 10, 391–95.

51. M. A. Farrow, *Index of wills proved in the Consistory Court of Norwich 1370–1550*, vol. 2 (London 1945).

52. D. King, *The Medieval Stained Glass of St Peter Mancroft Norwich* (Oxford and New York 2006), 140–41.

53. J. Bayliss, 'Brass of the Month, May 2008: William de Grey [1495] and his wives Mary and Grace, Merton, Norfolk', Monumental Brass Society website, http://www.mbs-brasses.co.uk/page148a.html [accessed June 2013].

54. J. L'Estrange, *Calendar of the Freemen of Norwich from 1307–1603* (London 1888), 73.

55. This suggestion is supported by the family connections between another 'Painter' and 'Goldbeater'. National Archives C 241/49/366 is a record of a debt owed by a Richard le Peyntour, son of Adam Orbatur (Goldbeater) in 1305, and is indicative of the close relationship between painting and goldbeating.

56. Baker, *English Panel Paintings* (as in n. 13), 224–25 suggests that the painter mentioned in North Elmham's churchwardens' accounts in 1548, William Tilney, may have been responsible for painting the screen. However, she was not aware of the 1474 date of the screen (see n. 30). For William Tilney, see A. G. Legge, *Ancient churchwardens' accounts of the parish of North Elmham 1539–1577* (Norwich 1891).

57. Bayliss, 'Brass of the month' (as in n. 52).

58. Greenwood and Norris, *Brasses* (as in n. 43), 22–30.

59. King, *Mancroft Glass* (as in n. 53), 138–41. For the individuals in question being made free, see L'Estrange, *Calendar* (as in n. 54), 55, 73, 130, 139.

60. King, *Mancroft Glass* (as in n. 52), 138.

61. Ibid., xcix.

62. The guild of St Luke in Norwich included the painters, stainers, bell founders, glass makers, brasiers, pewterers and plumbers. C. Woodforde, *The Norwich School of Glass-Painting in the Fifteenth Century* (Oxford 1950), 14.

Norwich Cathedral Spire: Why it Still Stands

A. RICHARD JONES

Norwich Cathedral's present spire, completed in the last quarter of the 15th century, is the second tallest in England, standing 318 ft high. An overview of the physical spire precedes a discussion of failure and an analysis of one particular failure, overtopping by wind. The methodology with which Jacques Heyman investigated the stability of spires is extended and adapted to the structure of this spire to see why it has withstood the elements for over five hundred years.

INTRODUCTION

ALTHOUGH this paper is not about history, a few dates from the Norwich Cathedral conservation plan provide context:[1]

1291–97	early spire built
1361–62	early spire destroyed in a storm
1463	timber replacement spire destroyed by a fire caused by lightning
1472–99	present spire built by Bishop James Goldwell; perhaps completed *c.* 1485

Evidently, the tower is well able to support the spire, the wall thickness of which diminishes with height.

THE PHYSICAL SPIRE

FIGURE 1a is a sectional drawing of Norwich Cathedral spire.[2] The spire's outer surface extends from its octagonal base to a geometrical summit — where the projections of the outer surfaces cross — 317 ft 10 in. (~96.9 m) above this drawing's base level. Above the roof of the tower, the same level as the crown of its interior floor, the spire rises 176 ft 6 in. (~53.8 m). The conservation plan (Section 9.5.1) gives the total height excluding the weathercock as 95.36 m (312 ft 10$^1/_3$ in.) above the floor of the crossing. This five-foot discrepancy must be due to different reference levels, not to, say, foundation settlement following the drawing. In the same section, the conservation plan's figure for the height of the spire itself is 52.64 m (172 ft 8$^7/_{16}$ in.), about 4 ft less than the height from the drawing. This, too, may be due to different reference levels, as the conservation plan does not rigorously relate reference levels to specific architectural details.

As shown in Figure 1b, the spire can be divided into upper, middle, and lower zones, designated zone 1, zone 2 and zone 3 respectively. Zone 1 has lucarnes (or dormers), no buttresses, and a thinner wall and steeper slope than zone 3, which has no lucarnes but does have buttresses. The short zone 2 is vertical, with the same thick wall and buttresses as zone 3.

The spire is actually brick with a stone facing, as the brick showing on a buttress reveals. A section of the wall in zone 1 reveals a serious problem: the stone had

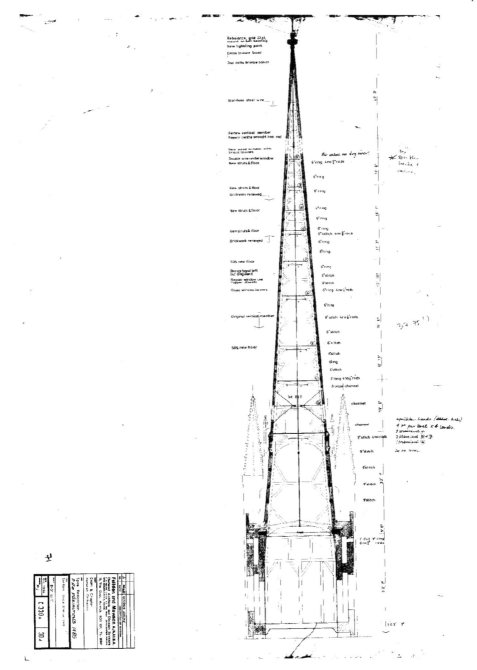

FIG. 1a.   Cross-section of Norwich Cathedral spire, Feilden and Mawson drawing
ref. 071-1964_Restoration_Sprinklers, Title 'Section Spire Sprinklers', dated October 1964,
revised March 1988

Used by permission

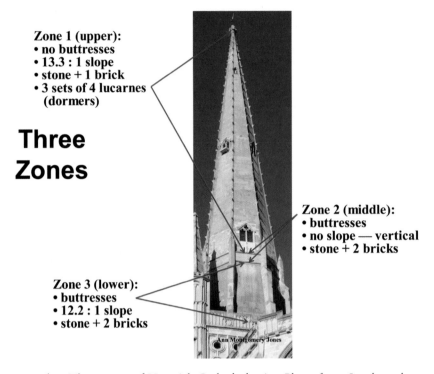

Zone 1 (upper):
• no buttresses
• 13.3 : 1 slope
• stone + 1 brick
• 3 sets of 4 lucarnes
  (dormers)

Three Zones

Zone 2 (middle):
• buttresses
• no slope — vertical
• stone + 2 bricks

Zone 3 (lower):
• buttresses
• 12.2 : 1 slope
• stone + 2 bricks

Ann Montgomery Jones

FIG. 1b.   Three zones of Norwich Cathedral spire. Photo from *Southeast* by
Ann Montgomery Jones, 14 September 2011, used by permission

detached from the brick, leaving an air gap. Bernard Feilden, the cathedral architect for many years, first involved at the cathedral in 1956, wrote a fascinating story of how, in 1962, the problem was addressed.[3] Grout and steel reinforcing replaced the air gap, with ties between the brick and the stone. Inside the spire a timber structure, supporting a series of platforms, allows access to the full height of the interior. It looks quite new, and is certainly no older than 1773 (see below). There is a gap between the timber structure and the masonry, which means that the timber structure does not significantly reinforce the masonry structure, and does not contribute to the spire's stability. Interior brickwork has been covered by a thick whitewash, which hides detail. However, the coursing and bond are visibly irregular and the courses are sometimes out of level. The corner braces are not original, being from the 1963 repairs. Numerous rectangular indentations are, as is said, an opportunity for future scholarship. What appears to be a filled-in putlog hole is occasionally seen on the interior and on the exterior along with some probable putlog holes.

CONSTRUCTING THE SPIRE

BUILDING a spire, of necessity, involves scaffolding. One method of erecting scaffolding is to support horizontal beams — putlogs — by embedding them in the structure being built. Usually, but not always, vertical poles support the other ends of these putlogs. The putlogs then support the platforms — planks or hurdles — from which the work is accomplished. The lacunae in the masonry where the putlogs were embedded before being removed at the end of the job are called (what else?) putlog holes.

It appears that, up to the tops of the lowest lucarnes, Norwich spire was built using both internal and external scaffolding. At greater heights, the evidence for an external scaffold diminishes, and it would be reasonable to conjecture that around that height the advantages of an internal scaffold outweighed the utility of further external scaffolding. At the very top, of course, external scaffolding would be mandatory, but this could have been supported by timbers extending out through the upper lucarnes. The same lucarnes would also have provided the access from the interior scaffold to the external scaffold necessary to complete the spire.

The ironwork at the top of the spire supports both a vertical iron bar that extends nearly to the bottom of the spire and an iron bar that extends through the capstone to secure the weathercock. A close-up view shows more details, but they are hard to see, so Figure 2a, traced from the close-up, helps. This can be deconstructed into conjectural pieces (Figs 2b–2e). The large and small crosses probably have legs, as shown, to anchor them in the masonry. It looks as though the claws on the vertical bar are part of a fastening scheme which involved raising the bar through the cross with its claws extending around and above the cross, dropping pins above the cross into the opening of the claws, then moving the pins sideways to engage the claws, thereby securing the bar to the cross. The piece shown in Figure 2d looks to be two pins held apart in locking position by a strap. The lack of top views surely hides some interesting and essential details of this scheme. Again, here is an opportunity for future scholarship.

One of the Feilden and Mawson drawings has an interesting handwritten note that gives the weight of one-eighth of the spire as 62 tons, or a total of about 500 tons. Each stone of zones 3 and 2, and the lowest part of zone 1, is identified in the eight

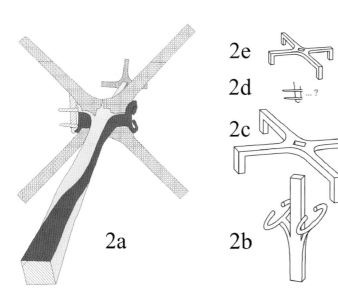

2e

2d

2c

2a

2b

FIG. 2. Norwich Cathedral spire top ironwork. (a) view from below, after Tim Tatton-Brown photo 17 Mar 2012, used by permission; (b–e) proposed dissection
A. Richard Jones

CAD (Computer Aided Design) drawings Feilden and Mawson prepared in 1994 for an extensive renovation, each showing the edge and two sides of a buttress and the spire facet to the right of said buttress. These drawings also specify every planned repair, stone by stone and the legend lists the types of stone found in the spire at that date. The original construction was of Weldon stone, a relatively light limestone — 142 pounds per cubic foot.[4] A large repair of Portland stone is clearly visible at the base of zone 1 in Figure 1b and, perhaps more clearly, in a photograph in the conservation plan, Section 9.5.1, p. 1.

There have been numerous repairs since the spire was completed around 1485. Here are the repairs mentioned in the conservation plan:[5]

1601	Lightning-damaged upper 6m replaced
1629	Storm-damaged upper part replaced
1760	Damage by lightning
1770	First lightning conductor installed
1772–73	Internal timber "framing" replaced
1793–94	Major repairs using Portland stone
1842–43	Major repairs
1899	Repointing upper part
1929	Repointing and adding three iron bands
1950–52	Add copper bands (replacing iron)
1962–63	Major structure repair and improvement
1993–96	Major repairs, base to lowest lucarnes

Lightning was an early problem which apparently was solved by the later lightning conductors. Notice that the upper part of the spire was replaced at least three times.

SPIRE FAILURES

SPIRE failure follows a loss of structural integrity: slow in the case of exterior weathering, fast in the case of an internal fire. Failure modes, many of which are indistinguishable after the event, include overtopping and collapse, either of which may involve the whole structure or just the uppermost sections. The 21 February 1861 failure of the spire at Chichester Cathedral is one of the best documented; Robert Willis' essay later that year on the collapse is a classic.[6] A paucity of proprietary prudence in any part can be avoided by a properly conceived, properly built, and properly maintained structure. But the structure is still subject to incidents. Fires due to human error are avoidable, but lightning is another matter. However, as already noted, the use of lightning conductors, the first installed in 1770, seems mostly to have disposed of this problem. Earthquakes are beyond the scope of this paper. That leaves wind, which can only be mitigated by prayer. The question, then, is what upper limit on winds to pray for. That is, how strong a wind will topple the spire? The remainder of this paper addresses that question.

A MODEL FOR WINDS

THE 'model' derived below yields the resistance of the spire to wind. As J. E. Gordon puts it so nicely, 'We hope that this [...] model will perform in a way which resembles the real thing sufficiently closely to widen our understanding and [...] enable [...] useful predictions'.[7] Jacques Heyman's treatment of a spire as a monolithic entity informs the present analysis.[8] Only the inception of teetering, not tottering, is the failure criterion used here. The failure contemplated is a monolithic topple, or actually, just the beginning of one — even less than one degree. The analysis is fairly straightforward: it would be possible just to present the result, but there are two reasons for not doing so. First, the result will be more or less wrong — guaranteed. Second, if the analysis is shown, knowing how it was conducted will allow it to be refined and corrected.

The balancing act

THE inception of a monolithic topple occurs when the force of a steady wind — gusts do not count — just balances the resisting force of the spire's weight. When this balance occurs, the compressive force holding the masonry together at the windward side of the spire has diminished just to zero, and failure is imminent. Heyman approached the stability of a spire against wind with an analytical model that informs the following treatment. The core principle is that a strong enough wind will blow a spire over. Heyman concentrated on finding a condition sufficient for the stability of a spire against a given wind. I shall instead ask what wind is required to topple a given spire. The answer results from the balancing of two opposing forces, just as on a see-saw, or, as Americans call it, a teeter-totter, the 'totter' part being particularly apt here.

Let us begin by imagining a teeter-totter with a small child sitting on one end. As everyone who has see-sawn knows, to balance the child, an adult must sit closer to the pivot. Stated more formally, the condition for balance is that each user's distance from the pivot multiplied by that user's weight must be the same. Some terms useful in the discussion are *moment* — a force times its distance from the pivot — and *moment arm* — that distance. It is the moments that are equal at balance.

For wind against a spire, revisions to the see-saw are required. It must be bent 90 degrees at the pivot, yielding a horizontal moment arm balancing a vertical moment arm. The spire's mass on the horizontal arm then resists the wind pressure on the vertical arm. Because the wind is a force instead of a mass, the force due to the spire's mass must be used. This was not necessary when masses were balancing. So the people's masses on the teeter-totter become the weight force and the wind force here. Failure is deemed imminent when a steady wind becomes strong enough that balance is achieved.

In the case of wind blowing against a spire, the two forces are sideways pressure from the wind, which is countered by downward pressure from the mass of the spire. So, in balancing wind versus a spire, there are five things to figure out:

- Where is the pivot?
- How far from the pivot does the weight force act?
- How large is the weight force?
- How far from the pivot does the wind force act?
- How large is the wind force?

The location of the pivot depends on an assumption, namely that the spire is cohesive, and so reacts as a monolith to the wind force. Thus, spire failure would begin on the side facing the wind with a small crack at its base, which would then propagate to the side opposite the wind direction. The pivot — around which the spire just begins to teeter, but does not yet totter — is therefore at the base of the spire opposite the direction of the wind. In fact, in order for a spire actually to totter, its centre of gravity must be pushed (reckoning vertically) beyond its base. As already noted, only the inception of teetering, not tottering, is the failure criterion used here.

Each force can be taken to act at a single point. The weight force acts downward at the familiar centre of gravity. The symmetry of a vertical spire locates its centre of gravity on its centre-line, with all the downward force transmitted to the centre of its base. So, the distance of the weight force from the pivot is the distance from the spire's centre-line to the side of its base. Already it is clear that more mass will confer more stability: all other things being equal, mass matters.

The wind force acts sideways at the less-familiar centroid of the presented area. The presented area is what the wind 'sees'. You can think of it either as the horizontal projection of the spire onto a flat screen — the 'shadow' cast by a distant windward searchlight — or, what is the same, as a windward vertical cross-section. Either way, the presented area is a triangle from base to apex facing the wind. The centroid is just the centre of gravity of this triangle, located on its centre-line, one-third of the way up from its base, which is therefore the distance of the wind force from the pivot. The weight and wind forces balance on an imaginary see-saw that is bent into a right-angle at its pivot.

THE SPIRE (OR PYRAMID) ON A SQUARE BASE

THE simple case of a solid square-base spire of height H based on a square of side $2 \bullet R$ is examined first. The results will then be used to treat the actual hollow octagonal-base spire. The words 'spire' and 'pyramid' are used interchangeably in this section.

Weight force

THE weight force is due to gravity acting on the spire's mass. Mass is found by figuring the volume of material and then multiplying by the material's density — its mass per unit of volume. The volume of this (or any) solid pyramid, in a result known to Euclid,[9] is the area of its base, here $(2 \bullet R) \bullet (2 \bullet R)$, or $4 \bullet R^2$, times $1/3$ its height. That is:

$$\frac{4 \bullet R^2 \bullet H}{3}$$

So to take a concrete — or rather limestone — example the weight force is:

$$\rho \bullet g \bullet \left(\frac{4 \bullet R^2 \bullet H}{3} \right) \quad \text{where:} \quad \begin{array}{l} \rho \text{ is the density of limestone, perhaps 2720 kg/cubic metre} \\ g \text{ is the strength of gravity, 9.80665 m/second/second} \end{array}$$

Wind force

THE wind force is taken to be the wind pressure acting on the presented area. The total force is found by multiplying the presented area by the pressure. The expression used for wind pressure is:

$$\frac{\rho' \bullet v^2}{2} \quad \text{where:} \quad \begin{array}{l} \rho' \text{ is the density of air in kg/cubic metre} \\ v \text{ is the wind speed in metres/second} \end{array}$$

For dry air at 15° C and 760 mm Hg (mercury) pressure, ρ' is 1.2256 kg/cubic metre.

This expression for pressure is ubiquitous in the literature for simple problems. Both the expression for wind force, and the use of the presented area, are approximations which are easy to deride, but hard to improve. Yes, the wind will likely be stronger at the top of the structure. Yes, there will be effects from turbulence. And, yes, if this were an engineering design, it would be replaced with far more complex computations. And so on. But the approximations allow the system's behaviour to be understood without being badly wrong on the exact numbers. The reader is free to replace this clarity of comprehension with the complexity of correctness, if desired.

In this case, the presented area is a triangle of base $2 \bullet R$ and height H. This triangle's area, from another of Euclid's results, is: $R \bullet H$. So the wind force is:

$$\frac{\rho' \bullet v^2}{2} \bullet (R \bullet H) \qquad \text{the wind pressure times the presented area}$$

DISCUSSION

THE spire will be stable if the weight force multiplied by its distance is more than the wind force multiplied by its distance, thus favouring the weight end of the see-saw over the wind end of the see-saw. Using the distances from the pivot, R for the weight force, and $H/3$ for the wind force, the balance at the inception of failure is between:

$$\left(\frac{4 \bullet \rho \bullet g \bullet R^2 \bullet H}{3} \right) \bullet R \qquad \text{the weight force times its horizontal distance from the pivot}$$

and

$$\left(\frac{\rho' \bullet v^2 \bullet R \bullet H}{2} \right) \bullet \frac{H}{3} \qquad \text{the wind force times its vertical distance from the pivot}$$

Equating these and solving for v, the wind speed at which teetering begins,

$$v = \sqrt{\frac{8 \bullet \rho \bullet g \bullet R^2}{\rho' \bullet H}} \qquad \text{for a pyramid of height } H \text{ and square base of side } 2 \bullet R$$

Just as a matter of interest, for the great pyramid at Giza, for which H is 146.71 m and $2 \bullet R$ is 230.35 m, v would be 3,968 m/sec, or 8,875 miles per hour, rather more than the initial wind speed of a nuclear explosion.[10]

Now, refer to Figure 3. So far, by taking the side of the square as the base for the presented area, the wind has been assumed parallel to the sides of the base as in Figure 3a. What if it blows parallel to a *diagonal* of the base, as in Figure 3b? The presented-area triangle's base would then be the diagonal facing the wind, and the pivot would be at the leeward end of the other diagonal. It is well known that the diagonal of a square is $\sqrt{2}$ times its side, thus the presented area increases by a factor of $\sqrt{2}$, but, as the height remains the same, so does the distance of the wind force above the pivot. The distance of the weight force from the pivot is now half a diagonal, more by the same factor of $\sqrt{2}$, but the weight force itself remains the same. So the two sides of the balance have each increased by the same factor, the wind side in its force, and the weight side in its distance from the pivot. The remarkable result is that the balance stays exactly the same, although the moments increase, because each moment increases by the same factor, the square root of 2. (The presented area's

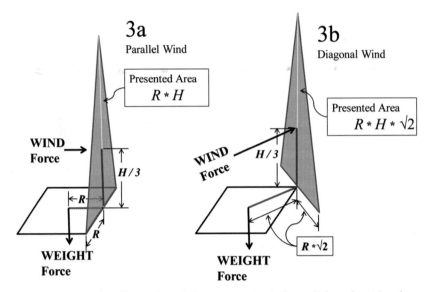

FIG. 3.   Investigating the effect of wind direction. (a) wind parallel to the side of a square;
(b)3b: wind parallel to the diagonal of the same square

A. Richard Jones

base and the weight force's moment arm both increase by a factor of the square root of 2 but maintain their 2:1 ratio.)

It turns out that, as the wind direction rotates, the base of the presented area and the moment arm of the weight remain in the ratio 2:1 for all directions for a square base. This is not true for a hexagonal base, but is again true for an octagonal base, and indeed, for any base with a multiple of four sides. This is a significant, perhaps unexpected, result: for bases with a multiple of four sides, stability does not depend on the direction of the wind — wind direction does not matter.

Note also that if the ratio is R/H fixed at a constant value, then all items in the equation are constant except for a leftover R, so v is proportional to R's square root (or to H's square root because the fixed value of R/H means that H is proportional to R). This interesting result means that the wind stability of a solid pyramid of a given shape increases as the square root of its absolute size. Thus, taking sand to consist of tiny pyramids, blown sand dunes exist, whereas pyramid dunes do not. Size matters.

One more manipulation: recalling that the half-angle of the pyramid is denoted α, the ratio R/H is, by definition, the tangent of α, written symbolically as $R/H \overset{\Delta}{=} \tan(\alpha)$. So the solution for the balance velocity can be rewritten:

$$v = \sqrt{\frac{8 \bullet \rho \bullet g \bullet R \bullet \tan(\alpha)}{\rho'}}$$

Suppose that for some reason R is fixed at a particular size, but α can vary. Then because $\tan(\alpha)$ increases with increasing α, the balance velocity will increase with increasing α. This means that a stumpy pyramid will be more stable than a taller pyramid erected on the same base. Squatness matters.

GENERALITIES

IT is worth reiterating the four general conclusions above. Three of them will apply to any spire, to confer stability, other things being equal:

- Mass matters
- Size matters
- Squatness matters

And the fourth applies to any spire based on a figure with a multiple of four sides:

- Wind direction does not matter

THE SPIRE ON AN OCTAGONAL BASE

PREVIOUS expressions applied to a solid pyramid on a square base. For other bases, the only change required is to revise the area of the base. For three base geometries of interest, the area of the base bounded by a square of radius r (i.e. a side of $2 \bullet R$) is:

$4 \bullet R^2$ for a square

$(8/(1+\sqrt{2})) \bullet R^2$ or $3.31371... \bullet R^2$ for an octagon

$\pi \bullet R^2$ or $3.14159... \bullet R^2$ for a circle.

Substituting these in the previous result gives, for a solid pyramid of height H:

$$v_{square} = \sqrt{\frac{2 \bullet \rho \bullet g \bullet R^2}{\rho' \bullet H} \bullet 4}$$
         for a square base of 'radius' R

$$v_{octagon} = \sqrt{\frac{2 \bullet \rho \bullet g \bullet R^2}{\rho' \bullet H} \bullet \frac{8}{\left(1+\sqrt{2}\right)}}$$
         for an octagonal base of 'radius' R

$$v_{circle} = \sqrt{\frac{2 \bullet \rho \bullet g \bullet R^2}{\rho' \bullet H} \bullet \pi}$$
         for a circular base of radius R[11]

The previous general conclusions remain valid for these additional base shapes because the various base shapes do not alter the progression of the argument in any way.

    These expressions still apply only to a solid spire/pyramid. To treat a hollow spire of interest, it is necessary only to re-compute the mass by subtracting an interior pyramid from the outer one. Figure 4 illustrates this process, and also illustrates the corresponding process for a ring with straight sides. Both processes are used in the Norwich spire model.

    The other refinement to the previous treatment is to remove the assumption that the spire acts as a monolith, with the failure occurring at its base, leading to a single value of v applicable to the entire spire. This is certainly an unwarranted assumption, as it completely ignores how well or poorly the spire is constructed. It amounts to saying the only weak joint in the spire is at the base, and the structure elsewhere hangs together regardless. The solution is to remain agnostic as to the place the spire might break, by finding a v for every possible level, from the tip down to the base. In essence, this involves considering a sequence of miniatures of the spire, formed by

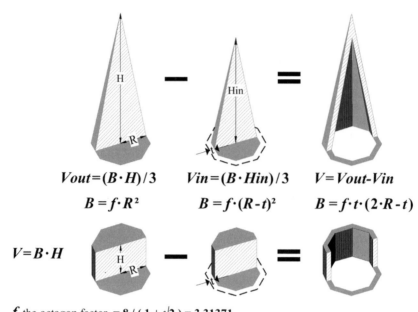

$$Vout = (B \cdot H)/3 \qquad Vin = (B \cdot Hin)/3 \qquad V = Vout - Vin$$

$$B = f \cdot R^2 \qquad B = f \cdot (R-t)^2 \qquad B = f \cdot t \cdot (2 \cdot R - t)$$

$$V = B \cdot H$$

f, the octagon factor, $= 8 / (1 + \sqrt{2}) = 3.31371...$

FIG. 4.   Shell volumes obtained by subtraction, (above) spire; (below) vertical shell

A. Richard Jones

cutting it at each possible height from top to bottom. The earlier findings that weight and size matter already indicate that these miniatures will be less stable — that is, the balancing wind velocity will be slower — than for the spire as a whole.

The meaning of these velocities is that if the spire, for whatever reason, breaks (only) at a particular level, the v found for that level applies. This is the v which places the windward side at that level just at the boundary between compression and tension, with the structure above that level behaving as a unit, i.e. monolithically. But at any level above the level which breaks, the structure is a miniature of the miniature spire, which will therefore have its windward side in tension. So it is an implicit requirement that above the level which breaks, the structure must resist tension well enough to behave as a monolith.

To accomplish this refinement, two relations are necessary: the radius *at* each level, and the mass *above* each level. These can be expressed in terms of a quantity h, which is defined as the distance from the top of the spire down to the level in question. So h varies from zero at the top of the spire to H at the spire's base. The usual notation writes (h) after quantities that vary with h, pronounced 'of h', to indicate that relationship. For example, in the expressions to follow — using lowercase r for the radius at an intermediate height — we write $r(h)$ (pronounced r of h) to mean the value of r at a given h. For a uniform solid spire, the radius will be directly proportional to h, being zero at the top where $h = 0$ and R at the base, where $h = H$. Thus, $r(h) = h \bullet (R/H) = h \bullet \tan(\alpha)$. The mass above h is: $\rho \bullet 4 \bullet [r(h)]^2 \bullet (H/3)$. This could be called $m(h)$, i.e. the mass above the distance h from the top.

The next step is to move from a solid spire to a hollow one. This is actually fairly simple, as Figure 4 shows. The volume of a solid spire exactly filling the void is subtracted from the volume of a solid spire conforming to the exterior of the spire. The difference between these volumes is the volume of the hollow spire, which may then be multiplied by the density of the material to obtain the mass. If these volumes are evaluated at an intermediate height, h, then $m(h)$ is readily computed.

THE NORWICH SPIRE MODEL

THIS result is now used to model Norwich spire as follows. The square base is morphed to an octagonal base by multiplying by the ratio of an octagon's area to its containing square, $2/(1+\sqrt{2})$, or 0.82847... , or, what is the same, replacing the 8 in the final equations with $16/(1+\sqrt{2})$, or 6.6274... . Then a spire with the dimensions of the inner surface is subtracted from a spire with the outer dimensions to yield the volume of the actual spire. The outer radius determines the presented area, the volume determines the weight, and the previous result then determines the wind velocity at balance.

The model in Figure 5 is derived from a copyrighted CAD drawing, used with permission of Hugh Feilden, which has a section of the wall. The incredible advantage of the CAD drawing is its precision, not to be confused with accuracy. It is possible to extrapolate it safely to find a cross section of the spire for carrying out the modelling scheme.

The process was as follows. With the wall section from the CAD drawing aligned at its correct level, zone 1 was extended to the top to determine its outer apex, and

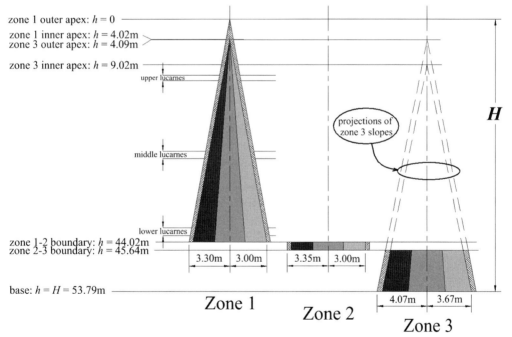

note: horizontal scale is expanded to 2.5 times vertical scale.

FIG. 5.   Norwich Cathedral spire model sectioned views

A. Richard Jones

249

mirrored to determine its inner apex. Zone 3 was treated the same way to determine the inner and outer apexes of its imaginary extension to a complete spire. This resulted in an initial CAD-derived model and a problem. Using another Feilden drawing (not a CAD drawing) of a section of the spire, isolating the modelled portion and superimposing the initial CAD-derived model showed it was too wide. The problem is that the CAD drawing is across the points of the octagon, but the non-CAD sectional drawing is across the flats. To change the initial CAD-derived model to a model across the flats its horizontal dimensions were multiplied by the ratio of a regular octagon's flats diagonal to its points diagonal, resulting in agreement with the non-CAD drawing. Thus it became possible to compute the radius at, and volume above, any level of the spire, and hence the wind required for it to break at that level.

A complication to the simple model is the lucarnes and buttresses. The lucarnes subtract weight from the levels containing them; similarly, the buttresses add weight. These differences are determined separately from the main model. The outcome is a *very* complicated expression (Fig. 6). It gives M at any h, optionally including the effects of the lucarnes and buttresses. A further option of extra weight is also provided, but not shown in Fig. 6.

Symbolic (rather than spreadsheet) expression for mass, M; commentary in italics

$M(h) = \rho \cdot \Big\{$ *Mass as a function of h is ρ, the density of Weldon stone, times the sum of all volumes above that height*

$+ F8 \cdot 4 \cdot \big[$ *Basic spire volume is octagon factor times four times outer volume minus inner volume*

$IF\big[\ h<HO_{12}, 1/3 \cdot [h-AO_1]^3 \cdot \tan^2(\alpha_1), IF[h<HO_{23}, 1/3 \cdot [HO_{12}-AO_1]^3 \cdot \tan^2(\alpha_1) + [h-HO_{12}] \cdot RO_2^2, 1/3 \cdot [HO_{12}-AO_1]^3 \cdot \tan^2(\alpha_1) + [HO_{23}-HO_{12}] \cdot RO_2^2 + 1/3 \cdot [[h-AO_3]^3 \cdot \tan^2(\alpha_3) - [HO_{23}-AO_3]^3 \cdot \tan^2(\alpha_3)]\ ]\ \big]$ *Outer volume*

$- IF\big[\ h<AI_1, 0, IF[\ h<HI_{12}, 1/3 \cdot [h-AI_1]^3 \cdot \tan^2(\alpha_1), IF[\ h<HI_{23}, 1/3 \cdot [HI_{12}-AI_1]^3 \cdot \tan^2(\alpha_1) + [h-HI_{12}] \cdot RI_2^2, 1/3 \cdot [\ [HI_{12}-AI_1]^3 \cdot \tan^2(\alpha_1)\ ] + [HI_{23}-HI_{12}] \cdot RI_2^2 + 1/3 \cdot [[h-AI_3]^3 \cdot \tan^2(\alpha_3) - [HI_{23}-AI_3]^3 \cdot \tan^2(\alpha_3)]\ ]\ ]\ \big]$ *Less inner volume*

$\big]$

Plus buttress volume if the buttress flag is on

$+ IF\big[buttresses, IF(\ h<HO_{12}, 0, (h-HO_{12}) \cdot Bmpm\ \big]$

Less lucarne volume if the lucarne flag is on

$- IF\big[lucarnes, IF\big[\ h<HL_{1t}, 0, IF\big[\ h<HL_{1b}, VL_1 \cdot [h-HL_{1t}]/[HL_{1b}-HL_{1t}], IF\big[\ h<HL_{2t}, VL_1, IF\big[\ h<HL_{2b}, VL_1 + VL_2 \cdot [h-HL_{2t}]/[HL_{2b}-HL_{2t}], IF\big[\ h<HL_{3t}, VL_1 + VL_2, IF\big[\ h<HL_{3b}, VL_1 + VL_2 + VL_3 \cdot [h-HL_{3t}]/[HL_{3b}-HL_{3t}], VL_1 + VL_2 + VL_3\ ]\ ]\ ]\ ]\ ]\ ]\ \big]$

$\Big\}$

Where

HO_{12} is the value of h at the outer junction of zones 1 and 2; HO_{23} is h at the outer junction of zones 2 and 3.
HI_{12} is the value of h at the inner junction of zones 1 and 2; HI_{23} is h at the inner junction of zones 2 and 3.
AO_1 is the outer apex height for zone 1, AO_3 for zone 3; AI_1 is the inner apex height for zone 1, AI_3 for zone 3
α_1 is the apex (half) angle for zone 1, α_3 for zone 3
RO_2 and RI_2 are the outer and inner radii of zone 2
$Bmpm$ is total buttress volume
HL's are h's for lucarnes 1, 2, and 3: t is top height, b, bottom height. Thus, HL_{1t} is the value of h at the top of lucarne 1.
VL's are total volumes of all four lucarnes in a set, VL_1 for the highest set, and so on.

FIG. 6. Norwich Cathedral spire model: mass, M, as a function of distance below apex, h. Symbolic (rather than spreadsheet) expression for mass; commentary in italics

A. Richard Jones

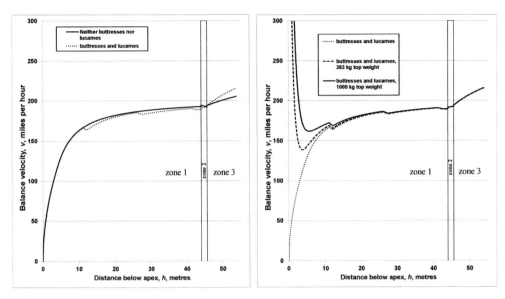

Fig. 7. Norwich Cathedral spire model results
Fig. 7.   Norwich Cathedral spire model results
A. Richard Jones

At last, the model yields the results of Figure 7. There is no *a priori* way of know-ing where the spire might break, so the graphs show how much wind will be needed for teetering at each distance below the apex. The solid curve of the left graph shows the simple model without lucarnes or buttresses. Notice the decrease in *v* in zone 2, between 44 and 46 m below the apex. The decrease in zone 2 is due to its vertical sides. Then in zone 3 the curve steepens because of the greater wall thickness in this part. This curve also serves to explain the proclivity for failures near the top of a spire: the lower balance velocities there require more robust vertical reinforcement than is needed lower down if wind is to be resisted.

In the dotted curve of the left graph the lucarnes and buttresses are added, causing a decrease in *v* over the span of each of the three sets of lucarnes, and an increase where the buttresses occur. The right graph shows the effect of adding weight at the top, another common strategy to mitigate low *v*'s near the top. The dotted curve of the right graph duplicates the dotted curve of the left graph. The dashed curve then shows the effect of adding 383 kg of weight to the top, a weight chosen because it approximates the weight of the iron bar presently suspended from the top of Norwich Cathedral's spire. The solid curve shows the effect of still more top-loading. If the break is higher up, the required wind is seen to be generally less, but extra weight at the top (a capstone, say), or suspended from the top, alters the curve. The high wind velocities in these charts indicate why the spire has stood for centuries, even with unrepaired damage. Norwich spire was built sturdy to last.

Finally, it may be interesting to know that the Met. Office website has a list of the highest recorded wind gusts in several parts of the UK. These, generally, are between 100 and 125 mph, with outliers in Scotland of 136 and 142 mph. Sustained winds rather than gusts would be necessary actually to topple a spire, and those sustained winds would clearly be slower than the gusts. It appears that Norwich Cathedral spire has a comfortable margin of safety.

NOTES

1. Dean and Chapter of Norwich Cathedral, *Conservation Plan for Norwich Cathedral* (2010), section 10.5.1, 1.

2. Copyright Feilden and Mawson, used by permission.

3. B. M. Feilden, 'Restorations and Repairs after World War II', in *Norwich Cathedral 1096–1996*, 728–44.

4. Peter W. Dunn, Weldon Stone Enterprises, pers. comm., 2012.

5. Dean and Chapter, *Conservation Plan* (as in n. 1), section 10.5.1, 1.

6. R. Willis, *The Architectural History of Chichester Cathedral: with an introductory essay on the fall of the tower and spire* (Chichester 1861), reprinted in P. P. B. Minet, *Architectural History of Some English Cathedrals, Vol. 1* (Chicheley 1972).

7. J. E. Gordon, *Structures: or Why Things Don't Fall Down* (New York 1978), 63.

8. J. Heyman, *The Stone Skeleton: Structural Engineering of Masonry Architecture* (Cambridge 1997), 127–38.

9. Euclid, *Elements*, Book XII, Proposition 7 and its corollary, as applied in general.

10. Metric dimensions converted from H of 5776.0 in. and $2 * r$ of 9068.8 in. See W. M. F. Petrie, *The Pyramids and Temples of Gizeh* (London 1883), reprinted by Kessinger Publishing (Whitefish, MT 2007), 43.

11. To reconcile this with Heyman's formulation, which approximates an octagonal spire with a spire based on a circle, note that q is $\sqrt{\dfrac{\rho' * v_{circle}^2}{2}}$, or $\sqrt{\dfrac{\pi * \rho * g * r^2}{H}}$, which is equivalent to the reduced form of Equation 7.3, Heyman, *The Stone Skeleton* (as in n. 8), 130. Heyman reckons density in Newtons/m^3 instead of kg/m^3, so the g here is absent in Equation 7.3, having been absorbed into the density in Equation 7.3. Also note that r/H is the tangent of an angle, α, which is the half-angle at the apex of the circular spire. $\dfrac{r^2}{H}$ can be written as $H * \dfrac{r^2}{H^2}$, or $H * \tan^2(\alpha)$. This substitution yields an equivalent to Equation 7.4, in Heyman, *The Stone Skeleton* (as in n. 8), 130.

The Integration of Church and City: The Development of Norwich City Centre in the Late Middle Ages

DAVID KING

This paper discusses the civic and ecclesiastical programme of rebuilding in late medi-eval Norwich, concentrating on a group of civic and ecclesiastical buildings in the central area in and around the market place and including the church of the College of St Mary in the Fields and the parish churches of St Peter Mancroft, St Andrew, St Stephen, St Giles and St Gregory. They were paid for largely by the wealthy civic elite and built and decorated by a common pool of urban craftsmen. The contrasting roles of the cathedral priory, often in dispute with the city, and the College of St Mary in the Fields with its close links to the civic administration, are analysed, the latter body being much more active in promoting the rebuilding of churches. It is suggested that both church and city, whose governance was reformed in 1452, saw the rebuilding programme as part of an effort to increase control over the citizens of Norwich in both religious and civic matters.

In recent years it has become generally agreed that the late medieval period, from about 1370 to the Reformation, in Norwich was marked by an extensive programme of renewal involving both the structures of governance and the buildings pertaining to it. This paper will examine how far the programme of civic, political and economic reform was linked to the widespread rebuilding and decoration of churches which occurred at the same time. The secular civic aspects of these developments have been examined in recent years, as has to some extent the rebuilding of churches, but little has been done to bring the two together.[1] This renewal was seen in many areas of the city, but the most important area around the market-place, from the castle in the east to St Giles' church in the west and from the church of St Andrew in the north to the College of St Mary in the Fields in the south, will be the focus of attention here (Fig. 1). This omits the largest single civic building project, the city walls with their gates, built with defence in mind but also to control entrance to and egress from the city. However, this was largely complete before the period under discussion.[2] A key point will concern the role at this period of the College of St Mary in the Fields, to which I shall henceforth refer as the College of St Mary. The civic dimension will be examined first. Penny Dunn has analysed the so-called Norwich Domesday Book initially compiled around 1396, and has demonstrated that it was an urban cartulary containing copies of all the avail-able property deeds belonging to the city between 1285 and 1507.[3] Most of the deeds relate to purchases in the period 1378–80 when a concerted effort was made to bring into public ownership the main commercial and trading facilities in the city. These included market stalls and shops, and legislation was passed to control the sale of meat,

FIG. 1. Plan of central Norwich, showing sites referred to in the text.
① St Giles; ② St Mary in the Fields; ③ St Stephen; ④ St Peter, Mancroft; ⑤ Guildhall;
⑥ St Gregory; ⑦ St Andrew; ⑧ St Peter, Hungate

Nick Warr

poultry and fish. The site of the common inn to the north of the market was bought and a wool seld established next to it. All trading in wool was supposed to be carried out there and merchants from outside the city engaging in this trade had to reside in the common inn. Control over goods coming via the Wensum was enabled by the purchase of the old and new common staithes, and the tower by the river, now called the Cow Tower, which was rebuilt in 1398–99. The process of consolidating power in the hands of the city administration was greatly enhanced in 1404, when the city was granted a royal charter according it the right to govern itself, elect a mayor, twenty-four aldermen and a common council of eighty (later reduced to sixty). It was also given county status and allowed to elect two sheriffs each year. As Penny Dunn and Ruth Frost have shown, the civic reforms were under the control of an elite group of wealthy merchants and tradesmen, both before and after the 1404 charter.[4]

The programme of building civic facilities which followed the purchase of land took an important step forward after the granting of the charter. The building of the guildhall (Fig. 1) began in 1406, the roof was raised in 1409 and prisoners were installed in the gaol in 1412, but additions continued to be made until 1453, when the mayoral council chamber was glazed. In 1411 the market cross was built (it was replaced in 1501–03) and in the previous year the new mills across the river at Heigham and owned by the city were completed, although they did not become operational until 1430.

As a possible reason for this radical reform of trade, administration and the built civic fabric, Dunn points to a warrant of Richard II in 1378 which endorsed the programme of financial reform and gave as its rationale that the community was 'greatly oppressed, injured and brought to ruin' by the burden of taxation, presumably because of the reduced number of taxpayers following plagues. She gives evidence for this

FIG. 2.   Norwich Guildhall, from the south

assertion from the city accounts. The major reduction in population and the conse-
quent redundancy of some buildings such as parish churches may have made it easier
for the city oligarchs to persuade their fellow citizens of the need for change. Thus the
reforms were at least partly undertaken to improve the financial stability of the city by
allowing it to receive rents from the acquired properties and taxes from the control of
trade and commerce. Subsequent financial records and the evidence of the new buildings such as the guildhall, the largest in the country outside London, show that these
measures were on the whole hugely successful both in the short term and the long,
despite the disruptions caused by the loss of liberties following civic disorder in the
1430s and 1440s. It is commonly stated that there was an economic recession in the
mid-15th century which was at its worst in the period 1440–60, a time of political disruption both on a national and local scale, but the evidence is unclear as to how far this
affected the overall prosperity of the city.[5]

We turn now to the ecclesiastical programme of renewal. Norman Tanner has
shown convincingly that, if it cannot be proved that Norwich was the most religious
city in medieval Europe, it can be confidently asserted that it was one of exceptional
piety.[6] Jonathan Finch characterizes the campaign of parish church building as '[a]
regeneration of civic identity' and 'the material expression of [. . .] faith and fortune',
which neatly links the prosperity and piety of the period, and it can be safely said that
this campaign of church building was a reflection of both the wealth of the city and
the religious fervour of its citizens.[7] Clive Burgess has stressed the importance of the
increasing participation of the laity in commemorative practices in churches, especially
in the provision of chantries, for the growing prosperity of parish churches in the late
Middle Ages. Any surplus income derived from endowments of property to fund
chantries after running costs had been paid was available to the parish church and
could have been used for rebuilding or further decoration.[8] Of the many churches

renewed at this period in the city, those in the area defined for discussion fall into two groups, the first comprising St Peter Mancroft, St Peter Hungate and St Andrew (Fig. 3), which were in the patronage of the College of St Mary, and the second, St Giles (Fig. 5), St Gregory and St Stephen (Fig. 4), whose advowsons were owned by the cathedral priory. In addition, the long-destroyed church of the college itself will be considered, and with this we begin.

The College of St Mary was founded a little before 1248 by John le Brun. Its original endowment included the advowsons of the city parish churches of St George Tombland, St Andrew and St Mary Unbrent.[9] At first intended to be a hospital, the college was soon transformed into a centre for the provision of mainly intercessory liturgy. By the late 14th century the existing accommodation needed to be extended and in 1374 money was given towards a common kitchen and precinct wall, and in 1377–79 further bequests supported this work and the construction of a cloister. Rebuilding of the church followed, beginning at the east end with the chancel, which was started about 1410 and was ready for a lead roof in 1428, as was the choir in 1433. Having completed the eastern arm, which included two transepts, the college decided to replace the nave and aisles, money for which was given in 1444 and 1458. The plan of the church as recovered by excavation and published in 1904 shows a building 186 ft long and 60 ft wide, greater than St Peter Mancroft, the largest parish church in the city.

The college was led by a master with prebendaries, chaplains to serve the chantries, other clerks not in holy orders and a boys' choir. Some gentlemen resided at the college, eating together and living in a collegiate manner. Several chantries were founded there by lay men and women and other members of the laity were buried there, although

Fig. 3.   Norwich, St Andrew: interior looking east

FIG. 4.   Norwich, St Stephen: exterior from the north-west

burial there was never as popular for the laity as in the churches of the mendicant orders. Some of the city guilds met at the college, including the most important 14th-century one, the confraternity of the Annunciation of the Blessed Virgin and its successor the company of St George, which became after 1452 effectively the city corporation. On Corpus Christi day the mayor, sheriffs and aldermen processed to St Mary's with thirty-two guilds carrying their banners. Before the guildhall was built in the early 15th century the city government often met at the college and the city records were housed there. From 1456 it held a solemn annual memorial service for civic benefactors. Apart from the advowsons of city churches the college also held Moulton, Bowthorpe and Field Dalling in Norfolk and Fressingfield in Suffolk. In addition, several of its prebends were the incumbents at various times of other churches such as St Stephen in the city and Great Massingham in the county. The most important example was John Saresson, alias de Wygenhale, 'first prebend' of the college in 1433 and dean from 1436–40 and from 1444–59. In 1429 he was appointed abbot of West Dereham and rector of Oxborough, in 1435 he became vicar-general to the bishop of Norwich, in 1436 he was presented to the rectory of Yaxham, from 1444–52 he was rector of Great Massingham and in 1452 was made archdeacon of Sudbury. He may be depicted in a window in St Peter Mancroft.[10]

The college's influence was increased by its close links with the clergy serving the city churches. It appointed its own members and others as chaplains to the churches of

257

FIG. 5.   Norwich, St Giles: interior looking west

which it was patron and sometimes as incumbents of churches with other patrons. At St Peter Mancroft, for example, at the bishop's visitation in 1492 Sir Robert Beverle was the parish chaplain.[11] In addition there were the two chantry priests, who acted as his assistants and nine other stipendiary priests.[12] It received income from several other city churches and it was the home of the guild of Corpus Christi, the priests' guild. The college also had close links with the diocesan administration based at the cathedral; several of its members holding office therein: John Derlington was 'first prebend' in 1376, vicar general in 1371 and archdeacon of Norwich in 1387, John Saresson, alias de Wygenhale, as mentioned above, and Robert Honeywood was dean in 1502, vicar-general in 1499 and archdeacon of Norwich in 1497; he was also at various times master of Bek Hospital in Billingford, rector of Coltishall and canon of Windsor.[13]

The first project undertaken by the college after the work on its own site was the rebuilding of St Peter Mancroft.[14] In 1388 the advowson had been transferred to the college from the abbey of Gloucester and work soon began, starting with a fashionable western tower perhaps to replace a central one, which was demolished.[15] The lower stages were completed by about 1431, and attention turned to the eastern arm of the church, whose completion was marked by its consecration in 1455. The nave was then rebuilt from east to west and joined rather awkwardly onto the new west tower and porches, and the top stage of the tower completed the building campaign in the early 16th century.

The 1455 consecration may have marked a point of strain in the finances of the college, for in 1458 it sold the advowson of one of the smaller parish churches in Norwich, St Peter Hungate, to the Paston family.[16] The chancel at Hungate had recently been rebuilt by the college and within two years the Pastons had rebuilt the nave and transepts, complete with glazing, some of which survives. The vicar during the Paston campaign had been appointed by the college and probably supervised the glazing programme, perhaps with input from the college. The 15th-century stained glass which survives there is by the same workshop as that at St Peter Mancroft.[17]

As soon as the nave and aisles at St Peter Mancroft were completed, by *c.*1480, a start was made on rebuilding the parish church of St Andrew situated some distance to the north of the market-place opposite the Dominican friary and also under the patronage of the College of St Mary. The west tower was under construction by 1478 and completed by *c.*1496. In 1500 a royal licence was granted for rebuilding the chancel, necessary because it was thought desirable to extend it by one foot, thus obtruding onto the royal highway. Rebuilding began in 1506 and by 1518 work was drawing to a close. Extant glass from the east chancel window dates from *c.*1510–20 on style.[18]

The resulting new churches of St Peter Mancroft and St Andrew have many points in common. Of relevance for the present argument is the evidence for close cooperation between the patron and the parishioners. At St Peter Mancroft, the fact that work began on the tower very shortly after the transfer of the advowson to the College of St Mary strongly suggests that the rebuilding was encouraged by the new patron. However, the church was a *Marktkirche*, and the largest of the many parish churches in the city. So updating of the market-place area may have been a factor in the decision to rebuild the church, and indeed the transfer of the advowson itself may have been prompted by the overall plan for renewal. Although the church today gives the impression of a unified build carried out in one campaign, close examination of the fabric and the documentary record shows that it was built in a number of phases and the decision to rebuild completely came quite late.[19] The most probable scenario is that the college and parishioners from the 1390s desired a total rebuild, but the decision to implement this depended on funding, so that a step-by-step approach had to be made as money became available. The economic downturn of 1440–60 may have played a part here. At St Andrew's finance seems to have been less of a problem, hence perhaps the shorter building time. In both churches, the fact that a complete rebuild involving chancel and church was eventually carried out does imply the intention of both patron and parish to work together, especially as the two buildings, along with other churches in Norwich, share the new style of continuity between nave and chancel, the latter being reduced to a single bay.

The parishioners who worked with the college on these projects and who provided much of the funding lived in two of the wealthiest parishes and were not surprisingly often members of the civic elite which governed the city. For example, at St Peter Mancroft, the leading merchant Robert Toppes gave one of the most important windows and helped equip the chapel in which it was placed. Toppes was mayor of Norwich on four occasions and also its member of parliament.[20] Another window there was given by Thomas Bumpstede, also a member of the civic elite, and several other donors to the fabric were mayors, aldermen or councillors. Also the Life of St John the Evangelist window, originally in the north-east window of the north chancel chapel, may have been given by William London, mayor of Norwich in 1482 and 1491, or, more probably, by William Elys, recorder of Norwich in 1517–20, in memory of his father Thomas Ellis, mayor in 1460, 1465 and 1474, and who died in 1487, when the window may have been made.[21] Much the same applies to the church of St Andrew where, for example, in his will proved in 1508, Robert Gardener, three times mayor, left £10 to glaze the north aisle. He also provided for seating in the new church and a new rood loft. Robert Jannys, who gave a legacy of £10 to the high altar, was twice mayor and also paid for one of the windows in the guildhall. The college as patron paid for the chancel and two of its masters, Nicholas Goldwell, and his successor Robert Honeywood, probably provided the glazing of the east window as a memorial to Nicholas' brother James Goldwell, bishop of Norwich, who died in 1499.[22]

As at St Peter Mancroft, a model of the college acting as a project manager for the rebuilding of a church in its patronage and thereby going beyond its legal obligation to maintain the chancel may have emerged at St Andrew's, although direct evidence is lacking. I have suggested elsewhere that in the case of St Peter's William Wode, rector of Salle church from 1428 to 1441, was responsible for directing and rebuilding the chancel there, which was glazed in 1440. He then became a prebendary at the College of St Mary and may have been head-hunted to oversee the work at St Peter Mancroft, where the decision to rebuild the chancel was made in 1439–41. Both the architecture and glazing of the eastern arm of St Peter Mancroft show influences from Salle.[23] That the rebuilding was also a joint enterprise of patron and parishioners is demonstrated not only by the many legacies left for the work by Norwich citizens and their wives, but by the fact that when Robert Pert left the large legacy of £20 in 1445 to the making of the new east wall of the chancel he specified staged payments and entrusted the money to the parishioners rather than the church.[24]

Another city church in the vicinity of the market-place which shows the influence of the college is St Stephen's. This was not in the patronage of the college, even though it stood almost next door to it, but was one of twenty-three city churches collated to the cathedral priory. The history of St Stephen's church raises the issue of the role of the cathedral priory and the bishop in the late medieval renewal of the city and its churches. It was the last medieval church to be rebuilt in the city. At the beginning of the 16th century the benefice was impoverished and in 1522 plate was sold for the new building of the church which was in such bad condition that its collapse was feared. The chancel was eventually rebuilt in 1520–34. Donations for the nave and aisles occur from 1533 to 1545, one of 1540 providing £10 for finishing the clerestory and a frieze above the west doorway bears the date 1550. One connection with the college comes with the glazing of the east window. Parts of the original three-light Crucifixion with flanking typological scenes from the Old Testament survive *in situ* and include the date 1533 and formerly the name of Thomas Cappe, vicar, as donor; he died in 1545 and had a brass in the chancel. He was a doctor in the decrees and prebend of the Mass of the Blessed Virgin Mary at the College of St Mary, and contributed an important part of the church's decoration. The design of the east window glass is clearly borrowed from that of the east window at St Andrew's, parts of which are also extant. Thus the choice of subject and the design of both these windows were determined by priests from the college. Parallels can also be drawn between the glazing programme at St Stephen's and that at St Peter Mancroft, including the former presence of a window depicting the Life of St Stephen in the north chancel, comparable to the similar window dedicated to the patron saint of the church in a side chancel at St Peter Mancroft, and also a lost Life of the Virgin cycle from the east window of the north aisle at St Stephen, similar to the Toppes window at St Peter Mancroft.[25]

The third church originally built in the French borough in addition to those of St Peter Mancroft and St Stephen was St Giles. This was also in the patronage of the cathedral priory. The nave and aisles were built in the late 14th and early 15th century; Pevsner and Wilson date them to the late 14th century, with some support for this from a bequest of 1386 of 30s. for the emendation of the nave. The chancel was demolished in

1581 and we know little of its date or appearance, although it appears to have been built on the footprint of the former building. There was also a legacy of £5 to the tower in 1424 and in 1455 there was a request for burial in the porch as the 'newest' part. Brasses for Robert Baxter of 1432 and for Richard Purdance of 1436 also suggest completion by this date.[26] The obedientary rolls record very low income from the church and no expenses on repairs after 1441, giving perhaps some indication that the cathedral priory was again rather negligent of its responsibilities to maintain the chancel. In general the obedientary roles indicate very little rebuilding of chancels undertaken by the cathedral priory in churches under its patronage, and repairs appear to have been minimal.[27]

The final church in the central area to be discussed is that of St Gregory, where the cathedral was again patron and did here initiate a rebuild of the chancel. In 1394 the cathedral cellarer's roll recorded a payment of £4 towards making the chancel and in 1401 the high altar was dedicated, indicating the completion of at least the sanctuary.[28] The nave, aisles and clerestory have been dated *c.*1425 on style.[29] However, the high altar was dedicated in 1401 and some fragments of glass gathered together in a panel in the north aisle and some *in situ* eyelets in the north-east aisle window are certainly of very late-14th-century date rather than the 1420s. The significance of this church for my argument is that the role of the cathedral priory, the patron of many of the city's churches, in contributing to the programme of renewal of the city centre cannot be ignored, but overall appears to have been less than that of the College of St Mary. Once again, at St Gregory's, many parishioners buried in the church or donors to it were councillors, aldermen and sheriffs, but I have found only one mayor, John Rede. He bequeathed his funeral pall to the church and has been suggested as the donor of the magnificent wall-painting of St George there (Fig. 6). He was a member of the guild of St George, which was assimilated to the city administration after 1452 and is said to have met in this church.[30] John Westgate, who gave £2 to repairing the leading of the chancel in 1525/6, was sheriff of Norwich in 1520 and alderman for St Giles in 1524–26.[31]

What conclusions can be drawn from this examination of the two programmes of civic and church renewal? In both cases improvements had occurred before the late 14th century, but around 1380 there was a definite increase in momentum which lasted in the case of the civic renewal until the mid-15th century, with churches being rebuilt up to and even beyond the Reformation. The close links between the city administration and the College of St Mary and the fact that the city began its programme of acquisitions in 1378 at the same time as the college was extending its own premises, and then in the 1380s gained the advowson of St Peter Mancroft, where the campaign of rebuilding began in the next decade, shows that civic and church improvements started at the same time and suggests, but does not prove, that they were coordinated in some way. In the case of the city, although the initial stimulus may have been the desire to increase its income to improve a difficult financial situation, the building campaigns which soon followed at the guildhall, common inn, market and mills, although also primarily carried out to provide for the practical functions of government and commerce and to enhance the ability of the civic government to control them, would also have had an element of increasing the status of the city by enhancing the visual appeal of its centre. Still today we can appreciate the ensemble of market-place, guildhall and *Marktkirche* and the castle overlooking from its mound to the east, and when the College of St Mary with its huge church was also visible the view would have been all the more impressive.

FIG. 6.   Norwich, St Gregory:
wall-painting of St George

If the college and city made a coordinated start on the refurbishments, the former certainly played an important role in promoting several of the later campaigns of church building in the area, providing expertise from its highly educated members and the experience it had already gained; note the much smoother progress of the campaign at St Andrew compared with that at St Peter Mancroft. But all its expertise would have been in vain without the continuing financial support of the parishioners, and above all the wealthy elite who were also the very same citizens responsible for governing the city and renewing its civic assets. Royal assistance in the form of charters and licences was needed at various points, but these were countered by the many heavy financial demands on the city from the crown. For example, when Queen Margaret of Anjou visited Norwich in 1453, the king and the queen each received 100 marks from the city.[32]

Not only were the civic elite involved in the work of both church and city in building and decoration, the craftsmen who constructed and decorated the resultant buildings were often the same. The workshop of John Wighton was the key to the glazing of both civic buildings and churches, and I have shown elsewhere that it was the workshop of choice for the College of St Mary, both within the city and in county churches under its patronage or influence.[33] John Marwe, mason, who worked with his brother Thomas on the guildhall in 1407 and 1411 and undertook in 1432 to rebuild Conisford Quay, also made a new window for Thurlton church in Norfolk; whether he worked on any of the city churches is not known.[34] John Doraunt, carpenter, supplied timber for the repairs of the common inn in 1426–27 and in 1439–40 worked for the cathedral. He is probably the same person as John Durrant, carpenter, who made a new roof for Thurlton church in 1441.[35]

What was the role of the cathedral priory in all this? Although it was patron of many more churches in the city than the college, it was physically remote from the centre around the market-place and there is evidence that it did the bare minimum in many cases to fulfil its duty as patron of parish churches. One reason for this is that relations between cathedral and city had been problematic since the riots of 1272.[36] However, it is important to distinguish between the cathedral priory and the diocesan administration. The animus in the city government at certain periods including the 1430s and 1440s was directed at the liberties of the priory, which conflicted with the claims of the city, not against the bishop and his officials. This is reflected in the fact that the College of St Mary worked closely with the city fathers in many ways, but its members also became diocesan officials working closely with the bishop.

Another aspect relevant to this discussion is that of civic and ecclesiastical control of the citizens of Norwich. How far was the building campaign discussed above linked to and a reflection of the desire by the church and civic elite to maintain control over the beliefs and behaviour of the population? Philippa Maddern has demonstrated the complex and well-developed system of oversight and control by which the city governed its citizens. She makes the point that the concept of civic disorder did not just refer to the riots and unrest which broke out at a number of points in the city's history, but applied equally to all aspects of behaviour, including '[p]rivate quarrels, tax grievances, breaches of economic regulations, failures to undertake civic responsibility, disagreement among the governing classes, arson, domestic violence and infidelity [...] and what was vaguely termed "lak of good governaunce"'.[37] After the city's incorporation in 1404, at least 155 officials were required every year to administer the political and legal bureaucracy, and in the 15th century between one in ten and one in twenty-three of all adult freemen took part at some stage in these functions.[38] Another engine of civic control was the guild ordinances. Many of these were designed as quality-control measures for the goods produced by each craft, but some went beyond these immediate functional requirements. The most important guild was that of St George, whose members included many of the leading citizens, but also figures of more modest status. In 1417 it issued a list of ordinances which included detailed provisions for such matters as the settling of disputes and the need for decorous behaviour.[39] According to Ben McCree, when the civic government was refashioned in 1452 following years of upheaval and loss of liberties and involving an assimilation of the guild of St George with the city governing body, the main purpose of the agreement was the preservation of civic order and the most important section of it contained measures to ensure the good behaviour of guild members and city officials.[40]

The Church was equally concerned to promote good behaviour and exercise control. The archdeacon's court gave judgements on matters of church law affecting the citizens when breaches occurred, but the parish churches were in the best position to encourage right living through sermons, confessions, and also through the didactic functions of stained glass, wall-paintings and other media. Churches were centres of control, where parishioners were taught what to believe and how to behave, and where expectations were confirmed by social pressure and ecclesiastical sanctions against those who offended. Perhaps most importantly, the lessons of the consequences of non-compliance in terms of the torments of hell and purgatory would have been a powerful disincentive to those inclined to err and a positive encouragement to provide churches with items of material culture. Images in different media and liturgical items at the same time memorialized the donations of individuals, elicited prayers for their souls and ensured that the teachings of the Church became available to all in a visual form.[41]

In addition to the parish churches, the civic buildings such as the guildhall, wool seld, murrage loft and common inn were places designed to facilitate civic control on the activities of the citizens both as players in the commercial life of the city and members of a crowded community living together. Stained glass was used in at least one civic building, the mayoral council chamber of the guildhall, as propaganda for the exercise of good government and justice, a function exercised in medieval town halls on the Continent in a variety of media.[42] The original glazing of the chamber in 1453 coincided with the election of the leading glazier in the city, John Wighton, as an alderman. Several panels of glass by his workshop are in the windows of the council chamber and, while it is possible that they come from elsewhere, it seems highly probable that they are part of the original glazing. The most important panels are four figures from a set of the twelve apostles. This iconography, which is also to be seen in the glazing of the guildhall at Boston, built in 1450, may have alluded to the apostles as the trusted ruling elite of early Christendom in comparison to the aldermen who met in the chamber as the governing body of the city.[43] A few fragments of the later glazing scheme made c. 1534 after the collapse of the roof are still to be seen, but much more was extant when Blomefield described the glass in the 18th century.[44] The windows had scenes telling such stories as the Corrupt Judge and the Judgement of Solomon and two of the surviving pieces depict personifications of Justice and Prudence. Here the ruling elite were again referred to, this time by name as the donors of the window. At the end of the Middle Ages panels of glass with a moralizing content were also to be seen in the houses of the wealthy. In the house of John Belton and later John Bassingham, both goldsmiths, was an inscription encouraging obedience to the king and charity to one's neighbour:

Goddes ordynance ws yn scriptur doth lede
To obaye wr kynge as supreme hede,
Wyth feare, love, honour, and subcyone,
And to thy neybor be in charite.[45]

In the house of Augustine Steward in Elm Hill, Norwich was a series of roundels depicting the parable of the Prodigal Son.[46]

Thus it is evident that the control of the citizens was a joint enterprise involving church and laity in public and private spheres and facilitated by the buildings provided in the late medieval campaign of renewal and reinforced by their decoration. The overall picture is of a tightly organized regime which by and large, and with a few notable exceptions which although significant have perhaps distorted the overall picture, was successful in maintaining good order in the city in both religious and civic spheres.

The motto, 'A fine city Norwich', conveys the enduring perception of it as an attractive place to live.[47] The earliest reference to this known to me is in one of the windows given by Robert Gardener to St Andrew's church in 1508. In the 18th century John Kirkpatrick recorded an inscription in it which reads in translation: 'Robert Gardener, alderman and mayor of this most pleasant city', but perhaps the seeds of this view were sown by those from both city and church who together started the process of civic renewal in the late 14th century, thereby helping to ensure the good order which was an important aspect of what the elite at least saw as the good life in Norwich.[48]

NOTES

1. An exception to this is C. P. Graves, *The Form and Fabric of Belief* (Oxford 2000). This book came late to my attention and requires a much more detailed response than can be given here. It is an important contribution, particularly in its ideas on the role of civic processions in late medieval Norwich, but is flawed in some details of interpretation. For the civic aspects, see J. Kirkpatrick, *The Streets and Lanes of Norwich: a memoir*, ed. W. H. Hudson (Norwich 1889); W. H. Hudson and J. C. Tingey, *The Records of the City of Norwich*, 2 vols (Norwich 1906 and 1910); B. McCree, 'Religious Gilds and Civic Order: The Case of Norwich in the Late Middle Ages', *Speculum*, 67 (1992), 69–97; B. Ayers, *Norwich 'A Fine City'* (Stroud 2003); B. Ayers, 'The Urban Landscape', in *Medieval Norwich*, 1–28; P. Dunn, 'Trade', in *Medieval Norwich*, 213–34; B. Ayers, 'Understanding the Urban Environment: Archaeological Approaches to Medieval Norwich', in *Medieval East Anglia*, ed. C. Harper-Bill (Woodbridge 2005), 68–82; P. Dunn, 'Financial Reform in Late Medieval Norwich: Evidence from an urban cartulary', in C. Harper-Bill, *Medieval East Anglia* (Woodbridge 2005), 99–114. For the religious sphere, see Cattermole and Cotton, 'Church Building'; N. Tanner, *The Church in Late Medieval Norwich 1370–1532* (Toronto 1984); N. Tanner, 'The Cathedral and the City', in *Norwich Cathedral 1096–1996*, 255–80; J. Finch, 'The Churches', in *Medieval Norwich*, 49–72; D. King, 'Glass-Painting', in *Medieval Norwich*, 121–36; N. Tanner, 'Religious Practice', in *Medieval Norwich*, 137–56; D. King, *The Medieval Stained Glass of St Peter Mancroft Norwich*, Corpus Vitrearum Medii Aevi, Great Britain, V (New York and Oxford 2006).

2. See Ayers, *Norwich* (as in n. 1), 87–91; Ayers, 'Urban Landscape' (as in n. 1), 23.

3. The Norwich Domesday Book is in Norwich, NRO, NCR, 17b. See Dunn, 'Financial Reform' (as in n. 1); this was based on her doctoral thesis: 'After the Black Death: Society and Economy in Late Fourteenth-Century Norwich' (unpublished Ph.D. thesis, University of East Anglia, 2003).

4. Dunn, 'Financial Reform' (as in n. 1), 106–09; R. Frost, 'The Urban Elite', in *Medieval Norwich*, 235–54.

5. Frost, 'Urban Elite' (as in n. 4), 236.

6. Tanner, 'Religious Practice' (as in n. 1), 155.

7. Finch, 'The Churches' (as in n. 1), 49.

8. C. Burgess, 'Obligations and Strategy: Managing Memory in the Later Medieval Parish', *Monumental Brass Society Transactions*, 18.4 (2012), 289–310.

9. For the college, see Blomefield, *Norfolk*, IV, 169–84; G. E. Hawes, 'Recent Excavations at the college of St Mary in the Fields, Norwich', *NA*, 15 (1904), 293–315; VCH, *Norfolk*, II, 455–57; C. Harper-Bill and C. Rawcliffe, 'The Religious Houses' in *Medieval Norwich*, 73–119.

10. Blomefield, *Norfolk*, III, 632, 648; IV, 171, 172; IX, 11; X, 283; VCH, *Norfolk*, II, 418; D. King, 'Glass-Painting in Late-Medieval Norwich: Continuity and Patronage in the John Wighton Workshop', in *Patrons and Professionals in the Middle Ages*, Harlaxton Medieval Studies, 22, ed. P. Binski and E. New (Donington 2012), 347–65. For the possible depiction, see D. King, *Glass of Mancroft* (as in n. 1), ccxvii.

11. It is not known whether Beverley was a prebend, as the list given by Blomefield is incomplete, but he would have been appointed by the college. For the list see Blomefield, *Norfolk*, IV, 171–74.

12. Blomefield, *Norfolk*, IV, 186; Tanner, *The Church in Norwich* (as in n. 1), 184; King, *Glass of Mancroft*, lxxxii–lxxxiii.

13. For Derlington, see Blomefield, *Norfolk*, III, 632, 639; IV, 172; for Saresson, see n. 10; and for Honeywood, see Blomefield, *Norfolk*, III, 633, 640; IV, 171.

14. F. Woodman, 'The Rebuilding of St Peter Mancroft', in *Essays presented to J. C. Barringer on his retirement*, ed. A. Longcroft and R. Joby (Norwich 1995), 290–95; Finch, 'The Churches' (as in n. 1), 63–64; King, *Glass of Mancroft* (as in n. 1), li–lxiii.

15. See F. Woodman in the present volume.

16. Blomefield, *Norfolk*, IV, 329–34.

17. For the glass at St Peter Hungate, see G. A. King, 'On the Ancient Stained Glass Still Remaining in the Church of St Peter Hungate, Norwich', *NA*, 16 (1907), 205–18; D. King, CVMA catalogue entry 'Norwich, St Peter Hungate', http://www.cvma.ac.uk/publications/digital/norfolk/sites/norwichhungate/history.html [accessed 11 June 2013].

18. Finch, 'The Churches' (as in n. 1), 66–67; King, 'Norwich, St Peter Hungate' (as in n. 17).

19. See F. Woodman in the present volume.

20. King, *Glass of Mancroft* (as in n. 1), clxxxiv–clxxxv and Appendix 2.

21. Ibid., lviii, ccxiii–ccxiv.

22. D. King, CVMA catalogue entries for Norwich, St Andrew and Norwich, Guildhall, Mayoral Council Chamber: http://www.cvma.ac.uk/publications/digital/norfolk/sites/norwichstandrew/history.html [accessed 11 June 2013]; http://www.cvma.ac.uk/publications/digital/norfolk/sites/norwichguildhall/history.html [accessed 11 June 2013]; D. King, 'Five case studies on parish churches in Norwich', in *The English Parish Church through the Centuries*, DVD, ed. D. Dyas (York 2010).

23. King, *Glass of Mancroft* (as in n. 1), lxxvii, cxiv, cxcvi.

24. Tanner, 'Religious Practice' (as in n. 1), 143; King, *Glass of Mancroft* (as in n. 1), 146.

25. D. Harford, 'On the East Window of St Stephen's Church, Norwich', *NA*, 15 (1904), 335–48; King, 'Five case studies' (as in n. 22).

26. Cattermole and Cotton, 'Church Building', 258; B/E, *Norfolk*, I, 236; personal communication from Simon Cotton. See also H. Lunnon, 'St Giles' in the present volume.

27. Unpublished typescript: P. Cattermole, 'Some Norwich Churches as seen in the Obedientary Rolls of Norwich Cathedral Priory, 1276–1536' (1985), 20 and passim; copy in possession of the author.

28. Ibid., 21–22.

29. Unpublished typescript: F. Woodman, 'Survey of Norwich Churches', 65–67; copy in possession of the author.

30. For John Rede, see D. Park in *Gothic. Art for England 1400–1547*, exhib. cat., ed. R. Marks and P. Williamson (London 2003), 409, cat. 297.

31. TNA, PCC 14 Porch; T. Hawes, *An Index to Norwich City Officers 1453–1835*, Norfolk Record Society LII, (Norwich 1986), 163.

32. *Paston Letters and Papers of the Fifteenth Century*, ed. N. Davis, (Oxford 2004), 248–49.

33. King, *Glass of Mancroft* (as in n. 1), cxliv–clii.

34. J. Harvey, *English Medieval Architects: a biographical dictionary down to 1550* (Gloucester 1984), 197.

35. Ibid., 85, 88.

36. For the medieval relations between the cathedral and the city, see N. Tanner, 'The Cathedral and the City' (as in n. 1), 255–80.

37. P. Maddern, 'Order and Disorder', in *Medieval Norwich*, 189–212.

38. Ibid., 191–93.

39. B. McRee, 'Religious Gilds and Civic Order: The Case of Norwich in the Late Middle Ages', *Speculum*, 67 (1992), 69–97.

40. Ibid., 92–93.

41. Burgess, 'Obligations and Strategy' (as in n. 8).

42. U. Lederle, 'Gerechtigkeitsdarstellungen in deutschen und niederländischen Rathäusern' (unpublished Ph.D. thesis, Heidelberg, 1937).

43. P. Hebgin-Barnes, *The Medieval Stained Glass of the County of Lincolnshire*, Corpus Vitrearum Medii Aevi, Great Britain, Summary Catalogue 3 (Oxford 1996), 41–49.

44. Blomefield, *Norfolk*, IV, 229–30; King, CVMA catalogue entry for the guildhall (as in n. 22).

45. W. C. Ewing, 'Notices of the Norwich Merchant Marks', *NA*, 3 (1852), 177–228, at 195–96; J. Sayers, 'Bell and Ton: The Beltons, Goldsmiths of Norwich c. 1450–1517', *NA*, 46 (2012), 357–69.

46. For Kirkpatrick, see Norwich, NRO, MC 500/19, and D. King, 'Le vitrail anglais et la Réforme. Déstruction, préservation et continuité à Norwich', *Revue de l'art*, CLXVII.1 (2010), 41–50, at 48, 50, n. 57.

47. C. Rawcliffe, 'Introduction', in *Medieval Norwich*, xix–xxxvii, at xix–xxi.

48. The panel in window nIV, 2b in the north aisle shows the kneeling Robert Gardener with an inscription rather different from that in Kirkpatrick's careful note. The glass is almost entirely or completely 19th century in date, but was presumably based on that seen by Kirkpatrick. Norwich, NRO, shelf T 150D; King, CVMA catalogue entry for Norwich, parish church of St Andrew (as in n. 22).

St Peter Mancroft and Late Medieval Church Building in Norwich

FRANCIS WOODMAN

St Peter Mancroft is an outstanding example of a late medieval parish church appar-ently rebuilt according to some 'master plan': one leaving no trace of the previous church, its layout, or indeed its architectural history. Given that Norwich possesses a remarkable collection of medieval parish churches, one of the largest in Northern Europe, can the thirty or so survivors help restore some of this 'lost history' and suggest methods for the process of the reconstruction that occupied both parish and patron of St Peter's for the best part of one hundred years? This paper will argue that the church grew from a simple addition to the old building, but was then developed with the cooperation of both parish and patrons until the present church was realized.

NORWICH churches range from the very modest to the big and extravert. St Peter Mancroft is the most obvious of the latter, dominating the market area. The church appears one complete, managed and purposeful rebuild, with almost uniform stone facing, matching tracery and that essential 'thru-build' of all the smartest and most expensive late medieval projects (Figs 1 and 2). Inevitably, the story is somewhat differ-ent and St Peter's needs examining and placing within the context of other Norwich churches, many of which were extensively and expensively rebuilt between *c.* 1400–1550.

St Peter's has a straightforward plan (Fig. 3); an extended east end with a multi-storey vestry block attached (Fig. 4), north and south chancel chapels leaving one aisle-less high altar bay, one-bay north and south transeptal chapels projecting at the junction with an aisled nave, north and south porches and a west tower. The tower is one of a group in the region where a processional route passes beneath the structure, leaving the west door into the church beneath the east face of the tower.

The constructional history of the building is uncontroversial, though in need of some clarification and refinement.[1] Beginning with a new tower against the old church in the 1390s, presumably the present west tower for reasons detailed below, the bulk of the rest of the structure developed from a new chantry chapel added to the north side of the previous chancel. A bequest for the glazing of the east window of the adjoining new north transeptal chapel occurred in 1445.[2] This single-bay chapel, for the confraternity of the Mass of the Name of Jesus, projects north at the junction of the western end of the north chancel chapel at the nave/chancel division. The present extended chancel and south chancel chapel can be dated from documentation between 1441 and 1455, and the nave was evidently complete by 1479.[3] The west tower remained unfinished at the beginning of the 16th century.[4]

There can be no doubt that the earliest part of the existing fabric is the lower sec-tion of the west tower, dated by documentary evidence to the last decades of the

FIG. 1.   Norwich, St Peter Mancroft: exterior from the south

14th century. The progress of this work may be gauged by the amount of standing structure requiring adaptation to accommodate the later mid-15th-century nave. The eastern tower buttresses that form the western responds of the existing nave arcades have base mouldings buried quite deep in the present floor. The buttresses have also been massively redressed from about 4 m above the modern floor level, and the repair work continues the full height of the nave elevation. The intrusion of the new eastern tower buttresses into the old nave may explain the reference to 'new clerestories' in a bequest of 1431, and other repairs carried out in the early 15th century.[5] Similarly, the eastern tower arch into the nave has been refaced for much of its upper section, suggesting the existence of a lower previous tower arch, presumably one accommodating a lower roof level of the former church. However, raising a tower arch within an existing structure must have represented considerable technical difficulties had much of the tower superstructure already existed. Equally, the four faces of the tower may not have been built evenly, the nave-facing eastern wall perhaps well ahead of the rest to seal the old nave against the weather.

The present west tower strides over a processional path to reach the western limit of the churchyard. Such thru-routes are not uncommon in East Anglia — Dedham (Essex), Cambridge, All Saints (lost) and Great St Mary's, March (Cambs.), East Bergholt (Suffolk), to name a few — and are commonly associated with a shortage of churchyard space, and in the case of both Cambridgeshire churches, allowing actual

Fɪɢ. 2.   Norwich, St Peter Mancroft: interior looking east

pedestrian traffic beneath. Another well-known example exists in Norwich beneath the west tower of St John Maddermarket. At Mancroft, the new west tower raises the question 'where was the old one?'. Of course, it might have been exactly on the existing site, though no evidence of an earlier tower has ever been uncovered. Was it further east against the west wall of a shorter nave? This is indeed a possibility. A site flanking the church attached or otherwise seems unlikely — the churchyard being very constricted both north and south. The final and perhaps most likely position of an earlier tower is in the middle, making the original church cruciform in the manner of East Dereham (Norf.), or a grand three-cell such as South Lopham (Norf.). The removal of a central tower for a western replacement often leaves visual evidence as at Newark (Notts.), but if done with skill or as part of a complete reconstruction of the church will leave little to show short of excavation, as at Saffron Walden (Essex), or detective work as with Long Melford (Suffolk). Sometimes the parish never got round to it, leaving an old central tower stranded amid an abandoned rebuilding project as at Ashbourne (Derbys.).

The evidence that the construction of the main body of the present church began as a result of the addition of a new north chancel chapel is also in need of clarification. It is now clear that the east window to be glazed within four years after 1445 was that of the north transeptal chapel not the adjoining chancel chapel, and this has implications for the progress of the entire project. That the north chancel chapel was begun against the old building cannot be doubted: the original floor level was well below that of the

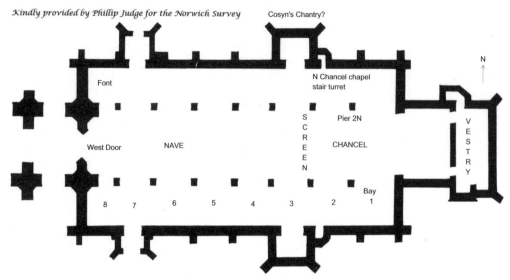

FIG. 3.   Norwich, St Peter Mancroft: schematic ground plan

FIG. 4.   Norwich, St Peter Mancroft: exterior, east end with three-storey vestry

present church and the arcade piers that open into the chancel are partially embedded in the floor. Further, the piers take no account of the new enhanced levels of the chancel reconstruction initiated in 1441. As a reconstruction of the chancel was mooted as early as 1439, the initial date of the north chancel chapel should be pushed back to the 1430s.[6] The project for the new northern transeptal chapel, at least proposed by 1445, may have been the inevitable result of the removal of an altar at the eastern termination of the old nave north aisle, this being perhaps a flat terminal wall or a transeptal feature. This chapel undoubtedly housed Cosyn's chantry, first mentioned in 1322, as there is good evidence that this altar was moved next door into the new north transeptal chapel.[7] The sequence of these decisions is made clear within the treacherous north chancel chapel stair turret, built initially to serve as access to the vaulted under-croft below, but adapted somewhat crudely to provide a rood turret perched rather precariously on the roof of the initial stair housing. On the exterior at this point, the resulting turret appears part of the entire angle between the north chancel and north transeptal chapels, which might suggest that the rebuilt Cosyn's chantry may have been intended initially merely to project from the old nave aisle. As ever, the structural evidence at this point is contradictory — the new north rood exit is too low, as may be seen by a comparison with the post-1441 south rood exit, yet the floor level of Cosyn's chantry in the north transeptal chapel seems to accommodate the existing floor level, which was not the case in the adjoining chancel chapel. However, as the 1445 east window bequest for the north transeptal chapel comes four years after the agreement to build a new chancel, apparently mostly funded by the parish, a decision on the entire reconstruction of the church had clearly been signalled by that date.

In summary, the structural and documentary evidence for this complex area suggests a new north chancel chapel, begun in the 1430s, was an addition to the old church. This must have involved a decision to move Cosyn's chantry elsewhere, but not neces-sarily at first into a new north transeptal chapel. The decision to raise, rebuild and extend the chancel in 1441 must coincide with the addition of the north transeptal chapel as shown by the raised floor levels throughout. Thus this transeptal chapel is the first part of the new scheme to be undertaken. This work may also have included the first eastern section of the north aisle wall, where the moulding details are unlike other parts of the nave and the aisle roof wall-plate is higher (Fig. 5).

But what may we discover from all of this about the previous church? There is sub-stantial evidence suggesting that the tower in building in the 1390s is the present west tower. The eastern buttresses that project into the church again confirm a lower floor level than at present, and also that the central vessel of the previous church was at least as wide as the present nave. The north chancel chapel, apparently intended to be added to the old building confirms the length of the previous parochial space while indicating that the lost chancel was at least as long to the east as its new flanking chapel. It is also possible to argue that the old church was at least as wide north to south at the parish/chancel division in order to accommodate the width of the new north chancel chapel, perhaps some transeptal feature, and that the earlier church had a substantially lower floor level than at present.

The north chancel chapel includes a stair turret that is now a danger to life and limb. The truncated door (1.59 m high) opens into a void, with more than a metre drop (1.02 m) before footfall is achieved. The turret appears to have been built with the chapel, indeed, it provides the sole original access to the brick rib-vaulted burial under-croft below. Some half metre before footfall another door opens into a turret for a rood access, one that could never have been utilized without some wooden insert or access

FIG. 5.   Norwich, St Peter Mancroft:
interior, south aisle showing change in
wall-plate level

FIG. 6.   Norwich, St Peter Mancroft: interior,
showing junction of north arcade and west
tower buttress

ladder from the initial stair. Howsoever this arrangement was intended to function, the
turret suggests that the east end of the previous church had at one time a substantially
lower floor level than at present.

While footfall is now only achieved 1.02 m from the present chapel floor, the original
stair may be seen to have continued at least another two steps upward, ending in a
stone platform, now all but trapped within the later enhancement of the chapel floor.
An original iron-peg door hinge also survives at this lower level. This provides clear
evidence that the turret stair not only encroached into the chapel as a potentially
dangerous hole but also that the chapel floor was then was some 0.5 m below current
floor level. That this represents the pre-1441 floor level in this part of the church may be
surmised from the addition made to this turret after its initial construction, when a
secondary door was cut into the brick lining, leading to a new rood stair turret perched
somewhat precariously on the roof of the original crypt stair. The cill level of this
secondary door is also 0.5 m below the present floor level, though it is also now impossible to reach from the earlier stair, being left high and dry. This additional door may
have taken advantage of a widening of the original turret at this level, resulting in a
noticeable setback in the brick lining. This ledge was surely used to support a moveable
wooden floor with direct access from the original chapel floor to the rood turret. How
often was access needed to the undercroft? The rood turret provided an upper loft
door, but one well below the level required by the 1441 rebuild, as may easily be seen by
a comparison between the opposing loft door head, the higher southern door interfering with the aisle roof corbel, something that does not happen on the lower northern

door. Thus the northern rood door may offer evidence for the height of the pre-1441 rood loft.

Had the north chancel chapel work initially included the existing two-bay arcade from the start, then a lower original floor level could mean that there are pedestal bases buried to some extent within the present floor level. This does indeed appear to be the case, though the damage inflicted upon the lower levels of the church by the various replacements floors renders certainty impossible. The exposed moulded elements of pier 2N currently reach a height of 0.8 m — was that originally 1.30 m? On close inspection, the eastern respond half-pier and the first free-standing pier both have moulded elements just visible peeping up through the present floor. The third pier, at the nave/chancel divide, has had elements at floor level chiselled off. When compared with the nave piers, the lowest pedestal moulding is 140 mm above the existing floor level. This is exactly the height of the single step up into the chancel. If this is deducted from the north chancel chapel floor level, the resulting chancel piers would match in design those of the nave though not rising so high overall. If 140 mm were to be deducted from the chancel chapel floor level, the footfall within the stair turret would be reduced to 380 mm, a not impossible step.

The most significant questions, however, must be how was the floor level raised to its present height and by how much? Has St Peter's really been lifted by half a metre or so and for its entire length? The new chancel shows one way this could be achieved: brick barrel-vaulted supports, providing the lift necessary for the altar area and allowing the multi-story vestry to be accessed direct from the raised sanctuary. Are there more such supports unseen beneath the church? Various repairs or heating ducts might have revealed evidence, though given the original floor levels in the north chancel chapel such work may never have penetrated deep enough. Whatever, the sheer effort in both engineering and financial terms suggests that the underpinning of the present church must have consumed huge amounts of time and money.

If how the present floor level was achieved can only be guessed at, 'why?' also springs to mind. It would have been easier to extend the church eastward at what appears to have been its previously lower ground level given that the churchyard falls away noticeably around the chancel. One possible answer is the sheer ambition of the whole project — not a church sinking into the city but one standing proudly over the market, as indeed it now does. Was it this that encouraged the parishioners to undertake the major responsibility for the non-parochial chancel, the cost representing a poor return for the patron alone? How common was this in late medieval Norwich, or indeed in England?

In 1441 the patron, the College of St Mary in the Fields, agreed terms for the building of the existing chancel of St Peter's, one longer than before, with a southern chapel matching that already built on the north, and a multi-storey vestry block against the east end.[8] One year's revenue was granted back to the parish towards the work. Apart from the documentary dating evidence, the chancel aisles arcades show that when the north chapel was built there had been no intention to raise the chancel floor as at present, whereas the south arcade bases rise with the new chancel steps. Similarly, the south rood stair built adjoining the new southern chancel chapel starts at the present floor level, with no access to any vaulted area below. A consecration is recorded in 1455, usually taken to be the new chancel.[9]

The annual revenue from St Peter's for the patron was at most about £30 so the 'grant' of one year's income to the chancel project would not have gone very far, given the enormous underpinning the work required.[10] Even if the grant was renewed annually, for which there is no evidence, the greater financial burden was clearly shouldered by the parish, probably through some *ad hoc* committee of the great and the good. St Peter's was not short of those. In granting the income back there must have been some group or organization to grant it to. Similarly, will bequests for the chancel must have been paid to someone or something, the churchwardens having no legal responsibility beyond the parochial nave. In 1445, the year that the east window of the north transeptal chapel was proposed, a most informative parish bequest proves a virtual running commentary on the progress of the new chancel. Robert Pert left £20 for the building work on the chancel in three lots: 10 marks when the chancel gable wall was built level with the churchyard (foundations complete), 10 marks when the east chancel wall reached the cill level of the great window and a final 10 marks when they reached the top.[11] Of course, assuming the previous chancel was shorter to the east than at present, all this work — vestry, east gable wall and some of the altar bay — could have proceeded without disturbing the older liturgical space. If the consecration of 1455 was indeed that of the chancel, then sufficient money must have flowed in at a considerable pace, given that only a decade earlier the east wall foundations may not even have been in place.

The apparent speed of the chancel build suggests some substantial donations from parishioners, perhaps on a par with the £1,000 'under the bed' cash offered to St Mary Redcliffe by William Canynges (d. 1474), following the collapse of their unfinished nave clerestory in 1446.[12] Robert Toppes (d. 1468) was one such wealthy Mancroft parishioner, but while buried in the church in the north chancel chapel that he may have paid for in part, no money is left for the completion of St Peter's in his will, despite leaving 'repair' money to around seventeen other churches in Norfolk in what is a very generous will.[13]

While the financial arrangements of the new chancel build at St Peter Mancroft are open to interpretation, it is clear that the parish, not the patron, bore the major responsibility for this part of the church. How common this was in late medieval parishes is but one question raised by St Peter's. The parish then proceeded to rebuild the nave, but apparently in fits and starts. Indeed, it is not clear from which end it was built, remembering that a new west tower had been under way for half a century or more, nor whether both sides were built at once. While the 'collision' between the older buttress piers of the west tower and the new nave arcades (Fig. 6) might suggest an east–west build, the damage inflicted on the tower was unavoidable if the new arcades were taller, and if the placing of the nave piers was dictated by earlier foundations reused and raised in the rebuild. Financial priority for the parish had clearly concentrated on the non-parochial chancel, with the nave following on as best it could. The Battle of St Albans and the outbreak of civil war in 1455 cannot have helped either with building or fundraising. References to 'new leading' and to the screen both in 1479 are perhaps indicative of slow progress in the later stages of the project.[14] Clearly, the deal of 1441 indicates that both parish and patron had decided by at least that date upon a total rebuild, one based upon the style of, and incorporating the newly built north chancel chapel.

The west tower of St Peter's is another area of potential information regarding the previous church and the process of constructing the new one. The internal eastern buttresses of the present tower have moulded features now deeply buried beneath the existing nave floor level, with only the topmost 300 mm of the base moulding now showing. Yet the west door, located beneath the east wall of the tower, opens to the outside only slightly below the present exterior ground level. As the door appears to be original to the build from the 1390s, an internal stair must have been present in order to allow this entrance to function, continuing the steps down from the processional passage that still exists outside the door. Documentary evidence suggests that the tower was under construction from at least the 1390s. How much was achieved may be judged from the amount of the built structure requiring major modification in the mid-15th century. The tower famously strides over the former processional path in a way found in a number of other East Anglian churches, though St Peter's may be the earliest to survive. The lowest areas of the tower include the linking sections between the buttresses of the eastern tower piers and the current north and south nave aisles. Hence, at these points, the 1390s meets the 1460s. These sections of the 14th-century work are decorated with flushwork panelling, something the later stages rejects emphatically. The existing 'joins' between the two periods are less than happy but, inside, it is the eastern faces of the earlier buttress piers that provide a rich source of information. The tower was built against the old nave, the width of which was demonstrably the same as at present. That the old nave arcades abutted against the new tower cannot be doubted — the sheer scale of the redressing of the buttresses indicating the work necessary after their removal. The south-eastern pier is the easiest to read, and may be examined from the modern organ stair. Above a height of 4.18 m from the present nave floor, the 14th-century mouldings have been cut away and replaced with matching mouldings that carry on to the (presumably) higher level necessary for the capital and respond for the new nave arcade. Curiously, these capitals alone within the whole church are decorated with diamond fleurons (Fig. 6). This suggests that the old arcades were somewhat lower, not surprising if the floor level was also some 0.5 m beneath the present. The great eastern arch beneath the tower has been similarly extended to accommodate the higher level of the new nave. Thus the refurbishment of the tower in the mid-15th century suggests that it had reached the roof level of the old nave by the time the new nave was begun after 1455.

Stair turrets seem to have been a constant problem dogging any reconstruction of the older church at Mancroft. The west tower has three doors in the 1390s work — the west door, an exterior door to the tower turret in the south-eastern tower pier, and an interior door facing diagonally into the south nave aisle. At present, none of the doors is fit for purpose and that may always have been the case. The west door seems to have been placed at roughly the mid-height between the exterior processional pathway and the old nave floor, necessitating steps both inside and out. The exterior stair turret door is 320 mm above the modern ground level, access now being assisted by a loose intermediate block. The problem door is in the south aisle. The doorhead shows obvious signs of being a rough insertion; indeed, the jambs are also disturbed near their tops, especially on the left side. However, the lower sections of the jambs are very well behaved, with smooth, continuous ashlar lines from the tower piers, and mouldings and bases compatible with the remaining 14th-century work. The cill is currently 240 mm above the aisle floor. If the door opened from the earlier aisle floor level some 0.5 m down, then the step would be almost 0.75 m. Given that neither of the other 14th-century doors is at appropriate levels, either for the former or existing church, is the south aisle turret door any different? It might be thought that opening the door would resolve whether it has been inserted or not. Think again. The door opens into an irregular lobby from which stairs ascend to a higher lobby with shared access from the exterior turret door. The aisle entry door jambs immediately within appear to continue smoothly for some distance within the lower lobby until on the right-hand side, the wall becomes roughly made up and now rises in an attempt to prop up the stairs above.

It is clearly not an original feature of the stair. The left wall jamb disappears at a crucial point behind electrical ducting. At the lower lobby floor level, three steps perhaps best described as 'rough-and-ready' lead up to a triangular upper lobby where the floor is at the level of the exterior turret door cill. These lowest steps have brick and rubble risers with sections of stone as treads, though the first is of timber. These makeshift steps adjoin two round stone blocks, not newels as such, but giving that appearance. They are not made in the same manner as the remaining newels above, but would obviously be necessary to underpin the newel if it had had to be lowered for a new interior access lobby. The impression from within is that the interior turret door entry has been hewn from within the tower pier, the rustic stairs providing the lift necessary to access the original floor level and commencement of the stair from the exterior door. The evidence from inside the south aisle turret door is at odds with the outward appearance of the entry within the aisle. There would appear to be no way of resolving the point. The turret interior has also had its share of 'refurbishment' with a blocked window and a large doorway(?) about halfway round the first turn. This appears to coincide with an area of smooth repaired ashlar on the north-eastern diagonal face of the tower pier that might otherwise pass for the scar of a removed wall monument. Was this an access point into some raised feature within the west end of the previous nave?

The existing 15th-century nave of St Peter's poses a number of problems of its own. The arcade bases on the north are lower than those on the south (an average of 0.94 m on the N, 0.98 m on the S). Why? In addition, there are slight variations in the mouldings of the aisle window jambs, in the arcade capitals and arch mouldings. While these factors may indicate the spasmodic progress of the work, could such basic 'mistakes' or changes of mind have occurred in what had clearly become an attempt at a single unified interior? St Peter's has eight arcade bays overall, two in the chancel and six in the public nave space (Fig. 3). They have significantly different bay lengths. Measurements are difficult due to furnishings and other obstructions, but it is possible to take readings at mid-pier height at roughly a metre above the floor, so the measurements given here are from the cardinal shafts east and west at this level. The first three bays counting from the east are roughly similar, the widest, bay 2N at 4.46 m the narrowest, bay 3S at 4.41 m. Thereafter the bays differ considerably with the widest bay 6N at 4.25 m, the narrowest bay 8N at only 2.26 m. On some occasions the nave bays differ from side to side, bay 7N being 3.62 m, while that opposite is 3.76 m. The westernmost bay, crashing as it does into the west tower, is 2.26 m on the north, 2.33 m on the south. The bay lengths confirm that the chancel was eventually carried out as a set piece, the southern arcade conforming closely in its measurements with the north, already existing. The nave is more problematic. The first bay, 3, does try to emulate the chancel but thereafter the bays get shorter, reaching only 4.01 m in bay 5S, then leaping to 4.25 m in the next, bay 6N. While this may indicate no more than the reuse of the foundations at a lower level of the previous nave piers, it does confirm a rather haphazard building campaign on this part of the church. Had a more consistent bay length been chosen for the nave, one nearer the 4.5 m mark of the chancel bays, then the nave could have had a more consistent bay length throughout though with one less bay, five instead of six. This would have avoided the 'collision' at the west end and would have helped to give the appearance of a planned single campaign, more like St Andrew's or St Stephen's were to have. Clearly, the nave campaign on St Peter's was patchy, with no overall view of the potential result.

How was the whole process finally achieved? If the chancel was consecrated in 1455, it was presumably roofed. Was that with the present roof or with a temporary roof beneath an as yet unbuilt clerestory? If the chancel was consecrated at its present height in 1455, then what supported the western end of its high roof? One answer might be the stump of a previous central tower. The widest of all the nave bays, bay 3 at 4.41 m, might also suggest some problems in layout during the nave construction caused by just such a surviving obstacle. The building of an entirely new western tower and the wider first bay east of the parochial nave might well signify the removal of an older central tower, a not uncommon feature in East Anglia. Given that the only potential for the parish to increase the footprint of their nave was eastwards, removing a central tower is an easy option.

Verbal reports from the 1960s, when the entire church was in scaffolding, suggested a break in the present high roof at the nave/chancel division but this is not clear from the floor today. The restoration of the roof was not well recorded, but two structural engineers, E. W. H. Gifford and P. Taylor, published some of their observations in *The Structural Engineer* of 1964. They made the interesting, if infuriatingly vague, comment that

The inspection also showed that whereas one half of the length of the roof was built with a cranked hammerbeam in one piece across the top of the wall and cantilevering out over the nave, the second half had been built with the beam in two sections, dependent for stability entirely on a few oak pins and curved brackets. The iron straps on this section were of a very early date with hand-cut threads and nuts.[15]

The report does not indicate where the two 'halves' of the roof meet, or whether the reference to the 'nave' means exactly that or merely the central vessel of the church. However, it does confirm the verbal reports that have endured for more than half a century that the high roof of Mancroft was built in two apparently very different structural campaigns. Sadly, the crucial structural evidence lies hidden once more above the false-work vault sections. The report also details where the crack or break at clerestory level actually occurs — not along one of the arcade walls as in popular memory but above the east window. The two flanking walls had departed so far from the plumb that the end gable just opened up.

Having seen the exterior of the clerestory stripped of its facing stone at the eastern end of the south side some thirty years ago, the writer can confirm that the structure at this level is of very poor construction. Rough, broken stone, rubble and some brick set in very thick mortar — hardly sufficient for the great weight and stresses of the high roof, as it was to prove. The facing is well-cut Ancaster but very thin, with bevelled backs to extrude the surplus mortar upon application. Considering the quality of brickwork in Norfolk in the 15th century — witness the aisles of Loddon — the quality of the work briefly visible at the chancel end of the clerestory of St Peter's is lamentable.

Parochial chancel projects cannot have been common. What was the possible return for the parishioners other than aggrandizing their church by creating a 'thru-build'? But there are other examples in late-medieval Norwich. St Gregory's, owned by the cathedral priory, was rebuilt completely in the last decades of the 14th century.[16] It, too, has a raised chancel over vaulted undercrofts. Will evidence is lacking so it is impossible to establish how or why this particular thru-build came about, nor what financial responsibility fell upon the parish. The monks of Norwich Cathedral were not noted for their extravagance when it came to their parochial responsibilities, yet Blomefield records that they did indeed pay for the new chancel, though he adds, 'and such benefactors as they could get to contribute to it'.[17] At the end of the 15th century both St Andrew's and St Stephen's (Fig. 7) saw new, complete thru-builds. St Andrew's,

FIG. 7.   Norwich, St Stephen: interior looking east

which like Mancroft belonged to the College of St Mary, seems to have been totally rebuilt against an earlier tower and was completed by 1506.[18] A simple, box-like structure, there being no architectural expression dividing parochial nave and patronal chancel; indeed, without a screen, the whole interior reads as a single space. Such a project must have involved the closest liaison, both financial and managerial, between the parish and rector, the swiftness and completeness of the whole project rendering all the usable spaces inoperative for the duration.

St Andrew's was rebuilt against an existing west tower, though one only just completed. St Stephen's, which belonged to the cathedral priory, appears to have been a more radical rebuild. Both churches are short of ground space to the east, both east chancel walls now standing 'on the road'. St Andrew's is also restricted to the west, adding to its box-like interior, whereas St Stephen's could and evidently did expand westwards. Preliminary findings from the recent restoration of St Stephen's suggest that foundations of a previous west tower now lie beneath the westernmost bays of the nave. If this proves correct, then the church offers a rare example of a west tower sacrificed for nave space, the tower function eventually transferred to the slight structure raised over the earlier north porch. The patronal arrangements at St Stephen's as detailed by Blomefield serve as a warning against any attempt to generalize financial liability for chancel reconstruction.[19] Commonly, rectors in receipt of the greater part of the parochial income would pay the greater part of any costs for repairs or reconstruction of the chancel. Vicars, chaplains and others would not. But the arrangement at St Stephen's, where Norwich Cathedral priory held the rectory, gave the whole income to the vicar yet maintained the arrangement that reconstruction costs should be paid two-thirds by the priory. Given that St Stephen's was one of the wealthier incumbencies, it is not surprising to find a vicar able to contribute, but puzzling how he and the parish squeezed so much from the priory, given the comparatively lavish cost of the thru-built church. The speed of the work is shown by the grant of lead for the chancel roof in 1521 and the glazing recorded as being in the west window, giving a date of 1536/7.[20]

A continuous flow of funding was clearly a problem for 'total' church reconstructions. But Norwich provides ample evidence of an alternative 'make-do-and-mend' policy, reusing substantial sections of a previous church where possible, and on occasion making little effort to hide the fact. St Stephen's not only preserved the 13th-century north porch, later used as a base for a new tower, but the north aisle was also preserved, complete with its projecting chapel. St George Colegate was more subtle, retaining the west tower and south porch from a mid-15th-century rebuild, whilst adapting the nave north aisle by extending the windows upwards through the original brick/flint over-arches, and inserting new tracery heads of a more depressed, four-centred design.[21] While it appears that little concern was given to the northern, less public exterior, the interior is more surprising as the window jamb mouldings change quite blatantly from the older lower sections to the extensions above. Adapting and remodelling of older sections of a church was clearly beneficial to the budget, but at St Peter's, other than the 'new' and still unfinished west tower, only the 1430s 'model' north chancel chapel survives from the pre-1441 church.

Adaptation may also have mitigated the disruption brought about by major thru-build projects. At St George Colegate the entirely new south aisle could have been erected on the open ground without disturbing the old nave. Even the modernization of the north aisle could have been accomplished without closing the church. But at some point the building of new, matching nave arcades, clerestory and high roof would surely put the public space completely out of action. How did the parishioners cope and how were such campaigns carried out?

St Michael Coslany provides one of the most revealing (and scary) examples of how a new nave might be 'installed' a section at a time.[22] The church had been substantially rebuilt in the 1420s with a new west tower and a broad, aisle-less nave. A simple scissor braced roof covered the nave, but with no clerestory the new church would have been somewhat dark. The lateral windows were of a flowing design still favoured in Norwich at that time, though the west window within the tower is of a more 'modern' design.[23] In the late 15th century a campaign began to add aisles to the parochial nave, together with sumptuous chancel chapels.[24] The work is very lavish, both aisles having elaborate and extremely costly flint and stone flush-work designs. The north aisle stands complete but the south aisle is missing its completion at the west end (Figs 8 and 9). Thus, one 'bay' of the previous church survives. Perhaps the most surprising feature of the unfinished aisle is the way it was being undertaken — one or more bays at a time from the east end, with a temporary north–south wall sealing the unfinished work at each stage. Thus the last complete bay towards the west still has its 'temporary' terminal wall awaiting the building of the westernmost bays. It has been a long wait.

Inside, two pieces of evidence are most surprising; the new south aisle arcade was being punched through the previous south wall one or two bays at a time. The last pier at the west end is in fact complete on all four sides, the remaining older wall to the west being patched up against the new pier to provide a temporary weather-seal.[25] Further, the springer block for the last, unbuilt western bay of the arcade can be seen dug into

FIG. 8. Norwich, St Michael Coslany: exterior from the south-west

the old wall fragment (Fig. 10), ready and waiting for the last arch. Rather than demolish the old nave south wall, it was removed a section at a time but had both sides been completed all evidence of this process would have been lost. The advantage for the parish was that much of the work could proceed without disrupting seriously the use of the nave and it enabled the retention of the old nave roof until the day that a new clerestory would sweep it away. That day never came. This is a great shame as a clerestory and potential flat roof as at St George Colgate, both products of the same workshop, would have given St Michael's perhaps the most splendid late gothic interior of all the Norwich parish churches. Was constructing a new arcade piecemeal beneath an existing main roof normal practice in late medieval Norwich? Did all churches undergoing reconstruction go through a period when they looked like St Michael's? Did St Peter Mancroft? It has been noted that the nave arcades at St Peter's are not identical. Equally, the evidence of the aisles suggests a haphazard progression.[26] Were the nave arcades rebuilt only to the base of the clerestory under an older or temporary roof before the whole nave interior was raised in one campaign and the new roof added? The problem with St Peter's is that it *was* finished, and nearly all stages of its late medieval constructional history lost in the process.

It is possible to make a general reconstruction of the previous St Peter Mancroft church, albeit with some uncertain elements. Before the 1390s, the parochial nave was as long as at present, appears to have had clerestories, and had a central vessel the width of its successor. There is no evidence of a western tower before the present, leaving a strong possibility that the previous church had a central tower, perhaps with

FIG. 9.   Norwich, St Michael Coslany: interior
looking south-west

FIG. 10.   Norwich, St Michael Coslany:
interior, detail of unfinished south arcade

adjoining transeptal features. Either way, the parochial space extended far enough to the north to accommodate the original 1430s intention for a new chancel chapel. In turn, the length of this addition gives some idea of the length of the lost chancel. The whole of the previous church seems to have had a floor level at least 0.5 m lower than at present.

It is not the purpose of this paper to complicate the constructional history of St Peter Mancroft. For the most part it is quite straightforward. While the parochial interest in the chancel is surely uncommon, the funding and project management of the scheme is pretty much as expected. However, the north chancel chapel stair evidence reveals that even the most 'ordinary' of projects has secrets hidden away that are perhaps difficult to grasp. As a parish church St Peter Mancroft represents an almost perfect example of a late medieval total rebuild. Everything is in its place, the spaces are clear and un-ambiguous, the result almost mechanical. Pevsner once said it took half an hour to see the most modest Romanesque English parish church, five minutes to see the best Perpendicular one. It is a common sentiment but, hopefully, this analysis of St Peter's demonstrates that even the 'best' is worthy of a little more than five minutes.

ACKNOWLEDGEMENTS

I would like to thank the vicar, staff and volunteers of St Peter Mancroft for their great assistance and forbearance during the preparation of this paper. I would also like to thank the vicar, staff and volunteers of St Stephen's. I am grateful to David King for his generous help and advice.

NOTES

1. See F. Woodman, 'The Rebuilding of St Peter Mancroft', *East Anglian Studies: Essays presented to J. C. Barringer on his retirement August 30, 1995*, ed. A. Longcroft and R. Toby (Norwich 1995), 290–94. Important modifications and corrections appear in D. King, *The Medieval Stained Glass of St Peter Mancroft, Norwich*, Corpus Vitrearum Medii Aevi, Great Britain, 5 (Oxford 2006), liv–lxii.

2. Ibid., lviii: the will of Thomas Bumpsteade, NRO, NCC Wylby 29.

3. Blomefield, *Norfolk*, IV, 186, 191.

4. Ibid., 214.

5. Will of William Setman, NRO, NCC Surflete, 124–25, and will of John Herries, NRO, NCC Surflete 78. For references to documentary evidence for the rebuilding, King, *Glass of Mancroft* (as in n. 1), Appendix 2 145–54.

6. Blomefield, *Norfolk*, IV, 212.

7. Ibid., 201.

8. Ibid., 186.

9. Ibid., 191.

10. Ibid., 186; N. P. Tanner, *The Church in late Medieval Norwich, 1370–1552* (Toronto 1984), 176.

11. Will of Robert Pert, NRO, NCC Wylby 58, 1445.

12. For William II Canynges, see *Oxford Dictionary of National Biography*, 9 (2004), 970–71.

13. Will of Robert Toppes, NRO, NCC Jekkys 97-99, 1467.

14. Will of Thomas Kempe, NRO, NCC Aubry 32.

15. E. W. H. Gifford and P. Taylor, 'The Restoration of Ancient buildings', *The Structural Engineer*, 42.10 (1964), 327–39. The team responsible for the work, R. Hare and R. Potter, are long deceased and their Salisbury practice no longer operating.

16. For St Gregory's, see Blomefield, *Norfolk*, IV, 273, and various payments in the Infirmarer Rolls, NRO, DCN Inf, e.g. dedication of altar, 1401: Cattermole and Cotton, 'Church Building', 258.

17. Blomefield, *Norfolk*, IV, 273.

18. For St Andrew's, see ibid., 303–04; Cattermole and Cotton, 'Church Building', 257.

19. For St Stephen's, see ibid., 259–60; Blomefield, *Norfolk*, IV, 145.

20. St Stephen's north chancel chapel east window was glazed in 1522, ibid., 154–55. The arms of Henry VIII and Queen Jane Seymour occurred in the west window, ibid., 160.

21. For the dating of St George Colegate, see ibid., 467; Cattermole and Cotton, 'Church Building', 257.

22. The west tower forms part of a rebuilt west gable wall and, given the scissor-braced roof of the nave, probably constituted a new-built nave and tower of the early 15th century. Various bequests for the west tower of St Michael Coslany, including the will of Robert Ardenne of 1422, NRO, NCC Hyrnyng 97 and a will bequest of 1428 by John Dowe for 'emendation of tower, NRO, NCC Surflete 35: Cattermole and Cotton, 'Church Building', 259.

23. The surviving south window in the nave of St Michael's Coslany may at first sight look 14th century, but it should be compared with the chancel windows of St Saviour's, contracted between 1424–26. See J. Harvey, *English Medieval Architects: a biographical dictionary down to 1550*, 2nd edn (Gloucester 1984), 357 (John Wyspenade).

24. Various will bequests, see wills of Robert Thorpe, TNA, PCC Moone 19, 1501, Richard Harte, NRO, NCC Ryxe 84, 1504: Cattermole and Cotton, 'Church Building', 259.

25. The author revealed this pier during an examination of the church in the 1980s.

26. There are other indicators of the piecemeal development of the present church; most obvious being the various wall thicknesses of each 'build' (as can be seen by eye from the various depths of the internal window splays). The thickest wall is the north wall of the NE chancel chapel (the first work of all), with an average total depth c. 0.92 m. The outer wall of the S aisle of the nave averages c. 0.90 m, while the SE chancel chapel south wall has an average total depth c. 0.75 m (part of the second campaign) and the outer wall of the N nave aisle averages c. 0.74 m (all measurements taken from the exterior to the interior). The S aisle exterior wall also places the aisle roof support corbels at a slightly higher level than those on the north wall, and throughout the church there is a variety of internal window hoodmoulds. The nave aisle evidence does not assist in establishing a sequence of construction, though the 'thinner' north aisle with simpler mullion mouldings might suggest a 'lean period', perhaps during the civil warfare 1455–61. However, it should be remembered that with the north side hemmed in behind a narrow alley of houses (now mostly gone) the south side of the church giving on to the Haymarket might be expected to be somewhat more substantial. I am obliged to Oliver Chinn at Purcell, Norwich, for providing the measurements.

Defining Porches in Norwich, *c.* 1250–*c.* 1510

HELEN E. LUNNON

The city of Norwich possesses thirty-two parish church porches. Collectively, they offer an opportunity to consider the scope of architectural forms applied to a single type of structure built across an extended chronological period but within close proximity. This paper is an attempt to define architecturally what a parish church porch could be and demonstrates how until c. 1400 *little consistent definition is possible. In the 15th century a greater sense of uniformity can be observed, and it is here argued that the repeated use of elements in particular ways, namely facades and stone vaults, constitute something akin to a Norwich church porch type.*

INTRODUCTION

THE aim of this paper is a simple one: to examine the architectural range of church porches built within the city walls of Norwich between the mid-13th and early 16th centuries. An essentially chronological approach therefore frames the discussion, with the first part concerned with the period up to *c.* 1400.

Despite their prominence and prevalence, porches have been little studied, and it is therefore appropriate that their architecture is analysed more fully. For Norwich, the most notable examination to date is that by Pevsner, who wrote in 1962 that '[t]he parish churches of Norwich are predominantly Perp and in every respect a Norfolk Perp. They have however also certain details which, whilst not absent in Norfolk otherwise, are more typical of Norwich than of the county'.[1] Except for the treatment of tower parapets, the differences Pevsner noted were all concerned with porches: '[...] porches continuing the aisles instead of in front of the aisles, porches two-storied, porches vaulted, and porch entrances with figures in relief in the spandrels'.[2] However, not all of Pevsner's points bear close scrutiny: two-storey porches are common throughout Norfolk (and likewise Suffolk and elsewhere), and figuratively carved spandrels are proportionally more prevalent in the county than in the city. But whilst the general trajectory of changes in church porch architecture in Norwich was not dissimilar to that seen in the county at large Norwich examples do, as Pevsner implied, favour particular architectural forms. There are two elements which in the 15th century distinguish city from county, and which are given emphasis in the second part of this paper: the manner in which stone vaulting is used and the emphasis on plain exterior surfaces.[3] It will be argued that these elements constitute an identifiably urban aesthetic.

NORWICH PORCHES *c.* 1250–*c.* 1400

THE earliest extant porch in Norwich is that at St Helen's parish church in Bishopgate (formerly Holme Street). In 1270, the decision was taken to abandon the existing parochial church, then located immediately inside the perimeter wall of the cathedral precinct, in favour of its integration into the site of St Giles' Hospital, founded in 1249 on the opposite side of Holme Street by Walter Suffield, bishop of Norwich.[4] The architectural chronology of the hospital site before the late 13th century is little known, and whether the porch was originally built to serve the hospital chapel or for parochial use is currently uncertain. The porch did, however, always provide a covered way into the westernmost bay of an aisled nave and its architectural form and detail support a dating in the second half of the 13th century, with alterations made in the first half of the 14th century, as will be argued below.

The south facade of the porch is effectively a part of the hospital's perimeter wall and thus links the street to the church. The internal space is wide and low, covered by three bays of quadripartite vaulting with thick, chamfered ribs (Fig. 1). Like other 13th-century Norfolk porches, notably the open arcaded porch at Great Massingham (built c. 1280), St Helen's porch is reminiscent of a cloister walk or vaulted passageway. Most unusually, however, it has four points of ingress or egress, as opposed to the more standard two. This may suggest a change in the access arrangements of the hospital chapel and parish church. Doorways in the side walls, apparently of the same date as the walling (i.e. second half of the 13th century) but with no evidence for valves, allow one to pass through the porch from east to west within the boundary wall of the hospital precinct. In the first half of the 14th century the main entrance, that leading from the street, was altered: the doorway arch was certainly remoulded; to judge by the profile of the arch mouldings this was done c. 1320–40, during a phase of works which

FIG. 1.   Norwich, St Helen: interior of the south porch

included the building of the lower stages of the bell tower. Significantly, the entrance arch is clearly rebated to allow for doors — hence the facade of this porch could be closed, a highly unusual arrangement for a Norfolk parish church. The layout and form of St Helen's porch can, however, be explained by the necessity for it to serve both the hospital chapel and the parish church, including the enclosing function of the former and the sacramental functions of the latter.

The porch at St Helen's is, and probably always has been, a two-storey building, and although the way to the upper chamber has been altered over time, it seems that the original arrangement had a stair turret accessed either from within the church or externally, but not from within the porch. The thickness of the walling at ground-floor stage is approximately 5 ft, but the walls of the upper storey are substantially thinner and as a result a prominent off-set exists. To date this has been explained as evidence of a building break,[5] however, that fails to account for the thickness of the lower walling and consistency of building materials and techniques between the two storeys. These elements suggest that the porch always had a vault supporting an upper chamber and that the more slender upper storey obviated the need for buttressing. The reduction in wall thickness maximizes the internal dimension of the upper chamber, which is commodious by medieval porch standards in height as well as plan. By the 15th century the upper chamber at St Helen's functioned as a chapel and muniment room; evidence for its use before this date is, however, lacking.[6]

The deep narrow plan of St Helen's porch (approx. 22 ft × 11 ft) compares with the lost porch of the College of St Mary in the Fields (founded as a hospital *c.* 1248) which measured 10 ft in width and a remarkable 42 ft in length.[7] Like that at St Helen's, it physically linked the street to an aisled nave. The elongated form was presumably dictated structurally by the distance from street to church. Perhaps more interestingly, the arrangement indicates the architectural means of regulating access to an enclosed precinct, which might imply the need for doors on the front of the porch. The evidence for the spatial arrangement at the College of St Mary therefore adds weight to the suggestion that the porch at St Helen's originated in conjunction with the building of the hospital, only later being appropriated as part of the parish church.

The north porch at St Stephen's could hardly be more different from those just discussed, and it is, given the foregoing argument, plausibly the earliest surviving specifically parochial church porch in Norwich (Fig. 2). It is one of seventeen lateral porch towers in Norfolk, a building type which developed in the late 13th century and continued to be constructed into the opening decades of the 15th century. Despite being renovated around 1600, the original form of the porch tower at St Stephen's is evident. In accordance with others of its type, the lower two stages of the tower were buttressed, whereas the uppermost (or bell) stage was not. The central belfry opening, fashioned as an unglazed mullioned window, is a later medieval alteration and the Y-tracery window below may well be a much later intrusion, although this is not certain. The carefully selected dark flints and the 'blind' windows in flushwork are, however, part of the original design, an indication of the burgeoning interest in the visual effects of contrasting materials which can also be seen in the spectacularly adventurous crocketed pinnacles and arches on the upper stage of the porch tower at Little Ellingham, built *c.* 1300.

In its external form, the porch tower at St Stephen's is very much like those in the county. Internally, however, it is quite a different building. To the best of my knowledge it has the earliest historiated bosses of any porch in Norfolk but, whilst this is a development for porches, it fits into a pattern of architectural activity in the city around

FIG. 2.   Norwich, St Stephen: view of the porch tower from the north

the same date. For example, as will be discussed shortly, it is approximately coeval with the initial campaign to rebuild the cathedral cloister from 1297, an early phase of which included a sequence of historiated bosses in the east range leading to the prior's door.[8] In forming a preparatory architectural experience which anticipates an entrance, this is not dissimilar to a church porch. This architectural mode — vaulted entrance building decorated with figurative bosses — came to have a particular currency in Norwich in the first quarter of the 14th century, occurring at the Ethelbert gate and the porch to the bishop's hall. Although they are insufficiently similar to support the suggestion of a shared designing or carving mason, it is probable that they have a shared patron — John Salmon, bishop of Norwich from 1299 to 1325.[9]

Although by no means the only challenge he inherited, St Stephen's exercised Bishop Salmon to a considerable degree in the early years of his episcopate, being one of several prestigious parish churches in the city of which the cathedral priory acted as patron. In 1304 the management of, and religious provision for the parish was re-ordered; a vicarage was instituted and Clement de Hoxne installed as the first incumbent.[10] Given his toponym, Clement perhaps served Salmon at the episcopal palace at Hoxne in Suffolk and was thereby known to be a suitable appointee for the position at St Stephen's. Seemingly Salmon was re-founding the parish and placed great importance on doing so in the right manner. Circumstantial evidence suggests that the porch tower was envisaged and constructed as part of a project with greater scope than architectural renewal, and was likely completed by 1304, the year of Clement's installation and an archiepiscopal visitation to the diocese.

Internally, the porch measures 150 in. × 120 in.[11] A stair rises within the thickness of the west wall from a doorway in the south-western corner; the threshold interrupts the lateral stone bench and is therefore evidently the original arrangement. The porch is divided into two bays, covered by a stone vault incorporating a large central oculus to allow bells to be raised into the upper parts of the tower (Fig. 3). The simple hollow-chamfered vault ribs at St Stephen's are essentially the same as those at St Helen's, but here figuratively carved bosses are introduced. The plain form of the ribs jars somewhat with the tri-lobe wall shafts and the finesse with which the bosses were carved, suggesting a construction date before either the Ethelbert gate or Salmon's hall porch, where the ribs have more complex profiles. In a typological sequence these elements would place St Stephen's in advance of Salmon's better known commissions. Equally, the capitals share with those in Salmon's hall porch the distinctly vertical (rather than concave) central section between a thick collar and quite complex capital, but there an abundance of carved foliage covers what at St Stephen's remains a moulded capital.

St Stephen's north porch tower is a remarkable encapsulation of architecture in the service of politically backed religion (or perhaps vice versa), an outward facing manifesto in stone; an achievement which, I suggest, bears the hallmarks of John Salmon, a politically astute courtier and intellectually engaged prelate. As his later architectural projects demonstrate, Salmon developed a portfolio of grand entrances which visually convey tales of social morality lightly sheltered under a biblical cloak; that at St Stephen's resulted from a set of circumstances sufficiently dramatic to inspire the introduction of sculpted biblical imagery into the repertoire of porch architecture in Norfolk.

The axial boss closest to the church door is widely held to represent the martyrdom of St Stephen, whilst its counterpart, that closest to the porch entrance, has been described as an atypical martyrdom of St Laurence.[12] In fact, this boss shows an episode earlier in the account of St Stephen's martyrdom. Having been accused of blasphemy,

FIG. 3.   Norwich, St Stephen: detail of the porch tower interior

Stephen is brought before the high priest and council, where false witnesses are set up against him (Acts 6:12–13). In specific detail, as well as in general terms, neither composition at Norwich St Stephen's is 'typical', with two elements being particularly instructive. In the first scene (the 'trial'), a centrally located thin pillar vertically dissects the image. Although now barely discernible, on top of this pillar is an idol; an allusion to the man-made golden calf to which the Israelites, disbelieving Moses and turning away from God, had offered sacrifice (Exodus 31:1) as retold by Stephen (Acts 7:41). The thrust of Stephen's long exposition before the high priest is twofold: the failure of God's people to remain true to his Law, setting up idols and glorying in the work of man, and a demonstration of Christ's propitiatory truth. Evidently both narratives were pertinent to the patron of the porch.

The parish of St Stephen, along with St Peter Mancroft and St Giles, was part of the 'French borough', the area of Norwich where the incoming Norman-French community settled in the late 11th century. Accompanying the new Norman population was a small community of Jews who settled in the same part of the city: an informal Jewry, including a synagogue, existed within the bounds of St Stephen's parish. During the 12th and 13th centuries Christians and Jews lived as neighbours in St Stephen's, a relationship which, at an inter-person level of trading and financing, was mutually beneficial.[13] On the larger corporate civic stage, however, Christian/Jewish relations were fraught with tensions, fuelled in large part by the formation and manipulation of the cult of St William. In the national context, the expulsion of the Jews in 1290 provides a likely explanation for the concentration of Stephenic iconography that was produced in England between *c.* 1270 and 1325.[14] St Stephen's porch is, to the best of my knowledge, the only surviving example in stone, but iconographically and stylistically the carved imagery fits well with contemporaneous examples in manuscripts and a mural painting at North Stoke, Oxfordshire, also dated to *c.* 1300. From these comparable representations of his martyrdom, it is reasonably certain that the porch tower at St Stephen's was built *c.* 1300, supporting my proposition that the tower was a focused response to the re-ordering of the parish at this time.

As mentioned, St Stephen's porch is the earliest surviving example in Norwich of porch architecture being used in this manner. It implies a change in the conception of what a porch interior could be; it is certainly a very different sort of place from that built at St Helen's a few decades earlier. These two parish porches, and the buildings to which they can be related, evince a fluid exchange of design ideas amongst masons working in Norwich, experimenting particularly with notions of entrance architecture, exchanges which were aided by the involvement of the cathedral priory as the common overseer.

During the 14th century Norwich's interest in entrance architecture extended beyond the patronage of the cathedral priory, as can be seen in the north and south porches of St John Maddermarket. Although suppression of the upper stages was necessitated by the addition of the nave clerestory in the 15th century, the considerable thickness of the walls and the interior arrangement of the north porch testify to the original scheme having been a porch tower.[15] Internally, the porch is covered by a masonry vault at the centre of which is a large circular opening, provided to allow the raising of bells into the tower above, as at St Stephen's. Applied to the surface of the masonry ribs are wooden mouldings and carved bosses which are of a piece with the timber 'plug' filling the central aperture. Whilst the figurative elements of the decoration in this porch tower could have been later additions (added to the masonry ribs when the porch was truncated), the south porch at Maddermarket (originally two-storey) was designed with a tierceron vault including large scale heads at the intersections of the ribs. Although much of the detail has been lost beneath layers of whitewash, the scale and disposition of the head-bosses is reminiscent of the Ethelbert gate and suggest a construction date in the early 14th century. St John Maddermarket follows the configuration of St Stephen's very closely but, although the vaults include carved bosses, neither porch at Maddermarket achieves the prodigious iconographic narrative scheme adopted at St Stephen's.

The development of porch architecture in the city continued at St Gregory's in the decades either side of 1400.[16] Here, features by now familiar are repeated whilst new elements which subsequently became prevalent are added. St Gregory's has north, south and west porches all vaulted and all of which clasp the base of the pre-existing west tower; as a result the depth of each lateral porch is subsumed by the adjacent aisle (Fig. 4). Porches built at the western end of an aisle (see also St Margaret's and St Andrew's) are not necessarily the result of restricted sites as in all cases there is sufficient open ground for the more common projecting form to have been built. Yet regardless of the continuum between aisle and porch in plan, in elevation the two elements are architecturally distinct structures. This is most apparent in the additional height of the porches and their gable roofs, as opposed to the single-pitched roof of the aisle. Like

FIG. 4.   Norwich, St Gregory: view
of the south porch

the south porches at St John Maddermarket and St Laurence's, access to the upper
chamber at St Gregory's is provided by way of a straight stair built within the wall
thickness, here the east wall of the south porch, and accessed from within the church.

   Both the north and south porches at St Gregory's have a central image niche flanked
by a pair of windows. This arrangement became commonplace in the city and county
more widely, but there is little extant evidence to indicate its use in Norwich before the
building of St Gregory's. Also, the niche, windows and buttresses rendered in ashlar, set
against uniformly black knapped-flint, give a variety of surfaces which, when new, contrasted the matt white limestone with what would have appeared as reflective, even
iridescent flint. The gloss-black walling had already been used on the porch tower at
St Stephen's, and has been more widely understood as evoking the jewel-like qualities
of the Heavenly Jerusalem (Revelation 21:11). In more prosaic terms, the flint work at
St Gregory's, which is not restricted to the porches, was evidently undertaken during
a period in which skilled flint working in the city was at a high point, with the wall
at Mayor Appleyard's house (today the Museum of Norwich) being a highly refined
example of the technique. Unlike the use of flint-flushwork which has been identified as
a technique solely used in ecclesiastical contexts,[17] the application of square-cut flint as
a walling veneer was not so restricted.

The relationship between the vault and the plan of the south porch at St Gregory's is complicated by the depth (approx. 4 ft 6 in.) of the west wall where 'seating' is recessed into the embrasure, set back from the wall shafts of the vault. Although when measured into the window embrasure the porch is square in plan (approx. 15 ft 8 in.), each vault bay is only 10 ft 9 in. wide by 7 ft 10 in. deep. The vault shafts on the west side rest on the ground, whereas the corresponding shafts on the east side of the porch are supported on a stone bench. The ribs no longer have the hollow-chamfered form of St Helen's and St Stephen's; they are altogether more refined and elegant in their profile. However, as at St Stephen's and St John Maddermarket, the vault is used for the display of figurative imagery, and, as in the case of the former, the iconography of the two principal bosses at St Gregory's may suggest the context of the porch's construction.

The boss to the north is traditionally interpreted as showing St Gregory teaching boys music,[18] that to the south is essentially unidentified. I suggest that both bosses in fact relate to the martyrdom of St George, although identification remains speculative.[19] The south boss clearly shows a bearded male, apparently wearing only a loin cloth, standing with a post or column at his back, behind which his arms are fastened (Fig. 5). To either side semi-human figures attack the central figure with unidentifiable implements, likely to be either whips or flesh-hooks. Before the mid-14th century the Life of St George rarely included the maiden or the dragon, but rather centred on the martyr's seven years of trials and tortures as meted out by 'Dacyan the tyrant', the late-13th-/early-14th-century copies of the *South English Legendary* being good evidence of this. However, even the early-16th-century *Life of St George* by Alexander Barclay gives an extensive recital of George's torments, including him being bound, his body stretched out and attacked with hooks and nails, although other versions have him being whipped. That

Fig. 5. Norwich, St Gregory: boss in south porch showing a depiction of St George(?) tied to a pillar

George's tormenters were less than human is a textual motif and also identifiable in the composition of the south boss at St Gregory's.[20] Whatever the specific detail (and written accounts of St George's experiences suggest a narrative freedom which may well have been maintained in visual representations), imagery of St George's trials are subsequently less common than the better-known rescue of the maiden or slaying of a dragon, but one example of a twelve-scene composition is found in the parish church of St Neot in Cornwall.[21]

If identification of the iconography as relating to the torments of St George is plausible, it is likely that the porch was built at the expense of the guild of St George, which was established in this parish in 1385.[22] The newly founded guild, undoubtedly inspired by the royal foundation of St George's College at Windsor in the mid-century, would be interested in their patron saint's defence of Christianity, suffering and ultimate martyrdom. In the absence of documentary evidence for the guild's involvement in the building of the porch, and until identification of the south boss has been possible, these suggestions have to remain tentative. The elongated canopied image niche centrally placed above the entrance arch might well have been occupied by a figure of St George, and perhaps it was here that the saintly warrior defeated the satanic dragon,[23] leaving the niche in the north porch facade for an image of St Gregory. What is more certain is that St Gregory's took on a similar role in establishing the desirability of certain aspects of porch form in the city, as did North Walsham and St Nicholas at Lynn in the county around the same time.[24]

PORCHES BUILT IN THE 15TH CENTURY

In order to investigate particular preferences which are more commonly found in urban parishes than in rural ones, the next part of this paper is concerned with the occurrence of two architectural features: stone-vaulted ceilings and 'unadorned' exterior elevations. It is not uncommon for porches to be stone vaulted, but there does appear to be a greater occurrence in Norwich than in Norfolk, as Pevsner noted in 1962. Is this simply a numbers game? I suggest not; rather the distinct ways in which Norwich porches were vaulted can be associated with an aesthetic particular to an urban context. Similarly, it is conjectured that the 'plain' facades of porches built in Norwich during the 15th century indicate a taste for simplicity which was rarely embraced in the county.

The south porch at St Giles-on-the-Hill is of two storeys with an ashlar facade (Fig. 6). Knapped-flint walls east and west have centrally placed traceried windows, the sills of which align with a base course present only on the buttresses. These diagonal buttresses have three off-sets, the middle one aligns with a string-course running directly beneath the large first-floor window which is flanked by niches. A projecting moulding creates a square frame for the entrance arch and the resulting spandrels are filled with spurred quatrefoils and shields. The set-piece entrance is otherwise isolated within the ashlar facade; it is not connected to any other feature of the porch (the niche above being a later addition). Compared with a broad range of mid-15th-century Norfolk porches, the surface detailing of the exterior of St Giles is remarkable in its austerity. However, in Norwich it is only one of a number which, as will be discussed later, indicate a preference for simplicity over superfluity.

Inside, St Giles porch is well lit from the entrance arch and two reasonably large, low, side windows. The door into the church is framed by a flat four-centred arch, the mouldings of which run without alteration or interruption from the plinth to the

FIG. 6.   Norwich, St Giles: view of the porch from the south

FIG. 7. Norwich, St Giles: detail
of the porch interior showing the
fan vault

apex and even the label protrudes only ever so slightly beyond the arch. The room is
sheltered by a fan vault, the conoids of which are formed of trefoil headed cells
arranged in two tiers delineated by horizontal bounding ribs (Fig. 7). Each of the four
roundels recessed within the central circle is composed of a regular quatrefoil with
cusped lobes which are recessed further still. Between the large framing circle and this
cusping the surface is set back four times which, with the addition of mouldings and
angled surfaces, creates a fluid and undulating effect; clever games are being played by
contrasting geometric formality with curved mouldings and subtle layers of detail.

This porch was clearly an ambitious project and is, as far as I am aware, the only
medieval fan-vaulted building in Norwich. It is not, however, the only fan-vaulted
porch in Norfolk, though that designed and intended at Shelton remains unfinished,
presumably owing to the lack (or reassignment) of funds. By the time the porch at
Shelton was being designed and built (c. 1487), the vaulting technique was well established; its use at St Giles was altogether more precocious, given its construction date of
not later than 1455.[25] As I have suggested elsewhere, the porch at St Giles was seemingly a specific architectural response to John Brosyard's desire to be interred there.[26] In

his final testament, dated on the morrow of the feast of the Annunciation to the Blessed Mary 1455, Brosyard requested that his body be buried in the porch of the church of St Giles in Norwich.[27] Implicitly the testator was aware of the type of place the porch was, and, given the building chronology of the church, it is possible that he influenced its design. It is not without significance for the current discussion that Leedy noted that '[a]bout half the fan vaults built before 1450 were located in chantry chapels, which is important in explaining why the fan vault gained acceptance'.[28]

Fan vaulting is based on geometric, not figural, design patterns and this design priority epitomizes the architectural interests of those building church porches in mid-15th-century Norwich. Whilst St Giles is the only fan-vaulted example, I suggest that elsewhere tierceron and lierne vaults were used in ways that create a similar architectural effect. An instance in the city also probably designed as a tomb canopy is the north porch at St Laurence, built *c.* 1459.[29] The simplicity of the exterior offers little indication of the star-like vault within (Fig. 8). It would be going far too far to suggest that the only impetus for vaulted porches was monumental. There is, however, a mid-15th-century preference for plain (i.e. without bosses), not necessarily simple, vaults in porches in Norwich, and this phenomenon may have been stimulated and perpetuated by a monumental context, as understood at St Giles and St Laurence. Beyond the association with burial, the city's 15th-century stone-vaulted porches emanate from a tradition in which architectural confidence was placed in the geometric design of the vault — the rib patterns and the articulation of the walling — as opposed to figuratively carved bosses. This approach to vaulting may well reference tabernacles and other such

Fig. 8.   Norwich, St Laurence: detail of the north porch interior showing the vault design

honorific structures, and in this sense can be seen as enlargements of microarchitectural forms rather than diminutive versions of larger buildings.

Another vaulted church porch in Norwich which served as, and was possibly constructed to be, a monumental tomb is that at St Mary Coslany (Fig. 9). Whereas St Giles' porch is without close comparators, Coslany is one of several Norfolk examples built close to the middle of 15th century to an essentially similar design, identifiable by the form of buttressing, an entrance arch including framing spandrels, and the arrangement of niche and windows in the upper storey. A *terminus ante quem* for the Coslany porch of 1457 is based on the request by John Wyghton, glazier, to be buried there.[30] The building's basic form is also seen in the city at St Margaret Westwick, and in the county at Colby, South Walsham, East Tuddenham and Acle. Although externally these porches present considerable architectural similarity, none of the examples in the county has a vaulted ceiling whereas both city examples do.

To refine the hypothesis that in the 15th century stone vaulting was associated with a patron's sense of their urbanity, it is necessary to consider a broader span of church porches built in Norwich at this period. Essentially, 15th-century porch vaults can be divided into two groups — those with and those without carved bosses (for more details, see Table 1). It might be anticipated that the example set by St Stephen's and

FIG. 9. Norwich, St Mary Coslany: view of the porch from the south

TABLE I.   Vaulted Porches in Norwich (all measurements are in inches)

Church*	Porch location	Approx. construction date	Vault code	Plan (north/south × east/west)	Floor area
St Helen	South	Second half of C13	RR, DR, TR	264 × 134	35,376
St Stephen	North	c. 1300	RR, DR, TR, B, Ca, WS	150 × 120	18,000
St John Maddermarket	North	c. 1320–40	RR, DR, T, L (ring), B, Co	118.5 × 87.5	10,369
St John Maddermarket	South	c. 1320–40	RR, DR, T, B, Ca, WS	133.5 × 118	15,753
St Gregory	South	c. 1385–1400	RR, DR, TR, B, Ca, WS	188 × 129	24,252
St Gregory	North	c. 1385–1400	RR, DR, TR, T, B, Ca, WS	191 × 161	30,751
St Peter Mancroft	North	c. 1445	RR, DR, 2DR, L (ring), B, WS	128.5 × 138	17,733
St Peter Mancroft	South	c. 1445	RR, DR, T × 2, B, Ca, WS	73.5 × 136	9,996
St George Tombland	North	c. 1447–61	RR, DR, Ca, WS	127 × 127	16,129
St John Sepulchre	North	mid-C15	RR, DR, T, WS	122.5 × 125	15,313
St Margaret	South	mid-C15	RR, DR, T, Co	113 × 114	12,882
St Giles	South	c. 1455	F	157 × 120.5	18,919
St Mary Coslany	South	c. 1457	RR, DR, T, WS	117 × 132	15,444
St George Tombland	South	c. 1457–1500	RR, DR, T, B, Co	125 × 109	13,625
St Laurence	North	c. 1459	RR, DR, T × 2, L × 2, Ca, WS	161 × 153	24,633

RR: Ridge Rib, DR: Diagonal Ribs, 2DR: Secondary Diagonal Ribs, TR: Transverse Rib
T: Tiercerons, L: Liernes, F: Fan, B: Bosses, Co: Corbels, Ca: Capitals, WS: Wall Shafts
* The porch at St John Timberhill, although vaulted, has been excluded from the sample as its date of construction, particularly the vault, is uncertain.

St Gregory's would be continued into the 15th century, particularly given Norwich's renown for the sculptural treatment of this architectural element. However, Bishop Lyhart's vaulting in stone of the cathedral nave post-dates the 1463 fire, and Bishop Goldwell's similar work in the presbytery was carried out at the turn of the century.[31] Neither is early enough in date to have served as a catalyst for such treatment of porch ceilings. In fact, only at five of the eleven churches with vaulted porches (St Stephen, St Gregory, St John Maddermarket, St Peter Mancroft and St George Tombland) were figuratively carved bosses deemed necessary or appropriate and, although this amounts to a total of nine out of fifteen porches, only the south porch at Tombland could have taken a steer from the cathedral nave and presbytery.[32]

In the north porch at St Peter Mancroft the bosses are a coherent part of the whole interior (Fig. 10) rather than a dominant feature. Furthermore, the scope of the imagery is narrow, essentially doing little more than reinforcing the presence of the dedicatory saint at the entrance to the church. The same concerns are seen in the rather smaller south porch, too. The distinction between city and county in terms of how stone vaults were treated centres on the subject matter of the bosses. The bosses of 15th-century city porches do not display the historiated sequences explored in the earlier porches at Stephen's and St Gregory's, in the gates, cloister, nave and presbytery of the cathedral, or the Marian cycles depicted in several 15th-century Norfolk porches.[33] This conception of a porch vault is absent even at Mancroft, the most ambitious of Norwich parish churches. But is this to be read as evidence of conservatism and reserve, as opposed to overt display and ornament, or is what we see a display of technical virtuosity? The success of the geometry, the precision with which the porch is built, the cutting and jointing of the rib stones are all exposed, and set at a viewable height in the prominent location of the church entrance.

Porch vaults in Norwich were not necessarily of complicated or elaborate design, even in the mid-15th century. Although presumably always more expensive than a simple form of timber ceiling, a 'cheap' masonry vault seems to have been preferred to an elaborate timber one. St George Tombland is an interesting case, having very different vaulted porches on north and south (Figs 11 and 12). The former emphasizes

FIG. 10.   Norwich, St Peter Mancroft: detail of the north porch vault

FIG. 11. Norwich,
St George Tombland: detail
of the north porch vault

FIG. 12. Norwich,
St George Tombland: detail
of the south porch vault

the vault design, whilst the latter is a vehicle for figurative decoration. Whereas in the north porch (built no earlier than 1447 but before 1461) the shafts link the vault to the wall benches and therefore ultimately the floor, the south porch vault (built after 1457 and before 1500) seems almost to float in the air, visually resting on only a small corbel at each corner. In one church it is therefore possible to notice a variation in the formal characteristics of 15th-century vaulted porches. The earlier example has physical continuity with the rest of the building in being supported on shafts which rest on grounded stone benches, whereas the later instance is a canopy suspended over the space, something more akin to canvas stretched over a frame than having architectural solidity. Other extant examples in Norwich of 15th-century 'floating' vaults are to be found at St Margaret and St Giles, whereas beyond the city many prominent mid-15th-century porches follow this form, for example Wymondham and Attleborough. In the majority of 15th-century porches in the city, seven out of the eleven, architectural continuity ensures the vault is connected to the ground. Even simple vaults, like that at St John Sepulchre, sit on corner shafts and the two elements combined form wall arches to frame the windows.

It has so far been argued that the form and decoration of vaults distinguish urban examples from those in the county at large, and that an apparent interest in forms over decoration is to be seen as a particularly urban architectural mode. The exterior materiality of porches can be read in like manner. Whilst Pevsner's suggestion that carved imagery in the spandrels of porches is more commonplace in the city than in the county cannot be sustained, it is possible to identify a strong preference for unadorned exteriors.[34]

Although the porch at St Mary Coslany has an ashlar facade and that at St Margaret Westwick is of flint, they were designed very much along the same lines. Essentially the negative of Coslany's white ashlar, the carefully selected and squared black flint used at St Margaret's makes the surface of the porch appear polished, absorbing and reflecting light as though a gemstone or sheet of glass. The widespread use of indigenous flint is well known in Norfolk and Suffolk, both as a basic building material and as a worked stone cladding, and the porches in the city are no exception. Two options predominate — either white ashlar or black flint rather than elaborate combinations of the two. In all examples it is apparent that the walling material and its treatment is part of the brief, presumably the client's own choice, but perhaps guided by the mason because of their experience and expertise.

At St Giles, St Mary Coslany and St Michael at Plea the enhancement of the front by means of ashlar cladding is in stark contrast to the side walls of the porches and the churches to which they are attached. Alternatively, at St Gregory, St Laurence and St Margaret the walling material is the same on all three sides, but detailing on the facade is used to differing degrees. St Gregory's is essentially unelaborated, at St Laurence spandrels are introduced, and at St Margaret a frieze is inserted between the apex of the portal hood mould and the sills of the upper windows. It is only at St Michael at Plea where all of these elements, an ashlar facade, figuratively carved spandrels and a frieze (here adorned with flushwork monograms) are brought together and result in a 15th-century porch which looks architecturally more towards the county than the city (Fig. 13). Flint flushwork was rarely used on porches in Norwich, with the only other notable surviving example being St John Sepulchre. The widespread use of monograms, inscriptions and decorative panelling in flushwork and carved ashlar on the facades of East Anglian porches such as Loddon or Swannington is not evident in

FIG. 13. Norwich, St Michael at Plea: view of the porch from the south

the city, and Norwich generally is noticeable by its almost complete absence from publications such as Blatchley and Northeast's *Decoding Flint Flushwork*.[35]

Other means of designing imagery into porches, such as canopied niches and carved spandrels, are also either absent or used sparingly in Norwich. For example, niches are restricted to one of two formats: most commonly a single niche centrally placed in the gable above the entrance arch (for example, at St Peter Hungate, St Mary Coslany and St Laurence) or, occasionally, a pair of niches flanking the entrance (as at St Peter Mancroft and formerly at St George Tombland). The diversity or multiplicity of niches seen on many porches across the county, such as the defining example at St Nicholas, Lynn, is not found in the city. Similarly, tiers of blind or shallow niches adorning buttresses or figuratively carved pinnacles, as at Salle, are also rarely found in the architectural repertoire of urban porches. Some caution is necessary when considering the latter, however, as alterations to roofs have removed much evidence.[36] On the whole, the porches of Norwich present restraint in the richness of their design, a sense of decorum based on simplicity. A case in point is the pair of two-storey unvaulted porches at St Andrew's (Figs 14 and 15): the buttresses are ashlar faced but without detail or ornament, the entrance arches are framed by spandrels, but these are principally of geometric pattern with small shields at the centre, and whilst the image niche on the north

FIG. 14. Norwich, St Andrew's: view of the south porch

FIG. 15. Norwich, St Andrew's: view of the north porch

porch is elegantly elongated it is the only niche on the porch, and the figure it housed must have been relatively small and set high above the porch entrance (the companion niche on the south porch is lost). St Andrew's encapsulates the ways in which Norwich parish church porches present a rather more disciplined version of county taste.

As the difference in taste between porches in the city and county might be regarded as a result of different masons being employed, it will be well to conclude with evidence that in some cases the same men were employed in both contexts. The design of St Mary Coslany is associated with the man dubbed by Richard Fawcett the 'Wiveton Mason'. In 1982, Fawcett published a study of buildings attributed to, or influenced by, this mason based in most part on moulding profiles; but he also discussed other architectural features which can be used as identifiers of a shared origin, such as the use of ashlar facades as foils for the elaborate mouldings of the entrance jambs. He compared the porch at St Mary Coslany to the north porch at Wiveton and the south porch at Great Cressingham, showing identical or near identical arch details but noting that 'in other respects the porch [St Mary Coslany] could hardly be less like those at the other churches [Wiveton and Cressingham]'.[37] This is an important point. Even where carved masonry features can link buildings to one designer, that person's influence on the building was inevitably tempered by the specific circumstances of each project, and very different buildings can and did result. If Fawcett's attributions are correct, the designer of these three porches had professional exposure to both city and county. In their shared plain ashlar facades and the flushwork-monogram plinths at Coslany and Cressingham we are presented with buildings which contain an amalgam of urban and non-urban architectural characteristics. However, whilst both Wiveton and Cressingham have characteristically understated 'urban' facades, neither has a stone vault.

In the same discussion Richard Fawcett offered the porch at St Margaret Westwick, also in the city, as 'an elided version' of his other examples, including St Mary Coslany, and discussed issues of how both inventiveness and the scale of buildings can be accommodated within a single mason's portfolio of works. What matters for current purposes, however, is that, although the Coslany and Westwick porches can be situated in an architectural group comprising seven examples associated either by details such as the moulding profiles used or by an overall architectural design, they are the only ones with stone-vaulted ceilings, both were built within the urban context of Norwich, and yet in terms of exterior elaboration urban simplicity is tempered by a degree of county influence. It seems, therefore, that much of what Fawcett recognized as a mason's inventiveness stemmed from him (the mason) being exposed to, and working in, both urban and rural architectural contexts. The buildings attributed to the 'Wiveton Mason', including the porches discussed here, are therefore unusual in that they blur the architectural distinction between city and county.

SUMMARY

THE approach adopted in this paper has been twofold: to chart the development of porches built in Norwich from the mid-13th century to *c.* 1400, and to investigate two characteristic architectural features of 15th-century examples, namely facades and stone-vaulted interiors. The city of Norwich retains thirty-two parish church porches with fabric essentially of medieval date. Several are either architecturally unremarkable or have been heavily restored and now offer little to our understanding of the building type, although they do add to an impression of the apparent desirability of church porches in the 15th-century city. Owing to the major rebuilding of so many Norwich churches in the 15th century, evidence for the form of earlier porches is lacking and conclusions have to be drawn from a small sample. There is no doubting, however, the diversity in architectural form which late-13th- and 14th-century porches could take, as those extant at St Helen's and St Stephen's demonstrate. Such range is in keeping with the development of parish church porches in Norfolk generally, although the city examples are particular in their details. In the 15th century porch architecture in the city diverges from that in the county. The foregoing paper has argued that church porches built in Norwich during that period present a particular urban taste for a sophisticated simplicity when compared with examples built contemporaneously in the county. Thus they imply a particular concern with architectural refinement, which would conceivably have been part of a more comprehensive system of collective behaviours in which propriety was achieved through restraint rather than exuberance. It is well attested that the royal charter of incorporation granted to Norwich in 1404 marked a watershed in the city's history and it was no less significant in the architectural story of Norwich. If, as other authors in the current volume have discussed,[38] architecture was one means by which citizens of Norwich defined themselves and their city, then it is perhaps to be expected that, as a visually eminent feature of most parish churches (themselves the paramount group of buildings in the city), porches display confidence through a refined simplicity. The same architectural ideal can be seen applied in the 'through-build' churches of St Andrew and St Peter Mancroft, for example. Independence in the form of self-government had come to Norwich; to a remarkable extent the manifestation of this new condition was architectural and nowhere is this more apparent than in the prominent restraint of the city's parish church porches.

NOTES

1. B/E, *Norfolk*, I, 230.

2. Ibid.

3. The 31 extant parish churches within the medieval city walls feature 32 porches, of varying degrees of original and rebuilt fabric. Of this number, 15 (47%) are vaulted. This compares to 17 (18%) of the 95 porches in Norfolk (including Norwich) for which primary or antiquarian documentary dating evidence survives.

4. C. Rawcliffe, *Medicine for the Soul: life, death and resurrection of an English medieval hospital, St Giles's, Norwich, c. 1249–1550* (Sutton 1999), 110.

5. For example, Purcell Miller Tritton, *The Great Hospital, Norwich: Condition Survey* (2002 unpublished), 2.

6. Rawcliffe, *Medicine* (as in n. 4), 111 and 286 n. 61.

7. The width being 10 ft is taken from the published plan; the length from the accompanying text and commentary, which reads: 'Of the porch or gallery you have found enough to show that its length was probably 42 ft, as given in the estimate of the timber, than the 12 ft in the account of the lead. The width, 18 ft, represents the two slopes of the roof, which must therefore have been of a high pitch'. G. E. Hawes, 'Recent Excavations at the College of St Mary in the Fields, Norwich', *NA*, 15 (1904), 313. Evidently, by the 1540s this porch had been reduced in depth to just 12 ft., ibid., 307. My thanks to Dr Claire Daunton for providing this reference. See also D. King in the present volume.

8. F. Woodman, 'The Gothic Campaigns', in *Norwich Cathedral 1096–1996*, 166–67.

9. For discussion of Bishop Salmon's artistic patronage, see V. Sekules in the present volume.

10. 1304 was an important year for Salmon. Following the archiepiscopal visitation of the Norwich diocese, Robert Winchelsey opposed Salmon's claim on the first-fruits from parishes in the care of the cathedral priory, a dispute settled by papal intervention in 1307 in Salmon's favour, despite a weight of evidence to the contrary. See J. H. Denton, *Robert Winchelsey and the Crown 1294–1313: a study in the defence of ecclesiastical liberty* (Cambridge 1980), 47–48.

11. The width therefore amounts to 80% of the depth. This compares with the porch towers at Hardingham (*c.* 1300), 130 in. × 94 in., width/depth equals 72%, Little Ellingham (*c.* 1300), 124 in. × 103 in., width/

depth equals 83% and Holme-next-the-Sea (*c.* 1405), 145 in. × 131 in., width/depth equals 90%. The other porch towers in Norfolk are square in plan.

12. A. Nichols, *The Early Art of Norfolk: A Subject List of Extant and Lost Art Including Items Relevant to Drama* (Kalamazoo 2002), 209 and 228.

13. For discussion of the often over-looked positive aspects of the Jewish community in Norwich, see E. Rutledge, 'The Medieval Jews of Norwich and their Legacy', in *Art, Faith and Place in East Anglia: from prehistory to the present*, ed. T. A. Heslop, E. Mellings and M. Thøfner (Woodbridge 2012), 117–29, esp. 122–23.

14. Four manuscript examples are particularly relevant here: London, British Library, MS Egerton 1066, f. 10v, *c.* 1270–90; London, British Library, MS Stowe 12, f. 20v, 1322–25; British Library MS Royal 2B VII, ff. 233v and 234r, *c.* 1310–20; British Library MS Yates Thompson 13, f. 84, *c.* 1325–35. All include images either of Stephen's trial or a vividly active stoning scene, in which the martyr kneels in prayer as leaping Jews gleefully pelt him with rocks. The first two manuscripts almost certainly had East Anglian origins, the other two probably London. For Egerton 1066, see N. Morgan, *Early Gothic Manuscripts: A survey of manuscripts illuminated in the British Isles, Vol II* (London 1982), 186–87, cat. 182. For Stowe 12, Royal 2B VII and Yates Thompson 13, see L. F. Sandler, *Gothic Manuscripts 1285–1385: A Survey of manuscripts illuminated in the British Isles, Vol II* (London 1986), 86–87 cat. 79; 64–66 cat. 56; 107–09 cat. 98 respectively.

15. The ground-floor stage of the now two-storey north porch at St John Maddermarket was observed as 'the fragment of a tower porch of c. 1320' by the Norwich Survey. See 'St John Maddermarket' in 'The Norwich Survey' (unpublished), 7, copy in the author's possession.

16. Pevsner and Wilson describe the church as 'Substantially of late C14 date', the nave roof as 'late C14', the arcade piers as 'a date between Dec and Perp', and the chancel as having been 'rebuilt in 1394 at the expense of the Cathedral Priory, probably by *Robert Wodehirst*'. B/E, *Norfolk*, I, 237.

17. J. Luxford, 'Symbolism in East Anglian Flushwork', in *Signs and Symbols*, ed. J. Cherry and A. Payne, Harlaxton Medieval Studies XVIII (Donnington 2009), 119–32.

18. Nichols, *Early Art* (as in n. 12), 201.

19. For a compositional comparison, see La Vitre de St-Georges, Eglise Fertre-Bernard, available at: http://www.flickr.com/photos/biron-philippe/5606088517/sizes/l/in/photostream/ [accessed 17 July 2014].

20. 'The tourmentours / and wretches inhumayne', A. Barclay, *Life of St George*, ed. W. Nelson, Early English Text Society, OS 230 (London 1955), 75.

21. For the St Neot glass, see J. Mattingly, 'Stories in the Glass — Reconstructing the St Neot Pre-Reformation Glazing Scheme', *Journal of the Royal Institution of Cornwall*, 3 (2000), 9–55. Another example of the flagellation of St George is a mid-14th-century mural painting at Decani Monastery in Serbia.

22. J. Jessopp, *History and Antiquities of St Gregory's Church, Norwich: with account of recent restorations and existing condition* (Norwich 1886), 9.

23. Little material evidence survives to indicate the subject matter of statuary which occupied image niches on porch exteriors. Although it has long been accepted that they would display an image of the church's dedicative saint, there are other factors to consider. Perhaps relevant here is the observation that excluding the Virgin, the range of saints carved into the spandrels of Norfolk porches is limited to St George, St Margaret and St Michael, all dragon slayers. Suggesting the placement of St George in combative mode would, therefore, be within this tradition.

24. For discussion of this development in Norfolk, see H. E. Lunnon, 'Making an entrance: studies of medieval church porches in Norfolk', 2 vols (unpublished Ph.D. thesis, University of East Anglia, 2012), I, 111–14.

25. Leedy observed that the complexity of the rib profile suggests a date of *c.* 1450, and on the same basis relates it to the north porch at St Peter Mancroft. W. C. Leedy, *Fan Vaulting: A Study of Form, Technology and Meaning* (London 1980), 189.

26. H. E. Lunnon, '"I will have one porch of stone ... over my grave" — Medieval parish church porches and their function as tomb canopies', *Church Monuments*, 27 (2012), 53–65.

27. He left the customary 6s. 8d. to the high altar and 20s. for the reparation of the church, but nothing to the porch. Norwich NRO, NCC Brosyard 1.

28. Leedy, *Fan Vaulting* (as in n. 25), 13.

29. Lunnon, 'one porch of stone' (as in n. 26), 58.

30. Norwich NCC Brosyard 84. The will of John Wyghton does not include any bequest to the building of the porch, which suggests that it had already been constructed by 1457. My thanks to Julian Luxford for this reference.

31. M. Rose, 'The Vault Bosses', in *Norwich Cathedral 1096–1996*, 375–76.

32. The south porch at St George Tombland was apparently built after 1456 when Sir William Balle requested burial in the churchyard by the south door, and before 1500 when Rob. Harneys requested his body to be buried 'by the south porch'. Blomefield, *Norfolk*, IV, 362.

33. Lunnon, 'Making an entrance' (as in n. 24), 129–34.

34. 26 (33%) of the 78 extant documented porches in Norfolk (including Norwich) have spandrels with some sort of figurative, heraldic or geometric design carved in relief, of which 7 are figurative (27%). In Norwich 4 out of 16 (25%) carved spandrels are figurative.

35. J. Blatchley and P. Northeast, *Decoding flint flushwork on Suffolk and Norfolk churches: a survey of more than 90 churches in the two counties where devices and descriptions challenge interpretation* (Ipswich 2005). Despite Blatchley and Northeast's suggestion of a Norwich-based workshop, the only examples of flushwork in the city they note are the tower parapet at St Clement's and the porches at St Michael at Plea and St John Sepulchre, with comment that elements of the latter are commonly found on 'Wiveton' churches. As Julian Luxford has noted, the relationship between East Anglian flushwork and late medieval religion has bearing 'on such weighty issues as the decorum of ecclesiastical decoration as opposed to secular, the definition of regional aesthetics, and attitudes to secular function, appearance and contemporary understanding of church exteriors'. See Luxford, 'Symbolism in East Anglian Flushwork' (as in n. 17), at 119. That flushwork designs were not widely used to decorate Norwich porches is therefore a remark on how this building type was perceived in the city.

36. For example, the late-15th-century south porch at St George Tombland, despite several episodes of restoration, retains what appear to be crenelated statue plinths of medieval date; a photograph taken by George Plunkett shows that as late as 1938 the porch at St James Pockthorpe retained three figuratively sculptured pinnacles, although of what date is uncertain. See St James' south side from Cowgate [2266] 1938-04-07 at www.georgeplunkett.co.uk/Norwich/mediaevalcitychurches.htm.

37. R. Fawcett, 'St Mary at Wiveton in Norfolk, a group of churches attributed to its mason', *Antiq. J.*, 62 (1982), 35–56, at 42.

38. See papers by D. King, F. Woodman and C. King in the current volume.

The Chancel Passageways of Norwich

KATHERINE M. BOIVIN

The parish churches of St Gregory Pottergate and St Peter Mancroft in Norwich each include a chancel passageway that tunnels beneath the elevated space of the eastern sanctuary. Commonly dismissed as a practical response to site topography, these passageways dramatically elevate the high altar above the level of the nave and provide a processional space accessible from outside the church. Like many of the comparable examples from England and continental Europe, the Norwich passageways lie alongside auxiliary crypts, and I suggest that the function of these parallel spaces was related. The disposition and scale of the passageways suggest that churchyard processions moved through these spaces. Situated within their respective cemeteries and alongside rooms that functioned as treasuries or ossuaries, the chancel passageways of Norwich provided a point of contact between city and church, between living and dead.

PASSAGEWAYS were a common feature in medieval architecture. City gates, church porches, and municipal buildings often included vaulted throughways beneath upper chambers. In many cases, the act of passing through these liminal voids carried an associated symbolism in the public consciousness. In the city of Rothenburg ob der Tauber (Bavaria), for example, the street that passed beneath a building of the Franciscan monastery became popularly known as *Höllgasse*, a play on the German homophones meaning 'hollow' and 'hell'.[1] Passageways that cross beneath the sanctuary of a church or chapel, however, are relatively scarce.[2] Nevertheless, examples can be found scattered throughout western Europe, from Sos del Rey Católico (Spain) to Walpole St Peter (UK) to Rostock (Germany) and from the 12th through the 16th centuries. Although characterized by differences in form and finish, scale and disposition, something may be said for considering the chancel passageways throughout Europe as a loosely classified group. In particular, the repetition of spatial arrangements and the chronological clustering of examples around the first half of the 15th century suggest that these passageways fulfilled analogous functions and carried similar symbolic connotations. Accordingly, this article considers patterns that emerge among comparable passageways throughout Europe, focusing in particular on the two extant examples in Norwich: the chancel passageways of St Gregory Pottergate and St Peter Mancroft (Figs 1 and 2).

Vaulted spaces located beneath sanctuaries but accessed from outside the church have been called *Stollenkrypta*, *Pilgergang*, *Kavate*, *Durchgang*, *Schwibbogen* and *Krypta* in German and *undercroft*, *vault*, *crypt* and *passageway* in English. I use *chancel passageway* to refer to a vaulted, ground-level space that tunnels beneath a medieval sanctuary perpendicular to the dominant east–west axis of the church. In form these passageways relate to a second type, which I term *outdoor-access crypts*.[3] Outdoor-access crypts are crypt-like spaces that follow the plan of the above-lying apse and open on multiple sides to the surrounding churchyard.

FIG. 1.   Norwich, St Gregory Pottergate: view from the north

FIG. 2.   Norwich, St Peter Mancroft: view from the north

The function of chancel passageways and outdoor-access crypts was twofold: to elevate the sanctuary above and to accommodate circulation in proximity to the high altar from outside the church. It is this outdoor access that most strikingly separates both types from traditional crypts. In later centuries, this difference was often 'corrected' by walling up the original access points and by breaking through an entry from within the church. This tendency may, for instance, explain the walled-up arch visible on the south side of the chancel of St Swithin in Norwich, and the conversion of the chancel passageway of St Peter Mancroft into an enclosed coatroom for the Octagon coffee shop is a late example of such alterations.[4]

Although they share much in common, chancel passageways and outdoor-access crypts differ in their spatiality. While the directional form of chancel passageways emphasizes movement through the passageway, the often spacious, room-like quality of outdoor-access crypts encourages a more stationary focus. Consequently, it has been suggested that outdoor-access crypts may have fulfilled a liturgical role.[5] By contrast, a possible liturgical role for chancel passageways has not been considered. Although this article concentrates primarily on the passageway type, outdoor-access crypts are closely related, and a more thorough study of both types is needed to fully understand their role and relationship.

The highest concentrations of surviving chancel passageways are found in England and Germany and date from the last quarter of the 14th century through the third quarter of the 15th century. The repetition of similar spatial arrangements both in England and in Germany suggests a connection between the scattered examples rather than the independent development of the form in multiple places. However, in only a few cases can a more direct relationship between sites be posited, and passageways beneath churches never became a popular architectural genre in either country.[6]

Chancel passageways commonly are situated directly beneath an altar, in some cases beneath a sacrament house or tabernacle. Though occasionally included in cathedrals and in monastic and collegiate churches, many chancel passageways are located in parish churches, as is the case with both the surviving examples in Norwich. Regardless of the identity of the associated community, in the majority of cases, an enclosed crypt lies alongside the passageway. Access to this neighbouring crypt is frequently from the churchyard or passageway, and in several examples also from within the church by means of a north stairway. The majority of chancel passageways are barrel vaulted, however some possess more elaborate rib vaulting. Less common are benches, niches, window openings, or painting programs that articulate the walls of the chancel tunnel. These features likely relate to the site-specific construction and use of each example.

Traditionally, chancel passageways have been dismissed with a few summary remarks as to site topography.[7] As a result, the interesting relationship they establish between the interior and exterior spaces of the church, between the high altar and those passing beneath, remains largely unexplored. While the textual record provides little information as to the exact ceremonies staged in these spaces, processions almost certainly made their way through chancel passageways on feast days that called for the circumambulation of the church. Moreover, the scale and disposition of the passageways argue for their possible use in a wider range of festivities and commemorative practices.

Like most churches that include a passageway, the two examples in Norwich are situated on sloping ground. The inclusion of a passageway elevates the east end of the church where the ground falls away. The practicality of this solution is one that should not be overlooked, but the desire to compensate for an uneven site can only partially explain the Norwich chancel passageways as built. The vast majority of medieval churches built on uneven terrain in Norwich as elsewhere negotiate the unevenness of the site by building up the foundations of the church or by including a more traditional enclosed crypt.[8] Moreover, the chancel passageways of St Gregory and St Peter in Norwich overcompensate for the slope of the ground, causing the sanctuary above each passageway to be raised from the floor of the nave by means of steps.[9] This tendency to raise the above-lying space higher than the nave is evinced by many of the comparable examples throughout Europe as well, the most extreme of which raises the above-lying chapel to the level of a gallery within the church.[10] The inclusion of the passageways, therefore, was a choice that impacted the interior as well as the exterior space of the church, and, while it clearly responded to site topography, it was not simply compensatory.[11]

As a result, there must have been additional motivations behind the construction of these passageways. It is perhaps impossible to determine whether the *raison d'être* is synonymous with the later use of the passageways, in other words, whether form followed function or function form. In what follows, I will look at the particular arrangements of the Norwich passageways in order to hypothesize a set of functions and connotations for their use in the context of 15th-century Norwich.

Built by the cathedral priory around 1394, the brick, barrel-vaulted passageway of St Gregory Pottergate in Norwich is 2.45 m wide and 2.64 m high.[12] It is situated beneath the easternmost bay of the chancel and thus directly beneath the high altar. Both the north and south arches leading to the passageway are articulated with alternating stone and flint striping. On the north side, an encased ogee-arch niche sits directly above the passageway (Fig. 3). The niche probably once held an image of a saint, as the comparable examples of St Burkhard in Würzburg (Bavaria, *c.* 1494) and St Nikolai in Rostock (Mecklenburg-Vorpommern, *c.* 1431) suggest. By contrast, the south side of the chancel of St Gregory in Norwich is unadorned and the pathway crowded by a small structure used as a vestry, which was added to the east of the south aisle after the construction of the church. The niche thus identifies the north side as the preferred entrance to the passageway, and it is likely that any ritualized traffic through the chancel passageway moved from north to south.[13] The natural approach was therefore from St Benedict's Street and the natural exit towards Pottergate.

A rectangular window on the north side of the chancel (a feature absent from the south side) provides the only light to a barrel-vaulted crypt that lies alongside the passageway of St Gregory to its west. In scale and form the crypt resembles the adjoining passageway, except that, while the passageway allows for open access, entry to the adjacent crypt is more restricted. The crypt does not communicate directly with the church interior. Instead, two doors, one from the vestry and one from the passageway, open onto the space (Fig. 5).[14] For this reason, the barrel-vaulted chamber should not be considered a traditional crypt but instead an auxiliary space, the function and symbolic meaning of which are related to the neighbouring passageway.

The builders and patrons of St Peter Mancroft in Norwich had the passageway of St Gregory as a model, and they replicated not only its position beneath the sanctuary but also its association with a neighbouring auxiliary crypt (Figs 4 and 6). With its smooth skin of ashlar facing, the passageway of St Peter Mancroft (*c.* 1441) is more elegantly finished than its earlier counterpart at St Gregory. It is also somewhat larger. At 2.99 m wide and 3.12 m high, the passageway is about 0.5 m wider than the passageway of St Gregory and at least 0.25 m taller.

FIG. 3.   Norwich, St Gregory Pottergate:
view of the chancel from the north

FIG. 4.   Norwich, St Peter Mancroft: view
of the chancel from the north

The cemetery of St Peter Mancroft, which extends both north and south of the chancel passageway, underwent several expansions in the late medieval period. In 1367 land was bought to increase the area of the churchyard, which was newly consecrated in 1375.[15] In 1441, the overseeing College of St Mary in the Fields granted a full year of profits and priests' stipends to the rebuilding of the chancel.[16] If construction proceeded from east to west, and the chancel passageway was planned from the start, it would predate the grander passageway through the west tower of the church.[17] When a consecration of the church was recorded in 1455, the east end with its chancel passageway was certainly complete.[18]

To the east of the chancel stands a three-storey medieval extension, the vestry building, which communicates both with the passageway and with the elevated sanctuary. From within the church two doors, one on either side of the high altar, lead into the uppermost floor of the vestry building. The medieval function of this floor and of the middle floor below is known, for a 16th-century inventory not only lists the holdings of these two rooms but also the locations of individual items within them.[19] Accordingly, the upper storey of the building still retains its original function of sacristy. The middle storey once served as the treasury, secured by barred windows positioned high above the city street and by a solid door accessed from the sacristy above. It is this treasury room that lies directly alongside the chancel passageway and now communicates with it through a modern door.

FIG. 5.   Norwich, St Gregory Pottergate: interior view of the crypt from the north
Photo courtesy of Zachary Stewart

George Edmund Street called the lowest storey of the vestry building 'a sort of crypt'.[20] In scale and disposition it resembles the crypt of St Gregory Pottergate, except that instead of being situated to the west of the passageway it is positioned to the east, and instead of lying at the same level as the chancel passageway it lies the equivalent of a storey below. This arrangement negotiates the steep slope of the ground in the eastern part of the churchyard, and responds to the presence of an urban street just to the east of the vestry building. It is thus fundamentally related to the particular site, which allows for a more complex ensemble of spaces than that at St Gregory.

The oldest Ordnance Survey plans of Norwich show the passageway through the east end of St Gregory as the continuation of an urban lane.[21] The passageway of St Peter Mancroft, by contrast, clearly belongs to the space of the surrounding churchyard. Already in the 15th century, a street ran directly to the east of the church complex alongside the three-storey facade of the medieval vestry building.[22] The passageway beneath the chancel of St Peter Mancroft, located on higher ground, provided a parallel path in close proximity to this street, one which would have been redundant had it not performed an important role in churchyard-related circulation. While Weavers Lane would have carried urban traffic around the east end of St Peter's, the parallel chancel passageway beneath the high altar and alongside the treasury of the church provided a more restricted space for ritualized passage within the church grounds. At the same

FIG. 6.   Norwich, St Peter Mancroft: interior view of the passageway from the south

time, the antiquarian evidence of Francis Blomefield suggests that the passageway may have been generally accessible. Blomefield notes that,

under the high-altar, which is very advantageously raised to a good eminence above the rest of the church, is another arch, formerly a common passage, but now stopped up, and made a convenient place for workmen to make mortar and such like in, for the church repairs.[23]

Although it is impossible to say for certain who would have used the passageway on a day-to-day basis, the idea that the passageway was 'common', or generally accessible, is probably correct.

    With its connection to the system of urban streets in Norwich, the chancel passageway of St Gregory, too, was generally accessible; however, it also likely featured in churchyard processions. The desire to maximize church length within the confines of the crowded urban centre meant that many churches in Norwich were built to the edge of the available plot of land. This was the case at St Gregory Pottergate, where arches visible in the east wall of the chancel demonstrate that other structures abutted against it. The chancel passageway was thus the sole means of passing around the east end of the church and, together with St Gregory's Alley to the west of the church, connected the north and south areas of the churchyard. As a result, the passageway was probably used for liturgical processions, such as those commonly held at Rogationtide or on Palm Sunday. Although sources related to the celebration of such processional liturgical feasts are not known for St Gregory or St Peter in Norwich, those from other sites provide circumstantial evidence for celebrations likely held in the parish churches of Norwich. Roger Martin's 16th-century account of pre-Reformation processions at the parish church of Long Melford (Suffolk), for instance, includes a description of the Palm Sunday procession.[24] As David Dymond and Clive Paine suggest, the Palm Sunday procession at Melford split into two groups upon entering the churchyard. One group carried the sacrament around the east end of the church, while a larger second group passed around the west tower. The groups joined up again outside the church before entering together.[25] Such highly structured ritual performances usually stopped at multiple stations and followed appointed paths through the churchyard and around the church. Melford church does not include a chancel passageway, but, if similar processions are to be imagined for St Peter and St Gregory in Norwich, they would by necessity have passed through the respective chancel passageway as they made their way around the east end of the church.

Processions on other occasions, such as Church Dedication, Corpus Christi, and All Souls Day, also commonly moved through the churchyard. In Rothenburg ob der Tauber, for instance, a procession held on the feast of Church Dedication passed through two passageways on its way around the churchyard. As Ludwig Schnurrer has argued, entries in the financial accounts of the parish for sweeping the church, the surrounding cemetery, and the stairs leading from the north-west portal down to the street that passed through the west passageway, relate to preparations for this procession around the church on Dedication Day.[26] This procession passed through the passageway beneath the western architectural choir of the church and likely also through the passageway of the free-standing charnel-house of St Michael at the eastern edge of the churchyard.[27] The western passageway in Rothenburg also featured in the procession that circulated through the wider city on the feast of Corpus Christi.[28]

In Norwich, similar celebrations likely animated the chancel passageways of St Peter Mancroft and St Gregory Pottergate at points throughout the liturgical year, though the particular form these processions took would have been site specific. As in Rothenburg, it is possible that the passageways of Norwich participated both in processions localized within the churchyard and in parades that wound their way through the city. One example of a city-wide procession that was particularly important during the second half of the 15th century in Norwich was the annual parade organized by the guild of St George on the feast day of its patron saint. Unfortunately, the otherwise rich surviving textual sources relating to this elaborate procession do not allow the path of the procession through the city to be traced. However, it is possible to speculate that this annual celebration may have included one or both of the Norwich chancel passageways on its route.

The guild of St George, responsible for the procession on its titular saint's feast day, was founded in 1385.[29] In 1452, a royal charter issued by Henry VI sought to amend relations between the guild and the city of Norwich by effectively merging the governing body of the city with the guild. Thereafter, all the city aldermen were to be members of the guild and the outgoing mayor was to become the head of the guild of St George.[30] The consequence of this charter was that the procession on the feast of St George became a major civic event. What may have begun as a small procession of the fraternity after 1452 became an organized parade of over two hundred of the city's wealthiest and most influential citizens, many of whom were parishioners of St Peter Mancroft.[31]

It is known that the splendidly dressed participants gathered at an appointed meeting spot and that the procession ended in the cathedral with an offering of wax at the high altar and the celebration of a mass.[32] I submit that the logical starting point for the procession after 1452 would have been the guildhall (1404–53), which functioned as the seat of municipal authority in Norwich. St Peter Mancroft, the largest parish church within the city, prominently located across from the guildhall on the southern edge of the market-place, almost certainly featured in these festivities. The two passageways of the church, one beneath the west tower and the other beneath the east chancel, may have allowed the procession to pass from the market-place, around the church, and back towards the river on its way to the cathedral. Whether the chancel passageway of St Gregory Pottergate also featured on the parade route is impossible to say. Its location near Pottergate, one of the main roads leading towards the cathedral, and the presence of the grand wall-painting of St George in the north aisle could point to its inclusion.[33] The final destination of the procession was the guild's chapel on the south side of the cathedral ambulatory.[34] Because of this, the procession may also have passed beneath the reliquary arch in the presbytery aisle of Norwich Cathedral.

In the context of city-wide processions, chancel passageways would have made possible a 'visit' to the principal altar of the church without the necessity of entering the church. This would have been particularly convenient for processions involving mounted participants, like the procession honouring St George. At heights of 2.64 m (St Gregory) and 3.12 m (St Peter) and widths under 3 m, the Norwich passageways were clearly not intended for a full range of urban traffic. However, both the Norwich chancel passageways would have been passable not only for those on foot but also for those on horseback.[35] The relatively intimate scale of the passageways would have made them an appropriate space for the experience of proximity to the altar during processions. It would seem, then, that the passageways of Norwich may have been specifically designed to accommodate equestrian as well as pedestrian passage.

At St Peter Mancroft, the chancel passageway provided a moment of proximity not only to the high altar but also to the neighbouring treasure of relics.[36] The arrangement of spaces at St Peter Mancroft, which associates a treasury or vestry with a passageway, is not unique. The 12th-century treasury, or *vestiarium*, of Canterbury Cathedral, for instance, incorporates a vaulted passageway beneath its upper storeys. This passageway led to the cemetery and served as a gateway to this sepulchral space, as Peter Fergusson has shown.[37]

The desire to provide passage in proximity to a relic was also formative for one of the early German chancel passageways. Now converted into a traditional crypt, the barrel-vaulted chancel passageway of St Lambert in Bechtheim (Rhineland-Palatinate, *c.* 1200) was built in response to the acquisition of a relic of St Lambert in 1195.[38] The chancel passageway in Bechtheim lies beneath the sacrament house and parallel to the flat terminus of the chancel. The pilgrimage function of the Bechtheim passageway clearly continued through the late medieval period, for around 1400 a new painting program decorated the passageway with a procession of saints.[39]

In Norwich Cathedral, the treasury arch in the north aisle of the presbytery, the so-called ante-reliquary chapel, also allowed for passage beneath displayed relics.[40] Here, processions could pass *sub reliquiis* and a quatrefoil window communicated between the passage space and the neighbouring sanctuary. As Paul Binski has shown, the collection of relics was one of three major sources of income for the church: money given in relation to relics reached thirty-five per cent of total receipts in 1319–20.[41] For the comparable example of St James in Rothenburg ob der Tauber, surviving financial accounts demonstrate that nearly half of the church's income from donations related to the principal relic housed in the elevated chapel above the passageway.[42] At a time when physical access to such relics was limited, sight of them or knowledge of their proximity functioned as a substitute.[43] Allowing for passage beneath relics and important altars may have encouraged donations. In this way, processional passageways would have provided not only spiritual but also financial benefits for the church. The public use of the Norwich chancel passageways during urban parades would have widely marketed the importance of these parish churches, just as processions were often used to perform the status of participants.[44]

While the inclusion of the Norwich passageways in specific city-wide celebrations, such as that held on the feast day of St George, must remain highly speculative, a stronger case can be made for their inclusion in localized ceremonies staged to commemorate the dead. During commemorative services (another major source of income for parish churches in particular) processions commonly moved from an altar within the church to specific gravesites in the cemetery outside.[45] Chancel passageways that facilitated access to both the north and south sides of a divided churchyard, such as those beneath St Peter, Walpole (Norfolk, c. 1420) and the Lady chapel of Gloucester Cathedral (c. 1470), may have been built with both the practical and connotative potential of the space in mind.[46] Passing beneath the high altar through a chancel passageway would have actively performed the desire for burial in proximity to an altar.[47] Hence, one connotation of chancel passageways likely lay in the complex relationship they established between the high altar, the surrounding cemetery, and neighbouring crypts.

An outdoor-access crypt beneath the polygonal apse of the parish church of St Michael in Jena (Thuringia) is illustrative of the link between such spaces and commemoration of the dead (Fig. 7). Construction on St Michael in Jena began during the last decade of the 14th century and proceeded from east to west. The outdoor-access crypt at Jena is thus an exact contemporary of the chancel passageway of St Gregory Pottergate in Norwich. Located beneath the polygonal terminus of the choir, the outdoor-access crypt in Jena accommodates foot traffic through three arches and beneath an elegant tri-radial rib vault. Like the passageway of St Peter Mancroft, the space in Jena lies parallel to a street immediately to its east. Again, a duplicate pathway only metres away from a parallel street cannot have been required for urban traffic. Instead, the open space provided a place for processions beneath the high altar and within the consecrated grounds of the cemetery.

An enclosed two-bay crypt with an altar, a wall grave, and a sacrament niche lies directly to the west of the outdoor-access crypt in Jena. In an arrangement akin to St Gregory in Norwich, the closed crypt of St Michael in Jena has a small window piercing its north wall. A 'Baroque' wall now divides this crypt into two rooms, the northern of which still serves as a burial vault (Fig. 8). Post-medieval alterations also block a corridor that lies to the west and once connected the enclosed crypt to a long low room beneath the north aisle of the church. The function of this space as an ossuary is certain. It is documented that in 1839–40 over seventy cartloads of bones were removed from this part of the crypt and reburied in a cemetery outside the city.[48]

As Friedrich Möbius has argued, the proximity of the outdoor-access crypt to the burial vault and ossuary chamber is likely what made this space an important station for funerary processions.[49] The last blessing of the individual dead before interment was performed here, but the collective dead were also commemorated in the passageway beneath the sacred space of the church sanctuary. The sources record that the outdoor-access crypt of Jena served as a station for processions that circled the church on All Souls Day and on Easter morning.[50]

FIG. 7.   Jena, St Michael:
view of the choir from the
north

With its close parallels to the Norwich examples, the composition in Jena may provide a key to understanding the relationship between the Norwich passageways and
their neighbouring crypts. As in Jena, it is likely that the Norwich enclosed crypts
housed charnel and that the passageways alongside provided a space for the ritual commemoration of the dead. Medieval Norwich had several spaces reserved for charnel. In
the 14th century Carnary College, built in the cathedral Close, received 'the bones of
persons buried in the city of Norwich'.[51] However, it is unlikely that the chapel actually
accommodated all the bones disinterred in the city's many over-crowded cemeteries.
Instead, each church would have found its own solution to house the bones of the
parish dead. Antiquarian evidence has long indicated that the elongated crypt of
St Gregory Pottergate served as an ossuary. In the 18th century Francis Blomefield

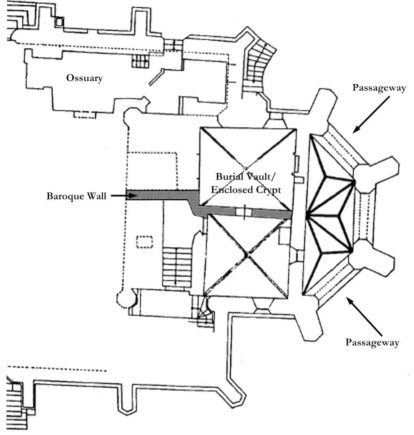

FIG. 8.   Jena, St Michael: plan of the east end basement storey, after Möbius, *Symbolik*
(as in n. 7)

referred to 'the vault under the chancel, which was a charnel', and 19th- and 20th-century guides to the church of St Gregory continued to claim that the long dark crypt was 'formerly used as a charnel' or a 'mortuary'.[52] At the time these accounts were written, the crypt was being let out as a lumber-room.[53] Although it is unclear how Blomefield knew of the charnel-house function of the space, there is no reason to doubt his assertion.

The door that connects the crypt to the neighbouring chancel passageway at St Gregory suggests a connection between the functions of these two spaces. Doors communicating between chancel passageways and neighbouring crypts are common, though it is not always easy to determine whether they are original to the medieval composition. At St Gregory, however, an older hinge visible behind the current door points to an early association between these spaces. This close connection is also supported by the presence of a walled-up window communicating between the passageway of St Gregory Pottergate and the neighbouring crypt. Since it once opened onto the middle of the dark passageway, this window shaft would have been a poor solution to lighting or aerating the crypt; the window on the north side of the crypt would have better served these purposes. The opening between the crypt and the chancel passage-way, then, may have had the function of providing visual (or symbolic) access to the crypt from the passageway akin to a *memento mori* opening. Such openings were a common feature of many charnel chapels, like Carnary College in Norwich and St Michael in Ochsenfurt (Bavaria).

In the Middle Ages, it seems to have been relatively common to associate passage-ways beneath altars with ossuary chambers. The 13th-century chancel of St Leonard's church in Hythe (Kent) is a rare example where a passageway itself serves the func-tion of an ossuary. It is clear from a preliminary analysis of the remains, conducted in 1910, that the passageway was used as an ossuary at least during the 14th and 15th centuries.[54] More common than the use of a chancel passageway as an ossuary was the arrangement of a passageway adjacent to an ossuary chamber. Free-standing charnel-house chapels, like those of Kiedrich (Hesse) and Rothenburg ob der Tauber (Bavaria), often included space for the bones of the dead alongside a processional passageway and beneath an elevated altar.[55] These two-storey charnel chapels were invariably located within the consecrated space of the cemetery and frequently had multiple points of entry to facilitate circulation.

This penchant for pairing ossuaries with passageways during the late medieval period was not ubiquitous, but nevertheless common enough that it may account for the spatial arrangement of the chancel passageways in Norwich. The east end of St Peter Mancroft was constructed over a complex system of basement-storey spaces and crypts analogous to that of St Michael in Jena. This close spatial parallel strongly suggests a corresponding desire to accommodate a processional space in proximity to provision for charnel and in relation to commemorative services for the dead. One of the crypts of St Peter Mancroft, now used as the vault for the Black family, lies beneath the north choir aisle in a similar position to the ossuary chamber in Jena (Fig. 8). Delanoy Saberton informs us that a corresponding crypt also lay beneath the south choir aisle of St Peter Mancroft before the extension of the current choir vestry in 1911.[56] As in Jena, the crypt beneath the north aisle of St Peter Mancroft is accessible from inside the church via a spiral staircase, in this case situated in the north wall. Similar stairways communicate with crypts alongside the chancel passageways of St Matthew in Walsall (West Midlands, *c.* 1462) and St Mary Redcliffe in Bristol (mid-15th century). The crypt beneath the north choir aisle of St Peter Mancroft in Norwich also communicated directly with the churchyard through a now blocked opening, an arrangement also akin to other passageway churches (including in Jena, Walsall, and Bristol). This would have provided an efficient means of transferring remains from the cemetery to the charnel crypt. The lowest storey of the vestry building of St Peter Mancroft, now used as a boiler room, may also have been part of this network of crypt spaces.

The significance of the passageways of St Peter Mancroft and St Gregory Pottergate may lie in their intermediary position between cemetery, charnel-house, and high altar. Here, commemorative processions could pass alongside the stacks of bones in the neighbouring crypt without disturbing them. Prayers for the dead may have been proffered beneath the high altar in this space in the hope of alleviating the sufferings of the souls of the ossuary's dead in purgatory. Situated as they are beneath the principal altars of their respective churches, the chancel passageways of St Peter Mancroft and St Gregory Pottergate made possible physical proximity to the sanctuary above without the necessity of entering the church. In the 15th century, when rood-screens still par-titioned off the east ends of both churches, this alternative access to holy materials would have been significant. Certainly, for civic processions, frequent stops within churches would have proven cumbersome. On the other hand, the symbolic passage beneath a church would have been a compelling and efficient gesture.

In recent years, a growing body of literature has added to our understanding of the *mise-en-scène* of liturgical and devotional rituals within and around Gothic churches.[57] At the heart of this literature, and of the artistic compositions it treats, are questions of access and visibility. Particularly in the 14th and 15th centuries, the politics of church space became complex, with various communities competing for access (visual, physical, or through artistic self-representation) to the sanctuary of the church.[58] At the heart of this struggle over space were the materials of the Eucharist, dramatically staged in the architectural choir or chancel of the church. A complex programme of visual substitutes, stimuli, and accentuations was developed to regulate access to the real presence of Christ in the form of the eucharistic bread and wine.[59] As physical contact with the sacred materials became progressively the prerogative of the clergy (the chalice, for instance, was increasingly withheld from the congregation), sight of holy matter, whether the Eucharist or relics, became a powerful substitute for the laity.[60] At the same time, the real presence of Christ in the eucharistic bread and wine remained an invisible concept, reliant on faith and supported by more tangible indicators like the gesture of elevation, the ringing of bells, and the multi-media artistic programs of altarpieces, chasubles and stained glass.

A passageway beneath the chancel of a church would have contributed to this tension between physical and visual access, between sensory perception and invisible presence. Within the church, the sanctuary was lifted above the level of the nave and the high altar set on this pedestal. Although the altar itself was not visible from outside the church, those passing beneath through the passageway would have been aware of the presence of the principal altar above. Crossing beneath the main altar simulated well-established rituals of pilgrimage, where devotees passed beneath a tomb or relic in the hope of benefitting from proximity to the holy materials. The void of the chancel passageway, therefore, could become a space for ritual performance. This performance was in many ways conditioned by the materials that bordered the passageway: the cemetery, the church sanctuary and neighbouring crypts. The creative architectural compositions of chancel-passageway churches harnessed their physical conditions to create a liminal space that participated in a complex network of relationships. Chancel passageways that tunnel beneath church sanctuaries provided a point of contact between living and dead, city and church that allowed for meaningful circulation in proximity to the high altar.

ACKNOWLEDGEMENTS

My first thanks go to the two excellent reviewers whose guiding comments helped reshape the article. I would also like to thank Paul Binski for first drawing to my attention the chancel passageways of Norwich during a conference in Cambridge in 2011. This article would not have been possible without the cooperation of the staff of St Gregory's Centre for the Arts and the parish of St Peter Mancroft, especially Reverend Janet Wyer, who kindly provided me access to the relevant spaces. My gratitude also goes to the German Academic Exchange Service (DAAD) and the Fulbright Commission for the fellowships that supported much of my research in Germany.

My attendance at the 2012 conference in Norwich was supported by a BAA conference travel grant for which I am truly grateful. Many thanks, also, to members of the BAA for their feedback during the conference, especially John McNeill, David Stocker, Tim Tatton-Brown and Brian

Ayers. Many of their suggestions for expansion have not found room in this article but are proving instrumental for my extended study of church passageways throughout Europe. For their help in editing and researching this article, I am also greatly indebted to many of my colleagues, including Jeffrey Miller, Zachary Stewart and Jérôme Zahn.

NOTES

1. The monastic building with the passageway beneath it was torn down in 1843. See A. Ress, *Die Kunstdenkmäler der Stadt Rothenburg ob der Tauber: Kirchliche Bauten*, Die Kunstdenkmäler von Bayern, VIII (Munich 1959), 234.

2. Thus far I have identified fewer than one hundred examples that either survive or are known from sources. These are largely located in current-day Germany and England. France, by contrast, seems to have had very few chancel passageways and those that still survive are often quite late, dating to the 16th or even 17th centuries. I have yet to fully explore examples in Spain, Italy and Eastern Europe.

3. This should not be confused with the German 'Außenkrypta', which refers to true crypts that extend beyond the walls of the upper structure and are accessible from within the main church. On *Außenkrypta*, see A. Verbeek, 'Die Aussenkrypta: Werden einer Bauform des Frühen Mittelalters', *Zeitschrift für Kunstgeschichte*, 13 (1950), 7–38; B. Schütz and W. Müller, *Deutsche Romanik: Die Kirchenbauten der Kaiser, Bischöfe und Klöster* (Freiburg 1989), 85–88.

4. On the churches of Norwich, see J. Finch, 'The churches', in *Medieval Norwich*, 49–72; N. Groves, *The Medieval Churches of the City of Norwich* (Norwich 2010).

5. This suggestion has never been fully explored, despite the occasional reference. See W. Götz, *Zentralbau und Zentralbautendenz* (Berlin 1968), 241. W. Stopfel, U. Fahrer, E. Grom, P. Klug and H. Metz, *Das Breisacher Münster* (Regensburg 2005), 13.

6. For example, St Peter Mancroft in Norwich had been impropriate to St Peter's abbey, Gloucester. It is therefore possible that the passageway beneath the Lady chapel in Gloucester resulted from a familiarity with the earlier Norwich passageways, though no particular similarities between the two passageways beyond the more general genre indicate a direct copying. D. King, *The Medieval Stained Glass of St Peter Mancroft Norwich*, Corpus Vitrearum Medii Aevi, V (Oxford and New York 2006), liv.

7. The one exception to this is the scholarship of Friedrich Möbius on St Michael in Jena (Thuringia). F. Möbius, *Die Stadtkirche St. Michael zu Jena: Symbolik und Baugeschichte einer spätgotischen Stadtpfarrkirche* (Jena 1996); F. Möbius, *Die Stadtkirche St. Michael zu Jena: Eine Einführung in die Baugeschichte und die Kunstwerke* (Jena 1983).

8. Examples include St Stephen, St Lawrence and St Giles in Norwich. Groves, *Medieval Churches* (as in n. 4).

9. J. Hooper, *Notes on the Parish Church of St. Peter Mancroft, Norwich* (Norwich 1895), 15; B/E, *Norfolk*, I, 250; B. Ayers, *Norwich: 'A Fine City'* (Stroud 2003), 130.

10. St James in Rothenburg ob der Tauber includes a passageway beneath the elevated sanctuary of its western architectural choir. The chapel above opens onto the nave as a western gallery and is accessible from within the nave by means of two steep staircases. Ress, *Kunstdenkmäler* (as in n. 1).

11. Instead, further research is needed to understand these passageways in relation to the practice of elevating the high altar, particularly in the context of eucharistic devotion in the late medieval period.

12. In 1394, £4 was spent on the chancel of St Gregory Pottergate. Cattermole and Cotton, 'Church Building', 258–59; A. B. Whittingham, 'St Gregory's Church, Charing Cross', *Archaeol. J.*, 106 (1949), 95.

13. I am not the first to suggest this. See N. Groves, *The Church of St. Gregory Pottergate* (Norwich 2010), 6.

14. The current door from the passageway is modern but an older hinge, visible from inside the crypt, demonstrates that it replaced an older predecessor.

15. The purchase of new land for the churchyard of St Peter Mancroft may be related to the outbreak of the plague in 1349 and again in 1361–62. Hooper, *Notes* (as in n. 9), 1–4. King, *Glass of Mancroft* (as in n. 6), liv.

16. Ibid., 146.

17. A more comprehensive study of chancel passageways will need to consider the relationship between such western porch or tower passages and passageways beneath the east end of a church.

18. William Fen gave 10 marks to the new chancel of St Peter Mancroft in 1439, and in 1441, the College of St Mary in the Fields granted a year of profits and priests' stipends to the construction project. On the debate as to whether the consecration date of 1455 corresponds to the completion of the entire church or just to the completion of the chancel and transepts, see King, *Glass of Mancroft* (as in n. 6), lx, 146; C. Wilson, 'Norwich,

church of St Peter Mancroft, nave and chancel', in *Gothic. Art for England 1400–1547*, ed. R. Marks and P. Williamson (London 2003), 259; F. Woodman, 'The rebuilding of St Peter Mancroft', in *East Anglian Studies. Essays presented to J. C. Barringer on his retirement, August, 30, 1995*, ed. A. Longcroft and R. Toby (Norwich 1995), 290–99.

19. London, British Library, MS Stowe 871.

20. G. E. Street, 'Extracts from the report upon the state of the fabric of St Peter Mancroft church, Norwich, and upon the repairs required', in *Restoration of St Peter Mancroft Church, Norwich: Second Statement* (Norwich 1880), 9.

21. Sheet 63:11, Ordnance Survey 1:25, 1st edn (1886).

22. This street to the east of St Peter Mancroft appears in the oldest ordnance surveys of Norwich. The presence of the elegantly finished facade of the vestry building corroborates the existence of this street in the 15th century. Sheet 63:15, Ordnance Survey 1:25, 1st edn (1887).

23. Blomefield, *Norfolk*, IV, 192.

24. 'The Blessed Sacrament was carried in procession around the church-yard, under a fair canopy, borne by four yeomen; the procession coming to the church gate, went westward, and they with the Blessed Sacrament, went eastward; and when the procession came against the door of Mr Clopton's ile, they, with the Blessed Sacrament, and with a little bell and signing, approached at the east end of Our Ladie's Chappel, at which time a boy, with a thing in his hand, pointed to it, signifying a prophet, as I think, sang, standing upon the tyrret that is on the said Mr Clopton's ile doore, ECCE REX TUUS, VENIT, etc.; and then all did kneel down, and then, rising up, went and met the Sacrament, and so then, went signing together, into the church'. D. Dymond and C. Paine ed., *The Spoils of Melford Church: The Reformation in a Suffolk Parish* (Ipswich 1989), 5.

25. Ibid.

26. L. Schnurrer, 'Das Fronleichnamsfest "Corpus Christi" in mittelalterlichen Rothenburg', *Die Linde*, ns, 89 (2007), 42–43, 49–56. On Rogationtide, see S. Hindle, 'Beating the Bounds of the Parish: Order, Memory, and Identity in the English Local Community, c. 1500–1700', in *Defining Community in Early Modern Europe*, ed. M. J. Halvorson and K. E. Spierling (Aldershot 2008).

27. K. M. Boivin, 'Holy Blood, Holy Cross: Architecture and Devotion in the Parochial Complex of Rothenburg' (unpublished Ph.D. thesis, Columbia University, 2013), 278–79.

28. Ibid., 265–80.

29. For this and the following information on the guild of St George, see M. Grace ed., *Records of the Gild of St. George in Norwich, 1389–1547: A Transcript with an Introduction*, Norfolk Record Society, 9 (Norwich 1937).

30. J. Good, *The Cult of Saint George in Medieval England* (Woodbridge 2009), 110.

31. D. King, 'Art in an Urban Context: The Toppes Window in St Peter Mancroft, Norwich', *Glasmalerei im Kontext: Bildprogramme und Raumfunktionen. Akten des XXII. Internationalen Colloquiums des Corpus Vitrearum. Nürnberg, 29. August–1. September 2004* (Nuremberg 2005), 198; King, *Stained Glass* (as in n. 6), li–lxii.

32. *Records of the Gild* (as in n. 29).

33. The wall painting was discovered in 1861 during a restoration of the church. E. A. Kent, 'St. Gregory's Church, Norwich: Compiled from Notes by the Late Rev. John Jessopp', *JBAA*, 31 (1925), 70. The prevalence of dedications to and images of St George throughout England at this time, however, means that the image is not necessarily specific to the guild of St George in Norwich. See Good, *Saint George* (as in n. 30), 95–121.

34. *Records of the Gild* (as in n. 29).

35. The average height of a man on horseback in the late Middle Ages may be estimated at roughly 2.4 m, based on J. Clark ed., *The Medieval Horse and its Equipment, c. 1150–1450* (London 2004), 23–29.

36. The treasure of relics is listed in a 16th-century inventory. MS Stowe 871 (as in n. 19).

37. P. Fergusson, 'Modernization and Mnemonics at Christ Church, Canterbury: The Treasury Building', *Journal of the Society of Architectural Historians*, 65 (2006), 50–67.

38. J. Sommer, *Bechtheim: St. Lambertus* (Königstein im Taunus 1980), 30.

39. This was eventually covered by a second painting programme. Ibid., 26.

40. P. Binski, 'The ante-reliquary chapel paintings in Norwich Cathedral: the Holy Blood, St. Richard, and All Saints', in *Tributes to Nigel Morgan: Contexts of Medieval Art: Images, Objects & Ideas*, ed. J. M. Luxford and M. A. Michael (Turnhout 2010), 241–61.

41. Ibid., 244.

42. K. Borchardt, *Die Geistlichen Institutionen in der Reichsstadt Rothenburg ob der Tauber und dem Zugehörigen Landgebiet von den Anfängen bis zur Reformation*, 2 vols (Neustadt/Aisch 1988), II, 55.

43. This is related to what Kees van der Ploeg has called a 'growing need for visualization' in the late medieval period. It can also be connected to the complex politics of church space surrounding the materials of the

Eucharist. K. van der Ploeg, 'The spatial setting of worship: some observation on the relation between altar-pieces and churches', in *Images of Cult and Devotion: Function and Reception of Christian Images in Medieval and Post-Medieval Europe*, ed. S. Kaspersen (Copenhagen 2004), 149–59. A. Timmermann, *Real Presence: Sacrament Houses and the Body of Christ, c. 1270–1600*, Architectura Medii Aevi, 4 (Turnhout 2009).

44. See, for instance, E. A. R. Brown and N. F. Regalado, '*Universitas et communitas*: The Parade of the Parisians at the Pentecost Feast of 1313', in *Moving Subjects: Processional Performance in the Middle Ages and the Renaissance*, ed. K. Ashley and W. Hüsken (Amsterdam 2001), 117–54.

45. As Jonathan Finch has demonstrated, the late medieval period, particularly the end of the 15th century, witnessed a notable increase in levels of commemoration, which 'appears to have been part of a wider movement that saw an increasing focus on patronage upon the parish church'. J. Finch, 'A reformation of meaning: commemoration and remembering the dead in the parish church, 1450–1640', in *The Archaeology of Reformation, 1480–1580: Papers given at the Archaeology of Reformation Conference, February 2001* (Leeds 2003), 437–49.

46. B/E, *Norfolk*, I, *North-west and South* (Harmondsworth 1970), 362–64; B/E, *Gloucestershire*, I, *The Vale and the Forest of Dean* (Harmondsworth 1976), 209.

47. Further research is needed to determine if chancel passageways themselves were ever the site of tombs.

48. Möbius, *Symbolik* (as in n. 7), 43.

49. Ibid., 40.

50. Ibid.

51. Ayers, *Norwich* (as in n. 9), 130.

52. Blomefield, *Norfolk* (as in n. 23), 273.

53. Kent, 'St. Gregory's Church' (as in n. 33), 68.

54. The bones belong to an estimated 4,000 medieval citizens of Hythe, men, women and children. Pottery sherds dating to the 14th and 15th centuries found among the bones support their medieval origin and suggest a more precise period of use. H. D. Dale, *St. Leonard's Church, Hythe, from its Foundation, with Some Account of the Life and Customs of the Town of Hythe from Ancient Sources, etc.* (London 1931), 55–62.

55. For more on free-standing charnel-house chapels, see S. Zilkins, *Karner-Kapellen in Deutschland: Untersuchungen zur Baugeschichte und Ikonographie doppelgeschossiger Beinhaus-Kapellen*, Veröffentlichung der Abteilung Architektur des Kunsthistorischen Instituts der Universität zu Köln, 22 (Cologne 1983). The charnel-house in the churchyard of St Nicholas in Great Yarmouth, now destroyed, is an English example. *Pictorial Guide to Great Yarmouth: Containing its Early History, and a Succinct Account of the Public Buildings and Other Objects of Interest in the Town and Neighbourhood* (Great Yarmouth 1854), 47.

56. D. Saberton, *St. Peter Mancroft, 1080–1930* (Norwich 1931), 15–18.

57. Timmermann, *Real Presence* (as in n. 43); J. Jung, *The Gothic Screen: Space, Sculpture, and Community in the Cathedrals of France and Germany, ca. 1200–1400* (New York 2013); J. Tripps, *Das handelnde Bildwerk in der Gotik: Forschungen zu den Bedeutungsschichten und der Funktion des Kirchengebäudes und seiner Ausstattung in der Hoch- und Spätgotik* (Berlin 1998); J. Kroesen and R Steensma, *The Interior of the Medieval Village Church*, 2nd edn (Leuven, Paris, Walpole 2012).

58. On the politics of church space and the role of tombs and chantries in this dynamic, see P. Binski, *Medieval Death: Ritual and Representation* (London 1996).

59. Timmermann, *Real Presence* (as in n. 43); C. W. Bynum, *Wonderful Blood: Theology and Practice in Late Medieval Northern Germany and Beyond* (Philadelphia 2007).

60. M. Rubin, *Corpus Christi: The Eucharist in Late Medieval Culture* (Cambridge 1991), 70.

Thomas Gooding or Goodwin, a Norwich Freemason

JON BAYLISS

A combination of documentary and physical evidence is used to associate a workshop producing funeral monuments and other stonework with a particular Norwich freemason. This group of monuments has been recognized previously and is here attributed to Thomas Gooding or Goodwin.[1]

THOMAS GOODING'S DOCUMENTED WORK

ON 29 April 1604 Henry Armiger wrote to Nathaniel Bacon reporting progress of building work at Stiffkey Hall, Bacon's house on the north Norfolk coast:

Sir accordynge to your worshypps dyrectyon by your letter, I caused Goodwyn presentlie to goe over to Wallsyngham to se the freestone to be solde, which he lyked & bowght at for 18s. beinge 3 lodes of verie good hard stone as he sayth fytt for steppynges at the gate & suchelyke purposes.

Later in the same letter he continued: 'The fre mason hath begun to sett up the gate & the dores of bothe lodges [...]'.[2]

The Stiffkey database includes this man as Thomas Goodwin, a stonemason from Norwich, and notes that he is not recorded among the freemen of Norwich.[3] The gatehouse erected in 1604 survives and prominently features Bacon's shield of arms in a distinctive strap-work surround. Thomas Gooding, mason, is listed in the 1595 Norwich muster roll under St Giles' parish and he was involved in property transactions in the parish in 1583 and 1594.[4] He was working at St Peter Mancroft in the city in 1595, where 30s. was 'P[ai]d Gooddon the fremason for setting upe of the West windowe in the Ille'. Gooding also worked in the same church in 1605:

Itm. payd to Thomas Godyng for the pilleres makeng upp to the owlde heade of the wendow agreed for by the pishernes [...] v^{li}. Itm. payd more to Tomas Goodyng for takeing downe of the heade for the stepell windows and makinge it upp agayne from the piller before specified as aperithe by his billes and payed unto him by Mr. Lionell Claxton the som of viij^{li}.[5]

There are also records of work done by him on the nave and west tower of Wymondham Abbey in 1584–85 and 1599–1600, Norwich School in 1604–05 and 1606–07, and St Stephen's church in Norwich in 1605–06.[6] Thus there are surviving records of Gooding working from at least 1584 through to 1607. He lived for a further twenty years, dying in January 1627/8, predeceasing his second wife Barbara and his brother Robert, and apparently leaving no children. He requested burial in the cathedral near his late wife, Elizabeth.[7] Gooding's first marriage, to Elizabeth Condlye on 29 May 1575, took place at St Stephen's, Norwich. He married his second wife, Barbara Ryall, on 12 April 1624 at All Saints, Norwich.[8] The spelling of his surname can vary not only

BAA Trans., vol. XXXVIII (2015), 324–340
© British Archaeological Association 2015

from record to record but also within the same record. 'Gooding' occurs more frequently than 'Goodwin' and is the name used both in his will and on his monument, although the parish burial register records him as 'Goodwin'.[9]

GOODING'S STYLE

THE shield over the gatehouse at Stiffkey, which carries the date 1604, shares the form of its strap-work surround with a number of shields on funeral monuments in and around Norwich bearing dates of death between 1574 and the 1610s (Fig. 1). These surrounds occur in combination with a number of other motifs that mark these monuments out as being the product of a single workshop with a period of production coinciding with Thomas Gooding's recorded biography. Other monuments lacking the distinctive strap-work surround but having combinations of the other motifs can also be identified as part of the same group, and products of the same workshop. Given that Gooding was always identified as a freemason, rather than a tomb maker, and that the documentary evidence given above is for other types of work, it is likely that Gooding produced monumental work in the winter months when outside building work could not be undertaken. Besides the monuments, the workshop produced fireplaces and other architectural features. Gooding used the elements of classical architecture in much the same way as his contemporaries, as a set of patterns to pick and choose from rather than a strict set of rules. Thus descriptions below of columns or pilasters on his

FIG. 1.   Stiffkey Hall, Norfolk: shield in strapwork over gatehouse, 1604

monuments as Doric or Ionic are indicative of their approximate appearance rather than of any systematic adherence to architectural rules by Gooding.

The distribution of monuments clearly indicates their origin is in Norwich as a considerable proportion is found within the city and few are further than twenty miles distant. With the possible exception of the tomb-chest at Westhall of Nicholas Bohun (d. 1602), none have been found in Suffolk. This is surprising, as Norwich-made monumental brasses of the period between the mid-15th century and the Reformation are found in north-east Suffolk.[10] The patrons of the workshop range from the diocesan, city and county elites to those of lesser note. A couple commemorate members of the newly established immigrant community in Norwich, Dr Martin van Kurnbeck and Anna, wife of Jacques de Hem.

WORK IN NORWICH CATHEDRAL

An early patron of the workshop was George Gardiner, dean of Norwich. Gardiner put up the monument in the cathedral to John Parkhurst, bishop of Norwich, who died in February 1574/5. This monument has an early version of Gooding's characteristic strap-work surround on the shield surmounting the panel set against the pillar over the east end of the tomb-chest. The chest itself is decorated with shields (without surrounds) in plain panels and has a lid of polished limestone with an indent for a brass.[11] A spandrel from a fireplace with a shield of Gardiner's arms survives in the cathedral stone collection (Fig. 2) and a shield of the same arms with the same strap-work surround is to be found over a door of the deanery.[12] Gardiner himself died around June 1589 and was commemorated by a monument set against the wall of the south nave aisle of the cathedral (Fig. 3). His monument has a simple panelled chest with plain shields either side of an indent with wooden plugs and a simple strap-work surround. The wooden plugs indicate that the now missing brass inscription was set there after the tomb was erected rather than fitted while the panel was laid flat, as in the latter circumstance lead would have been used to fix the rivets. While the panelled construction

FIG. 2. Norwich Cathedral stone collection: fragment of a fireplace with Dean Gardiner's arms

FIG. 3. Norwich Cathedral: monument to Dean George Gardiner (d. 1589)

resembles that of the Parkhurst memorial, the two monuments differ in a number of respects. The Gardiner monument is set at a higher level and the lid is made up of several pieces of polished limestone, in contrast to the single piece used for Parkhurst. There is a back wall consisting of a round arch framing three incised black-letter inscriptions flanked by fluted Ionic pilasters supporting a plain entablature below a pediment, in the centre of which is a shield of Gardiner's arms in a strap-work surround characteristic of the Gooding workshop. The spandrels of the arch, like the lettering, are a throwback to Gothic designs. The use of such lettering, while not invariable, persists throughout the workshop's existence.[13]

The tomb-chest of Miles Spencer, chancellor of the diocese (d. 1570), has plain shields in plain panels and may be another work erected at the same time as Parkhurst's, which it closely resembles, having a low chest with similar mouldings and shields. However, it has a heavy black marble top with the indent of a brass figure, inscription and shield. Sir Thomas Browne's description in *Repertorium* noted that 'The top stone was entire, but now quite broken, split, and depressed by blows',[14] suggesting that another stone has been found to fit the chest. As Browne recorded, the blows came from men trying money on it, so the choice of a heftier stone to replace it would have been sensible and its thickness is in particular contrast to the thin slabs used for the monuments of both Parkhurst and Gardiner, and that of Elizabeth Calthorpe, also in the cathedral. The latter (described in detail below) stands against the north wall of the ambulatory and commemorates a lady who died in December 1582, a member of the county elite with a house in the Norwich parish of St Martin-at-Palace.[15] The inscription indicates that she was the widow of Sir Francis Calthorpe and then wife of John Culpepper.[16] The heraldry of the monument suggests she had connections to the Barney family.

There are two further memorials in the cathedral from the Gooding workshop. One of these, placed here in 1585, commemorates Osbert Parsley who spent fifty years as a singing man at the cathedral. It is a mural tablet, mounted against one of the piers of the north aisle of the nave, with a small battered standing figure, now headless, presumably representing Parsley, in a scarlet-lined robe against a painted ground under an arch which tops the monument. Whether the painted background once represented the interior of the cathedral is no longer clear. Blomefield found the inscription almost illegible and the modern repainting reproduces his transcription.[17] The rest of the tablet is also covered in modern paint, which, however, serves to highlight the pattern carved on the frieze running across the entablature, supported at either end by Ionic columns which frame the inscription. Three painted roundels below are no longer decipherable but beneath each column is a plant (parsley) picked out in paint. The frieze consists of a row of quatrefoils each containing two trefoils facing each other. This frieze is of the type used most frequently by this workshop and will be referred to here as Frieze B (Fig. 4), although it varies somewhat in execution between different monuments. Osbert Parsley's figure has something in his hands, now impossible to decipher, but it may be that he was depicted holding or playing a viol. The final memorial from this workshop is discussed later.

WORK IN THE CITY AND COUNTY

TURNING to consider the monuments in Norwich and the rest of Norfolk, the county elite are represented by, among others, members of the circle around Gooding's employer at Stiffkey Hall. Nathaniel Bacon, born 1547, was the second son of Sir Nicholas Bacon, Lord Keeper under Elizabeth I.[18] Sir Nicholas purchased Stiffkey in 1571 and Nathaniel took up residence there in 1574. Nathaniel sat as MP for Norfolk

FIG. 4. Frieze pattern (Frieze B)

in three parliaments and for King's Lynn in another and was seen as a leading light of the puritan faction in the governance of the county. His uncles by marriage included the brothers Sir William and Thomas Butts. Their niece and heir was married to Nathaniel's elder brother Nicholas, whose estate was at Redgrave in Suffolk, close to the boundary with Norfolk. Sir William Butts died in 1583, and Thomas in 1593. Both brothers were commemorated by monuments from the Gooding workshop, at Thornage and Great Ryburgh respectively, both in north Norfolk. Bacon's brother-in-law was Francis Wyndham, steward of Norwich for five years from 1570, and recorder of the city in 1575, working closely with both Nathaniel and Sir Nicholas Bacon. When Wyndham died in 1592, he was commemorated by a monument in St Peter Mancroft, Norwich, with a large half-effigy in judge's robes, probably of plaster. It is very different from any other effigial representation in this group. The stonework structure of the tomb is, however, typical of the Gooding group, including the form of the frame which surrounds the achievement atop the monument which subsequently appeared on other monuments. The monuments to Sir William and Thomas Butts both consisted of tomb-chests, standing against the wall, with fluted Ionic pilasters dividing the front into three main panels, each containing a shield. Sir William's monument at Thornage, has the date 1583 painted so that each numeral is above each pilaster. Above the chest stands a back panel comprising a four-centred arch on fluted pilasters, a central round-topped achievement panel with S-shaped scrolls on either side, and flanking vase ornaments at either end (Fig. 5). There were once kneeling effigies under the arch but no sign of these remains.[19] At Great Ryburgh, the monument to Thomas Butts, erected in his life-time following the death of his wife, has a row of three low flat-topped arches in a row in place of the arch above the tomb-chest. A prominently dentilated architrave is sup-ported at either end by fluted Doric columns. This monument is mutilated: much of the tomb-chest, above the base, and the entire cover slab has been removed, so that the front of the chest is now placed against the wall beneath the back plate. This arrangement led Pevsner to suggest that what remains comprises parts of two different Elizabethan monuments, although the original format seems plain to me and Blomefield mentioned one monument only.[20] The tomb-chest of the Wyndham memorial differs in using Doric columns in place of pilasters.[21] The entablature of the chest has a different pattern on the frieze, termed here Frieze C, but at the corners single elements adapted from Frieze B are used (Fig. 6). The shields in the panels of the chest have the char-acteristic strap-work surround. The back plate has panels with plain pilasters set either side of the half-effigy of the judge. Above the effigy there is a projecting canopy, now unsupported at its front corners, with simple relief decoration on its frieze. At the top level, an achievement in a bold frame sits between two shields each with its own frame. The form of the frame around the achievement is one that reappears on some later monuments from the workshop.

The monument in the cathedral to Elizabeth Calthorpe, mentioned earlier, forms an interesting comparison with that to William Cantrell (d. 1585) at Hemingstone in Suffolk. They are obviously made to the same design but executed by different hands, as the handling of the decorative details indicates. Cantrell, as a native of Thorpe-next-Norwich, is likely to have known Elizabeth Calthorpe's monument and may have persuaded Gooding to pass the design to a Suffolk mason. There being no date of death in the inscription at Hemingstone is suggestive of the monument being erected before Cantrell's death.[22] Both have tomb-chests with pilasters dividing the front into three panels, the pilasters having Ionic capitals and tapering sides widening to a shoulder below the capitals. While the Calthorpe monument has a lozenge of the arms of Barney

FIG. 5. Thornage, Norfolk: monument to Sir William Butts (d. 1583)

in the central panel of the chest with decorative ornament in the flanking panels, Cantrell's monument has shields in all three panels. The Calthorpe chest is topped by a thin slab of polished limestone, but the thicker stone atop that at Hemingstone is unpolished. The back panel of each has an entablature supported by columns at either side; Doric for Calthorpe and rather spindly Corinthian ones for Cantrell. Both back panels have an inscription and three shields, but the arrangement of the two elements is reversed: the shields being at the bottom on the Norwich example with the inscription above in a strap-work surround, at Hemingstone the inscription (without surround) is below the shields. Surmounting both are semi-circular pediments with a large shell surrounded by a ring of dentils. The entablatures above the back panels have different friezes. The form of frieze on the Calthorpe monument also occurs on the monument of Elizabeth Gurdon at Blickling, who died on a visit there in 1582 at the age of seventeen.[23] The monument was erected by Sir Edward Clere, a man prominent in the

FIG. 6. Norwich, St Peter Mancroft: detail from the monument of Sir Francis Wyndham (d. 1592), showing frieze pattern (Frieze C) and shield in strap-work surround

governance of the county but generally opposed to the Bacon faction. This frieze pattern, termed here Frieze A, is a forerunner of Frieze B, having overlapping tendrils in place of trefoils. It appears to have been more difficult to cut correctly as both friezes are a little uneven. The front of the Gurdon tomb-chest is divided into two panels by polished grey limestone columns with Ionic capitals and bases in the same light-coloured stone as the chest. The frieze is on the entablature of the chest. Recessed into the wall above is a round arch flanked by columns of the same material as those on the tomb-chest but with Ionic capitals. Under the arch is the kneeling figure of Elizabeth, cut in alabaster. Although this is the only identified use of alabaster by the Gooding workshop, there is no reason to believe that the figure was brought in from another workshop; the carving is of much the same standard as figures to be discussed later, and notably no earlier monuments in the group include figures in their design. The entablature above the arch includes a modillion frieze. Above, the round-topped panel containing a shield with the characteristic strap-work has S-shaped scrolls either side. The inscription, in Roman capitals similar to those of the Calthorpe monument, is on a panel within square mouldings under the canopy.[24]

In the church of St Martin-at-Palace, just outside the cathedral Close, is a monument to another Elizabeth Calthorpe, who died in 1578.[25] Unlike her namesake in the cathedral, she was born a Calthorpe, but made three very advantageous marriages, to Sir Henry Parker, son of the 10th Baron Morley, Sir William Woodhouse and Dru Drury.

Drury and Sir Philip Parker (Elizabeth's son by her first marriage) were both members of the puritan faction, both sitting on a commission in Norwich with Nathaniel Bacon at around the time of Elizabeth's death. Her monument is of substantial size; the tomb-chest divided into four panels by pilasters with recessed centres. In the frieze of the chest's entablature are recessed panels edged by modillions. The top slab is made of the same stone as the rest of the monument. Above it a four-centred arch, with roundels and foliage in the spandrels, frames an inscription in two adjacent panels set in a frame surrounded by strap-work. Either side are fluted Ionic pilasters. Surmounting this back plate are three panels. The central one is round-topped and contains a shield of nineteen quarterings in a large strap-work surround. The outer panels have open pediments which contain achievements of arms, the crest of which matches those in the roundels of the spandrels below. The lettering of the inscription panels differs from any other monument in the group, but may be original. The letter forms are those introduced earlier in the century by Italian writing masters, familiar from other media but very rarely found on monuments.

Three monuments that have kneeling family groups are found at Bixley, Reedham and Wickmere. That at Bixley is currently *ex situ* following an arson attack on the church in 2004.[26] Edward Ward, son of a Marian MP for Norwich, died in 1583, leaving ten surviving children of twelve.[27] On the monument Ward and his wife, Anne Havers, are depicted kneeling and facing each other at a prayer desk, she with three daughters behind her, he with serried ranks of sons behind him. They are carved in relief on two panels that join in the middle of the prayer desk. Above them is a shield of arms on a separate stone and below an inscription panel. The whole is set into the back wall below a four-centred arch flanked by Ionic pilasters which support an entablature with Frieze B. Above this is a triangular pediment with an achievement of arms in the centre. The tomb-chest has a geometric pattern on the front rather than the more usual panels. In 1981, the monument to Henry Berney (d. March 1584/5) and his family at Reedham also survived a fire, the heat from which changed the light-coloured stone to red. Similarly to the Ward monument at Bixley, the figures of Berney and his wife kneel facing each other over a prayer desk, their sons and daughters behind them.[28] Unlike Bixley, the figures sit against the back wall and on the surface of the tomb-chest. They are grouped under a four-centred arch and above them is the inscription panel in a plain moulded frame. The inscription, prior to the fire, was an excellent example of the black-letter script employed by the Gooding workshop and also had two lines in Roman capitals (Fig. 7). The spandrels contain roundels, one with the Berney crest (a reed sheef), the other with initials HB embedded amongst foliage. The entablature supports a pair of round-topped panels containing an achievement of the arms of Berney on one side and a shield of the arms of Berney's wife, Anne Appleton, in the characteristic strap-work surround on the other. These panels are flanked by S-shaped scrolls and there is an ogee arch above. The tomb-chest is divided into three by Doric columns that support an entablature with Frieze C. The third monument in this group, found at Wickmere, no longer has a legible inscription but is known to commemorate William Dix, a servant of the Howard family.[29] Late in life Dix returned to his family home at Wickmere. Here he made his will, in June 1591, and his body was buried in the chancel of the church in 1596. He is represented kneeling at his prayer desk, facing east, his two wives kneeling at another desk behind him. The now blank inscription panel is above them on the back wall under a round arch, either side of which stand Ionic columns. The figures are now without heads, but were not so when the present author saw them in March 1979. The frieze on the entablature consists of alternating diagonal

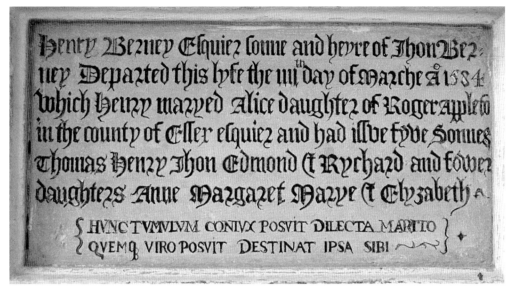

FIG. 7.   Reedham, Norfolk: inscription of the Berney monument, prior to the 1981 fire

strips. Like the Reedham tomb-chest, that at Wickmere is divided into three by Doric columns and there are three shields with arms, each in the characteristic strap-work surround. The chest has Frieze B on its entablature. Above the tomb is an achievement of the Dix arms in a surround like that on the Wyndham tomb. There are also bases for now lost obelisks.

A tomb that takes a rather different form to those described so far is that commissioned by Thomas Blundevile, who succeeded his father Edward in 1568. Three years later he commissioned a London-made monumental brass depicting his father, grandfather and great-grandfather each kneeling in armour at a prayer desk, with ten lines of verse which he no doubt composed himself. He later incorporated this plate into his own memorial at Newton Flotman (he died in 1606). It is a wall tablet and consists of a three panel mid-section flanked by Doric columns and divided by Doric pilasters, above which there is a semi-circular pediment with obelisks with tiered bases at either side. Beneath each column and pilaster are corbels with a plant carved in a shaped recess, as on the Parsley monument in the cathedral, but here not of any apparent significance. The central and left-hand panels have sculpted figures of Thomas, his two wives and two daughters, while the right-hand panel incorporates the earlier brass and shields pertinent to the three generations of Blundeviles depicted thereon. Six more shields set in pairs below each panel carried other Blundevile related painted heraldry in Farrer's time but are indecipherable now.[30] Thomas Blundevile had been employed as a mathematics tutor to the Bacon and Wyndham families. Another monument that has brass components is a small, apparently London-made, mural tablet at Hedenham to Henry, son and heir of Robert Bedingfield, who was buried on 2 February 1594/5, but Gooding was evidently called in only to add an inscription on the frame.[31]

The monument at Morningthorpe to Richard Garneys, who died on 3 January 1585/6, and his wife Margery Tyrrell is a further instance of work by Gooding. The form is familiar but not identical to any other example, having a four-centred arch as the back plate above a tomb-chest and a panel with an achievement flanked by S-scrolls. Beneath the arch is a later panel with the arms of Raworth, in commemoration of Martha (d. 1694), who was daughter of John Garneys and wife of Robert Raworth. Blomefield associated an inscription to her with this monument with the words 'On an altar monument in the chancel', but there is now no such inscription on the tomb.[32] The other arms on the monument establish that it commemorates Richard Garneys and Margery Tyrrell.[33] Presumably the large inserted Raworth panel replaced an inscription, or even figures like those at Bixley. Frieze B decorates the entablature of the chest. Other monuments dating from the late 16th century in the group include that to John Symonds (d. 1584) at Suffield. It has a tomb-chest against the wall similar to those discussed above, but the only upper component is a small inscription panel set into the wall. Two panels on the front of the chest also carry inscriptions and the monument has Frieze C on its entablature. At Ellingham, John Hamond, a gentleman who died in 1590, is commemorated by a wall monument with a triangular pediment framing a largely illegible inscription. A small wall monument at Ranworth to Thomas Holdiche (d. 1579) is a version on a reduced scale of the top portion of a number of the monuments discussed. It has a four-centred arch framing a panel with a black-letter inscription and flanked by Doric pilasters. The entablature carries simple ornaments in the frieze, while a shield of the Holdiche arms is at the centre of the triangular pediment. A larger monument of approximately the same design in St Mary Coslany, Norwich, has incised figures representing Dr Martin van Kurnbeck, who died in 1578/9, and his wife Joan, who died a few months later. They kneel, facing each other over a wide prayer desk, and an inscription in a frame is above them. Roundels in the spandrels carry crests of bull heads. In addition, there were once two figures of other family members added in paint on the back plate. This raises the question of the extent to which painting contributed to the original design of this group. Notably, the Blundeville monument at Newton Flotman once had a depiction of Noah's Ark, presumably painted on its pediment.[34] This question is particularly apposite to some of the 17th-century memorials discussed below.

A monument to the south of the high altar at Ashmanhaugh commemorating Honor, daughter of Edmund Bacon (d. 1591) takes a form analogous to that of Bishop Parkhurst, with a back panel against the east wall over the narrow end of the tomb-chest. Honor died at about the age of eighteen 'before her Mariage night', and her intended husband, Thomas Themilthorpe, erected the monument.[35] While it has various black-letter inscriptions and shields of arms, the triangular pediment above the back panel is the only architectural feature of note.

The other works made by the Gooding workshop at this time are most apparent within Norwich itself. In 1578, a brewer called Robert Gibson had a water supply, mainly for his own use but with text emphasizing his beneficence, set up in Westwick Street in the city. The surviving stonework, much renewed, employs the same motifs as used on the monuments. A strap-work surround enclosed the royal arms and its encircling garter was also used around the same time by an Irish mason from Galway, presumably both deriving from the same unidentified continental print.[36] The characteristic strap-work around a shield was also used on another conduit, the spring at Bishop's Bridge near Norwich Cathedral, known from 18th-century prints. This conduit was built in 1611 by Sir John Pettus, whose arms were on the shield.[37]

While fireplaces are difficult to date without documentation, a number in and around the city give every indication of coming from the Gooding workshop. The building currently known as the Dolphin Inn at Heigham, a Norwich suburb, has a doorcase with ornament like that found on some of the tombs. The doorcase carries the date 1587 and thus provides an approximate date for the fireplace within the building. Strangers' Hall has a number of fire-surrounds and some of these have designs in their spandrels, like those at the Dolphin Inn, that relate very closely to those on the arch of the standing wall monument commemorating Thomas Southwell (d. 1609) at Morton-on-the-Hill, a few miles west of the city. These are in the form of dragons with long plant-like tails and shields. Similar fireplaces can also be found in the Strangers' Club on Elm Hill in Norwich, and in a shop next door.[38] The Southwell monument has a tomb-chest with three shields in the familiar strap-work surrounds and Frieze B.[39]

Closely related to each other by their incised effigies are the monument to Anna de Hem (d. 1603) and her husband at St Michael-at-Plea in Norwich, and that to Anne Bulwer (d. 1604/5), at Guestwick, although the monuments themselves take different forms. The de Hem monument is set into a corner at the west end of the church, the two halves on different walls, meeting in the centre of its triangular pediment on which a spade and skull are incised into the left-hand side, crossed bones on the right.[40] The left-hand side of the main panel beneath has a black-letter inscription, on the right-hand side numerous figures of the family kneel either side of a prayer desk, above which is incised an hourglass. Anne Bulwer's memorial is a floor slab, incised with her figure standing on a pedestal, her children kneeling either side and looking very like the de Hem children (Fig. 8).[41] A black-letter inscription in an incised frame is set in the midst of the pedestal.

The only two monuments erected after 1600 to have sculpted effigies are that representing Christopher Knolles (d. 1610), his wife Elizabeth Barney and their children at Sprowston, and that to William Johnson (d. March 1611/2) in St Etheldreda's, Norwich, but originally from St Peter's Southgate.[42] The sculptural quality of the Knolles family is no higher than that found on earlier figurative monuments, but the Johnson effigies suggest that Gooding could by now call on the services of someone more talented as a figure sculptor when necessary. The Knolles tablet has the same frieze as the Parsley tablet, while the Johnson tablet has a shield in the now familiar strap-work surround. Both tablets have aprons of a form not seen in this group before. This suggests that Gooding had been looking at contemporary London work, of which there are a number of examples in Norwich, for example to Christopher Layer (d. 1600) in St John Maddermarket and Thomas Pettus (d. 1597) in St Simon and St Jude. The same sort of apron is seen on the tablet of John Rawlyns (d. 1614) at Attleborough, where he was the puritan rector.[43] He had also been entrusted with the education of Thomas Knyvett, Nathaniel Bacon's grandson. The tablet has the characteristic shield in strap-work surround and frieze and it has the form of superstructure that first appeared on the Wyndham monument. It retains all three obelisks around it, as does the Johnson monument and the monument to the brewer Edward Nutting (d. 1616), who held the office of sheriff for Norwich in 1602.[44] The inscription of the Nutting tablet in St Saviour's church in the city has been replaced by another on wooden boards, presumably after the death of his widow in 1634/5, about whom the new inscription has much to say. This suggests that the surviving paintwork may date from the time of this modification, but otherwise the characteristics are as those of the Rawlyns example at Attleborough.

Monuments to prominent members of the city elite include those which commemorate Francis Rugge (d. 1607), MP for Norwich and three times mayor of the city, and his wife Ann Aldrich (d. 1611), who was daughter and sister to successive city MPs, and Henry Fawcett, sheriff in 1608. Heavily repainted, the Rugge memorial in St Andrew's church is of the form dominant in the workshop's output in the previous century:

Fig. 8. Guestwick,
Norfolk: incised slab of
Anne Bulwer (d. 1604)

a standing wall monument with a tomb-chest divided into three panels, each with a
shield in the characteristic strap-work surround, a canopied backplate surmounted by a
round topped panel containing an achievement flanked by S-scrolls, and with the bases
of obelisks or other ornaments outside them.[45] The pattern of the frieze is, however,
one not encountered before, having triangles with fleur-de-lis within. The inscription
panel, in the centre of the back wall, has strap-work reminiscent of that of the
Calthorpe monument in the cathedral. The remains of Henry Fawcett's monument in
St Michael Coslany, Norwich, are a sad memorial to a major benefactor of the city.
Fawcett died in 1619 and by the first half of the 18th century the tomb-chest had been
removed to make way for a passage through to a vestry. This work left a back panel
with a four-centred arch below a semi-circular arch containing the achievement of
Fawcett's arms.[46] So much of the stonework of the monument has gone that it is only
included in this group on the balance of probabilities.

A monument that was certainly in better condition in Blomefield's time is that in the church of St Michael-at-Plea to Rebecca Playford (d. 1614/5), wife of John Playford, mercer.[47] It is a small tablet set against a column and has as its central feature a partially legible inscription. It is surmounted by a semi-circular pediment that, together with the frieze, must have contained all the missing components, presumably painted, that Blomefield recorded. The figures of John and Rebecca faced each other over a prayer desk, each with wording above them, her dead children behind her, his living ones behind him. There were six lines in Latin and English in addition to the remaining inscription. There is no trace of this now and it must have been depicted on a fairly small scale. Another wall monument on which the features seen by Blomefield can no longer be seen is now hidden away in the tower of the church at Honingham, smothered under layers of whitewash. However, a touch of red paint seen by the present author in February 1979 suggests that the figures of Sergeant Catelyn in his scarlet robes with his three sons and his wife in black with her three daughters could emerge one day from under the whitewash. This monument, according to the verses Blomefield recorded, was erected by Thomas Catelyn in 1618 to replace the original, put up sixty years earlier to his father.[48] Its removal from the chancel is likely to have caused damage to the painting, which also included texts over the heads of the children detailing their marriages. A final example is the monument at Elsing commemorating Dame Anne, wife of Sir Anthony Browne. It resembles closely the tomb-chests in the cathedral to Bishop Parkhurst and Chancellor Spencer of around fifty years earlier.[49] Above it is a panel set into the wall with a characteristic black-letter inscription.

GOODING'S OWN MONUMENT, HIS INFLUENCES AND LEGACY

SET into the wall of the south nave aisle of Norwich Cathedral, between two Roman-esque shafts, are two flat stones forming a monument, the top part of which has the incised image of the upper part of a skeleton above an incised panel with a black-letter inscription. Below is a portion with three vertical incised lines extending into the lower stone, terminating at the horizontal incised outer line enclosing the Roman capital inscription to Thomas Gooding (Fig. 9). Thomas Gooding, freemason, made his will in 1625.[50] In it he requested burial in the cathedral near his first wife Elizabeth, made bequests to his second wife Barbara, his niece Elizabeth Bollerd, his godson Thomas Alyn and his brother Robert, who was named as his executor. Robert proved the will on 23 January 1627/8, three days after Thomas's burial. Gooding is likely to have been in his late seventies, if not older, when he died, and how long before his death he prepared his own memorial is a matter of speculation. The general assumption has been that this monument was Elizabethan, reinforced no doubt by the proximity of the similar lettering on Dean Gardiner's memorial.

The main influence on Gooding in respect of his career as a monumental mason must have been the series of monuments erected by the Howard dukes of Norfolk at Framlingham, Suffolk. Earlier but recently made monuments to Henry Fitzroy (d. 1536), and the third Howard duke, Thomas, made in the latter's lifetime, had been brought from the Howards' previous burial site at Thetford Priory and re-erected with new components in the 1550s once the chancel at Framlingham had been rebuilt. Alongside them, tombs to the fourth Howard duke, also Thomas, and probably to his daughter Elizabeth were constructed from scratch in the 1550s and 1560s.[51] A small number of related monuments were made in East Anglia at this time. The tomb of Sir Richard Southwell (d. 1563) at Wood Rising is one indication that there were other monuments

FIG. 9. Norwich Cathedral: incised monument of Thomas Gooding

of a similar architectural form to those of the 1550s Framlingham style being made for local clients. Southwell named the duke of Norfolk as one of his executors. Richard Codington's monument at Ixworth in Suffolk, erected after his death in 1567 is also an adaptation of the 1550s Framlingham type and seems to have been erected before Codington's widow died in 1571.

Relatively small numbers of funeral monuments were being erected in East Anglia at this period. The earliest in the Norwich area that can be associated with Gooding is the tomb-chest of John Tompson (d. 1574) at Colney. It includes motifs that are not found on later examples but does have the general form of a chest divided into panels by the use of classically styled pilasters that Gooding copied from the Framlingham monuments. Apart from the monuments described above, there are a number of black-letter inscription panels that were presumably monuments in themselves rather than the remnants of larger structures. A mason called Thomas Gooding bought his freedom at Ipswich in 1559/60, but is unlikely to be the same man, unless he was well over eighty years old when he died in 1627/8.[52] Interestingly, the Suffolk Record Office at Ipswich holds records of masons with the surname Gooding living at Framlingham during 1630–40. For most of period during which Gooding worked in Norwich he was the only freemason, as opposed to mason, in the city. His absence from the list of freemen and the initial flourishing in the cathedral of his monumental work suggest that he was the cathedral's master mason. Unfortunately, little relevant Dean and Chapter documentation survives from the period to confirm or refute this supposition.[53] Certainly, Gooding's workshop was a prolific, adaptable and successful mason's yard, and the monuments discussed here are testament to his achievements.

NOTES

1. J. Finch, *Church Monuments in Norfolk before 1850: an archaeology of commemoration*, BAR British Series 317 (Oxford 2000), 96–98; J. Bayliss, 'Stone with pitch decoration', in *Two Medieval Churches in Norfolk*, EAA, 96, ed. O. Beazley and B. Ayers (Gressenhall 2001), 40–41. Finch provides an excellent summation of the characteristics of this group of monuments and Bayliss gives a list.

2. V. Morgan, E. Rutledge and B. Taylor ed., *The Papers of Nathaniel Bacon of Stiffkey*, V, Norfolk Record Society 74 (Norwich 2010), 105–06.

3. Ibid., see fn. 299 for the Stiffkey database.

4. P. Eade, *Some Account of the Parish of St. Giles, Norwich* (Norwich 1906), 463, 490, 493 and 494.

5. W. Rye ed., *The Norfolk Antiquarian Miscellany*, II.ii (Norwich 1883), 330–31.

6. J. Wilson, 'Wymondham town book 1585–1620', in *Country and City, Wymondham, Norwich and Eaton in 16th and 17th Centuries*, ed. J. Wilson, P. Howard and A. Hinkley, Norfolk Record Society 70 (Norfolk 2006), 13, 73; H. W. Saunders, *A History of Norwich Grammar School* (Norwich 1932), 31–32; A. E. R., 'Account books of St Stephen's church & parish', in *East Anglian, or, Notes and Queries on Subjects Connected with the Counties of Suffolk, Cambridge, Essex, & Norfolk*, ed. C. H. Evelyn White, 3rd series, 8 (Norwich 1899–1900), part CXXXII, 215.

7. F. F. Starr ed., *English Goodwin Family Papers*, II (Hartford 1921), 693.

8. Parish registers of St Stephen's, Norwich: NRO PD484; parish registers of All Saints, Norwich: NRO PD74.

9. He was buried on 21 January 1627/8, according to the parish register of St Mary-in-the-Marsh, NRO PD499. After the demolition of the church in 1570, parishioners held their services in the cathedral.

10. N. Norris and R. Greenwood, *The Brasses of Norfolk Churches* (Holt 1976), 15.

11. Blomefield, *Norfolk*, III, 555 gives the inscription once on the brass.

12. Another fireplace with the initial G in each spandrel has recently been uncovered in the cathedral library. Although simpler and smaller than other fireplaces discussed here, it is compatible in style.

13. Blomefield, *Norfolk*, III, 640 gives the inscription.

14. S. Wilkins ed., *The Works of Sir Thomas Browne*, III (London 1889), 280.

15. Finch, *Monuments* (as in n. 1), pl. 49.

16. Blomefield, *Norfolk*, IV, 31.

17. Ibid., 27.

18. Details of the lives of Bacon and others involved in local politics have been derived from A. Hassall Smith, *County and Court: Government and Politics in Norfolk 1558–1603* (Oxford 1974).

19. Blomefield, *Norfolk*, IX, 446: a tomb for Sir William Butts, with his effigy in armour, kneeling, his helmet at his feet, and his lady by him on her knees.

20. B/E, *Norfolk*, II, 369–70; Blomefield, *Norfolk*, VII, 166. There are faint traces of a date analogous to that on his brother's monument but now illegible.

21. Blomefield, *Norfolk*, IV, 220–21; Finch, *Monuments* (as in n. 1), pl. 48.

22. S. Cantrill Christie, *The Cantrill-Cantrell Genealogy* (New York 1908), xiii–xiv.

23. Finch, *Monuments* (as in n. 1), pl. 46.

24. Blomefield, *Norfolk*, VI, 405.

25. Finch, *Monuments* (as in n. 1), pl. 56; Blomefield, *Norfolk*, IV, 373–74.

26. It seemed to have survived in a reasonably complete state when viewed *in situ* through protective wire fencing a few days after the fire.

27. Blomefield, *Norfolk*, V, 452.

28. Blomefield, *Norfolk*, XI, 127–28.

29. Blomefield, *Norfolk*, VI, 458; Finch, *Monuments* (as in n. 1), pls 55 (shield in strap-work surround) and 57.

30. E. Farrer, *The Church Heraldry of Norfolk*, I.i (Norwich 1885), 179; Blomefield, *Norfolk*, V, 69.

31. Blomefield, *Norfolk*, X, 146. Parkin's transcription of the verse on the brass is incomplete, but the line immediately after, giving Robert's own burial date as 5 November 1600, may be the now illegible wording on the bottom of the frame.

32. Blomefield, *Norfolk*, V, 288; Finch, *Monuments* (as in n. 1), pl. 54, giving the death date of Garneys as 1571. J. Corder ed., *The Visitation of Suffolk, 1561*, New Series II, Harleian Society (London 1984), 285, cites the Norwich Consistory Court will made by Garneys on 20 October 1585 and proved 19 February 1586.

33. Blomefield, *Norfolk*, V, 292, where the nine quarters of the 'full coat of Garnish' that Richard Garneys placed over the 'portal' of Boyland Hall, finished in 1571, correspond exactly with those on the achievement over the monument. Two of the shields on the tomb-chest, Garneys impaling Berney and impaling Tyrell, represent his father's marriage and his. As he had no children, the monument cannot be for anyone else.

34. Blomefield, *Norfolk*, IV, 488. See Finch, *Monuments* (as in n. 1), 85 for the van Kurnbeck painting.

35. Blomefield, *Norfolk*, XI, 2.

36. A. L. Harris and J. Bayliss, 'An Unusual Memento from 16th Century Galway', *Journal of the Galway Archaeological & Historical Society*, 52 (2001), 120–26.

37. Blomefield, *Norfolk*, IV, 427–28.

38. 20 Elm Hill.

39. Blomefield, *Norfolk*, VIII, 238.

40. Finch, *Monuments* (as in n. 1), pl. 53; Blomefield, *Norfolk*, IV, 325.

41. *Monumental Brasses: The Portfolio Plates of the Monumental Brass Society 1894–1984*, introduction by M. W. Norris (Woodbridge 1988), pl. 445; Blomefield, *Norfolk*, VIII, 218.

42. Sprowston: E. Farrer, *The Church Heraldry of Norfolk*, II.iii (Norwich 1886), 262–63; St Etheldreda's: Finch, *Monuments*, pl. 50.

43. J. T. Barrett, *Memorials of the Parochial Church, the Collegiate Chantry, and the Chapel of St. Mary Commonly called Mortimer's Chapel in the Parish of Attleborough* (London 1848), 48.

44. Finch, *Monuments* (as in n. 1), pl. 47; Blomefield, *Norfolk*, IV, 447.

45. Blomefield, *Norfolk*, IV, 307.

46. Ibid., 498.

47. Ibid., 323.

48. Blomefield, *Norfolk*, II, 447.

49. Blomefield, *Norfolk*, VIII, 203.

50. Norwich, NRO PRDC 1/2/5 fo. 319.

51. L. Stone and H. Colvin, 'The Howard tombs at Framlingham, Suffolk', *Archaeol. J.*, 120 (1965), 159–71; R. Marks, 'The Howard Tombs at Thetford and Framlingham: New Discoveries', *Archaeol. J.*, 141 (1984), 255–57.

52. J. Webb ed., *The Town Finances of Elizabethan Ipswich: Select Treasurers' and Chamberlains' Accounts*, Suffolk Record Society, 38 (Suffolk 1996), 26.

53. Norwich, NRO DCN 12/5 and 12/6, the earliest surviving 17th-century auditors' papers, covering 1613–16, have no trace of him.

Private Lives and Public Power: Norwich Merchants' Houses Between the 14th and 16th Centuries

CHRIS KING

This paper discusses the surviving examples of large merchants' houses in the city of Norwich dating between the 14th and 16th centuries. These were the residences of families who dominated the economic and political life of the medieval and early modern city, and possess impressive domestic accommodation arranged around an open hall, alongside extensive undercroft spaces for the storage and display of merchandise. The eight remaining examples of great halls, with their screens-passages and bay windows, are a unique survival for an English provincial city. It is argued that these were important not simply for the expression of private status but as locales for the negotiation of shared cultural identities and public, civic authority within the mercantile elite. In the 16th century, many mercantile residences in Norwich were rebuilt adopting innovative plans and decorative elements, whilst other merchants chose to retain their medieval great halls as self-conscious symbols of personal and corporate honour and legitimacy.

INTRODUCTION

ALONGSIDE the impressive medieval monuments of its castle, cathedral, guildhall and parish churches, the city of Norwich retains a significant number of historic domestic buildings, including several examples of large merchants' houses constructed between the 14th and 16th centuries. In the medieval and early modern period the city government was controlled by wealthy townspeople belonging to the high-status trades of mercer, grocer, draper, dyer or goldsmith. These men dominated the highest civic offices as one of the four city bailiffs in the 14th century or, after the city gained its charter of incorporation in 1404, as sheriffs, aldermen and mayor.[1] They formed a well-integrated civic elite connected by ties of kinship, intermarriage and apprenticeship with each other and with local gentry families, and their large houses contained impressive suites of domestic rooms alongside extensive storage spaces for valuable merchandise. This paper will describe some of the most prominent surviving examples of wealthy merchants' houses in the city, seeking to understand not simply their plan and form, but to explore how their architectural design was used to express social status, corporate identity and political authority within the city between the 14th and 16th centuries.

Several of these buildings are already well known to architectural historians, forming part of the early typologies of medieval urban house plans created by W. A. Pantin and

Margaret Wood.[2] In the 1970s and 1980s the Norwich Survey (led by the late Alan Carter and Robert Smith) recorded over 200 pre-1700 domestic structures, including the remains of these large merchants' houses, and more recent surveys have been undertaken by the current author developing on these earlier efforts.[3] Archaeological excavations conducted by the Norwich Survey, and more recently by the Norfolk Archaeological Unit, provide further evidence for medieval and early modern housing across the city.[4] These surveys highlight the complex sequence of development of many of these properties, meaning that the idea of a rigid typology of urban houses is too simplistic.[5] Nonetheless, the surviving examples of merchants' houses in Norwich share common features which can be used to interpret their chronological development, form and functions, and highlight some of the multiple ways in which domestic spaces were implicated in private and public social identities.

THE MEDIEVAL MERCHANTS' HOUSES

THE majority of Norwich houses before the 14th century were built of timber, beginning with earth-fast construction and later developing the use of timber-framing. Archaeological excavations across the city have also revealed a large number of clay-walled houses, ranging from single-cell properties to larger dwellings and workshops.[6] There were, however, a small number of stone houses in the city from at least the 12th century, the dwellings of wealthy merchants, officials and the townhouses of the secular and ecclesiastical aristocracy. Elizabeth Rutledge has tracked references to eighteen examples before 1300 in documentary sources, which made up one component of large messuages with halls, chambers, solars, gateways, stables and shops.[7] Two rare surviving examples of 12th-century stone buildings are both associated with commercial sites, and have vaulted ground-floor rooms with first-floor accommodation. One of these is Wensum Lodge on King Street, for a long period known as The Music House. The two-storeyed north range at right-angles to the street is of mid-12th-century date, extended to the south by a single-aisled hall in *c.* 1175–80.[8] The property was owned by Isaac, son of Jurnet, and his descendants in the 13th century.[9] The second example was excavated in 1981 on a site bordering the Wensum on St Martin-at-Palace Plain, and the foundations are now preserved in the basement beneath the Magistrates' Court; it may have belonged to a cathedral official.[10]

The most substantial standing remains of houses of prosperous merchants date from the mid-14th century onwards and are clustered in the central parishes of the city. They adopt the common spatial arrangement found in the high-status houses of most English medieval towns with domestic, service and commercial spaces arranged around one or more courtyards.[11] There was usually a timber-framed range along the street frontage, which may have been leased separately as commercial rents. In almost all cases the street ranges have undergone significant modernization, making it difficult to establish their original appearance and functions with any certainty. Norwich retains one surviving example of a timber shop-front dating to the early 16th century at no. 15 Bedford Street, with two large openings with mortises for counters on either side of a central doorway.

Only a small number of medieval domestic buildings from lower down the social scale survive as standing structures, and the majority of houses recorded by the Norwich Survey post-date 1500. The most complete example is The Britons Arms on Elm Hill, a three-storeyed, probably ecclesiastical building of the 15th century which stands in the north-west corner of St Peter Hungate churchyard.[12] Archaeological excavations have shown that the tradition of clay-walled construction continued in the poorer suburbs of the city throughout the 14th and 15th centuries, whilst in the wealthier central parishes houses were increasingly built of timber-framing with dwarf-wall foundations and often ground floors and party walls of flint and brick rubble.[13] This shift in building construction was underway by the late 15th century, and was probably accelerated by the two catastrophic fires of 1507 which are estimated to have destroyed 40 per cent of the city's housing stock.[14] The most common surviving elements of late medieval domestic architecture in the city are more than fifty brick-vaulted undercrofts. These are often relatively modest structures with one or more small side chambers, and they are almost all concentrated on the sloping ground on the south bank of the River Wensum. As well as providing fire-proof storage, they also seem to have acted as level building platforms for clay and timber-framed houses.[15]

Within this general picture of domestic building drawn from excavations and fragmentary survivals, the houses of the wealthy mercantile elite of the city stand out as a distinct group for their scale, materials and architectural form. Norwich retains a larger collection of standing medieval houses belonging to the specific group of aldermen and wealthy merchants than any other English medieval city. In these properties the main domestic ranges are commonly built of full-height rubble or coursed flint, and they all retain evidence for a large open hall, located on the ground floor or raised above an undercroft. In total, there are eight standing examples of these halls in the city, and several more are known from records or have been excavated. The earliest examples were constructed in the second half of the 14th century, and a further group were built in the late 15th or early 16th century. The halls share certain architectural features which mark them out as a distinct building type, adopting the formal, hierarchical, spatial arrangement that characterizes the halls of the rural gentry and middling sort.[16] The merchants' houses also contain impressive storage and commercial spaces in the form of large, multi-chambered undercrofts with ample provision for access and lighting. Together, this group of houses presents an unparalleled opportunity to study the ways in which domestic space was configured to play a significant role in the everyday and ritual lives of elite urban households.

Strangers' Hall

STRANGERS' HALL, standing on Charing Cross, is the best known of these Norwich merchants' houses, having long been recognized as one of the most complete surviving examples of a medieval town-house in England. The house has a complex construction history, created over four centuries through a process of gradual extension and rebuilding. After a post-medieval period of divided ownership the property was rescued in 1899 by local antiquarian and Norwich diocesan registrar Leonard Bolingbroke, and was opened as one of Britain's first museums of domestic life; the house passed into the care of Norwich City Council in 1921. The broad architectural development of the house has been established by previous scholars, most recently Alan Carter and Robert Smith, and need only be summarized here.[17] The earliest surviving phase is a three-bay vaulted undercroft running north–south, approximately 12 m behind the present street frontage. The house is built on a sloping site, so this undercroft is partially above ground at the north end facing the courtyard but fully below ground to the south. It has hollow-chamfered stone ribs rising from semi-octagonal wall-piers with scroll-moulded capitals which place it in the late 13th or early 14th century, when the property was owned by the wealthy merchant Ralph de Middleton. The undercroft is well appointed with three large windows in the side walls, and seems to have been designed for the display as well as storage of merchandise.

Strangers' Hall underwent at least two phases of significant expansion in the 15th century, when the house was owned by wealthy merchants William Bayley (sheriff in 1451) and Thomas Caus (mayor in 1495 and 1503).[18] The undercrofts were extended to the east and west, incorporating a pre-existing range along the east side of the courtyard. These rooms supported domestic accommodation on the main living floor, approached by a staircase from the central courtyard but at ground level to the rear. At the core of the house is an L-plan arrangement with a great hall, over 10 m long and 6 m wide, placed transversely across the south end of the earlier undercroft. This has a two-storeyed service block at the east end, and a parlour-and-chamber block to the north. The south-west wing of the house was also added in the 15th century, connected to the corner of the great hall by a newel staircase of which only the window survives. The brick undercroft of this range is supported on its north side by an open arcade of wide arches, to allow the loading and unloading of merchandise, so it may originally have had a warehouse function. Already by the 15th century the house provided a complex sequence of spaces for commerce on the undercroft floor with impressive domestic rooms above, linked by a staircase at the rear of the hall.

By the third decade of the 16th century Strangers' Hall was owned by Nicholas Sotherton. Originally the son of a yeoman family from Ludham, Norfolk, Sotherton was apprenticed as a grocer and quickly prospered, becoming sheriff in 1530 and mayor in 1539.[19] He rebuilt the 15th-century great hall, heightening its walls and inserting a crown-post roof with his merchant's mark and the cross of St George painted in the carved wooden spandrels — a significant pairing in a city where the guild of St George was intimately tied to the civic government, and where the mayor of the city automatically became master of the guild in the year following his mayoralty (Fig. 1).[20] At the same time Sotherton inserted a fine traceried bay window at the high end of the hall, which has clearly been brought from another property (the stone jambs on the exterior clearly having been chiselled away from their original setting). Given that this rebuilding almost certainly occurred in the years 1539–40, as argued below, this impressive architectural fragment may have been salvaged from one of the recently dissolved monastic houses. The low end of the great hall was also rebuilt with a pair of stone-framed service doors inserted into the east wall; before this there is no evidence that the hall possessed the standard arrangement of two service rooms, and even at this point the two rooms were connected by an arched opening and provided access to the commercial area of the house below.[21] The hall screen contains four carved wooden panels with coats of arms which date to the Sotherton period, although the screen is a modern fabrication and this is not their original location: they are the arms of the Merchant Adventurers, Sotherton's personal coat of arms, the arms of the Grocers impaling his merchant's mark, and the arms of the city of Norwich — all means by which Sotherton proclaimed his familial, commercial and civic prestige and authority.

In the same period, Sotherton also extended the north parlour block, and added the brick and timber-framed west courtyard range, although most of the surviving 16th-century features in this wing were in fact brought from other Norwich buildings by Bolingbroke.[22] The fireplace in the ground-floor room has a massive bressumer bearing Sotherton's mark and the Grocers' arms, but this is in fact the top of a carriage arch and presumably once stood over a wide external entrance (Fig. 2). Finally, Sotherton rebuilt the upper storeys of the south-west range above the open arcade to create an impressive

FIG. 1.   Norwich, Strangers' Hall: the great hall roof with mayor Nicholas Sotherton's
merchant's mark and the cross of St George, and bay window, both inserted *c.* 1539

Photo: author

FIG. 2.   (*top*) Norwich, Strangers' Hall: the fireplace bressumer in the west courtyard range, originally an external carriage arch with Nicholas Sotherton's merchant's mark and the arms of the Grocers' Company. (*left*) Detail of left arch spandrel carved with the arms of the Grocers' Company. (*right*) Detail of right arch spandrel carved with the initials 'N' and 'S' and Nicholas Sotherton's merchant mark

Photo: author

great parlour with a finely moulded wooden ceiling (which is no longer visible but has been described by several earlier observers).[23]

Archaeological study of the building suggests that the bulk of this significant rebuilding occurred in a single campaign, which was closely tied to Sotherton's attainment of high civic office; one piece of evidence allows us to date this specifically to the years 1539–40 when he was mayor of the city, supported by the prominence of civic imagery in his refurbished great hall. At the centre of the vaulted entrance porch to the great hall is a boss carved with a woman's head in a veil and wimple. Sotherton died in 1540, the year following his mayoralty, and it appears that the rebuilding was completed by his widow Agnes. If the hall was a symbol of the public, civic authority of the head of the household in a specifically urban context, this is a striking material statement. Whilst a wealthy mercantile widow might continue their husband's business, she had only limited access to the wider economic and political institutions that structured elite male social interaction, particularly craft or trade guilds, and of course could not hold public office.[24] Through the placement of this sculpture, Agnes Sotherton was appropriating the 'public' connotations of this space in the service of her new private role as the head of a family and business.

Other medieval merchants' houses

THE remaining examples of wealthy merchants' houses in Norwich share many of the same architectural characteristics as Strangers' Hall, although the small number of examples and more fragmentary survival makes the interpretation of their development more tentative. Considered as a group, however, they shed light on the form and chronology of elite housing in the late-medieval city.

One of the earliest examples is Suckling House, which is also the closest parallel to Strangers' Hall in terms of layout. The standing building contains an open hall parallel to St Andrew's Plain and vaulted west range at right-angles to this along St Andrew's Hill. The hall originally stood between two courtyards, the northern courtyard having been demolished in 1889. It was built in the mid-14th century, as suggested by its north and south entrance doors with wave-moulded two-centred arches and scroll-moulded hood-moulds.[25] These form a cross-passage against the west range, which has four bays of vaulting with chamfered brick ribs on the ground floor. There is a blocked pair of plain two-centred arched service doorways between the hall and west range, but (as originally noted by Smith) the doors sit awkwardly against one of the vaulting ribs, suggesting that the traditional paired services are a later insertion, as at Strangers' Hall.[26] The great hall has a scissor-braced common-rafter roof, with a slender tie-beam and crown-post which may be a secondary insertion (Fig. 3). A large bay window has also been inserted into the south wall, with a two-centred rendered-brick archway (the current timber bay window with its stained glass is a 20th-century replacement). Suckling House was the home of several prominent medieval merchants, including the Paulet, Cambridge and Steward families, members of which regularly served as bailiff and mayor. In the 16th century it continued as the residence of the Suckling dynasty, retaining its impressive medieval great hall at the heart of an extensive double-courtyard property.[27]

The Bridewell is another impressive late-14th-century elite residence, containing the city's largest medieval undercroft. The house was built by the Appleyard family; William Appleyard (d. 1419) was bailiff three times, became the city's first mayor in 1404 and served again as mayor a further five times.[28] The house served as the city Bridewell and gaol from 1583 to 1828, and now houses a museum. The core of the medieval house survives as an L-shaped range, with an undercroft of six quadripartite brick-vaulted chambers, lit by windows at street level.[29] The street façade of the north range is constructed of remarkably finely cut, coursed and galleted flint blocks, creating an impressive glossy black surface, set with two-light windows on the ground and first

FIG. 3. Norwich, Suckling Hall: mid-14th-century great hall with scissor-braced roof, with a crown-post probably inserted in the mid-15th century, and inserted low-end service doors

Photo: author

floors, the latter with ogee-shaped heads. Very little remains of the internal arrangements but there was a great hall in the central range between two courtyards, evidenced by the pair of service doors which originally led into the north range, where there was a stair to the undercroft below.

Dragon Hall on King Street is a unique medieval building in both form and function, incorporating the remains of a large 14th-century great hall that was owned by two prominent city families, the Pages and the Middays. It forms the south range of the standing structure and has a pair of ogee-headed service doors connecting the low end of the hall to the street-front west range, one of them leading to a brick-vaulted undercroft below. In 1427 (dated by dendrochronology) the earlier house was incorporated into an expanded courtyard complex by its new wealthy merchant owner Robert

Toppes. This appears to have functioned as a private trading hall. The new building consisted of a street-front range with an open arcade at the rear of the ground floor, spanning a pre-existing road leading up from quays on the River Wensum, supporting a tall seven-bay timber-framed hall on the first floor divided into two rooms. A carved and painted dragon in the spandrel of one of the crown-post trusses gives the building its present name. This building was not Toppes' personal residence, although the earlier hall appears to have been retained in use, perhaps providing accommodation for a steward or as a suitable place to entertain guests and customers.[30]

Alongside these examples of large open halls constructed in the mid- to late-14th century, there are several examples in Norwich of halls constructed in the late 15th or early 16th century. These tend to have a smaller floor area, but they are finely detailed with carved and moulded roof trusses and full-height bay windows with flat four-centred arches. One example is Pykerell's House on St Mary's Plain, north of the Wensum, which was constructed by Thomas Pykerell, mayor in 1525, 1533 and 1538, although it was heavily restored after bombing in 1942. It has a pair of opposing bay windows at the high end of the hall, and queen-post roof trusses with cambered tie-beams and carved spandrels (Fig. 4).[31] A similar building survives with a single bay window and queen-post roof at the great hall on Oak Street, although this house is located towards the northern edge of the city and is not associated with any known mercantile or mayoral family.[32] Both of these halls are placed at right-angles to the street, with doorways leading into the two-storeyed street ranges.

Bacon's House on Colegate is a large flint and timber-framed courtyard house which was substantially rebuilt by mayor Henry Bacon in the mid-16th century. The heightened west range incorporates a 15th-century great hall constructed of coursed and galleted flint blocks, with an entrance at the low end. The moulded arch of a bay window is preserved facing the courtyard, its crenellated capitals matching those in St George Colegate parish church located opposite, rebuilt *c.* 1480–1500.

Finally among the standing examples of medieval open halls, nos 19–22 Bedford Street contain the remains of an extensive mercantile property, although the names of its owners are unknown. The present street-front range has a brick and flint ground floor and a close-studded jettied first floor with a roll-moulded and carved bressumer; this suggests a date in the early 16th century, and the range may have been rebuilt after the fire of 1507. Behind and at right-angles to the street range is an earlier 15th-century flint and brick-rubble wing. This has a large brick-vaulted undercroft of four quadripartite bays supported on a central octagonal stone column (Fig. 5). There are trefoil-headed lamp niches in the side walls, and a large moulded-brick arch leading to further undercrofts beneath the street range. Above the undercroft the building has been sub-divided, but the first floor preserves the roof of a large open hall, with a scissor-braced common-rafter roof and a massive central cambered tie-beam with mortises for a crown-post and substantial arch-braces.

The eight surviving examples of great halls can be supplemented by archaeological evidence. One almost complete hall-house was excavated by the Norfolk Archaeological Unit in 1981 on the north side of St Martin-at-Palace Plain (standing beside the 12th-century stone building described above). Constructed in the late 14th century, the hall was placed at right-angles behind a two-storeyed street range containing a vaulted undercroft entered from the cross-passage. In the late 15th century the property was occupied by Robert Everard, master mason to Norwich Cathedral, and at this time a stone bay window with four-centred-arched lights was inserted at the high end of the hall; it survives attached to no. 10 St Martin-at-Palace Plain.[33] Excavations across the

FIG. 4. Norwich, Pykerell's House: great hall with queen-post roof and bay window constructed by mayor Thomas Pykerell in the early 16th century

Photo: George Plunkett © 2004 G. A. F. Plunkett

city have revealed several further examples of houses with open halls and central hearths. These are generally more modest than the houses described above, constructed of clay walls or timber-framing on rubble foundations. One L-plan house on Oak Street is believed to have been a town residence of Creake Abbey, but the other examples on Oak Street and Pottergate were probably occupied by middling traders and artisans rather than the civic and mercantile elite.[34]

PUBLIC AND PRIVATE SPACE IN THE MEDIEVAL CITY

THE majority of the standing medieval houses in Norwich, then, can be directly or indirectly associated with members of the wealthy mercantile civic elite. The smallest of the surviving great halls, in terms of floor area, is Pykerell's House, and this is a finely

FIG. 5.   Nos 19–22 Bedford Street: four-bay brick vaulted undercroft in the rear range,
supporting an open hall above

Photo: author

detailed space built by one of the leading merchants of the city. Other examples of open
halls may not have been directly associated with the civic elite, such as the Great Hall
on Oak Street or the excavated hall at Everard's House, and these may represent the
homes of wealthy townspeople who emulated the spaces found in wealthy merchant
properties. Nonetheless, despite the small sample size, there is a general association
between the possession of a large open hall and the prominent mercantile families
whose members held high office in the city.

The halls themselves possess distinctive spatial and architectural characteristics. The
largest halls are those built in the late 14th century at Suckling House and Dragon Hall,
and the 15th-century hall at Strangers'; the halls built later in the 15th century are
generally smaller in floor area but finely detailed. The halls adopt the traditional hierarchical spatial arrangement, with a low-end cross-passage, paired service rooms and a
high end marked by features such as bay windows and access to private accommodation.[35] However, it is significant that none of the urban halls replicate this rural or
aristocratic pattern exactly, and in many cases this does not seem to have been the
original arrangement. In several examples, such as Strangers' Hall and Suckling House,
the paired service doors have been inserted into the low-end wall, and it is not known if
there was any original connection between the hall and the 'service' range. At Dragon
Hall, the Bridewell, and the excavated Everard's House, there may not have been a pair

of rooms at the low end, and the service area has direct access to the vaulted undercroft below. At several of the earlier halls, features such as bay windows and cross-passages have been inserted at some point in the 15th or early 16th century, to create the *appearance* of a 'traditional', formal great hall which masks the continuation of a more complex arrangement of domestic and commercial spaces within the property.[36]

Recent work on medieval urban dwellings by Jane Grenville and Sarah Pearson has challenged the argument originally put forward by W. A. Pantin that medieval town-houses are adaptations of rural forms. They highlight the complex and unique spatial arrangements which characterized urban houses, reflecting not simply the crowded pattern of buildings on tightly packed urban tenements, but the need to accommodate complex social relationships and varied domestic, service, storage and retail spaces within urban properties.[37] Large open halls are fairly rare in medieval town centres, as they take up a large amount of valuable space on urban plots; where open halls with central hearths do exist, only in the largest properties are they ranged parallel to the street with a traditional cross-passage arrangement. In towns such as York, Salisbury or Sandwich, halls are adapted to the building plot in varied ways, often placed at right-angles to the street without a full cross-passage, encroached on by upper chambers and galleries, with windows placed high up in the wall or roof-space.[38] Norwich is thus unique among English provincial cities for the grandeur of its surviving medieval mercantile residences with their impressive open halls. This reflects the wealth and social rank of the mercantile class in England's 'second city', whose members were often drawn from and intermarried with local gentry families. Similar large masonry halls are known to have existed in London and Bristol, but here they rarely survive as standing structures.[39]

One interpretation might see the move to create 'traditional' formal halls within the homes of Norwich merchants as the emulation of gentry houses to mark their social connections. However, we must question who might be the audience for such a material statement, and how this might accommodate the social constitution of the mercantile household as an effective economic and political unit. The merchant's household operated as a commercial enterprise, and was embedded within a series of distinctive political and cultural discourses that governed urban life. Mutual sociability was an important aspect of social relations among the urban elite throughout this period, and these events often combined elements of private and public ritual, where civic festivities, such as those surrounding mayoral elections or Christmas celebrations, frequently incorporated feasting and banquets given in private homes.[40] At Strangers' Hall, it can be demonstrated that the rebuilding of the house was closely associated with Nicholas Sotherton's rise to the mayoralty in 1539. The new great hall, with its cross-passage, bay window and crown-post roof decorated with commercial and civic insignia, provided a suitable setting for the large-scale formal hospitality which was an important element of public authority. This association between house building and the attainment of high civic office remained a consistent feature of Norwich houses throughout the 16th and 17th centuries.[41] In order to fully understand this phenom-enon, we must explore the meaningful connections that were made between public and domestic contexts and discourses in the late medieval and early modern city.

In the late 14th and early 15th centuries the municipality made wide-ranging efforts to increase the city's revenues and enhance their independence and authority, buying up extensive properties in the great market-place and establishing a new seld for the worsted trade, improving the public quays, building new mills on the Wensum, and enhancing the city's defences with a brick artillery fort, the Cow Tower.[42] After a campaign beginning in the 1370s, the city finally obtained a royal charter of incorporation in 1404 granting full county status and establishing a civic government of mayor, sheriffs, aldermen and a common council. Throughout the remainder of the 15th century merchants dominated the *cursus honorem*, and a large proportion of the men who served as upper office-holders were linked by blood, marriage or apprenticeship.[43] The city's new status was marked by the construction of an impressive new guildhall in the great market-place, between 1407 and 1412.[44] However, this triumph was followed by a period of tension and conflict within the city government. In the 1430s and 1440s factions emerged within the elite seeking to control the corporation, in part maintained through urban religious guilds and supported by members of the local nobility and the cathedral clergy. After a series of disputed elections and two major riots, including an attack on the cathedral in 1443, the city's liberties were revoked by the crown for four years. In 1452, royal justice William Yelverton was appointed as arbiter; his mediation resulted in the formal incorporation of the powerful guild of St George as a civic fraternity, with the aim of binding factions together as guild brothers under the mastership of the outgoing mayor.[45]

Religious and guild processions and civic festivals served to publicly define the membership of the civic community by tying together significant locales in the urban landscape. In Norwich, the magnificent parish church of St Peter Mancroft on the south side of the market-place was completely rebuilt in the 1440s and 1450s and became the chief civic church for the corporation, expressing the close interrelationship between religious and secular authority that underpinned late medieval urban culture. Many of the city's parish churches underwent significant phases of rebuilding and re-edification, principally paid for by the more prosperous townspeople and guilds. In these spaces the merchants of Norwich displayed their public honour and domestic virtues in stained glass and brass monuments, thus constituting themselves as an integrated governing elite in the earthly city below and the heavenly city above.[46] Public and private buildings shared a common architectural vocabulary. The dense layering of imagery, encompassing family status, commercial institutions and civic authority that is present at Stranger's Hall is also found in other mercantile residences, and was shared across civic, religious and domestic contexts.

One of the reasons why Norwich in particular preserves so many large medieval halls may lie in the unusually centralized nature of its government. There were over sixty craft guilds in the city, and fifty religious confraternities. However, none of the Norwich guilds possessed their own halls for feasting, a rather different situation from cities such as London or York, which may reflect the perceived need to control guild activities after the conflicts of the mid-15th century.[47] Guild feasts were often provided in the halls of religious houses and in the many public inns, but in this context feasting and sociability within elite residences may have taken on a further layer of significance as a primary locale for the negotiation of political identities in the late-medieval city. Investment in domestic buildings, and the shared lifestyle and culture they imply, was a significant material expression of the status of the urban elite, and a means of binding together a new civic oligarchy that was fractured by ongoing factional conflict. However, private sociability could also be contested; as early as 1414 the 'commons' of the city complained that members of the Bachelery guild, which was allied to the newly established civic government, had prevented them from freely electing the mayor and sheriffs, and diverted business away from the public worsted seld into their private houses.[48] Private magnificence thus had to be tied to legitimate public authority and reputation.

353

THE EARLY MODERN MERCHANTS' HOUSES

IF we extend some of these themes into the early-modern period, we can identify both strong elements of continuity and some dramatic changes in the architectural forms and social meanings of mercantile residences. Continuity can be demonstrated in the basic courtyard plan of elite houses into the later 17th century, the intermixing of commercial and domestic functions within the same property, and often in the physical structure of the buildings themselves. The retention of traditional medieval great halls at the centre of domestic space was not simply an expression of the innate conservatism of the mercantile classes, however, but a conscious strategy on the part of certain families to draw on architectural heritage in the service of social and political identities.[49]

This is clear if we compare Strangers' Hall to other aldermanic residences in the city. The Sothertons are an unusual example of a long-lived mercantile dynasty, with Nicholas and Agnes Sotherton's eldest son, Thomas, becoming mayor in 1565, followed by their grandson Thomas in 1605. The family are commemorated by a series of wall monuments in St John Maddermarket parish church, displaying a public emphasis on their dynastic connections in rural and urban society and their prominent role in civic life.[50] Strangers' Hall itself was an equally important material statement of dynastic status; throughout the 16th century private rooms in the house were improved with large fireplaces and frieze windows, whilst the medieval great hall was retained unaltered at the heart of the property as a symbol of familial antiquity and honour. Later owners of the house followed the same pattern; the grocer Francis Cocke inserted a staircase into the great hall the year before his mayoralty in 1628; and Sir Joseph Paine purchased and refurbished the house in 1659, in advance of his mayoralty in 1660.[51]

Elsewhere in the city, however, between c. 1530 and c. 1570, there was a widespread phase of reconstruction of elite residences. The majority of the medieval open halls described above were ceiled over by the end of the 16th century, and new houses adopted innovative plans providing suites of accommodation on two stories. At nos 22–26 Elm Hill, the Strangers' Club occupies the surviving street range of the house of Augustine Steward, three times mayor and one of the city's leading citizens in the mid-16th century; the first floor contains an impressive six-bay chamber with a roll-moulded and panelled ceiling, and a brick stair-turret to the rear (Fig. 6).[52] On Colegate, the medieval hall described above was incorporated into a fully two-storeyed courtyard house by the grocer Henry Bacon, mayor in 1557 and 1566. This provided two parlours on the ground floor and a sequence of four large first-floor chambers, all with moulded ceiling beams, connected by a large staircase decorated with plaster friezes.[53] At the home of Edmund Wood, mayor in 1548, now the King of Hearts gallery, survives a ground-floor great parlour, lit by a thirteen-light frieze window and provided with a magnificent battened timber ceiling (Fig. 7), beneath a first-floor chamber with a roll-moulded panelled ceiling painted a vivid yellow and red.[54]

These mayoral residences of the mid-16th century are geared to new modes of social life. They parallel contemporary changes in aristocratic and gentry building with a shift towards more private and specialized reception spaces, with first-floor suites of rooms accommodating more formal modes of elite sociability. The mercantile class of this wealthy provincial city were at the forefront of architectural innovation, strongly suggesting the strengthening of the shared social milieu of urban and rural elites.[55] However, in the specific context of the mid-16th-century city, we must also understand these changes as responses to wider conflicts over the forms and meanings of urban public spaces in the wake of the Protestant reformation. The dissolution or attenuation of

FIG. 6.   Nos 22–26 Elm Hill, now the Strangers' Club: a large courtyard house constructed by mayor Augustine Steward in the mid-16th century with this eight-bay first-floor chamber along the street frontage

Photo: author

traditional religious institutions and ceremonies represented a significant challenge to civic order, and in response urban elites sought new ways to maintain and reinforce both social cohesion and their own political authority.[56] In Norwich, the elite guild of St George was re-established as a civic company dedicated to secular feasting, and in 1540 the corporation purchased the medieval Dominican friary and converted it into a common hall where these guild and corporate feasts were held. Public ceremonial thus shifted from religious institutions to a monumental civic setting.[57] Whilst it would be wrong to suggest a direct, causal relationship between the Reformation and architectural change in the domestic sphere, elite hospitality may have become increasingly centred on established social and familial networks, away from public religious conflict. Sociability in a private, secular context could thus act to reaffirm the shared corporate identity of the civic elite in a time of significant religious and political upheaval.

Throughout the late medieval and early modern periods, the merchant elite of Norwich invested heavily in their domestic spaces as an expression not simply of personal and familial status, but in the service of a shared corporate identity and the maintenance of their political authority. The provision of formal open halls in the medieval merchants' houses provided spaces for the reception of guests and business partners and, perhaps, the performance of civic rituals, becoming an essential element of 'public' status within the city. These houses were prominent and long-lasting components of the urban landscape, and subsequent generations of merchant families acquired and

FIG. 7.   Nos 17–19 Fye Bridge Street, now the King of Hearts gallery: a medieval property rebuilt by mayor Edmund Wood in the mid-16th century with this large great parlour on the ground floor with a great chamber above

Photo: author

remodelled these properties as expressions of civic power. Over time, medieval spaces were incorporated into new modes of domestic life and sociability, becoming conscious symbols of the legitimacy and traditional values of the provincial mercantile class.

NOTES

1. R. H. Frost, 'The urban elite', in *Medieval Norwich*, 235–53.

2. W. A. Pantin, 'Medieval English town-house plans', *Med. Archaeol.*, 6–7 (1962–63), 202–39; M. Wood, *The English Medieval House* (London 1965).

3. R. Smith and A. Carter, 'Function and site: aspects of Norwich buildings before 1700', *Vernacular Architecture*, 14 (1983), 5–18; R. Smith, 'An architectural history of Norwich buildings, *c.* 1200–1700' (unpublished Ph.D. thesis, University of East Anglia, 1990); C. King, 'Houses and society in an English provincial city: the archaeology of urban households in Norwich, 1370–1700' (unpublished Ph.D. thesis, University of Reading, 2006).

4. A. Carter ed., *Excavations in Norwich 1971–1978: Part I*, EAA, 15 (Norwich 1982); M. W. Atkin, A. Carter and D. H. Evans ed., *Excavations in Norwich 1971–1978: Part II*, EAA, 26 (Norwich 1985); M. W. Atkin and D. H. Evans ed., *Excavations in Norwich 1971–1978: Part III*, EAA, 100 (Norwich 2002); B. Ayers, *Norwich: 'A Fine City'* (Stroud 2003).

5. Smith and Carter, 'Function and site' (as in n. 3), 10–14; Smith, 'Architectural history' (as in n. 3), 191–212.

6. M. W. Atkin, 'Medieval clay-walled buildings in Norwich', *NA*, 24 (1991), 171–85.

7. E. Rutledge, 'The early stone house in Norwich: the documentary evidence', in *The Medieval House in Normandy and England*, ed. D. Pitte and B. Ayers (Rouen 2002), 103–10.

8. The base of a moulded stone pier on the south wall of the earlier vaulted block is dated to *c.* 1175–80 by comparison to the piers of Norwich Cathedral priory infirmary; this was originally seen as the entrance to an external stair porch but has been reinterpreted as the respond for the arcade of a single-aisled hall: Smith, 'Architectural history' (as in n. 3), 47–69.

9. Wood, *Medieval House* (as in n. 2), 5–6; A. Carter, 'The Music House and Wensum Lodge, King Street, Norwich', *Archaeol. J.*, 137 (1980), 310–12; J. I. Dent and J. S. Livock, *Wensum Lodge: The Story of a House* (Norwich 1990).

10. B. Ayers ed., *Excavations at St Martin-at-Palace Plain, Norwich, 1981*, EAA, 37 (Norwich 1987).

11. A. Quiney, *Town Houses of Medieval Britain* (New Haven and London 2003).

12. The Britons Arms may be a rare example of an English 'beguinage', as a company of 'holy sisters' is believed to have resided in this parish in the 15th century: see R. Gilchrist and M. Oliva, *Religious Women in Medieval East Anglia* (Norwich 1993), 71–72.

13. A sequence discovered on Pottergate: D. H. Evans and A. Carter, 'Excavations on 31–51 Pottergate (Site 149N)', in *Excavations: Part II* (as in n. 4), 8–85; and Alms Lane: M. W. Atkin, 'Excavations on Alms Lane (Site 302N)', in *Excavations: Part II* (as in n. 4), 144–260.

14. C. King, '"Closure" and the urban great rebuilding in early modern Norwich', *Post-Medieval Archaeology*, 44/1 (2010), 54–80.

15. Smith and Carter, 'Function and site' (as in n. 3), 6–10.

16. M. W. Thompson, *The Medieval Hall: The Basis of Secular Domestic Life 600–1600 AD* (Aldershot 1995).

17. A. B. Whittingham, 'The Strangers' Hall', *Archaeol. J.*, 106 (1949), 80–81; A. Carter, 'Stranger's Hall, Norwich', *Archaeol. J.*, 137 (1980), 360–61; Smith and Carter, 'Function and site' (as in n. 3), 12–13; King, 'Houses' (as in n. 3), 74–89. I have published a phased plan of Strangers' Hall in C. King, 'The interpretation of urban buildings: power, memory and appropriation in Norwich merchants' houses c. 1400–1660', *World Archaeology*, 44/3 (2009), 471–88.

18. B. Cozens-Hardy and E. A. Kent, *The Mayors of Norwich 1403 to 1835: Biographical Notes on the Mayors of the Old Corporation* (Norwich 1938), 36.

19. Ibid., 50.

20. M. Grace, *Records of the Gild of St. George in Norwich, 1389–1547*, Norfolk Record Society 9 (Norwich 1937).

21. Smith and Carter, 'Function and site' (as in n. 3), 13.

22. Smith, 'Architectural history' (as in n. 3), 81–84.

23. Ibid., 13; English Heritage National Heritage List (No. 1372755); the moulding profile of the ceiling is shown in a mid-20th-century sketch by the city architect now held by the Norfolk Historic Environment Record (No. 606).

24. C. Barron and A. Sutton ed., *Medieval London Widows 1300–1500* (London 1994).

25. F. R. Beecheno with H. J. Green, 'The Sucklings' House at Norwich', *NA*, 19 (1920), 197–220b; F. R. Beecheno, 'The Sucklings' House at Norwich (II)', *NA*, 20 (1921), 158–78; the Norwich Survey mistakenly dated the hall to the 15th century.

26. Smith, 'Architectural history' (as in n. 3), 134–38.

27. E. M. Colman and H. C. Colman, *Suckling House and Stuart Hall, Norwich* (Norwich 1926); Cozens-Hardy and Kent, *Mayors* (as in n. 18), 22, 41.

28. Cozens-Hardy and Kent, *Mayors* (as in n. 18), 15.

29. Smith and Carter, 'Function and site' (as in n. 3), 10–11; Smith, 'Architectural history' (as in n. 3), 179–90.

30. A. Shelly and E. Rutledge, 'Excavation results and documentary evidence', in *Dragon Hall, King Street, Norwich: Excavation and Survey of a Late Medieval Merchant's Trading Complex*, EAA, 112, ed. A. Shelly (Norwich 2005), 29–88; R. Smith, 'Dragon Hall: description and interpretation', in ibid., 15–28.

31. Cozens-Hardy and Kent, *Mayors* (as in n. 18), 46; J. F. Williams, 'Pykerell's House, St Mary's Plain, Coslany', *Archaeol. J.*, 106 (1949), 82–83.

32. G. N. Barrett, 'The Great Hall, Oak Street, Norwich', *NA*, 41 (1991), 202–07.

33. Ayers, *Excavations* (as in n. 10).

34. Evans and Carter, '31–51 Pottergate (Site 149N)' (as in n. 12); M. W. Atkin, 'Excavations in Norwich — 1977/8: The Norwich Survey Seventh Interim Report: 351N. 70–78 Oak Street', *NA*, 37 (1978), 19–55.

35. See J. Grenville, *Medieval Housing* (London 1997), 89–114 for a complete description of the 'tripartite' great hall arrangement which became standard between the 13th and 14th centuries.

36. King, 'Interpretation' (as in n. 17).

37. Pantin, 'Town-house plans' (as in n. 2); Grenville, *Medieval Housing* (as in n. 35), 157–93; S. Pearson, 'Rural and urban houses 1100–1500: "urban adaptation" reconsidered', in *Town and Country in the Middle Ages: Contrasts, Contacts and Interconnections, 1100–1500*, ed. K. Giles and C. Dyer (Leeds 2005), 43–63.

38. RCHME, *The City of Salisbury* (London 1980); RCHME, *The City of York: vol. V: The Central Area* (London 1981); S. Pearson, 'Houses, shops and storage: building evidence from two Kentish ports', in *The Medieval Household in Christian Europe c. 850–c. 1550*, ed. C. Beattie, A. Maslakovic and S. Rees Jones (Turnhout 2003), 409–31.

39. J. Schofield, *Medieval London Houses* (London and New York 1995); R. H. Leech, 'The symbolic hall: historical context and merchant culture in the early modern city', *Vernacular Architecture*, 31 (2000), 1–10.

40. F. Heal, *Hospitality in Early Modern England* (Oxford 1990), 300–51; V. Morgan, 'The construction of civic memory in early modern Norwich', in *Material Memories*, ed. M. Kwint, C. Breward and J. Aynsley (Oxford and New York 1999), 183–97.

41. See King, 'Houses' (as in n. 3), 245–52.

42. J. Campbell, 'Norwich', in *The Atlas of Historic Towns, vol. II*, ed. M. Lobel and W. H. Johns (London 1975), 15; P. Dunn, 'Trade', in *Medieval Norwich*, 216–17, 228–33.

43. Frost, 'Urban elite' (as in n. 1), 236–40. For the formation of merchant oligarchies in late medieval towns, see S. H. Rigby, 'Urban "oligarchy" in late medieval England', in *Towns and Townspeople in the Fifteenth Century*, ed. J. A. F. Thompson (Stroud 1988), 62–86; and J. Kermode, 'Obvious observations on the formation of oligarchies in late medieval towns', in ibid., 87–106.

44. I. Dunn and H. Sutermeister, *The Norwich Guildhall* (Norwich n.d.).

45. N. P. Tanner, *The Church in Late Medieval Norwich, 1370–1532* (Toronto 1984), 143–55; B. R. McRee, 'Religious gilds and civic order: the case of Norwich in the late middle ages', *Speculum*, 67 (1992), 69–97; Grace, *Records* (as in n. 20).

46. Blomefield, *Norfolk*, IV, 184–238; J. Finch, 'The churches', in *Medieval Norwich*, 48–72; D. King, 'Medieval glass-painting', in ibid., 121–36.

47. The corporation issued a new set of craft guild ordinances in 1449 establishing authority over their economic and spiritual activities: Tanner, *The Church* (as in n. 45), 67–82. The two exceptions to this were the Goldsmiths who had a hall on the north side of the market-place: Blomefield, *Norfolk*, IV, 227; and the guild of St Luke in the cathedral precinct: Gilchrist, *Close*, 102.

48. Tanner, *The Church* (as in n. 45), 78. The contested dynamic between public and private is explored for early modern London by L. C. Orlin, *Locating Privacy in Tudor London* (Oxford 2010).

49. See King, 'Interpretation' (as in n. 17), 481–83.

50. Cozens-Hardy and Kent, *Mayors* (as in n. 18), 50, 68; Blomefield, *Norfolk*, IV, 293–94.

51. Cozens-Hardy and Kent, *Mayors* (as in n. 18), 76, 90; King, 'Interpretation' (as in n. 17), 483–84.

52. Cozens-Hardy and Kent, *Mayors* (as in n. 18), 48; King, 'Houses' (as in n. 3), 134–35.

53. Cozens-Hardy and Kent, *Mayors* (as in n. 18), 56; Smith, 'Architectural history' (as in n. 3), 107–33; King, 'Houses' (as in n. 3), 119–23.

54. Cozens-Hardy and Kent, *Mayors* (as in n. 18), 53; Smith, 'Architectural history' (as in n. 3), 151–60; King, 'Houses' (as in n. 3), 125–29; C. Carus ed., *Edmund Wood House: The Home of the King of Hearts* (Norwich 1995).

55. M. Girouard, *Life in the English Country House: A Social and Architectural History* (New Haven and London 1978), 81–162; N. Cooper, *Houses of the Gentry, 1480–1680* (New Haven and London 1999), 273–322; for the close connections between Norwich merchants and local gentry in the 16th and 17th centuries, see J. F. Pound, *Tudor and Stuart Norwich* (Chichester 1988), 80–82.

56. R. Tittler, *The Reformation and the Towns in England. Politics and Political Culture c. 1540–1640* (Oxford 1998); K. Giles, *An Archaeology of Social Identity. Guildhalls in York, c. 1350–1630*, BAR British Series 315 (Oxford 2000).

57. M. C. McClendon, *The Quiet Reformation: Magistrates and the Emergence of Protestantism in Tudor Norwich* (Stanford 1999), 88–110, 121–29.

Site Reports

St Nicholas, East Dereham

T. A. HESLOP

THE Anglo-Saxon Chronicle for the year 798 records the translation, 'fifty-five years after she departed this life', of the incorrupt body of St Wihtburh at Dereham, where later legend held her to have founded a monastery. She was understood to be a daughter of King Anna of East Anglia, and thus sister to SS Æthelthryth and Seaxburh. Royal lineage would indeed help make sense of otherwise unexplained 'facts'. One was the removal of her body to Ely by Abbot Byrhtnoth in 974. With it came jurisdiction, noted in Domesday Book, over the hundred and a half of Mitford, presumably originally part of the endowment of the church at Dereham.[1] The long reign of Wihtburh's cousin Ealdwulf saw the creation c. 673 of the see of Elmham just a few miles from Dereham (supposing this to be North Elmham). Both imply the very close co-operation of the king, creating an extended ecclesiastical enclave in central Norfolk in the late 7th century. The earliest elements of Dereham church visible today *in situ* are on the interior at ground level on the south and east sides of the crossing tower and the lower reaches of the chancel arch. They date from the early 12th century, when control passed from the monastery at Ely to the bishop of the see created there in 1109. The dedication to Nicholas is possibly coeval. The remains imply a cruciform plan, with eastern transeptal chapels. The detailing was elaborate, including a west door deriving from Ely[2] (now reset as the south door) and spiral columns flanking the entrance to the chancel. Chevron voussoirs and other stones carved with incised geometrical designs can be seen reused around putlog holes in the present chancel and presumably come from its Romanesque predecessor.

In the second quarter of the 13th century the chancel was rebuilt, probably under the aegis of Bishop Hugh Northwold of Ely. It is long and has two doors in the south wall, one towards the altar, the other at its west end implying that it functioned almost as an independent church. Furnishings include contemporary sedilia, piscina and an aumbry in the north wall, perhaps for an Easter sepulchre, unusually rich provision for the period. The windows are plate tracery (those to the north are extant, on the south they are copies); the size of the outer frame of the original east window suggests at least five lancets.

Also from the 13th century comes the bulk of the nave arcading (the Romanesque nave was presumably unaisled). In the early 14th century the arcade was extended one bay further west and a new facade provided overlooking St Wihtburh's Well in the churchyard. From this period several traceried windows also survive, although subsequent campaigns in the 1460s provided the south aisle with new fenestration, and work was undertaken on the aisle roofs (that on the north made by William Bishop, carpenter of Norwich) and on a new font, carved with the Seven Sacraments.[3] Payments for much of this are included in the extant churchwardens' accounts, including a breakdown of the costs for the font: £10 'to the mason for workmanship' plus a 20s. 'reward', 5s. split between another mason, a plumber and a smith, and 30s. on materials and transport.[4]

The impressive south porch is inscribed with the names of Roger Boton and his wife Margaret. She left money in her will of 1481 for glazing two windows in the porch, so building work was presumably complete, or nearly so, by that date.[5] The principal project of the next generation was the freestanding belfry. The foundations of the central tower had long been a cause for concern, but attempts to sustain it clearly proved inadequate and a new tower was begun around 1502 in the churchyard to the south-east. This solution may well have been prompted by the belfry (no longer extant) near the Erpingham gate at Norwich Cathedral. The large and impressive structure that stands at Dereham today is again well documented with donations from around fifty townspeople, though it seems construction came to a halt at the Reformation, before a parapet had been built.[6] This omission adds to the grand and rather austere impression conveyed by the sheer black flint walls and modest doors and window openings.

NOTES

1. T. Pestell, *Landscapes of Monastic Foundation: the establishment of religious houses in East Anglia* (Woodbridge 2004), 89–91.

2. G. Zarnecki, 'Some Observations Concerning the Romanesque Doorways of Ely Cathedral', *Studies in Medieval History Presented to R. Allen Brown*, ed. C. Harper-Bill, C. J. Holdsworth and J. Nelson (Woodbridge 1989), 345–52, reprinted in G. Zarnecki, *Further Studies in Romanesque Sculpture* (London 1992), item IX.

3. Cattermole and Cotton, 'Church Building', 244–45; J. Harvey, *English Medieval Architects: a Biographical Dictionary down to 1550* (2nd edn, Gloucester 1984); A. Nichols, *Seeable Signs, the Iconography of the Seven Sacraments 1350–1544* (Woodbridge 1994), 335.

4. As transcribed in Blomefield, *Norfolk*, X, 211–12.

5. Testament of Margaret Silverin (alias Boton) Norwich NRO, NCC Caston 111.

6. Cattermole and Cotton, 'Church Building', 245; P. Macaleer, 'Surviving Medieval Free-standing Bell Towers at Parish Churches in England and Wales', *JBAA*, 156 (2003), 70–103.

The Parish Church of St Mary, North Elmham

STEPHEN HEYWOOD

BEFORE the foundation of the present building, the parish church of Elmham was housed to the north in a timber chapel which had been the cathedral of East Anglia from the 10th century until 1071, when the seat of the bishop was moved to Thetford. Bishop Herbert de Losinga (1094–1119) founded the present church as a replacement using the site of the former cathedral to build a private chapel belonging to the manor which the bishop held in demesne. The lower walling of the chapel is extant.[1]

Of Herbert de Losinga's parish church only a pair of responds remain visible. These have double half-shafts and were designed to support Romanesque main arcades. The present arcades, standing on alternating cylindrical and octagonal piers, are, however, of *c.* 1200 and have two-centred arches with typical small, undercut and keeled, roll mouldings. At this point in its history the nave arcades were at the height of the arches still standing in the easternmost bay, with small clerestory openings centred above the spandrels.

The north and south doors have oddly shaped, depressed two-centred arches. This is because the arches are formed out of reused arcade arches which probably belonged to a further bay which was replaced by the present west tower. Also from this demolished part of the church are several finely carved crocket and stiff leaf capitals preserved beneath a shelf above the north door. The only place that such an array of early-

13th-century architectural sculpture could have been used in the building would have been a monumental west doorway with *en délit* shafts such as the west door at West Walton of a similar period. This raises the likelihood of there not having been a west tower, leaving the possibility of a former axial tower in front of the chancel; there are twenty other Norman parish churches in Norfolk with this arrangement.[2]

In the early years of the 14th century a major alteration took place, demonstrating a remarkable feat of engineering. The arches and capitals of the nave arcade were carefully taken down, the piers were heightened with new masonry and the capitals and arches re-erected, but in the present elevated position. The aisles were rebuilt and have fine Decorated tracery windows with some glass of the 1320s *in situ*. The roof over this first heightening of the nave is marked with a dripstone on the east wall of the tower and indicates there was just enough room for a low 14th-century clerestory, probably with foiled circular windows.

A late medieval refurbishment brought about the present arrangement of the (now Victorianized) chancel. The Norwich Dean and Chapter rolls record the reconstruction and re-roofing of the chancel to 1382–87.[3] Chapels were added to the chancel, replacing the eastern ends of the aisles. The north chapel, dedicated to St John, has a cusped Y-traceried east window which could be the former aisle east window re-set. The large five-light north window is a 15th-century insertion. The south chapel, of slightly different dimensions, is dedicated to St James. It has straightforward panel-traceried windows of mid-15th-century date. There is also a panel-traceried window above the chancel arch with some glass of the same date.

Until the second heightening of the nave in the mid-15th century, by the addition of a new clerestory, the chancel would have been as tall as the nave. Following this final upward extension, new furnishings were provided. The impressive painted screen across the east end of the nave incorporates part of the original chancel screen with the apostles (seven survive), which had a date of 1474.[4] A screen with virgin martyrs and a third screen with Benedictine saints look closely contemporary.[5] These fragments have all been carpentered together, but differences in mouldings and panel sizes show they were originally separate. Further research is needed to establish their original locations.

NOTES

1. See S. Heywood, 'The Ruined Church at North Elmham', *JBAA*, 135 (1982), 1–10.

2. See S. Heywood, 'Round-Towered Churches', in *An Historical Atlas of Norfolk*, 3rd edn, ed. T. Ashwin and A. Davison (Chichester 2005), 60–61.

3. See Cattermole and Cotton, 'Church Building', 246.

4. Recorded in Blomefield's notebooks in the Bodleian Library: David King, personal communication.

5. A. Baker, *English Panel Paintings, 1400–1558: A Survey of Figure Paintings on East Anglian Rood Screens* (London 2011), 26–27, 165–66. Also P. Hurst and J. Haselock, *Norfolk Rood Screens: An Illustrated Guide to the Medieval Splendour of Norfolk Church Screens* (Andover 2012), 50–51.

The Nave of St Margaret's Church, Cley-next-the-Sea

CHRISTOPHER WILSON

CLEY was one of the most successful of the small ports on the north Norfolk coast which became wealthy in the late Middle Ages from local and international maritime trade, the latter centred on the importation of dried fish from Iceland.[1] The nave of St Margaret's church has a claim to be considered the most ambitious work of English parish church architecture dating from the first quarter of the 14th century. Its only rivals are the naves at Bottisham in Cambridgeshire and Howden in the East Riding of Yorkshire and the chancel at Winchelsea in East Sussex,[2] and like those other exceptional buildings, Cley can with some confidence be attributed to one of the outstanding architects of the time, in this case John Ramsey, to all appearances East Anglia's foremost master mason from the 1290s until his probable death in the early or middle 1330s. Ramsey's works include a string of major buildings at Norwich Cathedral dating from the late 1290s to the mid-1320s, even more ambitious projects undertaken at Ely Cathedral between 1321 and the mid-1330s, and at least two top-flight parish church buildings of c. 1330, namely the chancel of Mildenhall church in Suffolk and the nave of Snettisham church in north-west Norfolk.[3] The only earlier architect who was similarly prolific was Michael of Canterbury, master mason to Canterbury Cathedral priory from the mid-1270s until at least the first decade of the 14th century, and designer of the most important royal ecclesiastical project of the age, the rebuilding of St Stephen's chapel in Westminster Palace from 1292. Ramsey made a certain number of borrowings from Michael of Canterbury's idiosyncratic formal repertory, but his most important debts were his eclectic approach and his readiness to treat each project as an opportunity to create a distinctive and innovatory design.

Comparison of Cley's interior elevations with those of Howden, Winchelsea and Bottisham (the last very possibly an early work of Ramsey's) serves to highlight the singular use made of the considerable resources which must have been available. Whereas arcades carried on widely spaced octagonal piers are a commonplace of 13th-century parish church architecture in England, the idea of canopy-topped standing figures occupying every spandrel of the arcades was unprecedented, and the clearstorey was almost certainly among the very earliest of countless examples in English late medieval parish churches which have twice as many windows as there are arches in the arcades below. It is likely that these horizontal-stressing bands of windows were originally complemented by low aisle walls lit by straight-headed windows resembling that which still survives in the blocking wall installed after the demolition of the north transeptal chapel. This consists of a row of lights with elongated ogee heads and foiled spandrels, effectively a scaled-up version of the blind tracery on the high altar sedilia in Canterbury Cathedral. The other obvious borrowings from Michael of Canterbury's works are also in the realm of tracery design: the two-light windows of the south clearstorey, which are simplified versions of the central sections of the lower chapel windows at St Stephen's chapel, and the large wave-sided diamond crowning the tracery in the splendid and unique window in the end wall of the south transeptal chapel. There are some striking resemblances to Bottisham, particularly of the double ogee mouldings forming the outer order of the arcade arches, the single lancets at the east and west ends of the clearstorey, and the odd way in which the lateral foils of the quatrefoils in the two-light south clearstorey windows are treated as extensions of the inner arcs of the lights below.[4] Details evidencing continuity with Ramsey's earlier work at Norwich include the extensive use of concave chamfers and the very large foiled but

FIG. I.   Cley-next-the-Sea, St Margaret: north nave arcade and clearstorey

unsubdivided circular windows, close relations no doubt of the circular windows in the cathedral's belfry, for whose making he had been paid in 1305–06. If large round windows had been a feature of the old belfry, which is extremely likely given that they are present in the Romanesque crossing tower of the cathedral, those in the new belfry and the Cley clearstorey could be considered Ramsey's nearest approach to 'archaisms' in the Michael of Canterbury manner. The lavish use of decorative and figural sculpture, so exceptional in a parish church, is only one among several features of Cley which foreshadow Ramsey's later buildings at Ely. The work of some of the Cley sculptors can be seen in the east cloister walk of Norwich Cathedral.

The early-14th-century work at Cley remains incomplete, for the north-west corner is still occupied by a modest earlier tower which has prevented the installation of the westernmost parts of the north aisle. The intention will have been to replace the tower by a freestanding belfry, and the failure to carry out this final phase of the project suggests that the prosperity of the town peaked in the first quarter of the 14th century.

NOTES

1. J. Hooton, *The Glaven Ports. A Maritime History of Blakeney, Cley and Wiveton in North Norfolk* (Blakeney 1996), 30.

2. As is the case with most English Gothic parish churches, the literature on the Cley nave (other than guidebooks) is exiguous; it is not mentioned in any of the modern surveys of Decorated architecture. The building was first attributed to John Ramsey in A. B. Whittingham, 'The Ramsey Family of Norwich', *Archaeol. J.*, 137 (1980), 285–89, at 285.

3. For the documented careers of John Ramsey and the likely architects of Winchelsea and Howden (Michael of Canterbury and Simon respectively), see J. Harvey, *English Mediaeval Architects. A Biographical Dictionary down to 1550*, rev. edn (Gloucester 1984), 240; ibid., 45–46, 239–41, 274. The oeuvres of these men are reconstructed and analysed in a work I have in preparation on late-13th- and early-14th-century English architecture.

4. This tracery and that of the south transeptal chapel is illustrated in C. Tracy, *English Gothic Choir-stalls 1200–1400* (Woodbridge 1987), pl. 63.

St Mary's, Wiveton

NICK TREND

ST MARY's Wiveton stands about 100 yards west of the River Glaven, directly across the meadows from St Margaret's, Cley. The two form a pair of showpiece churches, built by prosperous communities when the meadows were salt marshes and both towns, along with neighbouring Blakeney and Salthouse, were thriving seaports. High-specification flushwork panels on the exterior of the chancel at Wiveton suggest that an earlier, probably 14th-century church was finished to impressive standards — perhaps a response to, or spurred by, the contemporary aggrandisement of St Margaret's. St Mary's was then substantially rebuilt in the 15th century; a wider, higher nave being constructed between the chancel and the tower. New windows were inserted throughout, new chancel and tower arches were built, and porches added.

Perhaps the motivation came from the work at Blakeney — the most prosperous of the Glaven ports — where the church was being rebuilt in 1434.[1] Even in 1437, however, there was apparently some lack of resolve in Wiveton. That year, the wealthy land- and ship-owner, John Hakon, bequeathed 200 marks for the 'making of the new church',[2] which was to be reduced to £40 for repairs to the old church, should the new one not go ahead. Heraldry on the apexes of the south-east and south-west aisle windows suggest that other wealthy sponsors did help fund what must have been a high-budget project with exceptional attention to detail. Particularly noticeable is the high quality of workmanship of the nave arcades, door mouldings and window traceries.

Richard Fawcett commented on the subtlety and complexity of this work in 1975.[3] He found close matches between mouldings and/or arcade pier designs in Wiveton and several Norfolk churches, including Great Cressingham and Blakeney (north porch); the tower of St George Colegate, the naves of St John Maddermarket and St Peter Hungate in Norwich; and in the lower stages of the west tower of Wymondham Abbey.

He also pointed out similarities in tracery designs — notably at Hungate, Maddermarket and Cressingham. Particularly compelling are the comparisons between the porches at Wiveton, Great Cressingham, Hilborough and St Mary Coslany, which all have entrance arches cut from an identical template. They are of notable sophistication and subtlety, and he assumes a single highly skilled mason must have been responsible — one who was working in Norwich and Norfolk between about 1420 and 1460. In his thesis,[4] Fawcett tentatively identifies James Woderofe as the most likely candidate to be the 'Wiveton mason'. Woderofe was the most prominent mason working at Norwich Cathedral priory during this period — a series of payments was made to him for robes and works at the cathedral between 1415/16 and 1450/51 — and he was regarded highly enough to be sent for by Henry VI to work on the new chapel at Eton in 1449.[5]

Fawcett is hampered to some extent because he had no documentary reference to Woderofe's work in parish churches, only his rather different work in the cathedral, mainly in the cloisters. But in 1995 Birkin Haward was, with some caveats, also tempted by the attribution. He focused on a particular detail of the Wiveton tracery — the 'shouldered' ogee arch above the principal lights of the main windows.[6] This unusual figuration is also found in Woderofe's east window in the chancel at Wighton (*c*. 1441), some seven miles from Wiveton — which, as Cattermole and Cotton pointed out in 1983, Woderofe was commissioned to build in 1440/41[7] — and a handful of other churches. These Haward dates mainly between 1440 and 1470, tentatively attributing them to Woderofe's workshop and that of his successor at the cathedral, John Everard.

Is this attribution convincing? Clearly, the project supervisor at Wiveton was a highly skilled and inventive mason with a decent budget. He must have worked elsewhere in Norfolk during this period, and Fawcett's stylistic and design links surely cannot all be coincidental. But Woderofe's dates do not quite tally. Fawcett and Harvey were unaware that he died in 1450, when the masons John Jekkys and Nicholas Berkyng and the fuller William Shyrwen were confirmed as executors of his will.[8] The earliest likely dates for Hungate and Coslany are in the late 1450s,[9] so Woderofe could not have been directly responsible for the work. But it seems perfectly feasible that what must have been a successful workshop would have continued to operate, using familiar patterns and templates. Jekkys had certainly worked with Woderofe — he travelled to Eton with him the year before Woderofe died. The evidence is circumstantial, but Woderofe was clearly a talented and respected mason who, in a long career, must have produced a significant body of work. Wiveton must have been built by such a man, and he is the only potential candidate we have.

NOTES

1. Cattermole and Cotton, 'Church Building', 239.
2. Ibid., 274.
3. R. Fawcett, 'Later Gothic architecture in Norfolk: an examination of the work of some individual architects in the fourteenth and fifteenth centuries' (unpublished Ph.D. thesis, University of East Anglia, 1975) and subsequently summarized, though without the attribution to Woderofe, in R. Fawcett, 'St Mary at Wiveton in Norfolk, a group of churches attributed to its mason', *Antiq. J.*, 62 (1982), 35–56.
4. Page 341 (Cattermole and Cotton noted the link between Wighton and Woderofe in 1983, after Fawcett's 1975 thesis and 1982 publication).
5. J. Harvey, *English Medieval Architects, a biographical dictionary down to 1550* (Gloucester 1987), 343.
6. B. Haward, *Norfolk Album, Medieval Church Arcades* (Ipswich 1995), 14–19.
7. This reference was noted by Cattermole and Cotton, 'Church Building', 273, a year after Fawcett's publication.
8. Norwich NRO, NCC Aleyn 7.
9. See T. A. Heslop, 'St Peter Hungate, Norwich', in the present volume.

St Giles on the Hill, Norwich

HELEN E. LUNNON

THE church of St Giles, only a few yards inside the medieval city wall, occupies the highest point in Norwich, some 26 m above sea-level. Those responsible for the 15th-century rebuilding apparently appreciated this topography, enhancing the natural belvedere by constructing the tallest church tower in the city, measuring 120 ft (approx. 36.5 m).

Except for the 19th-century window tracery, the nave is essentially that built between *c.* 1386 and *c.* 1429, a phase of works to which several testamentary bequests pertain. In 1386 Stephen de Holt bequeathed 30 shillings for the emendation of the nave, suggesting work was being planned and funds raised, although nothing material indicates building had begun.[1] In 1424 Robert Dunston bequeathed £5 to repairing the tower.[2] Eight years later, Robert Baxter, Dunstan's close associate, was buried in the nave, where his memorial brass (bearing the date 1432) is extant. A mercer by trade, Baxter held several important civic offices: chamberlain (1415–16), sheriff (1418–19) and mayor (1424–25 and 1429–30).[3] Writing his testament in 1429, Baxter's concerns were for equipping St Giles: £20 for a suit of vestments, 12 marks for a missal and 7 marks for a gilt silver cup.[4] Presumably building works were almost complete and the church was coming back into use. Dunstan, Baxter and Richard Purdance (another parishioner, also a sheriff and mayor of Norwich, who was buried in the nave in 1436) were consummate negotiators and skilled businessmen with overseas contacts.[5] In such capable hands the church of St Giles was substantially remade; a bequest of 40 shillings to the emendation of the church in 1444 was probably for the upper parts of the tower.[6]

To find an architectural context for St Giles one must look beyond the city. The arcade piers have more numerous and elaborate mouldings on the nave face than on the aisle side, thus creating an overtly asymmetrical plan also found in Norfolk at Blickling and Carbrooke. In also having tiers of crenellated niches flanking the chancel arch, Carbrooke initially appears directly to imitate St Giles, but in terms of the pier dimensions Blickling is closer to the Norwich church and perhaps by the same mason.[7] The conventional window tracery at Blickling is also likely to be early-15th-century. The nave at Carbrooke can be dated by circumstantial evidence to *c.* 1424, and is thus coeval with St Giles.[8]

The aisle glazing at St Giles is recorded as displaying the arms of close political and military comrades, namely Thorpe (d. 1418), Felbrigg (d. 1442) and Shelton, men who shared a commitment to the architectural renewal of parish churches in their care (Sir Nicholas Dagworth of Blickling could be included easily in the group).[9] However, the most striking heraldry at St Giles is that displayed on the shields born by the roof angels. These include Leon and Castile impaling England, for Edward of Langley, 2nd Duke of York (d. 1415). The others principally show the royal arms quartering France 'modern', which dates the roof after 1404.[10] The roof structure (doubled-framed rather than hammer-beam) also suggests a design date not far into the 15th century. Unlike other early Norfolk angel roofs, St Giles with its heraldic emphasis is more akin to Westminster Hall than to its regional contemporaries.

St Giles contained many altars, images and accompanying lights. By 1448 a chapel with an image of St Catherine was located at the west end of the south aisle.[11] There was also an 'altar of the Virgin of Pity' (the altar of the guild of St Mary) though its location is unknown. The window at the west end of the south aisle contained scenes of

Christ's passion,[12] and records of payments made for the burning of lights evidence images of St Mary, St John the Baptist, St Giles and St Christopher. The latter was a large wall-painting on the north nave wall, rediscovered in 1723 but subsequently lost. A Trinity image occupied a niche on the west face of the tower, before which Richard Gosselyn, husbandman, requested burial in 1496.[13]

The medieval chancel was demolished in 1581 by order of the Dean and Chapter. The present one, designed by R. M. Phipson, was funded by William Ripley, vicar of St Giles, in 1866. However, above ground remains were seen and noted by John Kirkpatrick in 1712, and a pre-restoration interior photograph shows an apparently early-15th-century window under the chancel arch, perhaps the original east window reset.[14] Further investigation might well reveal more about the medieval chancel's form and indicate whether it was coeval with the nave.

NOTES

1. Norwich NRO, NCC Harsyk 78.

2. Blomefield, *Norfolk*, IV, 239; Norwich NRO, NCR Case 4i/7.

3. http://www.historyofparliamentonline.org/volume/1386-1421/member/baxter-robert-1431.

4. Norwich NRO, NCC Surflete 86.

5. Richard Purdance's brass remains in St Giles. His testament is not known to survive. For his biography, see http://www.historyofparliamentonline.org/volume/1386-1421/member/purdance-%28spurdaunce%29-richard-1436.

6. Testament of Henry Pykyng, Norwich NRO, NCC Wylbey 48. At least three of the extant bells are the work of Richard Baxter, d. 1457 (see P. Cattermole, *Church Bells of Norfolk* (East Harling 1995), 60). Bells were certainly in place and able to be rung by 1457, see Norwich NRO, NCC Betyns 27.

7. B. Haward, *Norfolk Album: Medieval Church Arcades* (Ipswich 1995), 30. The pier widths are St Giles: 21.5 in. × 30 in., Blickling: 21.5 in. × 30.5 in., Carbrooke: 23.5 in. × 30.75 in. Blickling has been dated *c.* 1460 on the basis of Geoffrey Boleyn's will: 'The bequest makes clear that if work was complete, the money was to be spent on ornaments, giving an approximate completion date for the rebuilding of the aisled nave' (Cattermole and Cotton, 'Church Building', 277 n. 12). The relevant part of the testament reads: 'Also I will that 20 pounds sterling of my goods be dispersed upon the work of the body of the church of Blickling aforesaid or upon ornaments of the same church or on both as shall be thought most necessary by the discretion of my brother master Thomas Boleyn and of my executors'. TNA PROB/11/5.

8. See T. A. Heslop, 'Swaffham Parish Church: Community Building in Fifteenth-Century Norfolk', in *Medieval East Anglia*, ed. C. Harper-Bill (Woodbridge 2005), 246–71, at n. 13.

9. Blomefield, *Norfolk*, IV, 246, recorded Scales, Thorpe, Clifton, Caily, Shelton, Calthorp and Vaus, plus *or*, a lion rampant *gul.* (for Sir Simon Felbrigg, d. 1442); *gul.* in a bordure *or*, a cross *arg.* (for John or Robert Carbonell); *gul.* on a chevron *arg.* three roses proper (for Robert Knollys, d. 1407). Dagworth was summoned to the Privy Council on 21 July 1401 along with Simon Felbrigg, Ralf Shelton, Thomas Gerberge and Edmund Thorpe. See Sir H. Nicolas ed., *Proceedings and Ordinances of the Privy Council of England*, 7 vols (London 1834–37), I, 163. In 1712, John Kirkpatrick also noted the 'paintings of various colours but now scare visible' included the arms of Erpingham (d. 1428). See Kirkpatrick's notes as reproduced in P. Eade, *Some Account of the Parish of St. Giles, Norwich* (London 1886), 209.

10. The shields as painted today do not display the same heraldry as that recorded by John Kirkpatrick in 1712. The angels have replacement wings, arms and hands and therefore the shields may also be replacements, or at the least have been repainted. It is clear, however, that the royal arms were the main emblem on the roof in 1712 as they are today. Kirkpatrick recorded heraldic details from 11 of the 12 shields and the only exception to the royal theme was 'St George's Cross'. See Eade, *The Parish of St. Giles* (as in n. 9), 208.

11. In 1448 Henry Pykyng was buried by the south nave door by St Catherine's altar. Blomefield, *Norfolk*, IV, 239.

12. In 1493 Thomas Smith was buried before the window of Christ's passion, at the west end of the south aisle. Blomefield, *Norfolk*, IV, 246.

13. Norwich NRO, NCC Multon 48.

14. Eade, *The Parish of St. Giles* (as in n. 9), 199.

St Peter Hungate, Norwich

T. A. HESLOP

ST PETER HUNGATE is located in central Norwich between the cathedral precinct and the Dominican friary, the chancel of which lies within the bounds of the parish. That effectively reduced the space for housing and parishioners, to the detriment of St Peter's income. The presence of the preaching order also offered an alternative focus for devotion and benefaction, in recognition of which the friars paid compensation.[1]

The church stands at the highest point of the parish with its churchyard to the north. Also on the north side is the great 'house', now known as the Britons Arms, which seems to have served as the home of the sisters of St Peter, a community of women devoted to charity and in character perhaps rather similar to beguinages on the Continent.[2] There was apparently direct access from the house to the churchyard and thence to the north door of the nave. That may explain why it was on the buttress beside the north door that John Paston recorded his role as patron and the date 1460.[3] He had acquired the advowson from the College of St Mary in the Fields in 1458.

The building as it stands today is mostly 15th century. The modest west tower and chancel were paid for by a wealthy parishioner, the cloth merchant and former mayor of Norwich Thomas Ingham, the tower in 1431, the chancel apparently finished by 1451.[4] The present aisleless nave and transept sponsored by John Paston has a similar layout to work of the same period, c. 1460, at St Mary Coslany, in that nave and transept are the same height and the intersection of their roofs is marked by elaborate timber-work.[5] At Hungate the central boss shows Christ in Judgement between the Virgin and John the Baptist, and the surrounding bosses carry half-length angels. This crossing arrangement is supported on four corbels, each with the image of a winged evangelist. So, for example, a winged St Mark stands with his lion at the north-west corner. The corbels for the nave roof are carved with seated figures of the four Doctors of the Church. There is apparently a 'programme' here: the nave is constituted as concerned with the authority of the Church on earth and the crossing area as the realm of heaven.

The transept arms contained the chapels of the Virgin (north) and St John (south) the Baptist, echoing their positions on the central judgement boss. In his will of 1479, Walter Paston asked to be buried in front of the image of the Baptist, the niche for which still exists in the south transept. In the corresponding position in the north transept is the door (now blocked) to the rood loft staircase. The most striking remaining imagery is the stained glass. Most is from the period of Paston's nave and transepts, including several half-length angels bearing scrolls with texts used in the liturgy, such as *Nunc dimittis*, from the tops of the main lights. On a larger scale, there is also a head of Gabriel from an Annunciation, now in the east window but perhaps originally from the north transept. All this work has been convincingly attributed to the workshop of John Wighton, responsible for glazing many churches in Norfolk and Norwich in the middle decades of the 15th century.[6] The original chancel scheme included the four doctors (again), but only St Gregory's head survives, and the four evangelists (again), but these are from the early 16th century.

Overall, the figurative imagery demonstrates the desire to counter the 'heretical' opinions of the Lollards. They criticized church building and decoration in general, but singled out figures of authority, such as the doctors, and representations of incorporeal beings such as angels.[7] The Pastons clearly wished to express their impeccable orthodoxy. Curiously, St Peter scarcely features in the rich extant material, unless we suppose that the continuous transept alludes to the basilica in Rome where his body rested.

NOTES

1. R. Young and G. Goreham, *St Peter Hungate, Norwich* (Norwich 1969), 3–4.
2. Blomefield, *Norfolk*, IV, 333–34.
3. Paston's shield and ragged staff were accompanied by an inscription, recorded in ibid., 331, as 'Fundata in anno domini mcccclx'.
4. See the account of the church's history given by D. King at http://www.cvma.ac.uk/publications/digital/norfolk/sites/norwichhungate/history.html
5. For the dates of St Mary, see Cattermole and Cotton, 'Church Building', 258 — the south transept was 'new' in 1464.
6. D. King, 'Glass-Painting in Late-Medieval Norwich: Continuity and Patronage in the John Wighton Workshop', in *Patrons and Professionals in the Middle Ages*, ed. P. Binski and E. A. New, Harlaxton Medieval Studies 22 (Donington 2012), 347–65, at 361 dating the work to 1460–65. See also for a fuller description http://www.cvma.ac.uk/publications/digital/norfolk/sites/norwichhungate/catalogue.html
7. E. Duffy, 'The Four Latin Doctors in Late Medieval England', in *Tributes to Nigel Morgan. Contexts of Medieval Art: Image, Objects and Ideas*, ed. J. M. Luxford and M. A. Michael (London and Turnhout 2010), 33–42. For Wycliffe's objection to representing angels, see M. Aston, *Lollards and Reformers, Images and Literacy in Late Medieval Religion* (London 1984), 139, citing his *De Mandatis Divinis*.

The Church of St Laurence, Norwich

JULIAN LUXFORD

ST LAURENCE'S is a large, aisled church with a tall west tower, north and south porches at the west end, and a stubby, projecting chancel of a sort common in East Anglian Perpendicular. With the exception of minor details, all of it dates from the second half of the 15th and the first years of the 16th century, when some wind of patronage, anonymous apart from ancillary sums recorded in wills, blew the previous (and of itself richly appointed) structure down and raised up a new building that could assert its quality amidst the architectural variegation of late medieval Norwich.[1] The main vessel is of five bays, and has a clear width of about 14.3 m, while the church's total clear length is around 38.7 m. Heavier buttressing and thicker piers in the third bay from the west, along with a polygonal rood-stair projecting on the south side, mark the transition from nave to liturgical chancel. The original high altar, like its modern replacement, was elevated on a vaulted undercroft over 2 m above the level of the nave, a design gesture which the High Anglican congregation using the church in the early 20th century (who contributed the remaining furnishings, along with a vestry at the east end) evidently enjoyed. Apart from the undercroft and the lierne-vaulted north porch, the building is entirely roofed in timber.

Externally, the tower, porches, aisles and chancel are faced with knapped flint, and the clerestory and eastern terminations of the aisles and chancel with freestone. The tower, around 34 m high and of four stages, has the usual stone-dressed buttresses and parapets with flushwork panelling. In the spandrels of the west door are relief sculptures showing the martyrdoms of St Laurence (to the north) and St Edmund: the holocaust and blood-sacrifice set like seals over the ceremonial entrance to advertise the mandate of spiritual and temporal patron alike, the latter the powerful abbey of Bury in Suffolk.[2] The lateral aisle windows, slightly richer on the south side, have four ogee lights and heads with reticulations and quatrefoils set beneath depressed arches. Over the sites of the altars at the eastern ends of the aisles are similar windows of three lights, that on the north side containing what is left of the church's medieval glass. The chancel window is modern, but the west window original, deeply set and distinctive in its tracery of four ogee lights surmounted by sub-arches, lozenges, and, centrally, a large sexfoil with slightly pointed lobes. As normal in an ambitious Norfolk church of this date, the clerestory has four windows per bay, with uniform Perpendicular tracery of three lights under more of the depressed arches. Both porches are of two storeys: that on the north side juts out from the building above Westwick Street, while the south porch is reached from St Benedict's Street by descending a flight of steps. The steeply sloping site means that the flanks of the building have markedly different airs: abrupt and massed to the north, couched and accessible to the south.

Within, the lack of furniture and coloured glass means that the formal qualities of the architecture assert themselves strongly (Fig. 2). Line and light are the dominant accents, and volume the dominant impression. The chancel is elegant and dramatic, the nave lofty and luminous. There are correspondences and effects arranged for the gaze of the attentive or serial viewer. The nave has piers of octagonal section, answering the form of the font and the large polygonal motif of the west window.[3] In the chancel there is a pair of lozenge-section piers whose form seems designed — as also elsewhere — to create the minimum possible obstruction to front-on views of whatever imagery occupied the aisle walls and window-glass.[4] The outstanding qualities of linearity and spatial clarity, together with the subtle modulation of light, particularly in the nave where the piers have soft angles and concave facets, suggest a clever, imaginative designer. Probably, however, they do not reflect the conscious concerns of the

FIG. 2.   Norwich, St Laurence: chancel and nave

church's original users, who had east-facing devotional and commemorative goals centred on specific objects. The church contained at least three altars (dedicated to St Laurence, the Virgin Mary and the Holy Cross), a roodscreen, wooden parcloses and no fewer than six votive images: the Virgin and Child, Assumption and Our Lady of Pity, plus saints Christopher, Nicholas and one of the Johns. There was also the rood-group, of course, figures of saints Laurence and Edmund at the high altar, and whatever imagery was displayed in the glazing, vestments and altar-cloths (St Laurence, the Virgin and the Crucifixion are recorded on altar frontals). Rectorial tombs, clustered together in hopeful fellowship, inhabited the chancel pavement, while the nave pavement was populated by the slabs and brasses of laypeople. Votive lights flickered on the rood-loft, before the images and also, no doubt, at the extremities of some of the tombs.[5] These ornaments and the enclaves around them were the focus of most of the church's ritual and social life.

Yet the parishioners were subject to the gestalt of the architecture, whether or not they were conscious of it. The building's straight lines ran vertically, up and down the piers and griddle-like mullions of the windows, horizontally, through the high altar-steps and broad sections of the chancel piers (not to mention the screens), and recessively, along the central vessel, window sills, wall-heads and purlins. These lines articulated spiritual axes which were calculated and important. Perhaps the most obvious of these is the axis of font, rood and high altar, so popular for burials. This was flanked by implicit lines connecting the figures of saints Laurence and Edmund at the west door with those at the high altar, the two pairs of images being set at a similar height and occupying the same sides (with Laurence to the north). The order in which people stood or sat, what and how they saw and where they chose to be buried were all conditioned by the structural accents of the building. This is not to suggest that function followed form at St Laurence's. On the contrary, form always followed function in buildings of this sort, for no element could be conceived independently of some function, whether utilitarian, symbolic or otherwise. Rather, it is to propose that those architectural properties which assert themselves so clearly with the extrusion of the medieval fittings, and whose modern appreciation is thus often considered anachronistic by historians, were in fact part and parcel of lived experience at St Laurence's, and other churches, in the late Middle Ages.

NOTES

1. For the copious ornaments and books at St Laurence's *c.* 1368, see *Archdeaconry of Norwich: Inventory of Church Goods* temp. *Edward III*, ed. A. Watkin, 2 vols, Norfolk Record Society 19 (Norwich 1947–48), I, 15–16.

2. It seems likely that Bury had some decisive part in the church's reconstruction. It is also probable that the tabernacles over the porch doors accommodated sculpted figures of St Laurence on the north and St Edmund on the south, standing on elongated pedestals.

3. The current octagonal font must be modern, but it is surpassingly likely that the original shared its form.

4. For the chancel piers (and a ground-plan), see B. Haward, *Suffolk Medieval Church Arcades, 1150–1550* (Ipswich 1993), 426–27.

5. All of the information on bequests, lost images, tombs and lights is taken from Blomefield, *Norfolk*, IV, 260–72.

INDEX

Page references in **bold** refer to illustrations

Previous Volumes in the Series